C000043279

W111 WOODSTOCK 304132

304132

E8 LS wrc 43

£22 —
e

James Orchard
Halliwell-Phillipps

The Life and Works of the
Shakespearean Scholar and Bookman

Frontispiece: Halliwell-Phillipps in his later years.
By kind permission of his great-grandson, Lt. Col. William Walcot Stewart

James Orchard Halliwell-Phillipps

The Life and Works of the Shakespearean Scholar and Bookman

Marvin Spevack

OAK KNOLL PRESS &
SHEPHEARD-WALWYN

2001

First Edition.

Published by **Oak Knoll Press**
310 Delaware Street, New Castle, Delaware, USA
and **Shepheard-Walwyn**
Suite 604, The Chandlery, 50 Westminster Bridge Rd.
London, SE1 7QY, UK

ISBN: 1584560517 (USA)
ISBN: 0 85683 193 X (UK)

Title: James Orchard Halliwell-Phillipps
Author: Marvin Spevack
Typographer: M. Spevack
Publishing Director: J. Lewis von Hoelle

Copyright: © 2001 by Marvin Spevack

Library of Congress Cataloging-in-Publication Data

Spevack, Marvin.
    James Orchard Halliwell-Phillipps: The Life and Works of the Shakespearean
    Scholar and Bookman / by Marvin Spevack.
        p. cm
    Includes bibliographical references and index.
    ISBN: 1584560517
    1. Halliwell-Phillipps, J.O. (James Orchard), 1820-1889. 2. Shakespeare, William,
    1564-1616--Criticism and interpretation--History--19th century. 3. Shakespeare,
    William, 1564-1616--Criticism, Textual. 4. Literary historians--Great
    Britain--Biography. 5. Bibliographers--Great Britain--Biography. 6.
    Lexicographers--Great Britain--Biography. 7. Scholars--Great Britain--Biography. I.
    Title.

    PR2972.H3 S64 2001
    822.3'3--dc21   2001016425

British Library Cataloguing-in-Publication Data
A CIP Record is available from The British Library

ALL RIGHTS RESERVED:
No part of this book may be reproduced in any manner without the
express written consent of the publisher, except in the case of brief
excepts in critical reviews and articles. All inquiries should be
addressed to: Oak Knoll Press, 310 Delaware Street, New Castle, DE 19720

Printed in the United States of America on 60# archival, acid-free paper meeting the
requirements of the Standard for Permanence of Paper for Printed Library Materials.

To Edmund Daniel Spevack

Contents

Preface

This is the first book-length presentation of the life and work of James Orchard Halliwell-Phillipps (1820-1889), the eminent Shakespearean factotum and bookman, whom critics of widely diverse orientation recognize as the greatest contributor of his age to our knowledge of Shakespeare's life and times. Outstanding among his hundreds of works dealing with Shakespeare and early modern English literature are his luxurious sixteen-volume folio edition of Shakespeare (1853-65) and his indispensable *Outlines of the Life of Shakespeare* (7th ed. 1887). Complementing his prolific publications and voluminous manuscripts were his efforts to establish Stratford-upon-Avon as a fitting memorial to Shakespeare, beginning with his purchase of Shakespeare's house, New Place, and his role in organizing a National Shakespeare Fund, and continuing with his founding and supporting its library and museum

Halliwell was a man of prodigious energy and wide interests. Some six hundred publications deal not only with Shakespeare and early modern literature but also with mathematics, lexicography, the history of science, archaeology, dialectology, history, and theology. He was founder or council member of the Shakespeare Society, Percy Society, Camden Society, among others, as well as member of numerous local, national, and international organizations. Before the age of twenty he was Fellow of the Royal Society and the Society of Antiquaries. In the course of his career he received many other honours, at home and abroad: at one end, at age eighteen he was the youngest Fellow ever elected to the Royal Society; at the other, he became the first honorary member of the Shakespeare Society of New York. He was active as a bookman and antiquary. His vast collections—rare books and manuscripts, hundreds of volumes of literary correspondence and scrapbooks, Shakespearean rarities (artifacts, engravings, and suchlike)—are found in the Folger Shakespeare Library in Washington, the Edinburgh University Library, the Shakespeare Centre in Stratford, not to mention other major national and university libraries.

From beginning to end, his life was colorful as well as productive: his exclusion in the mid 1840s from the British Museum Library for purportedly stealing manuscripts from Trinity College, Cambridge (where he had been a student), caused a national uproar, as did his involvement toward the end of the century, along with Swinburne, in a controversy with F. J. Furnivall and his New Shakspere Society over the direction of literary studies. Very Victorian was Halliwell's long conflict with his father-in-law, the renowned collector Sir Thomas Phillipps, who was enraged and unforgiving because Halliwell had eloped with his daughter. The tragic death of his wife in 1879 and his split with Stratford not long after are moments of great poignancy.

With such widely diverse interests and activities, Halliwell's life affords a panoramic as well as a personal view of Victorian literary theory and practice, the founding and organization of scholarly societies, popular education, the book trade, and, not the least important, the domestic everyday of England in the nineteenth century.

Since a biography tells its own story, the biographer would apparently need only indicate the sources of his material. This biography is based on some 15,000 letters mainly to Halliwell which he bequeathed to Edinburgh University, some 1,500 from him which have found their way into the Folger Shakespeare Library, and, in the manner of a frame-tale, the four-volume manuscript diary–an almost unbroken daily record of the years 1836 to 1875–of his wife, Henrietta, also in the Edinburgh University Library. Complementing this massive material is a vast number of printed and manuscript documents in the form of letters, accounts, records, lists, scrapbooks, catalogues, and illustrations, not merely in Edinburgh and Washington but also at the stations of Halliwell's career in London, Cambridge, Oxford, and Stratford-upon-Avon. To these sources must be added Halliwell's more than six hundred printed books, editions, and articles.

This biography is essentially a documentary life. But reconstructing a life on the basis of the material at hand is admittedly precarious. For one thing, there are very few documents relating to Halliwell's early years. For another, there is the danger of relying on letters, of which Halliwell himself was aware when in 1876 he wrote to his friend Charles Roach Smith: "Letters are ... to some extent a test of character but are often *unfairly* used for that purpose, for you must recollect that the characters of many people are undergoing a continual kaleidoscope change and a letter of one year may convey a very *unjust* impression of future temperament." To this more or less psycho-philosophical view must be added the fact that the vast majority of the letters have no match, thus leaving much open in the construing of motive and context. Furthermore Mrs. Halliwell's diary is also one-sided in its lovingly protective representation of her husband. Not to be forgotten too is the fact that since the immense and dense corpus obliged me to spend most of my energy as pioneer–sifting, ordering, and preparing it for evaluation–a pervasive critical stance or distance was difficult to attain, much less maintain. The almost natural tendency of a biographer to look kindly upon his subject was, admittedly, unavoidable.

The marshalling of this material, a prime responsibility of the biographer, could only be accomplished with the help of others. It is my duty and pleasure to acknowledge them. My debts are so extensive that my listing of names must be understood as a gesture of deep gratitude to many–libraries, public institutions, societies, and individuals for many things. They are varied and far-flung, constituting a kind of map of Halliwellian activities and enterprises, as well as a log of my own attempts to chart the course of his life. Foremost are the great depositories of Halliwelliana, which generously put at my disposal masses of manuscripts, books, and other related material: the Edinburgh University Library, the Folger Shakespeare Library in Washington, the Trinity College Library in Cambridge, the Bodleian Library in Oxford, the British Library and the British Museum in London, the University College Library in London, and the Shakespeare Centre Library and Records Office of the Shakespeare Birthplace Trust in Stratford-upon-Avon. I am much indebted to them for permission to quote from their collections. Further support in answering queries, supplying photocopies, and the like came from the Ashmolean Museum in Oxford, the Birmingham Central Library, the Cambridge University Library, Chetham's Library in Manchester, the Guildhall Library in London, the Library of Jesus College Cambridge, the John Rylands University Library in Manchester, the Library of Lincoln's Inn, the National Library of Scotland, the Reading University Library, the Royal Military Academy, the Victoria and Albert Museum, and the Arthur and Janet Freeman Collection; in the United States the Beinecke Library of Yale University, the Boston Public Library, the Furness and University of Pennsylvania Libraries in Philadelphia, and the Tyrus G. Harmsen Collection in Pasadena. Additional noteworthy support came from the Athenaeum Indexing Project, the Cambridge Antiquarian Society, the Chatsworth Settlement Trust, the Grolier Club (New York), the Law Society, the Royal Historical Society, the Royal Society, the Society of Antiquaries, the Wellcome Trust, and the Public Record Office (Chancery Lane and Kew), as well as the Record Offices and Local Archives in Cambridgeshire, Cornwall, Cumbria, Dorset, East Sussex, Gloucestershire, Kent, Kingston upon Thames, Lambeth, Lancashire, Northamptonshire, Oxfordshire, Shropshire, Surrey, Sutton, Westminster, and Worcester.

For fellowships for longer stays at crucial locations I am grateful to

Peter Jones, Director of the Institute for Advanced Study in the Humanities of Edinburgh University; M. J. Crump, Director of the Centre for the Book of the British Library in London; John Sutherland, Head of the Department of English, University College London; and Werner Gundersheimer, Director of the Folger Shakespeare Library in Washington.

It would be idle of me to attempt to specify my obligation to all the individuals at these places who helped me. I thank one and all. Those I now name were of special assistance in making available their expertise generously and patiently: Jean Archibald in Edinburgh, Arthur and Janet Freeman in London, David McKitterick and E. F. Mills in Cambridge, Laetitia Yeandle in Washington, Robert Bearman and Mairi Macdonald in Stratford-upon-Avon. Among the host of friends and scholars who stood ready to help were those in London, Martin Davies, G. M. Furlong, Philip Harris, Hilton Kelliher, Christopher Michaelides, Bernard Nurse, Randolph Quirk, Nigel Ramsay, and Christopher Wright; in Edinburgh, Jo Drurie, Jean Jones, and Colin Munro; in Cambridge, Mark Nicholls, J. D. Pickles, Jonathan Smith, and F. W. Willmoth; in Oxford, Paul Morgan, T. D. Rogers, and Steven Tomlinson; in Stratford, Russell Jackson and Stanley Wells; in North America, Paul Bertram, G. Blakemore Evans, Donald Farren, Paul Korshin, E. Lorraine de Montluzin, Jacob M. Price, Robert Rockman, Alan Somerset, Edmund Spevack, and Georgianna Ziegler; in Münster, Bernhard Fabian, Peter Kollenbrandt, Marga Munkelt, and Silke Tandetzki. For details of the family I was fortunate to have the research of the great-great-grandson of Halliwell-Phillipps, Benjamin Bather, and the views of his great-grandchildren Désirée Hancock (née Muntz) and Lt.-Col. William Walcot Stewart. I am grateful to Jill Pamela Pringle, the great-granddaughter of Halliwell's sister, Louisa, for the letter of the thirteen-year-old Halliwell to his sister, and to S. C. M. Hawthorne, great-great-granddaughter of Halliwell's brother Thomas, for Halliwell's speech at the wedding of his daughter Henrietta Somerset.

Finally, I take special pleasure in thanking my colleague Horst Kruse for his valuable suggestions after an eagle-eyed reading of the whole manuscript. There are not words enough for my wife, Helga Spevack-Husmann, who was with me on every page of this work.

Marvin Spevack

Note

The present work depends very heavily on unpublished manuscript material and contemporary journals. For the convenience of the reader, references are normally given in the text directly following quotations. The sources most often used are:

LOA = Letters of Authors, followed by the date (if given), volume and letter number (Edinburgh University Library, Special Collections)
Folger = Folger Shakespeare Library (Washington, D.C.)
Phil-Rob = Phillipps-Robinson Collection (Bodleian Library Oxford)
EUL = Edinburgh University Library (Special Collections)
TCC = Trinity College Cambridge
UCL = University College London (Manuscripts & Rare Books)
BL = British Library (London)
SBT = Shakespeare Birthplace Trust (Stratford-upon-Avon)

In the treatment of letters no distinction is made between an original and a draft or copy. The identification of anonymous reviewers in the *Gentleman's Magazine* is taken largely from James M. Kuist, *The Nichols File of the Gentlemen's Magazine* (Madison, 1982), and of those in the *Athenaeum* from the files of the Athenaeum Indexing Project of the City University in London.

Since there is a paucity of works on Halliwell, there is no bibliography; those few of value that exist, mainly contemporary eulogies, are mentioned in the text (especially in the last chapter) or footnotes. Recommended complementary works are my *James Orchard Halliwell-Phillipps: A Classified Bibliography* (Hildesheim, 1997) and *A Victorian Chronicle: The Diary of Henrietta Halliwell-Phillipps* (Hildesheim, 1999).

Because this biography is essentially a narrative with a clearly defined chronological and thematic framework, the index lists (in the main) persons. Since they appear on almost every page, the names of Halliwell, his wife Henrietta, and Shakespeare, as well as their abbreviated forms (e.g. J., Jas., JOH, H., Mrs. H., S., Sh., Wm.) or affectionate forms (e.g. Jamie, Papa, Harriet, Mamma, Will, Billy), are not given. For the rest of the names, all variants are assigned to the regularized full forms. For certain minor figures—wedding guests, tradesmen, etc.–it has not always been possible to provide full names.

*Written into Halliwell's Commonplace Book
at Trinity College in 1836*

"I have lived to know that the great secret of human happiness is this—never suffer your energies to stagnate. The old adage of 'too many irons in the fire' conveys an abominable lie. You cannot have too many pokers, tongs, and all—keep them all going."

—Dr. E. D. Clarke

PART ONE

1820-1846

James Orchard Halliwell

Fig.1 A lithograph 'drawn from life' of Halliwell-Phillipps in his early
twenties. His publisher, John Russell Smith, had 100 printed on India
paper and in his catalogue of 1843 offered them for 2s 6d each.

· 1 ·

Beginnings: 1820-1840

The beginnings can be pieced together only sparingly. James Orchard Halliwell was born on 21 June 1820 at 94 Sloane Street, Chelsea, the sixth of seven children of Thomas Halliwell (1777-1849) of Chorley in Lancashire and his wife Charlotte Ann (1789-1849), daughter of Esau Marsh of Ealing, West London, and baptized on 4 July 1820 at St. Luke's in Chelsea. He was named for James Orchard, apparently a friend of the family and witness with Caroline White at the wedding of his parents on 20 June 1810 at St. Mary's in Ealing.[1] After the marriage the Halliwells returned to Chorley, where their eldest son, Richard, was born on 8 May 1812, and a daughter, Jane, born on 4 January 1814, was to die three days later. Thomas, Henry, Esau, and James Orchard were born in London in (respectively) 1815, 1817, 1819, and 1820–Henry dying in 1818 and Esau in 1819. A last child, Louisa Susanna, was born on 7 July 1822 in Sutton, Surrey, to which the family had recently moved. Once a linen draper from a rural background, Thomas Halliwell was enterprising and evidently prosperous in real estate dealings, with properties in London and elsewhere, both on his own and in association with his wife's father, Esau Marsh (after whom he apparently named his fourth son in 1819). It is not clear why Sutton was chosen, but Halliwell owned a house in the High Street and land there as well.[2]

1. Identifying James Orchard is difficult. Since there are quite a few with that name but little in the way of details beyond a date and place of birth or death, one can only speculate. Because there is no record of a James Orchard in Chorley or Sutton, a Londoner is likely. A James Orchard made a marriage allegation on 10 August 1810, shortly after the marriage of the Halliwells, in the parish of St. Dunstan in West London. There is a record of the burial of a James Orchard in St. George's, Holborn, in 1812. It is not certain that they are one and the same person, but the early death–nine years before the birth of Halliwell–might serve to explain the conspicuous fact that the name has not found in Halliwell's vast legacy of letters and documents.

2. Halliwell paid poor rates for a house worth £35 in the High Street in the early 1830s. From Mrs. Halliwell's diary entry for 4 July 1855, which records a visit to

There the young James spent his early years. All that exists of this formative time are two documents, both extremely revealing. The first is a letter of 20 August 1833 to "My Dear Louisa" from her "Affectionate Brother J. O. Halliwell." It is striking in its self-assurance and clarity, all the more so that it was written by thirteen-year-old to an eleven-year-old. In a firm and confident hand Halliwell devotes a page and a half to his experiences and needs at school and an equally long postscript on the same. A charming and disarming self-portrait, it must be quoted in full:

How do they all do at home, and all your friends. How does the General get on with his fishing, & has he caught the 7lb carp that he lost out of his landing net. If you write me an answer, don't ask me many questions as I dare say I shall not be able to answer them. Ask Thomas to send me Caesar. How do you get on with your gardens, mind and save the gourds carefully till I come home at Christmass [sic]. I hope you have saved the seed from Miss Butler's favorite flower the sunflower. How does your little room get on I suppose it is full of curiosities by this time. Perhaps we shall go to the Dyke on Michaelmas day, but it is very uncertain. Ask Papa to lend you the keys of my drawer in the store room, & in one of them you will find 'Blair's Lessons for every day in the Year,' take it & give it Papa to pack it up in the parcel that he is going to send to me. Lock the drawers & return the keys to Papa, & ask him to send me my instruments. Tell Papa I had to pay 5 shillings for the cricket ground, which every boy in the school pays & I hope he will send it me. Ask Papa to send me one of those interesting duodecimo books that he has on the top shelf of his bookcase. Tell Richard that Mr Butler is like him a noted Phrenologist, & that I have told him that his is one of the Members of the Council. P. S. We have none of that horrible suet pudding which is one comfort. Tell Mama that I shall be much obliged if she will send me another little box with lock & key, which I would rather have than a key to my desk. Ask my mother to send me two cakes & a large knife to cut them with, as I could not cut my last with my little one, plenty of apples & pears if they are ripe, some elder-flower or currant wine, with a glass, a bag to put my clothes in to bring home as Christmas, a small jar [of] Red currant jam, a quire of paper, plenty of pens & a Virgil with plenty of notes. I suppose that Thomas's wiskers have outstripped Mr Elliot's by this time. I want my instruments particularly, & some blotting Paper. Will you send me a

the house their friend Arthur Koch had taken in Sutton, "where James & his father & mother & family lived when he was a boy," it has been possible to identify the house as Haddon House.

collection of riddles, as the boys are very fond of them. I hope you will send plenty of letters to your

Affectionate Brother
J. O. Halliwell.

P. S. Tell my mother that instead of sending a bag she might send the box that she meant to have had made to take my clean clothes back in after the christmas holidays. How do you get on with your pigeons, & have you got any more. Papa was mistaken when he thought that there would be no boys with the same initials as I have, for there are two. Tell mama to send me plenty of apples, for there are a great many boys who will be very glad of them & likewise some pears. How is Mr Butler & Miss D°. I am in the second class in Latin, but I am in no class in the Mathematics, for the biggest boy has not yet done the 5th book of Euclid, & I am doing Conic Sections. Tell Mama that they did not put me back at all as she thought thy would, but only asked me questions on the preceeding rules to see whether I understood them. I like school a great deal better than I thought I should, as I don't much care about the eatables. A great many boys bring sugar like Thomas did. There is a boy whose mother used to live at Sutton, & another who knows Mr Veal very well. I intended to send you a double letter but I found I had not enough to say to fill it, though I began with it the first sunday I came. There was a grand cricket match the other day between Sussez [sic] & all England which we could see from our window by the assistance of a telescope. I have learnt to play at Cricket already, we have a match every Wednesday & Saturday afternoon, generally seniors against Juniors. I am one of the former. I get on very well with my French, & I am the 3rd in the 1st class. Our French Master is a funny old gentilhomme [crossed out] gentleman who talks hardly anything else but French. Tell Thomas if he wants to be edified he ought to come here every sunday evening to hear a sermon three hours & a half long, and part of the New Testament taking up another three & a half; making in all 7 hours, that is from 2 to 9 O'clock. I will write another letter on the first of September, to say what else I shall want.

The second document, viewing the early experience from another perspective, is an undated note by Halliwell attached to a letter of 16 August 1839 (LOA 1:18) from William Henry Butler of Brighton, thanking Halliwell for his "recollection of me" in sending him a copy of *Rara Mathematica*.

The Rev. W. H. Butler, at whose school at Brighton I was for about two years. This school was near the old church & at that time there was scarcely a house between his school & the Dyke. Mutton's eating-house was then nearly the extreme house to the West fronting the sea.

The note continues with further details and introduces another important figure in his life.

Previously to being at his [Butler's] school, I had no education to speak of, having been brought up under the care of old Charles Butler, who lived, when I was quite a child, at a small white cottage midway between Cheam & Sutton. C. B. was the author of some mathematical works. He had in his early days been at sea & had travelled a good bit about the world, I suspect in an inferior capacity. Instead of really teaching me anything the old fellow used to recount his early naval adventures. It was not his fault. He was too old to have had a pupil. A very good sort of old man who never gave me an unkind word.

It was surely more than the Dickensian atmospherics–the lonely seascape, the "very good sort of old man," the telling of tales–that moved Halliwell to want to collect and edit the papers of Butler; and it would be a mistake to underestimate his influence on the young boy. Despite Halliwell's avowal of not having been taught "anything" by Butler, he was doubtless affected by the "old man." Butler had been a mathematics teacher at Cheam School in Brighton: it can be no accident that the young Halliwell was a passionate mathematician. Charles Butler was to be the subject of one of Halliwell's earliest works, one of a series of eighteen brief biographies of "scientific men" which he wrote for the *Parthenon* in 1836-37. The sketch itself is revealing in a number of ways. It summarizes and evaluates Butler's contributions to mathematics, including him among such luminaries as Euclid and Pascal. It also displays some of the warmth of the relationship the admiring boy must have felt, the seventeen-year-old Halliwell concluding the sketch, "The latter part of his life was spent in quiet retirement at Sutton, and after a short illness he terminated an honourable and useful existence on the 23rd of January, 1836, beloved and regretted by his family, relations, friends, acquaintances, and neighbours." Less obvious, but nevertheless vital, was Halliwell's presentation of the outlines of Butler's life: it became a pattern of the lives to which he was attracted and with which he was to identify himself. His little preamble to the life of Charles Butler became his creed:

Surrounded by a multiplicity of teachers for every subject, with every means that can entice one to the pleasure of procuring knowledge, with every opportunity wherewith we can obtain that procurement, we forget the inconvenience that attended our ancestors in the progress of literature at the close of the last century. If, at that time, a boy had a peculiar genius for a particular study, in nine cases out of ten, there were no means for procuring him instruction in that branch, and frequently when there was no opportunity, some circumstance would prevent its availment; and so seldom is it that industry and talent are united in the same person, that few would struggle unassisted though in a study most congenial to their tastes. Often also their friends would not permit them, under a conviction that it would hinder them in a great measure from getting what many erroneously consider the only necessary for constituting happiness—money. But with all these disadvantages, with all these obstacles, which would at once discourage any ordinary person, a few have always been found to withstand every impediment, and even raise themselves high in their particular branches of learning—one of these few was the subject of this memoir (1:19 [4 March 1837], 299).

The elements of a reconstruction of that early time are present as well in the letter of the son of Charles Butler, William Henry Butler, whose Old Church Grammar School James attended before moving back to London about 1835. Butler's salutation—"My dear Friend"—to the then nineteen-year-old former pupil communicates something of the cordial relationship of man and boy and, as well, of the headmaster and the Halliwell family. "I am happy," he writes, "to find that your brother has attained the summit of his minds' [sic] late prospects wishing him much success in the prosecution of his new duties."[3] And he sends his thanks to Halliwell's "respected parents for their great attention to a part of our family."[4] Closing with "kind regards to you all," he does not forget to add Mrs. Butler's "best compliments" (16 August 1839; LOA 1:18).

The letter was sent to Halliwell at 35 Alfred Place, Bedford Square, London, to which the family had moved, the postal address of his brother Richard, the attorney. It was in London that Halliwell was able to pursue the concomitant to his passion for mathematics, book-collecting. "About the year 1836," he recalled some fifty years later in a letter to Justin Winsor, the librarian of the Harvard library, "when I first began hunting for old books at the various stalls in our famous London City, black-letter

3. The reference is most likely to James's brother Thomas, who was ordained priest in the diocese of Norwich in 1839.

4. The reference may be to his sister, Sarah Elizabeth, daughter of Charles Butler, who in 1840 married Thomas Stephens Davies, the mathematician, an intimate of the Halliwell family and friend of James.

ones and rare prints were 'plenty as blackberries,' and I have often found such things in unlikely places and amidst a mass of commonplace rubbish, exposed for sale in boxes labelled, '*These books and pamphlets, 6d. or 1s. each*,' outside an old bookseller's window, where another notice informed the passer-by that *Libraries were purchased or books bought*; and thus plainly showed how such, now, indeed, rarities came into the possession of an ignorant bibliophile!" (*Book-Lore*, 1 [Dec. 1884-May 1885], 85). It was in London that Halliwell began his career as author, signing himself in his contributions to the *Parthenon* "J. L." (i.e. using the first and last letters of his full name) of A. P. (i.e. Alfred Place). It was in London that Halliwell became the pupil of James William Worthington, who had been admitted as a ten-year man to Trinity College Cambridge in 1824, matriculated in 1833, and received a B.D. in 1834 and a D.D. in 1839. There is no direct evidence of how long Halliwell was his pupil or what he studied. But several of Worthington's activities will be seen to occur in Halliwell's life: his theological orientation–he was to become in 1838 the first vicar of Holy Trinity Church, Gray's Inn Road, which post he held until his death in 1879; his editorship of a periodical, the *Foreign Quarterly Review*; his connection with Sion College, of which he was president in 1859-60. And his Trinity College Cambridge background: for on 8 November 1836, so the record, James Orchard Halliwell, "son of Thomas Halliwell. Born in London, Pupil of Mr. Worthington. Age 16," was admitted pensioner of Trinity.

For the next four years, however, Halliwell was not fixed there, moving freely and often between London and Cambridge, London and Oxford–pausing in Alfred Place, the British Museum Library, Lambeth Palace, Sion College, the Public Record Office, Trinity College and Jesus College, the Cambridge Public Library, the Bodleian Library and the Ashmolean Museum. For at sixteen Halliwell was not so much launching his student days as pursuing his professional career.

+++

It may be said of James Orchard Halliwell in 1836, when he was sixteen, that he hit the ground running. Beginning in November 1836 he published a series of eighteen short biographical sketches of "scientific men": Isaac Newton, Roger Bacon, Edmund Stone, Edward Cocker, Robert Simson, René Descartes, Euclid of Alexandria, John Napier, Charles Butler, Johannes de Sacro-Bosco, Blaise Pascal, William Emerson, Bonaventura Cavalieri, Robert Recorde, Archimedes, John Wilkins (in two parts), John Flamsteed (in three parts), and Proclus. These were interspersed with brief articles, also of one or two pages each, on "scientific" topics: steam, the origin of steamboats, scientific controversies, the squaring of the circle, aerostation, the introduction and employment of steamboats upon the Thames, arithmetic, comets (in five parts), the first book printed in Aberdeen, the first book on surveying published in England, the commission of Henry VIII to take possession of Cardinal Wolsey's estate, Baker's Chronicle, the introduction of Arabic numerals in England. In addition he wrote nine letters to the editor in reply to various correspondents. By the time he concluded these contributions to the *Parthenon: A Weekly Journal of English and Foreign Literature, the Arts, and Sciences,* on 17 June 1837,[5] Halliwell was but three days short of his seventeenth birthday.

He signed himself "J. L."–perhaps to disguise his age, perhaps just a playful use of the first and last letters of his name. Whatever the case–and the alternatives will recur–there was no disguising of his engagement, nor was there frivolousness in his intention. His scholarly disposition was only too evident: an indivisibility of industry and ambition, determination and passion, mind and ego. Precociousness to the point of arrogance–the sweep of topics and the clangour of confidence–is undeniable. Still, it is equally undeniable that the boy Halliwell was totally devoted to scholarship: to history, to science, to literature, above all to books. Telling are his exchanges of letters to the editor of the *Parthenon* with one Jacques Cagzini. Halliwell's imperious rejection–"Mr. Gagzini [*sic*] is egregiously mistaken if he thinks that he has advanced any novelty in supposing Euclid and Eudoxus to be the same person"–is accompanied by his showy summoning up of learned evidence from a Latin work by Saville (1621), Gregory's edition of Euclid (1703), and a long passage from a "very correct Latin translation" of Euclid's *Elements* (albeit "the original Greek being very defective") by Barocius "published at Patavia, in folio 155, and 1569" (11 February 1837, p. 255). Halliwell's pen could be wicked as well. "The controversy between me and Mr. Cagzini, was, to all appearance, quite ended some time ago," he wrote a month later, "by Mr. C. confessing himself to be wrong; but Mr. C. now takes up the cudgels with fresh confidence in his own insignificant powers" (18 March 1837, p. 333). But there is no mistaking his idealism, however passionately haughty. Responding in a letter of 6 May 1837 (p. 30) to a letter (29 April

5. A handy index is provided by Douglas Wertheimer, "J. O. Halliwell's Contributions to 'The Parthenon'–1836-37," *Victorian Periodicals Newsletter,* 8 (1975), 3-6. It builds on the handwritten index apparently by Ernest E. Baker, Halliwell's nephew and executor, in the copy in the Natural History Museum (London).

1837, p. 16) from "F.D." addressed to all readers, Halliwell staunchly held that the "advantage of pursuing knowledge for its own sake, is evidently superior to the meanness of pursuing it for the useful, or to the casting it on one side because it does not yield so many bodily advantages as trade. The watch-word of 'the useful' in its obvious acceptation—without reference to the virtuous, the grand, the beautiful, in sentiment, in action, in the works of nature, and in those of art," Halliwell was certain, "if once received among the conventions of society, or the principles of science, would debase and uncivilize our species" (6 May 1837, p. 30).

Self-assurance is evident in his next publications in 1837, starting while he was a pensioner at sixteen of Trinity College Cambridge (he matriculated a year later on 13 November 1837). Three rather more substantial articles in the *Magazine of Popular Science, and Journal of the Useful Arts* are nothing less than a sketch of English scientific literature prior to and following the invention of printing to the end of the sixteenth century.[6] Although modestly admitting that "It must not be supposed that I have attempted to give a history of English science" (4 [1837], 103), he is confident enough not merely to describe some "unpublished scientific manuscripts ... in various libraries in Great Britain ... which have fallen under [his] own observation [as well as the] published works therein omitted" (p. 99) but also to make strong critical assertions. Robert Recorde's *Whetstone of Witte* (1557), he is certain, is "not only the first work on Algebra in the English language, but the first of its kind published in England" (p. 102). "The progress of science in this country," he wrote in the earlier installment, "has hitherto almost entirely escaped the pen of mathematical historians, both English and foreign" (3 [1837], 440), confidently concluding that "our Continental neighbours being, in most cases, unable to obtain inspection of the original works, have often misrepresented their merits" (p. 440).

It is obvious, of course, that Halliwell was trained in mathematics. Before he entered Trinity College he had been tutored by Charles Butler, one-time mathematics instructor at Cheam School. While at William Henry Butler's school in Brighton, he was not only preparing articles for the *Parthenon* and the *Magazine of Popular Science*, but was also visiting libraries and nurturing his appetite for early manuscripts and printed works, increasingly his main fare, if not sole occupation. In 1837-38 he

---

6. "A Brief Sketch of English Scientific Literature, from the Invention of Printing to the End of the Sixteenth Century," 3 (1837), 440-5; continued 4 (1837), 99-104. "A Brief Sketch of English Scientific Literature, Prior to the Invention of Printing," 4 (1837), 272-6.

produced a manuscript (BL Add. MS. 14061) entitled "Collections on the history of the Mathematics. Principally from Books and Manuscripts in the British Museum," a handwritten work of 142 leaves, written on both sides, in which he transcribed bibliographical and other information, added synopses, biographies, annotations, and comments and closed with an index of names. References to other collections, such as those in Lambeth Palace and Sion College, make clear that Halliwell was a much-travelled and prodigious young scholar.[7] In fact, the date of the work indicates that he must have had special permission to work in the library of the British Museum, for eighteen was the customary minimum age for admission. An entry in the commonplace book he kept while at Trinity (O.10a.24) reflects his pride: "In the spring of 1837 I obtained admission into the library of Sion-College and was a regular attendant there for several months until I got a ticket for the reading-room of the Museum-library which very far exceeds the former both in the quantity and quantity [*sic*] of its volumes" (48'). Another entry, dated 4 August 1837, reads: "Got admission into the Reading-Room of the British Museum a year before the proper period." Impressively, it was none other than Sir Frederic Madden himself, Keeper of the Department of Manuscripts, who was his referee.

At Trinity College his tutor was the eminent mathematician George Peacock, in 1836 treasurer of the Cambridge Philosophical Society. Halliwell could have hardly escaped contact with the secretary, William Whewell, tutor till 1838 and from 1841 Master of Trinity. Both men were interested in the history and philosophy of science. Peacock had a fine library of incunabula and early books on mathematics. Among Whewell's major works at the time were his *History of the Inductive Sciences* (1837) and *The Philosophy of the Inductive Sciences* (1840). Although characterized as "one of the most arrogant men of science" by the mathematician Robert Leslie Ellis, another of Halliwell's contemporaries and friends at Trinity, he exchanged letters with the young student on a subject of common interest, the tides, commenting, "Your collection ['of excerpts respecting the tides'] extended in the way I have mentioned would be an interesting portion of scientific history" (31 March 1839; LOA 6:5). John Hind, the renowned mathematician, gave Halliwell private lessons. Beyond Cambridge Halliwell had developed a close relationship with Thomas Stephens Davies, professor of mathematics at the Royal Military Academy, Woolwich, whom he visited frequently while a student. He had

---

7. Halliwell also produced a somewhat similar manuscript, now also in the British Library, on the Bodleian Library collection (BL, Add. MS. 10462).

started a correspondence with Baden Powell, Savilian professor of geometry, and Stephen Peter Rigaud, Radcliffe Observer and Savilian professor of astronomy, both of Oxford, and Augustus De Morgan of University College London. Most important, perhaps, was Halliwell's friendship with Thomas Wright, ten years his senior, which continued till Wright's death in 1877. Wright was an antiquary, an editor of early texts, and an energetic organizer. Although he was not a mathematician or scientist, he was, as antiquary, interested in philology, history and archaeological research. He was a man of the library and the society, so to speak. And it is there that the two men found a common and fertile ground. And it is there that the mathematician Halliwell gradually but surely moved. Whether in mathematics or literature, Halliwell's first and lasting commitment was to archaeology—that is, the discovery, the classification, and dissemination of the documents of historical evolution. Libraries, record offices, bookshops, churches, and attics were from the beginning his "digs." And publication was his mission.

Not surprisingly, Halliwell's infatuation with learning comprised an addiction to the acquisition of those documents and inevitably to the exquisite art and (as the case may be) artifice of buying and selling. "On Thursday, June 25th, 1840, and following Day, at One o'Clock, precisely," S. Leigh Sotheby announced the sale by auction of a "Selected Portion of the Scientific, Historical, and Miscellaneous Library of James Orchard Halliwell, Esq. F.R.S. F.S.A. and *English Correspondent of the French Historical Committee of Sciences*": 624 lots; for Saturday "A Collection of Scientific and Historical Manuscripts": 162 lots. And thereby hang a number of interrelated tales recapitulating, highlighting, and foreshadowing the career of the then just-turned-twenty collector. For Halliwell's library was—and continued to be—the man.

Halliwell began his collecting as a schoolboy. "As early as 1835," he reflected in 1845, "I was in the habit of purchasing MSS generally of a scientific character and relating chiefly to Mathematics, Geometry, Physics, Astrology, &c." (Case, f.50[8]). Not surprisingly, this passion is reflected in his contributions to the *Parthenon* and the *Magazine of Popular Science* in 1836 and 1837. They are based almost entirely on works he himself owned. Of the eighteen short biographies he wrote for the *Parthenon*, all but two can be traced to the items in Sotheby's sale—and those two, of Charles Butler and Pascal, may be safely assumed to have

---

8. "Case" refers to the legal documentation of the British Museum affair discussed on pp. 124-43. It is found in the library of Trinity College Cambridge: TCC Muniments Box 29. See also n. 71.

been within his ken: Butler had been Halliwell's tutor, whose papers Butler's daughter, Catherine, mentions (9 July 1838; LOA 2:7) he considered collecting; Pascal was ever his standard.

Halliwell's first separate publications, in 1838, follow a similar pattern. *A Brief Account of the Life, Writings, and Inventions of Sir Samuel Morland, Master of Mechanics to Charles the Second*, dated Trinity College Cambridge, February 1838, derives from his own copy of the *Tuba Stentoro-Phonica* (No. 604), as well as (if indirectly) numerous works on mechanics, inventions, and discoveries in his collection. It was for all intents and purposes his maiden work, and it is worth mentioning that it was produced with characteristic engagement and passion. Long stretches of it are found in his journal-like manuscript "Collections on the history of the Mathematics," which he compiled as a teenager in the British Museum Library, and also in his Trinity College commonplace book, also in 1837-8. In the latter he recorded the details and excitement of the process of publication. On 3 February 1838: "Finished my life of Sir Samuel Morland and sent it to the Printers: this is the first printing (Except my advertisement of Pappus) order that I have yet given: may it be successful!" (43ʳ). On 10 February he received the proof copy (52ᵛ). On 12 February: "Took my proof sheet of Sir Samuel Morland back & wrote an Appendix. I am promised it again on Wednesday morning. Young [most likely, his fellow student at Trinity, James Gavin Young, who also matriculated Michaelmas 1837] says–'Don't you wish you may get it.' I do indeed!" (99ᵛ). And finally on 1 March 1838: "Received my life of Sir Samuel Morland all finished–300 copies 150 in sheets. Published today by Johnson in Trinity Street" (99ᵛ). Halliwell's inclusion of a transcription and brief discussion of *A Treatise on the Numeration of Algorism, from a MS. of the 14th Century*, "which was found loose in an ancient manuscript on Astronomy in my possession, and is curious inasmuch as it is the most ancient piece on arithmetic in the English language that has hitherto fallen under my observation" (p. 21-2)–No. 147 of the second day sale–is inserted, not without a certain touch of self-indulgence, "not that it has any reference to the subject of our memoir, but because it appeared to be a seasonable opportunity for rescuing a curious piece of antiquity from destruction" (Advertisement, p. 3). And in addition to the learned references to manuscript collections and scientific and historical works–such as John Evelyn's *Numismata* (1697), James Welwood's *Memoirs of the Most Material Transactions in England* (1700), and Thomas Birch's *Life of Thurloe* (1742)–the work concludes with an appendix (pp. 27-31) containing a "short abstract" of the more important of John Pell's manuscripts in the Birch Collection in the British Museum. Halliwell's second separate publication in 1838, a transcription of Johannes de Sacro-Bosco's *De Arte Numerandi*, is of an original he purchased "at the sale of the Library of the Abbate Canonici of Venice" (v; second day sale No. 128). Although it is a simple reprint without so much as an introduction, thirteen footnotes attest to Halliwell's acquaintance with collateral Latin texts in books and manuscripts in various collections. Interesting too is Halliwell's handwritten correction of the title page's "nunc primum editit ex antiquo manuscripto": he inserted a slip reading "This is not 'now first published'. An edition without the author's name appeared about 1490. 4o. See B.M. catalogue under *Ars*."

If the years 1836 to 1838 are characteristic of the boyish precociousness of Halliwell, 1839 marks a transition to a mature professional career. That year he produced twenty-two publications, among them eight separate works and four articles in the prestigious *London and Edinburgh Philosophical Magazine and Journal of Science*, was elected Fellow of the Society of Antiquaries on 14 February (and admitted on 23 April) and of the Royal Society on 30 May. Indeed, his *Letter to the Right Honourable Lord Francis Egerton*, dated 10 August, proclaimed him (so the title page) "Fellow of the Royal Society; Fellow of the Society of Antiquaries; Member of the Royal Society of Literature; Fellow of the Royal Astronomical Society; Honorary Fellow of the Royal Society of Northern Antiquaries at Copenhagen; Honorary Secretary of the Cambridge Antiquarian Society; Scholar of Jesus College, Cambridge, &c. &c. &c."

Halliwell's publications in 1839 follow the same basic pattern: on the whole, descriptive rather than analytical, drawing heavily on works in his collection and so interrelated as to make multiple use and even repetition features of his professional manner. *Two Essays*, whose advertisement is dated 12 February 1839, makes no secret of the fact that the essays "will form an Appendix to the *Rara Mathematica*. They are printed in this form in order that they may be immediately and more easily accessible to any one interested in those portions of scientific history on which they treat." Not only that, but the second essay, "Notes on Early Almanacs"–on the title page as "Notes on Early Calendars"–was reprinted from the 1839 issue (pp. 52-7) of the *Companion to the British Almanac*. The first essay is "A Few Observations on the Numerical Contractions Found in Some Manuscripts of the Treatise on Geometry by Boetius"–on the title page solemnly as "An Inquiry into the Nature of the Numerical Contractions, Found in a Passage on the Abacus, in Some Manuscripts of the Geometry of Anicius Manlius Torquatus Severinus Boetius." Both are characteristically brief–the first of six pages, the second eight. Both are similar in being "observations" or "notes": along with "account" and "remarks" and preceded by "few" or "some," Halliwell's favourite designations. Both fulfill Halliwell's avowed procedure of presenting compilations from "notes collected at various times, and without any intention of placing a dissertation before the public" (p. 10). In both, Halliwell records his examination of various manuscripts and printed books found in his favourite haunts–the British Museum in London, the Bodleian and Ashmolean in Oxford, and in Cambridge the Trinity College and Public (i.e. University) Libraries, among others–describing ("The Metz MS. in the Arundel collection ... is probably an abridgment of one or more extensive treatises on the subject: the author ... quotes Boetius" [p. 7]); correcting ("M. Chasles has confused the sipos and celentis, the latter of which was seldom used as a cipher" [p. 6]); commenting ("The extracts from this calendar are wretchedly transcribed, and evidently by one who was totally unacquainted with MSS." [p. 15]); and parading "remarks" which have not "found a place in prior publications" (p. 5). Common too is Halliwell's avoidance, at this stage of his career, of making large critical claims–this despite his otherwise almost imperious confidence in what he has seen and judged. He is careful to employ the ameliorative "may" when it comes to conclusions. "It would be impossible, with the few materials yet brought to light, to conjecture with any great probability how far these Boetian contractions may have influenced the introduction, or co-operated with the Arabic system to the formation, of our present numerical notation" (p. 9). Equally characteristic, however, is Halliwell's persistent return to these subjects.

A few weeks later the two essays did indeed form the appendix of Halliwell's next work, *Rara Mathematica*, whose dedication is dated Jesus College, Cambridge, 1 March 1839. Although he refers to it as his "first public effort in literature" (iii), it includes as well two other works already published: paginal reprints of *De Arte Numerandi* and *A Treatise on the Numeration of Algorism, from a MS. of the 14th Century.*[9] As has been pointed out, both were from his own library, as was also a third, Johannes Robyns *de Cometis*. The subtitle of *Rara* is revealing: *A Collection of Treatises on the Mathematics and Subjects Connected with Them, from Ancient Inedited Manuscripts.* Indeed, the slim volume of 120 pages consists of transcriptions of thirteen tracts to be found in Halliwell's favourite libraries (as well as his own) with simple indications ("notes") in a sentence or two, only an occasional

9. And, of course, he had already published his life of Morland, which he designated on 3 February 1838 as the "first printing (Except my advertisement of Pappus [LOA 11:14]) order that I have yet given" (Commonplace book, 43ʳ).

footnote, and a short list of corrections (mainly of misprints in the Latin originals) and remarks (a mention of an "eminent classical scholar" or an acknowledgment of previous work on the subject). Halliwell's circumspection, apparent as well in his "hope of being able to fill up a chasm in history, being convinced that he has left the meritorious labours of later writers–Anderson, Fermat, Simson, and Playfair–in better and more able hands" (iv), is matched (as before) by the ambition evident in his decision not "to enter very fully into the history of the several treatises ... because it will be done at large in my history of early English Mathematics, now in the course of rapid preparation for the press" (v).

A third feature of what might be termed the Halliwell enterprise is his inscribing the work to his "best and most valued friend" Thomas Stephens Davies (1795-1851), the "best geometrician in England." It is difficult at this point to assess accurately the designation "valued": is it a personal or a professional judgment? In 1839 it was doubtless both. But an advantageous association with an eminent mathematician, one who gave his name to a new system of spherical geometry, cannot be ruled out, of course. Nor can the presentation of a copy with the "Editors [sic] best compliments" (BL: G.16648) to the Right Hon. Thomas Grenville (1755-1846), who on his death was to leave his magnificent collection of some 20,000 works valued at about £50,000 to the British Museum. In any event, the mention of two important personalities of the time is a sign of the widening circle of Halliwell's professional contacts and activities.

Another feature of the Halliwell enterprise is his keen competitiveness and, inevitably, his fearless (if not at times reckless) engagement in controversy. "I am not surprised," he writes in the dedicatory letter, "at the question [relative to the existence of the materials for writing a history of the early progress of science in Wales] when I take into consideration, that a man–or rather a boy–who arrogates to himself the title of the Welch mathematical representative of England,[10] once said in the dining-hall of my own College, when a dispute about Demoivre's theorem had arisen, that 'he thought Demoivre [unaware that he had died in 1754] a very clever man, having some praiseworthy articles on the expansion of series in the Philosophical Magazine!'" (iii-iv).

A further feature of the Halliwell enterprise, apparent again in *Rara Mathematica* and to continue later, concerns the matter of publication.

10. It is well-nigh impossible to identify this "boy": Two Welshmen who were contemporaries of Halliwell's at Trinity were Evan Lewis Davies, who migrated from St. John's on 17 October 1836, and Mesac Thomas, who migrated from St. John's on 31 January 1837. Neither seems to have had noteworthy distinctions, however.

Halliwell's economical use or recycling of his material is to be seen in the "Note" following p. 120 in which the reader is informed that the "foregoing volume was published at three several times: the first part (pp. 1-18) appeared on the 1st of June, 1838; the second (pp. 49-96) on the 1st of October, 1838; and the remainder on the 1st of June, 1839."[11] "By the same author," following p. 120, omits mention of Halliwell's *De Arte Numerandi* (1838), although listing *Two Essays* (1839), despite the fact that the contents of both works are included in *Rara*. And Halliwell is already listed as the author of *The Travels of Sir John Maundeville*, although it most likely appeared only in the previous month. Earlier publications are also clouded by apparent contradictions. In *Two Essays* there is a discrepancy between the wording of the title page and the actual titles of the essays: between the announcement "by the same author" of a "History of Jesus College, Cambridge," a work which did not appear until 1841 and then in Latin; between "In the Press" of a "History of the Mathematical Sciences in England and Wales, to the End of the 16th Century," a work which never seems to have appeared; and between "Preparing for the Press" of "An Account of Some Early Observations on the Tides" and "The Claims of the Rivals of the Invention of Logarithms Carefully Examined," both of which are not extant. Halliwell's supposedly earliest separate work on Samuel Morland in 1838 exists in a version printed by E. Johnson of Trinity Street, Cambridge, and Whitaker & Co., London, but in his presentation copy to the British Museum Halliwell wrote in his name, crossed out the publishers, and inserted "This tract was never published," although it was assuredly not a simple private printing.

There are different explanations for these puzzles, to be sure. Whatever the individual answers, and whatever the exact motivation of the publishers, it is fairly clear that they are connected with the dynamism—the drive, the restlessness, the ambition—of the young Halliwell. If the parade of honours which adorns the title page of the *Letter to Lord Egerton* (see p. 14) seems an inflation of a convention, even more so perhaps the concluding string of etceteras, it must also be acknowledged that Halliwell actually did belong and that he did contribute to these institutions, as well as promise to do so. It must also be apparent that a final feature of the Halliwell enterprise is the coexistence of ambition and modesty, of personal thrust and business acumen, which underlies serious and total devotion. In his commonplace book entry for

11. The work seems to have appeared in parts, the first up to the opening page of Chapter II; the second, through the third page of Chapter XIII; the rest through the Appendix.

27 October Halliwell outlines a prospectus for what he then called "Anecdota Mathematica," to "be published in parts at 3 shillings each":

The Editor neither expects or wishes to receive any pecuniary reward for his trouble but [crossed out: "to protect himself] at the same time not being willing to encounter any serious loss in the publication he will not send it to the press untill 150 subscribers' names are obtained.
One number or more may be subscribed for but to avoid the unnecessary trouble often occasioned at the delivery of such publications every subscriber will be reqd to pay the full price when he puts down his name. No copies will be permitted to be sold and therefore none but subscribers will be able to obtain it (65`).

Whatever his mind-set, Halliwell's titles and publications, furthermore, testify to the expansion of his scholarly horizon. And it becomes growingly apparent as well that while mathematics was still central in the circle of the history of science, that circle, as the titles of his works indicate, was expanding to interrelate science, history, language, bibliography, book collecting, and publishing: all founded in and promoted by archaeological research and discovery. The widening circle is apparent in the remaining publications in 1839. Of the four articles in the *London and Edinburgh Philosophical Magazine*, three deal with Halliwell's favourite themes in the history of science: comets in April (14:260-1), Pappus in July (15:85-6), and Boethius in December (15:447-9). The fourth, in October (15:284-5), on notices of America by Middle-age [i.e. medieval] writers, testifies to Halliwell's larger interest in learning, in history and geography. Indeed, the extract is from Halliwell's edition of The *Voiage and Travaile of Sir John Maundeville* (essentially a reprint of the 1725 edition with an introduction, a description of nineteen manuscripts, additional notes, a glossary, and illustrations by F. W. Fairholt), which appeared earlier in the year. Halliwell's attraction to the Middle Ages, and early literature in general, is further illustrated in his edition for the Camden Society of John Warkworth's *Chronicle of the First Thirteen Years of the Reign of King Edward the Fourth* (the introduction is dated 18 September 1839). His commitment to scholarship may be seen in the fact that the work is not a simple transcription in the manner of his earlier efforts but a full-fledged edition with an introduction of nineteen pages and fifty pages of notes and index to a text in fifteenth-century Latin of twenty-seven pages.
　　The circle could be overstretched, given Halliwell's energy and zeal. If works were announced as published before their actual appearance–be it

to attract subscribers, to protect topics, to bolster the ego, or whatever–there were also those which were envisioned or promised but which never appeared or were much delayed. A collaboration with C. H. Hartshorne called "Early Metrical Tales" seems never to have appeared, although Halliwell wrote that "in a month I shall have finished the transcripts." Nor did a new edition of *Hudibras*, which he mentioned in the same letter of 11 October 1839.[12] To the ghosts announced as "in the press" in *Two Essays*, Halliwell also "hope[d] shortly to be able to put in a form fit for publication some researches on the Leopoldine Numerical Contractions, which form a system of numeration that has hitherto entirely escaped the researches of every writer on the history of arithmetic. Thus within the space of four months will a completely new face be laid on the history of the Hindoo arithmetic in Europe during the middle ages."[13] These high promises were not empty, however. Halliwell had outlined the history of scientific literature in England in three earlier articles in the *Magazine of Popular Science*. He did send a manuscript on the tides to William Whewell, which drew an encouraging reply on 31 March 1839 (LOA 6:5). A paper of his, "An Inquiry into the Probable Origin of the Baden Numerical Contractions, and How Far They May Have Influenced the Introduction of Hindoo Arithmetical Notation into Western Europe," was read to the Royal Society of Literature on 13 June 1838 (but published in the Transactions in 1843). And if he did promise, but not produce, a catalogue of the oriental manuscripts in the library of the Royal Society, he did complete one of its miscellaneous manuscripts.[14]

Unpublished works need not be without importance, however. Two of Halliwell's most significant works of the early period were unpublished. The first has already been mentioned. The handwritten "Collections on

12. Hartshorne Papers, Northamptonshire Record Office, X7226, Album D, No. 87.

13. "On the Connexion between the Boetian and the Middle-Arabic Numerical Forms," *The London and Edinburgh Philosophical Magazine and Journal of Science*, 15 (1839), 449.

14. In a letter to Lubbock of 1 June 1840 (?) (Royal Society, LUB.H30) Halliwell reported that he had finished the arrangement of the oriental manuscripts, but on 11 October 1843 he wrote Lubbock (Royal Society, MC.3.304) that he regretted he was unable to make the catalogue. Later Halliwell added a revealing comment to the letter in which the Royal Society thanked him for his "obliging offer" (17 October 1839; LOA 3:22): "I had only just begun to study Oriental literature, & knew really nothing about it, although I fancied I did; & what little I did know has been long forgotten. Nothing but the vanity of youth will account for the temerity of my making an offer requiring real scholarship."

the history of the Mathematics. Principally from Books and Manuscripts in the British Museum" (BL Add. MS. 14061) is not simply a list of titles with some bibliographical commentary but a rambling record of his early interests and movements: citations and personal evaluations of works in various libraries, transcriptions of source works, quotations from works used in discussions of source works. In short, the collection provides a good picture of the young Halliwell's activities and directions. In fact, Halliwell's actual earliest separate work, his life of Samuel Morland, was assembled verbatim from the notes in one place or another in the collection. The second work of 1839–lacking a title page but one copy at least bearing Halliwell's handwritten "not published," apparently Halliwell's designation for a private printing–is *A Catalogue of Scientific Manuscripts in the Possession of J. O. Halliwell, Esq.*–just eight pages listing 136 works, perhaps the most important professional and personal document of Halliwell's early career. From these titles may be seen the sources of Halliwell's early publications–works by Johannes de Sacro-Bosco and Alexandre Villa Dei, for example–as well as authors dealt with in his early articles, such as John Flamsteed, Charles Hutton, John Blagrave. From the titles may also be seen the scope of Halliwell's interest in mathematics and science: e.g. Cavalieri's *Nuova Prattica Astrologia,* Cocker's *Arithmetick,* Barlowe's *Magnetical Advertisements,* Recorde's *Whetstone of Witte,* Dee's *Euclid,* Cyprian Lucar's *A Treatise Named Lucarsolace.* And from these titles may be construed Halliwell's intense engagement as collector, the profession which spanned his lifetime and the one which was the mortar for all his individual pursuits. It made him–and almost undid him, as shall be seen.

There were other activities too. On 6 April 1838 Halliwell migrated from Trinity, where he is said to have even catalogued several of its manuscripts, to Jesus College, where he was a Foundation Scholar and library clerk (an office that Coleridge had held some forty-five years earlier) and is also said to have catalogued manuscripts.[15] And there were the various societies so proudly listed in his *Letter to Lord Egerton* or simply paraded under the numerous etceteras which followed the "Esq." of his name on various title pages. Though they were not all based in Cambridge–most were in London and numerous in the

15. There is no evidence, however, for this assertion to be found in either library. All that seems to exist is a remark to that effect by Charles Warren, librarian of Trinity College in 1838, but since Warren admittedly did not know exactly what Halliwell was doing (see p. 131), the reference most likely applies to Halliwell's work on his *Manuscript Rarities of the University of Cambridge*, which included brief descriptions of selected items in the various college libraries.

provinces–Halliwell was by no means a passive member. His role in these societies requires separate treatment, for it is large and varied and says much about his personal and professional instincts and accomplishments. For the moment it is sufficient to point out that he began early in his career to publish under the aegis of the recently formed Camden Society, whose objectives seemed to match Halliwell's predisposition. Founded in 1838, the society aimed "to perpetuate, and render accessible, whatever is valuable, but at present little known, amongst the materials for the civil, ecclesiastical, or literary history of the United Kingdom." Moreover, it was less a learned society than a book-publishing club, whose members (limited to 1200) were able for an annual fee of one guinea to subscribe to a host of what were in the main edited print facsimiles on a wide range of topics drawn from early English sources.

Expanding his base of historical documentation to include more than the history of science, Halliwell edited for the Camden Society Warkworth's *Chronicle*. True to form, he chose a manuscript from his immediate environment, from the library of St. Peter's College, Cambridge, applied his customary description of manuscript and historical documents in the introduction, as well as "unpublished evidences I have collected relative to the transaction," corrected errors by such authorities as John Lingard and Sharon Turner, added a host of learned notes which included excerpts in early English and Latin from various and often "curious" tracts, and supplied a detailed index of names and places. The edition of 1839 gave him the opportunity to thank–and thus show his acquaintance with–the Master of St. Peter's, the Reverend William Hodgson (who was also Vice-Chancellor of the University), George Young (York Herald), and John Gough Nichols (founder of the Camden Society and editor of the *Gentleman's Magazine*). It also brought him into close personal and professional contact with important members of the Council of the Camden Society, such as John Payne Collier, Alexander Dyce, Henry Ellis, Joseph Hunter, among others, as well as strengthening his ties with Thomas Wright and T. Crofton Croker (who helped found the Camden Society, the Percy Society in 1840, and the British Archaeological Association in 1843, all important stations in Halliwell's career).

Halliwell's presence in the Society also, and not untypically, produced sharp conflict. His two remaining separate publications in mid 1839 amused some but stirred and even offended many of the figures of the establishment. One, from the scholar of Jesus College, aged nineteen, was entitled *A Few Hints to Novices in Manuscript Literature*, a patronizing title to many, not at all mollified by the fact that the phrasing was not at all unfamiliar in titles of short introductory works nor by Halliwell's avowal that "these elementary memoranda were unwillingly published" (p. 3). The "little pamphlet" itself is simple and straightforward, more helpful perhaps than harmful. One page explains that "this scrap of information" is not addressed to the antiquary but rather to "one whose studies are of a more modern nature, and yet occasionally wanting access to materials constructed previously to the invention of typography" (p. 5). The remaining six pages consist of a list of printed catalogues of manuscripts In England (pp. 6-9), a short list of initial abbreviations, with common ones for the letter A as illustrations (p. 10), and on abbreviations in general (pp. 10-12). Apart from the implications of the title, a few uncomplimentary but not necessarily incorrect assessments–e.g. of Samuel Ayscough's catalogue of the additional manuscripts in the British Museum and Henry John Todd's of the Archiepiscopal manuscripts in the library of Lambeth Palace[16]–and perhaps a certain haughty reference to the "uninitiated," Halliwell would seem no more "guilty" than one who produces a primer or textbook. William Jerdan was so delighted with it that instead of reviewing it he printed it *in toto* in the *Literary Gazette* (27 July 1839, pp. 476-7). But it was despised by some of Halliwell's "friends," among them Madden, Hunter, and Sir Thomas Phillipps. The ramifications of Halliwell's apparent presumption were to be considerable.

They were exacerbated by his publication of the open letter to Lord Egerton, president of the Camden Society, with a bloated string of six lines of memberships in various societies on the title page. It is dated 10 August 1839 (with a postscript dated one day later) from the Bodleian Library, Oxford. After an extensive presentation of his "most honest and best of motives," and an even more elaborate delineation of his awareness of the dangerous path he is treading–"I do for the time run the risk of creating myself powerful literary enemies among those leading members of the Camden Society who differ from me" (p. 4)–he proceeds to pronounce his dissatisfaction with the last publication of the Society, W. J. Thoms's *Anecdotes and Traditions*, which he feels "violates the very first law of the Camden Society" because the "greater portion" of it belongs to the latter half of the seventeenth century and cannot be "considered in any way as early." As if this were not enough, Halliwell goes on–wickedly lamenting in a gratuitous footnote b (p. 8), "I cannot help remarking here,

16. On Ayscough: "This is an absurd attempt at a classed catalogue, and without exception is the very worst failure at a classification that has ever come within the notice of the learned world" (p. 8). On Todd: "This is generally considered to be a good catalogue, but not, I think, by any one who has had occasion to examine many of the MSS. It is full of imperfections and errors" (p. 9).

that I think a succession of puns and jokes, however splendid and imposing, rather unsuited to a work with the head of the venerable Camden on the title page as its tutelar saint. Poor Camden! how melancholy would have been the prospect, could he have foreseen that the unfortunate name of his valuable book would have afforded a handle for the facetious to make vulgar in the court of Momus his venerated manes!" Purporting throughout to reflect the "expressed opinion of many of those Members who were most instrumental in its [the Society's] formation," he suggests that "we ought not to print any work that would cover its expenses in the common way of publication." And climactically: "This is the grand ultimate point of the question,–whether the Society ... would advance its true interests by flattering the popular taste for fun" (pp. 8-9).

Whether his own idea or whether he was being used by others, Halliwell was taking on a hornet's nest. Thoms was secretary of the Society. Kemp's *Nine Daies Wonder*, proposed for publication and "desirable" (so Halliwell in footnote c, p. 9) to be transferred to the pages of the *Mirror*, was edited in 1840 by no less an eminence than Alexander Dyce. As for "early" literature, in 1843 Henry Ellis produced *Original Letters of Eminent Literary Men of the Sixteenth, Seventeenth, and Eighteenth Centuries*, and Joseph Hunter, *The Diary of Thomas Cartwright ... August 1686 ... October 1687*. All four editors were members of the Council of the Camden Society. All were of another generation, ranging from seventeen to forty-three years older than Halliwell. And although all maintained at the time what might be considered a civil relationship with Halliwell, it is clear that there was not merely organizational controversy but, on the part of some, personal strife as well.

Halliwell, it is obvious by the very publication of this letter, was hurt by certain accusations and he does not disguise his feelings. He is "perfectly aware, that many Members of the Society will be but ill-disposed to pay attention to the suggestions of *a boy of under nineteen*." He has been taunted for pointing out a "most egregious and nepial error" in a recent publication of an "honourable and learned Member."[17] Halliwell's

17. The "error" and the "Member" have not yet been identified. A number of members had published recently, and well-nigh all were older than Halliwell. The most "eligible" candidates, leaders of the "opposing" faction, are W. J. Thoms and John Bruce, who wrote devastating anonymous reviews of Halliwell later on–this despite their temperate and fair correspondence with Halliwell. Another possibility might be William Chappell, whose *Collection of National English Airs* was somewhat patronizingly reviewed by the then twenty-year-old Halliwell in the *Gentlemen's Magazine* (n.s. 14 [1840], 273-4) and who was later mentioned by

postscript is almost paranoiac in its intensity: "Hardly a day passes, but what I am assaulted with some insult or another, under the impression of an almost universal doubt–What can a young person know of antiquarian matters?" He has in fact received a letter (as yet unidentified) "wherein the writer calmly stated, that no person under age should allow his name to appear in print!" The strife goes beyond the internal workings of the Society, for Halliwell closes with a reference to a Camden Society publication in the *Gentleman's Magazine*, expecting an "attempt at a refutation of the preceding calm remarks," one incidentally which does not seem to have appeared. What did appear in the October number (n.s. [1839], pp. 393-8) was a review of Thoms's *Anecdotes and Traditions*, which concluded: "We have said enough to prove how much amusement as well as advantage may be derived from Mr. Thoms's volume, which we have no doubt will be generally acceptable to the members of the Camden Society. They cannot but feel much obliged to him for the great pains and trouble he has taken in his illustrative remarks, many of which are derived from works of foreign scholars and antiquaries, with which, as he has remarked, the antiquarian students of this country are as yet too little acquainted" (p. 398). The anonymous reviewer has been identified by Kuist as, not surprisingly, John Bruce. It is likewise not unexpected that Halliwell's ally, Thomas Wright, comforted him by reporting that Collier "expressed uncommonly good feelings towards you. He says he likes you all the better because you say what you think, and are not afraid of anybody, and that it was shocking impudence to talke [*sic*] about your being too young" (26 October 1839; LOA 2:46). Almost a year later, in a letter of 1 July 1840 (LOA 3:23), Dyce would write: "Tell me if you have yet demolished the Camden ... cultivate brotherly love towards Thoms & [John] Bruce." To be sure, Halliwell was not unaware of the consequences of his action. "My silly little pamphlet did more harm than good," he admitted to C. H. Hartshorne in a letter of 11 October 1839. But for him conviction and solidarity took precedence. "There is much prejudice," he continued, "against young authors and their doings and whatever they say or do against any system is generally interpreted into an argument for its defence. I find that to be too much the case in every thing, and I am therefore so much the more obliged to you and those of my friends who do not discard me on that account." Obviously, there is more in play here

Collier to Peter Cunningham as one "who speaks even worse of him [Halliwell] than I think" (8 February 1851; Tyrus Harmsen Collection). Since there is no written work of the time by Halliwell in which he criticizes another member of the Society, it may well be that the remark was made orally, perhaps at a meeting.

than Halliwell's ego, as a discussion of Halliwell's relationship with the Camden Society will demonstrate.

Whether he was driven by devotion to self or to scholarship, or both, Halliwell was irrepressible in 1839. Just a few months after his election to the Royal Society, just a few weeks before his *Letter to Egerton*, and barely a fortnight after his nineteenth birthday, he offered a startling suggestion to the vice-president of the Royal Society and Vice-Chancellor of London University J. W. Lubbock. In a letter of 4 July 1839 (Royal Society, LUB.H25) he wrote:

It seems to me that there is a deficiency in the Professorships in the London University [–] one for Anglo-Saxon language and literature–and a deficiency which is not supplied by that for English Language & Literature, because the study of Anglo-Saxon has taken a most absolutely definite individual turn.

That there would be an advantage derived to the Professor is another question. If there are Professorships founded for Anglo-Saxon at both Colleges [University and King's], Professors must be found who care little or nothing for pecuniary interest, for a large class could not be found.

As far as University College itself is concerned, if any thing definite was arranged, and no scholar of note offered himself–for the love of the subject I would undertake it gratis to any one [crossed out] who might wish to join a class; but there is time enough to talk about that, if you think it advisable to urge the propriety of it, and I thought you would not think it supercilious of me to hint to you as Vice Chancellor what would I am sure be considered by many as a great improvement to the *generality* of the institution.

There is little doubt that Halliwell's suggestion was serious and forward-looking, perhaps revolutionary since not merely Anglo-Saxon studies but indeed English studies were hardly considered academic essentials. At Halliwell's Cambridge the core education consisted of mathematics and classics. But reform was in the air, and for the recently established London University–newly chartered only three years earlier in 1836–a wide-reaching curriculum was being developed and in liberal arts and sciences an opportunity for it to establish its own identity and distinguish itself from the older universities. Halliwell's tone is subdued; he is writing a private letter. But the drive is undeniable, the zealous engagement distinctive and enduring. Lubbock's immediate response is not known. But, although the first vice-chancellor and barely two years in office, he must have been only a little amazed, for Halliwell, man and reputation, were known to him. Halliwell did not become professor. Anglo-Saxon cannot be said to have become a rounded subject of study at University College until many years later, perhaps not until the appointment of W. P. Ker in 1889. But Halliwell was on his way, thrusting forward in 1839.

Although all of Halliwell's separate works but his edition of Mandeville emanate from his tenure at Jesus College, and Cambridge was to remain for a time at least the center of his professional career, it was to yield in 1840 to London, his birthplace. All of his nine separate books or pamphlets in 1840 have a London imprint. And as a kind of pendant, of his thirty-five publications–i.e. including articles, reviews, prospectuses, and catalogues–only eleven dealt in one way or another with the history of science, the longest separate publication, *The Connexion of Wales with the Early Science of England,* consisting of only sixteen pages. The rest dealt with early English history and literature and most prominently catalogues of libraries. Furthermore, the ever-widening circle of societies in London, to which he belonged and which he helped found, as well as his friends and family there, also motivated his move. Besides, he had always commuted between Cambridge and London, and his stay in Cambridge was not untroubled by strains with dons and fellow students, not to mention financial problems and illness, all of which contributed to his abrupt departure from Jesus College without a degree. And no inconsiderable factor must have been a passion for collecting books and manuscripts which demanded his presence in London. For it is not unreasonable to say that the most important publications concerning Halliwell in 1840, with reverberations thereafter, were the catalogues announcing the sale at Sotheby's on three days, from 25 to 27 June, a few days after his twentieth birthday, of 786 books and manuscripts "forming a portion of the library of James Orchard Halliwell, Esq. F.R.S. F.S.A."

The change from Cambridge to London, from 1839 to 1840, was not abrupt, of course. In a letter of 1 January 1840 (LOA 1:5) John Jones (known as Tegid) confessed to "not knowing whether to direct to you in London or Cambridge." Thomas Phillipps addressed a letter of 17 May 1840 (LOA 7:38) to Halliwell at Jesus College; Halliwell dated a letter from Collier 10 November 1840 (LOA 3:32) and commented, "addressed to me at Cambridge."[18] Halliwell was working on, perhaps had just finished with, material in Cambridge in 1839 which was then published in London in 1840. The "Lectori" of his edition of John Sherman's *Historia*

18. Robert Bowes's *Catalogue of the Books Printed at or Relating to the University, Town & County of Cambridge from 1521 to 1893* (Cambridge, 1894), p. 353, has Halliwell as having attended Jesus College from 1839 to 1842.

Collegii Jesu Cantabrigiensis is dated "Kalend. Mart. M.DCCCXL," from "Coll. Jes. Cantab." Even if the subject-matter were not proof enough of the Cambridge provenance, the prefatory tribute to the help of Thomas Wright and the actual printing by the Cambridge firm of Metcalfe and Palmer, as well as of the co-publisher Thomas Stevenson, point to the fact that the work was done by Halliwell while a student at Cambridge, who then moved to London, where Thomas Rodd published the work. The text itself is a simple reprint in Latin with no textual or editorial apparatus at all. This is unusual for Halliwell, leading to the impression that the work was an occasional one, perhaps produced as a quick token of gratitude to the College which had provided him with a scholarship and library post, perhaps just for money. Similarly–from a London base–although his *Catalogue of the Miscellaneous Manuscripts Preserved in the Library of the Royal Society* appeared in 1840, its preface is dated 17 October 1839, and must have been undertaken in connection with Halliwell's election on 30 May 1839. The simple listing of items with descriptions of a line or two is typical.

The rest of Halliwell's separate publications have a definite London origin. Both *A Few Notes on the History of the Discovery of the Composition of Water* and *The Chronicle of William de Rishanger* were published in London (the latter for the Camden Society), and emanating from 35 Alfred Place. Publishers of the other works were those with whom Halliwell was to have a long-standing relationship: *The Harrowing of Hell* and *The Merry Tales of the Wise Men of Gotham* published by John Russell Smith, and *The Early History of Freemasonry in England* by Thomas Rodd. The dedications or expressions of gratitude to friends and colleagues are further indications of the London orientation: the *Historia* to Joseph Hunter, the *Merry Tales* and *Freemasonry* to John Payne Collier, and the *Harrowing of Hell* to the Reverend Alexander Dyce.

Significant too is the noticeable shift of interest from mathematics and the history of science to the archaeological origins of English literary culture. True, his contributions to the *London and Edinburgh Philosophical Magazine* in 1840 and 1841–five of six of which deal with his favourite topic of Boethian numerical contractions–testify to his continuing interest in mathematical operations. But the historical framework, never absent in his treatment of earlier sources, becomes more foreground than context. A pamphlet is entitled *A Few Notes on the History of the Discovery of the Composition of Water*, another *The Connexion of Wales with the Early Science of England*. Both works are discursive rather than analytic. Both describe works which are neither technical nor of immediate interest in the current debates: the first draws on letters and papers of the eighteenth century, mainly by James Watt; the second briefly summarizes the life and work of Robert Recorde, a sixteenth-century mathematician and physician to Queen Mary (Halliwell employing, as was his wont, works he himself owned).[19] In a manifesto dated 6 March 1840 Halliwell announced the founding of the British Historical Society of Sciences. To overcome "the great deficiency of printed materials illustrating the history of Science ... long complained of," the Society would print "inedited documents relative to that subject." This objective, as well as the annual subscription of one pound, coincides with the handwritten note Halliwell added: "This is formed upon the principle of the Camden Society."[20] Among the works suggested for publication were treatises ranging from geometry to music to mechanical inventions to botany–based mainly on early manuscripts and on subjects Halliwell and his friend Thomas Wright had been working on.[21] The nominations for the Council are also recognizable both in their intellectual quality and as friends and important correspondents of Halliwell's: Charles Purton Cooper (to whom he inscribed *Reliquiae Antiquae*), Thomas Stephens Davies (to whom he inscribed the *Historia Collegii Jesu Cantabrigiensis*), Thomas Joseph Pettigrew (to whom he inscribed *A Brief Description of the Ancient and Modern Manuscripts in the Public Library, Plymouth*), as well as such mathematical luminaries as Augustus De Morgan of University College London and Baden Powell of Oxford, both of whom Halliwell was cultivating and both interested in the history of science and both–especially De Morgan–collectors on the subject.[22] Halliwell himself was secretary and treasurer. The society matched the scholarly interests and aims of a serious antiquary and bookman engaged in making available neglected older texts and popularizing them. For it

19. Halliwell's interest in Recorde brought him into contact with John Jones (aka Tegid), who invited him to assist in translating and editing the lives of the Welsh saints (13 February 1840; LOA 3:12). Halliwell does not seem to have complied, but his engagement with Wales as archaeologist and vacationer was lively, coming to fruition in his charming travel book *Notes of Family Excursions in North Wales* (1860).

20. Appended to the prospectus of 6 March 1840 of what was originally called the British Historical Society of Sciences, now among Dawson Turner's papers in the library of Trinity College Cambridge (O.14.25^{12}).

21. In addition to that in the prospectus of the Historical Society of Science, a list of the works suggested for publication is found in the *Gentleman's Magazine*, n.s. 14 (1840), 75.

22. Very early on, before he had even met De Morgan, Halliwell presented him with a copy of Edward Cocker's *Arithmetick*, according to a letter in the De Morgan collection in the University of London ([DeM] L.1.[Cocker]).

was not a society which had regular meetings for the reading of papers and other intellectual exercises. It was a publishing club. As such, it was very much in tune with the times in its attempt to rediscover the hidden culture of England and to educate a wider public.

Halliwell's edition for the Camden Society of *The Chronicle of William de Rishanger, of the Barons' War.* [with] *The Miracles of Simon de Montfort,* both from manuscripts in the Cottonian Library, continues that aim. After an obligatory note of thanks to J. G. Nichols, editor of the *Gentleman's Magazine,* to which Halliwell was a regular contributor, a sound and scholarly introduction of thirty-nine pages gives the necessary bibliographical and historical information, preceding a transcription of the Latin texts and some fifty pages devoted to Notes and Illustrations and an Index of Names. The inclusion of the *Miracles,* interesting enough, may have to do not merely with Halliwell's interest in early history or his engagement with Cottonian manuscripts in general or even with an attempt to rescue Montfort from obscurity or history's treatment of "his memory with severity." It may also reflect Halliwell's interest in religious matters and institutions, in 1840 looking back and later, as will be shown, dealing with the contemporary situation. A communication (dated June 1839) appearing in *Archaeologia* in 1840 (38:455-7) transcribes passages from the catalogue of Ramsey monastery, with some remarks on the catalogue of the library of Canterbury Cathedral in the British Museum and an indication that he has examined the catalogue of the library of the Monastery of Sion in Archbishop Parker's collection in Corpus Christ College, Cambridge, Halliwell adding typically: "It is my intention ere long to edit this volume with notes." Theology is also implicit in Halliwell's article (dated 18 April 1839) in the same 1840 number (pp. 444-7) on the antiquity of freemasonry in England. The "mystery" is only touched on in an article devoted mainly to extracts from early manuscripts, but Halliwell does admit that he leaves the matter "with hardly a perceptible hint as to the manner of degeneration from bodies of skilled architects to friendship societies ... The separation from the Roman Catholic church doubtless contributed ... to further the distinction" (p. 447). It is not surprising, at any rate, that Halliwell attempted in 1841 to found the English Theological Society, which though it never materialized was to provide him with still another topic for publication some years later.

Halliwell's remaining separate publications in 1840 confirm the direction he would take: on the one hand, editions or reprints of early popular literature undertaken for various publishing societies or certain lively publishers, like John Russell Smith, and on the other hand privately printed works, increasingly catalogues of early works in his collection, for subscribers and friends. The former is represented by editions of the miracle play *The Harrowing of Hell* and the collection *The Merry Tales of the Wise Men of Gotham*, both published by Smith. Both are relatively and not untypically slight volumes–the first of thirty-three pages, the second of twenty-four. The first, whose title page resembles those of the Camden Society publications, with Camden himself, the "Norwich of Antiquities," pictured, has a nine-page introduction, twenty pages of Middle English text and facing translation, and two pages of notes. It is a workmanlike job, despite its brevity giving Halliwell ample opportunity to display his scholarly way with older texts, as well as his knowledge of Middle English language and literature and of Latin, with illustrations drawn from his ongoing *Reliquiae Antiquae*. It also allows him to acknowledge debts and make known his relationship with important friends: Collier, David Laing (who had printed a limited number of copies earlier), and Dyce (who provided him with a copy of Laing's edition). The second work for Smith is an obvious occasional work, with a brief introduction and a simple reprint of twenty tales, most not quite a page long, of the early sixteenth century and of a popular folksy nature. A commercial enterprise to be sure, it nevertheless reflects what is to develop as Halliwell's continuous interest in dealing with and himself writing mild comic prose. It also enabled Halliwell to announce his connection with Joseph Hunter, who had lent him a copy of the work in modern English, and in a note (p. 24) to mention–perhaps by way of reconciliation for the charges in the *Letter to Egerton*–William John Thoms, who gave up his intention of printing the tales on learning that Halliwell wished to publish them. They too were members of the Council of the Camden Society and Fellows of the Society of Antiquaries, Hunter having proposed Halliwell for the latter in 1839. More ambitious is Halliwell's edition for the Percy Society of *A Selection from the Minor Poems of Dan Lydgate*: a brief seven-page introduction precedes a selection of forty-four poems (each with a brief bibliographical headnote) covering 264 pages, followed by seven pages of notes. Although admittedly modest in aim–the "few notes ... have been selected from material at hand, and without any attempt at continuous illustration, which, in a work of this nature, might be extended to any assignable length" (xi)–it is an independent selection from more than 250 poems and, though little more than a reading text, the first attempt to present even a selection of the poetry of John Lydgate to a modern audience. It is, in fact, the first reprint of Lydgate altogether and remained alone until well into the twentieth century.

Less immediately popular but more important in the long run was the string of Halliwell's publications–also often privately printed–of catalogues, inventories, handlists, and the like of libraries and increasingly of his own collection. This area of his career was prefigured not merely in his own collecting and dealing with books and his researches in various libraries but also in his reading while at Cambridge. At Trinity, the borrowing book of the library reveals, he was reading intensively. The very number of books is impressive: in the last week of November 1837 alone, just after his matriculation on the 13th, he borrowed twelve books, more than anyone else in Trinity. They are clues to his activities as well. On the one hand he seems to have been an earnest student preparing for his little-go. He was reading mathematical and what he understood to be scientific books, such as John Dansie's *A Mathematical Manual* (1654), Gerhardus Johannes Vossius's *De Quatuor Artibus Popularibus* (1650), Friedrich W. A. Murhard's *Bibliotheca Mathematica* (1797-1805), Copernicus's *De Revolutionibus Orbium Coelestium* (1566), Thomas Tredgold's *The Steam Engine* (1827), Noah Bridges's *Vulgar Arithmetique* (1653), Robert Hues's *Tractatus de Globis* (1594), and other tracts by Robert Recorde, Jacques de Billy, John Playfair, Edmund Wingate, John Wallis, Jean Etienne Montucola, among others.[23] For classical literature he borrowed Euripides and Hellanicus. He did not, however, neglect current projects. He must have had his colleague Thomas Wright's projects in mind borrowing *Piers Ploughman* and Joseph Bosworth's *Elements of Anglo-Saxon Grammar* and his own *Manuscript Rarities of the University of Cambridge* in borrowing C. H. Hartshorne's *Book Rarities of the University of Cambridge*. In all, he borrowed thirty-four books in four months at Trinity and was one of the most frequent users of the library. At Jesus he borrowed far fewer books, perhaps not needing to record his borrowings because he was library clerk or deputy librarian. But he did record four, and they show his professional direction: On 3 November 1838 he borrowed the first volume of the works of Bede (most likely in connection with Thomas Wright) and, strikingly, on 5 February 1839 catalogues of the Harleian and Cottonian manuscripts and *Reports from the Select Committee Appointed to Inquire into the State of the Public Records of the Kingdom* (1800).

One work of 1840 by Halliwell characteristic of this direction, *A Catalogue of the Contents of the Codex Holbrookianus*, is simply a list of thirty-

23. Although the number of borrowings is clear enough, determining the exact work can be problematic. Since the Trinity shelfmarks have been changed it is necessary to go through all the titles and volumes by an author (only the family name is given in the borrowing book) to find the original shelfmark. In a number of cases, moreover, an author or a title is no longer in the current catalogue or a work does not have the original shelfmark or its designation is too vague to be identified (e.g. Math tract).

one Latin items, with an occasional brief remark on some of them. Only
a hundred copies were printed, the title page explicitly headed "Not
Published." It reflects his Cambridge days. The manuscript (which
Halliwell had acquired) for the most part in the autograph of John
Holbrook, Master of St. Peter's College from 1418-31, and one of
Halliwell's most cherished possessions, was bought by Madden for the
British Museum in December 1840 for £16.16.0. More significant, and
coincidental with Halliwell's leaving Jesus College without a degree and
taking up residence in London, at 35 Alfred Place, were the catalogues of
two sales at Sotheby's of a portion of his collection—the first, of printed
books, on 25 and 26 June, the second, of manuscripts, on 27 June 1840.
Why they took place when they did, and their apparent lack of success,
and the short- and middle-term consequences therefrom, are matters of
speculation and of no small complexity. The sheer number of lots—624 in
the first and 162 in the second sale—speaks volumes about the young
Halliwell's activities. He was after all only twenty at the time. The overall
nature of the lots—"scientific, historical, and miscellaneous"—is further
evidence of his scholarly and business activities. Scientific and historical
topics are not surprising, but seven Burmese manuscripts, which Halliwell
had purchased at the sale of Captain Cox's Museum, were doubtless
objects for speculation. The bidders at the first sale afford some
indication of the attention it elicited. The most prominent buyer seems to
have been Augustus De Morgan, the eminent professor of mathematics
in University College London; others who made substantial purchases
were the mathematical bookseller and author Samuel Maynard, the
bookseller Henry Bohn, and Thomas Stephens Davies, the mathematician
and friend of the Halliwells, who bought forty-nine lots for a total of
£6.10.0. That the 624 lots of the first sale fetched but £130.0.6, a
disappointingly small sum, may be due to the as yet undeveloped sense of
the nature and importance of the history of science beyond the learned
societies[24] and the expanding horizon of influential popular publications
dealing with practical scientific matters like mechanics and technological
inventions or even the relatively modest achievements of, say, Lord
Brougham's and Charles Knight's Society for the Diffusion of Useful
Knowledge. That the second sale, consisting of 162 manuscripts, was
offered and then withdrawn is either very simple or very difficult to
explain. The customary explanation—that there was no interest or that the

---

24. A point discussed by A. N. L. Munby, *The History and Bibliography of Science in
England: The First Phase, 1833-1845* (Berkeley, 1968), pp. 17-19.

prices expected would be too low (a projection based on the disappointing first sale)–has merits.[25]

That Halliwell needed money is apparent. He left Trinity, where he was a pensioner, for Jesus, where he became a Foundation Scholar, a post which provided him with board and accommodation. As deputy librarian in 1839 he earned £22.2.6 to supplement the allowance he had from his father. Still, living expenses in Cambridge could be considerable. It was not uncommon for a bill for ordinary expenses to reach at least £50 per quarter, Halliwell lists one scrap of expenses, however modest, in his commonplace book as paid (100[r]:

Bedroom candlestick	2.6
Parcel Cat	1.3
Pst Letters 2	1.4
Lock picked	.6
College Porter from Bentley's	5.-
Porter. Wine	.6
Book. MS. Farmer	4.6

Some time later his tutor at Jesus, Thomas Gaskin, who was responsible for Halliwell's account, reminded him that he still owed £110.13.9 even after £15 caution money had been deducted (26 July [1842]; LOA 21:79). As a collector of books and manuscripts, he must have required ready cash: for the brief period it covers, his commonplace book at Trinity records £50.18.0 paid to booksellers and printers (69[v]). It is furthermore unlikely that his early publications, whose printing he may well have had to subsidize, produced much of an income; the reprinting of the same material and the hasty announcements of impending works point to a rather meager market. Even the appearance of a second edition could not be a guarantee of financial success; besides, the press-runs are not readily available, nor are details about possible remuneration. Still, Halliwell had a "large allowance" from his father and, as James Heywood later testified, he was "well off in worldly circumstances ... whilst at Trinity College" (28 February 1845; TCC Add. MSS. a.170.17).

But there are direct indications that Halliwell fell suddenly and heavily into debt. On 9 October 1839, citing "misfortune–dire and unexpected &

25. See A. N. L. Munby, *The Family Affairs of Sir Thomas Phillipps* (Cambridge, 1952), pp. 16-17. James Heywood, Halliwell's friend, later wrote to William Whewell, "The collection of M.S.S. were put up for sale by Mr. Sotheby, but were bought in by Mr. Halliwell's brother [Richard], as they were not selling well" (28 February 1845; TCC Add. MSS. a.170.17).

enough to crush me," he offered his manuscript collection in the catalogue of 1839 to Sir Thomas Phillipps for £250, less, he maintained, than their cost, and admitted in a letter to him of 11 October that "Now I think of nothing but a way of escape from the Shylock money-lenders of the City of London."[26] Though sympathetic, Phillipps did not agree to a purchase. Nor did Halliwell's tutor at Trinity, the mathematician George Peacock, who, on receiving the privately printed and distributed catalogue, asked whether Halliwell had written to John Lodge, librarian of the Cambridge Public Library, suggesting that if the Cambridge Syndics were not disposed to purchase the whole, then the British Museum should certainly do so (22 January 1840; LOA 77:26). It did not, Sir Frederic Madden also turning down the offer.

The degree of financial and emotional stress is explicit in a letter, headed "private," of Halliwell's to John William Lubbock, whom he must have known personally as vice-president of the Royal Society and Vice-Chancellor of London University. Although sent to the Royal Society, the letter is doubtless addressed to Lubbock as the banker of Lubbock, Forster, and Co., 11 Mansion House Street. It is dated only Monday evening but is doubtless of his Cambridge days:

I hope you will pardon me for applying to you on a matter of business but when I assure you I am in a great and (to me) a novel dilemma I hope you will pardon me.

The fact is that through indiscretions at Cambridge I am in an *immediate* want of 300£ or 400£ to pay some urgent bills and as a point of duty I feel I should be doing very wrong to ask my father for a large increase on an already large allowance.

If then you could conveniently accommodate me I should be very willing to engage to pay half of it back at the end of one year and the other half at the end of another year and of course the highest rate of interest likewise, and also feel most permanently grateful to you.

I am only nineteen and being most ignorant of money matters I am uncertain what security will be considered sufficient. My own personal security would not be sufficient but I feel certain that if I mentioned my difficulties to Prof Davies, my only intimate friend, he would readily become responsible for me; but I would not on any account ask him for the loan.

I know not exactly what prompts me to apply to you except the consciousness that your knowledge of my having once been very silly at

26. The letters are reproduced in Munby, *Family Affairs*, pp. 39-41.

Cambridge would never act as any drawback upon my future exertions (Royal Society, LUB.H33).

What the "indiscretions" were is not known. But it is unlikely that wine, women, and song were meant. There is hardly a reference, direct or indirect, to his participating in the raucous and indeed brutal undergraduate amusements: his description of a town versus gown row of 6 November 1837 involving 370 strong of Trinity and 165 of St. John's, the longest single personal entry in his commonplace book (59^v-61^r), is based on his having observed it from the window of his rooms. Gambling cannot be discounted, of course, but it is hardly mentioned in Halliwell's entire career. In a hastily written addition to the printed announcement of the Cambridge Antiquarian Society, "for want of better material," Halliwell explained to his brother Richard that he was unable to visit his father because he "went with [Duffield] to the Cavendish [a London club and hotel at 307 Regent Street] and flared up for 4 hours [crossed out: "3 hours & a half"] and came back minus 3s/6 in my pocket" (postmarked 16 November 1839, dated only "Friday evening"; LOA 10:34)—not exactly an indication of lavish expenditure or indiscretion. Other undergraduate expenses—gown, barber, butler, steward, tutor, and the like—can hardly be called "indiscretions." Nor, for that matter, can the fashionable dress Halliwell wore for the portrait he had made (and sold) of himself in 1843, since his sister Louisa's humorously badgering reference many years later to his "foppish" days at Cambridge was less a remark on his wardrobe than on his habitual fastidiousness.[27]

Halliwell's passion for books, his formidable appetite for collecting, is an attractive possibility. But the list in his commonplace book of sums paid to booksellers is composed of numerous small sums totalling a considerable but by no means extraordinary £50.18.0. And there is nothing in his catalogue or collection at this time, singly or together, which might account for "indiscretions" requiring £300 or £400—the "or" in fact implying that he may have needed perhaps more. Even speculation in book-dealing later in his life, when large sums were involved, was always cautious and conservative. A tempting possibility may be Halliwell's generosity. There are letters to Halliwell from contemporaries thanking him for kind deeds done or to be done. In the letter in which he asks Halliwell to pay the money owed for expenses at Jesus, his former tutor, Thomas Gaskin, goes on to say: "I am truly sorry to learn, that you

27. See n. 266.

are one of the numerous friends of my Brother, who from the best feelings of kindness & benevolence have been persuaded to advance him money, at a time when with ordinary prudence his resources were ample. For your kindness I shall ever be grateful, & I regret that it has been so ill repaid. Unfortunately he got into difficulties from which it was impossible for me to extricate him, & I was obliged to leave him to struggle with his fate" (26 July [1842]; LOA 21:79). If Halliwell could lend money to an undergraduate whom he could not have known very well–Robert Gaskin matriculated at Queen's in 1840–and the amount must have been considerable for Robert Gaskin's own brother to mention it and admit too that he could not help him, then to what lengths might Halliwell go to come to the assistance of his "only intimate friend" and mentor, Thomas Stephens Davies?

Davies had a long history of being in debt. Halliwell deleted a letter of Davies's of 20 January 1839 (LOA 2:34) from the collection he bequeathed to Edinburgh University, presumably in accordance with his wish to take "care to remove every thing at all to cause pain or annoyance to any one" (LOA 1:1). On 4 February 1839 (LOA 10:52) Davies wrote to Richard Halliwell: "I am always to be in debt: even in gambling with the only friend [the reference is to Halliwell's father, Thomas] I ever gambled with in my life. Gambling debts terminate in 'I.O.U.' given 'upon honour'; and these terminate, God knows how–but most commonly in ruin ... Most certainly, I am resolved to never give one to any other than to *him*: and I hope he will not be *very* impatient in wanting its payment." In resigning from the Society of Antiquaries for lack of funds, Davies (in a letter of 7 December 1848) recalled that "shortly after my admission [in early 1840], a momentous change took place in my circumstances, though with great difficulty, I made up my annual payments." On 22 February 1840 (LOA 31:20) Davies wrote to Halliwell that a certain "'Old Shirt' was I suppose out of humour, and told me he had just had a heavy loss &c. &c. &c. It was all a farce to get higher interest: and higher I would not give." In a letter dated only "Feb. 1840" (LOA 34:12) Davies wrote to him: "Never again during your whole life serve me such a trick again. I am still not three quarters dead but five! I feel as if I should never be well again. But a truce to this, I enclose the check. If you could hold it back for a week it would do me a service, as I have not yet got Whittaker's money. If you cannot, present it. All will be right: though a week hence it would be *more* right." Halliwell wrote a bill of exchange (or promissory note) dated 23 May 1840 (LOA 18:28*)–a month before the Sotheby sales–paying Davies £342, a very large sum indeed. Was Halliwell counting on repayment after the sale? What can be made of three bills from Davies dated 30 June 1840 (LOA 1:28*, 18:32*, 59:21*) amounting to only £140, another from Halliwell dated 18 August (LOA 18:20*) for £40? Or of Halliwell's sibyllic undated comment on his first bill: "The possession of this bill, so my brother [most likely, Richard, who was an attorney] notes, refutes statements respecting me made in Davies's bankruptcy case." Puzzling too is Halliwell's assertion which follows: "I forget all the circumstances." Why then, if not for financial reasons–default of payment–did Halliwell write to Lord Brougham some years later, "I dropped Mr Davies's acquaintance in the autumn of the year 1840, since which period I have never had any communication with him by letter or in conversation" (21 April 1846; UCL Brougham MSS.).

From whom did Halliwell get the money to cover his "indiscretions"? It is fairly certain that Lubbock did not respond to his request for a loan of £300 or £400, although no written response nor bank document seems extant. Only a short time later, for example, Lubbock's declining Halliwell's invitation to subscribe to the Historical Society of Science–"I do not wish to belong to any more Societies. The one you propose will require much pecuniary support I hope it will answer. Yours faithfully" (12 March 1840; LOA 100:28)–offers no clue. Nor is there any evidence that Halliwell did indeed go to the "Shylock money-lenders of the City of London." His reason for not accepting Thomas Phillipps's invitation to visit Middle Hill was that he was too busy *thinking* of how to escape them. What seems most likely is that Halliwell's family came to his rescue and to Davies's, who was after all their close friend. Halliwell's brother Thomas and his sister, Louisa, were to be the witnesses at Davies's wedding on 7 July 1840 in Islip, where the Halliwells had a house. James Heywood, a close friend of Halliwell's, explained that "being desirous to repay to his brother a sum of money which he had lent to him, he [Halliwell] made a printed catalogue of his M.S.S." (28 February 1845; TCC Add. MSS. a.170.17). The bills written by both Halliwell and Davies in payment and repayment of debts, were all marked "Payable at 4 Great Ryder Street. St James's," the address of the law firm of William Lovell and Richard Halliwell. Richard Halliwell was apparently the administrator of his younger brother's finances. It was he who must have made the arrangements for the sale at Sotheby's. For on 29 May 1840, shortly before the sale and just a week after James wrote the £342 bill payable to Davies, Leigh Sotheby sent Richard his bill of exchange for £200 "on Acct of the proceeds of the sale," agreeing to "attend to the instructions contained" in Richard's letter of 28 May.

Questions upon questions. If Halliwell needed money badly, why withdraw the sale of the manuscripts when he had previously failed to sell

the lot to individuals? Would not even a small sum be better than
nothing? Most likely Halliwell must have felt the disappointing results of
the first sale presaged the same for the second: only one volume, Edward
Cocker's *Arithmetic* (1678), brought at least one pound (£1.2.0); very few
of the single volumes surpassed two or three shillings. Even Sotheby must
have been concerned that he had advanced £200. At any rate the
manuscripts were withdrawn and offered once again to Madden at the
"very lowest valuation." Obviously, needing money urgently, Halliwell
suggested that if the Trustees of the British Museum were not consulted,
he would accept between £100 and £140 for the lot. When Madden
declined, Halliwell consigned the manuscripts to Thomas Rodd, who
offered the manuscripts again to Madden at the prices he would originally
have bid. On 13 August Madden selected thirty-three for a total of
£35.12.[28] On 18 August 1840 Halliwell gave another £40 to Davies.
Somewhat later Thomas Wright mentioned almost *en passant*: "I was at
Alfred Place yesterday evening. I understand a certain Woolwich
professor is in the Fleet. Sorry for it on one side, because some people
wont get paid, who ought not to be done out of their money" (11
February [1842]; LOA 36:24). This was not to be the end of the story,
however. Nor was it to remain a purely financial matter.

Noteworthy, at any rate, are the titles themselves of the printed works
put up for auction, for the library reflects the man. Although the emphasis
is on scientific works, one quarter to one third of the 624 books of the
first sale are devoted to history, philosophy, theology, literature, and art.
George Ballard's *Memoirs of Learned Ladies* (1770), Hugh Blair's *Lectures on
Rhetoric* (1793), Joseph Butler's *Anthology of Religion* (1827), Lord Byron's
English Bards (1811), Samuel Carr's *Sermons* (1817), Francis Douce's
Illustrations of Shakespeare (1839), David Hume's *Essays* (1825), Samuel
Jebb's *Life of Mary Queen of Scots* (1725), William Camden's *Remaines* (1629),
Albrecht Dürer's *Pittore* (1591), Malcolm Laing's *History of Scotland* (1800),
and Thomas Warton's *History of English Poetry* (1824) are representative of
the non-scientific titles as given on the catalogue. Halliwell obviously had
wide interests both as a reader and collector. Since only a portion of his
library was for sale, and scientific literature was dominant, it is not unlikely
that he was selling most of his scientific library and thinning out the non-
scientific works. In other words, the sale may indicate that he was turning
his main attention from his earliest passion, mathematics, to the broader

---

28. The details are from R. W. Hunt's "Additional Note" (pp. 278-9) to D. A.
Winstanley, "Halliwell Phillipps and Trinity College Library," *The Library*, III, 2
(1947-8), 250-82.

concerns of cultural archaeology, history, and increasingly, as the 1840s proceeded, to literature, more specifically to early literature and language and Shakespeare. This shift is evident perhaps in the fact that most of the books on sale were of the eighteenth and nineteenth centuries, none of them first editions.

Halliwell had more than money problems in Cambridge. There were tensions with other undergraduates and dons. If he hoped to escape the bustle of Trinity, which in 1840 had 448 students in residence, for the intimacy of Jesus, which had but sixty, he was disappointed. Robert Leslie Ellis, a former classmate at Trinity, records in his diary entry for 20 November 1838 that "Hallowell [sic] also called. Told me of the quarrels at Jesus. They shew great ignorance of what one is & is not entitled to expect & demand amongst gentlemen–Hallowel [sic] himself is in the thick of them–knows only 2 or 3 men out of 40 whom he knew once" (TCC Add. MSS. a.219^{1}[7]). Somewhat sardonically, Halliwell seems to be reflecting on his Cambridge difficulties in mentioning in his letter of 11 October 1839 to Hartshorne that if his son "*is not sent to a public school* he is *sure* to be a great man in after life." A London friend, J. H. C. Wright, hoped Halliwell had not had "quarrels & cabals with the Dean of your college [James Fendal] who, I fear, thinks that you take the impositions & restrictions rather too coolly, especially, when, without an exeat, you came up to town for a day" (26 November 1839; LOA 2:51). Another London friend E. H. Hunter, the son of Joseph Hunter, was "concerned to hear that you have not been well lately; let your *spill* be a warning to you to refrain for the present at least from indulging those rowing propensities" (15 February 1839; LOA 2:19). Halliwell seems in fact to have been seriously ill while at Jesus. He did not sit the examinations in May 1839, appearing on the list as *aegrotat*. Gibbes Rigaud, a friend at Oxford and son of the renowned mathematical historian and astronomer Stephen Peter Rigaud, cautioned, "Why go near Cambridge again–you will do nothing there, & you know, as well as I do, that anything like dissipation is the very worst thing for your health at present" (19 October 1839; LOA 2:45). In a letter of 11 October 1839 from Alfred Place to C. H. Hartshorne, Halliwell inflected a not uncommon undergraduate malaise: "The fact is that my health–my present low spirits–every thing about me only adds to the conviction that in a very limited period my name will for the last time appear before the public."[29] All things considered, it is not surprising that although entitled as Foundation Scholar to meals and accommodation, he was frequently absent from Jesus, as from Trinity, most often in London

29. See n. 12.

with his family or in Oxford at the Bodleian or in Woolwich visiting Davies.

Halliwell's professional ventures in Cambridge were not exactly prospering either. The Historical Society of Science, which he founded on 6 March 1840 "upon the principle of the Camden Society," may have lasted until 21 November 1846, but it can hardly be considered a success. True, Halliwell succeeded in enlisting prominent figures for the Council: Augustus De Morgan, Joseph Hunter, Francis Palgrave, among others. Joining the undergraduate were such luminaries as Beriah Botfield, John Bruce, Michael Faraday, Henry Hallam, Frederic Madden, George Peacock, and Robert Willis, as well as close friends and relatives, such as Samuel Charles (his intimate friend at Trinity and frequent correspondent), his brothers Richard and Thomas, and of course Thomas Wright. Nevertheless the Society seems to have existed mainly on paper. Of the fifteen works announced in the prospectus, only two actually were published: not surprisingly, one by Thomas Wright, *Popular Treatises on Sciences of the Middle Ages*, and the other by Halliwell himself, *A Collection of Letters Illustrative of the History of Science in England.* None of the twenty-two English "inedited" writers who were to "receive the marked attention of the Council" seems to have come past the prospectus. There are also indications of some internal problems. Baden Powell, whose name appears as a member of the Council, was at pains to stress in two letters that he could not "think it consistent to be on the *council* of a Society to which [he was] *not* a *subscriber*" (7 March 1841; LOA 34:46) and more emphatically a year later: "Being away from home I am unable to refer to any memoranda respecting the Historical Society of Science. But I feel confident that if I did join it in any way it was under an impression that I was not a *subscriber* as I have been obliged to decline subscribing to any institutions which I did not feel bound to support as belonging strictly to Science" (26 July 1842; LOA 16:49). Others whom Halliwell invited declined, among the most prominent, J. W. Lubbock and J. F. W. Herschel.[30] Notable too is the absence of the name of William Whewell of Trinity College, who was prominent in the professional British Association for the Advancement of Science. Interesting as well is the fact that Halliwell must have broken off his studies and left Cambridge at about the exact time he issued the prospectus announcing the Society. In any event the Society did not prosper. In his final statement dissolving it on 21 November 1846 (LOA 24:45), Halliwell did not shy away from

---

30. Herschel declined on 28 June 1840, although admiring Halliwell's efforts and the Society's "objects" (Royal Society, Herschel Papers, HS.10.147).

referring to the "ill success," attributing it to the lack of subscriptions: "500 at least" were "confidently expected," and of the 179 original members seventy-six never paid any subscriptions at all; 103 paid one year's subscription, thirty-nine paid the second year's subscriptions, and two compounded. It is to his credit and the integrity of his endeavor that certain members volunteered to help make up the financial loss incurred by Halliwell (£74.3.0), absolving him of personal responsibility for what may have been mismanagement. The Bishop of Durham gave £12, Pettigrew £10, and Heywood £5 (21 November 1846; LOA 24:45).

The Cambridge Antiquarian Society was another of Halliwell's creations. Established (so its prospectus of 1839) "for the encouragement of the study of the history and antiquities of the university, town, and county of Cambridge," it is still in existence. Halliwell was its first secretary and a Council member; his edition of John Sherman's *Historia Collegii Jesu Cantabrigiensis* was published under its auspices. Strikingly, Halliwell was the only undergraduate among the founders. The president was Ralph Tatham, Master of St. John's and Vice-Chancellor of the University, the treasurer was John James Smith, Tutor at Caius; among the Council members were John Lodge, University librarian, and Elwes Corrie, then Tutor at Catharine Hall and later Master of Jesus College. All the Council members but Halliwell and Sir Henry Dryden were divines; Corrie was Norrisian Professor of Divinity. Despite shared aims and the possible benefits of hobnobbing, as it were, with senior members–the early meetings were held in the Master's Lodge at St. John's–Halliwell was absent from Cambridge often, apparently not attending any meetings after 1840. His being elected only joint secretary in early 1842 was doubtless an indication of his being eased from the center of the Society's activities by the energetic J. J. Smith. In the very beginning Halliwell was very much concerned with the existence of the Society, confiding to C. H. Hartshorne as early as 11 October 1839, under the influence of "low spirits" but perhaps also with a sense of his imminent departure from Cambridge, "I am very much afraid of the future success of the *Cambridge Antiquarian Society*: it quite depends on the exertions of Mr Smith and he has no practical knowledge of the method of managing the *humbug* which every new society must necessarily possess." In 1840, desiring to enhance the stature of the Society, he (and the ever-present Thomas Wright) successfully proposed for honorary membership the foreign dignitaries F. P. G. Guizot and V. A. Huber, the ever-useful John Gough Nichols, and as ordinary members Thomas Phillipps and John Richards, jun. Although he continued his membership and his scholarly communications to the expanding Society into the 1850s, sending books and other gifts, and making suggestions about membership and publication policy,[31] he had to admit in a letter to Smith of 19 May 1852 that he has "been looking for anything on primeval Cambridgeshire but can find *nothing*." It is, he has no doubt, an "interesting subject," but as with his delay in answering Smith, he "can only excuse [him]self by pleading severe labour & business of various kinds," so with the attractions of London and, more specifically, new and more engrossing challenges.

The reasons for the move from Cambridge to London are many and interrelated. One may be his reaction to the tensions and turmoil, if not tedium, of Cambridge undergraduate life, combined with the fact that as an undergraduate he seems to have been alone professionally among seniors who, given the rigid hierarchy of college life, were hardly likely to give him his due. It may be that Halliwell realized his limits as mathematician. His professional debut as a sixteen-year-old mathematician, an article entitled "A Direct Demonstration of the Rule for the Multiplication of Negative Signs," was doubtless precocious and adventurous since algebra was not yet a well-developed field but nevertheless rather more clever than convincing or deep.[32] He never published in the *Cambridge Mathematical Journal*; Rigaud "avail[ed]" himself of the "privilege [of making alterations in a work of Halliwell's] by the omission of [his] own name" (26 October 1838; LOA 2:11); and there was his falling-out with his mentor Davies. His greater potential as a kind of cultural historian was recognized and nurtured by the antiquary Thomas Wright. And it may well be that London colleagues were more compatible, personally and professionally, than those in Cambridge, not to mention the comfort of his closely knit family in Alfred Place. It may also be that the unsuccessful Sotheby's sale caused Halliwell to see that the market

31. See the Cambridge Antiquarian Society letter book Nos. 46 and 102 for Halliwell's letters of 4 August 1845 and 13 June 1849 to C. C. Babington, the treasurer. Of special interest is Halliwell's response of 19 May 1852 (No. 123) to J. J. Smith's good opinion of his "Suggestions towards the Production of an Athenae Cantabrigiensis," which was read on 3 May 1852. Halliwell had in fact begun a series called "Collections for an Athenae Cantabrigiensis" which appeared in the *Literary Gazette* in twelve instalments between 6 March and 5 June 1847. It consisted of brief biographies of varying length of men of the sixteenth to eighteenth centuries, beginning with Abbot (Robert) and concluding with Aynsworth (Ralph).

32. *The London and Edinburgh Philosophical Magazine and Journal of Science*, 9 (1836), 540. A similar instance, more clever than convincing, is his "A New Game of Chess," *The Cambridge Advertiser*, 14 December 1842, p. [4].

value of scientific literature was meager, that, as Munby suggests,[33] there was little to be gained financially, certainly a consideration for a passionate collector and dealer. Nor, as far as the manuscripts were concerned, can the possibility be entirely overlooked–though it is pure speculation, arrived at with the benefit of hindsight–that Halliwell wanted to dispose of what turned out to be stolen goods (assuming but not concluding that he had indeed stolen manuscripts from Trinity College) and in leaving Cambridge cover his tracks, as it were. Whatever the exact explanation or combination of explanations, money was doubtless a vital matter, connected with Halliwell's "indiscretion" or, as he termed it in giving his reason to Hartshorne in October 1839 for his "unwilling refusal" of an invitation to examine Thomas Phillipps's manuscripts, "untoward circumstances." One thing is certain: Halliwell was changing, as were his interests and horizon.

33. See n. 24.

·2·

_____

The Young Professional: 1840-1845

By 1841 Halliwell's shift from science to the humanities was pronounced. For the Historical Society of Science he produced *A Collection of Letters Illustrative of the Progress of Science in England*. Since its preface is dated 15 January 1841 it was doubtless put together earlier and reflects his previous experience in the libraries of the British Museum, Sion College, Lambeth, and Oxford. Moreover, many of the writers of the eighty-three letters had already been dealt with by Halliwell in essays or were among his collection–Thomas Digges, Dee, John Bulkeley, Charles Cavendish, John Pell, Morland. The same is true of those works "suggested" for publication–such as those from Halliwell's repertory by Roger Bacon, Pappus Alexandrinus, William Bourne, and John Dee–none of which appeared under the aegis of the Society.

Halliwell's other publications in 1841 dealing with the history of science (including mathematics) consisted of three papers–or, more accurately, three separately titled parts of one paper on the Boetian numerical notation–read by the secretary of the Royal Irish Academy (of which Halliwell became an honorary member on 16 March 1841) on 17 January and 27 April 1840. Another, read by the secretary on 22 February 1841, was reprinted in the *London, Edinburgh, and Dublin Philosophical Magazine* in 1842 (20:595-9): "Collection of Notes on the Early History of Science in Ireland." Both subjects were Halliwell favorites: the first accounting for eight publications, the second another of his customary descriptions of manuscripts in the collections he knew so well in London, Oxford, and Cambridge.

The striking interest, one which persisted throughout Halliwell's career, was in catalogues, including his own. Whether called catalogues, handlists, calendars, or the like, they constituted the backbone of his scholarly and commercial activities. Many were integrated into discursive articles and pamphlets; most were straightforward lists with brief comments. They served, of course, to make the works known, as Halliwell had "promised" in his *Few Hints*, and thus help the experts and the novices. They served too to "correct" errors or fill gaps which Halliwell had found in library catalogues.

Two such works in 1841 provide instances of Halliwell's aims. The first, doubtless modelled on the *Book Rarities in the University of Cambridge* (1829) by C. H. Hartshorne, an antiquary with whom Halliwell had established and continued a cordial personal and professional relationship, is *The Manuscript Rarities of the University of Cambridge*. It consists of a simple listing in 170 pages of titles, with only rare and brief comment; Part II, five pages (171-5) devoted to remarks on the manuscript collections in the college libraries, is often little more than a mention of whether or not a catalogue exists, or whether or not an existing one is adequate. Halliwell seems to be addressing in this part an audience not unlike the one envisioned in the *Few Hints*, although apparently in a more subdued manner. Its scope is reduced, as the title indicates, from the advertised title—"A Catalogue of the Manuscripts Preserved in the Libraries of the University of Cambridge"—appended to his *Historia Collegii Jesu Cantabrigiensis* (1840). In fact his preface is so conciliatory as to suggest a certain adjustment to the problems he had encountered in Cambridge:

It was at one time my intention to have printed a catalogue of all the manuscripts in the various libraries of the University, but, upon consideration, I concluded that it would not be well for a private individual to undertake the accomplishment of such a work, unless it were published under the immediate superintendence of the University authorities. A Catalogue of the Cambridge Manuscripts by a Member of the University, would be liable to imperfect criticism out of doors, as proceeding from and sanctioned by the University itself. I was unwilling to subject my Alma Mater to the possibility of any attack being instituted on the ground of not performing its undertakings with proper effect; I was fully aware that I could not effectually guard against such an attack; and I have, therefore, preferred to offer the following pages to the reader, as mere rough notes of a few of the inestimable treasures, in the department of manuscripts, which our noble and ancient University possesses (iii-iv).

If the preface seems less than ingenuous, however, there is no mistaking the chastened reduction of eleven lines and three etceteras of associations and honors following Halliwell's name in the advertisement to the one line and one etc. of the published title page.[34]

The second, *Shakesperiana. A Catalogue of the Early Editions of Shakespeare's Plays, and of the Commentaries and Other Publications Illustrative of His Works*, is in the vein of popular education, an area Halliwell never neglected, combining his passion for bibliography, his growing devotion to literature, especially Shakespeare, and his desire to supply the critic and especially the student with "a manual of bibliographical information which is indispensable to the attainment of any correct knowledge in that department of literature" (p. 3). Not to be underestimated is Halliwell's pointing to the "scarcity" of a similar work of 1827 by John Wilson, *Shaksperiana. Catalogue of All the Books, Pamphlets, &c., Relating to Shakspeare*, and above all "the rapid progress which this class of literature has made since its publication," and thus seeing "sufficient reasons for the present undertaking." Published by John Russell Smith, noted for popular works of this kind, this little pamphlet of forty-six pages—pp. 5-19 on editions of the single plays, pp. 20-40 on "Commentaries, Essays, &c.," pp. 41-2 on the poems, and pp. 43-6 on Collected Editions—is serviceable and up-to-date: the collected editions ending with Knight's Pictorial, 1839-41; the commentaries, with Collier's *Memoirs of Edward Alleyn* of 1841. Smith's appended list of "Works Relating to Shakespeare" serves to complement the commentaries and to make available many of the items listed (even one offering the only judgment made by Halliwell: Andrew Becket's *Shakespeare's Himself Again* [1815], "a work of very little value"). It must be stressed that Halliwell does not simply update Wilson, as might be expected if his total of 233 entries of commentaries is compared with Wilson's 204. On the contrary, he omits some thirty entries found in Wilson—many of which are on the periphery of Shakespeare studies—and adds some thirty to the period (i.e. to 1827) covered by Wilson. Halliwell's entries are more accurate (although he mistakenly repeats Thomas Robertson's *Essay on the Character of Hamlet* [1788], most likely intending William Richardson's *Essays on Shakespeare's Character of Sir John Falstaff* [1789]). And he goes much further than Wilson in describing the individual and collected works, giving more detail and all versions—including those in French and Italian—into the nineteenth century. Although he omits Wilson's practice of giving prices obtained for certain editions and also the apocryphal plays, Halliwell produced an

---

34. Some disappointment may also be evident in the lack of a dedication. A year earlier, in a letter of 16 May 1840, Halliwell sent a prospectus to Lord Brougham asking for permission to inscribe the work to him, as the "talisman of your Lordship's name would be a means of rescuing my humble efforts from oblivion" (UCL Brougham Collection, 18,258).

independent and state-of-the-art work, one certainly living up to his and his publisher's avowed intentions.[35]

Significantly, the rest—and bulk—of Halliwell's publications in 1841 are devoted to more or less literary subjects. Of the nine remaining separate works, three were done for the Percy Society, one for the Shakespeare Society: these reflect Halliwell's permanent interest in reviving and reproducing early literature in accordance with the aims of both societies, of which he was a founding and active member. Two works attest to Halliwell's sharpening focus on Shakespeare. Both were published by William Pickering (who was also doing *Reliquiae Antiquae* and would do *The Foundation Documents of Merton College, Oxford* in 1843): *An Introduction to Shakespeare's Midsummer Night's Dream* and *On the Character of Sir John Falstaff* (dedicated to John Payne Collier, Halliwell's lifelong colleague and friend). They also are witness to Halliwell's entrance into the world of professional Shakespeare criticism. Twenty-one, with considerable ego, and doubtless buoyed by the honors he had received, his recognition by important people, his swirling activism in various societies, and last but not least his enchantment with Shakespeare, Halliwell—for the first time in his career—reveals not merely his professional methodology but also his personal—nay, intimate—response to literature. The very opening sentence of the *Introduction* is both a critical and a personal credo: "It remains to be seen, whether the labours of former commentators have, as some imagine, exhausted all the proper and useful annotation on the works of Shakespeare, which the lapse of two centuries, and the continual change in our language and manners, have rendered necessary" (p. 3). A few lines later Halliwell provides the answer: "We predict that many years must yet elapse, ere that complete inquiry into Shakespeare's language and allusion, without which the spirit of his writings can never be fully understood or appreciated, can be presented to the view of the general reader by means of a commentary" (pp. 3-4). Certain tenets are immediately clear: first, "illustrations"—that is, the scholarly, archaeological investigation of documents contemporary with Shakespeare—are a *sine qua non* for the understanding of Shakespeare and all writings for that matter; second, that understanding is of the "spirit" of Shakespeare's writing. Archaeological research is thus not an end in itself, but can—must—be the key to aesthetic appreciation. Halliwell is always aware, and did not hesitate to pronounce,

35. There was criticism, however, from William Pickering, who, Wright reported (1 August 1841; LOA 9:36), found it " full of very great errors and omissions, and he complains of the arrangement. He says if he were you he would burn it." Although Wright characterized Pickering as "rather fastidious," he advised Halliwell to be "shy" of such undertakings.

that Shakespeare was "truly the child of nature ... that we must receive his works as the production of a genius unfettered by the knowledge of more philosophical canons" (p. 5). This is bardolatry, of course, but not of the kind of those "who despise even the most minute illustration of our great dramatist" (p. 3). It does not deter Halliwell from observing Shakespeare's lack of classical rules or his anachronisms, but neither does it prevent him from employing archaeological research to provide illuminating details of Shakespeare's creativity and establish the proper context for study.

The various chapters follow the established pattern of such introductions: discussions of date, sources, stage history, textual authority for conjecture and emendation. They are distinctly Halliwellian in a number of ways. For one thing, they enable him to interweave his recent and current research: titles like Richard Tarlton's *Newes Out of Purgatorie* and Simon Forman's *Diary* (in the discussion of dating in Chapter II)). For another, they enable him to show his acquaintance with early literature, like Chaucer and Arthur Golding's translation of Ovid (in the discussion of sources in Chapter III). They also enable him to show his knowledge of the work of earlier scholars, like Thomas Tyrwhitt, contemporary ones, like Collier, and sites of scholarship, like the Bodleian (in the discussion of fairy mythology in Chapter IV). They enable him, further, to make known his presence in the contemporary theater and his acquaintance with important personalities, as in his agreeing with John Abraham Heraud (poet and dramatist, from 1843 drama critic for the *Athenaeum)* that *A Midsummer Night's Dream* is not unfit for the stage, that Charles Knight is wrong to say that it is, and that the alterations of his friend James Robinson Planché for the Covent Garden Theatre version are "few, and made with that good judgment which characterizes every thing that Mr. Planché undertakes" (in the discussion of the stage history in Chapter IV). Others in Halliwell's professional and personal circle are appreciatively or dutifully mentioned: Joseph Hunter is agreed with (in the discussion of emendation in Chapter VIII); Frederic Madden is disagreed with (in the discussion of the spelling of Shakespeare's name in Chapter IX). Furthermore they enable Halliwell to pursue what are to be topics of enduring interest—fairy mythology and popular knowledge—and to indulge his predilection for longish excerpts from his favorites, as in a few small-print pages (12-16) from Golding on Pyramus and Thisbe; as in six pages (28-37) from Collier's reprint of the black-letter ballad *The Merry Puck, or Robin Goodfellow*; as in six pages (61-6) from John Lane's *Triton's Trumpet* (although admitting doing so not only because it contains an "interesting allusion to Spenser's death, but also mentions other English poets" [p. 61]); as in six pages (82-7) from the quarto of 1600; as in the six-page appendix on the popular character of Robin Goodfellow. Noteworthy too is Halliwell's dealing with single readings in the longest chapter in the volume–an indication of his lexicographical bent to be realized in his various dictionaries and glossaries, a reflection of his editorial activities, and a prelude to the vast folio edition of Shakespeare he was to produce (1853-66) and also to his compendious *Hand-book Index to the Works of Shakespeare* (1866).

Running through the whole is the Halliwellian blend of the conservative and the radical. On the one hand, there is the dedication to facts and reason ("reasonable" is Halliwell's recurring and dominant adjective), nowhere more obvious perhaps than in his devotion to the textual authority of early printed versions: "no alteration from the original text of Shakespeare's plays is justifiable, unless it can be clearly proved that the typographical error which such an alteration must or ought necessarily to imply, could have been committed by the compositor of the time." Judging this as the "only safe method" (doubtless influenced by Edward Capell, to whose memory he was to dedicate his folio edition of Shakespeare), Halliwell did not hesitate to "most strongly deprecate the whole system of conjectural emendation employed by Theobald and a few other editors" (p. 69). And on the other hand, and existing simultaneously, is the Halliwell who regards Shakespeare as the "child of nature," ever his "greatest favourite." In a coda to the volume Halliwell underscores the "reasonable" in his attempt to extenuate his "presumption in entering a field of research already trodden by so many writers of established reputation" (p. 94) by asserting that he "cannot persuade [himself] to reject any illustrations ... however minute and comparatively trifling they may appear ... always endeavour[ing] to present the reader with new facts rather than adaptations of old ones" (p. 95). And yet in the same context he emphasizes the "fanciful" in his description of the works of Shakespeare as "wonderful" and "sublime" and "idolized": a seeming paradox, one to be continued and intensified in Halliwell's life and career. Framing, if not permeating, the whole in the young Halliwell's defence of his professional position is his defensiveness. For all his confidence there is once again at this stage of his career his extreme sensitivity in a hostile world. The close of the book is a revealing apologia, elegantly phrased and with great assurance, yet not disguising the personal insecurity:

I have perhaps ventured too far, and may be destined to receive the punishment due to presumption in the discovery of my error. If I am doomed to this, at least I may hope that in after many years, my unhappy attempt may escape the affliction of being converted into a testimony in favour of universal censure. Then, after a while, if it be permitted me, when the host of reviewers inimical to this class of learning shall have exhausted their criticisms,

> 'I'll break my staff,
> Bury it certain fathoms in the earth,
> And deeper than did ever plummet sound,
> I'll drown my book.' (p. 97)

By comparison Halliwell's other work, *On the Character of Sir John Falstaff, as Originally Exhibited by Shakespeare in the Two Parts of King Henry IV*, is perhaps less pedantic than its title but nevertheless slighter than the *Introduction*, not only in length–it is more an article than a book–but also in breadth and depth. For its objective is limited to proving that Falstaff was not "intended to represent a person equally historical with the other *dramatis personae*" and that it is "absurd" to hold "that its prototype [was] Sir John Fastolf" (p. 5). Still, Halliwell's methodology and personality are clearly demonstrated. His thesis is that Shakespeare "did not invent–he perfected a drama already ennobled by the labours of others" (p. 12). To prove his point, Halliwell employs unpublished documents, citing the dedicatory epistle to Richard James's *The Legend and Defence of the Noble Knight and Martyr, Sir John Oldcastel.* "Never published, but preserved with his [James's] other manuscripts in the Bodleian Library," it is a supporting testimony, for James was librarian to Robert Cotton and an intimate of Ben Jonson. Other contemporary documents cited in support of the tradition handed down by Nicholas Rowe in his *Life of Shakespeare*–"that this part of Falstaff is said to have been written originally under the name of Oldcastle; some of that family then remaining, the Queen was pleased to command him to alter it; upon which he made use of Falstaff"–are *The Meeting of Gallants* (1604), *The Wandering Jew Telling Fortunes to Englishmen* (before 1630), and *The First Part of the True and Honorable History of the Life of Sir John Oldcastle* (1600). Halliwell's thesis is now generally accepted. One recent edition, the Oxford Shakespeare, has gone so far as to substitute the name Oldcastle for Falstaff.

Equally characteristic are Halliwell's defence of his archaeological methodology–"a study so inadequately encouraged, and so little valued, that few have the courage to enlist in its cause" (pp. 10-11)–and his defence of "one of our most learned and acute critics [who] ... was pronounced a perfect barbarian ... because he fixed by historic wand the scene of Prospero's enchantments" (p. 11).[36] Approval of friends and allies, Joseph Hunter and John Payne Collier, mention of libraries visited and librarians consulted, are as typical of Halliwell as pointing out errors by formidable personalities, like George Frederick Beltz in his *Memorials of the Most Noble Order of the Garter* (1841), or an unidentified "reviewer ... in a literary journal of high pretensions" (p. 14), who held Fastolfe "guiltless" of cowardice (*Athenaeum*, 28 August 1841, pp. 660-1). And finally, and inevitably, there is his own (erroneous) certainty that this "drum and trumpet" play (p. 13) is not to be ascribed to Shakespeare and that "to tax Shakespeare with the character of *Fastolf*, as exhibited in that play, is an absolute libel on his genius."

Halliwell's personal procedures are irrepressible. For one thing, he makes economical use of the material he has at hand: the three contemporary documents cited he was himself to publish separately or make extensive use of. The larger subject-matter, the Yorkist and Lancastrian tetralogies, was among his main publications for the Shakespeare Society. His use of Rowe's *Life* as a starting-point did not prevent him from regarding its information as "valuable ... though evidently not always in a very accurate manner" (pp. 46-7); characteristically, aware "how little has hitherto been discovered," he cannot resist offering two "biographical particulars." They are not relevant to the matter at hand, of course, but are typical of Halliwell's making information public just for the sake of making it public, perhaps of just showing off what he has discovered. In the middle and long range he was previewing, in his criticism of Rowe, the *Life* he himself was to produce in 1848 and his *magnum opus*, *Outlines of the Life of Shakespeare*, which grew in his lifetime to seven editions in the 1880s to become the most comprehensive and authoritative collection of documents relative to the life and times of Shakespeare of his time and later.

The two remaining pamphlets in 1841 are likewise devoted to continuing interests. There is little to say about the slight volume *The Jokes of the Cambridge Coffee-Houses in the Seventeenth Century* that is not already explicit in its title. The collection is consonant with Halliwell's abiding preoccupation with early popular literature, especially jests, anecdotes, tales, and what might be called trivial literature–"fair specimens of books," so the advertisement, "that served in the place which our periodical literature has since supplied"–moving from the Middle Ages and the

36. The reference is to Joseph Hunter and his *Disquisition on the Scene, Origin, Date, &c. of Shakespeare's Tempest*, which was savagely reviewed in the *Gentleman's Magazine*, n.s. 13 (1840), 49-54. Hunter replied in 13 (1840), 166-8.

Renaissance to include the seventeenth century, where Halliwell drew the line. The volume seems to have sold well enough for it to be reprinted in 1842 and perhaps brought some financial gain. Halliwell's next pamphlet in 1841, *The Management of Covent Garden Theatre Vindicated from the Attack of an Anonymous Critic in a Letter to the Editor of the "Cambridge Advertiser,"* though but eight pages long and "Not printed for sale," is not uninteresting for a number of reasons. For one, it is evidence of Halliwell's engagement in the living theater: he was an active theatergoer and critic. For another, it displays his willingness to take sides publicly and passionately, to come to the defence of his friend James Robinson Planché (who was the adapter of Shakespeare's *Midsummer Night's Dream,* one of the productions being attacked), and to give evidence of his taste in supporting Mme. Vestris (Lucia Elizabeth Mathews), with her husband co-manager of Covent Garden Theatre. Above all, Halliwell reacts so indignantly to "Constant Reader" (the pseudonymous letter-writer), who finds fault with the views of the pseudonymous "London Correspondent" of the *Cambridge Advertiser,* as to reveal himself to be the London Correspondent and to be appalled not merely by the attacks from "outside" but by the moral laxity of the newspaper in laying its critical department "open to question by the multitude." That his letter was printed in the *Cambridge Advertiser* (on 13 October 1841) was not satisfaction enough for Halliwell. The privately printed pamphlet is a good measure of Halliwell's sensitivity. Not for the first or last time is his love of what he regarded as truth and "good report" (p. 6) animated and exacerbated by his sense of personal injury.

Halliwell's two editions for the Percy Society in 1841 conform with the others in the series. Although firsts of their kind, they are in the main simple reprints with little or no editorial apparatus. *The Early Naval Ballads,* a selection, follows the established pattern: a brief general preface of three pages, fifty-seven ballads (each preceded by a bibliographical headnote), but no notes. *The Meeting of Gallants,* first published in 1604, has a preface of four pages, a text of twenty-seven, and ten of notes. Both are examples of early popular literature, in the form of poetry and dramatic dialogue. Both have a historical context: the first, although Halliwell "apologise[s] for the incompleteness of its chronological arrangement," reflects the "national interest of the subject ... [and] the triumphs of our marine power cannot be too frequently recalled in our memories" (vii-viii); the second, in its depiction of the plague in London in 1603, offers "a curious picture of a very eventful occurrence in the history of our great metropolis" (v). Both incorporate the language and humor of their time, aspects which appealed to the lexicographer and humorist in Halliwell. Finally, the bare first reprint of *The Boke of Curtasye* is another example of Halliwell's interest in Middle English literature and language, being based on a fourteenth-century manuscript which Halliwell came across in one of his favorite archaeological "digs"–the British Museum Library, MS. Sloane 1986.

Halliwell's edition of the *Ludus Coventriae* for the newly formed Shakespeare Society is for many his most important work to date. It is the first edition of all the plays, not to be done again until K. S. Block's for the Early English Text Society in 1922. Its introduction is, as usual, a brief and not very detailed eight and a half pages and its notes only eleven, but it is nevertheless a major transcription of forty-three plays (totalling 405 pages) from a fifteenth-century manuscript in Halliwell's cherished Cottonian collection (Vespas.D.viii). Although he "endeavoured to give the reader as faithful a copy of the original manuscript as was possible, with all its errors and defects," Halliwell did attempt at least to correct some egregious errors in the notes and especially the "barbarous work of the few Latin passages" (xii). And aware that it "will be found useful to those who are learned in the philology of our early language, as there are many words of very unfrequent occurrence," Halliwell "constructed [a glossary] more especially with a view to the wants of those who have not made our early poetry a matter of study" (xiii). The glossary (pp. 419-34) is the most extensive one he had as yet published. It is consonant with Halliwell's literary bent (including parallels in Chaucer and other early writers and commentators, as well as Shakespeare); with the activities of his professional and personal circle (including references to work by Frederic Madden and Thomas Wright); and with his own predilection for dictionaries, glossaries, and other lexica, as manifestations of the all-encompassing archaeological research he represented.[37]

Bridging 1841 with 1842 was Halliwell's ambitious journal *The Archaeologist and Journal of Antiquarian Science*, which appeared in ten monthly numbers from September to June and then together in two volumes in 1842. Although the editorial "we" is the pronoun of the preface (dated 1 February 1842) to the first volume, the contributions are generally unsigned, and Thomas Wright played an important role in concept and content,[38] the journal bears all the hallmarks of Halliwell's personal and professional orientation. It is another reflection and

37. For a discussion of the edition and its reception, see Sylvia Stoler Wagonheim, "John Payne Collier and the Shakespeare Society" (diss. University of Maryland, 1980), pp. 151-6.

38. For instances of Wright's involvement, see 30 October 1841; LOA 9:19, 12 January [1842]; LOA 39:34, and May [1842]; LOA 14:76.

extension of the point of view expressed in his previous works. As the Address (dated September 1841) which heads the first number makes clear, the undertaking is an act of devotion to archaeological research and, consonant with Halliwell's choice and treatment of subjects like Samuel Morland, William Rishanger, and Simonds D'Ewes, an *apologia* for the value of history: "We will ... endeavor to imbue the public mind with a more favourable feeling than it has hitherto had towards antiquarian researches, the utility and importance of which, *when properly directed*, are unquestioned by every one who admits the value of HISTORY" (p. 2). The devotion is idealistic: "We do so fearlessly and sanguinely, because we write not for the sake of gain, or of reputation. but really and solely for the benefit of our favourite science" (pp. 1-2). It is youth-oriented, addressed to the "rising generation," knowing "too well the difficulties which young authors have to encounter, not to show every indulgence towards early errors, and cheer each one on in his labours" (p. 3). It is progressive and forward-looking, acknowledging the "rapid and essential changes [which have] taken place in ... the last few years ... in the study of antiquities" (p. 2). It is expansive and all-embracing, its contents ranging from the Round Towers of Ireland to Christmas Cards to Egyptian Antiquities to Jests to Catholicism at Oxford to Theatrical Prospects to Yorkshire Dialect. If the wide-ranging landscape has been influenced by Halliwell's membership in various societies, and doubtless by the panoramic scholarship and patronymic stance of Thomas Wright, it has also been shaped by Halliwell's personal experience. Youth may have been mistreated or misunderstood, and the older generation often guilty of abusing their science. But Halliwell's appeal, reflecting his personal decision, is for solidarity in the framing and understanding of the objectives of archaeology and for the "assistance" of "all classes of antiquaries" in "making advances towards excellence" (pp. 4-5).

Of Halliwell's ten articles published in 1842, only five were actually written in 1842. Three were read or communicated on 27 February and 19 and 26 March 1840 but appeared in *Archaeologia*, the journal of the Society of Antiquaries, in 1842. They continue his early interest in manuscripts dealing with history and religion, as well as mechanics and inventions. His "Observations upon the History of Certain Events in England," the most extensive of the three in *Archaeologia* (29 [1842], 127-38), reprints several documents pertaining to the life of Edward IV, Halliwell hoping to "furnish a few additional facts on a period of history, the obscurity of which has been admitted by every writer" (p. 127), and not failing to mention the productive work of Henry Ellis, W. H. Black, and John Bruce (all members of the Society) and correcting (pp. 137-8) in some instances errors in dating made by John Lingard in his *History of England*. Halliwell's second communication, "The Volvelle, and on Chaucer's Treatise on the Astrolabe" (29 [1842], 374-5), consists of three independent excerpts from some of his favorite collections–Lambeth, Ashmolean, and British Museum–explaining the volvelle and its uses as an accompaniment to a manuscript in his own possession being exhibited. The third, "Speculum Christiani" (29 [1842], 375-8), is a description of "one of the most sensible and least violent of the Lollardic writings" (p. 375), with an attempt to identify its author definitively but concluding that although John Morris is apparently the author, "further evidence would be acceptable" (p. 377), if discovered. The remaining two–slight notes of less than a page–deal with ancient paintings in an exhibition of drawings on 2 December 1841 and a brief biography (done anonymously) of Richard Norwood for the *Penny Cyclopaedia* in 1839.[39]

The articles written and published in 1842 are brief and insignificant, except as they attest to Halliwell's interests and methods. His little note on Nathaniel Torporley, quoting a passage he had come across in Aubrey's MS. collection in the Ashmolean, confirms Rigaud's conjecture about the anagrammatic spelling of the name (Poulterey) and identifies the source of his profession, showing thus "how little credit is frequently to be placed on unauthenticated relations." "Some Notices of the Manuscripts in the Chetham Library at Manchester," an unlocated communication to the Society of Antiquaries, is doubtless incorporated into his larger *Account of the European Manuscripts in the Chetham Library, Manchester*, which also appeared in 1842. Similarly, his note "Shakespeare's Merry Wives" was incorporated into his full-length *First Sketch*, both for the Shakespeare Society. The remaining two–each just a paragraph long–are a biographical entry on Richard Suisset in the *Penny Cyclopaedia* and a clever chess stratagem in the *Cambridge Advertiser* (14 December 1842, p. 4). A sure sign of Halliwell's diminishing engagement with purely scientific topics is obvious in one exchange of letters with J. W. Lubbock. Responding to his receiving manuscript notes on the tides which Halliwell described as "not being of any use to me" (26 March [1842]; Royal Society, LUB.H31), Lubbock did "not think them very remarkable" and "will take an opportunity of returning" them (26 March 1842; LOA 14:9).

Of greater general interest was Halliwell's reprint of the *Private Diary*

---

39. Halliwell contributed a number of such anonymous brief biographies to Knight's *Penny Cyclopaedia*, as did his mentors Thomas Stephens Davies and Thomas Wright. It was evidently Wright who arranged for them, as he did for those in the *New General Biographical Dictionary*.

of Dr. John Dee, covering the period from 25 August 1554 to 6 April 1601 (to which Halliwell provided a very useful index), and the *Catalogue of His Library of Manuscripts,* both in a volume for the Camden Society. Although the preface is dated 15 March 1842, it is likely that the catalogue is based on earlier research, while Halliwell was a student, in the collection of Trinity College. And both works accord with Halliwell's concern with the history and men of science, the catalogue containing names and works which recur in Halliwell's early writings: Roger Bacon, Boethius, Sacro-Bosco, among others.

Halliwell's *Account of the European Manuscripts in the Chetham Library, Manchester,* another briefly annotated contribution to "paleographical literature," reflects his interest in and journeys to provincial libraries on what he called "archaeological outings." And it serves as well to modify the brash stance regarding unqualified readers in public libraries evident in his earlier letter to the *Times*[40] and in fact to delineate a mature attitude towards popular education. He praises a Chetham Library which "has long been open to the public under singularly liberal regulations. It is, indeed, the only Library, I believe, in England which is accessible to men of all conditions of life, without the necessity of an admission ticket, recommendation, or qualification of any kind, save the simple one of being competent to inscribe their names in a visiting book" (iii). The work is also notable as the first result in print of Halliwell's long and productive relationship with James Heywood, one of the founders of the Manchester Athenaeum, at whose house in Acresfield, near Pendleton, he stayed, and to whom he was to dedicate the second edition of his *Early History of Freemasonry in England* (1844) and whose research he was to edit as *The Foundation Documents of Merton College, Oxford* in 1843

But literature was to dominate and establish the direction of his future scholarship. Drawing on his visit to the Chetham Library, he transcribed its unique manuscript of *Torrent of Portugal,* assisted by an earlier transcription made by Frederic Madden, to whom he dedicated the work. Since he had already given an account of the manuscript in two places—in his catalogue and in a paper communicated to the Society of Antiquaries on 17 February 1842 (but not printed in *Archaeologia* until 1844 [30:527-30])—Halliwell devotes the brief preface to a summary of the Scandinavian version of the legend of Veland, one of the heroes of Northern mythology alluded to in the fifteenth-century verse romance of Torrent, as well as in the romance of Horn and early German and French romances. There is no critical apparatus. The work must have been done

40. See pp. 72-3.

quickly for the popular series of John Russell Smith, although Halliwell does append a few fragments of an earlier printed edition in the Douce Collection in the Bodleian Library. Animating his preoccupation with literature and its focus in particular on Shakespeare was Halliwell's purchase at the George Chalmers sale in March 1842 of four later Shakespeare quartos: lot No. 946, *The Taming of the Shrew* (1631) (imperfect), bound with *Pericles* (1619) (wanting the title) for twelve shillings; lot No. 947, *Hamlet* (1637) (part of the bottom of the title cut off) for seven shillings; lot No. 948, *Richard II*, with new additions of the Parliament scene and the deposing of King Richard (1615) for £5; and lot No. 949, *History of Henry IV*, with the battle of Shrewsbury (1622) (the line containing the date cut off) for £1.1.0. Halliwell's investment was modest, to be sure–in the same sale Collier paid £105 for *The Sonnets* (1609)–but the direction and verve of the twenty-two-year-old were unmistakable.

Halliwell's print facsimile *The First Sketch of Shakespeare's Merry Wives of Windsor* is his first full-blooded encounter with editing Shakespeare, the first in his preoccupation with other "bad" quartos (the Henry the Sixth plays), and the continuation of his work on the English history plays of the Lancastrian tetralogy. His introduction is noteworthy for its almost exclusive attention to the occasion and the dating of the play, portraying his expertise and confidence in historical documentation and reasonable conclusion. He is "induced to hazard a conjecture which will satisfy all the authenticated parts of the tradition, by supposing *another reason* for the play having been produced before the court at a very short notice" (ix): the play was produced at Windsor in connection with the visit in 1592 by the Duke of Württemberg. The date as well as the setting would then be established as not in 1601 (Halliwell disagreeing with Edmond Malone and, as it turned out, the view now accepted) when the visit might be forgotten, nor "likely to be alluded to in 1596, four years afterwards" (xiv)–Halliwell disagreeing with Alexander Chalmers. Furthermore, since characters overlap with those in the Lancastrian tetralogy, Halliwell's examination of internal evidence makes him "inclined to believe that the two parts of Henry IV, like the Merry Wives, *originally existed in an unfinished state, and that, when the first sketch of the Merry Wives was written, those plays had* NOT *been altered and amended in the form in which they have come down to us*" (xxviii-xxix). And, returning to a topic he had already discussed, Halliwell concludes that the "amended" play was written after the change from Oldcastle to Falstaff, "in all probability not very long after the production of the two parts of Henry IV" (xxx). Halliwell's introduction shows confidence but not arrogance. His disagreements with Chalmers and especially Charles Knight are not abusive or haughty. And, as always, he attempts a cautious and reasonable point of view. He even warns the readers about the possible sources and analogues he appends. Still, he has pride enough to conclude his introduction with a reference to a manuscript he has discovered in the British Museum which alludes to the legend of Horne the hunter, the first to do so and the first to be dated. And after careful notes he adds, less conservatively, excerpts from Italian works (with translations) and, typically, from two works which he himself is to edit: Tarlton's *Newes Out of Purgatorie* and *Westward for Smelts*.

With *The Nursery Rhymes of England*, whose preface is dated in the coyly fashionable manner Feast of All Saints, 1841, Halliwell achieved wide popularity, if the number of editions is any indication. In quick succession John Russell Smith, who had taken over the publication from the Percy Society, brought out further editions in 1843, 1844, 1846, and then a "sequel," *Popular Rhymes and Nursery Tales*, in 1849. Smith was buoyant. Calling attention to an article in *Tait's Edinburgh Magazine*, "which will make [Halliwell] stare," he was sure "all this row will make them sell, you must be getting prepared for a new & *improved!* edition according to some of the critics" (2 February 1842; LOA 15:53).[41] "Look out on Sunday Morng for the best review of the Nursery Rhymes," Smith enthused early in 1843, "I am told its [*sic*] likely to sell 100 copies" (5 January 1843; LOA 15:3). Half a year later he informed Halliwell that Mark Anthony Lower "promises to try his hand at a design or two of the N. R." (27 July 1843; LOA 15:28). In November Smith has "just written to New York to offer a 1,000 copies at a very moderate price to counteract the Boston edition" (2 November 1843; LOA 15:51). Versions and reworkings of it are still available today. It is, moreover, not a simple potboiler, for Halliwell's original classification scheme—three hundred poems arranged in fourteen classes—was novel and adventurous. And he was wise enough—or had learned—to anticipate and thus deflect criticism by admitting in the preface that "in attempting a classification, I am well aware that much question may arise concerning the true appropriation of many of the nursery rhymes to their several classes, and I must claim the indulgence of my readers for any mistakes I have committed in this respect" (vii). He did not quite abandon his sensitivity and sharp edge, however, for he goes on to "take the opportunity of stating, that it was originally my intention to have introduced also a collection of merriments upon which many of

41. There appears to be an error in the dating of Smith's letter, for the review article appeared in *Tait's Edinburgh Magazine for 1843*, 10 (1843), 114-22. There is nothing of this nature from November 1841 to April 1842 to which Smith could have been referring.

these rhymes are founded, but the project was overruled by a gentleman, who gave it as his opinion that the Society would by their publication be involved in an awkward question of copyright. I was not previously aware that 'Goody Two Shoes', and romances of this kind, were regarded so jealously by the trade" (vii-viii). And his extravagance as far as true friends were concerned is not to be overlooked in the dedication he added when Smith took over the publication. Smith wrote that it "is found great fault with ... you should have said no more than what you said of Sir F. Madden in 'Torrente'" (5 January 1843: LOA 15:3). But Halliwell was determined to honor and support a friend, as a discussion of his role in the Shakespeare Society will demonstrate: "If it be not sacrilege to associate the name of an eminent writer with the traditional poetry of our childhood, the following collection is inscribed, as a trifling mark of esteem and friendship, to J. R. Planché, Esq."

The four articles published by Halliwell in 1843 were all presented to the Royal Society of Literature, of which (for financial reasons) he was no longer a member. In theme all stem from an earlier period and, with one exception, reflect earlier interests. Halliwell's special attention to that area of mathematics involving numerical contractions is reflected in three of them: "An Inquiry into the Probable Origin of the Boetian Numerical Contractions" had been read by the secretary on 13 June 1839; "A Few Observations on the Two Meanings of the Greek Word Pórisma" on 23 January 1840 (and mentioned in the Proceedings in 1837). Although "Observations on the Pórismata" was read by the secretary on 25 January 1844 and published in the Proceedings of 1843, it is clear that it merely adds a bit more detail to the earlier work and may be assumed to have been written before 1843. Only Halliwell's "On the History of the Monastery of Ely," read on 14 May 1841, reflects his continuing devotion to reprinting documents connected with early historical events, persons, and places. Similarly, the reprinting of selected *Foundation Documents of Merton College, Oxford* satisfies a Halliwellian preoccupation with universities, with manuscript collections, with the élite of English science–Walter de Merton was "probably intimate with Roger Bacon and John Holywood [i.e. Johannes de Sacro-Bosco], both of whom, it is said, were among the earliest members of Merton College" (viii)–and with the thirteenth century. It allows him, not untypically, to realize in print the collection made by his friend James Heywood, also Fellow of the Royal Society and also student at Trinity College, who inspired and supported Halliwell's *Account of the European Manuscripts in the Chetham Library*, which had appeared in the previous year.

Aside from a further contribution to the history and literature of early science, a controversial reprint *of A Selection from the Papers of Dr. Simon Forman*, which was set in type for the Camden Society but then cancelled,[42] Halliwell now concentrated on two main areas: popular and vernacular literature and Shakespeare. *The Pleasant Conceits of Old Hobson, the Merry Londoner*, another publication for the Percy Society, is a further contribution to the growing list of titles of mainly humorous anecdotes and jests of the sixteenth and seventeenth centuries. It consists of thirty-five "conceits," normally less than a page each: a loose collection of encounters which enable the legendary Hobson (of Hobson's choice, this or none) to display his wit. *A Collection of Pieces in the Dialect of Zummerʒet*, published by John Russell Smith, who must have sensed the popularity of this sub-genre and wished to expand his extensive list of books dealing with dialects, is in the same tradition but slighter: there is not even the customary two-page preface, only the reprint of ten short poems and prose tales, all mainly "merry," as the dialect perforce implies. What is of note is that Halliwell has selected them from manuscripts of the seventeenth century and printed works of the eighteenth–that is, following the practice of the Percy Society–and begins to develop further his penchant for lexicographical studies already evident in the texts and glossaries he had published and in his achieving wide-reaching importance in the *Dictionary of Archaic and Provincial Words*, on which he was working.

Halliwell's edition for the Shakespeare Society of the quartos of *2 and 3 Henry 6* continues his engagement with early and problematic texts. It follows the standard format of his edition of *The Merry Wives*: introduction, reprint, notes. As was the custom, the introduction provides a bibliographical description and history of the editions and proceeds to the main object: the "question ... whether Shakespeare was their author, or whether he merely borrowed from some older dramatist" (xiii). Reviewing the external evidence, Halliwell concludes that it favors Malone's theory (in his "Dissertation") that Shakespeare was not the author. The absence of Shakespeare's name on the title page, for example, and (internally) the "constant offences against grammar" (xvi) leave little doubt that the plays were published "piratically." Still, Halliwell is convinced that he can "place before the reader certain evidences, before unnoticed, which lead [him] to think that neither Malone, nor Knight [referring to his Pictorial Edition, 1838-42], nor Collier [his edition of 1842], are exactly right in the results to which they have arrived concerning the authorship" (xvi-xvii). Halliwell, it must be stated, was disagreeing with Malone's conclusion but only with elements of Knight's

42. See p. 120.

and Collier's evidence and procedure, for both supported Shakespeare's authorship. Knight especially is singled out for criticism: his collation only of the edition of 1619 (to Halliwell an "intermediate composition"); his assertion that "if Malone's theory be adopted, Shakespeare was the most unblushing plagiarist that ever put pen to paper" (xxix); in short, "the argument of authorship, as adopted by Mr. Knight, is at best but a *reductio ad absurdum*, where *possibilities* exist, that even, if the predicates be proved, two conclusions may be drawn" (xxxix). The mathematician in Halliwell concludes that although one of the mentioned candidates for authorship can be said to have had the talent, "it does not necessarily follow that there was no one of their contemporaries who was not capable of it," carefully adding, "though the presumptive evidence may be in favour of the first position" (xl). Halliwell does not produce any startling evidence in his argumentation, but he does follow that line which is to prevail and is especially alert not only to details from authors he himself will work on–like Robert Greene and Henry Chettle–but also to the stylistic or literary elements, especially the structural unity of the tetralogy. His close reasoning and overall information weigh more heavily than an occasional lapse, like his statement that there was no Shakespearean connection with the Earl of Pembroke's company, or his criticism of the unnamed editor of the Percy Society reprint of Chettle's *Kind Heart's Dream* for an "announcement [which] will be read with considerable astonishment by those who have paid any attention to this branch of literature" (xxiv, n. 1). Since the editor was Edward Francis Rimbault, a founder and secretary of the Percy Society, the criticism was doubtless ill considered. Collier and Knight were reconciled, but perhaps not all were forgiving.

Halliwell's *Account of the Only Known Manuscript of Shakespeare's Plays* takes up his interest in the *Merry Wives* and in making known early manuscripts (this one written during the Commonwealth) which he had purchased. Little more than a comparison of twenty-six parallel passages, it nevertheless poses the important question of textual authority "for the purpose of showing how very little early authority for the text of Shakespeare has yet been discovered, and the extreme importance given by the critics [agreeing with Collier] to evidence of this nature" (p. 23).

A crown of sorts to the year 1843 was the completion of *Reliquiae Antiquae*, a collection which appeared in four parts from 1839 to 1843 and in two volumes published by William Pickering, the first in 1841, the second in 1843. In a way it symbolizes Halliwell and his sphere. A collaboration with Thomas Wright–the original idea, however, was doubtless Halliwell's[43]—it reflects, as the full title—*Scraps from Ancient Manuscripts, Illustrating Chiefly Early English Literature and English Language*—makes clear, their common interest in older popular literature, in history, and in lexicography. It charts their excursions to manuscript sources, so many as to constitute a veritable map of English archaeological treasure sites—i.e. the major library and private manuscript collections at home and abroad. It enabled both to exercise their linguistic and lexicographical talent in the form of Anglo-Saxon, Middle English, Anglo-Norman, and Latin glosses and glossaries and to use or collect material for lexica they were working on. For Halliwell personally it spanned his youth—he identifies his contribution with "Hllll.," an abbreviation he had used for his letters to the editor of the *Gentleman's Magazine*, which grew out of the "J. L." he had used as a sixteen-year-old for his contributions to the *Parthenon*—and his student days, for many of the selections are from his Cambridge haunts, such as the Cambridge Public Library and Jesus College; and his tireless excavations in London, Oxford, Manchester, and other sites. It also incorporates as contributors some of his closest friends—like Samuel Charles of Cambridge and E. H. Hunter of Oxford, both of whom edited pieces from manuscripts Q.T.3 and Q.T.8, which Halliwell must have provided from Jesus College—and idols, such as Thomas Phillipps, who provided a number of manuscripts for transcription from his own collection and to whom the first volume of 1841 was dedicated but whom he had as yet not visited, and Charles Purton Cooper, former secretary of the second Record Commission, who "caused the libraries of the continent to be explored " and to whom the second volume was dedicated.

By 1844 Halliwell seems to have given himself up almost entirely to literary subjects. The second edition of *The Early History of Freemasonry* has a preface dated 3 August 1843; it is a reprint of the first edition with but a new glossary and a new dedication, this time to his friend James Heywood, whose collection of the foundation documents of Merton College, Oxford, Halliwell had edited in 1843 and who had supported the *Account of the European Manuscripts in the Chetham Library* (1842). Halliwell's two treatments of library holdings, "English Poetical Manuscript in the

43. In a letter of 7 February 1839 (LOA 2:17) Wright, "thinking a good deal about your proposed little quarterly publication," recommended a printer, gave a detailed estimate of what his suggested printing of 250 copies would cost (£5.5.0), recommended a publisher (Pickering) and even wrote to friends in Edinburgh (William Turnbull and David Laing) asking them to get "transcribers," himself promising to "work it up well in the Gentleman's Magazine and the Literary Gazette."

Chetham Library" and "The Chronicle of the Monastery of Abingdon," are products of 1842: the former communicated to the Society of Antiquaries on 17 February 1842, the second for the Berkshire Ashmolean Society, of which Halliwell was a member and local secretary at Cambridge. The first is a description of a unique manuscript Halliwell must have come across as he worked on the catalogue published in 1842, containing verse lives of the Virgin Mary, various female saints, the proverbs of Cato, and the *Torrence of Portyngale* (which he had edited separately in 1842). The second is a transcription of a copy of Hemingford's Chronicle in Latin with an English translation by an unnamed "graduate of Oxford," which Halliwell deems "occasionally inaccurate" (iii). It continues his attempt to make available "curious" manuscripts with early historical relevance.

With one exception–and that not in theme but in publisher only–all the rest of Halliwell's separate publications in 1844 were issued by the publishing societies: the Shakespeare, the Percy, and the Camden. Without exception, all deal with early popular literature, drama, and stage, mainly Shakespeare (not to mention his seven anonymous brief pieces on individual Shakespearean plays in the *Cambridge Advertiser*). For the Papers of the Shakespeare Society (III:1847), he contributed three articles, as many as the director, John Payne Collier (if only signed articles of the twenty-five are counted). They are brief, from two to five pages long, and are more notes than articles with a thesis. Their titles as listed in the Contents are enough to reveal their nature: "Remarks on the Similarity of a Passage in Marlowe's *Edward II*, and One in the First Part of *The Contention*" (pp. 5-7), tracing obviously from Halliwell's edition; "Observations on the Correct Method of Punctuating 'Too Too,' in *Hamlet*" (pp. 39-43), with a host of instances from numerous sources, including the Thornton manuscript on which he was working; and "On the Word 'Ducdame,' in *As You Like It*" (pp. 109-110), in which he suggests a reading from an uncollated manuscript of the "Vision of Piers Ploughman" in the Bodleian Library (edited by his friend Thomas Wright and which he reviewed in 1842) and finds fault with Charles Knight and the commentators except Collier. *Tarlton's Jests, and Newes Out of Purgatorie* is a more substantial contribution to the history of the early English stage. A forty-page introduction contains a repository of extracts from contemporary literature which provides information about the life of Tarlton, some of them from works Halliwell himself, always economical, was to publish separately, like *Westward for Smelts* (1848) and *The Tinker of Turvey* (1859). There is little attempt to do more than present a string of passages, but they are themselves of interest for the light they shed on

Renaissance literature and Halliwell's acquaintance with it through books and manuscripts and also the efforts of some of his contemporaries, such as Wright, with whose wish (15 December 1843; LOA 18:23) Halliwell complied in mentioning his "Essay on St. Patrick's Purgatory" (xxxix-xl), and especially Collier, who provided a copy of the unique manuscript of *Tarlton's Jigge* and lent (6 December 1843; LOA 23:34) a woodcut reproduced on p. 4, as well as commenting extensively on the notes. Halliwell's generous acknowledgment of Collier's "most valuable assistance" (xlvi) is not without a certain piquancy. In a letter of 5 July 1843 (LOA 18:9) to Halliwell, Wright gives a vivid picture of the interplay of persons and politics in the societies. He describes a meeting of the Percy Society at which "Lord Braybroke was there also, and we had another stir about indecent publications ... We began taking all indecent books off our list—your Tarlton's Jests must come off." With cunning tactical advice and impressive prescience, he continues:

I have some reason for believing that Collier was very desirous of doing Tarlton himself. If I were you, under all circumstances, I would send the transcript of Tarlton to Collier, I would say to him that I had accidentally heard something which led me to believe that he would like to edit it ... for the Shakespeare. By doing this you will lose nothing of any account, and I think you will make Collier your friend for ever. You will thus defeat some persons who I suspect try to put him against you, and you will also get a little reputation for having done a generous action which will singularly disappoint some persons that I know, and gain you more advantage than the editing of the book. I have known Collier about 9 years, and I have always found him a good friend, and ready to do me any service he could.

As it turned out, Halliwell found an outlet for his reprint in the Shakespeare Society, of which of course Collier was director (and of which, ironically, Lord Braybrooke, president of the Percy Society, was also vice-president). Furthermore, in another twist, Halliwell does not avoid mentioning the suppression of "indecent" material. But despite the resistance against it in the Percy Society—Dyce resigned from the Council in protest—and his having himself been the victim of such censorship in the Camden Society,[44] Halliwell is surprisingly conciliatory in his opinion,

44. The topic seems to have been widely and heatedly discussed. On 11 May 1843 "the anniversary meeting of the Camden Society," reported George Elwes Corrie, "was held this evening, at which there was a good deal of fun. An

as if wary of the ready hostility of certain colleagues or chastened by it or convinced by the counsel of Wright:

In concluding our collection of these scattered notices of Tarlton, which it is to be regretted are not more explicit and satisfactory, it may be necessary to observe that the grossness of two articles in the original edition of the 'Jests' made it requisite to diminish the present reprint 'lesser than a little' by rejecting them, purifying our own pages at the expence of destroying the purity of the ancient text. We are not for our own part very squeamish in these matters, believing that those who can read the whole of Shakespeare's works as they have come down to us may bear almost any thing in this way; but as the passages now omitted convey no information, and certainly are not worthy of preservation from their language, no real good purpose would have been answered by retaining them (xlv-xlvi).

It is also not unlikely that Halliwell, though avowedly not "very squeamish," did not condone the publication of such extreme material.

Halliwell was no longer a member of the Council of the Percy Society and held no office in 1844. But he was one of its most prolific authors. In 1844 alone he produced three works under its auspices: editions of *The Poems of John Audelay*, the *Romance of the Emperor Octavian*, and the satire *Friar Bakon's Prophesie*. Although of differing subgenres and theme, they have in common the fact that they are early popular texts in verse, that they are derived from unique manuscripts or printed copies (as is the case with *Friar Bakon's Prophesie*), and that they reflect, each in its own way, linguistic variety. They bear, of course, the hallmarks of Halliwell's engagement: ample illustrations of his activities in the Bodleian and the Cambridge and Lincoln Cathedral libraries, with references to others as well; his favorite tripartite structure: a brief introduction discussing the

amendment was moved to the Report, the effect of which was in fact a censure on the Committee for undignified expressions in the publications of the Society. The adoption of the Report was then moved and seconded. After a good deal of talk and interruption I asked permission to say a few words, to the effect that enough had been proved by the speakers on the amendment, to shew that caution was necessary, and that an opportunity had been given for bringing the objected matter under discussion. It seemed to me that the end of the mover of the amendment had been accomplished, and I took the liberty of suggesting that leave should be asked to withdraw it. This was readily acceded to and the amendment withdrawn. Thus the dispute was amicably settled" (*Memorials of the Life of George Elwes Corrie, D.D.*, ed. M. Holroyd, Cambridge, 1890, pp. 215-16).

provenance of the copytext and adding a few remarks on the underlying literary tradition, a clear and on the whole accurate reprint of the text, and finally a brief set of notes containing parallel passages, glossarial explanations, and corrections of the original text.

Halliwell's edition of the *Thornton Romances* has already been mentioned in connection with his edition of *Octavian*, reflecting his customary economy of effort. Parallel enterprises and parallel publications (even of the same material) mark his career. This one for the Camden Society, is, however, a considerable accomplishment. To his customary introductory structure dealing with four early English metrical romances, Halliwell adds a detailed description of the three Cambridge and Lincoln manuscripts (xxv-l), a discussion of the terminal contractions in early English manuscripts (li-lvi), and separate glossarial notes. The generously printed volume of 368 pages also illustrates Halliwell's growing linguistic and lexicographical disposition: the former with quotations from Anglo-Norman, Middle High German, Latin, and Middle English texts–although it is certain that he was simply quoting, not necessarily knowing, the first two languages–the latter with the glossarial index and his admission that he was collecting materials for a lexicographical work (doubtless, the *Dictionary of Archaic and Provincial Words*, which began appearing in parts in 1844 and was completed in two volumes in 1847). And, as usual, there is the parade of Halliwell staples: references to manuscripts in his favorite libraries, to his own published and in-progress works (such as his *Torrent of Portugal* and *Captain Cox's Library*), and to fellow antiquaries and acquaintances (such as Thomas Wright and Frederic Madden).

The one work which did not appear under the auspices of one of the societies, the *Nugae Poeticae*, is not in essence or substance an exception. Obviously another of the commercial undertakings for John Russell Smith, it is a slim volume reprinting twelve, so the title page, "select pieces of old English popular poetry, illustrating the manners and arts of the fifteenth century." It is a "little volume" in all the senses: barely three pages for a very general preface, sixty-nine pages of poems based on collections in Cambridge, Oxford, and London, and three pages containing eleven notes (somewhat inflated by longish quotations). In short, it is another example of what may be termed Halliwell's occasional endeavors.

The year 1845 was climactic, if not traumatic, for Halliwell. In a proceeding of great complexity (to be discussed below) he was banned from the library of the British Museum for purportedly having stolen–"abstracted" was the word used–manuscripts from the library of Trinity College Cambridge, some of which found their way into the collection of the British Museum. An added shock was the sudden death on 7 September 1845 of his eldest brother, Richard, aged thirty-three, to whom Halliwell was devoted and who was the law partner of William Lovell, who represented Halliwell in the British Museum affair.

Despite his understandable pleas that his work was being disrupted because of the ban, Halliwell continued to publish and, all things considered, abundantly. Five books, seven articles, and a lengthy pamphlet defending himself against the charges were published. In addition, of course, his already massive correspondence increased substantially, no doubt because of the numerous letters connected with the British Museum ban.[45] And the collecting of material for certain projects—such as the *Dictionary of Archaic and Provincial Words*, which was appearing in parts, the *Letters of Kings of England*, and the *Life of Shakespeare*—was so vigorously pursued that these works were completed within two years.

Halliwell's work took on a strong focus in 1845. Of the books, four appeared under the aegis of the publishing societies: for the Percy Society, *The Affectionate Shepherd* and *Poetical Miscellanies*, for the Shakespeare Society, *Illustrations of the Fairy Mythology of A Midsummer Night's Dream* and *Shakespeare's Play of King Henry the Fourth*. Another, the two-volume *Autobiography and Correspondence of Sir Simonds D'Ewes*, was published by Richard Bentley. Three articles were written for the Shakespeare Society, four for the British Archaeological Association. There were to be no more publications for the Camden Society, with which Halliwell had been involved in a notable dispute, or the Historical Society of Science, which had been dwindling so sharply that it was officially dissolved in the following year. Halliwell's titles indicate his concentration on the sixteenth and seventeenth centuries, especially Shakespeare. They also reinforce his employment of "archaeological" research to make available original documents. Mathematical subjects fade; the remaining articles for the British Archaeological Association are devoted to illustrations of life in earlier times as drawn from early manuscripts.

Four of the works had in fact been finished in 1844. The newly constituted *Archaeological Journal*, concentrating on the early and middle ages, mentions (1 [1845], 278) that at the first annual meeting of the British Archaeological Association at Canterbury Halliwell, on 13 September 1844, "made a few observations on some early MSS. preserved in the library of Canterbury cathedral" and that Thomas Wright followed

45. In addition to a considerable number of letters of support from his regular correspondents, Halliwell received very many others, which he bound among the 199 in Volumes 25 and 26 of the Letters of Authors in the Edinburgh collection.

with a "short communication from Mr. Halliwell, relating to the coronation of Henry VI. of England in Paris." The texts of these papers do not seem to be extant. A third, an excerpt form a manuscript in the Public (i.e. University) Library at Cambridge, gives a brief description of the interior of a chamber in a castle. Interesting is the fact that Halliwell economizes, once again: the romance of Sir Degrevant, the source of the excerpt, appeared as one of the Thornton Romances for the Camden Society in the same year.

The *Illustrations of the Fairy Mythology of A Midsummer Night's Dream* is a substantial collection of thirty-nine romances, tales, poems, dramatic scenes, and other "tracts" which reflect Halliwell's dominant interest in early literature and persistent activity in favorite libraries, the latter obvious in the fact that although the reprints are not annotated they are always introduced by a brief description of their provenance. What is striking is the personal delight Halliwell seems to take in the subject matter and the unabashed and continuing penchant–mathematics and sober scholarship notwithstanding–for humor and whimsy. How else can the opening of his introduction be explained?

Poor Puck's occupation, alas, is gone! Cream-bowls are safe, and slovenly servants freed from the persecutions of the noisy sprite. Money is no longer lent by a fairy or any one else without interest, and not a rat once caught in a trap seldom vanishes with the merry ho! ho! ho! of Robin Goodfellow. Times, indeed, are sadly changed–even fairy-rings are sacrilegiously subjected to the hypotheses of science–and if Shakespeare had lived some two centuries later, he must have had recourse to the sister island for a fairy creed that has long departed from his native shores (vii).

The mixture of sober scholar and pleasure addict is obvious in the other works published for the societies. Halliwell's edition of the Dering manuscript of *Henry the Fourth* (provided by the Reverend Lambert B. Larking on 23 October 1844) was certainly one of the Shakespeare Society's most important publications, for, but for a few passages in the fragment of the play of *Sir Thomas More*, it is the only extant contemporary manuscript version of a Shakespeare play. It was a sensational find. And Halliwell's introduction, written five months later, however measured in its cautious appraisal of the validity of the manuscript, does not disguise his excitement. That the transcription and printing–not to mention the brief notes–could proceed so swiftly is further evidence of Halliwell's eager engagement, his speed, and his sense of opportunities to be seized.

Not as sensational but in the same vein of scholarly discovery combined with personal pleasure is Halliwell's transcription for the Percy Society of an anthology of poems, *Poetical Miscellanies, from a Manuscript Collection of the Time of James I*. It is a slight duodecimo volume, forty-nine pages all told. But here too is the sense of an opportunity to be seized in Halliwell's assertion—however protectively phrased—that the pieces have not been previously published: at once a verification of the originality of the manuscript and, as well, an advertisement for the reprint, something at least to add more luster to the statement that of the "various collections of the like kind are to be found in our public libraries, bit I know of few more curious or interesting than the present (v)."

Halliwell's edition of Richard Barnfield's *Affectionate Shepherd* is, similarly, a transcription with a few notes of a rare Elizabethan work (1594) by a contemporary of Shakespeare's, one "remarkably free from the coarseness which disfigures so much of the Elizabethan literature,—an additional inducement, if any were necessary, for rescuing it from the liability to destruction which is of course incident to any book of such excessive rarity" (iv). Halliwell is not being prudish here, although he was not without a certain piousness: he is more likely referring, indirectly but undeniably, to the internal struggle within the literary societies over the publication of "indecent" works which led, for example, to Alexander Dyce's resignation from the Council of the Percy Society in 1843.[46]

Two one-page notes for the Shakespeare Society—one adding a few details to his edition of the Dering manuscript, the other pointing out a notice of *Henry the Eighth* in 1628—are of little significance, as are the unpublished fragments, "all that were printed," of a sketch of the Boar's Head tavern (which found their way into his later work). Finally, a communication of 30 April 1845 to the British Archaeological Association, of which Halliwell was now a member of the General Committee, is little more than a token of his diminishing presence as author for its journal: less than a page long, it is a "Curious Inventory of Goods in the House at 'Fyndyne'."

Perhaps Halliwell's most ambitious work of 1845 was his two-volume edition of the *Autobiography and Correspondence of Sir Simonds D'Ewes*. In its scope (the reigns of James I and Charles I) and in its topic (personal history and religious controversy) and in its material (manuscripts, "a

---

46. The Reverend Alexander Dyce's crusty humor and scholarly integrity were not spared the Percy Society. He quarrelled with the "Percy Asses"—playing of the name of the president, Lord Braybrooke—"who have determined to castrate the publications on account of indecency,—a determination," he wrote to Halliwell, "at which Collier was, as well as myself, indignant" (20 September 1843; LOA 16:54), and asked Rimbault to withdraw his name from the Council list.

sealed book to all but antiquaries" [vi], in the British Museum), it was only in a small way a surprising endeavor for Halliwell, who until then had dealt mainly with more limited historical and archaeological topics. Now twenty-five, a figure of some renown (John Russell Smith published a printing of one hundred portraits of him in 1843), and a *cause célèbre* for many because of his banishment from the British Museum Library in 1845, Halliwell, not known for reticence or hesitation, may have found in the subject matter a personal calling. For one thing, there may have been some special identification with D'Ewes, who spent more than twenty years collecting records and "other abstruse and exotic Monuments" for his history of Great Britain and ten years in writing it. D'Ewes was not only a scholar, like Halliwell, but also one who had suffered at Cambridge and was later persecuted for his religious beliefs and treated with severity by critics. For another, Halliwell was able for the first time to use his preface to speak out on what he believed to be "truth." In addition, Halliwell was obviously so moved by the substance of the work he was editing that he spoke out not simply for the importance of historical documentation—that is, for his profession as antiquary and archaeologist—but also passionately for the value of history both as a key to the understanding of the contemporary scene and for its very self as a course of study.

In D'Ewes we find an instance of one who invariably recommended conciliatory measures on both sides,—a rare example among the host of turbulent spirits who, having once felt their power, systematically refused concessions that would have more than satisfied them a short time previously, and who were generally desirous, in the words of one of their leaders, of effacing the memory of all previous governments, and commencing again the affairs of the nation de novo, on the democratic principles they vainly hoped to establish for future ages (xvi).

And even more fervently:

When will men learn wisdom from the follies and errors of their predecessors? Are the same shoals on which the latter have been wrecked to offer like dangers in times to come, or shall we rather distinguish these dangers in the chart of history, to be ever afterwards avoided by public navigators? If history is of any value, surely it must consist in this; and yet one would imagine, to see what is daily passing around us, that its lessons were entirely disregarded and overlooked,—or men of experience and talent would hardly endanger the safety of an establishment by pursuing the courses which occasioned its overthrow so recently. The lapse of two centuries, they may rest assured, has not destroyed the Protestant bias of the English people; and if its violence has been in some measure dulled, any return to the corruptions which occasioned the first great secession will be the signal for a movement that may in the end result in a severance still more alarming, though perhaps equally beneficial in its effects. What has been confiscated once, may be confiscated again. The same power that wrested mighty possessions from the Catholics may revest them in a newer and purer sect; and the warnings of D'Ewes will be found equally applicable to many circumstances that have recently afforded subject for general and severe animadversion (xii-xiii).

3

Persons and Policies
Professional and Private: 1840-1845

Halliwell's professionalism—his ability to write and write quickly on a wide variety of subjects—was doubtless the result of his scholarly devotion and ambition, which in turn were motored by his sensitivity and pride. Doubtless too is the impact of his attraction to those not understood or even oppressed by society, as in his not unemotional tributes to such apparently diverse personalities as Charles Butler, Samuel Morland, Simonds D'Ewes, and Falstaff, as well as his fervent letters to the editor of the *Parthenon* and of course his impulsive *Letter to Lord Egerton*. Whatever the exact psychological explanation, it is clear in both his professional and personal life that he was determined to make his way. That way was to be bumpy and stormy. But it was travelled with an overriding and unflinching faith in the value of humanistic research and the community of those with whom Henry Ellis placed him, the "labourers in the Vineyard of Archaeology" (2 September 1842: LOA 34:11), be it at the expense of professional and personal security and safety.

In the second of a lifetime of contributions to the *Times*—the first, some two weeks earlier, on the Corn Laws of 1800—Halliwell wrote, on 18 October 1841, an almost full-column-length Letter to the Editor on the library of the British Museum (p. 5). In response to a letter from "J. H." advocating the opening of the library to the education of the "rising and unformed minds of the metropolis," the twenty-one-year-old Halliwell countered, unequivocally, that the "legitimate object of the library of the British Museum is the promotion of literature, and it accomplishes this by affording scholars the facility of referring to books, manuscripts, and records, that would not otherwise be accessible to them, or at any rate not easily procured elsewhere." Admission of unqualified readers, he continued, is "really detrimental to the best interests of literature," illustrating the point with an episode in which such a person ordered a valuable "membranacean" copy of an early edition of Homer which he then "rejected ... with a remark that he had transcribed the first entry he found in the catalogue; that the copy before him was useless because he did not understand the contractions and that a modern school edition with a translation was the 'kind of thing he wanted'." As if the point were not clear enough, Halliwell adds: "The reading room is already filled, I am sorry to say, with too many persons of this class, and the constant whispering which is kept up almost entirely by them, is often a source of very great annoyance to those who frequent it for the purposes of real learning and research." Political fireworks from a Cambridge man, even if he apparently moved from Trinity to Jesus College for financial reasons. He enforces his message by referring to the stellar position in the world of the Bodleian Library, which, "with not more than a dozen readers daily," was founded for "research, and not education," and which its delegates "do not convert ... into a lecture-room for the undergraduates." Halliwell goes on to dismiss the charge that the "chief frequenters of the library of the British Museum are a *coterie* of professed *littérateurs*–men whose devotions are more paid to Mammon than to Minerva," perorating with political passion:

The only privilege that the historian possesses–a privilege shared in common with the most humble of his kind–is to be invaded by the deceptive outcry of 'rights to the million,' and universal suffrage as well as ballot permeate the ranks of literature. It was said long since that literature was a republic only because authors had not a sovereign amongst them; and I sincerely hope and trust that, under the present Government, this the only feasible reason for so styling it will be removed, and pestilential Radicalism no longer suffered to affect the exertions of a class of men, many of whom unquestionably confer so much honour on their country.

In a not uncharacteristic (and, in terms of what is to happen in a few years, eerily prophetic) coda he concludes:

I am induced, contrary to my general custom in such communications, to add my name to these brief observations–not that it is of any value, but because anonymous vindications of any large institutions are often vulgarly attributed to persons connected with the particular establishment, and I am desirous of giving the present one the weight at least of a disinterested advocacy.

Halliwell's "disinterested advocacy" was not likely to ingratiate him with a Panizzi whose often-quoted creed was "I want a poor student to have the same means of indulging his learned curiosity, of following his rational pursuits, of consulting the same authorities, of fathoming the most intricate enquiry, as the richest man in the kingdom." Besides, "disinterested" is somewhat disingenuous, for Halliwell was much involved in the affairs of the British Museum Library as reader and author and critic. We may not know exactly how much use–how often and to what extent–Halliwell made of the library as reader. But we do have some specific information about his relevant activities in the library. They began early. In 1837-8, at the age of seventeen, he produced a manuscript entitled "Collections on the history of the Mathematics. Principally from Books and Manuscripts in the British Museum," a work which presupposes not merely the presence in the library of a minor (eighteen was the customary minimum age for admission) but also permission from official sources: in this case Sir Frederic Madden himself, Keeper of the Department of Manuscripts, was referee. Halliwell was proud of his early admission. More impressive perhaps than pride and delight was the teenager's personal veneration of the library and its collections. "It is very lamentable," he records in his commonplace book, "to perceive the effects of that destructive element–fire–among the invaluable manuscripts in the Cottonian Collection in the British Museum: I never open a volume in that collection without a sigh: Alas! sighs can now avail but little–they are gone and gone *never* to be recovered: the most valuable are now preserved in fire-proof cases after the flames have almost done their last injury: after the horse is stolen they shut the stable-door: not a single candle is *now* allowed in the Museum on any pretense whatsoever" (21ʳ).

Halliwell's activities in the library were as intense as they were precocious. In a later report (and in another context) to the Standing Committee of the Museum (C10477) on 6 March 1845 Madden declared that "in the course of a twelvemonth," in 1840, Halliwell "came to the Reading Room *156* days and consulted no less than *1635* MSS., having had on the 10th of June *37* MSS. in one day!" In another instance, the Standing Committee was informed by Antonio Panizzi, then Keeper of the Department of Printed Books, on 25 July 1840 (C5433-34) "respecting the number of Books required by Mr. Halliwell and the manner in which they were left in the Reading Room." The matter was referred to Sir Henry Ellis, the principal librarian, who, on 10 October 1840 (C5472), "stated in a letter to the secretary dated 8th October that he had seen Mr. Halliwell in the Reading Room, and believed that no more cause of difference would arise respecting the return of his books." And, of course, in the tradition of readers before and after him, Halliwell was active for others who were not able to visit the library themselves. No lesser than Sir

Thomas Phillipps, his father-in-law-to-be, asked him on 31 March 1842 to "spare me a day at the Brit. Museum" (LOA 14:15) and thanked him promptly on 3 April 1842 (LOA 24:11) for what must have been Halliwell's speedy response.

By the time the library was presented with and acknowledged receipt of his "Collections on the history of the Mathematics" on 8 April 1843, he was well known in other ways as well to the highest officers of the library. Like Ellis and Madden, the young Halliwell was also a Fellow of the Society of Antiquaries and the Royal Society, among others. In the early 1840s he corresponded with them fairly regularly on professional matters. For by that time—when he was between twenty and twenty-three—he was busily productive and apparently knowledgeable in at least one of the ways of scholarly interaction: he was a keen distributor of his works. From Ellis he received "Many Thanks" for a copy of his "interesting little Volume of Old Letters illustrative of Science," with the comment "You work very hard" (29 January 1841; LOA 31:8); for the "obliging Present" of the romance, *Torrent of Portugal* (1842), with the florid comment: "You are one of the most industrious labourers in the Vineyard of Archaeology whom I know" (2 September 1842; LOA 34:11); for the "kind Present" of *The Manuscript Rarities of the University of Cambridge* (1841), with the flattering comment: "I find much that is new to me in the work, and am going carefully through it. The bookish world is under many obligations to you, as well as Your sincere friend Henry Ellis" (25 September 1841; LOA 31:34); and for numerous other works received between 1839 and 1844. Ellis also congratulated Halliwell on his marriage in 1842 and added, with a flourish, "Should any thing occur in which I can feel at liberty to aid your wishes, at any time, you may always rest assured of my kindness" (24 August 1842; LOA 10:14).

Egerton 2842 and 2843 contain ten letters from Halliwell to Madden between 24 April 1839 and 8 April 1843 which cover a range of scholarly concerns of special interest to Madden: in a note from the Reading Room, comments on a translation in St. John's College, Cambridge, of Harley MS. 694, which might be Wycliffe's (24 April 1839; Eg. 2842 f.26); a request for "further particulars" about Latin translations of Welsh romances and whether Madden intended to edit them (2 August 1839; Eg. 2842 f.66); thanks for information and "valuable advice" on various projects Halliwell was engaged in and even the loan of a transcription of *Torrent of Portugal* as well as the customary requests for permissions and copying, exchanges of opinion, offers of assistance ("I shall feel proud of being of any service ... in the libraries here [in Oxford] if I can" [11 August 1841; Eg. 2842 f.349]), and, *de rigueur* the presentation to the library of recently published works. Not completely customary perhaps–and however the motivation may be interpreted–was Halliwell's adding to his assertion that "every one knows that you are better acquainted with the early romances than any one in the world" a request for permission to publish *Torrent of Portugal* with the dedication "To Sir Frederic Madden, K. H. Keeper of the Manuscripts in the British Museum, etc. etc. etc. this volume is, with his kind permission, most respectfully inscribed" (20 July 1842; Eg. 2843 f.81). Madden did not object. And in addition to the dedication, the preface concludes with Halliwell's "best thanks" to Madden, "who most liberally lent me his own transcription of the romance, made in the autumn of 1835," not failing to mention, "I ought to add that when I made my transcript, I was not aware that a copy had previously been taken by a gentleman, whose very superior knowledge both of the language and the subject would have produced an edition of this romance much more satisfactory than the present one" (xii). For his part, in a dozen letters in the Edinburgh collection to Halliwell in the early 1840s, Madden gave advice, exchanged information, and addressed all matters promptly and courteously, even at one point writing to the twenty-one-year-old, "I am sorry I should have been so much engaged during the last week or more that I was unable to see you on the subject of your letter, until you had left town," and offering, "Any afternoon after two o'clock that you are at the Museum I shall be happy to give you any assistance in my power" (13 July [1841]; LOA 35:21). In short, these were apparently fruitful scholarly exchanges: a young reader's and author's dream.

But young Halliwell was not only productive, he was ambitious. By 1840, when he was twenty, he was already, as has been pointed out, a Fellow of the Royal Society and of the Society of Antiquaries. He was also secretary and treasurer of the Historical Society of Science, a member of the Camden Society, of the Oxford Society for Promoting the Study of Gothic Architecture, of the Ashmolean Society, to mention but a few of the dozen or so organizations, as well as founding and Council member of the Percy and Shakespeare Societies. Such a reader is not necessarily a cause of delight for a library, much less for such formidable personalities as Madden and Panizzi. Madden's diary (now in the Bodleian Library) reveals an unambiguous subtext. In regard to Halliwell's membership in societies, Madden's entry on 25 February 1841 records: "It is really too bad that this conceited young man should be allowed to figure in the Council of every Society, & be so utterly incapable of editing any work properly." On 5 January 1843 it reads: "Sir Henry Ellis informed me today, that Hallam had seriously proposed to Hudson Gurney, to elect

Halliwell Director of the Society of Antiquaries!!! What next? If so absurd a step had been taken, I would at once have resigned. But to Mr Hallam, a man of *no research*, no doubt Mr Halliwell appears a man of *great* research." Practically all of Halliwell's early works were savaged. Halliwell's *A Few Hints to Novices in Manuscript Literature* (1839), a "flimsy tract," elicits from Madden a revealingly personal response: "He professes that this is only the prelude to a larger treatise on the subject, which I hope is not the case, as I have always had the design of writing myself a work on the subject. Mr. Halliwell is certainly not qualified at *present* to do it" (17 March 1840). On 9 August 1841 at Rodd's (the bookseller) Madden met Dyce, who spoke of Halliwell's editions of the *Ludus Coventriae* (1841) and of the minor poems of John Lydgate (1840), "both of which [Madden] condemned in no very measured terms. In fact Mr Halliwell ought to go to school again, before he puts his name on the title page of a book." On 25 August 1841 Madden introduced further charges against Halliwell. Referring to the latter's *The Manuscript Rarities of the University of Cambridge*, which he termed a "miserable volume," and "done in a very jejune & meagre manner," he expanded his distaste: "I am thoroughly sick of the *Halliwelliana*. He is a puerile blockhead aiming at everything and able to do nothing." Even Halliwell's well-meant letter to the Secretary of State for the Home Department recommending the purchase by the government of a manuscript at Bright's sale (4 June 1844; LOA 17:35) "had done no good to the Museum, and had rather annoyed them," Madden told Wright (June 1844; LOA 19:10). And to incompetence and impertinence Madden added a strong hint of what he considered Halliwell's penchant for deception: "But it really is too vexatious for this meddler to occupy ground like this, procure a list of subscribers to carry so desirable an object into effect ... and then to find that he has deceived us all in this pitiful manner, and by way of crowning his folly, calling his volume 'The Manuscript *Rarities* of Cambridge'!" The hint became an accusation–not the first and not the last. Of a meeting of the Percy Society Council on 8 December 1842 Madden reported:

Above an hour was occupied in a very stormy discussion respecting Mr Halliwell, whose shameful (not to say swindling conduct) as Treasurer, ended by his quitting the Society altogether, and who now retains in his hands some transcripts paid for and belonging to the Society, & which he refuses to give up–saying in a letter to Mr Chappel [*sic*], 'he would see the Society damned first.' One of these transcripts he had sent to the printer, without the authority of the Council, & the Secretary having taking [*sic*] the transcript out of the printer's hands, this proceeding is now complained of by Mr Wright (on the part of Mr Halliwell) as an affront. A part of the members present wished to defer the consideration of the whole question till Mr Wright's return, but the majority (with whom I voted) declared that the Society had acted perfectly right. The *private* details I afterwards received from Mr Chappel (the present Treasurer) of Halliwell's conduct about money are really most disgraceful to the latter. He can have no right to be recognized or treated as a gentleman, and I sincerely pity little Miss Phillipps at having fallen into such hands. Among other of Mr H's proceedings, it appears that without leave of the Council, he actually printed a transcript *paid for by the Society* (of the tract intitled *Westward for Smelts*) for the Shakespeare Society! Is such conduct to be endured? I am sick of the very name of Halliwell. He is as much scoundrel as he is coxcomb!

It may not come as a surprise that even Halliwell's tribute to Madden in the dedication and preface of *Torrent of Portugal* could only be regarded as fawning bordering on mockery. A number of forces converge in Madden's intemperate reaction: Halliwell's youth and ambition, his ubiquitousness and self-seeking, his wheeling and dealing. These traits are, of course, contrasted with Madden's own long-enduring and painstaking scholarship and also reinforced by his obvious envy of the young man's vitality and perhaps his own disappointment at not having achieved important goals, goals which in fact may have been usurped. It may not be too much to say that Madden's diary is a revelation of his abiding bitterness, backbiting, and frustration.

It must not be overlooked, moreover, that much of the conflict was played out not overtly (as yet) in the library itself but in the various literary societies. In the entry for 9 February 1843 Madden's diary describes another dramatic scene. At a meeting of the Council of the Percy Society,

supposing that the affair of Halliwell discussed on the 8 Decr. could be again brought forward, but to my very great surprise, I found that there has been a meeting on the 12 Jany last, to which I received *no summons*, at which the Council stultified themselves by passing a resolution to *request* Mr Halliwell to edit for them Hobson's Jests! the work which they had previously, on account of his ill-conduct, taken out of his hands!!! I was perfectly disgusted, and soon left the Council, and in the morning wrote a letter to the Secretary, to resign my seat in it.

Within the societies there were, of course, factions and, as is inevitably the case, they were fractious. The personal rivalry between Thomas

Wright and Frederic Madden extended to alliances: Halliwell and Thomas
Pettigrew, for example, were of the party of Wright; Joseph Hunter and
Thomas Phillipps that of Madden. The company one kept was a source
of tension and, as it so happens, opportunities presented themselves for
an increasing animosity based on distrust, deception, even paranoia. The
history of these societies–including the implications of the overlapping
memberships–has yet to be written. And Halliwell's role in them, which
cannot be seen in isolation, is complex and elusive. But some of the
important aspects can be pieced together from the letters, personal and
professional, which define his early relationship with his colleagues and
friends John Payne Collier and Thomas Wright, both important motors
of literary societies. Their letters to Halliwell provide as well self-portraits
within a larger context and defining frame.

Although there are but eight letters from Collier in 1840, they are
enough to suggest the tenor and substance of the relationship. The first
letter from Collier to Halliwell is dated 30 January 1840. Collier had just
turned fifty-one (on 11 January), Halliwell was to turn twenty on 21 June.
By then, Collier had had a career as a reporter for the *Times* and the
Morning Chronicle; for the latter he was until 1847 law and parliamentary
reporter as well as an occasional dramatic and literary critic and writer of
leading articles. Although he had studied law and had various prospects
in the legal profession he turned more and more to literary activities. By
1839 he had written, edited, compiled, or translated some twenty-three
works, among which were the three-volume *History of English Dramatic
Poetry to the Time of Shakespeare* (1831), translations of two works by
Schiller, and the *Catalogue, Biographical and Critical, of Early English Literature,
Forming a Portion of the Library at Bridgewater House, the Property of Lord Francis
Egerton* (1837). He was, among other things, literary adviser to the Duke
of Devonshire, a Fellow of the Society of Antiquaries, a member of the
Garrick Club, and a founding member and councillor of the Camden
Society. Collier was, in short, an established figure in the London literary
scene by the time he wrote his first letter to the nineteen-year-old
Halliwell. By 1840 Halliwell had established himself as author of
numerous works, founder of organizations, fellow or officer of more than
a dozen learned societies, in Great Britain, Europe, and America. By 1840
Collier and Halliwell were both active in the newly formed literary
organizations in London; both were members of the Council of the
Camden Society, the Percy Society, and the Shakespeare Society.

Common aims and pursuits, obviously, motivated and invigorated the
correspondence. In that first letter of 30 January 1840 (LOA 3:10) Collier
mentions sending Halliwell a copy of his *Five Miracle Plays* (privately

printed and issued individually in an edition of twenty-five copies in 1835-36). He no doubt wished to show his good will and collegiality, for Halliwell must have consulted it in preparing his own edition of *The Harrowing of Hell*, which appeared in the course of 1840; Halliwell also made use for his 1840 edition of *The Merry Tales of the Wise Men of Gotham* of a copy which Collier (erroneously referring to Andrew Borde's *Merry Tales of the Mad Men of Gotham*) had lent him.[47] Collier's collegiality does not amount to a kind of bland noblesse oblige. For he comments (14 July 1840; LOA 3:25) on a "translation" of Halliwell's as being "not literal enough for me," referring perhaps to *The Harrowing of Hell* or more likely to the *Ludus Coventriae*, which Halliwell was to publish in 1841.

Receiving somewhat more attention in these first letters is the business of the literary societies. On 11 April 1840 (LOA 3:49) Collier writes that he has accepted an invitation to be a member of the Council of the Percy Society, remarking immediately that it should have more competition as to printers (not just one) and that the subscription should be two guineas, perhaps only one, although he would be willing to give five; on 16 June 1840 (LOA 1:13) that he will not join the Historical Society; on 2 July 1840 (LOA 1:16) that he has agreed to join the Shakespeare Society and be one of the Council. Some of the internal workings of the newly formed Shakespeare Society are evident in his letter of 10 November 1840 (LOA 3:32) in which he reports that since there is "not yet much money in hand," he must defer the transcript of Halliwell's *Ludus Coventriae*, "though all the members (& myself in particular) are anxious to give you every facility for the accomplishment of so desirable an object." More programmatic is Collier's opinion (2 July 1840; LOA 1:16) that Shakespeare's name should be spelled "as it was invariably ... spelt by contemporaries," a matter very dear to Halliwell's heart, one which he championed from the beginning of his career in *An Introduction to Shakespeare's Midsummer Night's Dream* (1841) to the very end in *Which Shall It Be? New Lamps or Old? Shaxpere or Shakespeare?* (1879).[48] Perhaps the

---

47. Halliwell's acknowledgement in his introduction to *The Harrowing of Hell* (p. 3) is gracious: "It is unnecessary to enter here into the history of this species of dramatic poetry, and more especially as the wide circulation of Mr. Collier's admirable work on the subject has left nothing to be wished for, save the discovery of fresh documents." It is worth mentioning too that Halliwell, in 1841, dedicated his *On the Character of Sir John Falstaff, As Originally Exhibited by Shakespeare in the Two Parts of King Henry IV* to Collier "as a slight testimony of respect and esteem."

48. Much later, after acknowledging this work as "extremely well done," Collier

most personally interesting letter in 1840 is that in which Collier, replying to Halliwell's request that he "puff" his *Early History of Freemasonry in England* (1840) in the *Morning Chronicle*, writes, "However many other proofs I may have given of my own quackery ... I never puffed myself, nor procured myself to be puffed in my life," (8 May 1840; LOA 3:35). Coming within the context of the letters already written, and given Collier's temperament therein, as well as the fact that both were within a month or two to become founders and then councillors of the Shakespeare Society, Collier's reply is perhaps milder than has been judged, or at least is not necessarily an indication that Collier was "taken aback" by a "brash letter" from a "callow youth of twenty."[49] Halliwell's original letter is in fact quite cordial and respectful: "You told me the other day that you thought every one a quack who wished for newspaper puffs. I suppose I am a quack, for I should be really *very* much obliged to you if you would give me a notice of my little work on Freemasonry in your newspaper."[50] The fact of the matter is that Collier did insert a "puff" in the *Morning Chronicle* on the very next day (9 May 1840, [p. 3]).[51] The episode offers a hint of the nature of their long-standing relationship. Throughout, both were what they were: Collier direct and at times bluff,

could not resist adding: "I care more for one letter of his text than for all the letters of his name" (10 December 1879; LOA 266:21).

49. S. Schoenbaum, *Shakespeare's Lives* (new edition, Oxford, 1991), p. 284.

50. This letter, dated only "Thursday" and bound in a copy of Halliwell's *Early History of Freemasonry in England*, is in University College London (Ogden Collection). Halliwell made a similar request in connection with the British Museum affair (10 July 1846; Folger Y.d.6 [135]), apparently not previously aware that Collier was about to lose the *Morning Chronicle* post or had indeed just lost it.

51. The "puff" is as follows: "A very curious, and, to all Masons, a very interesting tract has just been published by Mr. J. O. Halliwell, F.R.S. and F.S.A., under the title of 'The Early History of Freemasonry in England,' and it is illustrated by a fac-simile of an ancient and unprinted poem upon the subject, which has escaped the notice of all antiquaries, although in the royal library of the British Museum. It was misdescribed by Casley, the compiler of the catalogue, as "A Poem of Moral Duties," which perhaps led to the long concealment of it. Mr. Halliwell has given a fac-simile of the commencement of it, and states it as his opinion (with which it would be unsafe to differ) that it was 'written not later than the latter part of the fourteenth century.' It is a remarkable relic, and all the friends of 'the craft,' and, indeed, antiquaries in general, are much indebted to Mr. Halliwell for making it public. He is, if we mistake not, a young man, and we look confidently for much from his zeal and enthusiasm, as well as from his extraordinary acquirements. The poem itself is 'on the constitution of Masonry,' and the editor has furnished a great deal of illustrative matter in a small compass."

but not without a certain ambiguity; Halliwell direct and always civil, but not without a certain purposefulness.

Collier was director of the Shakespeare Society from 1841, when it first began issuing publications, to 1853, the year of its dissolution. Of the twenty-one original members of the Council, he is one of the five to have served uninterruptedly—the others being William Ayrton, Halliwell, William Harness, and F. Guest Tomlins (who was secretary throughout). Although he was a member of other societies, it is clear that he was especially active, energetic, and devoted in this one. Perhaps even more important than the fact that he was assured another outlet for his scholarly work was the evident pleasure he had in directing people and events. Numerous letters to Halliwell are concerned with the day-by-day business of the Council of the Shakespeare Society. Typical is Collier's letter of 11 November 1842 (LOA 23:52), in which he tells of having informed the members of the state of Halliwell's transcripts, of a resolution enabling Thomas Wright to commence printing the Chester Plays, of the payment for a German translation, of the state of Collier's reprints of *Pierce Penniless* and Henslowe's *Diary* and Barron Field's *Edward IV*. Others testify more directly to Collier's attempts to shape and control the society. Early on, in a letter of 8 January 1841 (LOA 10:20), he quotes, approvingly, the "correct" view of Halliwell that they should have "men on the Council known to the public as well as to ourselves," but adds: "My objection is to such a one as is *nimis notus omnibus*: he is worse than an *ignotus*—However, such we have avoided as yet." Indeed, personalities—harmonizing or conflicting—are the subject of numerous letters. In a P.S. of 10 November 1840 (LOA 3:32) Collier had been "very much obliged for the earnest & zealous manner in which you have so early stepped forward with your aid. It is in contrast with Mr [Joseph] Hunter's apparent reluctance, though he may have very good reasons for retiring from active duties." Collier expands on the matter on 8 January 1841 (LOA 10:20):

I am sorry to say that Mr Hunter has declined to re-join the Council of the Shakespeare Society. Perhaps he does not like some of the members of it; but I think he is wrong to let any personal feelings interfere with the attainment of a good object. Of course neither I nor any body else ever expected him to apply to the purposes of the Society any acquisitions he may have made & can profitably apply otherwise. If I were he, I would stand on my own learning & reputation and not care one straw for any member of the Council, however *dislikeable*. I think it a condescension on his part to be at all governed by such feelings & it is making others of a vast deal too much importance. It makes himself too little, and them too great.

Collier's apparent evenhandedness did not prevent him, however, from wondering (31 December 1841; LOA 33:19) whether Hunter could take over from Charles Knight, who had withdrawn from the Council, for Hunter might be the lesser of two evils. What is clear is that Collier wanted to rule the Council and that meant populating it with compatible members. Halliwell did become a member of the Council after Hunter resigned. Sensing in him a sympathetic ally, Collier mentions (30 March 1841; LOA 14:11) that "at the next Council we shall have to consider who shall come in instead of the five retiring members," and urges him to "turn this in your mind & let me know without reserve what your wishes are. I am confident that in the main we shall concur." Collier had a definite idea of whom he wanted (8 January 1841; LOA 10:20): "I want to get such a man as Mr [Henry] Hallam, if we can. I do not object to the young, who have often more zeal & sometimes more knowledge than the old. It would give me great satisfaction to have Mr C[harles] P[urton] Cooper among us, if he would consent." They would certainly be better than Thomas Campbell, who had withdrawn from the Council and the Society: "he is one of those who think that mines of information have yet been unexplored and that we ought to discover wonders unheard of respecting Shakespeare. Let him be one of the discoverers. He seems to have had some opium dream of 'treasures yet undug'." He has doubts about Halliwell's candidate, James Robinson Planché, who at the founding of the Society "refused not only that place [on the Council], but to subscribe at all, though pressed as far as good breeding would allow." Although "pledged" to Planché, Collier reports (19 January 1842; LOA 24:1) that he has not been elected to the Council and is sorry that Halliwell is "dissatisfied." A few days later (24 January 1842; LOA 24:7), he asks Halliwell to "reconsider" his decision to resign.[52] Shortly thereafter

52. Remaining or resigning was apparently a tactical device in the machinations of the societies. Within a relatively short period, moves and counter moves are referred to. On 13 December 1841, for example, a fragment of a letter from Collier reads: "me to return to the Percy Society after I had withdrawn. Let me now prevail with you. I shall miss you most grievously, for I always look up to you as a thorough-going antiquarian, who will support me in the right against all pretenders" (LOA 10:43). Two days later Collier is "sorry" Halliwell has withdrawn from the Percy Society: "What we shall do without you ... I know not" (15 December 1841; LOA 35:8). On 13 January 1842 Rimbault, the secretary, asks Halliwell to postpone retiring so as to show there are not "some dissensions ... in

(19 April 1842; LOA 24:16) Planché appears once again on Collier's list of candidates, along with Henry Hallam, Barron Field, T. J. Pettigrew, and John Oxenford: "Thus you will see that the wishes of both of us are so far accomplished & there can be no doubt of their election." By 1842 a considerable overhaul of the Council had taken place. Although the number of members remained twenty-one, Thomas Courtenay, C. W. Dilke, Thomas Campbell, Charles Knight, Douglas Jerrold, James Kenney, Frederic Madden, Thomas Noon Talfourd, and Charles Young were replaced by Peter Cunningham, Beriah Botfield, Frederick Watson, Barron Field, Henry Hallam, John Oxenford, Thomas Joseph Pettigrew, and Planché. Despite some later changes, Collier's power remained stable. As director from the founding to the dissolution of the Shakespeare Society he could respond to a move by Halliwell with a magisterial "Of course the Shakespeare Society would not for an instant think of standing in your way" (17 July 1852; LOA 56:40).

Halliwell was, it may be assumed, useful to Collier for the implementation and consolidation of his power as director. "As far as I am concerned," writes Collier on 30 October 1841 (LOA 31:22), "the more you interfere with the proceedings of the Shakespeare Society the better," explaining that Halliwell had helped him by pointing out Peter Cunningham's inconsistent editorial practices and indicating that it would be best not to mention the source of this information since "some authors do not like their copy to be examined & criticized by other authors." It would be inaccurate, however, to interpret Collier's role as merely power-oriented. For, as is apparent in some of the letters just quoted, Collier was not simply interested in personalities but was following a programmatic course. Not only were the members of the Council to represent various intellectual and literary views—antiquaries and bibliographers were as well represented as literati—they were also expected to exhibit solidarity. In a typical stance, Collier castigates one member, whose name (possibly, Dyce) Halliwell excised from the letter:

That kind are generally good: notwithstanding he does not think he can

the Council" (LOA 24:8). In another instance, Sir Frederic Madden's diary (now in the Bodleian Library) entry for 8 December 1842 gives a vivid picture of a meeting of the Percy Society Council: "Above an hour was occupied in a very stormy discussion respecting Mr Halliwell, whose shameful (not to say swindling) conduct as Treasurer, ended by his quitting the Society altogether." Be that as it may, Halliwell continued his publications for the Percy Society, became a Council member again in 1846, acting secretary in 1849, and then honorary secretary until its dissolution.

afford to say a good word of any body–but himself, I will say this of him. I told him many years ago that the true way was to give every man his due, and not to try to build up a reputation for himself by pulling that of other people down–& *using the materials* (4 January 1844; LOA 23:42).

Even more exemplary is Collier's

I only wish you understood me as I wish to be understood, & we should never have the slightest discordance. It is these petty disputes about nothing that render us Lit. Antiquaries as a body comparatively powerless. No two pull together; & the moment one appears to be getting a-head, the rest are for pulling him back & putting him down. We should act upon a more enlarged view & system, and then we might do something (14 January 1851; LOA 56:98).

The combination of the programmatic, the practical, and the personal is evident in Collier's reaction to Charles Knight's "distinct motion against me for my unanswerable (I still call it) note in Armin's tract" (13 October 1842; LOA 10:29), brought up by George Craik, "one of Mr Knight's employés."[53] Collier supported the Council's "resolution ... that in future a declaration should accompany the works of the Society, leaving the editors only responsible for facts, criticism or remarks," although "this course seemed to me on some accounts too much, but as I was a party concerned in the question, I expressed my approbation to a certain extent." Two years later, in a characteristic turn, Collier announces that he is responsible for putting the names of the writers of articles in the *Shakespeare Society's Papers* as signatures at the end (30 June 1844; LOA 17:15). (As it turned out, many of the names are fictitious, and Collier himself wrote several articles signed with other names.) Collier's standpoint is sharply illustrated in his response to Halliwell's conjecture about "ducdame" (*AYL* 2.5.54)[54] :"I do not concur ... but that is neither here nor there: neither you nor I denounce people for not concurring in an opinion. We know too well the difficulty of arriving at conclusions to insist upon others swallowing our nostrum willy nilly. It answers the purpose, however, to seem positive & dictatorial now & then since it

53. Knight was enraged at Collier's criticism of his "error" in both the *Pictorial* and *Library Shakspere* for "not having consulted the earlier editions of [*Much Ado about Nothing*]." The criticism is to be found in the introduction signed J.P.C. to the reprint of Robert Armin's *Nest of Ninnies* (Shakespeare Society Publications 10, 1842, ix).

54. *Shakespeare Society's Papers*, I:24 (1844), 109-10.

makes weak minds concur from the mere apprehension of differing. They think infallible those who affect to think themselves so" (3 July 1844; LOA 21:23). The irony, in view of what was to happen in their careers, is inescapable. But that is a matter which requires separate treatment.

An even more striking example of the interaction of policy and personality is found in Collier's reaction to the treatment of two tracts proposed for publication by the Percy Society, *Pleasant Quips for Upstart Newfangled Gentlewomen* (attributed by Collier to Stephen Gosson) and Charles Bansley's *The Pride and Abuse of Women.* "Finding a strong objection on the part of some members to coarse words (though some of our modern fine words are a great deal coarser)," Collier "left out some lines and terms in the reprints, rather to shew how much worse the blanks were, than the lines & terms which [he] had omitted" (20 October 1841; LOA 10:10). Nevertheless the Council cancelled the reprint altogether, substituting Collier's edition of *The Pain and Sorrow of Evil Marriage.* Collier felt "the sudden determination of the Council amounted to this–that I was unfit to be entrusted with the choice or editing of works for the Society." With not uncharacteristic self-pity he was "annoyed, not to say hurt, that what I have done (however little) [the parenthesis interlined] was treated with so little ceremony." Continuing, Collier was in fact almost lachrymose:

Without any overweeningness on my part (of which I should be ashamed) I think I was entitled to this sort of observation from some of the Council–'Here is a work on which some little pains have been bestowed: the work has merit in itself, independently of its rarity; & here are notes and an introduction, trifling in themselves, but still containing some knowledge: it has been prepared by one of our oldest & not least zealous members, and what we ought to do is to take copies of it home, read them, & on a future day decide whether we ought or ought not to cancel the whole impression'.

Collier, obviously, was angry at being caught acting single- and even highhandedly: his ever-present suspiciousness is evident in his remarking that "one or more Members" observed, "This ought to be a lesson to us, not to permit any work to be put to press without the previous sanction of the Council." Beneath the surface perhaps, his over-reaction may have served to cover his uneasiness or relief at not (yet) having been caught forging an inscription so as to establish the attribution of *Pleasant Quips* to Stephen Gosson. At any rate Collier threatened to resign. From the Lear-like pathos to the Coriolanus-like stance he thanks Halliwell (in a final burst added vertically above the salutation in the same letter of 20 October 1841) for his "good opinion" of him and for his "earnest wish that [he] should not leave the Society," convinced that "the Society has left me by taking a different road." At any rate, in what may be the most characteristic personal and programmatic gesture of all, Collier did not leave the Council, his name not missing from the list of members until 1848. Without doubt, Collier enjoyed the politics and personalities of the societies. "I shall not be tired of them as long as they are not tired of me," he wrote to Halliwell on 1 May 1852 (LOA 53:50), ironically the year which saw the dissolution of the Percy Society, to be followed in 1853 by that of the Shakespeare Society.

Collier's letters to Halliwell in this period on the projects they were engaged in are likewise programmatic, professional, and personal. In them Halliwell shares Collier's confidence, is regarded as colleague and competitor, and is treated with Collier's habitual cordiality and testiness. Typical of their collegial interaction is Collier's offer of his Robin Goodfellow ballad for use by Halliwell in his *Introduction to Shakespeare's Midsummer Night's Dream* (1841), although he has no illustrations for it (22 February 1841; LOA 11:42). In fact, he has no objection to Halliwell's reprinting it, adding that he has "in several places ... invented stanzas or parts of stanzas and lines or parts of lines, exactly fitting what is left of the original impression. These additions are invariably marked with brackets" (5 March 1841; LOA 11:40). Collier's generosity does not, however, prevent him from expressing his disagreement with Halliwell on the date of the play (20 April 1841; LOA 11:33) or asserting that he "cannot undertake to do what even you wish about your Introduction" (26 April 1841; LOA 11:32). Still, Collier would like a copy (11 April 1841; LOA 11:35).

Underlying these exchanges is a programmatic standpoint which Collier felt impelled to make quite explicit on several occasions. Praising their cooperation, he quotes the end of the ballad "From Oberon in Fairyland" (mistakenly attributed to Ben Jonson) and goes on: "I hate dog-in-the-mangerism above all things & cannot approve even the reply of those who say, 'I cannot communicate that because I am going to use it myself'" (24 November 1841; LOA 24:13). It is not just a question of exchanging material, it is more importantly a matter of critical give-and-take. Acknowledging a mistake pointed out by Halliwell, Collier replies, "I am glad you have found me out in an error which I will acknowledge the moment it is pointed out to me. I dare say it is only one of many, but I make as few as I can." And in a jovial counter he points to a mistake Halliwell has made and concludes, "You must not be too sore and thin-skinned about such matters. I am pretty callous, but I should like to know which twenty lines I omitted, that I may make a note of my blunder" (11 August 1841; LOA 10:40). Collier is much "obliged" by Halliwell's "remarks & corrections at all times, because ... they are the result of thought and reading, & are only offered in the best spirit–the spirit of arriving at truth" (25 January 1843; LOA 23:63). In the scholarly world, differences are to be expected and respected: "Our 'verbal Shakespearian differences' I know nothing of. What are they? and where are they? I can have no 'difference' with you merely because you are of one opinion on some philological point, and I of another. Each of us must think according to our several means of information.–If your means are more, or better, than mine so much the better for you" (27 November 1850; LOA 59:22). The coexistence of opposing positions is dramatically illustrated in Collier's response to Halliwell's edition of the *Ludus Coventriae* (1841):

The principle on which you have gone is in my judgment a mistaken one, but other people may think differently. My plan would have been to correct all the obvious and undoubted errors of the MS, & to have pointed out the corrections in the notes, thereby shewing how the ignorant transcriber had blundered without adopting his blunders in the text. Your mode accomplishes the same end in a different manner, and I am confident that people in general will be sensible of the obligation you have conferred by your disinterested labours (15 July 1841; LOA 10:45).

In fact, in a kind of internalized coexistence of opposing positions (similar to his writing of a "puff" although vowing never to do so) Collier's anonymous review of the work in the *Athenaeum* (4 September 1841, pp. 686-7) does not mention the "mistaken" principle, but finds the "editorial care ... entrusted to Mr. Halliwell ... to have [been] discharged ... with praiseworthy zeal, knowledge, and acuteness."

Given his apparent ambivalence towards Halliwell, it is perhaps not surprising that Collier is relatively tight-lipped in his remarks to Halliwell about his own first edition of 1842-44. He regrets not being able to present him with a copy, with a fairly lame excuse: "I wish the 'liberality' of the publishers enabled me to give you a copy of the Shakespeare" (30 January 1843; LOA 23:45). But he nevertheless awaits Halliwell's opinion of the seventh volume (9 February 1843; LOA 23:78) and, in returning Halliwell's "postponed, not rejected, papers [most likely, *Some Notes on Passages in Shakespeare*, 1847]," seems peeved enough to remark, "Do not think that I shall quarrel with you for not mentioning me or my

Shakespeare" (6 April 1845; LOA 23:18). His only other references in this period to his edition are used to attack Alexander Dyce. Collier did have a copy sent to Dyce but wishes

that I had never presented one copy to a quarter where it is only received for the sake of finding all possible fault with it, in the true spirit of an old friend turned new enemy. But no more of that, for I will continue to heap coals of fire on his head. I will venture to say that in many respects there is no man living under greater obligations to me than he is (30 January 1843; LOA 23:45).

Collier's almost congenital fear of betrayal is obvious in his complaining to Halliwell of "Mr Dyce who promised me the use of all his notes upon Shakespeare before I began, but when I asked him for them withheld them & now prints them in order to do me what injury he can" (12 March 1844; LOA 22:40). Collier's indignation–"This is not the conduct of a friend of twenty years standing"–is, however, to be balanced against his own penchant for withholding information, especially as (a bit later on) regards his *Notes and Emendations* and the Perkins Folio or indeed his sputtering and restrained response to Halliwell's edition.

Their relationship deepened in the following four decades. It also mellowed with the years. But since competition was inherent in the collegiality, it was never without a certain degree of personal and professional ambivalence. Moreover, Collier was thirty-one years Halliwell's senior. In fact, Halliwell's most important colleagues at this time belonged to an older generation: Henry Ellis was born in 1777, Joseph Hunter in 1783, Alexander Dyce in 1798, Frederic Madden in 1801, John Bruce in 1802, W. J. Thoms in 1803. Even Thomas Wright, Halliwell's closest adviser and collaborator, was ten years older. In the long run, Halliwell got along satisfactorily with most of them, meeting or exchanging letters well into the second half of the century. But there is little doubt that in his early career he was constantly made aware of his age by established personalities. And not merely his age but his drive was a source of irritation, as was his irrepressible sensitivity. With Thomas Wright, however, there never seemed to be any problems.

Halliwell's relationship with Wright, although in many ways similar, was in essence vastly different from that with Collier. The younger man moved in many of the same circles. All three were motors in the leading societies: Percy, Shakespeare, Antiquaries, and more. All three were prolific authors and editors, as well as founders of periodicals. All three were energetic and enthusiastic doers. And with the older men Halliwell developed a relationship which was to last almost half a century and to be capped by the emotional intensity which motivated Halliwell to come to the aid of the debilitated and financially stressed old men and in fact to seek to alleviate the situation of their surviving families. But Wright was closer than Collier to Halliwell and of a more profound influence. Ten years Halliwell's senior, Wright seemed from the outset to be clearing a path for Halliwell. From a family of modest means he managed to be admitted on 7 July 1830 sizar at Trinity College Cambridge; his tutor was William Whewell. Like Halliwell, he was precociously productive. As an undergraduate, for example, he began–among other things–his *History and Topography of the County of Essex,* which appeared in forty-eight monthly parts from 1831-6 and in 1836 in two folio-sized volumes totalling 1532 pages. In 1836, when Halliwell was admitted pensioner at Trinity, Wright was leaving Cambridge to take up residence in London, where his career seemed to continue to foreshadow Halliwell's: in 1837 he became Fellow of the Society of Antiquaries, in 1838 secretary of the Camden Society, in 1841 secretary and treasurer of the Percy Society. As the dates suggest, these professional activities not only foreshadow Halliwell's, they also overlap. For it was not only membership in these societies, as well as in the Shakespeare Society, the Royal Society of Literature, the Historical Society of Science, and numerous other local and foreign ones, but also works produced for them that bound the two men. A dozen or so works under the aegis of these societies emanated from Wright in the early 1840s; a similar number were produced by Halliwell.

And unlike Collier, who was essentially a colleague and competitor, often warmly congenial and yet often distantly ambiguous, Wright was completely direct and intimate in his dealings with Halliwell. It was more than college tie or the overlapping of honors and associations; it was not just that Wright was only ten years Halliwell's senior, whereas Collier was thirty-one years older. It was a certain chemistry which includes but surpasses common interests. It was, all in all, more a matter of personality than of collegiality. Nor were Wright and Halliwell competitors; they were collaborators whose wide spectrum of interests were similar and whose talents were at the same time complementary. Collier was essentially a literary man; Wright was from the beginning an antiquary, a historian, and a philologist. His focus was on the Middle Ages, its artifacts, events, and languages. The *Journal of the British Archaeological Association,* which he founded with Thomas Crofton Croker and Charles Roach Smith in 1843, was all-inclusive in its orientation, established, so its title page, "for the encouragement and preservation of researches into the arts and monuments of the early and middle ages." Although Britain was his speciality, he was also European in his outlook. It was not just that he was a member of foreign societies, had important connections with French colleagues, nor even that he had a French wife. It was more than his fluency in French or Latin or Greek. He was simply immensely active and social, with apparently unlimited energy and a limitless horizon. To Halliwell he was doubtless a model, mentor, and friend. In the beginning at least and for a considerable time thereafter he was Wright's protégé.

It is not clear whether they met in Cambridge or London, for they were both commuters, as it were, Wright from London to visit libraries in Cambridge and in 1836 for his M.A., and Halliwell to Cambridge, from 1836 as pensioner of Trinity College. They met early in their careers, in the spring of 1838 (Case, f.54), and must have struck it off immediately. Wright's first letter to Halliwell in the Edinburgh collection is dated 8 November 1838 (LOA 2:12) but presupposes a considerable professional relationship. In many ways it is revealing of the intensity of their interaction. Halliwell, as was his wont, had sent Wright copies of the second number of *Rara Mathematica*. One is "addressed" to Wright personally (for which he thanks "much"), the others, following what must have been a predetermined plan, Wright has "given to [William] Jerdan and John Nichols for the Lit. Gaz. and the Gents." Moreover, in a pattern of mutual reviewing to be followed assiduously over the next years, Wright "will probably notice it" himself in the *Gentleman's Magazine*, which he did indeed.[55] Halliwell is also thanked for having verified the *Lai de Cor* and for the "trouble" he took with parcels for further distribution in Cambridge (presupposing a circle of common acquaintances, James Hildyard of Christ's being mentioned), and is asked to copy songs from a manuscript in the Cambridge Public Library, Such matters are, of course, common to many other correspondents. But what begins to distinguish this particular relationship is Wright's detailed and personalized advice on both the content of Halliwell's work and importantly the strategy needed to secure its success in the arena of professional life:

55. According to the identifications of the anonymous reviewers in the *Gentleman's Magazine* made by Kuist, Wright reviewed Halliwell's *Rara Mathematica* (n.s. 11 [1839], 174-5]), Mandeville's *Travels* (n.s. 12 [1839], 45-8), and *Ludus Coventriae* (n.s. 16 [1841], 381-4). Halliwell reviewed *Reliquiae Antiquae* (n.s. 12 [1839], 165-6) and, according to the Letters of Authors, the *History of Ludlow* (n.s. 16 [1841], 174-6). For the *Literary Gazette*, according to the Letters of Authors, Wright reviewed the second and third editions of Halliwell's *Nursery Rhymes* (24 December 1842, p. 878-80, and 30 December 1843, p. 848-9) and the *Early History of Freemasonry* (30 May 1840, p. 344). Halliwell reviewed Wright's *Piers Ploughman* (26 November 1842, p. 804) and *Anecdota Literaria* (9 November 1844, p. 716).

In opening your second N⁰ at p. 91. I saw by chance in the 17th line *versa ince,* which evidently should be *versa vice (uice).* When you print your third N⁰ you would do well to mark it on the wrapper as an error of the press. In editing such documents as these there is nothing one is so apt to do as to overlook a little thing of this kind, but an ill-natured person might cry out about it, and by putting it in an errata you will disarm him (8 November 1838; LOA 2:12).

A veritable cascade of letters from Wright expands and intensifies the structure of the relationship. Nichols will notice both *Rara Mathematica* and *A Brief Account of the Life, Writings, and Inventions of Sir Samuel Morland* (20 January 1839; LOA 2:16), Wright reports, among other things, adding that he has "desired some of [his] friends to get it [*Rara*] reviewed in the Journals in Paris." A few days later he makes it known that he "has been thinking a good deal about [Halliwell's] proposed little quarterly publication—both how to get it done at as moderate an expense as possible, and how to make it repay itself as quickly as possible" (7 February 1839; LOA 2:17). Wright's advice is so precise, taking in all aspects from conception to distribution, as to be prescriptive and worth quotation for the information it provides about book production in 1839 and his ebullient personality:

With respect to the first point, after thinking of Whittingham, and Noyes, and Richard Taylor, I bethought me of a relative of mine who is a printer, and who has a good many prentices, and therefore, if we give him a bit at a time so as not to hurry him, it struck me that he would do it the most moderately of anybody. So I have just been to his office, and took with me a number of the German Publication—the Alt Deutsche Blätter. He will print it in the same type as that—a good bit smaller than your *Rara Mathematica,* with notes as may be necessary, at 250 copies (quite as much as you should print), composition, paper, and print included, for 3.15.0 a sheet, which I think is very reasonable—At the rate of your *Rara Mathematica* it would be at least 5.5.0, I am sure. The difference between 250 and 500 copies would be a very small matter, but I recommend you strongly to keep to the former.

I think Pickering will be the best publisher, and I have little doubt in my own mind that you will sell as many copies as will at least very nearly, if not quite, clear your expenses. I had occasion to write to Edinburgh three or four days ago, and I asked both [William] Turnbell [i.e. Turnbull] and David Laing if they would endeavour to get as many transcribers as they could. I will work it up well in the Gentleman's Magazine and the

Literary Gazette.

I should think *Reliquiae Antiquae*, &c. would do very well for the title. I think the content should be chiefly scraps of Old English, verse or prose, with here and there a piece of Latin or Anglo-Norman, when they are very curious as illustrative of Old English Literature or Manners and Customs. I have got several scraps ready transcribed which would do very nicely in the first number. I think the best way would be for different persons to put their initial or so forth to their communication–it gives an appearance of variety–you will see that after the first number we shall get several contributors. I have one or two scraps from Cambridge that I will give you to collate, and you can, if you find nothing better for the first number, put them in as your own, as you will not have much time for some few weeks to come. Within a few days, I will just think over and look over some of my notes, and then send you a list of a few pieces I will propose for the beginning, so as to make as good a show as possible.

After a page or so of other business Wright returns to the earlier subject with the promise that he "will talk of it among people who I think will be of use in contributing or buying. Adieu!" The idea for *Reliquiae Antiquae* may have been Halliwell's, but it is obvious that Wright was the guiding, if not the commanding, figure in what was to be overall a successful collaboration and lifelong friendship.

And there was more. For Wright was fostering other aspects of Halliwell's career. Evidently responding to a question of protocol by Halliwell, Wright advised, "You cant do wrong in addressing him [Sir Thomas Phillipps] in the same way he addresses you." Further: "I think next night will be your ballotting night [for election to the Society of Antiquaries], when I [Wright] will make a point of being there, and carrying as many votes as I can." A week later Halliwell was elected Fellow (14 February 1839; LOA 59:3). And a few days after that Wright was busy for Halliwell on all fronts: Evan Hunter, son of the highly regarded Joseph Hunter, "would be the best person to present you, and [as] he is generally pretty early ... If you will call on me, or, if you like, I on you in the evening, we will go down to Somerset House [the meeting place of the Society] together. I have asked Crofton Croker, who is a very excellent fellow, to be there on Thursday next that I may introduce you to him" (22 February 1839; LOA 2:20). The advice was focussed not simply on introductions, however, but on Wright's strategy of adding another member to the faction he represented in the various societies. And that involved as well, some accommodation with the opposition. In the same letter Wright mentioned having broached the plan of *Reliquiae Antiquae* to

Frederic Madden: "He thinks it will repay itself, and promises to be a contributor." He was to be one, and it did repay itself. Later in the year Wright reported that the "Reliquiae goes better than ever, so they [William Pickering, the publisher] tell me. Everybody likes No. 2. Sir Frederick [*sic*] Madden speaks very highly of it" (6 November [1839]; LOA 2:48).

By the end of 1839 Halliwell, not yet twenty, had been successfully launched. Wright paved the way for his election to the Royal Society of Literature, among others, as well as introducing him to important figures in the literary and publishing world. He also used his influence to develop the practice of mutual reviewing, making arrangements with John Gough Nichols of the *Gentleman's Magazine*, in which he reviewed Halliwell's edition of Mandeville's *Travels* (having promised a "Glowing review" in a letter of 24 May 1839 [LOA 2:28]), *Rara Mathematica*, and the *Ludus Coventriae*, and in which Halliwell reviewed *Reliquiae Antiquae*. With William Jerdan of the *Literary Gazette*, Wright arranged his review of Halliwell's *Nursery Rhymes* in return (so his letter of 5 September 1842 [LOA 36:7]) for Halliwell's review of his *Piers Ploughman*. He also saw to Halliwell's reviewing of his *Anecdota Literaria* (for he wanted it "pushed a little" [12 October 1844; LOA 18:90]), having said he would to do as much for Halliwell's *Early History of Freemasonry* (8 December 1843; LOA 19:8). The cultivation of important contacts involved more than reviewing. Wright attempted to reduce the tension that followed Halliwell's *Letter to Egerton* by speaking to Collier, who, he assured Halliwell, "likes you all the better because you say what you think, and are not afraid of anybody, and that it was shocking impudence to talke about your being too young" (26 October 1839; LOA 2:46)–not, however, losing sight of the reality of the situation: "I fear you will make many persons your enemies by it, who were or were inclined to be your good friends, which is a pity" (30 August 1839; LOA 2:39). "I wouldn't be too critical on Dyce['s book on Collier's and Knight's editions of Shakespeare]. The worst he says of you is that you are given to joking," he wrote on another occasion (6 June 1844; LOA 18:95).

It is obvious that Wright's advice for the furthering of Halliwell's professional career in the byzantine complexity of societies and publishing tends to be admonitory, stressing restraint, caution, and maneuvering. An exemplary instance of Wright's tactical skill in dealing with the Tarlton material in the Percy and Shakespeare Societies has already been detailed.[56] Also instructive and thoroughly typical is his reaction to the suppression by the Camden Society of Halliwell's edition of the Simon Forman papers.

56. See p. 64.

"I would take it all quietly–any blame is taken off your shoulders with regard to judgment, by the fact of Dr Bliss having so strongly recommended it" (dated only "Thursday Morning"; LOA 16:97). In another instance he counsels: "I should feel obliged if you will burn the inclosed. I would not be annoyed at anything–but it will help you to know with whom you have to deal. My opinion is that he will do anything he can to injure you; and that the best thing you can do is to keep aloof–make no advances towards him at all, and if he has in time an inclination to reconciliation let him make the advances himself" (14 November 1842; LOA 16:85). It may involve restraint bordering on duplicity. Wright continues: "Be so good as not to say how you came by your information relating to S.T.P. [Sir Thomas Phillipps]. If you should meet Rimbault in Oxford, speak to him as if you had not the slightest knowledge of what has passed." In any event caution can never be wrong: "Be very careful always about what you say in writing to [name deleted by Halliwell] for I see more and more every day to make me think it necessary to be very cautious in our dealings in that quarter" (21 February [1841]; LOA 39:23). In all, Wright never lost sight of the larger scene, of which he knew he was himself but one player.

This larger view was not impersonal, however. In the midst of the activism and turbulence of 1839 Wright never lost sight of the man Halliwell. For the student Halliwell, anxious about his examinations, there was concern from Wright about the little-go facing Halliwell: "It is not a thing to be lost sight of, but it is not a very difficult matter" (22 February 1839; LOA 2:20). Responding to an attack on Halliwell, Wright was quick to advise him not to "take any notice" of Bolton Corney's "Lucubrations" (4 December 1839; LOA 5:32). Given Wright's gregariousness and ebullience, it is little wonder that the relationship was lively and, as the years progressed, intensely personal. Wright's 1250 letters to Halliwell form the largest group in the Edinburgh collection. The script is minuscule, the lines tightly spaced, the letters long (even when they begin with a ritual "no news"). Without exception each one is animated–a mixture of news, gossip, opinion, description, tactics, dialogue, cartoons, jokes (almost half of LOA 24:68 is devoted to two long jokes), graphical oddities (LOA 36:18 Wright called a letter a "circular" letter, having written it in the form of a spiral); LOA 15:84 uses Greek characters to render an English text phonetically), characterizations, and what-have-you. They are, above all, forthcoming and direct–a measure of their intimacy being the large number of names Halliwell excised if "at all likely to cause pain or annoyance to any one" (LOA 1:1). Together, they present an insightful and rollicking picture of the mores and customs of the species *antiquarius britannicus.* Together, they present an illuminated life of an archetypal antiquarian activist. And together they portray the professional and personal compatibility of two fellow travellers and friends. For his part Halliwell must have matched the detailed letters he received from Wright, but they do not seem to exist. But from the tone of Wright's letters it is safe to conclude that he was always welcome for his self and his opinions. There were printed testimonies as well. At the outset of his career, in the prefatory remarks ("Lectori") to his edition of John Sherman's *Historia Collegii Jesu Cantabrigiensis* (1840), Halliwell singled out Wright: "Opem haud perexiguam ad hunc laborem subeundum debemus viro, in literis omnibus instructissimo Thomae Wright, A.M. ob quod ipsius meritum, aliaque nobis alias suppedidata auxilia, grates libentissime agimus."

As the years passed, the mentor remained the mentor, advising and dictating. As the years passed, and age no longer mattered, there was giving and taking. As the years passed, the bond became increasingly personal. Wright was always there, so to speak, writing, counselling, dropping by for a chat or dessert, inviting Halliwell to join him at a meeting or the theater or on a trip, inquiring after the family and jesting with the children, the first to spend the night at the Halliwells' just a few days after their marriage. Professional interactions in the 1840s–among them the *Archaeologist* and the *Dictionary of Archaic and Provincial Words*–were marked by the solidarity which comes only of deep personal respect and affection.[57] And so there can be little surprise that when the dam broke, as it were, when in 1845 Halliwell was accused of having "abstracted" manuscripts from Trinity College, it was Wright who took the lead in defending him. Loyalty and trust and affection spurred him to become the spokesman, the spin doctor, the campaign manager, so to speak, of his colleague and friend. And they spurred Halliwell so deeply that the decay and downfall of Wright some thirty years later were almost unbearable. The relationship lasted a lifetime, in a whirlwind of activity its stability

---

57. As always, Wright had a word, if not a last word. Finding the "last number [of the *Archaeologist*] was [not] a bad one," he nevertheless felt "there was perhaps too much out of the Table Book," adding judiciously, "I look upon it as a good rule, to a certain extent, not to make too extensive extracts from a cheap book, because the reader is easily tempted to buy the book itself, and then he does not value the review" (May 1842; LOA 14:76). As for the dictionary he was quick to advise Halliwell not to start with William the Conqueror but with the period since Chaucer and to use Robert Nares's *Glossary* and John Brand's *Observations on the Popular Antiquities of Great Britain* for popular customs (19 January 1843; LOA 16:87).

founded upon the dominance of personal affection over professional gain.

The critical reception of Halliwell's early work, which helped define his career, can to a considerable extent be understood within this network of personal and professional collegiality, group alliances, as well as general reviewing policy. What was to be published was a matter of the Councils of the societies and the publishers. Both bodies were often interrelated, the individuals could be members of both groups. John Gough Nichols, editor of the *Gentleman's Magazine*, for example, was a founding member of the Camden Society, as well as its publisher and close friend of Thomas Wright. And collegiality not infrequently took the form of by rivalry. Factionism was endemic. There were demonstrative gestures: threats and acts of resignation from societies, blackballing, open dissension and dispute in Council meetings. On the surface the waters were for the most part apparently calm. John Bruce and W. J. Thoms may have belonged to the opposing faction in the Camden Society, but Halliwell carried on a cordial and even touching personal correspondence with them for many years thereafter, indeed in their retirement when Bruce expounded his views on religion (as on 22 April 1859; LOA 67:66) and Thoms wrote that he would pass Halliwell's "kind remembrances" to Collier aged ninety-three (14 October 1882; LOA 261:77). Frederic Madden was infuriated by the behavior of Halliwell but was nevertheless the leading invited contributor to his *Reliquiae Antiquae*. For the most part disputes were not public, nor were they recorded in minute books; they were recorded in private letters, in personal diaries, in irrecoverable conversations. In other words, but for the occasional outburst–like Halliwell's *Letter to Egerton*, which was well-nigh unforgivable–discretion was the better part of malice. Better yet: anonymity recapitulated fraternity. This was especially evident in the contemporary practice of anonymous or pseudonymous reviewing, be it in the form of puffs, notices, letters to the editor of a journal or newspaper, or extensive critical treatments. It may not be too much to say that friendly reviews were done by one's own camp, unfriendly ones by the opposing camp.

If arrangements were made, an author could review his own work anonymously. Thomas Wright was able to place reviews in the *Gentleman's Magazine*, since its editor, John Gough Nichols, was his friend and "fellow traveller." In 1839 Halliwell took on the first part of his own and Wright's *Reliquiae Antiquae*. Not surprisingly he (using the editorial "we") could "rejoice that the very curious unconnected scraps, so common in middle-age manuscripts, and often so extremely interesting, have at last found place in a work constructed on an excellent plan, and, as far as we can judge from the number before us, conducted with great care and ability" (n.s. 12 [1839], 165]. Moreover, of his own brainchild he is "glad also to observe that a proper regard is had for the purse of the connoisseur in these matters: ... one number ... for three shillings" (p. 165). In 1840 after a long quotation from the poem which forms the major portion of his *Early History of Freemasonry*, "the principal value of this little volume" (n.s. 14 [1840], 161), Halliwell the reviewer agrees that Halliwell the author has proved the Leland document to be a forgery, disagrees on the connection between *Freemason* and *Freestone*, and is even "surprised" that "no notice has been taken of the curious allusions to Freemasons, Collected by Sir Francis Palgrave" (p.163).[58] In 1841 Halliwell uses his review of his *Collection of Letters Illustrative of the History of Science in England* to mention the articles he has written, as well as others by fellow members of his own Historical Society of Science, such as Joseph Hunter and Augustus De Morgan, in his campaign to overcome the "little attention from scientific men, either on account of that lamentable apathy towards matter of history which is too frequently characteristic of the lover of demonstration, or perhaps, let us hope, from the want of some general channel of communication, such as the Historical Society of Science now affords" (n.s. 15 [1841], 290)—and, it must be added, whose first publication is the work being reviewed. In closing, Halliwell does not miss the opportunity to recommend his *Brief Account of the Life, Writings, and Inventions of Sir Samuel Morland.*

A major contribution of the *Gentleman's Magazine* to the Halliwell enterprise was made by the joint editor himself. Although Nichols's reviews tend to be short, they can be more substantial certainly than the customary advertisement or puff. For one thing, they serve to introduce the young Halliwell to a wider public. From an oblique mention of the anonymous author of the *Life of Morland* as "gentleman of Trinity College, Cambridge," and a mere summary of the work, Nichols moves to find *Rara Mathematica* meriting "especial praise" (n.s. 11 [1839], 174), adding that the "very well and carefully edited" work (p. 175) is "we believe ... by J. O. Halliwell, Esq.. of Jesus College" (p. 174), that he is "glad to understand that its Editor, Mr. Halliwell, is preparing for publication a History of the Mathematical Science in England" (p. 175) and that *Two Essays* is a "valuable appendix to the Rara Mathematica" (n.s. 11 [1839], 404). And in 1839, 1840, and 1841 his reviews of parts II to VII of *Reliquiae Antiquae*, although mainly summaries, add weight to the reception, the final review beginning, "We do not know what we can say

---

58. Kuist's attribution of this review to Halliwell is questionable, given its content.

in addition to our former remarks in commendation of this work, except that the later numbers are distinguished by the greater number and variety of their contents, and that we are glad to see the Editors supported by several contributors of the first consideration" (n.s. 15 [1841], 395). Nichols did, however, find things to criticize, albeit benevolently enough to suggest honesty rather than diplomacy. Reviewing Warkworth's *Chronicle of the First Thirteen Years of the Reign of King Edward the Fourth*, he was skeptical of Halliwell's "grounds for attributing authorship" to Warkworth (n.s. 12 [1839], 617) and of his dating of a visit of King Edward's to Bristol (p. 618). Likewise, he praised the *Merry Tales of the Wise Men of Gotham* in 1840, but did point out that Halliwell was "incorrect in stating that the subject is at all noticed by Thoroton, the old county historian" (n.s. 14 [1840], 401). Halliwell's "illustrations" in his *Chronicle of William de Rishanger* are characteristic rather of his industry than his judgment–his industry, that is, in collecting, but not in examining and comparing" (n.s. 15 [1841], 399), albeit praising him for his "courage in undertaking the task" (p. 397). And while acknowledging a "faithful transcript of his MS." of *Torrent of Portugal,* Nichols in 1842 could not help mentioning that some annotations might have helped Halliwell's suggestion that the "Romance will be 'valuable to the philologist'," and that he has "noticed some words that should have been corrected ... and some others quite obvious to every reader" (n.s. 18 [1842], 403).

As reviewer of Halliwell for the *Gentleman's Magazine* Thomas Wright was naturally more buoyant and expansive. If these were his professional and personal traits, he applied them even more so for his friend and protégé. A "retrospective review" of the *Voiage and Travaile of Sir John Maundeville* enabled him to show his own learning on the subject of "middle-age geography" and set excerpts from Halliwell's work within a larger and more compelling framework. What defects there are–the philological inaccuracy of the facsimile text itself, etc.–may be attributed to the publisher. But this "valuable acquisition to the general ... is much enriched by the detailed list of manuscripts, and editions, given in Halliwell's introduction; as well as by that gentleman's supplementary notes and glossary" (n.s. 12 [1839], 47). In fact, "the publisher would have done well to put the whole care of editing into his [Halliwell's] hands." Wright was less restrained in his retrospective review of *Ludus Coventriae.* Whereas he had mentioned Halliwell's name but once in the Mandeville (and that more or less inconspicuously in the middle of the review), he opens this review with trumpets: "Mr Halliwell has presented us with a very valuable contribution to the history of the stage during the Middle Ages" (n.s. 16 [1841], 381). The subject enables him, quite typically, to give an overview of early drama which occupies almost the entire review. Not until the last paragraph does he feel he "must give our mede of praise" to the editor. First, in his most magnanimous manner, he provides the aureole. "Mr. Halliwell has already conferred great benefits on history, both political and literary, by his publications, and we trust he will not slacken in his exertions in this fair road." Then follows the precise professional praise: "He has published the text with great fidelity from the manuscript; he has prefixed to it an interesting preface, and in a few brief notes he has illustrated several curious allusions, and, which is more important, pointed out and corrected some of the errors of the manuscript which he considered it his duty to reproduce in the text; and finally, which is by no means the least useful part of the book, he has completed it by adding a copious glossary of the difficult and uncommon words, and such as are rendered obscure by their orthography" (p. 384).

A subtle but gradual modification of point of view, a move towards professional objectivity, was noticeable in the *Gentleman's Magazine*, however. Nichols's joint editor, John Mitford, was a literary person, editor and poet, more independent, it seems, than Nichols, who was deeply involved in the intricacies of the Camden Society and the Royal Society. Mitford's three reviews of works by Halliwell in this early period are business-like and objective. He submits Halliwell's *A Selection of the Minor Pieces of Lydgate* to three tests—"faulty or doubtful reading of manuscripts," "words wanting the explanation of a glossary," and what he considers "errors of the editor" (n.s. 15 [1841], 576)—and concludes his admittedly "casual," "time confined" reading with the somber assessment: "The poems are worthy of being more correctly edited, and illustrated with more care and learning than either the present editor has bestowed, or we have it in our power to contribute" (p. 579). In the same year he faulted Halliwell's edition of the *Early Naval Ballads of England* for lacking chronological order (n.s. 15 [1841], 570-1). He did, however, acknowledge that the "latter pieces are more fully illustrated." But there is a certain piquancy in his attributing this improvement to the "*deputy* editor Mr. Rimbault" (p. 571), secretary of the Percy Society and one not of Wright's camp. But Mitford could be evenhanded. For his review in 1845 of the *First Sketches of the Second and Third Parts of King Henry the Sixth* is long and detailed, involving a serious evaluation of the views of Malone, Knight, and Collier. Although suggesting "a trifle or so" of conjectural or emendatory criticism, In which he disagrees with Halliwell's readings, he nevertheless is of the opinion that this is a "curious and valuable republication, edited with care, and accompanied by useful and learned illustrations" (n.s. 23 [1845], 237).

The *Literary Gazette*, under the editorship of William Jerdan, was similarly, if not overwhelmingly, sympathetic to Halliwell and, by extension, to the Wright camp. It was in fact Wright who seems to have managed–so his numerous letters to Halliwell in which Jerdan is mentioned–the relationship between Jerdan and Halliwell. It was Wright who "got [Halliwell's] certif[icate] for [the] R[oyal] S[ociety of] L[iterature] made out and signed by Jerdan" (12 March [1839]; LOA 2:23); it was Wright who announced to Halliwell, "Did you see what a splash review of your Warkworth in the Literary Gazette on Saturday. Jerdan did it" (28 February 1839; LOA 2:52); it was Wright who advised Halliwell, "Do any thing you can for Jerdan. He is very much your friend. Has told me privately he esteemed you very much–and I know he takes your part whenever he hears anybody say anything against you" (20 February 1842; LOA 14:54). And it was Jerdan, a founder of the Royal Society of Literature in 1823 and Fellow of the Society of Antiquaries in 1826, who some years later proposed that Halliwell also join him on the *Literary Gazette*.

Its reviews were anonymous and, especially when considering minor work, in the manner of notices, informal and neutral. Such is the case, for example, in the reviews in 1839 of *Two Essays* (29 June 1839, p. 408), in 1840 of the *Early History of Freemasonry in England* (30 May 1840, p. 344), and in 1842 of the *Jokes of the Cambridge Coffee-Houses* (11 June 1842, pp. 395-6). Still, the reviews could be so enthusiastic as to exceed the bounds of sheer puffery. The reception of the first part of *Reliquiae Antiquae* in 1839 is so much a triumphal trumpeting that it is difficult not to believe that Wright or Halliwell did not have a hand in it. "We hail," so the opening, "with much satisfaction this little publication" (13 July 1839, p. 439) would seem to match the "We hail with pleasure ... " (p. 165) of the anonymous reviewer (i.e. Halliwell) in the *Gentleman's Magazine*. The latter's "excellence of the plan" is echoed by the former's "good arrangement and correctness" (p. 439), as is the "care and ability" of the editors by the "names of the editors are a sufficient guarantee" (p. 439). The *Literary Gazette*'s reviewer is more expansive, so setting the collection within the wider context of early literature, and making specific references to Latin and Anglo-Norman that the authorship may very well be attributed to Wright. The echoes and expansiveness of the review in 1839 of Mandeville's *Voiage and Travaile* are likewise familiar. Although in the main a summary, the reviewer's "we rejoice to see that the task has fallen into such competent hands" (1 June 1839, p. 342) calls to mind "we rejoice ... excellent plan ... conducted with great care and ability." Of course there is no doubt about the identity of the reviewer in 1842 and 1843 of the first and second editions of the *Nursery Rhymes of England*. Even if Wright had not mentioned that he was to review the work in exchange for Halliwell's reviewing his *Piers Ploughman* (5 September 1842; LOA 36:7), he would certainly be recognizable by the jaunty enthusiasm of "Well done, 'third edition!'" (30 December 1843, p. 848), the characteristic reference to the "great antiquity" of the rhymes, and the numerous illustrations which Wright, mindful of payment according to length, often employed.

Still, both the *Gentleman's Magazine* and the *Literary Gazette* were under pressure, as were other journals, to reduce party political or personal puffery or at least to reflect the independence, if not critical expertise, of its reviewers. Whatever the exact reasons, even partisan journals allowed a certain deviation from the party line and a measure of critical autonomy. The anonymous reviewer in the *Gentleman's Magazine* could in 1845 praise Halliwell's "very seasonable and valuable volume," the Thornton Romances, as being "in our opinion, by far the best edited that Mr. Halliwell has yet put forth" (n.s. 23 [1845], 61); in the same year the reviewer (identified as John Mitford) could write of the *First Sketches of the Second and Third Parts of King Henry the Sixth*: "This is a curious and valuable republication, edited with care, and accompanied by useful and learned illustrations" (n.s. 23 [1845], 237). Yet some months later an anonymous reviewer in the same journal, while acknowledging the "important matter" of the *Autobiography and Correspondence of Sir Simonds D'Ewes*, did not fail to mention the "foibles" and errors and haste, concluding that the "whole publication, and every separate part of it, is unworthy of so practised an editor as Mr. Halliwell" (n.s. 25 [1846], 272). Halliwell's ambitious *Dictionary of Archaic and Provincial Words*, with which Wright was so intimately connected, was severely criticized in the *Gentleman's Magazine* as being "totally deficient of any definite design or substantial conclusion" (n.s. 23 [1845], 62) and was offered pages of detailed criticism and suggestions for improving this "extensive and important undertaking." Even the review in the generally more sympathetic *Literary Gazette* tempered its high praise: "We think Mr. Halliwell's *Dictionary* may be considered one of the most remarkable productions of the day. He merits, at least, a full meed of praise and admiration for his zeal and labour" (4 January 1845, p. 6). Still, it is on the whole more measured, more balanced, and just—especially when the recurrence of the word "meed" (which had appeared in the review of *Ludus Coventriae*), the reference to *Piers Ploughman*, and the wide-ranging survey of earlier attempts seem to suggest that the reviewer was none other than Thomas Wright.

Puffery and partisanship were subsiding but in the early 1840's still potent. The opposing camp was represented by the *Athenaeum*, as much a rival of the *Literary Gazette qua* journal as of the Wright faction, although–a savory detail–its editor, Charles Wentworth Dilke, was with Halliwell one of the founding Council members of the Shakespeare Society. Its identified reviewers of Halliwell's work of his earlier period are numerous and diverse in speciality and personality.[59] Their reaction ranges from mild favor to hostile disapproval, the latter more often the case. Interesting is a comparison of the reviews of the same work in the *Gentleman's Magazine* and the *Athenaeum*. In 1841 Wright's "mede of praise" of Halliwell both as editor of the *Ludus Coventriae*, as well as of previous works in which he had "already conferred great benefits on history, both political and literary" is echoed by Collier reviewing in the *Athenaeum*, but in a somewhat muted form. Granting it to be a "necessary and valuable production [of the Shakespeare Society, of which Collier was director, it must be remembered] ... discharged ... with praiseworthy zeal, knowledge, and acuteness" (4 September 1841, p. 686), Collier nevertheless has reservations: "Here and there ... Mr. Halliwell appears to have gone a little out of his way in order to introduce information" (p. 687). There may also be too much in the way of glossing, he held, courteously modifying this criticism with "It is an error on the right side to be too copious" (p. 687). However considerate of his young friend and colleague, Collier was in effect criticizing the method of archaeological research, distancing himself from the massive accumulation of documents, artifacts, and other forms of data as an end in itself. "Illustrations" were doubtless necessary but not at the expense of order and discipline. Augustus De Morgan, another friend and colleague of Halliwell's, makes the same point in his review of *A Collection of Letters Illustrative of the Progress of Science in England.* Whereas Halliwell himself (reviewing anonymously in the *Gentleman's Magazine*) found the collection "a valuable addition to the few materials we already possess," and used the review to puff his newly formed Historical Society of Science, of which this was the first publication, De Morgan, himself a Council member and in the review a firm supporter of the Society, was aware of the archaeological "problem": "There is a vein which they are to open, and an ore which they are to extract. Whatever may be the per-centage of apparently useless matter which they bring up with the metal, it is not their business to make any final selection; and they could not fall into any more pernicious error, than publishing upon any definite system of rejection. Whatever there may be to dig up, let us at least have large specimens of everything" (7 August 1841, p. 589). Be that as it may, De

59. The identification of reviewers in the *Athenaeum* is based on the work of the Athenaeum Indexing Project of the City University (London).

Morgan can only come to the conclusion, restrainedly if not critically, that the "present collection is *miscellaneous*" [italics are mine], and taking direct exception to Halliwell's recommendation, he ends: "Matters which would interest the general reader, such as Sir Samuel Morland's autobiography, would not give any idea of the scientific contents of the work" (p. 589).

There is little ambiguity or courtesy in Henry Cole's review in the *Athenaeum* of the second edition of the *Nursery Rhymes*. Set between Wright's glowing reviews in the *Literary Gazette* of the first and third editions–their ample illustrations indicating Wright's delight and approval–Cole's illustrations serve to criticize Halliwell for having been overwhelmed by his material, for having been unable to control it and therefore to discover why it is "worthy of investigation." For all his energy, Halliwell lacks critical acumen and a plan. The result, Cole finds, is that "this edition may be received as perhaps the most ample collection which has hitherto been made; but for any other merit, we cannot bestow much praise on it. Mr. Halliwell deserves all the credit that may be due for printing whatever he could meet with, in any shape, oral or written (the latter without acknowledgment), and his materials may perhaps serve some future editor, who has more feeling and judgment for the task, a certain amount of labour; but this will, we suspect, be all the benefit he will derive from this collection" (29 April 1843, p. 409).

From friend or foe, the focus of critical attention was only to a degree on Halliwell's person or personality or even alliance. In the treatment of his early works the reviews did not fail to coincide on the matter of his lack of control and order. Thus Peter Cunningham, a fellow Council member of the Shakespeare Society and a longtime correspondent, was certainly motivated by more than professional rivalry in asserting in his *Athenaeum* review of *An Introduction to Shakespeare's Midsummer Night's Dream*: "It has not often been our lot to see so much reading turned to so little account, as in the volume before us" (29 May 1841, p. 420). It may not be a surprise that John Holmes, senior assistant in the Department of Manuscripts of the British Museum, and doubtless an ally of Frederic Madden on this matter,[60] should be hostile to Halliwell's *Manuscript Rarities of the University of Cambridge* for what was considered arrogance of tone and presumption, as also in *A Few Hints to Novices*. Still, Holmes, reviewing in the *Gentleman's Magazine*, is following what emerges as the general line of attack: Halliwell "has contented himself with the cheap labour of a list of

60. On 1 January 1845 it was Holmes who contacted the librarian of Trinity College, James Ind Smith, about the manuscripts Halliwell was accused of having stolen (TCC Add. MSS. a.170.1).

the MSS. contained in three presses in the Public Library alone. Why these particular presses are selected does not appear, nor are we told why [others] are omitted" (n.s. 17 [1842], 518).[61]

If the *Athenaeum* was hostile towards Halliwell, and continued to be so in crucial moments, it must be pointed out that its reviewers were themselves of widely disparate backgrounds and interests. To the views of Collier, De Morgan, Cunningham, and Cole may be added—however much the shadings, the core of their criticism is similar—those of the anonymous reviewer of *An Account of the Only Known Manuscript* ("The variations are not of such importance as ... to justify the publication" [29 April 1843, p. 812]) and of Samuel Astley Dunham's review of *Illustrations of the Fairy Mythology* ("None of these pieces have more than a distant, some a very dubious affinity with the immortal drama of 'A Midsummer Night's Dream'" [26 July 1845, p. 739]). In arriving at a common core although starting as it were from different points, reviewing was becoming more rational, it might be said. And since that was the case with differing journals, it might also be said that the discussion was not only about persons but about the objectives of learning and scholarship. John Abraham Heraud, in his review in the *Athenaeum* of the *Autobiography and Correspondence of Sir Simonds D'Ewes*, characterized the two octavo volumes as a "somewhat bold and hazardous venture" (13 September 1845, p. 900). He might well be characterizing Halliwell and his youthful enterprises. As Halliwell was to learn very early in his life and career, and that painfully, the glory of his call required discipline, persistence, and courage.

The interplay of professional ambition and personal sensitivity, of career and life, is otherwise and most dramatically displayed in the early 1840s in Halliwell's relationship with the eminent book collector Sir Thomas Phillipps. Still a teenager, Halliwell was impelled by his avid

---

61. Holmes was evidently not, at first at least, a reviewer of the work, and whether he was put up to writing a communication is not clear. In all fairness it is best to reproduce his letter to J. G. Nichols of 6 April 1842 (Folger Y.d.24, Box 23 [190]): "I have no acquaintance with Mr. Halliwell and cannot entertain any personal feeling against him nor I hope against any one else: the book however entre nous, is most contemptible and should be exposed. I think it would be better for what I have written to appear as a review and I have therefore marked all such passages in pencil which may be omitted as in any way personal to the author or harsh in expression. I do not fear a controversy but I sometimes think there is almost too much of it in your pages. Of course you are at perfect liberty to give my name to Mr. Halliwell as author of the review on his book. If I were to make it a communication I should certainly keep all the original strictures, but I think it is now so softened in tone that it may safely appear as a review."

bibliophile interests to seek out yet another grand personality. The attraction must have been mutual. As early as 1838, when Halliwell was eighteen, Phillipps invited him to Middle Hill to see his manuscripts (22 October 1838; LOA 2:9). In response to Halliwell's offer to examine manuscripts for him in Cambridge, Phillipps repeated the invitation just a day before Halliwell's nineteenth birthday, adding that he (a member of the Council) would be happy to sign Halliwell's certificate at the Society of Antiquaries (19 January 1839; LOA 1:33). That he seems not to have done so had little effect on their relationship. Halliwell became a Fellow shortly thereafter–the certificate initiated by Joseph Hunter and endorsed by other celebrities, C. F. Barnwell, Madden, Thomas Amyot, Wright, and John Bruce. A meeting was doubtless imminent, as is evident in Thomas Wright's response to Halliwell's animated question: "I think you cant do wrong in addressing him in the same way he addresses you," and adding the comforting "I have always found him a very good sort of a fellow" (7 February 1839; LOA 2:17). In any event the two must have struck it off quite well–amazingly well considering the well-known eccentricities of Phillipps and the impetuosity of Halliwell. To the common interests of collectors and antiquaries may be added common membership in various societies: by mid 1839 both were Fellows of the Society of Antiquaries and the Royal Society, among others. They had common views: Phillipps's complaints about the Camden Society–"There is so much trumpery among the Publications that I am half inclined to leave it" (23 August 1839; LOA 2:41); he would be in societies only if he had the "power of a veto upon what should *not* be printed" (24 December 1841; LOA 63:34)–doubtless found Halliwell's sympathetic ear. Further, in the manner of colleagues, they exchanged books and articles (17 May 1840; LOA 7:38); Halliwell inscribed the first volume of *Reliquiae Antiquae* to Phillipps; he agreed to Phillipps's request that he "spare me a day at the Brit. Museum" (31 March 1842; LOA 14:15). And they did business together. In the negotiation which was to have enormous consequences only a few years later, Halliwell on 8 October 1839 wrote to Phillipps offering him a collection of 136 scientific manuscripts for £250. That Phillipps did not take up the offer, nor agree to keep it confidential, did not, however, appear to affect the relationship. It continued and evidently prospered until the middle of 1842, when a clash of personal interests, with a powerful professional undertone, changed the relationship dramatically and unalterably.

Halliwell was finally able to accept one of Phillipps's cordial invitations to visit him at Middle Hill, the last one on 24 December 1841 (LOA 63:34), having smoothed the way with an extended apology for having possibly offended Dr. Gustav Friedrich Haenel (a scholar from Leipzig), itself a revealing self-portrait:

I regret very much too that my unworthy little pamphlet on MS. literature should be circulated now. I have withdrawn it a long time and burnt all the copies which were not sold. Mr. J. R. Smith has I believe a few copies, which I am sorry for, but he charges double the publishing price for them. I hope you will consider that it was published when I was only *eighteen*, and that excuse (a poor one I confess) is the only one I can offer for the unwarrantable and improper criticism on Dr Haegnel [*sic*]. All I can say [is] this that I will not again be guilty of the like offence against good feeling, but if you think that I *ought* to acknowledge my boyish error I will do so. I am sure I should be very sorry to let any one think I bore any ill will towards Dr Haenel. The fact is that the Few Hints to Novices in MS. Literature was written for the use of the Cambridge Society, and I heartily regret that so crude a production should have got out in the world at all (12 February 1842; Phil-Rob c.478:162).

The visit is mentioned, with notable understatement and compression, in her diary entry for 22 February 1842 by Henrietta Phillipps, his twenty-one-year-old daughter: "Mr James O. Halliwell arrived at Middle Hill from Manchester by invitation from Papa to look at some MSS. He stayed two or three days, after he left he wrote Papa for his consent to marry me & several letters passed between Papa & James's father–& Papa partially consented." As a matter of fact he stayed for eight days, according to "extracts from my Wife's Diary" preserved among Halliwell's letters (LOA 240:29). It seems to have been a week of intense work. "He arrived to dinner at 7 o'clock & looked over some of Papa's publications in the evening." The next day he "was engaged all day in examining some of Papa's MSS. and did not go out." On 24 February he "was engaged all day with the MSS. & neither he or Papa left the house." The same total engagement continued, with the exception of two afternoon walks, until 2 March, when the two men were "engaged with the MSS. in the morning" only, Halliwell leaving after dinner. The visit was evidently a great professional success. A few days later Phillipps wrote to ask for the "five *Visitations*" in Rodd's catalogue (11 March 1842; LOA 14:75), one day later thanking him for various things (12 March 1842; LOA 14:68)–in a P.S. "forward[ing] to you this Evening a Shirt which you left behind"–and a fortnight later (31 March 1842; LOA 14:15) to ask for the "pleasure of seeing" him again. In April there were further letters to Halliwell thanking him for his help in checking certain items in the British

Museum and expecting a visit from him on "Friday or Saturday" (3 April 1842; LOA 24:11). Henrietta's "other" diary extracts are very succinct about the visit and very enlightening. Recording Halliwell's stay from Saturday, 9 to 18 April (although not indicating exactly when he left, for the extracts simply break off with Halliwell's notation, "My Wife kept two diaries at this time, one brief, the other longer"), she mentions the daily engagement of the two men with the manuscripts. Noteworthy is the reason for their working so hard that they often "did not go out": on 12 April "Mr Halliwell & Papa were busy among the MSS. & I got out about 100 in order to see which way Mr. H. should arrange them for the Catalogue he is about commencing." The visit was known to Collier, who was curious as to whether Halliwell had "met with the M.S. of *Henslowe's Diary* in the library of Sir Thomas Phillipps" (19 April 1842; LOA 24:16), having hoped to borrow it "for our use" (7 April 1842; LOA 24:15), and to John Russell Smith, who was confident he could sell a hundred copies of Phillipps's catalogue (20 April 1842; LOA 14:43).

But this rather routine business success was overshadowed by what was, at first at least, a rousing and exhilarating personal experience and, almost simultaneously, a painful and enduring strain, to be climaxed just a few years later in 1845 by a personal and professional trauma.

Halliwell fell in love with Phillipps's eldest daughter, Henrietta. Although some may feel he was an opportunist—Phillipps was after all the greatest private collector England had known and a personality of considerable influence—there are many signs that the affection was mutual and sincere, confirmed by the fact that the marriage took place without Phillipps's blessing or presence, and that it remained loving and stable until Henrietta's death in 1879, although it led to the total estrangement of son- and father-in-law and personal and professional hostility towards Halliwell.

The attraction of the young lovers is testified to in letters from Halliwell's brother Thomas. On 31 March 1842 (LOA 14:16) he wrote that he "was very pleased to hear of your intended return to all the enchantments of Middle Hill & hope that it may prove equally delightful & enticing as before." Halliwell's youthful exhilaration is implied in Thomas's almost mock-serious response of 3 April 1842 (LOA 14:21) to Halliwell's letter, "just arrived," after the "necessary consultation has passed upon it": "imprimis I am to give you the information that the material for the handkerchiefs & collars which you name could not very easily be made up, washed & prepared for use in the limited time allowed by you—secondly, I can tell you for your satisfaction the remedy for this difficulty wch we propose—viz to send you ... some collars of mine of the newest cut & also some white pocket hdkchfs all ready for use–of all of which my Mother begs you will be very careful–remind Louy [Louisa, his sister] *before the last day* that you have plenty of proper shirts fit &c &c." He does not forget to add his "best wishes for a happy enjoyment of your proposed visit to Middle Hill." And, adding to the frothy atmosphere, is his reaction to another and recent outing by his younger brother: he "was very pleased to hear from Louy so delightful an account of your excursion to the present attraction at Strawberry Hill. She describes the pleasures of the whole day in raptures but appears I think more delighted with the gaiety & witticisms of the party than with the crowded heaps of curiosities" (13 April 1842; LOA 14:28).

From Middle Hill Halliwell sent a request of Planché, adding, in its almost comic awkwardness, another telling touch: "There is a great favour I have to ask of you, which I shouldn't have done, if I didn't think that if you had any objection to grant it we are too good friends to be in any way affronted at such trifles. The fact is I want very much for a lady's album a few lines in which Middle-Hill the name of this mansion is introduced, and as I can't write poetry you would by giving me a few verses as early as possible confer the greatest obligation on your sincere friend" (March 1842; Folger Y.c.1267[1]). Even Henrietta's laconic "extracts" from her "other" diary (LOA 240:29) hint at the developing personal relationship. For if the men were almost totally occupied with the manuscripts during the February visit, in April there is almost equal mention of Halliwell's giving them "some pieces of music in the evening" of his arrival (9 April), of his walking "with Mary & Kate & I to the garden in the morning & with Papa Mary & I to the Tower in the afternoon" (10 April), of his accompanying "Mary & I down to the garden & in the Bratch" (15 April), of his going "with us to the garden & also ... up the New Road" (16 April), and of his walking "down with Mary & I to see Miss Russell" (18 April). And even if Planché's verses never existed or have disappeared, Halliwell's do, and his charmingly amateurish "Acrostic"(a lone handwritten and undated leaf, Phil-Rob d.247:80) must capture some of his youthful rapture:

> Happy happy with thee ever
>   Eagerly the knot entwine!
> No power then our hearts shall sever–
>   Radiant joy for ever shine!
> Increasing love decreasing never
>   Entirely I'm thine and only thine!
> Thenceforth my dearest only love,

Through life, on earth, in Heav'n above!
Angel of angels, be mine! be mine!
JOH

If April was exhilarating, late April, May, and June were depressing.
After searching for and missing Halliwell in Oxford on 24 and 25 April
(LOA 10:13.1 and 113:35), Phillipps abruptly announced on 26 April
(LOA 105:5) that he had decided not have a new catalogue made of his
manuscripts, a step which may well have been connected with both
Halliwell's participation and especially his proposal of marriage to
Henrietta. From 24 May to 23 June an exchange of seven letters
(preserved by Halliwell) between Phillipps and Halliwell's father, Thomas,
concerning the conditions for a marriage settlement almost destroyed the
alliance. Following Halliwell's proposal to his daughter, Phillipps felt it
"incumbent ... to ascertain what are his means of living, & of supporting
her in a style consistent with her rank & the expectations she has been
brought up with" (24 May 1842; LOA 4:3). The icy tone was not assuaged
by Thomas Halliwell's assurance to "ever do all in my power to promote
the happiness of my children, & in this case shall, as far as my means
permit me, do all I can to forward the wishes of my son James" (30 May
1842; LOA 4:4). Referring to himself in the third person and not deigning
to sign his letter, Phillipps turned from ice to fire, accusing the young
Halliwell of saying he could provide £1000 per year but then in Phillipps's
"*absence, knowing* that he cd *only* obtain 500£ p[er] ann. & yet, *with that
knowledge*, he, very unhandsomely & ungenerously, *in Sir T. P.'s absence*,
proposes marriage to Miss P.!!" (7 June 1842; LOA 4:5). Thomas
Halliwell's disbelief of this report and unwillingness to accept without
reciprocation Phillipps's wish to secure £800 per annum for his daughter
(11 June 1842; LOA 4:7) led Phillipps to make further accusations against
James–his cheek in announcing he "*would marry her whether I want or
no*!!!"–and to declare, "*As to my Daughter's Expectations they are fallen to the
ground by my late marriage*" (13 June 1842; LOA 4:8). (On 2 June 1842
Henrietta's diary entry reads: "Papa" married Elizabeth Harriet Anne
Mansel, "The bride is very fair with tight ringlets, short & rather stout &
27 years old rather pretty and very amiable"; this was the second marriage
for Phillipps, who was fifty.) The haggling continued. Phillipps's
ultimatory "Allow me to ask if it is your final determination to give your
son nothing ... as such I, at present, understand to be the purport of your
last letter" (20 June 1842; LOA 4:10) was matched by the impatience of
his P.S.: "I should not have written, only my Daughter wishes it to be
decided one way or the other, that she may look elsewhere, if this can not

be accomplished." Thomas Halliwell's assertion was that he had been misunderstood: "Indeed the idea of giving my son nothing never entered my head & never will. If I recollect rightly I merely said I thought it too much to ask a man to settle a large sum of money upon a wife who brings him little or nothing."

At any rate, a settlement was never reached. Whether Phillipps needed money for his new wife or his collection—most likely the latter[62]—whether young Halliwell was attempting to make the best of improper behavior (the letters from his father to Phillipps are copies in his own hand), it is hard to say with certainty. What is clear is that Halliwell was determined to marry Henrietta and that both were willing to brave the rage of a Victorian father and a stormy personality at that. Numerous letters passed between the two, as Halliwell indicates in the opening of his letter to his "dearest" Henrietta of 28 June 1842 (LOA 208:11): "I am sorry I did not get your letter soon enough to answer it yesterday and now this morning I have received another." And the way, as the letter continues, was not smooth. For one thing, Halliwell admits to having "erred in being occasionally of a passionate temper" but denies having ever spoken ill of Sir Thomas although he thinks he has been "tirated [*sic*] by him in a manner only to be borne by the slave of an Oriental despot." He then explains the core of the negotiations: "I could not obtain a settlement on you *now* unless Sir Thomas does so also." But reacting to what in "her letter of this morning thus appears to me to be a distinct refusal of me as you insist in that letter on having a settlement," Halliwell assures her that his "income will not decrease, and that I will take care you shall be provided for in case of my death ["my share at least of my Father's property, with at least £2000 that I should insure my life for"], are points that you, having no fortune, oughts I should think to rely on my honour."

That Henrietta was equally under pressure—that her "refusal" was in part at least dictated to her by her father—is to be derived from tight-lipped remarks in her diary. At the head of 1842 she writes: "My diary for this year is in Papa's possession & I cannot get it. I will write down what I remember of it till the day I married." From the first mention on 22 February of the visit of Mr James O. Halliwell to Middle Hill to the recording of their marriage on 9 August, there are but seven entries. They are brief and not always revealing. Halliwell seems to have seen Henrietta

62. After the death of his first wife in 1832, Phillipps began the search for a new wife with a large fortune. "Do you know of any Lady with 50,000£ who wants a husband? I am for sale at that price," he wrote in 1833. Munby (*Family Affairs*, p. 28) counts "no less than seventeen abortive negotiations with the parents of heiresses ... during the next nine years."

at Middle Hill twice in April, visited her in the house in Welbeck Street in Leamington in May, seen her again once in June and again on 7 August at Middle Hill. Two days later they married. Also recorded is the fact that Phillipps in May was "paying his addresses" to Elizabeth Mansel, that on the first of June he had "long disputes" with Elizabeth's uncles about the marriage settlement, that the wedding was fixed for the next day, and that they returned home "uncertain whether it would really take place." On the next day, 2 June, it did. And on his return to Middle Hill soon after, Phillipps continued his correspondence with Halliwell's father, asking for £800 per annum for his daughter. The turmoil surrounding the marriage itself is not extensively described but with some interesting details. "James came down to M. H. & I saw him, Papa heard of it & was extremely angry, although he had partly consented to our marriage ... I saw James in the afternoon for Papa sd I might marry him or not just as I pleased only he wd not consent. When he first knew James in February he liked him very much indeed. Papa furious all day & I went to bed very sick & ill. He locked up all my clothes &c &c." The next day, 8 August, while Halliwell had gone to Worcester for a license and the rest of the family were off to dinner, Henrietta "packed as many of [her] things as [she] cd find wch Papa had not locked up." The day of the marriage, 9 August, "I got up early & walked through the plantation with Mary & I later met James at the end & walked with him to the church at Broadway. Lucretia and E. Marshall were my bridesmaids. We were married at 8 o'clock by Revd Wm Battersley. I parted with my sisters Mary & Kate in the plantation at M. Hill. After our marriage—which took place in presence of a great many people from Broadway—who wished us health & happiness & threw immense bouquets of flowers into the carriage, we started for Cheltenham & then posted to Cirencester whence we proceeded by rail to London. Called at Alfred Place & James introduced me to his father & mother."

The marriage was not secretive or solemn. From Charles Clark, proprietor of the Great Totham Press, came a printed "Acrostic," "*Composed Extempore on Reading the Announcement of the Marriage,*" entitled "Hail, Wedded Love!" (August 1842; LOA 23:57*):

> **P**–roceed, proceed, proud Hymen!
>   **H**–ow can we wonder why men
> **H**–ail more and more thy name now,
>   **A**–nd so resound thy fame now!
> **I**–nspired seem all around us,–
>   **L**–et belles or beaux but bound us,

L–o! How employed each tongue is–
    L–ouder thy praise still rung is!–
L–est some dolt his voice raises,
    I–nquiring *why* these praises,
I–n wedlock's bands, know, bound so
    W–e've now a pair, who're–crown'd so!–
P–lain 'tis that no connection
    E–'er blended more affection!–
P–rosperity, Fate, send them!
    L–ong from all ills defend them!
S–weetly from thy store still
    L–ife's blessings on them pour still!

For all its triviality the poem does reflect something of the context of these young people: it is cheerful and spirited. And congratulations came pouring in. From Wright: "I need hardly tell you that I wish you all the happiness and prosperity that this world can afford ... Pray give my sincere respects and congratulations to madame votre belle epouse" (12 August [1842]; LOA 16:71). From Collier, surprised but with "unfeigned pleasure," after praising Halliwell's *Merry Wives of Windsor* he hopes "you will have a Merry Wife yourself" (19 August 1842; LOA 23:53). And from Henry Ellis of the British Museum (24 August 1842: LOA 10:14), from William Henry Black of the Public Record Office (7 September 1842; LOA 12:20), from John William Burgon, and others. On their honeymoon the couple were joined almost immediately by friends, some of whom, like Wright and James Heywood, were mixing pleasure with business, doubtless furthering the projects they were working on with Halliwell. A few months later, in a letter of 7 December to her cousin Utretia Cotterell (preserved by Halliwell as he was destroying a volume of copies of letters made by his wife), written "when the circumstances were fresh in mind," since "several absurd reports & misrepresentations on the subject [were] current," Henrietta gives the most explicit description of the events surrounding the marriage:

You *must* have been rather astonished when you saw it in the papers, & particularly being married without Papa's consent & yet going to Broadway Church to be 'tied up' as the saying is. You little thought the quiet Harry wd run away tho' it can hardly be called that for nobody once attempted to stop me & Papa you must know was enchanted with my husbd when he first came to M. H. last February, because he was fond of literature (tho' by no means an Antiquary like his father in law) & wd have been delighted if he thought I shd like him for a partner thro' life, but I was looking another way then; besides I did not like having a husband recommended to me, when however matters came to a crisis by J. popping the question, I found I liked him whereupon Papa immediately turned round & found fault & kindly told me I shd never have his property if he cd help it. & to frighten me went off & married directly. Things went on in an extremely tiresome way, Papa opening all our letters, until J. came down to M. H.–where I met him in the plantation, was found out by Papa, blown up, & commanded to make up my mind one way or other & if I still continued determined I was to quit the house that day. After trying to compromise the matter & in several ways & finding all wd not do I made up my mind to give him up & was very ill &c &c. but the next morning changed my mind the other way. On Tuesday 9th Augst behold me quietly dressing myself at 7 o'clock in the morng with Mary & K & afterwards marching along the plantation to the top of the lane where I met my intended & walked with him down to the Church–Mary & K did not go with me but when they returned to the house found that Papa had been walking about the plantation while we were in it. He never asked any question except who gave her away–I had a lovely day & went very composedly thro' the ceremony there were a great many people in the Church & I had lots of flowers thrown into me & at 9 o'clock we were dashing off in a P. Chaise & four to Cheltenham where we stopped & then went on to Cirencester, went by Railroad to London, on to Southton where we finished that days journey. The next day we went over to Ryde where we spent a very happy H. Moon & I am just as happy now as I was then–This is the quiet Harry P. you must remember. & now as you wish it I must give you a description of my husband, Tall, thin, fair but pale, blue eyes & aged 22–younger than I am. Very good tempered & as kind as possible to me. Papa finding he had failed to frighten me into submission was of course very angry for some time but said little, & in two months wrote to say I might come down to M. H., but without James wch I did then, but will not again, if I can possibly help it. I don't approve of going about without my husband so I hope Papa will soon come to his senses & ask him as well (LOA 230:48).

Phillipps never did.[63] He was simply too obtuse even to recognize that

---

63. Phillipps's discontent extended to his other daughters and his new wife as well. In September 1842 (LOA 107:40*) Kate Fenwick wrote to "My darling Mr

Halliwell's struggle against parental opposition was almost the mirror of his own plight in his desire to marry Henrietta Molyneux.[64] Just a week after the wedding, while Henrietta and James were honeymooning at Ryde on the Isle of Wight and thereabouts, bathing and sailing and making small excursions until 21 September, Phillipps's anger was further ignited by a scurrilous anonymous letter postmarked "Holborn-Hill 18 August 1842" and "Broadway, 19 August 1842" in which Halliwell's "origin and connections" were attacked: His father "kept a Linen Draper's Shop"... his mother is the daughter of a publican ... his eldest brother ... married an illegitimate child, whose mother was a milliner, and dressmaker." Halliwell himself is charged with betraying his friends, with shady borrowing and lending practices. His character is thoroughly blackened by a series of rhetorical questions beginning with "ask" this person and that one. Convinced that Phillipps has been deceived and aware that his warning comes too late to save the "ill-fated" daughter, the writer closes with the hardly comforting, but surely taunting, "That he has great talent is undeniable, and had it not been employed in the way it has, he must have been a respectable man on his own ground, in spite of his origin."[65] Halliwell's reputation was once again at risk, for Phillipps lost no opportunity to disgrace him publicly–and for as long as he lived. It is little wonder that Halliwell preserved, "with great reluctance," the exchange of letters between his father and Thomas Phillipps, commenting, "there is something so despicable in the character of a fortune-hunter & something also not very creditable in surreptitious addresses,–& both these accusations have not only been industriously circulated respecting myself, but also, as I know, placed upon written & printed record–the presentation of these documents, which speak for themselves in refutation, is I hope justifiable" (undated; LOA 4:1). And how ironic a letter of 4 October 1842 (LOA 12:28) from a friend, John William Burgon, congratulating Halliwell on his marriage and the "*opportunities* you will now have in abundance–amid the treasures of your Father in law's Library" when Halliwell was never to be reconciled with his father-in-law,

Hally": "I wish we could say that we are [happy]. Papa has been very cross & angry with Eliza & she cries a great deal sometimes he is vexed at her having no child & will not let us go to church in consequence. He has not given us more linen that will make Mary & I two shirts & more of the other stuff." The rest of the letter has been deleted.

64. Only the death of his father made the marriage possible. See Munby, *Family Affairs*, pp. 12-16.

65. The author of the letter has not been identified. In a forthcoming article I suggest it may have been Thomas Stephens Davies.

who in fact was later to declare his library open to the public—except for his son-in-law, his wife (i.e. Phillipps's daughter Henrietta), and all Roman Catholics.[66]

Along with Thomas Wright's warning—"My opinion is that he will do anything he can to injure you" (14 November 1842; LOA 16:85)—were the unsettling rumors that were circulating. On the same day as Wright's warning, Collier (somewhat mischievously, as was his wont) wrote, "I heard it said that Mrs. Halliwell had returned to her father's, but it is no part of my character to give circulation to such matters. Besides, I have too much work to do to have time to gossip" (LOA 23:14). The word "father's" elicited from Halliwell a comment in purple ink: "It is astonishing how this foundless bit of gossip was generally spread about & believed." It is little wonder that Halliwell preserved his wife's letter to Utretia Cotterell, "several absurd reports & misrepresentations on the subject being current." More were to follow.

In fact the months leading up to the marriage were fraught with problems. There were irritations in the societies. In January Edward Francis Rimbault asked Halliwell to postpone resigning from the Percy Society so as to show there are no "dissensions ... in the Council" (13 January 1842; LOA 24:8). A few days later Collier informed him that James Robinson Planché, Halliwell's candidate, had not been elected to the Council of the Shakespeare Society (19 January 1842; LOA 24:1), and a few days thereafter asked Halliwell to re-consider his decision to resign (24 January 1842; LOA 24:7). On 29 March J. W. Lubbock reported that he did not think Halliwell's notes on the tides "very remarkable" and would return them forthwith (LOA 14:9). On 31 March his brother Thomas wrote to say he "was particularly sorry ... that the project of which we had talked so much had for the present failed" (LOA 14:16), evidently referring to a projected edition of Shakespeare which Halliwell's friend James Heywood was glad had been postponed "as the two editions of Knight & Collier, now coming out, will, I think glut the market, for the present" (12 February 1842; LOA 33:23). On 24 July Baden Powell of Oxford stressed that he did not wish to subscribe to Halliwell's pet Historical Society of Science, thus joining William Whewell of Trinity College Cambridge, who had done much the same two years earlier (12 June 1840; LOA 7:48), and others.

There were signs of soul-searching. Deeply sympathizing with [Halliwell's] yearning after literary fame, Burgon (later dean of Chichester) "cannot at all agree with [Halliwell's] idea concerning fame. Contemporary

---

66. Phillipps's will is reproduced in Munby, *Family Affairs*, pp. 106-15.

reputation is, as nothing, with me," he explains, "compared with a *lasting* & honourable celebrity. True, both of these commonly go together; but if they are to be disjoined, give me the more permanent blessing ... After all, it may I think be laid down as a principle–that in 99 cases out of 100, none but truly *good* books–I mean books really carefully & well written,–command the admiration & win for us the regard of our own function–& that it is from such work alone that a man can hope for the regard of posterity" (26 January 1842; LOA 33:22). There were signs of personal disappointment, if not disillusionment, too. A letter of 3 May 1842 (LOA 17:7) from the antiquary C. H. Hartshorne is revealing. "I heard of you from [John] Russell Smith when I was in town, being at Middle Hill. I suppose you overworked yourself there, and you have returned disgusted with literature and the whole business. But every body does that occasionally, and then thinks better of it. And I hope you will do the same." Hartshorne then touches on another troubling concern, the hostility of cliques and reviewers: "Or perhaps you are annoyed at the Gentlemans Review," referring to a savage anonymous review [n.s. 17 (1842), 517-19, identified by Kuist as by John Holmes of the British Museum] of *The Manuscript Rarities of the University of Cambridge*, its detail fitting Frederic Madden's contemptuous description: "a miserable volume ... done in a very jejune & meagre manner" (Diary, 25 August 1841). When the larger context is considered, Halliwell cannot have been very comforted by Hartshorne's "I would never let a scribler [*sic*] deter me from my purpose. No body thinks of those things an hour after they read them. I suppose it was penned by some of the Camden Men, whose opinion is not worth a rush." That may be so, but the Camden Society and reviewers were to be a constant source of pain

And the haggling with Thomas Phillipps over a marriage settlement threw into relief once again Halliwell's financial problems. One solution–a personal and professional one–was to seek a secure position. Responding to Halliwell's inquiry, Henry Hallam, although convinced of his "talents and ... remarkable acquirements," admits, "I do not quite perceive what species of permanent situation you contemplate. If it be in the British Museum, where you might imagine me to have influence, I can only say that the patronage of that institution is exclusively in the Archbishop of Canterbury; & moreover that the salaries of those who first enter are greatly below your claims. As to government offices, I have no sort of interest; &, in fact, if I had any, it must be exerted for those with whom I have connexion of some kind" (19 May 1842; LOA 17:10). A week or so before the marriage the financial problems, never distant, increased. A letter of 26 July [1842] (LOA 21:79) from Thomas Gaskin, his former tutor at Jesus, informed him that, as requested, his name will be removed from the College Board, entitling him to a deduction of £15 for the caution money but reminding him of a balance of £110.13.9 still standing against him. And since the major part of the debt was contracted "upward" of two years earlier, Gaskin feels "confident" that Halliwell "will make every effort to make the best arrangement for its speedy settlement"–by the end of September. A month after the wedding Halliwell received a letter from Thomas Grenville (7 September 1842; LOA 19:85), the great book collector: "I was naturally displeased at the little attention with which I thought myself treated. But your letter of acknowledgment & the circumstances of pecuniary embarrassment to which it refers cancels the debt in question, & I accordingly consider it as paid & enclose herewith the note of hand which you had sent me; neither can I be induced to permit you to make any payment to Coutts as you had proposed." Halliwell's offer of Shakespeare manuscripts Grenville "must altogether decline," however, because he does not "permit [him]self to purchase any Manuscripts." Two months earlier Collier could not afford to buy Halliwell's Alleyn Letters; nor would the Duke of Devonshire, whom he advised, "never layd out any money in that way" (30 June 1842; LOA 23:74).

Other, related, problems also continued. Searching for security, Halliwell considered returning to university for a degree. Having thought first of Oxford–he and his wife were living with his parents in Islip, where his sister, Louisa, had reminded him that his father "had rather you would remain at Oxford that is to say at Islip as Son," adding, "I could not help being selfish enough to be glad you were coming home again for I cannot bear you to be away long ... I do *so* want to see you" (19 April 1842; LOA 14:41)–he decided to return to Jesus. In a letter of 16 September 1842 (LOA 12:33) H. A. Woodham, Fellow of Jesus, indicated that Halliwell would have to keep seven more terms in order to go out in the Michaelmas term of 1844. Just two days later a friend, Elizabeth Strickland, daughter of the historian Agnes Strickland, with whom Halliwell had a lively correspondence, highlights his state of mind:

Henrietta has served so doleful an apprenticeship to antiquities that no one can wonder at her detesting with might and main every thing connected with the pursuit, but as to you I have no patience with you, for persecuting ruins and all the beautiful realities and idealities connected with them. As for defying and deserting your antiquarian pursuits that is sooner said than done. Indeed my friend when five or six years have passed over your head you will be able to appreciate the value of the number of steps you have already climbed into distinction and public view, steps which with patience and prudence lead men to wealth, honour and many other advantages. Now do control your whims and value properly the distinction you have deservedly obtained" (18 September 1842; LOA 12:35).

A month later, however, Thomas Wright wrote that he thought "before long there will be changes and vacancies in the best places about the Record Offices. And I see nobody," he comforted, "that have any great claims to notice except you and me. I think, in case you keep yourself before the public, nobody has so good a chance as you. Dont [*sic*] lose sight of this. Edit," continued the counsellor, "as you can find time, for the Camden Society, & some of the earlier historical documents, and show as much knowledge of records of history as you can–it will not be labour lost" (18 October 1842; LOA 36:33).

Still, the obstacles to "distinction and public view" were challenges. And Halliwell had a way not merely of surviving but indeed of thriving. In the turbulent, but not untypical, first year of his marriage, he managed to produce five separate publications, eight articles, at least one review, contribute to the *Times*, the *Athenaeum*, and the *Penny Cyclopaedia*, as well as continue his editorship of the *Archaeologist* (and doubtless writing much of it), his collaboration with Thomas Wright on the *Reliquiae Antiquae*, and maintain his active membership in numerous societies (though recently resigned from the Council of the Percy Society, he was in 1842 on the Council of the Society of Antiquaries and the Shakespeare Society), among other things. In the following year, 1843, ten and in 1844 fourteen publications attest to his industry and, notably, perseverance, for he had to overcome opposition of various kinds. There was always a certain amount of strain, if not conflict, in the publishing societies. Despite his troubles with the Percy Society, he did manage to produce for them *The Nursery Rhymes of England* in 1842, *The Pleasant Conceits of Old Hobson* in 1843, and *Friar Bakon's Prophesie, The Poems of John Audelay*, and *The Romance of the Emperor Octavian* in 1844. For the Shakespeare Society he produced *The First Sketch of Shakespeare's Merry Wives of Windsor* in 1842, *The First Sketches of the Second and Third Parts of King Henry the Sixth* in 1843, and *Tarlton's Jests* in 1844–no mean achievement when the internal intrigue and unrest of that organization are taken into account. For the Camden Society he produced *The Private Diary of Dr. John Dee* in 1842 and *The Thornton Romances* in 1844. That Halliwell published for the Camden Society at all is characteristic of his energy and tenacity. There was not only the storm over the *Letter to Lord Egerton* which he weathered. There was also the decided opposition from the Council to his proposal of the papers of Simon Forman as being in parts morally objectionable; even Thomas Wright, reporting that it had "shocked the feelings of the printers," advised Halliwell to "castrate" it (1 September 1843; LOA 18:37). And ever alert to the tactical aspects, he observed a few days later, "I think [W. J.] Thoms and [John] Bruce are afraid you should think they act hardly towards you, and will be the readier to support you on another occasion" (11 September 1843; LOA 18:34). The Forman project was suppressed, but Halliwell went on, managing in the end to publish *The Thornton Romances* in the next year with the approval of the main antagonists Thoms and Bruce. In fact, not letting go, Halliwell did not forget Wright's suggestion that he might make a "very nice little biography of Forman out of them" (Thursday, September 1843; LOA 16:13) by editing and publishing *The Autobiography and Personal Diary of Dr. Simon Forman, the Celebrated Astrologer* in 1849.

His reputation growing, Halliwell was not dependent upon the publishing societies as outlets for his work. His *Account of the European Manuscripts in the Chetham Library* (1842) was published by Simms and Dinham of Manchester, *The Foundation Documents of Merton College, Oxford* (1843) by William Pickering, *The Autobiography and Correspondence of Sir Simonds D'Ewes* (1845) by Richard Bentley. Above all, Halliwell developed what turned out to be a long-enduring relationship with the London bookseller John Russell Smith, who published Halliwell's periodical *The Archaeologist* (1841-2), and seven other works in the period between 1842 and 1845: *Torrent of Portugal* (1842), *An Account of the Only Known Manuscript of Shakespeare's Plays* (1843), *A Collection of Pieces in the Dialect of Zummerzet* (1843), *The Early History of Freemasonry in England* (1844), *Nugae Poeticae* (1844), as well as further editions of *The Nursery Rhymes of England* and the first parts of the *Dictionary of Archaic and Provincial Words, Obsolete Phrases, Proverbs, and Ancient Customs.* Smith's extensive correspondence with Halliwell—there are some 121 letters from him in the Edinburgh collection alone—provides interesting details of some of Halliwell's ideas and projects. In addition to establishing Halliwell's enduring interest in lexicography and popular culture, as well as Shakespeare, it demonstrates the interaction of author and publisher and anticipates, in its attention to such details of publishing as publicity and finances, Halliwell's career as publisher on his own. The dictionary, for example, seems to have been solicited by Smith. "I have been thinking," he wrote on 10 February 1842 (LOA 12:26), "of a work which is much wanted in the Literary world, and one I should like to publish, it is a '*Glossary of Words, Customs, Proverbs, &c from Gower & Chaucer to Shakespeare & his Contemporaries*[,]' it is a work which might easily be compiled with a little industry as there is an excellent basis in Nares, Toone &c &c ... it is a work you are fully competent to execute if you have the leisure to devote to it, and as it would be more than a labour of love in this case I must leave you to name a sum which you think would pay you for your trouble, if you coincide in my views I should propose to publish it in about 8 parts in 8vo with double columns making up about 500 to 600 pages, I do not think it would make much less." And to complete the archetypal construction, Smith adds the cautionary P.S.: "What I have here said let it be between ourselves for the present." Two years later he reports that a thousand copies of the first part had been printed (19 October 1844; LOA 15:39). By 29 December 1842 Smith was preparing a third edition of *The Nursery Rhymes* (LOA 15:10), and on 2 November 1843 (LOA 15:51) he offered a thousand copies to New York "at a very moderate price to counteract the Boston edition." Two weeks later he reports that the parties in New York "declined the N. R. as the reprinters of the 2nd Edit was their friend ... nevertheless I have written to another publishing firm & offered them 1000 for £50 in sheets ... At present I have sold about 800 of the new edition, chiefly to the trade" (11 January 1844; LOA 15:55). Moreover, aware of the need to beat the drum, as it were, Smith suggests that a prospectus be sent to the Philological Society, finding it "strange that no one there (some of my own customers) did not notice your attempt, so as it has been announced in my catalogues." And of course Smith was a valuable source of information: "I do really hear a deal of literary gossip a times in my shop which if it were to be related again would make queer history, of course you come in for your share, I hear much said about you pro & con but of course I hear all and say nothing." He does say something, of course: "Mr. R [Rimbault, most likely]," he confides, "has always underated [*sic*] your talents to me, I tell them all to wait a little & they will have cause to alter their opinions" (27 July 1843; LOA 15:28).

Domestically there was apparent stability, despite the continuing friction with Thomas Phillipps and the never-ending financial problems. Halliwell's family–his parents, brothers Thomas and Richard, and sister, Louisa–were constant in their devotion. His wife, the quiet Henrietta, seems to have been supremely content, a state which may be easily derived from the almost placid way she depicts activities and events, even those of some importance, in her diary. Three entries of the early 1840s illustrate her situation and manner:

3 August 1843: I was very poorly all day. My daughter Henrietta Somerset was born at 6 o'clock this evening & named shortly afterwards. The child

seemed weak & not very well & was named by Revd. W. Bowerbank after Aunt Somerset & myself. James busy with his Dict. Very wet.

9 August 1843: My wedding day. We have just been married a year - I spent it very happily with dear James who sat with me almost all day. He gave me Miss Stricklands Letters of Mary Q. of Scots in 2 vols & Bilberry Thurland a novel in 3 vols. The baby is improving. Mr Walker the doctor who attended me came & congratulated me. I worked & read. A tremendous storm of thunder, lightening [sic] & hail in the afternoon. James wrote to Aunt Somerset but did not send it on account of the weather. Sat up a long time.

9 August 1844: My wedding day. We are both as happy as we were when we married. James worked at his Dict. & Glossary to Thornton Romances. I trimmed a bonnet & wrote Lou, Lizzy Carew & Mr Bowell for patterns of paper. We packed up Lou's box and clothes.

If Henrietta appears rather subdued, then that is her manner. But that the emotional was not absent may be evident in the numerous responses of their friends. Collier was perhaps the first to congratulate Halliwell on the birth of his daughter: "You will have a son all in good time, I dare say; only do not bring him up to the unprofitable trade of an antiquary. It is all very well to be an antiquary but not to try to get anything by it" (10 August 1843; LOA 23:99). A fortnight later he continued what must have been the cheer of the moment: "You mistake when you say I congratulated you twice on the same event; but if it had been *twenty times* it would hardly have been too often, considering that it is your first. When the twenty first arrives, then perhaps even a single congratulation will be too much. Ask Mrs Halliwell" (29 August 1843; LOA 17:89).

Still, the times were turbulent. Thomas Phillipps, his daughter Kate wrote to Henrietta, "is become so odd this last month that we all have serious thoughts that he is going rather cracked," hoping for her rather than assuring her that though she "may not yet be rich yet I trust the day will come when you will be for I see at present no chance of his having any children which is I think one great thing which preys upon his mind" (23 August 1843; LOA 107:18*). Phillipps never ceased in his efforts against Halliwell. Using Greek characters to represent an English text, Wright advised: "If I ouere u I ouould be ueri kautious of Sir Th. Phillipps, and aboue all, enter into no agreement or kompromise about mone matters or the properti. In mi opinion he ouil be sure to plai u some trik. that u ouil repent." (1 September 1845; LOA 15:84 [literal transcription is mine: ou=w]). Living in Islip with his parents alleviated but did not eliminate Halliwell's financial problems. Even small amounts were taken into account. On 28 January 1845 (Folger Y.c.1267[3] he informed Planché that he was no longer a member of the Camden Society and was not "surprised at any one retiring, the incessant demands from the societies from 1£ to 6£6 having long since *tired* me. Two days later (30 January 1845; Folger Y.c.1266[7] he agreed to do some work for Pettigrew, but "the Camden must pay the 3.d a folio, as I am you see not so liberal in these matters as I used to be." And old ghosts were stirring. In a letter to Lord Brougham, Halliwell could "most safely & positively say that no statement whatever respecting a loan transaction between a Law Lord and Sir J. Banks [most likely, Sir Joseph Banks, president of the Royal Society from 1778 to 1820] has ever been repeated by me, nor have I even heard of any thing of the kind" (21 April 1846; UCL Brougham MSS.). The source of the rumor was apparently Thomas Stephens Davies. Nor were the professional conflicts ever really resolved or at rest. Sides were drawn up, each eying the other suspiciously. The bundled energy of it all came to a head and exploded in early 1845 when Halliwell was banned from the British Museum for reputedly having "abstracted" manuscripts from the library of Trinity College Cambridge, eleven of which were sold to them by the bookseller Thomas Rodd, who had had them from Halliwell.

4

The British Museum Affair: 1845-1846

Launched in the last days of 1844 and spent by mid-1846, what Mrs. Halliwell's diary entry for 2 February 1845 described as the "scandalous MS affair got up by the British Museum People" against her husband was for him a personal trauma and a fairly explosive event of the time. The minutes of the General Meeting of the Trustees of 8 February 1845 (GM1814) ordered "that the Principal Librarian repeat to Mr. Halliwell in the name of the Trustees the suggestion conveyed in the Principal Librarian's letter of the 29th January, namely that until the case of the Manuscripts improperly abstracted from Trinity College Library has been thoroughly investigated, he would probably think it proper to abstain from consulting the Museum Collections." On 15 February 1845 in the minutes of the Standing Committee (C10454) the Principal Librarian reported to the Trustees that "Sir Henry Ellis, Sir Frederic Madden, and Mr. Panizzi join in expressing their humble opinion to the Trustees, that Mr. Halliwell, under all the circumstances of his case as it at present stands, is not a fit person to have admission to the Reading Room" (although at the very time of the deliberations Madden was negotiating with Halliwell on the purchase of a "poetical volume" [30 December 1844; LOA 17:57]).

Individuals, factions, societies, and institutions were mobilized: sides were taken. Reports were written, statements were circulated, leading articles appeared. Rumors were swirling in a Kafkaesque atmosphere of suspicion and mistrust, Halliwell constantly protesting his innocence and demanding a public hearing, the British Museum and Trinity College determinedly stonewalling. After some six months Halliwell issued a widely circulated twenty-four page *Statement* dated 26 July 1845 defending himself. A letter from him to the Archbishop of Canterbury was read by His Grace's "desire" to the Board of the Museum (Standing Committee minutes of 9 August 1845, C6761-2). On 13 August 1845 Halliwell's lawyer, William Lovell, indicated that he would ask Disraeli about the *Statement* (LOA 22:12). Months passed, and in November a barrage of indignant and emotional letters supporting Halliwell–"Not only pending the litigation, but until the authorities of Trinity College shall have commenced the litigation, at however distant a period, Mr. Halliwell is to suffer all the penalties of a conviction! Really this is Lynch Law on the part of the Trustees of the British Museum ... a tyrannical abuse of power," wrote one person–appeared in the *Times,* beginning with one letter from Halliwell himself which appeared on 13 November and was followed by letters from A Lover of Justice and A Reader at the Museum (both on 14 November), from F.S.A. and A Poor Student (17 November), from Juvenis (18 November), from A Hater of Oppression (19 November), from Thomas Wright and Philo-Justitiae (20 November), from Presbyter (25 November), from Thomas Pettigrew (26 November), and from An Historian (27 November).[67] This doubtless well-organized barrage–accompanied by another letter to the Archbishop of Canterbury (which was recorded in the minutes of the Standing Committee of the British Museum on 8 November, C6801-3) and passionate leading articles in the *Times* of 15 and 22 November in which Halliwell was characterized as a victim of a "foul and scandalous conspiracy" and both the British Museum and Trinity College severely criticized for not substantiating their suspicions–brought results. On 5 December 1845, almost a year after Halliwell was accused of thievery, the *Times* announced under the title "A Curious Case" that "a trial of some interest in the literary world will take place in the Court of Exchequer, either in the present or the early part of the ensuing term ... It is an action brought by Trinity College, Cambridge, against the trustees of the British Museum, for their possession of a manuscript alleged to have been stolen from the library of the former. They have been intermediately in the possession of Mr. J. O. Halliwell, F.R.S., whose suspension from the library of the Museum has recently caused a painful interest in literary circles." (The *Times's* support of Halliwell may well have been political as well, as an attempt to embarrass the government and the person of Sir Robert Peel, Prime Minister and Trustee of the Museum.[68]) Six months passed, however. Early in June of 1846 Lovell consulted Disraeli again (3 June 1846; LOA 14:83); Charles Roach Smith asked Halliwell who was to present his petition to the Commons (6 June 1846; LOA 14:93). Finally, a trial was scheduled for Tuesday, 23 June, then postponed until the following Thursday. It never

67. In addition to a steady flow of letters of support from intimates, much of Volumes 25 and 26 of the Letters of Authors in the Edinburgh collection is devoted to statements of encouragement from outsiders.

68. W. H. Bond, "Henry Hallam, the *Times* Newspaper, and the Halliwell Case," *The Library,* V, 18 (1963), 133-44.

took place. The case of trover, with Trinity College as plaintiff and the British Museum as defendant, was suddenly dropped. Halliwell was issued a new reader's ticket.

The question of Halliwell's guilt or innocence, victory or defeat, is not answered easily or confidently, although there is considerable evidence, and opinion, against him.[69] Whatever the final verdict, it is clear that the dispute was intense and bitter, and not one arising from a simple case of theft. On the surface it ranged from cold to icy. And it is difficult not to have the impression of the pushy young man of questionable talent and ethics being ambushed, an impression reinforced and amplified by the refusal of the officials of the British Museum to provide Halliwell (if not the public) with details of its charges against him, even to indicate how long the investigation would last, much less to give him a hearing. Henry Ellis, who over the years had graciously acknowledged Halliwell's scholarly accomplishments and warmly congratulated him on his marriage, was obliged to close his letter banning Halliwell from the Reading Room with "You will excuse me if I decline any but written Communication with you in this delicate subject" (GM 8/2/45, No. 3). William Whewell, Master of Trinity College (who had previously corresponded with Halliwell on matters connected with the history of science and had recommended him for membership in the Royal Society), even asserted at one point, as Halliwell wrote to Thomas Pettigrew (19 December 1845; Folger Y.c.1266[13]), that "it is not in my power to answer the question" as to what the particular MSS. were, the recovery of which was the reason for the proceedings against the British Museum. Whewell's immediate, single sentence reply to Halliwell's request of 14 January 1846 was, drastically, "I have to say that I cannot furnish you with such a list" (15 January 1846; LOA 1:21a). And behind the scenes, the old personal and professional rivalries were bristling. In one of numerous utterances, Thomas Wright, no admirer of Madden as person or scholar, advised Halliwell: "I think I would take no further notice of Madden—he is only a clown at best" (10 September 1845; LOA 15:81). For his part, in a small but telling incident, Madden, sensing that one Charles Hook had been engaged by Halliwell to transcribe folios 11-27 of Add. MSS. 15,233, exerted such pressure that Hook wrote: "The unexpected and unnecessary enquiries of Sir F. Madden, relative to *Heywood*'s MS., and the bad feeling between you and the Museum Trustees, induced me (for Sir F. knew it was for you) to

69. For a comprehensive discussion of the affair and a presentation of much of the documentation, see D. A. Winstanley, "Halliwell Phillipps and Trinity College Library," *The Library*, III, 2 (1947-8), 250-82.

decline, *for the present*, by Note to make the transcription. This feeling of mine arose partly from shyness, partly perhaps from fear" (16 April 1846; LOA 27:43). For his part, Halliwell wrote on 24 August 1845 (Yale University Library, Osborn Coll.) to the printer William Shoberl concerning their plans to issue a series of historical letters: "I see Bentley has advertised another series of Sir H. Ellis's letters. I cannot help thinking we can make a far more interesting collection .... Don't you think it would be just as well to get our book out first? Sir H. Ellis has treated me so ungenerously in the recent MS. affair, that I owe him no courtesy in anything." Other instances, petty and considerable, abound. And it must be remembered that it was Madden himself who had bought the manuscripts, and to him fell the embarrassing and bitter task of exposing the fact that he had been duped. What is undeniable in the whole affair is that what was under way for eighteen months was not so much an investigation–Ellis, Madden, and Panizzi were convinced enough from the very beginning of Halliwell's guilt for him to be banned from the Reading Room–as an attempt by the Museum and Trinity College to figure out what to do.

And the conclusion of the affair can only be described as painful and ugly. A letter from Henry Ellis–a grudging verbatim repetition of the terse entry in the minutes of the Standing Committee (C6913-14)–is dated 27 June 1846: "Dear Sir,–I am instructed by our trustees to communicate to you, that if an application in the usual form for admission to the reading-room shall be made by you, the same will be granted in the usual manner." The reply by Halliwell is dated 29 June 1846:

Dear Sir Henry,–I beg to acknowledge the receipt of your note of Saturday's date, acquainting me that by the instruction of the trustees of the British Museum you had to communicate to me, that if an application were made by me for admission to the reading-room, it would be granted in the usual manner. I can only assure you that my readmission will be a source of great satisfaction to me, since my literary engagements have been most seriously obstructed by my exclusion, not to mention the distress of mind I have experienced for a period of a year and a half. I therefore request you have the goodness to send me a ticket of admission to the reading-room. I am not aware that any other form of application is necessary, but, if such be the case, you will perhaps be kind enough to inform me of it.

This exchange was followed by the terse note: "Sir H. Ellis at once forwarded a ticket of admission to the reading-room to Mr. Halliwell, unaccompanied by any further communication." The British Museum's frost was matched by the publication by Halliwell of both letters in the *Times* of 3 July 1846 (p. 5). Ellis's seemingly matter-of-fact "in the usual manner" was thus replicated in another and more drastic key by Halliwell.

From a certain point of view Halliwell's British Museum "affair" was not at all complicated, despite the long and apparently complex dealings that persisted over some eighteen months. It is indisputable that Halliwell possessed the manuscripts (among the three hundred or so he had collected by the time he was twenty[70]); that he had numbered and signed them in his customary fashion; that he had announced them in a privately printed and circulated catalogue in 1839-1840; and that he had put them up for sale, along with others, at Sotheby's on 27 June 1840. After withdrawing them from the sale for want of interest–"Few persons ... attending on the day of sale," he reported (557a.10[71])–he sold them to the bookseller Thomas Rodd, who on 13 August 1840 sold thirty-three manuscripts to Sir Frederic Madden of the British Museum, where they were duly catalogued and remain to this day. Madden later identified eleven of them as parts of manuscripts missing from the Trinity College Library.

A considerable part of the documentation of the affair is devoted to establishing these facts. That Trinity College initiated a suit against the British Museum in order to have the manuscripts returned is likewise indisputable, as is the fact that the suit was agreed upon by both plaintiff and defendant. The agreement, based on Frederic Madden's intensive investigations, also confirms their view that the manuscripts in question were indeed those "abstracted" from Trinity College. One significant aim of the suit, however, was the uncovering of the perpetrator of the crime–to some, at least as important as the demonstration of the authority of public institutions in the safeguarding of their treasures or, in the words of Josiah Forshall, secretary to the Trustees of the British Museum, "the object of affording better security to public libraries" (16 June 1845; Case, f.71). A case of trover was entered into in order to cause to testify and thus to expose Halliwell, whose reader's ticket had been withdrawn almost a year and a half earlier and whose guilt was from the beginning indisputable, to the Master and Seniors of Trinity College and the officers

70. In 1845 Halliwell wrote that he had begun collecting manuscripts "as early as 1835" and "engaged in this pursuit during four or five years, in which time [he] had accumulated a collection amounting to about three hundred M.S.S." (Case, f.50).

71. All items marked 557-571 are from TCC Muniments, Box 29. Much of the documentation is also to be found in "Case." See n. 8.

and trustees of the British Museum, despite their lofty profession of the need for a "thorough investigation" (8 February 1845; TCC Add. MSS. a.170.11) and, as it turned out, trial "as a service," so William Whewell, "to the general cause of guardians of libraries" (14 June 1846; 569e). His coda, "I have no care about Mr Halliwell, except so far as this object is concerned," intensifies rather than mollifies the cold distancing of many from Halliwell, indeed the personal animosity of some.

The guilt of Halliwell was never proved, however. He professed his innocence from the outset: immediately on receiving Sir Henry Ellis's letter of 29 January 1845 excluding him from the British Museum Library, which "caused [him] so much surprise, that [he] seize[d] the earliest opportunity" and wrote to Whewell on 1 February 1845 vowing to "do all in [his] power to assist any enquiries that may be made on the subject, and [to] immediately attend to any suggestions for that purpose with which [Whewell] may favour [him]" (557a.8).[72] Numerous letters having been unsatisfactorily answered, if at all, including one of 7 June 1845 in which he expressed satisfaction that legal proceedings were being contemplated (561a), Halliwell, feeling spurned "for nearly nine months" after his exclusion, issued "in self-defense" (he wrote to Whewell on 22 October 1845) a twenty-four-page printed *Statement in Answer to Reports Which Have Been Spread Abroad Against Mr. James Orchard Halliwell*, outlining the events and his position, was supported by a host of sympathizers (led by Thomas Wright), asked repeatedly to be heard by the authorities of the British Museum, welcomed the news of legal proceedings, volunteered through his lawyers to cooperate and share information with the lawyers of his accusers, and, in what must have been regarded as desperation, wrote to Whewell on 5 December 1845: "I have to demand of you as an act of justice due to me that you cause me to be summoned as a witness on the occasion" (565b). Whewell noted coldly at the foot of Halliwell's letter: "Dec. 7. Ans[were]d that the lawyers must decide what witnesses to call." Less than a fortnight before the trial was scheduled to begin, Halliwell pleaded on 10 June 1846 that he "would be ready to accept a subpoena to

72. Halliwell must have written first to Wright on the very day he received Ellis's letter. Sensing an emergency, Wright responded by return mail on 31 January 1845 (LOA 39:36) with detailed advice on how to react. Halliwell followed it almost verbatim. In quotation marks are some of the phrases taken over by Halliwell: he wrote to Whewell, was "surprised" at the report, was "totally unaware" that manuscripts in his possession had come from Trinity, had "bought a large quantity of manuscripts and never kept any account of the sources," "in a few days" he would be in town and "will then go and look at it," and other examples.

attend the Trial as a Witness" (Lovell's bill, f.45). In short, he seems to have done everything he could to implement his avowal of his innocence. He was met with stolid resistance, which offered only the small solace of his possibly being allowed to have his day in court. But neither the plaintiff nor the defendant, nor Halliwell himself, had a day in court. The suit, which, after many months of maneuvering, was scheduled for Tuesday, 23 June, and then postponed until 25 June 1846 (six years, almost to the day, after the Sotheby sale and more than eight years after the manuscript was reported missing), was suddenly withdrawn and Halliwell's reader's ticket restored. Despite cries of victory, vindication, and what-have-you, neither innocence nor guilt was ever proved. Business as usual was resumed, although Halliwell never even had the satisfaction of a legal pronouncement of *in dubio pro reo*, much less any acknowledgment, personal or institutional. And the shadow has remained up to the present day.

The shadow hovers not merely over Halliwell but over the whole affair, even if the strictly legal opinion pronounced by Trinity College's solicitor, F. J. Fuller, in consultation with the expert W. G. Humphreys as early as 22 May 1845, which questioned the identity and thus source of the manuscripts, is discounted—namely, that the "facts are all capable of proof, but inasmuch as the identity (if the work be the same) is destroyed by the abstraction of some leaves the substituting of others and by the new binding and more particularly as neither Mr. Warren [the librarian] nor Mr. Cranwell [the library keeper or sub-librarian] can identify with positiveness even that part of the Manuscript which remains by any mark tho there are some in it of a very extraordinary character we are of opinion that no criminal prosecution can be instituted with any probability of success" (560d). The shadow may be attributed to several factors. Most striking is the fact that the accusations arise seven years after the presumed event, that the Master, librarian, and testifying tutor of Trinity College were in 1845 no longer in office or even in Cambridge and had to rely on recollections of an event or events in which only the sub-librarian was apparently a direct participant but for which they were all directly responsible, and that their testimony is not merely retrospective and, inevitably, self-protecting but also not of a piece, in fact contradictory.

In his response of 21 February 1845 to the Master of Trinity, William Whewell, Christopher Wordsworth, Master of Trinity from 1820 to 1841, remembers reports laid before him and the Seniors by Charles Warren, the librarian. But he does not remember any special report of the MSS. Classes R and O, "such as to leave any impression on [his] mind that any considerable n[o] of MSS. were discovered by him, to have been missing, at least to have disappeared recently." "Had any such impression reached my mind," he continues, "I cannot but think, that I should have distinctly remembered it now; and that I should have called the attention of the Seniors to it, or the Bursar at that time in a very pointed way, and that we should have been anxious to have made the best investigation into the affair, that we could." He then admits that the "catalogues of the classes were indeed very unsatisfactory." As for Halliwell, he is "confident" that he had "never had any intercourse with him whatever," though he does remember one of the Fellows–he "inclines to think it was the present Dean of Ely [George Peacock]"–asking permission for a gentleman, "probably the Mr Halliwell in question," to transcribe, which he "understood afterwards" did indeed occur but without knowing whether in the library or not. And, in a not unexpected assertion, he is "pretty well persuaded that [he] gave no permission whatever for this to be done, without consulting the Seniors, and without communicating that permission to the Librarian: for that was [his] practice,[his] invariable practice, in such cases."

On 30 December 1845 Charles Warren, librarian of Trinity from 1838 to 1840, testified that after a few months in office he found it "quite impossible to adhere to the regulation" that he be present whenever any persons, even Fellows, were admitted to the manuscript classes. He did, however, give Halliwell access to the manuscripts but "depart[ed] from the rule upon which [he] before acted" because Halliwell had a note from the Master and, adding once again, that "up to the time of the calling over [i.e. for his first three months in office] of the M.S.S. [he] had uniformly acted strictly upon the before mentioned rule." He "recollect[ed]" calling over the Library but did not remember the exact time, thinking it to have been either in March or April 1838 and to have "missed" several manuscripts, among them O.8.16.[73] Although he remembered Halliwell saying he believed the manuscript had been in the library, he "cannot say that Mr. Halliwell had the possession of it." Halliwell was a frequent visitor, admitted into Class 0, but, Warren repeats, "Don't remember Mr. H. having the MS. O.8.16." Still, he inserts ("this is all nothing but added by way of explanation") in a footnote, "I entertained suspicion that Mr. H had stolen the M.S. in question & stated my suspicions to Cranwell [the library keeper] but I did not take any steps in the matter because I

---

73. Actually, according to the Librarians Register (TCC Add. MSS. a.166) Class O was called over on 9 April; missing were 1.72, 3.44, 3.49, 7.2, 7.17, 7.22, 7.36-44, and 8.16. The calling over of the rest of the manuscripts extended until December.

perceived from his manner that Mr. H was aware of my suspicions & that any steps without more evidence wd be useless–I therefore simply reported the M.S. as missing among others & mentioned my suspicions to Mr. H's tutor Mr. Thompson" (565f).

Warren's testimony speaks for itself. His relaxing the rules is understandable, of course–the Fellows were cranky and uncooperative–even considering the fact that Wordsworth was reputed to be a very strict disciplinarian. That he suspected Halliwell, although he admits not remembering his having MS. O.8.16, is less understandable. That he did not mention his suspicions to the Master or Seniors is unusual, to say the least; and his reason for not doing so–that he was aware that Halliwell was aware–is as whimsical as his saying he needed "more" evidence when in reality he seems to have had little, if any at all. And that he reported his suspicions to Halliwell's tutor, Mr. Thompson, borders on the far-fetched, for Halliwell's tutor at Trinity was George Peacock, who had asked the Master for the permission in the first place. (William Hepworth Thompson, only assistant tutor at the time, was appointed successor to Peacock in 1844; it is interesting to note that no testimony from Thompson is to be found in the extensive documentation assembled by the solicitors for Trinity College.) In his diary entry for 22 February 1845 Madden reports that Thompson "cautioned the librarian of Jesus not to allow Mr. H. free access to their library"–an apparently useless gesture since Halliwell was library clerk. Nor did the suspicions prevent Halliwell of Jesus from borrowing books from Trinity on at least ten different occasions in 1839.

The statement of Edward Cranwell is shorter, less rambling, but only apparently clearer. He dates the event: "In the Lent term of *1838*" [inserted above a caret: "Mr Warren told me"] the Master gave an order in that Mr. H might examine the M.S.S. [inserted above a caret: "& desired me to admit him"]–During that time," the statement continues, "he exam^d great many of the M.S.S. in Class O–I recollect Mr H about this time–examining O.8.16. Did not know its contents–Mr. H. had out an immense number of M.S.S. to inspect ... It was about the end of March or beginning of April in 1838. At this calling over I first missed the M.S. O.8.16" (565f). This testimony asks the reader to believe that Cranwell could remember that Halliwell, who had out an immense number of manuscripts, was examining "about this time"–i.e. seven years earlier–the specific manuscript O.8.16, a manuscript whose contents Cranwell did not even know. At any rate, Halliwell, despite the suspicions, continued to be a frequent visitor of the library, examining with the needed permission of a Fellow no fewer than fourteen titles (so the borrowing book) between

3 February and 3 April 1839. He was, in fact, one of the library's leading users. And, in what begins to suggest further uncertainty, Warren (in an undated letter addressed only "Dear Sir," but from the contents shortly before the trial, to a solicitor) wrote to deny that there is a discrepancy between Cranwell's evidence and his: "He says I think that we discovered the loss before the calling over the class. I do not at all deny this, and am rather inclined to think it may be so but I cannot state it upon oath ... I thought Cranwell rather inclined to doctor my memory. Now I had much rather not be doctored before going into the witness box." And in a striking prophecy, he concluded: "However if an uninitiated man may judge I should think there is but small probability of the cause ever being tried" (566a).

There is also a statement from George Peacock, a six-page letter to Whewell dated 25 February [1845] (559a). Halliwell, he writes, was his pupil for one year: "he always appeared to be a very respectable young man." After many discussions with Halliwell, who told him of the numerous manuscripts he had acquired, and who was "already acquainted" with the Trinity manuscripts, Peacock applied to the Master for permission for him to see the manuscripts at Trinity. "It never for a moment crossed my mind," he reflected, "that they could have been purloined." Peacock's order of events is mystifying. He seems to have been told about manuscripts *before* he asked for permission for Halliwell to see the Trinity manuscripts in question–the implication being that Halliwell had seen them on other earlier occasions, which would contradict the testimony of the Master and librarians or, embarrassingly enough for the college, if Halliwell had seen them earlier, he had done so without any official permission or record. At any rate, Peacock testified further that he had been offered Halliwell's manuscripts. He had in fact received one at Ely at £5, but did not purchase it because Halliwell did not wish to "break up his set." To the offer of 1839, Peacock ventures a qualifying opinion of 1845: "I judged from his correspondence [Halliwell's letters are not extant] that he was distressed for money." This *ex post facto* judgment matches the one he had made earlier, qualifying "very respectable young man" with "but I have since heard that he got into bad hands at Jesus & was very extravagant." If it were cheeky of Halliwell to offer stolen manuscripts to the British Museum which, according to Madden, had been bound at Halliwell's expense by the Museum's bookbinder, Charles Tuckett, in 1839 (GM 8/2/45, No. 2),[74] it would of

74. In a letter to Halliwell of 1 January 1840 (LOA 1:5) John Jones (aka Tegid), writing from Oxford, mentions that "Mr [likely, Henry] Gough has bound

course be brazen-faced of Halliwell to offer manuscripts stolen from Trinity College to the Trinity College mathematician George Peacock: Hudson Gurney, in an undated letter of the time and of which only the last page exists, was aware of the absurdity, a "proceeding nearly approaching to *Impossible*, If you had had any *Idea* of their Having been Ever abstracted from their Library" (LOA 9:35). It would be bordering on effrontery for Halliwell to offer the manuscripts to Peacock, who admits in his letter that while at Trinity he "could not read MSS and [knows] nothing whatever of those in [the] Library: when [he] was writing his history of Arithmetic, it was a subject of great regret to [him] that [he] could not read mathematical & other MSS." Be that as it may, Peacock in a letter to Halliwell of 22 January 1840 (LOA 77:26) hoped that "such a collection of MSS will not be dispersed" and asked whether Halliwell had written to John Lodge, the University librarian, about them. His concluding sentence is not without a certain unintended irony: "I trust that the British Museum will buy the whole of them, if the Cambridge Syndicate are not disposed to do so." There is no evidence of whether Halliwell did indeed offer his collection to Lodge, though they must have met on numerous occasions, at the Master's lodge of St. John's for meetings of the Council of the Cambridge Antiquarian Society or at the Public Library while Halliwell was compiling his *Manuscript Rarities of the University of Cambridge*, in whose preface he singled out for "respectful and grateful thanks" the "learned Librarian of the University, who has always most kindly and most liberally aided [Halliwell's] researches among the MSS. in the Public Library." Whewell and the Trinity solicitors did try to discover whether the offer had been made, but, curiously, they did not approach Lodge himself but Joseph Romilly, who in a note of 26 February 1845 reported that he had asked Lodge, who replied that he had "no recollection whatever of such a transaction"–a statement which cannot be taken as a denial since Lodge was seriously ill at the time and (on 17 March 1845) "complaining of forgetfulness," among other weaknesses.[75] Whether the offer was made or not has, to be sure, no substantive relevance to the matter at hand. There was no secret to the fact that Halliwell was circulating his catalogue among private buyers (like Thomas Phillipps) and public institutions (like the British Museum) and a short time later had announced a public auction at Sotheby's. Also apparently significant but likewise irrelevant is the fact that Halliwell was

[Halliwell's] MSS very neatly & well" in two folio and two quarto volumes.

75. *Romilly's Cambridge Diary, 1842-1847*, ed. M. E. Bury & J. D. Pickles (Cambridge, 1994), p. 128.

library clerk at Jesus College, where, as Peacock had later heard, he "got into bad hands ... & was very extravagant," but nevertheless no missing volumes were charged to him. Even Madden was disappointed in his tireless crusade against Halliwell: in his diary entry for 2 March 1846 he reports having "looked over the MS. Catalogue of the MSS. in Jesus Coll. library ... I could not trace in it any of the MSS. in H's collection."[76] Even Peacock's conversion quoted in a letter of Pettigrew's dated 7 October 1845 (LOA 27:21) to Halliwell, is irrelevant: "Dean Peacock says that he has read Halliwell's defence–that every thing he says in it of his offering the MSS to him is strictly true–that also he has ascertained that the Bookseller Halliwell mentions [John Denley] did deal in MSS of the sort [thus, and pointedly, disagreeing with Madden and agreeing with Wright]–& if he had known of the prices at which they were to be obtained, he certainly should have become the purchaser–that his view of the standing of the matter has been greatly changed."

What is relevant as far as the library of Trinity College is concerned is, as Whewell explained to his solicitors in a letter of 2 July 1845, that "we have no record of Catalogues or of the Library being called over, except what are contained in the catalogues themselves, which you have. Nor are there any records of the M.S.S. which have been consulted by Fellows or others till those of recent date ... The practice of consulting M.S. by fellows or others can easily be established but not with regard to any of the M.S.S. in question" (Case, f.74). What is relevant is that the statements of the librarians do not disguise the fact that the administration of the catalogues did not conform to the regulations and, as Warren wrote on 11 December 1838, his report was "necessarily incomplete ... as many changes have been made in the arrangement of the books in the last 50 years without any sufficient alteration of the Catalogues [and] several classes are in a state of utter confusion" (MS. Add. a.166, f.2). What is relevant is that seventeen volumes of manuscripts and not just O.8.16 were reported missing in 1838, as well as sixty-four books, with only the vaguest indication of just when they were missing since admittedly there had not been a comprehensive and reliable calling over since 1784. What is relevant is the fact that thefts from libraries throughout the university and elsewhere were common. In a comment on Whewell's letter of 15 January 1846 (LOA 1:21) in which he is refused a complete list of the

76. Madden also observed that Woodham of Jesus, who escorted him, "was inclined to think Wright worse than Halliwell." Like others, Woodham had his own agenda: he also migrated from Trinity to Jesus, had a strong dependence on Halliwell in the Cambridge Antiquarian Society, and encouraged him to return to Jesus to complete his studies.

missing manuscripts, Halliwell wrote: "In the discussion with Trinity College about the missing MSS., it was stated by me & was indeed a fact well known to Wright & other contemporary College friends, that College MSS. were constantly being pillaged by some of the underlings & getting into the market." As an example, he notes that "Albert Way borrowed Femina, one of their choicest MSS., in 1843, & restored it in 1844. This MS is now missing." The example, incidentally, is pointed, illustrating both the "pillaging" and the habit of cavalier borrowing, as well as highlighting Way, who was put up by Madden in February 1844 to ask where Halliwell had obtained the manuscript of Theophilus, one of those missing,[77] and who in 1845 was battling Wright and Pettigrew for control of the British Archaeological Association and its journal.[78]

What is purely circumstantial is that Halliwell collected manuscripts, used the Trinity College Library (and all other major college libraries and the university library as well), and may have suffered from a not uncommon undergraduate ailment, the need of money. None of this is disputed, none of it can be relevant. And all extrapolations are pure speculation. Suspicious but likewise irrelevant, it must be admitted, are some of Halliwell's assertions, among them that he "never thought of any necessity existing to write down the name of the bookseller or of the place of auction whence [he] obtained [the manuscripts], although [he] may have done so in some few instances" (557a.10)–whereas his commonplace book contains lists of payments to booksellers and throughout his career he kept financial records assiduously, accounting for practically every shilling–or that he "possess[ed] no bills or documents which relate to them" (557a.10)–a possibility but, given his temperament, unlikely. These doubts–such as personal attacks on his integrity, indications of debt, rumors of shady dealings or bad company–are at least balanced by others: such as that there just happened to be a calling over at the very time

77. It is hard not to miss the ambush mentality of Madden asking his "friend" Way to inquire and to learn from Way that Halliwell's answer "was not satisfactory." In a letter of 28 March 1845 (LOA 77:22) to his brother Richard, Halliwell asserted that "when Mr Way asked me about Theophilus I had not the least idea he alluded to the MS. on Painting, or I should have recollected having had it."

78. In a letter to Robert Willis (dated only "Friday" but very likely of 7 February 1845), Way remarked that Wright "had got into hot water by backing Halliwell" and had "resigned his place in connexion with the Journal, which was all we immediately wanted." In a letter to Halliwell of 14 March 1845 (LOA 15:99) Wright asked: "Have you received a certain printed Statement, sent by these *Way-ward* malcontents, against us?"

Halliwell was examining manuscripts; that Warren testified he had followed the regulation that he be present whenever any persons were admitted to the manuscript classes up to the time of the calling over and yet had noticed little; that Cranwell was always present, he claimed, while Halliwell was purportedly stealing numerous manuscripts; that after seven years Cranwell not only remembers Halliwell's examining, from an "immense" number, O.8.16 but in fact that even the outsider Frederic Madden could report that Cranwell "remembered getting down this very Volume from the Shelves for Mr. Halliwell's inspection" (23 April 1845; Case, f.64); and–to crown all and contradict most–that Madden in his diary entry for 22 February 1845 reports that Warren informed the Trustees that Halliwell was "allowed by special order of the Master, to have the freest access to the library ... and to *remain alone*, and have the keys; privileges not even enjoyed by a Fellow of the College."

Thefts were common enough. In most cases, then as now, little can be done beyond the report, the outrage, the condemnation, and the promise to tighten controls. At Trinity in 1838 even the report seems to have been received with little ado, despite Warren's understandable zeal in having a calling over at the beginning of his tenure and despite Master Wordsworth's reputation as a disciplinarian. Thomas Wright, ironically enough and long before there were charges against his friend Halliwell, recommended as "a rule" a bond for manuscripts taken out of the library (4 December 1839; LOA 5:32). At a meeting of Halliwell's Cambridge Antiquarian Society on 9 May 1845 H. A. Woodham, a close associate of Halliwell's, called for proper cataloguing and other measures to combat thefts, giving instances of manuscripts which had disappeared from the library of Jesus College (where incidentally no manuscript catalogue survives for the nineteenth century, nor any known list of missing documents). At Trinity Halliwell continued to be a regular user while at Jesus and thereafter. It was only in 1845 that Trinity expressed open outrage against Halliwell.

As a matter of fact it was not Trinity which was the first to do so, and despite the fact that many in Cambridge, for one reason or another, were not favorably disposed towards Halliwell during and after his college days. The alarm and the outrage originated in London, from the Keeper of Manuscripts in the British Museum, Frederic Madden.

The relationship between Madden and Halliwell in the early 1840s has already been outlined.[79] There is little doubt that Madden was eager to expose the "scoundrel" Halliwell. There is evidence too of an attempt to

79. See pp. 74-8.

implicate others. After a visit to the British Museum, F. J. Fuller, the solicitor to the Master of Trinity, reported on 18 February 1845 that the day before he had interviewed the secretary, Josiah Forshall, the Principal Librarian, Sir Henry Ellis, and their solicitor, Augustus Warren (of Bray, Warren, and Harding). He was also "closeted with Sir Frederic Madden from half past ten o'C. till past two o'clock," and concluded that "circumstances appear suspicious against Mr. Halliwell & Mr. Wright." (In his diary entry for 22 February 1845 Madden reported of the meeting that the Bishop of London "spoke his mind plainly and boldly against Halliwell and Wright.") Fuller, however, admitted that the "evidence wants strengthening very much," and that he should wish to know, among other things, "whether Mr. Wright was in the habit of using the manuscripts" and "whether Wilcocks was one of the party" (558b). As to Madden it is sufficient to add that Wright was not simply the friend and collaborator of Halliwell but also the leader of the opposition camp in various societies: as just one illustration, Madden resigned from the Percy Society "on account of the scandalous conduct of the Council," so his diary entry for 2 June 1845: "Messrs. Wright, Pettigrew, & Co. ... electing Mr. Halliwell a member, in spite of the stigma which rests on him." On 21 July 1845 he characterized Pettigrew as "a vulgar & half-educated man." The identity of Wilcocks is less clear and all the more intriguing. Since no Wilcocks of this spelling seems to have been associated with Trinity at the time, it is tempting to propose Charles Bonnycastle Willcox, who was admitted sizar at Trinity at age twenty on 11 October 1838 and matriculated Michaelmas 1838. In reply to a query from Halliwell, his Cambridge informant and friend Samuel Charles wrote on 28 October 1841 (LOA 9:20) that Wilcox [sic] "is not a member of our college, his name having been removed from the boards some time since. He *was* a sizar of Trinity and as such got very much in debt and absconded with some valuable books from our library: whether they have been returned or not I cannot say ... He belonged to a very bad set when he resided at Cambridge and affected a degree of eccentricity which was then considered to be absurd, and now seems to have been criminal. I regret extremely that you are placed in such an awkward situation by his rascality." The exact nature of the "awkward situation" is not stated but was doubtless financial, most likely a debt not repaid by Willcox. For in a letter to Whewell of 3 May 1850 Willcox admitted having "disgraced" himself by stealing a book from the library of the British Museum because he was "tortured by the pangs of hunger," to have sold it, and to have been imprisoned for one year and barely saved from the customary sentence, transportation. The association of Halliwell with Willcox was initiated by British Museum officials. Ellis informed Madden, who, despite his denial of having made public or private statements to the effect (in his diary entry for 4 September 1845), did not hesitate to condemn Halliwell for even the 'mere formality' of recommending the thief Willcox (whom Halliwell hardly knew) to the Reading Room[80] and of having associated as well with George J. Aungier, like Madden a contributor to the *Reliquiae Antiquae*, who had been transported for forgery.

Whatever Madden's exact motivation, there can be no doubt as to its extent: he was angry, lowering, unforgiving, and vindictive, even while admitting in his diary that there was "no legal proof of guilt" (8 January 1850). For years after Halliwell's reader's ticket had been restored and the uproar had subsided, Madden's diary is filled with attacks on Halliwell: on 1 January and 6 March 1850, 12 December 1852, 4 July and 19 September 1856, among which the references are to "that mean and dishonourable feeling which has marked his whole career," "if ever man deserved transportation, I believe H does," and "I should be glad if some of H's villainous tricks could be brought home to him." His reaction was not always rational, nor was a nimbus of suspicion that has hovered over Halliwell. In a letter of 28 March 1845 (LOA 77:22) Halliwell urged his solicitor to write to Thomas Rodd "and demand from him his authority for stating to Mr Dyce that 'my admission to the Bodleian Library was suspended'." On 10 August 1845 (Folger Y.c.1266 [10]) he complained to Pettigrew of Professor Adam Sedgwick's (one of the Trinity seniority) "rudeness to me at Ld N[orthampton]'s and his prejudice agt me when he confessed he had not read the papers on the subject." He made the same complaint in a letter of 14 August 1845 (TCC Add. MSS. a.170.27) to Whewell. In her diary entry for 24 February 1861 Henrietta Halliwell reported that "James awake in the night and said he had a bitter disappointment. He had asked to be allowed to see the Capell Collection at Trinity College himself and had been refused–he thought they wd be glad of the opportunity to be civil, in consequence of the way he was treated in the MS. affair years ago." Even in recent times two Rawlinson manuscripts referred to by Halliwell in his published works and missing from the Bodleian Library are now believed to have been stolen by him,

80. Wright also refers to Madden's interest in the connection with Willcox, advising Halliwell to add to a letter to Madden "what you say of Wilcox, that you only saw him once or twice, and that at the Museum. It will be quite enough. Pettigrew says that his son had met Wilcox at Cambridge, and that he brought him with them to dine in Saville Row, and that if he had asked him for a recommendation to the Brit. Mus., he should have given it him immediately" (1 September 1845; LOA 15:84).

although the only evidence against him is that he must have examined them. They were reported missing in the 1940s–i.e. at least a hundred years after Halliwell might have seen them; there is no record of who else might have looked at them. In fact, since inventory lists were kept only from the end of the nineteenth century, the only conclusion must be that the manuscripts, like countless others, cannot now be found.[81] The same kind of "when-did-you-stop-beating-your-wife" logic is also employed by W. H. Bond,[82] who uses extensive quotations from letters to the *Times* on behalf of Halliwell to suggest that a "vigorous and adroit campaign" (p. 134) and the "bias" (p. 135) of the *Times* went "far towards explaining why the case was permitted to wither and die" (p. 136). With further support from the correspondence of Henry Hallam and Robert Peel, the "strong suspicion" is that the letters to the *Times* were "not exactly spontaneous" (p. 140). The implication is somehow that Halliwell's defending himself in the press and his "other tactics in dealing with the crisis" (p. 140), as well as a possible "publicity scheme carefully planned by his faction" (p. 140), are signs of guilt. Bond's quoting but apparently overlooking Hallam's careful and constant use of *if* in qualifying Halliwell's "guilt" is topped by W. A. Jackson's use of the question mark in his note "Did Halliwell Steal and Mutilate the Phillipps Copy of *Hamlet*, 1603?"[83] His conclusion, although itself a question and employing the ever-useful *if*, points a finger of accusation but not an arrow of proof against Halliwell: "It cannot be proved that this copy which Halliwell bought from Boone, possibly taking care not to buy it directly from its 'discoverer', was the copy listed in the Middle Hill catalogue, but if it is not, then what has become of the copy, and what of Sir Thomas's accusation?" (p. 177). The question is, in fact, academic, for it has been shown that Phillipps did not own a copy of the *Hamlet* of 1603.[84]

To this day, nothing has been proved, nor has anything been forgiven or forgotten. Perhaps not even the quarrel between Trinity College and the British Museum not merely over the costs of the case but surely over the return of the manuscripts. Ellis's frigid letter to Halliwell on the restoration of his reader's ticket is no match for Fuller's fulmination to Whewell on 18 November 1846, months after the case was abandoned: "My dear Sir, On the other side I forward you copy of a most extraordinary letter I have received from Messrs Bray & Co the Soli[citor]s

81. See the *Bodleian Library Record*, 2 (1941-9), 237-8.
82. See n. 68.
83. Munby, *Family Affairs*, pp. 116-17.
84. See the article by Arthur Freeman, forthcoming in the *Library*.

of the British Museum. Our Counsel says that the only answer I can possibly give to it is—Do as you please—and let them take the consequences—It is certainly most unbecoming and outrageous conduct" (571c). The reaction was to a letter of 16 November in which "Bray & Co" have been "instructed ... to proceed according to the practice of the Court to post an end to the Suit and also to claim such Costs from the College as they are liable to bring in" (571b). Colder and more abrasive is "Bray & Co"'s letter of 7 September 1846 to Fuller: "In reply to your letter of the 21st of August requesting that the Trustees of the British Museum will restore to the Library of Trinity College the Manuscripts which form the subject of the action commenced by the College against the Trustees, we are directed by the Trustees to request that the Master and Fellows of Trinity College may be informed that the Trustees hold these Manuscripts on behalf of the public, and that they cannot allow them to pass out of their own possession until a legal right to them has been established by some other Claimant" (571b).

This last quotation does not appear in Winstanley's otherwise exhaustive and exemplary presentation of the documentation which makes it "possible to scrutinize his [Halliwell's] story a hundred years after the events it records occurred."[85] And his pinpointing of the inconsistencies and evasions of Halliwell's defence must be granted. Still, his concluding sentence—"after giving him the benefit of every doubt it is impossible not to believe that he stole the manuscripts from the college library" (p. 177)—is, perhaps not surprisingly, involuted. "Impossible not to believe" is more cautious than the comfortable aphorism which, a few lines earlier, opens his last paragraph: "When honest men fall out, rogues prosper." Even if one agreed that it is "impossible not to believe" that Halliwell stole the manuscripts, it is equally "impossible not to believe" that the case against him was never proved. For the burden of proof rests, then as now, with the accusers and not with the accused. The case against Halliwell must be considered as having been abandoned because there was insufficient evidence to convict him and not simply because the plaintiff and the defendant, who had agreed all along, suddenly disagreed on where the manuscripts belonged. If the proof were so damning—and the "envy, hatred and malice" as great as Halliwell's barrister had noticed (28 March 1846; LOA 25:93)—certainly criminal charges could have been—nay, should have been—brought. Even the view expressed by Winstanley that at the time "the prisoner could not give evidence" (p. 264, n. 3) would not hinder a criminal trial in which the accused does not testify and is still

85. See n. 69.

found guilty. But then the standard of proof in a criminal case was about ninety-five percent. And the fact of the matter, as was stated very early on by Trinity's solicitor, was that from a "strict legal point of view" there was no case. For the "moral point of view," with which he attempted to counterbalance the legal one, there was likewise no case. For it must be argued that it is not moral to accuse a person of a crime which has never been legally proved or even provable, no matter how seemingly damning the evidence or how apparently weak the defense.

For the documentation to be complete and perhaps for the case to come to rest, it is necessary to examine not merely the situation of the "rogue" but also that of the "honest men." Whewell and Madden are representative— as men, scholars, colleagues, and officers of institutions—of the opposition to Halliwell. That both were honest and high-minded is as much beyond doubt as the fact that both were authoritarian and arrogant. That both had a personal dislike of Halliwell long before 1845 is likewise beyond doubt. That both took opposing views in societies and associations is also indisputable. These factors of course are not explanations in themselves for the intensity of the campaign against Halliwell, but they are too pronounced to be ignored.

What also cannot be ignored, and which has hitherto been hardly attended to, is that both men were inflexibly convinced of the absolute power of their institutions. Trinity College was not merely outraged by a theft, it was humiliated by the exposure of its dilatoriness in managing its prized possessions—its manuscripts were neither marked nor stamped; there was inadequate supervision—and the behavior of its personnel and, as the years passed, the increasing exposure of the fossilization of its structure as an institution. It is "impossible not to believe" that the relentless eighteen-month persecution of Halliwell was to a measure a compensatory demonstration of the not-to-be-questioned supremacy of the institution. If its action did not constitute a cover-up, then it must at least be considered as an overreaction to its having been caught with its guard down. For its highminded intransigence Trinity College lost its manuscripts and its case, and was rewarded with a stately solicitor's bill of £271.14.8. The campaign of the British Museum was scarcely different. Madden was even more possessed than Whewell, for he had closer contact with Halliwell and more grounds for animosity. It is "impossible not to believe" that he was determined to assist in the destruction of Halliwell, so the catalogue of accusations and threats which his diary records over some twenty years. His passion was so aroused that he could agree on this matter at least with his arch rival Panizzi and even give credence to the egomaniacal and lunatic denunciations of Thomas

Phillipps. His crusade against Halliwell was also evident in the societies to which both belonged and was energetically directed against others associated with the opposition, especially Wright, who was only too aware that the "Museum people are very savage against [him]" (18 December 1845; LOA 29:5), as were the *Athenaeum* and the "Way-ward" party whose views Madden ardently shared. Above all, Madden mobilized the might of the institution, the British Museum, as defender of public trust and property with its sublime pronouncement that it will "hold the Manuscripts on behalf of the public ... and not allow them to pass out of their own possession until a legal right has been established by some other Claimant" and, of course, as an institution superior to Trinity College, to insist on the legality of Trinity College's paying the costs of the aborted attempt. The pronouncement is made in the name of the Trustees, but the Archbishop of Canterbury, to whom Halliwell had written, did not attend the crucial meetings, nor did others who wrote Halliwell more than half a year after his exclusion that "they had heard nothing about it and *never attended*" (10 August 1845; Folger Y.c.1266[10]). It is easy to understand the remarks of Halliwell's barrister A. J. Stephens: "I consider you a very persecuted man—and that a *powerful party* are determined, if they can, to ruin you" (28 March 1846; LOA 25:93). His characterization of the clash as "truth ... against might" (21 March 1846; LOA 26:15) may be an overstatement. But there can be little doubt that personal, professional, and institutional power—and that not totally honest or altruistic—was being flaunted.

For Halliwell the affair was over. But in the wake of his "triumph" and his accusers' bitterness could he at twenty-six achieve something like a status quo ante?

PART TWO

1846-1853

Fig. 2 Henrietta Halliwell-Phillipps with her daughters Henrietta Somerset and Charlotte in 1851. By kind permission of her great-granddaughter, Désirée Hancock, née Muntz.

·5·

Controversies

Continuity was never really interrupted, despite outward pressures and apparent changes. Although he protested that his work was being severely hindered by the British Museum affair, Halliwell continued to be remarkably active and productive. As is often the case, professional crises and personal calamities produced clarity. Friends and foes were unmistakably defined: Wright and Pettigrew continued as pillars of support and encouragement. Professional aims and alliances were strengthened and objectives delineated: early pursuits, manifold but often diffuse, gave way to more precise, more ambitious, and more significant ones. Halliwell founded no more societies; he continued only with those most essential to his interests. Within a year or two after the British Museum affair Halliwell published his most important works to date: the complete *Dictionary of Archaic and Provincial Words, Obsolete Phrases, Proverbs, and Ancient Customs, from the Fourteenth Century* (1847) and the *Life of William Shakespeare* (1848). In one way or another they are crystallizations of earlier activities and pathways for future ones. With them came new and long-lasting attachments, among them F. W. Fairholt, who provided the illustrations for the Shakespearean works, and W. O. Hunt, the town clerk who was a key in Halliwell's engagement with Stratford-upon-Avon. Similarly, the frustrating and hostile relationship with his father-in-law, Thomas Phillipps, served to strengthen Halliwell's marriage, as significant choices and decisions had to be made: for Henrietta, husband for father, for James, litigation for reconciliation. The sudden death in 1845 of Richard Halliwell, his eldest brother, and in 1849 of both his father and mother, tightened Halliwell's bond with his remaining brother, Thomas, and his sister, Louisa. His father's will, designating him and his mother as executors of the estate, had a decided effect on his financial situation and responsibilities, as did, of course, the birth of his daughters: Henrietta Somerset in 1843, Charlotte in 1847, Ellen in 1854, and Katherine in 1855. Even a change of address was a stabilizing factor: from such commuting points in London (35 Alfred Place and 10 Fitzroy Street) and Oxford

(Islip), Halliwell moved in 1846 to Avenue Lodge, Brixton, Hill, Surrey, where he consolidated his household and, till 1853, from which he continued to produce works for his favorite societies–eleven separate works for the Percy Society (which was dissolved in 1853), three for the Shakespeare Society (which was dissolved in 1853)–as well as eleven for John Russell Smith, four for other publishers and–in what was to be a defining feature of his career as author and bookman–twenty-four privately printed works. When the first volume of his remarkable and privately printed sixteen-volume folio edition of Shakespeare appeared in 1853, Halliwell was thirty-three years old, had become a major figure in the world of literary scholarship, and–*plus ça change plus c'est la même chose*–continued to be embroiled in controversies.

+++

During the eighteen months of the British Museum affair, and in its immediate wake, there were other shock waves. At the moment the officials of the British Museum were deciding to exclude Halliwell, a grand Victorian storm was brewing. In December 1844 at a meeting of the Central Committee of the British Archaeological Association a struggle between factions led by Thomas Wright and Albert Way reached a climax of sorts, leading to the resignations of Wright and Charles Roach Smith from the Publishing Committee, further disruptions in early 1845,[86] and finally a split which led to the creation of the Way faction's Archaeological Institute. The outlines of this "classic Victorian row" are readily

---

86. The severity of what was to come may not have been fully understood by all the participants, as is evident in this excerpt from a poem by Stephen Isaacson (26 February 1845; LOA 19:83):

> My dear and learned friend Roach Smith,
> I'll come with all the men of pith,
> To make a-way with Albert Way,
> And all who join him in the fray.
> Shall Wright be wrong, & wrong be Wright,
> And justice yield her scales to might?
> And power usurped by would be wise 'uns,
> Who look as fierce as *Yankee Bisons*,
> Upset the Archae-o-logical,
> Or hold our *Wrights* and *Smiths* in thrall?
> –'Forbid it, all ye gods and fishes!
> Forbid it, pots, and urns, and dishes!!'

available.[87] What is of concern here is the composition of the alliances and their scholarly objectives. The names associated with the Wright faction should not be surprising, if not entirely predictable: among them Charles Roach Smith, Thomas Pettigrew, and of course Halliwell. Among the followers of Way, including those who left the Wright faction, were Henry Ellis, William Whewell, and Frederic Madden. The *Athenaeum*, as to be expected, was strongly in support of Way, as was to a considerable extent the *Gentleman's Magazine*, their respective editors, Charles Dilke and John Gough Nichols, among the initial subscribers to the new organization. Underlying the clash of personalities, power-grasping, and petty jealousies were deep social and intellectual differences between the factions. The schism was described, albeit superficially, by J. H. Parker (no ally of Wright's):

It became evident at Canterbury [the meeting of the BAA in December 1843] that the society consisted of two distinct classes of persons–the one, gentlemen of property and amateurs of Archaeology, who wished to have opportunities of communicating to others the information they had collected, that it might not die with them, as had frequently been the case with many of their friends. The other party consisted of professional archaeologists.[88]

It is not without a certain irony that the so-called amateurs were led by Way, whom the recent president of the Royal Archaeological Society and historian of the Society of Antiquaries (of which Way was director) characterized as "an admirable example of the leisured archaeologist, the learned amateur, of the old school,"[89] and were composed to a notable

87. See David Wetherall, "From Canterbury to Winchester: The Foundation of the Institute," in *Building on the Past: Papers Celebrating 150 Years of the Royal Archaeological Institute*, ed. Blaise Vyner (London, 1994), pp. 8-21.

88. Quoted by Wetherall, p. 17.

89. Joan Evans, "The Royal Archaeological Institute: A Retrospect," *Archaeological Journal*, 106 (1951), 2. Although acknowledging some talent and engagement in them, Evans is not without a certain bias in her characterization of Wright as a "Grub Street medievalist," of Charles Roach Smith as a "self-educated egotist of litigious tendencies," and of Pettigrew as a surgeon who "had not gone so far in his profession as he might have done, because of a tendency to quarrel with his Boards of Management." Way, on the other hand, was "of completely different stamp" (pp. 1-2), as were the committee members of "our Society": "the Marquess of Northampton, President of the Royal Society, as President, seven Fellows of

extent of leading members of the establishment–a veritable phalanx from the British Museum, the clergy, and the academic world.[90] ("Amateur," it should not be forgotten, was not used in a depreciatory sense. In a typical instance Wright wrote that he did not "pretend to judge, as I am not an amateur of bibliography" [1 August 1841; LOA 9:36].) Surely Wright and Halliwell (essentially freelance writers), Pettigrew (a surgeon), and Roach Smith (a chemist) were as much amateurs as Way, Madden, and Whewell. The larger irony, the social and intellectual one, is that the former were not a private clique but were from the beginning open and popularizing in outlook. Their aim was to bring together those individuals throughout the country who shared a common interest in antiquity: local secretaries and provincial correspondents were instituted, no subscriptions were exacted at the outset. By the end of 1844, a year after its founding, the British Archaeological Association had over a thousand members. Way's amateurs, on the other hand, were exclusive and selective at the core, despite avowals of disinterested pursuit and dissemination of the valuable national heritage. Their outlook is undisguised in the plain talk of the *Athenaeum* (1 March 1848, p. 221): "It was high time for the 'better spirits' of the council to look a-head ... The *traders* must go ... We must have no repetition, at Winchester, of the Canterbury cockneyisms of last year ... The Secretaries must be disinterested men, of name and standing ... men who can write good English and speak it correctly when it is written." A vivid example of the hostility was provided by the Reverend Richard Garnett (the elder), Assistant Keeper of Printed Books in the British Museum, and a philologist, who in the *Quarterly Review* (82 [1848], 309-42) surveyed and attacked the work of both Halliwell and Wright over the years. He prefaced his criticism thus: "we have our reasons for distrusting everything done under the superintendence of those two gentlemen, if the task demand the smallest possible amount of critical skill or acumen" (p. 316). After pointing out various deficiencies in Halliwell's edition of *The Harrowing of Hell*, he can only conclude: "Such are the fruits of people meddling with matters they have neither learning to understand nor wit to guess at" (p. 319). He grants Wright industry, but "his activity is so counterbalanced by want of scholarship and acumen, that he can never be more than a third or fourth rate personage, bearing about the same relationship to a scientific philologist and antiquarian that a law-stationer

the Royal Society, as members, and a strong representation of the British Museum, the R.I.B.A. and the Antiquaries" (p. 4).

90. For demographic statistics see Philippa Levine, *The Amateur and the Professional* (Cambridge, 1986), pp. 48-9.

does to a barrister, or a country druggist to a physician" (p. 319). The substance of the criticism may not be completely unwarranted but is doubtless mollified by Garnett's absolutist stance and strident tone, as well as by his unqualified praise of Way's *Promptorium Parvulorum* and Madden's edition of *Layamon*, not to mention his social bias.

Halliwell was a valued member of the Wright faction, ideologically as well as personally. More important than his not inconsiderable efforts on its behalf—as author, officer, and organizer—and his opposition to the Way faction, was its compatibility with his personality and scholarly perspective. For all his apparent early elitism—as in his defence of the exclusiveness of the British Museum Library and the rigorous requirements of scholarship itself—Halliwell was in a constant struggle with authority and establishment, as an eager if not aggressive young man producing the *Letter to Egerton* and *A Few Hints to Novices* and choosing as subjects those who had not been appreciated in their time or in fact had been persecuted, such as Morland and D'Ewes. And, to be sure, at the height of the battle of the factions for the control of the British Archaeological Association, Halliwell was in conflict with the establishment in the guise of the British Museum and Trinity College. It is in this context that his *Letters of the Kings of England*, his first major publication to take form and emerge from that cloud, must be understood. Although a relatively simple and straightforward undertaking, a collection of letters ranging chronologically from Richard I to Charles I for the edification and amusement of a general audience, it caused a storm which exemplifies important features of Halliwell's personality and career as well as the swelling tide of the times.

First there were the circumstances surrounding the publication. Halliwell's edition of the *Autobiography and Correspondence of Sir Simonds D'Ewes* was published by Richard Bentley in two volumes in 1845, apparently to the consternation of Henry Colburn, who had also planned to publish it. "*Very much annoyed at Bentley's getting this publication out of his hands,*" wrote Thomas Wright (22 January 1845; LOA 15:97), he offered to let Halliwell have his transcript for £50 and, if accepted, he would give up the project. As always, Wright dictated a solution: Halliwell should write to Colburn that he was "sorry that this should have happened, but that when you arranged with Bentley [he] had no idea of his [Colburn's] intentions to publish this book" and also to Bentley to ask if "he is willing to give the fifty pounds." Bentley responded immediately: "Pray let not an instant be lost in proceeding with the printing that we be not anticipated by Mr. Colburn" (24 January 1845; LOA 20:88). And, as it was later attested to, the owner of the transcript, Sir Charles Young, made a present of it in return for two copies of the published work (27 July 1846; LOA 24:31). This brief episode is a prelude to one which develops and highlights elements of literary and publishing enterprise, especially the practices of competition, in Halliwell's career. At the same time as he was producing the D'Ewes volumes for Bentley, Halliwell was preparing a collection, *Letters of the Kings of England,* for Colburn. In addition to the delicacy required in negotiating simultaneously with competing publishers, Halliwell was having problems with the assembling of the material. He was informed, in one instance, by Markham J. Thorpe that he must get permission himself from the Secretary of State before certain royal letters could be copied (1 March 1845; LOA 22:20). A few months later, Sir James Graham, Home Secretary under Robert Peel, refused Halliwell permission to transcribe letters of kings in the State Paper Office (18 June 1845; LOA 20:69). Collecting letters presented problems as well. Naively, William Shoberl, the printer of the work, volunteered to forward a request from Halliwell to Thomas Phillipps, "trust[ing] a good understanding will shortly be restored between yourself and him" (10 October 1845; LOA 24:38). Not surprisingly, a few days later Shoberl reported Phillipps's answer: "When Mr. Colburn condescends to write to Sir T. P. Sir T. P will know how to answer him" (16 October 1845; LOA 29:11). Phillipps's refusal was to be expected; that of the Home Secretary was also not entirely unexpected if Peel's position as Trustee of the British Museum is considered.

Competition in the field had also to be taken into account—enough for Thorpe to agree with Halliwell that the project be kept "as secret as you like" (1 March 1845; LOA 22:20). Halliwell did not have to worry about the work of Agnes Strickland, the friend to whom he dedicated his *Letters* "as a slight testimony of esteem and respect," whose use of modern spelling (in her *Lives of the Queens of England*) he adopted. But there was obvious concern about the appearance, also in 1846, of the third series of *Original Letters, Illustrative of English History; Including Numerous Royal Letters; from Autographs in the British Museum, the State Paper Office, and One or Two Other Collections. With Notes and Illustrations,* published by Bentley and edited by another of Halliwell's antagonists, Sir Henry Ellis.[91] "I hope all the

---

91. The opposition to Ellis's work began earlier, of course. On 5 April 1843 (LOA 18:50), for example, Wright noted that "Ellis's vol. of letters of literary people is just ready. Between you and me, its a poor affair." In the same letter Wright commented on Way's *Promptorium Parvulorum.* "He has put a Latin title page, and went hawking it about to hear if it was good Latin, as I hear. This is great foppery. By what I see, poor Way is getting filled with conceit—this information is confidential!" Incidentally, Halliwell did not consider it harmful

required transcripts will be quite finished by the end of next week,"
Halliwell wrote to Frederick Shoberl on 27 October 1845 (Folger Y.c.
1242[3], "as it would be terribly provoking if Sir H. got the start of us."
And in a clear reference to the desire for novelty and the awareness of
obstacles, features of the competitive situation, he agreed with Shoberl to
include all Edward VI letters: "as it is we shall make a very good show of
new unedited letters, even if we are disappointed with getting into the
S.P.O." The sense of competition may indeed have motivated William
Shoberl to print the work "somewhat after the fashion of Sir Henry Ellis's
Royal Letters which do not contain so much matter in a page" (10
October 1845; LOA 24:38). And a sense of the market was certainly
behind his plan for a third volume: "I think of publishing *the two volumes*
(so as to get the start of a certain party) & at the end of Vol II to
announce that the third & concluding volume of this Work will be
published about the ____ ____ of ____ next. The sale of the whole will
be, I consider, promoted by not giving the public too large & expensive
a dose at first" (26 March 1846; LOA 27:95).

To insure the rapid completion and success of his work, both in itself
and in competition with Ellis's and a number of other collections then en
vogue, Halliwell took the advice of friends and, for details of the
production, Frederick and his brother William Shoberl. Halliwell always
got along well with printers and listened as attentively to their
recommendations as he expected them to adhere to his directives.
Modest–"I hope you will not consider me presuming or impertinent"–but
not reticent, William Shoberl mediated some of the transcripts and had
definite views about their presentation. In a typical example he wrote on
26 May 1845 (LOA 22:21):

I think the notes, (which in my opinion need not be very heavy) should
appear solely at the *foot* of the pages to which they refer, as in the case of
Miss Strickland's 'Lives of the Queens', as readers never like to turn to the
end of a volume for illustrations of the text by doing which distracts their
attention from what they are reading. As respects the Authority for each
letter I think it should always be given like the "Letters of Mary Queen of
Scots," a proof sheet of which I have forwarded with the transcripts.
Obsolete words should not be changed but their meaning given (perhaps
in the text in parentheses) as any alteration in this respect would destroy
the *vraisemblance* & integrity of the documents. Quaint & curious phrases,

enough to excise it, as he did for the name of the author of a book Wright
described as "miserable" (20 December 1845; LOA 18:79).

which often give a peculiar character to the letters, should also for the same reason be retained. In short the *words* themselves should always be retained but *not* their *antiquated orthography*.

And final details of the publication—concerning proofs, portraits, paper supply—were outlined by his brother, Frederick, a year later (30 March 1846; LOA 27:51). In addition, it was natural for Shoberl to assume the role of coordinator in the preparation and transmission of transcripts of letters from home and abroad, especially since Halliwell was "rusticated" at Islip at the time.

Although on the whole more restrained in tone, Halliwell's introduction is not without the polemics of earlier statements of his ideological position. The collection is admittedly popular and educative in conception and address. That relatively little of English history was widely known Halliwell does not hesitate to attribute to "our limited and confined system of public and University education, which leads our Students to place greater importance on the deeds of Xerxes, or Alexander, than on those of later heroes, whose triumphs or reverses have been productive of more sensible effects on the constitution of society and nations in more recent times" (v-vi), as well as to undervalue or neglect the national literature, even the "sublime writings of the Bard of Avon." Also at fault are "our antiquaries [who] seem for the most part to have been obstinately bent on either not admitting, or overlooking," the needs of the general reader in their "presentation of documents in an antiquarian form [which] precludes the hope of any extensive benefit being derived from their publication" (vii). To help make the documents "properly read and explained," and thus to enhance their value, Halliwell has adopted modern spelling—in the same way that Shakespeare has been treated—and translated documents in foreign languages. Having criticized the educational and scholarly establishment, Halliwell cannot resist, as usual, the pull of pen, the rhetorical apostrophe so common in his prose style:

The Utilitarian spirit of the age decides against that ancient race of antiquaries who would make a mountain of a trifling departure from an original paper, and at the same time be nervously alive to the slightest ridicule of any favourite conjecture, however absurd, useless, or inconsistent with facts. Such men not infrequently made mighty preparations of learning in pursuit of worthless objects. Let us hope that we shall descend or ascend the stream of rational criteria, not by the minutiae of antiquarianism; and that the race of whom we have just spoken may find no more followers, for they can in sooth only be compared to Caligula, who alarmed the whole world by raising a mighty army, and then led it to gather cockle-shells (x-xi).

The two-volume work was published early in the spring of 1846, its first important reviews appearing in May 1846, as the British Museum affair was nearing a conclusion and in time for it to be reviewed almost simultaneously with Ellis's *Original Letters*. William Shoberl was quick to recognize the commercial advantages of the publicity which Halliwell's case evoked. "I congratulate you much," he wrote on 21 April 1846 (LOA 27:41), "on the able Article in the *Times* in your behalf, and also upon that in the last Lit[erar]y Gazette,–both of which will serve to herald in the Kings." A month later, however, he had to console Halliwell "to take no notice of the attack in the Athenaeum" (22 May 1846: LOA 25:48). Given the almost passionate interest in history–as evidenced in the flood of letters, memoirs, biographies, and the like–the divisions within the ranks of scholarship, and the climaxing British Museum affair, the reviews of Halliwell's work could not be expected to be impartial, nor could the extent of the reception and the extremity of the positions taken. The review in the *Athenaeum* extends over two issues and devotes fourteen columns (2 and 9 May 1846, pp. 448-50, 473-5) to Halliwell's collection. Acknowledging the general interest in the subject, the reviewer (most likely Samuel Astley Dunham, according to the Athenaeum Indexing Project) provides long and detailed excerpts. Although he points out the dangers inherent in epistolary presentations–e.g. the "self-love" of the authors that may distort reality–he does not single out Halliwell but rather applies his censure, "merited by nineteen-twentieths of all the letters ... that have yet issued from the press" (p. 448), to the genre itself. He does not overlook the fact that one volume instead of two would have sufficed, and that "the places of many documents were not supplied by others of a more important, more interesting, or less suspicious character." And in his most specific criticism, although acknowledging advantages and disadvantages, he takes only mild exception to Halliwell's modernization of spelling and translations, proposing a glossary to deal with obsolete words and phrases and an appendix for the latter group (pp. 448-9). There is little restraint, however, in his assessment of the work as "really, on the whole, a valuable addition to the mass of our historical materials,–as valuable, no doubt, as almost any other that has appeared in our time ... Comparing him with others, [Halliwell] is entitled to high praise" (p. 448).

Such benevolence towards Halliwell from the pages of the *Athenaeum* was surprising, if not unthinkable. In the next issue (16 May 1846, pp.

500-1), however, it was countered by a scorching attack by another
historian, Thomas Hudson Turner, an antiquary who happened to be a
resident secretary of the Archaeological Institute which had emerged from
the Way faction's split with the British Archaeological Association. From
his ironic employment of the rhetorical *praeteritio* device—"Passing in
silence the blunder with which this truly extraordinary collection opens,
viz. the attribution of a letter written by Henry II. to his successor,
Richard I."—Turner proceeds with heavy sarcasm to challenge Halliwell to
"produce any *authentic* evidence whatever of the genuineness of this
document," contradicting Halliwell's statement that it is in the Tower and
asserting that it could not have been translated from the Anglo-Norman
since "in the time of Richard Anglo-Norman was not used either in public
or in private letters." The criticism becomes even harsher, as Turner
points out errors in dating, attribution, and translation. Not satisfied with
exposing Halliwell's lack of historical knowledge, Turner, increasingly
exasperated, charges Halliwell with deception: citation without accurate
acknowledgment or even plagiarism, presenting documents as letters
which are in reality something else, falsely purporting documents to have
been seen in the original, and falsely claiming documents as being printed
for the first time. And in a final blow Turner accuses Halliwell of what
amounts to fraud in averring that "he had, in almost every instance,
examined the original MSS. of these letters, when accessible" and
dishonestly thanking Thomas Duffus Hardy, Keeper of the Records of
the Tower (and also a member of the Way faction), for his assistance.
"Mr. Hardy," Turner proclaims, "has authorized me to state, that he
neither directly nor, to his knowledge, indirectly, rendered Mr. Halliwell
any assistance whatever." More virulent is the implication of Turner's
concluding lines: Hardy expressed "great surprise" at receiving from Mr.
Shoberl a copy of the work, accompanied by a note in which he calls it *his*
collection of letters, which he had been so fortunate as to obtain Mr.
Halliwell to edit!"

Halliwell was quick to reply, obviously furious not merely at Turner's
charges of "editorial inaccuracy brought against his supposed labours"—so
the phrasing of the *Athenaeum*, which printed only extracts from his letter
on 13 June 1846 (p. 605)—but also at the "moral implications which Mr.
Turner's criticism involves." Halliwell countered that he "thanked *no one*
for assistance; but ... merely [gave] a list of names, which was handed to
[him] by the publisher, consisting of gentlemen who had facilitated the
progress of the work, rather by throwing no impediments in the way of

collecting the materials, than by other assistance."[92] Hiring transcribers was a common practice, he continued, "an editor [having] as much right to employ a copyist, as a solicitor to engage the services of an amanuensis." The *Athenaeum* could not accept Halliwell's "special pleading" or accept that adornment is not uncommon in such contexts, finding that Halliwell's acknowledgment contains "ordinary expressions of men who *have* enjoyed exclusive facilities;—and are initiated here, for the purpose of raising a similar presumption ... Mr. Halliwell ... cannot ... play with language at his pleasure." This harsh accusation of deception is compounded by one of cynicism and fraud. Exposing the implications of Turner's final reproach, the *Athenaeum* has "reason to know that the Collection is not *his* at all, but Mr. Shoberl's ... and bearing of Mr. Halliwell's editorship *only his name*, lent to it for a consideration! ... Other names," the *Athenaeum* continues, "were bid for, before Mr. Halliwell was applied to,—but the mercenary sponsorship was, of course, refused ... Mr. Halliwell may rest assured that it is not by such means that he will take the place amongst honourable and distinguished antiquarians of which he is ambitious."

This was ten days before the case of trover was to take place. Three days before it, on 20 June 1846, the *Athenaeum* continued its attack (p. 629), responding to another letter of protest from Halliwell first by not printing it in full "because it is not couched in the language accepted amongst gentlemen" and then by affirming its own integrity and condemning, with a selected excerpt from Halliwell's letter, his "skirmishing" with the full text of a letter from Hardy asserting that "neither Mr. Halliwell, nor Mr. Shoberl, nor any other person for them, paid one *farthing* for copies of any document at the Tower, for the work in question; nor has either of these gentlemen, or any agent for them, searched for, seen, or copied, any original letters in the Tower." "If, therefore," concludes the *Athenaeum*, "Mr. Halliwell thinks he can rally from a fresh defeat like this, and means to take up new ground, he must do so through some other agency than that of the *Athenaeum*."

That was not the end of the altercation, however. A week later, in the next issue (27 June 1846, p. 656)–two days after the postponement and then abandonment of the case of Trinity College versus the British Museum and on the very day Halliwell was granted permission to apply

92. Halliwell received the list in a letter from Shoberl dated 26 March 1846 (LOA 27:95). He mentioned all the names, including Hardy's, as well as, in Shoberl's words, "a host of other persons which you will be better able to specify than I am."

for readmission to the library of the British Museum–the *Athenaeum* responded to an assertion of his honesty that Halliwell had "advertised" in the *Times*, "demur[ring] to his recommending his own character, after the fashion of quacks in general, by depreciating that of his neighbour." Rejecting the charge that it had ever denied Halliwell's being editor of the *Letters* ("every article of ours on the subject has been headed with his name in connexion with the work") and that it had been unfair and garbled his replies ("the questions of *fairness* and *gentlemanly criticism* are not of the kind which the *Athenaeum* will argue with such men as *Mr. Halliwell*"), the *Athenaeum* closes the affair by condemning "that gentleman's incapacity for seeing straight or walking directly," having taken as an avowal of its imputation that the work was not Halliwell's at all his statement: "I was requested by Mr. Colburn to *edit* a collection ... with an historical introduction ... Transcribers and translators were to be furnished for me ... My business as Editor was merely to direct the researches of the persons employed,–to select from their copies the letters which seemed most interesting, and to illustrate them by notes, &c. in the best manner I could." This excerpt, quoted in the *Athenaeum*, seems to accord with the correspondence of Halliwell with Colburn and Shoberl: in fact, Halliwell's direct engagement is obvious in Shoberl's writing that he is "very glad to find you expect to meet with some Letters among the Rawlinson MSS." (24 May 1845; LOA 20:75). And it illustrates a common enough practice of publishers suggesting or commissioning works and of authors responding–Halliwell the freelancer, it must be remembered, had to support himself and his family. Still, it is clear that swords were drawn and slashing. Parallel to the reception in the *Athenaeum* was that in the *Literary Gazette*, which ran a series of five notices: on 9 May 1846 (pp. 417-18), 16 May (pp. 446-8), 23 May (pp. 470-2), 30 May (pp. 495-6), and 6 June (pp. 518-19). Not unlike the first review in the *Athenaeum*, that in the *Literary Gazette* was favorable, recognizing that the work is intended for a general audience and successful in its aim of "forming as interesting a selection of royal letters as any that has ever issued from the press" (p. 417). The benevolence of attitude is evident in its mild notice of "slight" errors and especially in its filling the notices with generous specimens of letters from Henry VIII, James I, and Charles I, among others, which it held together in the manner of popular serial publications, such as "And so we dismiss Henry the Eighth. Our attention will next be directed to the more amusing, if not more interesting, correspondence of James I.; and we think we see some anecdotes and old scandal in prospective which will be worth the selecting for our readers' entertainment. To quote Prince Hal, there is more than one of James's letters which will be an 'argument for a week, laughter for a month, and a good jest for ever'" (p. 448).

The apparently casual and benign approach is not without an awareness of criticism from other sources. For one thing, it attempts to defuse the charge of errors and blunders by calling them not serious. In a clever tactic the reviewer anticipates and so dissipates errors which so anger Turner–e.g. Richard I's addressing, in 1196, Henry V, who died in 1125–by dealing first with this letter and stating mildly: "Mr. Halliwell has committed a slight error in the address of the letter [and] the date also may be somewhat too late" (p. 471). For another, he attempts to diminish the attack on Halliwell's lack of scholarship by stressing throughout that this interesting and amusing work is aimed at the general reader. In this spirit the reviewer, in the manner of a peroration, concludes the fifth notice with a comfortable confirmation of Halliwell's intent and accomplishment:

On the whole, although there are a large number of important documents in this work hitherto inedited, it will somewhat disappoint the literary antiquary. In truth, Mr. Halliwell seems to have thrown overboard all his antiquarian notions in this work, for there is really nothing antiquarian in it. Everything is popularised in the true book-selling spirit of the age to fit the work for our numerous book-clubs. And we think the endeavour has been successful; for although we have seen many works of the kind more learned, and far more valuable for the professed student, it has never fallen to our lot to peruse a collection of historical letters so readable and interesting, or so likely to prove a favourite with the general reader. Amusement and instruction may be culled from its pages, and a cursory knowledge of English history gathered, where larger treatises would too frequently present a formidable appearance not readily to be encountered (p. 519).

And lest there be no mistake about the side being taken, the editor of the *Literary Gazette*, William Jerdan, intervenes and at the end of the third notice (pp. 471-2) responds directly to Turner's attack:

A letter has been published, signed by Mr. T. Hudson Turner (secretary to the Archaeological Institute), in which our corrections are adopted, with a few trifling additions, and, we are sorry to say, urged in a spirit of acrimony which cannot but be disapproved in one literary man or antiquary towards another engaged in similar pursuits. Mr. Turner has boldly put his name to this concoction; and Mr. Hardy, of the Tower, appears as a coadjutor, charging Mr. Halliwell (as far as he knows) with never having made the research among the records in his charge, referred to in the preface. We think Mr. Halliwell's signature to the preface affords grounds for his enemies to offer this allegation; for though the plural 'We' is used throughout, the signature at the end seems to individualise the statement. But this is taking advantage of a mere ambiguity. The collection was not made, nor pretended to be made, by Mr. Halliwell; and his 'editing' could not imply that he must personally consult or inspect every document referred to, any more than if a literary man edited (for example) travels in the interior of Africa, he should be bound to visit all the localities! In the present instance it was more discreditable to step out of the way to assail such oversights as the ignorance of the Vicecomites being the Sheriffs of London (the single blemish, in addition to ours, pointed out), as Mr. Halliwell has already been as cruelly persecuted as any individual could possibly be. And it seems to us at the moment that to blame him for not having examined MSS. in the British Museum is rather too gross in those who abet his exclusion from that Public Library, on an accusation which he is denied the opportunity to meet or refute.

There were other ramifications as well. In a time in which collections of letters were abundant, Halliwell's appeared in direct competition with Henry Ellis's. The inevitable clash of persons, positions, and politics was highlighted in the *Gentleman's Magazine*, which in the same number (n.s. 26 [August 1846], 137-44, 145-9) reviewed both works, "frowning brow to brow" (as it were). There is little need to analyze the reviews themselves since they are preceded by editorial forewarnings:

In reference to the first of these collections [Halliwell's] we have felt ourselves obliged to speak strongly in condemnation of the carelessness and inaccuracy which pervade it from beginning to end. The book comes forth with an air of assumption and pretence, and is puffed in many quarters with extraordinary diligence, but we would entreat its Editor to beware how he permits himself to be misled into again taking part in such a publication. He possesses a zeal which, if employed in an honourable service, would render him distinguished; but no zeal, nor any other good quality, can withstand the evil influence of several such books. If he would sink into a Ned Purdon, he will proceed; if he would hold a place amongst the labourers who do credit to literature, he must retrace his steps. No one will be more delighted than ourselves to forget that he has ever had a share in such a worthless publication (p. 137).

Nichols's paternalistic stance–in some ways it was he who had introduced the young Halliwell to the scholarly society by calling attention to his earliest works[93]–may on the surface be his attempt to mollify the viciousness of the review itself, which concludes: "Faults of all conceivable kinds could be adduced without end. Text, references to authorities, glossary, notes, introduction, all teem with blunders totally destructive of authority: all give proof of every kind and variety of ignorance." But this is not enough; it is but the prelude to a crescendo of charges against the whole career of Halliwell: "his carelessness and inaccuracy [which] have been long painfully obvious to all persons who have examined any of his books," "his obvious incompetency for many of the tasks he has undertaken ... as marvellous as that he should have condescended to play the part of a mask, and sell the authority that may attach to the many initials which he appends to his name, to an ignorant compilation and to a titlepage devoid of truth." "Such things," this settling the score with Halliwell as person and as scholar culminates, "discredit literature and literary men, cast wide upon the world the seeds of almost ineradicable errors, and stamp lasting discredit upon every one concerned in them" (p. 144).

The author of this philippic has been identified as John Bruce, who in 1841 denied ever having reviewed a book of Halliwell's and vowed "unless I very much change my mind, I shall never do so" (6 April 1841; LOA 30:57). Its intensity is doubtless based upon a long-endured frustration and anger: echoes of the heated reaction to the *Letter to Egerton* and the *Few Hints to Novices*, the political maneuvering within the various societies, especially in the Camden Society (of which Bruce was a Council member), and what-have-you are undeniable. Coming so soon after the end of the British Museum affair, the explosive vituperation is understandable as a loosing of collective grievances and resentments, exacerbated by a deep disappointment at the outcome. Why it–as well as a letter from Philalethes containing a long list of errors[94]–should appear in the *Gentleman's Magazine*, long friendly to Halliwell, is a matter of speculation: Nichols became a member of the Way faction; there was friction (as shall be discussed) with the Camden Society. One thing is sure. The times were slippery, events unforeseeable and alliances fickle. Still, and not unexpectedly, the companion review of Ellis's collection is sober and moderate, stressing Ellis's long experience ("some twenty years ago [he] first entered the field of literary labour" [p. 144] and notable accomplishment ("the first editor of letters who endeavoured, by proper historical illustration ... [to make]

93. See pp. 98-9.
94. n.s. 26 (August 1846), 154-5.

his collections popular, and certainly rendered them more generally useful than any similar publications" [pp. 144-5]). And, after commenting approvingly on selected letters, the review concludes with an unmistakable swipe at Halliwell's work: "The explanatory introductions [not found in Halliwell] contain valuable information, and the book is throughout an honest book, made up of matter neither borrowed nor stolen, but collected together by the intelligent and hard-working pains and industry of the editor. It will sustain his previous reputation in this branch of literature, and be found a useful book by all classes of historical inquirers" (p. 149). Reflecting the pressure of the past, the last and honest word on the subject was uttered by Halliwell himself some forty years later. Responding to a request from H. Maxwell Lyte for information on the Mordant MS. of which "I have now no more idea than the babe unborn," Halliwell confessed. "The materials for the Letters of the Kings were not collected by me but by a person employed by the publisher–it was altogether a booksellers job–a stupid book of which I am ashamed but I wanted money at the time & had a good sum for the Preface, & hinc &c." (9 July 1884; EUL E.97: 19:1).

+++

In the immediate wake of the British Museum affair there was still another assault on Halliwell's character and ethics. Things were never quiet in the societies. It might be expected that the Camden Society, for instance, would be an exception: Halliwell was auditor and Council member from 1841 to 1843 and an active proposer and contributor to its publication series between 1839 and 1844; he had survived the furore over his *Letter to Egerton* and the suppression of the Forman papers with the support of strong allies. But another apparent misstep led to stormy meetings and a public letter of 4 February 1847 accusing him of a "fraud" which has "damaged [his] character ... greatly ... and with it the characters of Mr. Pettigrew, and Mr. Wright, who undertook his defence at the Camden Council yesterday, and conducted it in a very boisterous manner." Its author, the prominent Joseph Hunter, with whom Halliwell had had an extensive though at times not untroubled relationship: in mid 1843 there were tensions regarding the "indecent" Forman papers, and at the end of 1844 a vigorous disagreement about the dating of the Dering manuscript of *Henry IV*, which led Lambert Larking to remark that "you have hit Mr Hunter *hard*–but I fear will have made an enemy of him" (18

November 1844; LOA 22:96).[95] Hunter was incensed that Halliwell had used for publication a transcript which was not the one described as MS. Bright 276, the diary of Sir Henry Wotton, but rather a copy of a transcript made from a manuscript in the British Museum. Hunter's fury had not been abated by Collier's attempt at mediation. Writing earlier to Halliwell on Hunter's "fuss," Collier, also a member of the Council, reported: Hunter "is generally 'a day after the fair' with his discoveries: he does not often make them until other people have found them out. I gave it as my opinion that the Diary was not by Sir H. Wotton at the last Council of the C. S. and referred it to Mr Hunter on that very account. I merely said you believed it to be Wotton's" (26 January 1847; LOA 59:14). This was also Halliwell's explanation. And he could hardly follow the resolution of the Council meeting of 3 February 1847[96] that the printed sheets be collated with MS. 276, which was believed to be in the possession of his contentious father-in-law, Thomas Phillipps. At any rate the matter seems to have been resolved rather quickly, for Halliwell's manuscript appeared promptly in the *Camden Miscellany* (vol. I) in 1847 with the title *Journal of the Siege of Rouen, 1591*, but edited by John Gough Nichols. There is but one distant reference to the "fuss": "The true author of this Journal [Thomas Coningsby] has not been ascertained without much difficulty. It has been attributed in one quarter to the celebrated sir Henry Wotton" (p. 4), to which is added the footnote: "Sale Catalogue of Mr. Bright's Manuscripts, Lot 276: which was evidently another copy of the same Journal, as shown by the passage there given, which is the same as that in p. 44, though slightly differing in language. It is supposed to have passed into the collection of Sir Thomas Phillipps, Bart." There seem to have been no resignations or other dramatic gestures. Halliwell's association with the Society was unimpaired and continued for years thereafter.[97]

95. LOA 22:62 consists of Hunter's position of 15 November 1844 and a draft of Halliwell's strident response of 17 November 1844.

96. Of some interest are the names of those Council members who were present: Beriah Botfield, Collier, William Durant Cooper, Charles Purton Cooper, Bolton Corney, Henry Ellis (in the Chair), Joseph Hunter, Pettigrew, Thomas Stapleton, W. J. Thoms, and Wright.

97. Although he appears to have resigned in 1859, he was elected to the Council in 1874 and again in 1876.

6

Family Relations: 1846-1847

During the professional crises from 1845 to 1847 it is not to be doubted that Halliwell's energy and ambition found their greatest support in the stability and shelter of his immediate family. For a number of years after his marriage in 1842 he lived with his parents, spending much time with them in London at 35 Alfred Place, then with his brother Richard at 10 Fitzroy Street, with his parents in Islip, and finally at Avenue Lodge, Brixton Hill. That James, the youngest, was his parents' favorite can easily be deduced, for he was provided with private tutors, sent to Cambridge with a generous allowance, helped when in financial trouble, urged to take up residence in Islip, aided in his intricate negotiations with his father-in-law—all testifying to intensity of affection. That he, the youngest son, was made executor of his father's estate in 1849 is no surprise, nor is the fact that his mother, who was joint executor, willed him as sole executor at her death, also in 1849. Their actions were not only an act of love but also of faith in his judgment and ability to assume responsibilities. Louisa—Louy, as she was affectionately called—was a faithful and adoring sister: only two years younger, she was able to share in Halliwell's bachelor days, often accompanying him on his social outings, later befriending Henrietta, and always acting the loyal daughter (her father referred to her as his "Town Housekeeper" [20 June 1847; LOA 55:41]), beloved aunt (to the children of Richard, Thomas, and James), and doting sister, who, alone, often addressed her brother as "Ort," as intimate and particular a salutation as their father's "Orchard."

Halliwell's relationship with his brother Thomas was also singularly cordial. A graduate of New Inn Hall, Oxford (BA 1837, MA 1840), he was ordained priest in 1839 and became curate of Christ Church Wrington (Somerset) in 1844. Like Richard, he too was a member of his younger brother's Historical Society of Science and took an active interest in his career. He was especially encouraging of the *Dictionary of Archaic Words*, animating friends and colleagues to submit contributions and providing some himself. He knew his brother well, inquiring at one point, "Have you anything else in the stocks to fill up the gaping void when your present labor shall be completed?", then answering himself, "doubtless several irons are already in the fire," and adding an essential note, "I hope the next may be a very lucrative one" (20 February 1845; LOA 21:16). His numerous chatty letters convey family news and birthday congratulations, acknowledge letters and gifts, and offer advice. "I wish that you could indulge in the sport [haymaking]" he wrote, "as a little recreation from your upper story both of house & body" (20 June 1845; LOA 20:26). Although there seem to be no extant letters to him from James, Thomas's eighty-two letters in the Edinburgh collection make reference to them and attest to the closeness of the family ties, which was carried on as well in the next generation in the correspondence between Halliwell and his nephew Thomas, the son of his brother Thomas.

A measure of the intensity of the family ties was Halliwell's—and the Halliwells'—response to the unexpected death of his eldest brother, Richard, eight years his senior. Like the other members of the family, Richard was an active supporter of Halliwell's scholarship, himself a Fellow of the Society of Antiquaries and a member of the Historical Society of Science and the British Archaeological Association. He provided Halliwell with residence at his home at 10 Fitzroy Street and the company of his wife and two sons. He was, with William Lovell, Halliwell's lawyer and financial adviser. His sudden death on 7 September 1845 in the midst of the British Museum affair was deeply felt. Mrs. Halliwell, normally sketchy and reserved in her diary, describes his last days with unstudied detail and frankness:

1 September. Richard seem easier & more cheerful all the afternoon.
2 September. Richard so ill we think he cannot last long ... Richard had a dreadful night last night. James wrote for his brother Thos. to come from Wrington in Somersetshire.
3 September. Richard very faint & weak all the morning ... Dr Wootton & Mr Turner came in about 1/2 p. 12 & both agreed as to Richards complaint which seems to be dropsy. Dr W. gave him over. Thomas arrived at 6 o'c. & found Richard much altered. James quite overcome about his poor brother & was hysterical at night.
4 September. Richard is getting rapidly worse. He slept a little last night but it was through taking an opiate & he is very faint and weak today ... Got James & Lou to work a little to distract their attention. Mrs Lovell left. Mr Lovell & I & James met Mrs Chard [Richard's mother-in-law] at the Railway.
5 September. James & I called up at 2 o'c this morning to see poor Richard

who called us one by one into his bedroom & took leave of us. He prayed
with Thomas & seemed quite happy all day & wishing to die. He made us
all drink tea up in his room & at night I asked Thos to read the Visitation
for the Sick & the Burial Service which he did. We all prayed for him.
After it was over he knew us all & took leave of him. It was a very
affecting scene - he was much exhausted & wandering & prayed to die
soon.

6 September. Richard suffers dreadful agony, but is conscious & knows us.
He had a presentiment he should die at 5 o'c this morning ... Mr Turner
came and gave Richard a very strong opiate which eased him & caused
sleep. I sat up with him till 12 o'c with Sarah's mother tonight & then
woke Sarah [Richard's wife].

7 September. Richard easier & quite cheerful & would have some dessert set
out on his table. Mr Turner came & found him apparently better & gave
him medicine–he sunk afterwards however & died in Church times about
1/2 p. 11 in Mr Turners arms without a sigh ... Richard was prayed for in
Church this morning. Saw Richard after he had been dead for a short time
... Poor Mr H & all the family sadly afflicted at their loss.

10 September. Copied out the verses James wrote on Richard.

13 September. Mr Halliwell, Thomas and James went with Richards corpse
to London by railway. They met Mr Lovell at Paddington & they all went
to Kensal Green Cemetery where they buried him. They all lunched at
Mrs. Ords in Upper Berkeley Street & returned to supper this evening at
9 o'c. We all went into mourning.

The extent of the family's being "sadly affected at their loss" is further
illustrated in a letter of Halliwell's from Islip a month later to his father,
who with his wife was attending Sarah and the children in London: "Louy
I fear is not quite well. She does not sleep well, and her nerves have
evidently been much shaken by the recent sad event. I did not mention
this before, but as she does not seem to get better, thought I had better
tell you of it, as I am rather at fault what to do. There is nothing to be at
all uneasy about in any way, as she is not ill; it is only the nerves, the least
noise frightening her, especially in the evening, and the house has been
much more untied since you left. Henrietta thinks if it is not inconvenient
to you a short visit to London might dispel these glooms; but if you can't
very well have her we must manage to amuse her as well as possible" (19
October 1845; LOA 10:6). Richard died so suddenly that a will was never
completed (or, if so, never found). It remained for the family to provide
for his widow, Sarah Ann, and her two children. This was done willingly
by the Halliwells.

Letters of consolation from his friends followed: from Wright (9 September 1845; LOA 15:83), Pettigrew (10 September 1845; LOA 22:35), and Planché (10 September 1845; LOA 21:93). But the sustaining force in Halliwell's life and career in these years, as later, was his wife, Henrietta, who provided him with congenial domesticity, a well-run household, and a constant flow of friends and visitors, as well as skillful and willing scholarly assistance in the form of reading, collating, and copying. One letter from a host at this time is enough to illustrate their particular intimacy:

My dearest Jamie

You are a dear good fellow to write so soon. I wanted to hear very much how you got down to Warwick, for after you left we had a tremendous storm and thunder and lightening is not so nice to travel in. And now about the contents of your epistle. I dont care about going to old Newdegates, so dont you think you had better go alone there and have the day to yourself and then meet me at Coventry in the evening this would do if I came by a later train and if you were not at the station when I arrived I could get out and sit in the waiting room with my boxes till you came. I could if you thought it better come by the early train and meet you at Coventry & we cd go to Newdegates together but I think that wd entail more expense because we should want a fly I suppose to go in and there would be my boxes though perhaps I could leave those at the station. I think altogether it would be better for me not to go there and then I should not interfere with any of your plans for the day. Will you write and tell me what you think about my coming by a later train & whether it would not be better. Your father is not at home but your mother thinks I had better do as I say come in the evening only you must be very particular and tell me what o'clock I must start from Euston Square and *be sure and say whether the ticket is only to be made out to Coventry* as the Governor will be in a fantigue.

I have not heard from Mary [her sister] so I suppose all is right–if anything occurs I will write tomorrow. I am quite well and have not watered the garden once since you left. Baby too is quite well and sends a kiss to Papa. Mrs Wright is not arrived but we expect her every minute. No letters at all for you.

Did you see in Saturdays Lit. Gaz. in the Notice to Correspondents a letter about Shakespeare's marriage Bond & Sir R. Phillipps which I presume means Papa. They seem to insinuate that he has prigged it dont they? It is a great shame for he was so particular to leave it where he found it in Edgars Tower. Now pray dont forget & write all about the train. I dont mind a bit waiting for you at Coventry & if I was hungry could easily get something to grub–and it wont signify how late we get to Mary's. When you have *fixed* I will write and tell her. Adieu with our united best love and wishes for you to have a capital week of fun & believe me ever, Yr most affectionate wife H Halliwell (19 July 1847; LOA 55:42).

Henrietta was, ironically enough, both a source of strength and also of vulnerability. Her irascible father, Thomas Phillipps, could never come to terms with her marriage to Halliwell. Or, more precisely, from the very beginning he could only accept the marriage on his own terms. After the initial negotiations relating to the marriage had failed–they were in the main financial–he did not give up his campaign to blacken the name and so ruin the career of his son-in-law. And at the same time he persisted in torturing his daughter with charges of filial disrespect and disloyalty, challenging her repeatedly to choose between her husband and him. He did not hesitate to refer to the British Museum affair as a "judgement against you for having broken the 4th Commandment by disobeying your Father" (25 August 1845; Phil-Rob d.247:116). In the same letter he fanatically suggested (crossed out but thoroughly legible), "I think your best plan will be to obtain a divorce before the Trial comes on," adding maliciously, "for if he is convicted and transported your children [there was only one in 1845] will not be able to inherit anything." Henrietta's constant attempts at reconciliation–her unceasing pleas for forgiveness, her grief at missing certain appointments with him and their unsatisfactory meetings, all expressed with a contriteness as excessive as it was unnecessary, were toyed with by a heartless father whose questionable compassion was apparent in his avowing, as always, that he was sorry to have afflicted her but "thought it better to give you a hint of what the world thought than let the blow come upon you suddenly" (20 January 1846; Phil-Rob d.139:4). It is a testament to her love of Halliwell and the stability of their marriage that Henrietta, full of distress and heavy with remorse, should resist her father and stand by her husband–and that over a period of some thirty years of relentless, even vicious intimidation and persecution.

That persecution also took the form of tantalizing negotiations. There was always the tease of closeness and then the squelch of rejection, even among those not directly involved. Thus William Shoberl could have no "objection" to forwarding a letter from Halliwell to Phillipps, "trust[ing] a good understanding will shortly be resolved between yourself and him" (10 October 1845; LOA 24:38); Wright could suggest, "Perhaps I might bring him [Phillipps] to see you for half an hour" (30 August 1846; LOA 25:55). And yet at the same time Halliwell and Henrietta were not simply passive in their response or weathering the storm with stoic fortitude. It is not too much to say that Phillipps was more desperate for money than for affection.[98] At one point, as the British Museum affair was reaching its climax, Phillipps sought £50,000 from the Halliwells (Diary, 19 March 1846), insisting that Halliwell had promised it. And so, as such events dictate, the matter became still another legal one. Lovell had hardly finished with the British Museum affair when he was already involved in what was to be the long-lasting litigation of the Halliwells versus Thomas Phillipps. For all the charges evident in the "injured" father's megalo-maniacal attacks on his daughter,[99] the reality of the matter was that since he had no male heir his entire estate would fall to Henrietta. And the Halliwells were examining the legal details. Lord William Somerset replied to Henrietta's inquiry that he could not say who was co-trustee with him in her mother's marriage settlement and referred her to the solicitor J. C. Straford (31 August 1846; LOA 27:98). Straford in turn sent a copy of the marriage settlement to Halliwell (14 September 1846; LOA 14:96) and acknowledged receipt of £3.15.6 for his charges (26 September 1846; LOA 25:38). A letter from the father of one of Henrietta's friends, D. C. Moylan, a solicitor, answered Halliwell's inquiry as "best I can without waiting to consider it or to Enquire the particulars of the V.C.'s Judgment" and clearly established the legal arena in which a long battle was to be staged: "You are aware that any restriction upon Marriage is against the general policy of the Law of England. A Husband has a special Interest in the widowhood of his wife, which may be held to counter-balance the public Interest. Not so however with a stranger, & I should think in the case you put, a Court of Equity would consider the limitation as a restraint upon Marriage & consequently invalid" (9 September 1846; LOA 25:26). The case was to continue, and for many years.

98. Henrietta's sister Kate was also a victim of her father's avariciousness. In a letter about this time to Henrietta, Emma Molyneux reported that Mrs. Fenwick "does not like her son to marry Kate unless yr Papa will settle £3000 upon her & besides this give her 100£ p. annum–it is not likely he will do this–particularly since yr account of his recent purchases" (17 November 1846; LOA 221:9).

99. In a not untypical example he wrote: "You are just mistaken in saying that I had declared I wd blast all yr prospects in life. I never sd any thing of the kind, & some enemy of yours must have told you otherwise. But I might have said that *you* had blasted all *my* prospects in life, which you have, as well as yr own for nobody will esteem you hereafter in the same degree, as they wd have done had you not committed this *faux pas*" (17 June 1845; Phil-Rob d.135:116).

7

Labors in the Vineyard
Literary Archaeology and Lexicography

Despite the pressures of the British Museum and British Archaeological Association affairs, as well as other professional and personal strains, Halliwell worked on, producing as separate works in 1846, in addition to the *Letters of Kings*, editions of *The Marriage of Wit and Wisdom* for the Shakespeare Society and *The Romance of Sir Tryamoure* for the Percy, and in 1847 the two-volume *Dictionary of Archaic and Provincial Words* for John Russell Smith, *The Most Pleasant Song of Lady Bessy* for the Percy Society, and *Morte Arthure*, which he published privately. The sponsors are significant, for they were, on the whole, sources of support during the crises Halliwell was undergoing. He was still a member of the Council of the Shakespeare Society: as the British Museum affair was reaching a climax, he was informed by the secretary, F. Guest Tomlins, that the Society "unanimously resolved that your continued & invaluable services to the Society quite placed you beyond the general rule and therefore your name was not entered on the lists of those to retire. This was nothing but the commonest acknowledgement of your attention and incessant services to us" (14 April 1846; LOA 9:39). Bolton Corney added, "I doubt if there was a single vote against you" (15 April 1846; LOA 26:46). Collier, who was director, had said a few words in his favor, and Corney "followed his example"; and Halliwell could always count on his loyal friends Pettigrew and Planché, among other Council members. He would continue to contribute books and articles until its dissolution in 1853. He was also a member of the Council of the Percy Society, for whom he produced eleven works before it dissolved in 1853 and where he could rely on many trusted friends on the Council, such as W. H. Black, T. Crofton Croker, Fairholt, Jerdan, Pettigrew, and of course Wright, who was secretary and treasurer. And for his favorite publisher, the enterprising John Russell Smith, with whom he had developed an open and reliable relationship, he produced eleven works until 1853.

Halliwell's edition of *The Marriage of Wit and Wisdom* hardly reflects any of the external tensions he was undergoing. The reprinting of this "ancient interlude" continues his interest, as well as the Society's, in early popular literature, especially drama. A brief seven-page introduction and fourteen pages of notes provide the customary frame. Halliwell's tribute to Lambert Larking for discovering the manuscript, as he had the Dering manuscript of *Henry IV* (which Halliwell edited for the Shakespeare Society in 1845) and to the generosity of Edward Dering enables him to touch on the current discussion of the nature of antiquarian pursuits: for one thing, to open "to the world the treasures deposited in the rich archives of our ancient families" (v) and, for another–and pointedly–the necessity "to pause before they [literary antiquaries] substantiate conjectures and probabilities as matters of fact, and hesitate at assertions respecting the identity or non-existence of MSS. and rare books" (vi). Halliwell even points a finger at the much-respected Alexander Dyce, also a member of the Council, for asserting in his edition of *Sir Thomas More* that "no such drama ever existed" and chastises an anonymous defence of Dyce's view"[100] as "one of the many instances of the want of sufficient discrimination in antiquarian conjectures–conjectures which not unfrequently prove of incalculable injury to the interests of real science" (vii-viii). Since the very existence of the manuscript is proof enough, Halliwell was able to avoid offending Dyce. And it is noteworthy that the "striking lesson" he teaches does not lead him to the dead end of intransigence. While acknowledging the pitfalls of the "enthusiastic inquirer," he is nevertheless captive of his calling, for, he all too humanly concludes, "however we may deprecate the danger of hasty deductions, and the liability of falling into them sometimes imperceptibly, which the greatest caution cannot always avoid, there is a charm invested in the subject that renders the pursuit one of those most engaging entertainments in literature" (xi-xii). The immediate reference is of course to Halliwell's indirect identification of himself as the "enthusiastic inquirer [who] might see in this the germ of a character [Dr. Caius] introduced in the 'Merry Wives of Windsor'" (xi)–an almost whimsical touch noted by the otherwise friendly reviewer in the *Literary Gazette*, who "suspect[ed] ... it is a fanciful conjecture, and must be left to Mr. Halliwell's own imagination, too prone to find models for Shakspere which never entered the study of our great dramatist" (4 July 1846, p. 597). Finally, even the addition of twenty brief "illustrations of Shakespeare and the early English drama" constitutes a familiar feature of the Halliwell enterprise, enabling

100. A Ballad-monger, "The Marriage of Wit and Wisdom," *Shakespeare Society's Papers*, 2:10 (1845), 76-8.

him to almost double the size of the volume and to make use of material from his ample supply (both tried economic factors). Characteristically, he drew from his projects past, present, and future. Among the examples from the past, "Forman on Shakespeare's Plays" (pp. 111-16); from the present (his forthcoming *Life of Shakespeare*), "Shakespeare's Birth-Place" (p. 116) and "The Property of Shakespeares" (pp. 143-5); from the future (his folio edition of Shakespeare), "Shakespeare's Tempest" (pp. 81-4) and a ballad on Troilus and Cressida (pp. 101-5).[101] And the manuscript sources illustrate, as always, his presence in such favorite haunts as the Ashmolean Museum and the Bodleian Library, visited often during his residence in Islip. Interesting too is the appearance of an engraving of the seal of Sir Thomas Lucy (p. 142) by Fairholt, who was providing pictorial material for the *Life of Shakespeare* and the folio edition.

Halliwell's two publications for the Percy Society in this period are of little importance beyond demonstrating his and the Society's uninterrupted interest in reprinting rare manuscripts of early popular literature. *The Romance of Sir Tryamoure* (1846) is a simple reprint of a piece from a collection in the Cambridge Public Library, identified in a scant note "To the Reader" and followed by two and a half pages of spare notes. Of added but unsubstantiated interest may be a fragment from the Rawlinson collection in the Bodleian which Halliwell has been suspected of stealing.[102] *The Most Pleasant Song of Bessy* is fairly insignificant, with a barely four-page preface and no notes at all. Both works, appropriately enough, received little attention in the main journals. There were, to be sure, also occasional efforts, done with the left hand, so to speak, such as the slight notes in 1846 and 1847 on Shakespeare, old jest books, John Claptone the alchemist, and the catalogue of Thomas Markaunt's books.[103]

The apparently routine reprint in 1847 of *Morte Arthure: The Alliterative Romance of the Death of King Arthur* resembles the works illustrating early

101. See Volume 1, p. 332, and Volume 12, p, 307, of the folio edition.
102. See pp. 139-40.
103. "Lime in Sack: Shakspere," *The Literary Gazette*, 11 April 1846, pp. 346-7; "Old Jest-books," *Bentley's Miscellany*, 20 (1846), 594-8; "Some Account of the Life and Writings of John Claptone, a Philosopher and Alchemist of Winchester, in the Reign of Henry VIII," *Proceedings of the British Archaeological Association*, August 1845, pp. 40-4; "A Catalogue of the Books Bequeathed to Corpus Christi College, Cambridge (A.D. 1439), by Thomas Markaunt," *Publications of the Cambridge Antiquarian Society*, No. XIV (1847), Miscellaneous Communications, Part I, No. III, pp. 15-20; "Notes on Passages in Shakespeare" and "A Poem Containing Notices of Ben Jonson, Shakespeare, Massinger, &c.," *Shakespeare Society's Papers*, 3:36 (1847), 33-9 and 172-4.

English popular literature which were a staple of Halliwell's efforts for the various societies: a brief preface, a text based on a manuscript from a literary archaeological site (Lincoln Cathedral), brief notes. Evident also are other hallmarks of the Halliwell enterprise: the overcoming of initial resistance–his proposal had been declined by the Roxborough Club (5 March 1845; LOA 17:75), the suspicion being that the decision was somehow connected with the rupture of the British Archaeological Association–and the judicious dedication to Lord Conyngham, the president, at once a declaration of loyalty to the Association and the discipline, which reads, "It is a source of great satisfaction to me to be the means of rescuing it from its unmerited obscurity, and more so in having the opportunity of inscribing it in its modern dress to one who will appreciate its literary importance, and whose strenuous exertions in the cause of archaeology merit the respect of every antiquary" (vii). What is striking, however, is that the work was privately printed, limited to seventy-five copies, twenty-five on thick paper and fifty on thin paper. It is the first such venture to emerge from Brixton Hill and represents not only Halliwell's impatience and dissatisfaction with some publishers and the wrangling in some societies,[104] but, and perhaps mainly, his desire for independence, artistic integrity, and commercial advantage. For as a bookman he was not only interested in the technical aspects of printing–he had his own little printing press, and he even handset, however crudely, a small item which he was later to reprint more lavishly[105]–but began to develop a theory about the connection between rarity and commercial value based on his understanding of the market and his experience as producer, buyer, and seller. It is also not unlikely that he began to see the limits of the most popular of the publishing societies or perhaps even foresaw their diminishing prospects. He had only recently announced the demise of his Historical Society of Science. Furthermore it is interesting to note that the *Literary Gazette* devotes most of its review (11 September 1847, p. 658) to what it calls an "introduction of aristocracy into a literary republic." While it has "ever been the foremost to encourage cheap literature, and [is itself] an example of the public taste in that direction [it] contend[s] that a taste for the privately-printed books of limited circulation has been of great advantage to literature, for the simple reason that they would, in all probability, have remained in manuscript."

104. For example, Colburn, according to Shoberl, turned down a work on the Civil Wars as not being profitable (11 August 1845; LOA 22:25), as well as the diary of "[Humphrey] Mildmay, and a translation of Matthew Paris" (29 June 1846; LOA 26:30).
105. *Harry White His Humour So Neare as It May Be Set Forth by M. P.*

For his taste and risk-taking, Halliwell is extended the "best acknowledgements for the splendid volume he has just produced." And it is hard to deny that, being anchored in a harmonious and increasing family, he was in need of personal financial resources. As he wrote to his wife, "my dearest Harry," from the momentous Winchester meeting of the British Archaeological Society on 6 August 1845 (LOA 221:3), "It is going on very well but I am rather sick of it, and it is an inconvenient affair for ladies, as well as too expensive." Most of all perhaps, he seemed ripe for larger challenges.

The first of these was the *Dictionary of Archaic and Provincial Words, Obsolete Phrases. Proverbs, and Ancient Customs, from the Fourteenth Century*, which was published in four parts starting in 1844 and reached two volumes of more than a thousand pages on publication in 1847. It is a prime example of Halliwell's methodology. The most obvious aspect is, of course, Halliwell's preoccupation as cultural and literary archaeologist with early texts, especially early popular literature, his sense of the development of the English language over the centuries, and the necessity for compilation, illustration, and explication. As literary archaeologist he was confronted with texts written before the emergence and standardization of English. As archaeologist he was perforce a traveller and thus constantly in contact with the peculiarities of local customs, dialects, and provincialisms. The full title of his dictionary is in fact an explicit summary of his entire *oeuvre* and professional career. Hardly an edited work of his, from the very beginning, does not contain a glossary. It is not too much to say that he was inescapably a lexicographer.

Halliwell's lexicographical disposition was recognized, motivated, and nurtured by his favorite publisher, the energetic John Russell Smith. Smith was enterprising, anxious to expand his list of works dealing with the provincial dialects of England. His catalogue of 1843 lists nineteen such works. "I have been thinking of a work which is much wanted in the Literary world, and one which I should like to publish, it is a '*Glossary of Words, Customs, Proverbs, &c. from Gower & Chaucer to Shakspeare & his Contemporaries*'," he wrote Halliwell on 10 February 1842 (LOA 12:26).[106] For one reason or another, Halliwell did not take up the offer immediately, leading Smith to repeat on 6 October 1842 (LOA 33:40) that "a work of the kind [he] once proposed to you would sell," but now conceding that "it would be a work of much labour & time, and you would want no few books as you are at present situated [in Islip]." And with a bit of motivation for Halliwell's competitive instinct, an eye to the

106. See pp. 120-1.

market, and an indication of the scope the work should have, Smith
mentions that "Mr Way is doing a work of this nature for the Camden
[the *Promptorium Parvulorum*] but from what I can learn it will [be] too
much of a DuCange sort of book to suit the general reader."

Halliwell took on the assignment and with it the directions of his
publisher. "When I advertise the Dictionary," Smith did not hesitate to
say, "I shall take the liberty of dropping its Latin title, although very good
to literary men it will in haste be passed over by the 'Million'[,] the more
simple and plainer the better" (5 January 1843; LOA 15:3). His shop at 4
Old Compton Street a hub of communication and his ears open to the
gossip of his customers, Smith found it "strange that no one there [at a
"Society called the Philological Society, who meet at the London Library
rooms every month or so"] (some of my own customers) did not notice
your attempt, so as it has been announced in my catalogues ... It would be
as well to send the Secretary one of the prospectuses." Smith was
concerned about his investment and did not neglect to remind Halliwell
that if a work is to appear over a period of time, it must be "regular," for
"if the work is not brought out without disappointment to its purchasers
it will be a great drawback" (11 January 1844; LOA 15:55). But he could
be understanding and flexible as well: "I was sorry to hear you were
indisposed but I hope you are now convalescent," he assured Halliwell,
"don't fash yourself about the Dictionary, you are not tied down to
complete it by a certain day" (16 May 1844; LOA 15:18). As the work
progressed, Smith was forthcoming in his views: "The last N° strikes me
as being very brief in explanations & quotations ... In *my* opinion many of
the words beginning with *Dis* might have been left out, *I* could have
guessed what they meant" (26 August 1845; LOA 15:34). And he did not
spare the financial details. "I owe my Stationer so much money," he
admitted, "till I pay him I do not mean to order any more paper so the
Dictionary will not appear perhaps for a month" (23 May 1846; LOA
26:48). And so the collaboration functioned, and so the work came into
being.

There were others involved as well. The experience of Thomas Wright
as archaeologist, historian, and philologist was vaster than Halliwell's, and
Wright's influence on his younger friend and colleague was as
forthcoming as it was profound. In all their many collaborations and
contacts, Wright was always dominant, pouring out information, gossip,
and advice, and dictating strategy. "Now for your Dictionary," he wasted
no time in beginning a letter of 19 January 1843 (LOA 16:87) to the just-
turned- twenty-three-year-old Halliwell,

I advise you strongly to lay aside the idea of beginning with William the Conqueror. You will save yourself a great deal of trouble, and your book will be much better for it. Up to the end of the thirteenth century the whole language, all the words, and all the phrases, are obsolete, so that, since for a century after the conquest pure Saxon was spoken, and for the other century and a half semi-Saxon, you oblige yourself by the words of your title to include not only a complet [*sic*] Anglo-Saxon Dictionary, but also a Dictionary of semi-saxon and Early English. Even for the customs, allusions, &c. it would be a tremendous task to make a dictionary for this period.
If I were you I would confine it to the period since the time of Chaucer. Take Nares' Glossary—use Brand for popular customs (you might get a good deal from Hone's Every Day Book, &c.)—take the provincial words—and as many collections of proverbs as you can. Fill up from the Glossaries to Chaucer, Piers Ploughman, Weber's Romances, Ritson's publications, Percy, and as many similar works as you can get. Always give references, extracts, &c. which will triple the value of the book.

As always, he is not sparing of specific criticism and is ever alert to the larger context of reception. Responding to the actual entries, he opens a letter with "You put A.S. and A.N. after words which I doubt if they ever existed. Most people will say you invented them to fill out your book, if you dont say where you got them from. The Philological Society people will pitch into you terribly about them" (25 August 1845; LOA 15:82). And, as always, Halliwell could count on Wright's affection for him—not solely in the countless charming letters full of jokes and gossip but in times of stress, as in the attempt in a single letter (14 March 1845; LOA 15:99) to lighten Halliwell's burden with a smile ("I dreamt last night I had bought a MS. which was stolen from Trin. Coll.!") and a push ("Get on with the Dictionary, and dont fidget yourself"). It is little wonder that Halliwell capped his preface with an acknowledgment of his "chief obligations" to Wright, "whose suggestions on nearly every sheet of this work, as it was passing through the press, have been of the greatest advantage, and whose profound knowledge of Anglo-Saxon and Anglo-Norman has frequently been of essential service when the ordinary guides had been ineffectually consulted" (viii).

Works of this kind do not emerge *ab ovo* or full blown; they are necessarily cumulative. And Halliwell made full use of Wright's advice. But that does not mean he simply copied entries from existing glossaries. A comparison of his with entries in works Halliwell mentions—such as John Ray's *Collection of English Words Not Generally Used* (1674) and Robert

Nares's *Glossary* (1822)–reveals that he was relatively independent, often adopting information but then often modifying, expanding, predating, citing more specifically. The same is true of his use of Toone,[107] whom Smith had recommended: the Toone headwords may appear, but Halliwell's spellings are more standard, the definitions more precise, and the citations more extensive. And since collecting was one of his passions, Halliwell made use not only of the works that had been published but also appealed through advertisements in newspapers and periodicals to individuals throughout the country for assistance. They responded in great numbers and with intensity. Their suggestions were acknowledged, collected, evaluated, and included in the three hundred volumes of Letters of Authors he bequeathed to the University of Edinburgh. Among them are also comments from immediate colleagues and friends. Collier, for example, received the installments regularly and did not hesitate to put his finger on one of the sore points of lexicography: "The only material fault I can find ... (others may not think it a fault) is the repetition of the same words under different forms. It seems to me to occupy space needlessly, though it makes reference more easy" (14 March 1846; LOA 24:49). And if Halliwell did not seem to have had contact with the newly formed Philological Society–as he was to have later–he was nevertheless in correspondence with lexicographers like Charles Richardson, in addition to numerous others mentioned in his preface. That he was comfortable with lexicography is evident in his taking on the reviewing (anonymously, as was the practice) in the *Literary Gazette* of 23 December 1843 (pp. 822-3) of Albert Way's *Promptorium Parvulorum*.[108] His dependence on others would not be complete without mention of his wife, to whom he was much indebted for her professional assistance in all his projects, although it was not the custom to publicly announce it. As her diary amply indicates, the Halliwells, man, wife, and children, were totally dedicated to his scholarship. Almost from the moment of the marriage in 1842 entries attest to the collecting, copying, checking, and evaluating suggestions for

107. William Toone, *A Glossary and Etymological Dictionary of Obsolete and Uncommon Words* (1832).

108. That Halliwell was able to combine possible sources, financial need, and self-advertisement may be derived from his offering to write a "careful notice" of J. T. Brockett's *Glossary of North Country Words* in the *Literary Gazette* (Bodl. MS Eng.lett. d.113:233). He is likely to have written the anonymous review (19 September 1846, pp. 805-6) with its tell-tale conclusion: "Mr. Halliwell's larger undertaking, which we are glad to see so nearly completed, will, we are inclined to think, amply supply its intended place of a general glossary, to which Brockett's and others will form useful and valuable adjuncts."

the dictionary. The work was continuous and of high priority. On Christmas Eve of 1842 Mrs. Halliwell reports work on the dictionary. On 2 August 1843 "James & I worked at Dict."; on the next day "My daughter Henrietta Somerset was born at 6 o'clock this evening ... James busy with his Dict." On 9 August 1844 she notes: "My wedding day. We are both as happy as we were when married. James worked on his Dict. & Glossary." In April 1846 they are working on the dictionary "letter by letter - writing out one, correcting proofs of another." On 15 December 1846 they are "finishing off the Dict." Even Halliwell's brother, Thomas, was involved, sending word, in one instance, that his Co-Curator was contributing examples from the Somerset idiom and dialect and that he himself "hope[d] that it may very fully reward you for all your great trouble bestowed upon it" (20 February 1845; LOA 21:16).

Halliwell did not have to be reminded of the great trouble involved in such a work. His preface clearly reflects the criticism which the earlier publication of the parts in 1844 and 1845 evoked—mainly the lack of a defined philological system. He does not attempt to deny the various charges, especially the neglect of etymology which caused him to include "numerous forms the etymologist will properly regard corrupt, and which might easily have been reduced to their original sources" (vii). The perennial lexicographical challenge, the constitution of the lemma (or headword), is answered (or avoided) by a statement of the "real value of provincial words ... the important assistance they continually afford in glossing the works of our early writers" (vii). A decade before Richard Chenevix Trench published his two seminal papers presented to the Philological Society under the title *On Some Deficiencies in Our English Dictionaries*, Halliwell did not intend to prepare a dictionary—the original title was "glossary"—but a helpmate for the ad hoc understanding of certain words in certain texts. This does not exclude the application of the gloss to other texts but very considerably limits it, resembling the glosses Halliwell customarily supplied for his edited reprints. At the same time, however, and for the same reason, the work addressed to "unskilled readers"–"unskilfull persons," interestingly enough, were also the target of the first hard-word dictionary, Robert Cawdrey's *Table Alphabeticall* (1604)–and its organization is appropriately simple and direct. Faced with a "vast quantity of words which had escaped the notice of all the compilers of provincial glossaries [whose] arrangement added immeasurably to the labour" (vii), Halliwell avoided the "trouble of arranging long lists of words, and separating more dialectical forms" (vii) by designating graphic units as words and then merely alphabetizing the proudly announced 51,027 he had collected and evaluated. As a result, there is an unavoidable inflation of headwords, as in *alder, alder-best, alder-first, alder-formest, alder-highest, alder-last, alder-lest, alder-liefer, alder-liefest, alder-lowest, alder-mest, alder-truest, alder-werst, alder-wisist*. That this alphabetical list is interspersed with different etymological forms, such as *alder, alderes, aldekar, alderlings, aldermanry*, and *alderne*, may, Halliwell admits, not foster the "literary entertainment of professed students" (vii), but as Collier remarked on noting the repetition, "it makes reference more easy." This would apply to other structural features, such as a lack of systematic or predictable cross-references (as, for example, between *armyte* and *eremite*, or *arnd, arrand*, and *hernde*).

The entries themselves share only one feature: a brief, often one-word, gloss. It depends upon the particular sensitivity of the compiler to the nuances of synonymy in determining the particular meaning in a particular passage. Halliwell's alternatives "Foolish; stupid; dull; strange" for *nice* ("It occurs in Shakespeare," he remarks) may not coincide with "unimportant, trifling" (as required in *Romeo* 5.2.18). Generally, but not always, the gloss is followed and concluded by an indication of the dialect–e.g. Devon, North, Chesh., and the like. Although Halliwell made a point of stating that the "greatest care has been taken to render the references and quotations accurate" (vii), they are most often simply the name of an author–e.g. "Bulled. Swollen. *Jonson*" or a work–e.g. "Frouze. To curl. Florio, p. 247." Halliwell is best, not unexpectedly, in the citations from manuscripts, which consist of quotation, manuscript identification, and folio number.

Halliwell also included a survey, "The English Provincial Dialects" (ix–xxxvi), listing a few of the main phonetic or grammatical characteristics of the various counties. Once again, the same reservations apply. "Believing that the principal use of the study of English dialects consists in the explanation of archaisms," Halliwell "has not attempted that research which would be necessary to understand their [the dialects'] history" (x). Furthermore, recognizing the "probability, many cases the certainty, of an essential distinction between the language of literature and that of the natives of a county" (xi), and with it the "want of authentic specimens," he is able to justify (however lamely) his resorting to an alphabetical listing of the counties instead of attempting a philological structure. Seizing the moment, Smith extracted the survey and published it separately in 1847 as *An Historical Sketch of the Provincial Dialects of England.*

From the beginning of its appearance in parts the reviews of the dictionary in the main journals were all aware of the limitations of the undertaking. They all acknowledge the remarkable engagement of the author and the great need for a work of this nature. But, as was to be expected, they were divided in their estimation of the competence of the author and the success of the enterprise. The anonymous—and as yet unidentified—reviewers in the *Athenaeum* and the *Literary Gazette* were, for once, in agreement in their appraisal of Halliwell: "Mr. Halliwell, though habitually too off-handed to be altogether satisfactory, is ... as well qualified, by industry, ability, and previous study, to be the editor as any man living" (*The Athenaeum*, 16 November 1844, p. 1046); "Mr. Halliwell ... has performed his task in a manner that far exceeds our best hopes" (*The Literary Gazette*, 4 January 1845, p. 6). Both agree as well that this "very laborious undertaking [is] a task in which it is difficult to succeed, and almost impossible not to leave some room for criticism" (*The Literary Gazette*, pp. 5-6), that "it is a work ... that, in the first instance, must be imperfect" (*The Athenaeum*, p. 1046). Both come to much the same conclusion: "We are not inclined to seek very curiously for faults in a work of such obvious difficulty, when, even if it be imperfect, it cannot fail to be useful" (*The Athenaeum*, p. 1046); "[It] deserves, merely on account of its general and great utility, what we hope it will have, an extensive circulation ... We think [it] may be considered one of the most remarkable productions of the day" (*The Literary Gazette*, p. 6). In briefer notices both the *Spectator* (2 November 1844, p. 1050) and the *Critic* (1 January 1845], pp. 266-7) also stressed the utility of the work, while admitting the obvious shortcomings.

The anonymous reviewer in the *Gentleman's Magazine* was not, however, so generously indulgent. In a long review–n.s. 23 (January 1845), 61-6–he is unwilling to concede utility and popularity priority over a lucid and scholarly arrangement, devoting much of a colorful–"Mr. Halliwell is the victim of a very extraordinary passion ... he is absolutely enamoured of a very ugly and derepid [*sic*] old witch, Cacography" (p. 62)–and detailed criticism of what he considers the inflated, diffuse, misleading, and wasteful features which result from the "want of etymological arrangement and connection" (p. 64). The rejection is all the more intense because it applies only to the letters A and B, despite the cold comfort of the reviewer's assurance that after this first notice of an "extensive and important undertaking" he "shall be glad if we find that our remarks in any respect conduce to greater caution and consideration, and above all to a more lucid arrangement, in future portions of the work" (p. 66). But Halliwell was, of course, committed to his plan and could hardly alter it. And it is fairly obvious that the reviewer, even if correct in his appraisal, was reacting to the person and career of Halliwell. His very opening is a salvo:

Mr. Halliwell has now for some years made his name exceedingly conspicuous in antiquarian literature, not only by his appearance in most of the associations intended for its advancement, either as an actual or an honorary member, but more particularly in the title-pages of various publications, which must be accounted, even by himself, rather by their number than their importance (pp. 61-2).

It is followed by volleys:

· Mr. Halliwell's Dictionary we can only assimilate to a tessellated pavement, or a patchwork counterpane. Contenting himself with putting together an alphabet of archaisms, provincialisms, technicalisms, and solecisms, with a sprinkling of 'proverbs' and 'customs,' he performs a task not very different to those wherein he has previously distinguished himself, whilst editing his multifarious succession of *libretti*, and, it must be feared, as totally deficient of any definite design or substantial conclusion (p. 62).

It is tempting but futile to guess the name of the reviewer. But even if the date were not considered–the British Museum affair was beginning to bubble–and the personal bias ignored, it is all too obvious that he comes from the long-established opposing faction. What is also undeniable is that he and they oppose the pragmatic, if not programmatic, view of scholarship as consisting of collecting and accumulating documents and then mainly disseminating them. What may be at issue here–as in the establishment of publishing and learned societies, the trend toward expanding educational opportunities, and the reform of their institutions–is the propagation and popularization of learning. They were never far from the center of Halliwell's thinking as scholar and freelancer and were to be an issue throughout his life.

Never content to do one thing at a time, Halliwell was also busy with his *Life of Shakespeare*, among other projects. As always, whether researching or attending meetings of various organizations in and outside of London, he was constantly underway. In 1847 his concentration on Shakespeare involved visits to Stratford-upon-Avon and signalled the beginning of a long relationship and voluminous correspondence with W. O. Hunt, the town clerk. For his *Life of Shakespeare* Halliwell needed Hunt's help in getting copies and transcripts, as well a making the acquaintance of the members of the Corporation in Stratford and Birmingham. Letters to and from Hunt were over the years normally long and detailed, a mixture of precise business and casual cordiality. Two early

ones, of 21 October 1847 (Folger Y.c.1236[1]) and 27 October 1847
(Folger Y.c.1236[2]) are typical, containing Halliwell's inquiries (on
Shakespeare's mark), requests (transcripts), reports (on the progress of the
Life), and thanks (for introducing him to Birmingham). From the
Shakespeare Inn he wrote enthusiastically to his wife on 26 September
1847 (LOA 221:1):

My dearest Harry
I had expected to have finished my work yesterday but could not manage
it so you will probably not see me till Wednesday. Mrs Jeaffreson sent me
a pressing invitation to stop there two or three days which I
decline–Stratford having superior attractions. It is impossible for the
people here to have shown me greater kindness or attention–all the chests
of records in the Council Chamber have been opened for me, besides the
large box Mr Hunt has that I came for principally. Mr Hunt is the leading
man here and has made it his business to assist me in every possible way–I
dine with him today, & Dr Thompson has asked me to dinner on Tuesday
which I have only conditionally accepted, as I am thinking of leaving her
by the evening coach on Tuesday, sleeping at Dr Jeaffresons, and so
returning to Town on Wednesday, when I hope to find you all well–My
best love to all & Believe me My dearest Harry
Yr attached husband
J. O. Halliwell
A grand dinner at the Stratford Club (at the old White Lion in Henley
Street)–venison with fat nearly an inch thick in the grand cut. It was lost
on me–I didnt think it half so good as a haunch of mutton.

And it was in July 1847 that Halliwell's presence at the meeting of the
British Archaeological Association in Warwick and Stratford to discuss
the Shakespeare properties must also have helped nurture the germ of an
idea of establishing and shaping a proper national shrine to Shakespeare
in the form of accurately restored buildings, a museum and a library. The
impetus came from several directions, The news in 1847 was that
Shakespeare's birthplace was put up for sale. Following the lead of the
Royal Shakespearean Club of Stratford, a London Committee for the
purchase of the house was formed, and at a general meeting at the
Thatched House Tavern on 26 August 1847 it began mobilizing sentiment
and funds. The president was Viscount Morpeth, the vice president the
Earl of Ellesmere; Peter Cunningham was treasurer and F. G. Tomlins
honorary secretary. The chairman was Collier and among the well-known
personalities on the Committee were Dickens, Leigh Hunt, Bulwer

Lytton, Macready, Thomas Moore, and Tennyson, as well as the prominence from various societies and public life. Halliwell was among them, as was Thomas Wright, who characteristically was only too aware of the frictions and fractions such efforts evoke: "I should think they have not got money enough to do anything. I am cautious of showing myself, as I dont want to subscribe. As far as I can hear, Theodosius Purland is the man who figures most at these committee meetings. [Charles Roach] Smith is very angry with him, for the way he troubles him about it. Purland says he is going to give a subscription to the Shakespeare House *in the name of his cat!* Only fancy 'Purland and his cat' glorified among the worshippers at the 'temple'" (12 September 1847; LOA 39:37). Still, money poured in. As patrons of the Shakespeare Memorial Queen Victoria contributed £100 and Prince Albert £250; among others the Earl of Ellesmere, the Corporation of Stratford, Matthew White Ridley, and J. Spear gave £100 each. The sale took place on 25 September 1847. Peter Cunningham's offer of £3000 on behalf of the committee secured the house. Halliwell was present at the sale, standing between Collier and George Godwin in a drawing by J. W. Archer which appeared in the *Illustrated London News* (25 September 1847, p. 208). It cannot be said that Halliwell played a role of any significance in the purchase. But he was present, was establishing his contacts, had projects which connected him with Stratford. And as Cunningham's report of 6 December 1847 of the finances indicated, the £4400 in liabilities for the purchase and other expenses were not covered by the £2900 in subscriptions and the £1000 from a benefit performance. The future was open and inviting, and not just for the collection of the £500 still wanting. For it was the wish of the Committee "before making the Property over to the Crown," continued Cunningham, "to place it under the superintendence of some Person honourably connected with Dramatic Literature, and to remove certain premises adjoining, which injure the appearance, and endanger the safety of the House" (SBT ER 1/129:189). And of course there were other properties as well which needed rescuing and structuring. Not long after, Halliwell was already travelling regularly to Stratford to arrange the records of the Corporation. Given his interests, abilities, and ambitions, it cannot be surprising that Stratford and Halliwell were to be inseparable for the next forty years.

+++

The next five years, 1848 to 1853, were enormously productive. Having survived one crisis after another, and apparently resolved to master any that might arise, the twenty-eight-year-old Halliwell increased the tempo and sharpened the focus of his enterprise. The forty-six separate works which emerged from Avenue Lodge, Brixton Hill, Surrey, are at once a continuation and a development of his professional skills and horizon.

His work for the Shakespeare Society enhanced his earlier efforts. *The Moral Play of Wit and Science* (1848) is of much the same mold as the *Marriage of Wit and Wisdom* (1847). The fifty-four page text, based on a single manuscript of the time of Henry VIII, is framed by a short preface (v-x) and brief notes (pp. 122-8). Much of the preface and notes is devoted, however, not to the play but to a "remarkably curious" by John Heywood and other Elizabethans which are also found in the manuscript. This is all recognizable, as is Halliwell's equally characteristic *apologia pro vita sua* in his swipe at "some writers who deal in generalization, and who seem to forget that, by the incessant collection of minutiae, information of real value is almost invariably elicited" (viii). Not immediately recognizable but of growing importance is Halliwell's awareness of the vastness of documentary sources and the limitations of personal resources. Referring to the notices of John Redford, the author, which are preserved in the "voluminous records at the Rolls' House Record Office, and at the Chapter House," Halliwell is "obliged to confess that the time and patience required for the faithful prosecution of such inquiries can scarcely be willingly expended on names of inferior note" (viii). The confession is at once, and perhaps for the first time, an admission of the laboriousness of the work of the antiquary and a clear setting of priorities on the part of one who had hitherto worked joyfully and indiscriminately, in Ellis's phrase, as one of the "Labourers in the Vineyard of Archaeology." "For it requires," he continues his self-revelation, "no small exercise of self-denial to tear one's self away from the tomes of Marlowe, Shakespeare, and Jonson, to be choked for weeks together by musty rolls of ancient vellum, or to wade through centuries of indices. This is a service I have compelled myself to perform for Shakespeare" (viii). It is difficult to deny that this confession may be interpreted as an excuse for the numerous hasty and often careless works he produced and would continue to produce. Even the benefits of simply making older texts readily available in modern reprints for a modern general public may not be enough to justify the relaxation of the strict stipulations of scholarship. The review in the *Literary Gazette* (20 March 1848, p. 215) severely criticized the Shakespeare Society for having only "produced in eight years *six* works directly illustrating Shakspere" and instead of being "very active in hunting up trifles about the wives and children of the old actors ... had

better turn their attention to matters of real utility, and publications that
bear some reference to their patron saint." Be that as it may, Halliwell's
vocabulary is one of addiction and devotion: "This is a service I have
compelled myself to perform for Shakespeare, but can we name one other
writer whose personal history is sufficiently important to be purchased at
so dear an expense?" (viii).

The focus of Halliwell's "service" was Shakespeare and the approach
was that of the literary archaeologist. Shakespeare's personal history could
only be determined through exploration, documentation, and
reconstruction. The indivisibility of objective and method is apparent in
the articles Halliwell wrote in the period in which he was preparing his *Life
of Shakespeare* and the folio edition of his works. Of the articles in the
Shakespeare Society's Papers (4:1849), three are illustrations of early
vernacular domestic literature and contemporary figures and events.[109]
They are the archaeologist's contribution to the study of early English
literature and thus supply elements of the context in which Shakespeare
can best be understood. Similarly, and by now not surprisingly, although
only two of the twelve papers for the British Archaeological Association
deal more or less directly with Shakespeare,[110] many of the others could
well have been published by the Shakespeare Society as collateral
information. The account of Captain Cox's library, for example, is to be
found in both journals, as well as in a separate publication.[111]

Halliwell's emphasis on documentation for the understanding of
Shakespeare had his highest priority. And Halliwell had applied it early
and consistently. The one article for the *Shakespeare Society's Papers* (4:13
[1849]) in which Shakespeare is directly treated, "A Few Observations on

109. "Some Account of the Popular Tracts Which Composed the Library of
Captain Cox, a Humourist Who Took a Part in the Hock Tuesday Play Performed
before Queen Elizabeth at Kenilworth, in 1575," pp. 17-35; "Extract from a
Manuscript at Oxford, Containing a Memorandum of the Complaints against
Dethick, the Herald Who Made the Grant of Arms to John Shakespeare," pp. 57-
62; and "Dispute between the Earl of Worcester's Players and the Corporation of
Leicester in 1586; from the Records of that City," pp. 145-6.

110. "On the Credibility of Traditional Anecdotes Respecting Shakespeare, More
Especially Regarding the Story of His Stealing Deer from Sir Thomas Lucy's
Park," *Journal,* 3 (1848), 164-7, and "The Passages of Shakespeare's First Love,"
Proceedings of the Fifth Annual Congress, August 1848, pp. 339-42.

111. It was read on 21 July 1847 at the Congress of the British Archaeological
Association at Warwick and reported in its *Journal,* 3 (1848), 160. It appeared also
in the *Shakespeare Society's Papers*, 4:40 (1849), 17-35, and was separately published
by John Russell Smith in 1849.

the Composition of the 'Midsummer Night's Dream'," is a statement of Halliwell's critical position: "Shakespeare's object in writing was to please an audience–to fill a theatre. We are not even to presume that he disregarded the opinion of the denizens of the gallery" (p. 130). This would explain and justify the introduction of Bottom and his fellows. "For," Halliwell concludes, taking his stand against those who would treat Shakespeare *in vacuo*, "it is inconsistent with every known fact of his life to suppose that his dramas were formed without a reference to the taste of the individuals before whom they were to be produced" (p. 132). This position, it must be stressed, does in no way dampen Halliwell's appreciation of the "unlimited extent of his [Shakespeare's] imagination"; on the contrary, the various groups in the play are "wonderfully connected ... the inexplicable work of a mind that has passed the 'thin partitions' which separate genius from insanity" (p. 131). "Wonder" has a firm place in Halliwell's critical vocabulary. it may well have supplied the dynamism of what his friend and colleague Charles Roach Smith called his "archaeological criticism."

Halliwell was, in fact, attempting to integrate various, apparently conflicting, elements into his archaeology. In the preface to his *Remarks of M. Karl Simrock, on the Plots of Shakespeare's Plays* (1850), his last work for the Shakespeare Society, he very clearly states that criticism consists of interrelated points of view: "Criticism on the works of Shakespeare may be classed into three principal divisions: I. *Philological*, including the grammatical construction used by the poet, idiomatic phraseology, explanations of obsolete words, and the systems of metre. II. *Philosophical*, including every kind of aesthetic or psychological commentary. III. *Historical*, including inquiries into the sources of the plots, local and contemporary illustrations of realities (not words), costume, and all that relates to history, geography, chronology, &c." (vii). Halliwell never wavered in his belief that the "earnest" or "intelligent inquirer" must be versed in "each of these departments," however much he was aware that a "capability, indeed, for research and minute criticism, and a power to philosophize the information so obtained, seldom occur united in the same mind," as he, a twenty-one-year-old, had stated in his *Introduction to Shakespeare's Midsummer Night's Dream* (p. 96). In this, Halliwell was describing the mold of editions past and present and to come. And he judged them on how appropriately all the departments were handled.

They were not equal in importance, however, to Halliwell. His own talent and disposition, as well as his awareness of what had already been done or not, led him to conclude that the philological was most in need of attention, while "passing over" but not undervaluing the philosophical, "which has the advantage of employing the pens of some of the most able writers of the present day" (ix), or that "curious branch of inquiry which is the subject of the present volume, and which indirectly illustrates the history of the poet's mind, in exhibiting to us the simple materials [sources and analogues] from which his wonderful dramas were constructed" (ix). While not denying that Shakespeare's plays can be enjoyed "without the assistance of a line of commentary" (v), Halliwell, not surprisingly, devoted much of his energy to commentary, as is evident in the introductory and glossarial notes he provided in his edited texts, in his lexicographical works, and in the enormous correspondence regarding readings, conjectures, provincialisms, and the like which he participated in throughout his lifetime.

Halliwell's nine works for the Percy Society from 1848 to 1850, the last he was to contribute, deal exclusively with early popular literature. Three are devoted to early English drama (*The Interlude of the Disobedient Child* [1848], *The Interlude of the Four Elements* [1848], *The Interlude of the Trial of Treasure* [1850]), three to collections of prose tales (*Westward for Smelts* [1848], *The Man in the Moone* [1849], *A Manifest Detection of the Most Vyle and Detestable Use of Dice Play* [1850]), one to seventeenth-century songs (*The Loyal Garland* [1850]), and two to catalogues of collections of prose works with brief and informal summaries and bibliographical descriptions (*Descriptive Notices of Popular English Histories* [1848] and *Notices of Fugitive Tracts and Chap-Books* [1849]). As was the custom his productions for the Society were often little more than reprints of texts, preceded by an almost uniform one to one-and-a-half-page preface and accompanied occasionally by spare footnotes or, rarely, endnotes. Although they illustrate his preoccupation with popular literature and his continuing engagement with professional societies, they contribute little more than quantity to Halliwell's development. A passing questioning of dating conjectures by Collier in the *Trial of Treasure* and *Westward for Smelts*, a reference in the *Man in the Moone* to Philip Bliss's not having noticed two tracts, an omission of a few songs, "*causa pudoris*," from the *Loyal Garland* are of small interest. Although the two catalogues deal with the same subject, and the brief descriptions are little more than the brief prefaces they would receive if reprinted separately, they are nevertheless worth a mention. For one thing, they are drawn or printed mainly from works of the eighteenth century. For another, they are works to be found in his own expanding collection, illustrating his continuing occupation and, as he confesses in not having presented others, his lack of "leisure ... to permit a course of research in our public libraries." Book-collecting was also his business, and making catalogues was an obvious means of self-celebration and of course attracting buyers and sellers. It is not surprising that, in addition to soliciting communications in a footnote in *Descriptive Notices* (iii), he republished both works privately as a *Catalogue of Chap-Books, Garlands, and Popular Histories, in the Possession of James Orchard Halliwell,* also in 1849.

Perhaps the most interesting aspect of these seemingly harmless works was the reaction they evoked in the *Athenaeum.* Three, we now know, were reviewed by W. J. Thoms, two by Collier. Like Halliwell, both were Council members of the Shakespeare Society; Thoms, as Halliwell had been, was Council member of the Camden Society and one of his works, as will be remembered, the object of Halliwell's attack in the *Letter to Egerton,* almost ten years earlier. Thoms apparently never forgave Halliwell. His review of the *Interlude of the Disobedient Child* (19 August 1848, pp. 827-8) begins with an attack on the Percy Society (in which the not too admired Wright was the prime mover as secretary and treasurer) for the "abuse" of its otherwise useful objectives, a charge not unlike that levelled against the Camden Society by Halliwell for their publishing Thoms's *Anecdotes and Traditions.* But whereas Halliwell had concentrated on the work, Thoms moves quickly to an assault on Halliwell: the Council could "have a veto on the publication of any trifling work which an editor ambitious rather for the number of books that he edits than for the editorial skill applied." Thoms proceeds with the "only serious mode of treating such a publication," a list of thirty-four inane notes, first having "copied the titles with which Mr. Halliwell presents himself on his title page, that our readers may judge of the value of diplomas and associations." The notes–e.g. "sepulchre. *Burial. From the Latin*"–are followed by Thoms's sarcastic "Whatever University produced Mr. Halliwell may justly be proud of etymological discoveries like these." Listing as well all the thirteen honorary titles on the title page of Halliwell's *Dictionary,* which he was not reviewing, enables him to conclude, "We know not what additional the mysterious '&c. &c.' ... may stand for, but if it mean 'competent editor,' we are bound, on such authority as the pamphlet before us, to pronounce it an unwarranted usurpation." Thoms's review of *Westward for Smelts* (28 October 1848, p. 1073) continues the attack on the abuses of the Percy Society and the editor of the work. As before, Halliwell's "editorship consists of a Preface which is the merest trifling, and just such a series of trivial or erroneous notes as signalized" in the previous review. Once again, numerous examples are listed, followed by exclamations of exasperation and a concluding "If the Council are tired of the existence of this Association, and desirous of bringing it to a close, let them entrust a few more such books to the present editor and they will be likely to accomplish their desire." Although Thoms reacts (21 April 1849, pp. 398-9) —to the Percy Society's choice of *Descriptive Notices of Popular English Histories* "with pleasure," and Halliwell's editorship "does not call for such animadversions" as previously, he is nevertheless "bound" to point out that Halliwell "has not been altogether successful in his manner of treating it. We regret to say, he has not done full justice either to his materials or to his own ability to illustrate them." Once again, Halliwell is charged with the "unequal, irregular and hurried manner in which he has put together the various notes he had collected." Oversights and errors are duly mentioned, however much Thoms finds it "an ungracious task to point out defects." The tone may be somewhat milder, the intent however is clear.

Collier's review of the *Loyal Garland* (5 October 1850, p. 1039) and the *Interlude of the Trial of Treasure* (20 October 1850, pp. 1112-13) are less emotional but no less critical. The opening sentence of the first review sets the tone: "We apprehend the editor is mistaken as to the extreme rarity of the original from which this small volume is reprinted." Collier is authoritative and haughty. He is also slyly ironic. He grants the scarceness and merit of the work, and adds, "the copy which Mr. Halliwell followed appears to be his own,–and we give him credit for the liberality of feeling which would not allow him to keep it merely for his own use and selfish gratification." Faint praise is more than balanced by outright and indisputable criticism: Halliwell has omitted not only whole songs ("the absence of which is nowhere specified") but also lines and words–and the "fault applies to at least twenty or thirty places in the course of considerably less than a hundred pages." Other faults are likewise due to Halliwell's "editorial doings": "too little labour has been bestowed on a volume which really merits a good deal of the pains-taking illustration that he is no doubt qualified to supply." A similar charge against both the Percy Society and Halliwell as editor is unmistakable in the opening sentence of Collier's review of the *Interlude of the Trial of Treasure*: "We must own that we do not quite like the way in which the Percy Society has lately brought out its books:–too little pains have been taken with the editing of them." In addition to criticizing the poor copy Halliwell had chosen and the attendant omissions and errors–"Mr. Halliwell must know that this is not the way in which a reprint ought to be edited"–Collier, evidently piqued at Halliwell's having taken exception to his dating of the work, cannot resist responding on behalf of "Mr. Collier [who] called attention to this interlude twenty years ago and showed how much older it was than the date it bore" and adding a lesson:

"an editor in our day has therefore less excuse for not availing himself of the most perfect copy that he could procure." Picking up and twisting Halliwell's own expression against him, Collier concludes that the work is worth "a great deal more than perhaps his leisure (we say nothing of his knowledge) permitted him to afford." Less than a month before these reviews, Wright saw Collier, "who asked very anxiously after you [Halliwell], where you were, how Mrs. H. was, how many children you had got, wether they were boys or girls, &c. &c. &c." (Friday, September 1850; LOA 42:31). A month after the review Collier acknowledged Halliwell's consolatory feeling that he (Collier) merits a pension of more than £100 per year and also insists that he has no "difference with you [Halliwell] merely because you are of one opinion on some philological point, and I of another" (27 November 1850; LOA 59:22). Two months later on 8 February 1851 Collier wrote to Peter Cunningham, "I never dined at Halliwells, for ... I was always shy of him and his. Beware of him: he is slippery and insincere."[112] As always, there was a text and a subtext which marked and would continue to mark the relationship between Halliwell and certain friends.[113]

That subtext was not merely concerned with the person Halliwell and the fraction to which he belonged. It was also directed by certain quarters against the commercialization of antiquarian research. The response to Halliwell's *Popular Rhymes and Nursery Tales* (1849) is typical. While the *Literary Gazette* (26 May 1849, p. 390) found it sufficient to show that it was charmed by its "random dips and remarks into this welcome addition to our nursery antiquities, stories, songs, game-rhymes, riddles, proverbs, and superstitions, &c.," the *Athenaeum* (2 June 1849, pp. 568-70), although admitting the value of the subject matter, quoted many examples at length in order to conclude: "When will the author produce one really well-edited volume, instead of issuing a number of crude and imperfect books that serve only to show him capable of better things?" (p. 570). This was to be expected of W. J. Thoms, now identified as the reviewer, who must have been infuriated by Halliwell's prefatory evasiveness, his persistent and

112. The letter is in the collection of Tyrus Harmsen.

113. See my articles in the *Library* under the general title "James Orchard Halliwell and Friends": I. John Payne Collier, *The Library*, 18:2 (June 1996), 126-53; II. Alexander Dyce. III. Thomas Keightley, *The Library*, 18:3 (September 1996), 230-45; IV. Howard Staunton, V. Samuel Weller Singer. VI. Charles Knight, *The Library*, 19:2 (June 1997), 122-37; VII. Richard Grant White. VIII. Horace Howard Furness. IX. William James Rolfe, *The Library*, 19:3 (September 1997), 221-41; X. Frederick James Furnivall. XI. William Aldis Wright and William George Clark, *The Library*, 20:2 (June 1998), 126-44.

lame substitution of "rescu[ing] in order to restore" for a thorough and systematic presentation. If not completely predictable, then certainly logical, is Thoms's charge that "it is impossible to turn over twenty pages without feeling convinced that the work has been undertaken rather as a bookseller's speculation—as a trade-companion to the 'Nursery Rhymes of England'—than with any well-considered purpose" (p. 568). John Russell Smith, the publisher, doubtless initiated the sequel, as he had the original, and had, as was his custom, a large say in its contents. That Halliwell was engaged in a commercial project is likewise undeniable. The work, in modified form, is still in print. Halliwell and not Smith, however, bears the brunt of the attack, as he had in the review of the original work which Thoms sees fit to repeat: "'The book will not suit any class of readers—either children, adults, philosophers, poets, or antiquaries'" (p. 569). But Smith and other publishers who exercise their power must be thought to be included. The issue is faced squarely by a review of Halliwell's relatively slight reworking of George Ellis's *Specimens of Early English Metrical Romances* (1848) for Bohn's Antiquarian Library. The as yet unidentified reviewer—most likely Wright or Jerdan—in the *Literary Gazette* (8 July 1848, pp. 454-5) devotes all but the opening paragraph to quoting a specimen which "has hitherto been too expensive to have found its way to the multitudinous recesses of our present cheap literature." That opening paragraph, however, is a position paper, if not a creed:

A very judicious choice for Mr. Bohn's cheap series, but a work that might have been most easily spoilt by the professed antiquary. An edition of this popular work, loaded with the dry antiquarian details on the subject which half a century has accumulated, might have been acceptable to a few, but would undoubtedly have smothered the original design of the author, and rendered the volume incapable of continuing a mission similar to that accomplished by *Percy's Reliques*, and which it has hitherto relished. Ellis, in fact, did for early romances what Percy had previously effected for ancient poetry. Both subjects were first made popular by those writers, and we are glad to find that Mr. Halliwell's additions and corrections in the present edition are in no way calculated to embarrass the general reader by the discussion of learned subjects, which, however valuable to archaeologists, would have been positive blemishes in Ellis's charming narratives.[114]

114. This was a friendly echo of Halliwell's programmatic assertion: "In the present edition, care has been taken not to diminish the popular character of the work by an unnecessary exhibition of archaeological learning. It has been

Halliwell was offered £25 by Bohn for supplying some prefatory and descriptive connecting material. There is no doubt that although the subject matter was of great interest to him he was engaged in a commercial venture, as he was when he accepted Bohn's offer of updating Henry Ellis's revision of John Brand's *Observations on the Popular Antiquities of Great Britain* (1849), attended to Bohn's suggestions[115] (6 September 1848; LOA 38:37), and added numerous references to his own *Dictionary of Archaic and Provincial Words*. Nevertheless it would be a mistake to charge Halliwell solely with crass commercialism or with attempting to cover up his lack of patient scholarship or even knowledge. On one level at least it must be granted that Halliwell was generally interested in popular education, that he could produce items for mass consumption and at the same time luxury items for those with wealth. In this he was very much a man of his time.

Admittedly Halliwell had and was to have problems with works commissioned by commercial publishers and was increasingly wary of them. But they were useful since they reached a wide audience and, especially in the case of John Russell Smith, with whom Halliwell had excellent relations and who had numerous special lists, might also be receptive to occasional more exclusive proposals. Thus it is likely that in the context of the commercial success of such works as the *Dictionary* and the *Nursery Rhymes* Smith could be persuaded to publish such Halliwell delicacies as *Some Account of the Vernon Manuscript of Early English Poetry Preserved in the Bodleian Library* (1848), *Notices of the History and Antiquities of Islip, Oxfordshire* (1849), and *Some Account of the Popular Tracts Formerly in the Library of Captain Cox, A.D. 1576* (1849). These are essentially pamphlets, the first two of fifteen pages each, the third of twenty-one, resembling private publications with the first two limited to fifty copies. They enabled Halliwell to recycle, as it were, work he had already done or to expand

sufficient to amend silently the various philological errors into which Ellis had fallen, without pointing them out to special attention, and the editorial additions and corrections will tend, it is believed, to facilitate the reader's progress, without distracting his attention" (iv).

115. "Mr. Bohn has been looking at Brand's Popular Antiquities, and finds that it will be quite impossible to get the remainder into one volume. He must therefore be content to let the work extend to three. The first volume, he finds, relates entirely to fast and festival days, and he thinks that if any thing more is contained on this matter in the other two, it would be better to extract it, so as to make the subject complete. Perhaps the second volume may as well comprise all that relates to sports, pastimes, customs, &c.; and the third be limited to sorcery, witchcraft, and vulgar errors, as at present" (6 September 1848; LOA 38:37).

what he was to present. In the case of the Vernon Manuscript, Halliwell in fact admits that he did not even intend to publish these "imperfect" notices from his memoranda, but–with his customary rationale–"they will enable the student to form an estimate of the nature of the contents of this remarkable collection" (p. 3). In another instance, his high-sounding pamphlet of fifteen pages, *Notices of the History and Antiquities of Islip, Oxfordshire, the Birthplace of Edward the Confessor*, "merely consists of a few notes" (and also appeared in the *Journal of the British Archaeological Association*, 5 [1850], 39-51). For his part Smith was doubtless most interested in Halliwell's *Life of Shakespeare*, which he published with considerable fanfare, and was naturally amenable to doing a by-product like the facsimile of Shakespeare's will (1850), "with a few preliminary observations by J. O. Halliwell," limited to one hundred copies, and enthusiastically three controversial pamphlets by Halliwell on Collier and the Perkins folio.

Most noteworthy, not so much for their content as for their very existence, were the twenty-four separately printed works which Halliwell published "for private circulation" between 1848 and 1853. Fourteen are reprints of early popular literature, three are catalogues of library collections (of Halliwell, Chetham, and Plymouth), four deal with Shakespearean records or illustrations (including the first volume of Halliwell's folio edition in 1853), one describes a collection of fifty-four volumes presented to the Smithsonian Institution illustrating the history of prices between 1650 and 1750, one contains the autobiography and diary of Simon Forman, and a last, slight pamphlet deals with book value and preservation. With the exception of the *Catalogue of Chap-Books* (1849) and the last two mentioned works, the rest tend to be luxury editions on thick or ordinary paper, limited in number, and printed by Thomas Richards or C. & J. Adlard. The uniformity of size (large quarto) has a practical as well as aesthetic function. It enabled Halliwell to employ the material flexibly–that is, to use the same plates in various combinations. *Contributions to Early English Literature Derived Chiefly from Rare Books and Ancient Inedited Manuscripts, from the Fifteenth to the Seventeenth Century* (1849) contains six works which also appeared separately; *The Literature of the Sixteenth and Seventeenth Centuries Illustrated by Reprints of Very Rare Tracts* (1851) contains works which he was to reprint later. Other evidences of Halliwell's "husbandry" are his refreshing of material from his past–*The Autobiography and Personal Diary of Dr. Simon Forman* (1849); Robert Grosseteste's *Castle of Love* (1849); *A Catalogue of Chap-Books, Garlands, and Popular Histories* (1849); and his collecting and later reprinting of records "illustrative" of Shakespeare's life and works–*New Boke about Shakespeare and Stratford-on-Avon* (1850), *Some Account of the Antiquities, Coins, Manuscripts, Rare Books, Ancient Documents, and Other Reliques* (1852). The former, one of whose "chief objects ... was the gradual collection of facsimiles of every document of any real importance respecting Shakespeare" (v), is a loose collection of documents and facsimiles ranging from ballads to Shakespeare's marriage-bond and will. The latter is essentially a descriptive catalogue–its head-title is "A Catalogue of Shakespearian Reliques"–of items in his possession, as are the catalogues of works from his library which he presented to the Chetham Library in Manchester (1852)[116] and his description of manuscripts in the Public Library in Plymouth (1853). What may not be so obvious from the titles alone is that Halliwell was not only continuing his preoccupation with early popular literature, collecting, and cataloguing but also integrating his archaeological and philological interest in provincial customs and language, as evident in collections relating to the North of England (*A Catalogue of Chap-Books, Garlands, and Popular Histories*, 1849), Lancashire and Cheshire (*Palatine Anthology* and *Palatine Garland*, both 1850), Yorkshire (*The Yorkshire Anthology*, 1851), Norfolk (*The Norfolk Anthology*, 1852), and again Lancashire (*The Poetry of Witchcraft*, 1853). What is all too obvious is the absence of a scholarly apparatus and, even where necessary, of any systematic arrangement. Halliwell does not attempt to hide this. On the contrary, what little there is in the way of prefatory information is devoted prominently to elegant variations of his admission. With litanical predictability he confesses that the "only object proposed in works like the present, and for which their mode of circulation is so especially suited, is the collection of useful materials, not the formation of them into critical disquisitions or popular narratives" (*Palatine Anthology*, xiii); that "the Catalogue having been gradually compiled, and a classification found to be almost impracticable, it was finally arranged to print it without regard either to arrangement of subject or chronological order" (*A Catalogue of Proclamations, Broadsides, Ballads, and Poems*, x); and "In plainer words, perhaps the absolute reason for presenting the tracts without the accompaniment of editorial display, in the shape of copious notes, might be found in the idea, that the limited space to which we were confined, if partially so occupied, would have lessened the number of the texts themselves, and so materially decreased the value of the work. It has always appeared to us that, in the great majority of instances, the student who is interested in remains of this kind, finds the texts constitute the

---

116. For details see *Proclamations, Broadsides, Ballads and Poems, 1357-1830*, ed. A. C. Snape (1990), pp. 17-27.

chief value; and, wherever space is a consideration, would prefer a second text to an appendix of notes" *(The Literature of the Sixteenth and Seventeenth Centuries*, pp. 3-4). What is indisputable is that Halliwell was generally recognized as an important exponent, even champion, of early popular literature. His wife's diary entry for 1 September 1852 records that "James brought home Punch [xxiii (1852), 96] there is some fun in it about his paper on Robin Hood [published as "The Era and Character of Robin Hood," *Journal of the British Archaeological Association*, 8 (1853), 223-9] - James is called Dr Rummage."

Doing his own publishing was a commercial as well as an archaeological venture. Authors were expected to bear the cost of paper and printing, and often had no copyright privileges but were paid only a flat sum by publishers. And publishing, despite the intense activity, was an unstable and risky business: Charles Knight, one of the most prolific publishers, was on the verge of bankruptcy in 1841;[117] publishing societies like the Shakespeare and the Percy folded in 1853. Halliwell was only too aware of the problems he was facing. In issuing the thirty-two-page *Autobiography and Personal Diary of Dr. Simon Forman* (1849), he admitted his caution: "To the student their [these pages] value is unquestionable, and it was therefore thought that a small impression of them would be an acceptable offering to the curious reader, although they will not, it must be confessed, bear the light of a large circulation, which was at one time proposed" (iii-iv). In 1852 he laid bare his experience and aspiration: "The impression is strictly limited, with the view of protecting the interests of those who support the design by their subscriptions; but it is scarcely necessary to say the Editor has no personal interest in printing works of this description, it being almost invariably accompanied (as in the present instance) by a pecuniary loss" *(The Norfolk Anthology*, viii). Still, for a passionate scholar and dealer like Halliwell the possibility of controlling the whole process from discovery to dissemination was undoubtedly irresistible. And it is no wonder that very early in his career he was writing on the various aspects of book research and collecting. In 1839, at nineteen, he had caused a bit of an uproar with his *Few Hints to Novices in Manuscript Literature* (1839); not a few of his works contained prefatory remarks on his experience in libraries and the market. And as he was establishing his private publishing business, he issued *Notes on Ascertaining*

---

117. On 1 August 1841 (LOA 9:36) Wright informed Halliwell: "Knight is certainly gone—no help for him. I am told his debts amount to nearly £200,000. They tell me he owes his printer Clowes the trifling sum of £75,000!!! I understand his business is to be put in trust and carried on for the benefit of the creditors, who are to receive 4/- in the pound yearly for five years."

the Value, and Directions for the Preservation, of Old Books, Manuscripts, Deeds, and Family Papers (1851), a primer "to afford, in the simplest form, such information on the subject as can be compressed into a very limited compass, divesting it of all technicalities" (p. 3). In essence Halliwell was appealing to the greater public not to "despise" and "neglect" "repiques of the olden time." His readiness to receive communications—a standard feature of the works he was producing—was a scholarly gesture of solidarity and at the same time an effective bit of commercial enterprise, as was his issuing of works like *A List of Privately Printed Works* (ca. 1851), which was essentially a priced catalogue of seventy-one works, and numerous prospectuses, as well as his proposal in about 1852 to form the Brixton Hill Club, to launch "a series of privately-printed works, uniform in size with those of the Roxburgh Club, to consist entirely of antiquarian texts, bibliographical reprints, and collections of old tracts and ballads." In 1854 he issued another small pamphlet, *On the Means Adopted to Insure the Rarity of the Privately Printed Works*, in which he revealed financial details, on the basis of his experience with twelve of the privately printed works just discussed, which led him to conclude that the "only possible method of sustaining the pecuniary value of a work printed by subscription, is a by adhering strictly to an impression of a limited number" (p. 3). This was to be the theme of further pamphlets and was to figure largely, as will be shown, in the management of his sixteen-volume folio edition of Shakespeare (1853-65), of his proposals for "an unique collection of reprints of curious old English books, and lists of such books to be found in various libraries" (announced in 1861), and facsimiles in small quarto of Shakespeare's dramas and poems printed before 1623 (announced in 1862), among others.

· 8 ·

Shakespeare: Fact and Fiction

• *A Life of William Shakespeare*

In the midst of all the turbulence of his professional and personal life Halliwell produced his greatest work to date. Beset with financial problems, besieged by law suits, he continued his searches and accumulated documents and records in the service of his idol Shakespeare. The preface to his *Life of William Shakespeare* is dated 21 November 1847; Halliwell must have finished the work when he was about twenty-seven. Precociousness cannot then be ruled out, but the presentation is so secure and comprehensive as to be clearly the work of a mature and major scholar. It is the epitome of the type of scholarship Halliwell represented and advocated. It is caviare to the general, preferring "rigid authenticity" (xiii) to imaginative reconstruction. Schoenbaum is perhaps overstating in delineating Halliwell as "antiquarianism incarnate" and characterizing his style as "spare, dry, graceless—rarely ris[ing] to the level of banality."[118] Halliwell could write otherwise, but chose not to. His aim was to make available new information and to consolidate what already existed and not to be one of the "authors of almost every description [who] have attempted this for Shakespeare, each one bitterly complaining of the paucity of facts, but making ample amends by conjectures of their own; for, as the great dramatist excelled all in imagination, his biographers have exceeded all other biographers in the facility with which they have regarded him in all imaginable and imaginary positions" (vi). The fact of the matter is that Halliwell "entertained the humbler project of publishing [his] discoveries separately ... [with] little idea of becoming one of Shakespeare's biographers" (x). But, he confides, "the publishers, those arbiters of the destinies of authors, refused to accept my collections unless presented to the public in a consecutive narrative, and I was obliged to make an essay which, under the circumstances, would probably not have been attempted" (x).

118. *Shakespeare's Lives*, p. 291.

What the *Life* presents is a unique collection of eighty-nine authenticated documents, printed at length if of any importance, and with "no more ... attempted beyond placing before the reader an unprejudiced and complete view of every known fact respecting the poet" (x). To some, of course, this may be still another instance of Halliwell's avoiding critical evaluation and the responsibility which comes with it. But as his particular brand of criticism dictates, the evaluation is implicit in the exploration, discovery, selection, authentication, and relevance of the records and documents. Such a stance does not exist to avoid interpretation and error; they are integral to the process of discovery and presentation. The papers, which Halliwell lovingly described as "attractive bundles, filling large boxes, chests, drawers, and cupboards" (vii), he found in the Council Chamber of Stratford-upon-Avon and in the various Record Offices (Chapter House, Rolls Chapel, Herald's College, among others) in London. They are permanent and, like Halliwell's collection, for all times. And they are ample and wide-reaching, for Halliwell had sense and experience enough to realize that the man could only be understood within his total environment. As Halliwell's subtitle makes clear, included are "many particulars respecting the poet and his family." Among the fifty-seven documents Halliwell marks as not having been printed in any other work, and representative of the wide horizon, are Extracts relating to the Shakespeares, from the Register of the Guild of St. Anne Knolle, a MS. at Longbridge House, near Warwick; Inventory of the goods of Agnes Arden; Abstract of the title of the Swan Inn; Extracts from the Chamberlains' Accounts, 1564; Fine relating to the will of Roger Sadler, 1578; Inventory of the goods of Henry Field, 1592; List of tenants in Bridge-street Ward; The eighth sonnet from Bright's MS.; Grant mentioning the Boar's Head Theatre; Fine levied on property purchased by Shakespeare; Will of John Combe; Order relating to the Blackfriars Theatre. The sweep is considerable, the selection perceptive. The "same star of rigid authenticity" is to be found in the seventy-six illustrations—woodcuts and facsimiles—executed by Halliwell's friend and colleague F. W. Fairholt, to whom Halliwell had written, "Remember my motto is *authenticity* & *reality* what actually was or is not what some fancy might have been" (14 October 1847; Folger W.a.81[7/1]). And there can be very little doubt that this time Halliwell took the greatest pains to assure accuracy. A surviving proof copy of p. 299 (EUL Hc. 6.35) reveals almost fifty hand corrections, the result of a collation "noted by me from the original MS," although they did not appear in the printed version, which tended to modernize spellings. Very little of the material presented, or of Halliwell's connecting text, has been challenged to the present day.

The work continues to be a seminal source for the study of Shakespeare and Stratford.

It was not conceived *in vacuo*, however. Although avowedly "unprejudiced" in the presentation, Halliwell was only too aware pf his predecessors and contemporaries, and did not hesitate to mention them. He was experienced enough by then to be circumspect, and he was concerned about giving every man his due.[119] Malone and Collier are praised for their "laudable diligence in examining records for notices likely to throw light on the poet's history" (vi). Even Knight, for whom Halliwell had no special regard, is acknowledged "as the only one of late years who has referred to the originals" (vii). Still, they were competitors, and Halliwell's zeal did not allow him to suppress his opinion that, for all their "distinguished and valuable researches," they "never properly examined" the "repositories of documents most obvious to any enquirer as likely to contain information relating to Shakespeare" (vi-vii). "Collier ... contented himself with Malone's researches [in the records of Stratford] ... [as for Knight] the very slight notice he has taken of them, and the portentous mistakes he has committed in cases where printed copies were not to be found, would appear to show that they were unintelligible to [him]" (vii). Malone, he grants, with a sideswipe at Knight, "with all his errors, possessed some knowledge of palaeography" (although in a footnote Halliwell could not resist adding, "but not in a very profound degree"), especially of Latin (vii). Other biographers of Shakespeare, "those who exceeded all other biographers in the facility with which they have regarded him in all imaginable and imaginary positions," Halliwell does not mention by name. He does, however, point out that in the will of Agnes Arden, "as printed by Mr. [Joseph] Hunter, which occupies not quite two octavo pages, eighty-seven errors have been committed," but his moderating "these are mostly literal, and do not affect the sense" (xii) was not likely to appease that venerable figure who had recently issued a public letter accusing Halliwell of misdeeds in the business of the Camden

---

119. He wrote to W. O. Hunt, anxious that he may not have mentioned him sufficiently in the Preface, "I rely on your judgement to believe how anxious I am to give every one that assisted me the best acknowledgement in my power" (18 December 1847; Folger Y.c.1236[4]). And that consideration extended to his publisher as well. Sending prospectuses to Joseph Clarke, whose institution might be interested, he added, "not that I have the slightest interest in the sale of the work, which is the publisher's exclusive property, but R. Smith has expended a large sum on it, and I am anxious he should reap the benefit of his spirited speculation" (26 January 1848; Folger W.a.81[8]).

Society.[120]

Presenting an "unprejudiced and complete view of every known fact respecting the poet" is obviously not simply reprinting documents and leaving the rest to the reader. The records must be found, evaluated, selected, transcribed, and arranged in a chronological sequence, and the text that binds them must consist of more than simple connectives. Halliwell must justify their existence and express an opinion of the evidence as well as reflecting, where necessary, on the opinions of others. "I have ventured," he announces, "to submit in every case the best evidence I could obtain, frankly grounding my opinion in every instance on testimony or reasonable probability" (xi). The work is thus a test of Halliwell's scholarship, intelligence, and tact. His treatment of Collier, whose *New Facts* (1835) he called a "little mine of valuable detail" (x) and second only to the present volume for new information, reflects careful evaluation and, as needs be, independence of judgment. Thus Halliwell can point to a stronger reason than Collier's for believing that Richard Shakespeare was Shakespeare's grandfather (p. 8), or, in discussing John Shakespeare's mark, he can attribute Collier's holding that it does not occur in an inventory either to his having overlooked it or—generously— "what is more probable, [having] used a different copy of the document" (p. 69).[121] He can hold that Collier's opinion that Shakespeare had something like a legal education is "entitled to great consideration," but nevertheless be of the opinion that the "frequent and correct use Shakespeare made of such terms may have been readily taught by the numerous legal transactions in which his parents were implicated" (p. 108). He can disagree with Collier's attributing some verses entitled "Shakespeare on the King" to Shakespeare as not being "sufficiently elegant" (p. 207). And he can agree unequivocally with Collier that Shakespeare had a permanent interest in the Blackfriars theater (pp. 162-3); that an anecdote that Burbage played Richard III was current in 1602 (p. 196); that *Twelfth Night* was performed at the Middle Temple in 1602 (p. 197), among other instances. "In fairness" to Collier, Halliwell could point out that the letter of H.S. discovered by Collier among the Egerton papers was believed to be genuine by several competent judges at the Council of the Shakespeare Society (p. 225). But he did distance himself from Hunter's doubting the authority of all the Shakespeare documents

120. See p. 162-3.
121. On 5 November 1847 (LOA 11:1) Collier had written that he had no evidence "to *prove* that John Shakespeare made a + for his mark" but had "the best reason for thinking that he did, and [his] recollection is strong almost certain from the point."

in the Ellesmere collection: "how much reliance is to be placed on his [Hunter's] conclusions may be inferred from the fact that the paper of the spuriousness of which he is most positive is preserved, not in the nobleman's library, but in the archives of the city of London, enrolled in books unquestionably authentic" (p. 225). Knight does not come off too well either: for inaccuracy (p. 20), for want of "evidence of weight" (p. 132), among other things. A conjecture by the prominent Shakespearean William Harness is deemed "most improbable" (p. 31); discoveries by Peter Cunningham which exhibit the popularity of Shakespeare's plays are considered of "so much curiosity and importance" that Halliwell reproduces those Audit Office entries which relate to them (pp. 205-6). In short, Halliwell was operating critically, with careful and reliable scholarship, in his documentary life of Shakespeare.

And, as to be expected, the overall reception of Halliwell's work in the leading journals was not surprising. William Jerdan's *Literary Gazette*, generally friendly to Halliwell, after an early puff in which "we look forward with great interest to the time, which we hope is not far distant, when Mr. Halliwell will give the public the result of his labours" (2 October 1847, p. 706), did not have to wait very long to declare it was "unfeignedly of opinion that no work on the personal history of Shakespeare has yet been published so full of curious, novel, and interesting matter as the present," despite "many points on which we are at issue with the author" (1 January 1848, p. 7). In a continuation (8 January 1848, pp. 38-40) the reviewer lists further new facts and "novelties," concluding that "excepting the obvious errors of author as well as artist in falling into too great detail, we may repeat our conviction that the present attempt to collect the scattered remnants of the biography of the great dramatist into an intelligible form, is one of the most successful that have yet appeared" (p. 40). The reviewer may very likely have been Jerdan himself since he was very anxious to have Halliwell join him on the journal.

The importance attached to the *Life* by the *Gentleman's Magazine* may be judged from the fact that its review is twenty-one pages long (n.s. 29 [May 1848], pp. 459-79). The reviewer, now identified as John Mitford, who had dealt fairly with some of Halliwell's earlier works,[122] devotes most of his review to a "popular summary of the Biography, for the use of our country readers, who have no opportunity, like Mr. Halliwell, of inspecting the Record Office in London, or of taking lodgings, like Mr. Harness, at Stratford in the summer months, and who must therefore

122. See p. 100.

derive their information solely from this volume" (p. 461). Despite the somewhat patronizing tone of this prelude, Mitford gives not only a reasonable summary but also spices it with enough personal comments to indicate his critical engagement. He is impressed–the "volume contains some new and interesting materials" (p. 459)–so much so that it warrants extended treatment. But Mitford's increasing superciliousness cannot be overlooked:

Amidst the pleasing variety of these biographical traditions it is no wonder that an inexperienced person like ourselves should perchance lose our way, and be led by our 'blind guides' into much doubt and discontent. We are therefore thankful for a new Life of our bard which should remove anomalies and reconcile differences, restore something that is lost, and correct much that is amiss. Mr. Halliwell certainly is not wanting in zeal, industry, and extensive investigation of the subject. He has travelled many miles, turned over many manuscripts, consulted many volumes, detected many errors, rectified many mistakes, contradicted some of his contemporaries (to which we have no kind of objection) and agreed with others (p. 459).

Mitford himself disagrees and agrees, but almost always with an assertion–something on the order of "the matter is, we think, rather doubtful" (p. 462) or "we think this might have been a little more definite" (p. 472)–and hardly ever with evidence. In fact, it is difficult not to believe that Mitford is mocking the kind of scholarship Halliwell represents. Typical of Mitford's attitude towards what he regards as the small-minded fixation on minutiae is, for example, his response to Halliwell's rhetorical comment–"Thousands will breathe their fervent thanks that the lowly roof in Henley Street was one of the favoured spots where the hand of the destroying angel was stayed"–on the plague which visited Stratford in 1564: "True! for had there been no Shakspere (sc. Shaxper)[123] there would have been no commentators, and about six-and-twenty gentlemen would have lived and died in vain, finding nothing upon earth to do!" (p. 463). Even more unrestrained is Mitford's comment on Halliwell's giving a "notice [of 1578] from the corporation records on the subject of defensive preparations for the security of the country, in which Mr. Shakspere is a *defaulter* to the amount of three shillings and four pence":

123. These spellings of Shakespeare's name were likely to irritate Halliwell, who from the beginning to the end of his career was a strong advocate of the now accepted spelling. See pp. 556-9.

What is most worthy of notice in this matter is, that, though this extract consists only of about a dozen lines, Mr. Malone has made no less than thirty-one errors, and Mr. Knight, professing to see the value of accuracy on such matters, and to correct his predecessors, falls into twenty-six more, being at the rate consequently of one error for every three words!! O! criticorum gens perfida! may we well cry out. Our confidence in them is gone utterly! and as Lord Chatham says, 'confidence is a plant of slow growth,' we think it will not likely to be soon restored. In 1578 and 1579, John Shakspere was mortgaging and selling away in a spendthrift manner: we hope *Shakspere junior* was not at the bottom of all this, but we have our fears (p. 463).

There is nothing supercilious about Peter Cunningham's review in the *Athenaeum* (8 January 1848, pp. 32-3). Whereas Mitford used the rapier, Cunningham used the sword. Although admitting that Halliwell's book is a "valuable contribution to the long shelf of works relating to Shakespeare," he is nevertheless convinced of a previous conclusion: "how little it is that we know of Shakspeare!" If Mitford, however coyly, could detect "some new and interesting materials," Cunningham can nevertheless adamantly declare, "We have read and re-read the whole of Mr. Halliwell's book,–and cannot for the life is us, find more than three new facts in his thick octavo volume." Moreover, he accuses Halliwell of a "good deal of loose writing," of "sometimes drawing on his imagination for facts," of committing blunders in his transcriptions, of making erroneous statements, and–after asserting he could add to these errors "were we willing"–concludes with a triumphant "piece of mis-information": "the mortgage deed of Shakspeare's property in the Blackfriars, containing Shakspeare's signature," has not been lost or mislaid, as Halliwell contends, "but belongs to Mr. Troward, and was exhibited at the last general meeting but one of the Shakespeare Society!" (p. 33).

Cunningham had said as much in his *Athenaeum* review of Halliwell's *Introduction to Shakespeare's Midsummer Night's Dream* (29 May 1841, p. 420): "It has not often been our lot to see so much reading turned to so little account, as in the volume before us." Once again, Halliwell is accused of simply and senselessly collecting material, of not properly assessing its relevance or importance, and, when making decisions, of coming to dubious conclusions. And, once again, it is hard to deny that personal as well as professional motives were involved in the critical reception of Halliwell's work. Shakespeare was the focus of Halliwell's attention, as it was of many of his closest colleagues and acquaintances. Lives of

Shakespeare had been produced by Dyce, Collier, and Knight, among others of the Shakespeare Society. Who cannot help but speculate on the motives that lay behind, say, Collier's writing, "I shall wait with impatience for the appearance of the volume" (5 November 1847; LOA 11:1)? Or Halliwell's writing to Fairholt, "I am nervously fidgetty at the thought of being anticipated in the minutest particular" (9 November 1847; Folger W.a.81[7/2])? Or Halliwell's sending Collier one copy of only ten free copies he had had from the publisher (18 December 1847; Folger Y.c.1236(4) and hoping that he could rely on Collier's "usual candour" not to be affronted by plain speaking" (18 December 1847; Folger Y.c.1207(1)? Or Wright's reporting ten days later that Collier had not seen the work but had asked "anxiously" about it (18 December 1847; LOA 39:48)? Or Collier's asserting, after receiving the work, that Halliwell need not make any apology for differing but that he expected only "ordinary literary courtesy" (20 December 1847; LOA 11:21)? If Shakespeare was the attraction for so many, he was also the trap.

Halliwell's colleagues also produced editions–that fatal Cleopatra of Shakespeare scholarship. It is little wonder that the *Life* had hardly appeared when Mrs. Halliwell recorded in her diary entry for 1 February 1848 that Halliwell was "to allow himself 10 years to complete a new edition of Shakespeare, from this time, he is now reading for it." The first volume appeared five years later in 1853, as the Shakespeare trap was being sprung.

+++

• *The Tallis Edition*

Halliwell's concentration on Shakespeare extended beyond the assembling of records and documents. It involved as well the reproduction of original texts and inevitably the editing of the text of Shakespeare. While his folio edition was taking shape in his mind and filling the cabinets he had specially constructed to hold his material, and as he was establishing himself as a major figure of the Shakespearean scene and a reputed collector-dealer of early literature, and as he was always in need of financial support for his family and his professional expenses, he was easily lured into the maze of commercial Shakespearean publishing. In a letter from Wright (which Halliwell dated 28 January 1850) he was informed that "Mr Tallis ... seemed decided on having his own book [an edition of Shakespeare], which he wants you to do, and not Knight's" (LOA 44:20). Interestingly enough, Tallis "intends it to be composed here and sent over [to America] in stereotype plates," Wright continued. As usual, Wright had advice about the nature of the work and the tactics of proceeding: "I cannot help thinking that with a modest statement in the title that it is 'illustrated from the notes of former editors selected by ___' &c, it would throw credit on your name without exposing it to any serious discredit." After some hesitation about whether to permit his name to appear on the title page (Diary, 17 February 1850), and then asserting he could not do so for less than £250 (Diary, 21 February 1850), on 11 April 1850 Halliwell entered into an agreement with Frederick Tallis to edit the complete works of Shakespeare with an introduction and notes to each play and a life of the poet, to furnish sufficient copy to enable Tallis to produce one sheet per week after the publication had commenced, and to receive two hundred pounds in four equal payments and twenty copies of the work as published (SBT ER 1/50/40:122). On 28 August 1850 (LOA 42:38) Halliwell heard from Wright that the Shakespeare was selling well in America. On 14 October 1850 (LOA 56:75) he received from Charles Tallis, partner of Frederick, an advertisement announcing an edition with Halliwell's name "attached, as Editor," to be published by John Tallis, their brother, and urging him to contact him, as he was about to communicate with the solicitors to the firm and "our house" in New York. Halliwell lost no time in reacting on two fronts. On that very day, "very angry ... very much displeased" (Diary, 14 October 1850), he wrote to the *Times* (15 October 1850, p. 8) tersely disclaiming any connection with an edition advertised by George Vickers of Holywell Street, London. On 17 October he sent a statement to the *Times* (of 18 October 1850, p. 3) protesting against another unauthorized edition, an American one that had been advertised both in England and America by Messrs. Tallis and Co. of St. John Street, London, "styling themselves 'John Tallis and Co., London and New York' ... informing the public that it is 'guaranteed' to be completed in 30 Parts at 1s. each, being a saving of at least 12s. or 30 per cent., on the New York copyright edition." Halliwell disavowed any connection with this edition and lamented the "defective state of the law": "As the law stands at present," he declared, "it seems that not only may the works of any English author be pirated in America, but if he attempts to secure an American circulation by publication in that country, he is liable to have his book reprinted in England without his consent; producing a sad illustration of the fine old line (which is [Halliwell is unable to suppress his pedantry], by the way, so often misquoted)–'Incidis in Scyllam, cupiens vitare

Charybdim'."[124] Halliwell discontinued his work on the edition after a portion of the Histories was printed in 1851. Frederick and Charles Tallis brought suit for an injunction against their brother John's "Halliwell's Edition of Shakespeare," which was continued under the editorship of Henry Tyrrell, reaching fifty-two parts or a fourth and final volume (of the "doubtful" plays, including *Titus Andronicus*, *Pericles*, and *The Two Noble Kinsmen*) in 1854. In 1853 Halliwell was released from the contract with Frederick Tallis (2 May 1853; LOA 49:71). On 3 January 1854 (LOA 59:39) Halliwell received from Frederick Tallis a printed statement (and documents) that the suit–"*In Chancery*. Between John Tallis, Plaintiff, and Frederick and Charles Edward Tallis, Defendants"; and "In the *Queen's Bench*. Between John Tallis, Plaintiff, and Frederick Tallis, Defendant"–for an injunction against "Halliwell's edition of Shakespeare" had been "*dismissed* by mutual consent" on 15 December 1853. And a few days later Wright confirmed that he had seen Frederick, who had "made up the dispute with his brother ... so that he can now sell it [the Shakespeare]" (12 January 1854; LOA 44:77). Mrs. Halliwell's diary entry for 18 February 1854 mentions that Mr. Hodgson, the auctioneer, about to sell the stereotype plates, asked Halliwell whether he meant to go on with the Tallis edition and Halliwell "declined unless well paid for it."

Attempting to salvage a modicum of satisfaction from the ordeal, Halliwell privately issued a volume of the Comedies, "reprinted from the American edition" (so the title page), attaching a new title page to the twenty copies he had received as honorarium from Frederick Tallis and (in an added preface dated 3 February 1854) hoping "any student of Shakespeare into whose hands a copy of the present volume may chanced to be placed, will particularly oblige by considering it to contain all really belonging to me to be found partially repeated in the cheap editions hitherto issued under my name."[125] The preface also enabled him to mention his "regret" at his "inability to make a more extensive publication, not merely from the fact of the pirated edition of Messrs. John Tallis and Co. being replete with oversights not to be ascribed to myself, but also because many of my notes have been almost literally adopted by an

124. Copyright also played a role in the readiness of Willoughby & Co., the publishers of an edition edited by Samuel Phelps, to make amends for any "injurious or improper" use of Halliwell's notes or in any way infringing on his copyright (18 February 1851; LOA 59:34).

125. Comparing the two editions, Joseph Crosby found them as different as "chalk" [and] "cheese." See *One Touch of Shakespeare: Letters of Joseph Crosby to Joseph Parker Norris, 1875-1878*, ed. John W. Velz and Frances N. Teague (Washington, 1986), p. 178.

American editor,–the Rev. Mr. Hudson,–without the slightest acknowledgment." Thus to his distress at the inadequacy of protection of copyright was added that of plagiarism–both issues of major concern in Halliwell's career. Halliwell's indignant conclusion, not new to him, was one he was to repeat often: "The system of Editors of Shakespeare adopting notes of their predecessors, and availing themselves of the results of their reading, as if it were their own, cannot be too strongly deprecated. Whatever is worth taking does, at least, also deserve a line of recognition."

The appearance of the Tallis edition in America caused embarrassment to at least one other Shakespearean. Richard Grant White congratulated Halliwell on its "magnificent appearance ... the excellence of the introductory matter & the purity of the text" (23 November 1853; LOA 230:87), not realizing that he had seen the "cheap" Tallis edition and not the luxurious folio edition. In another twist, White was asked by one of those "catchpenny" publishers to examine an incomplete edition of which they had purchased the stereotype plates. To White's surprise it turned out to be Halliwell's first edition, and he was quick to apologize for his "inadvertance," as these "cheap-illustrated-publication houses" are so regarded that "no man of literary taste, not to say, no man of letters, would dream of having one of their publications upon his table" (25 September 1854; LOA 59:36). A short while later White was quick to offer his sympathies at the "shabby treatment" Halliwell had received at the "hands of these publishers, & trust[ed] that you will not consider the edition I am looking after an aggravation of your wrongs," continuing, "I do very little to it ... I could not afford to *edit* the edition for five times the sum which the publishers wish to pay" (14 December 1854; LOA 48:67). Joseph Crosby, another American Shakespearean, was more direct. With more distance and honesty, he explained the situation in a letter of 6 September 1876 to his friend and fellow Shakespearean Joseph Parker Norris: "I presume the American edition was also continued to the end by another editor or two. I wonder if the one that I have, pubd. by Martin & Johnson, New York, n.d., but about 1852 or 3, in 3 volumes quarto, is not the one. If so, it was continued & finished by Grant White, as I learned from a letter of his to me, in which he said that he collated it; but was not responsible for the text, nor would he allow his name on the title page."[126]

The experience with the Tallis edition had a deep and permanent effect on Halliwell's relations with editors of Shakespeare, their editorial

126. *One Touch of Shakespeare*, p. 179.

disposition, the transmission of scholarship, and–as one engaged in private publishing for a select group of subscribers but also interested in educating a wider public through inexpensive publications–the nature and aims of publishing itself.

+++

• *The Collier Controversy*
    The first twenty-five or so years of Halliwell's career, which coincided with those of the reign of Queen Victoria, saw the appearance of new and/or revised important editions of Shakespeare by Charles Knight, John Payne Collier, Samuel Weller Singer, Alexander Dyce, Howard Staunton, Richard Grant White, Thomas Keightley, and Halliwell, among the more than eighty recorded in the British Library catalogue. Then as now, Shakespeare was a popular author and a fiercely competitive product for both scholars and publishers. Since there were difficulties with copyright, there were piracies. It was an open market, and it put a strain not merely on publishers but heavily on editors, especially those in England (which meant essentially London), who belonged to the same societies and knew each other more or less personally. On the whole, it would not be unfair to say they got along well enough with each other, surviving often harsh criticism or the intrigues of cliques with the veil of collegiality if not the cloak of indifference which distinguishes the true professional. All the major Shakespeareans were put to the test–and that over a period of a dozen years–by the discovery by Collier of a second folio edition (1632) of Shakespeare's works with what was purported to be contemporary handwritten corrections. The whole story took years to unfold, but Halliwell was implicated from the beginning, even before what was considered a modern forgery was attributed and proved to be the work of Collier himself.
    Collier's discovery, appearing in his *Notes and Emendations to the Text of Shakespeare's Plays* (1852), caused a sensation among Shakespeareans, not the least of which was the fact that Collier refused at first to allow others to examine the original and more importantly held that he alone had copyright to them and of course issued them in 1853 as a supplemental volume to his eight-volume edition of Shakespeare.[127] Thus several key

127. In explaining in his introduction (xxv) that his edition did not include the new readings and thus "will remain an authentic representation of the text of our great dramatist, as it is contained in the early editions," Collier was having his cake and eating it too.

issues of the day were highlighted: the integrity of discoveries, the collegiality of scholars, the question of copyright, the competitiveness of the market. All touched Halliwell in one way or another. But one important topic, generally receiving slight attention in the discussion of the controversy, was thrown into relief by Halliwell's publications at this time. It was provoked by the Collier question and one devastating review of the first volume of his own folio edition of Shakespeare. For all the editing of Shakespeare, there was relatively little written or discussed about editing itself. There were models, of course, and heroes. But a theoretical base was hardly developed. To be sure, there was a turning away from the view that the old texts—the quartos and the folio—were simply imperfect relics, "dangling apricocks," which required the salutary intervention of the editor (or the careful pruning of the gardener) to restore their pristine perfection. And that existed in the guiding intelligence, if not the vigorous imagination, of the editor alone. In the mid nineteenth century Charles Knight was influential in countering this attitude by insisting on the absolute authority of the First Folio and thus helped establish a principle of editorial theory and a mode of practice. In his *Reasons for a New Edition of Shakespeare's Works* (1841), Collier called attention to the necessity of collating multiple copies of the same edition and of considering press variants. Both features were to be incorporated, albeit not bodily, into the dominant editorial practice established in the early part of the twentieth century. Even in their own context, however, Knight's view was too rigid, if not simplistic; Collier's too fragmentary, if not impressionistic. The whole question of a coherent editorial rationale was opened up by Collier's discovery of what came to be known as the Perkins Folio.

It is hard to deny that those who took the forefront against Collier—among them Singer, Dyce, and Halliwell—had personal motives: all were, or were in the act of, producing their own editions of Shakespeare. For Halliwell not only the Perkins Folio but also the Bridgewater House documents were a special source of irritation, for he had accepted Collier's findings in the *Life* and, when they were found to be forgeries, he was "disappointed" and, so his wife's diary entry for 10 February 1853, "had to alter the sheets of his new Shak. in consequence." And there were other sources of irritation as well which might account for a prejudiced evaluation.[128] Still, Halliwell attempted in his pamphlets of

---

128. One such may be deduced from Collier's assertion, "As to calling upon you to sacrifice any notes or criticisms on Shakespeare to me, I never contemplated such a thing—Neither did I ever dream of asking you to furnish me with

1852 and 1853 not to attack Collier personally or to minimize his contributions to the study of Shakespeare and indeed to scholarship itself. All, he repeated, was done (so one reviewer) in a "spirit of friendliness and truth"–at least in the first publication, *A Few Remarks on the Emendation, "Who Smothers Her with Painting," in the Play of Cymbeline* (1852).

What emerges from the first few pages of this slim fifteen-page pamphlet are the outlines of editorial principles which Halliwell was to continue in the next two pamphlets on the Collier controversy, also published by John Russell Smith in 1853. For one thing, Halliwell accents philology as the main determinant for editorial procedure. His lexicographical experience with early English texts, not to mention his linguistic bent and knowledge and his close association with Thomas Wright, made him especially sensitive to what he termed the "language of idiom" as a way of perceiving and evaluating the "phraseology" of the sixteenth and seventeenth centuries.[129] Historical linguistics was hardly developed in the early 1850s, and Trench had not yet made the proposals which inspired the Philological Society to take up the challenge of preparing a new English dictionary based on historical principles. Yet Halliwell was confident enough to state that the "English language underwent greater changes between 1600 and 1630" (p. 5) than in the two centuries that followed. Nevertheless, he continued, the "idiom of the language" has not undergone any "sensible variation, certainly no important change" since then, however much semantic variation there may have been or however many new words may have been created. Freely admitting the necessity of correcting errors of importance which perforce exist in the original works (given their history), and pointing to the absence of contemporary authorities, Halliwell cannot but welcome Collier's discovery. For it appears to be the sole surviving witness of a "person evidently acquainted with the author he attempts to correct," one whose "corrections are as nearly contemporary with the work itself" (pp.

information respecting any of your Shakespearean discoveries" (8 April 1852; LOA 47:30).

129. Collier seems to have anticipated this criterion and attempted to defuse it in the introduction to *Notes and Emendations*: "I shall probably be told, in the usual terms, by some whose prejudices or interests may be affected by the ensuing volume, that the old corrector knew little about the spirit or language of Shakespeare; and that, in the remarks I have ventured on his emendations, I prove myself to be in a similar predicament. The last accusation is probably true: I have read and studied our great dramatist for nearly half a century, and if I could read and study him for half a century more, I should yet be far from arriving at an accurate knowledge of his works" (xxvi).

6-7). Thus the apparent instability of the text would be to an extent counteracted by a kind of synchronic philological control. Interpretations would be simultaneous, as it were, with the work itself, thus apparently stemming the diachronic flux.

But–a crucial reservation–from a textual and logical point of view, that errors may exist does not necessarily mean that the corrections are of those particular errors. And from a philological point of view, since Halliwell believed that "it may fairly be questioned whether the idiom of the language has undergone any sensible variation, certainly no important change" (p. 5) in the last century and a half, emendation which cannot be proved to be authorial–and that is the case with Shakespeare's works–cannot rest solely on one witness, even if contemporary. The emender or editor must in all instances submit to a law "well known to every student that in philology, as in science, there are systematic boundaries which, when confirmed by evidence and observation, must not be violated without the strongest proof of the cases being exceptional" (p. 7). Halliwell then postulates the "two circumstances under which no manuscript emendation of so late a date as 1632 will be admissible":

1. It will not be admissible in any case where good sense can be satisfactorily made of the passage as it stands in the original, even although the correction may appear to give greater force or harmony to the passage.
2. It will not be admissible in any alteration of an idiomatic passage, where a similar turn of language can be produced in any contemporary writer; and it must be at once rejected, if the like idiom can be discovered in other parts of the works of Shakespeare himself (pp. 7-8).

Applying these criteria to Collier's volume, Halliwell can only conclude that in many of the emendations Collier "almost unhesitatingly adopt[s] readings that merely have the merit of variation, and give[s] his immediate attention to others which admit of the greatest doubt" (p. 8). Although repeatedly affirming his respect for the person and work of Collier–"It is only a student who can really appreciate the labours of a student; and Mr. Collier's exertions ... have been so arduous, so meritorious, and ... so successful, it is ... quite unnecessary to disclaim any idea of controversy beyond the gentle one of suggesting what we imagine to be the path of Truth" (p. 8)–Halliwell's close examination of one "correction" in *Cymbeline*, comparing similar locutions in older plays, confirms for him the necessity of "ascertaining whether or no we are departing from the phraseology of the poet and his contemporaries" (p. 14). Accordingly, he cannot accept the emendation.

The response of the *Athenaeum* (10 April 1852, p. 403) to Halliwell's work was, unexpectedly perhaps, straightforward. In what was more a summary than a review, Thomas Kibble Hervey, the editor, simply outlined the salient points without further comment. It was not likely, however, that Collier or his cohorts were pleased or conciliatory. There were too many things going on—too many rivalries, too many intrigues, too many publications: Byzantine would seem to be the most appropriate adjective to describe the attitudes and activities of the Shakespeareans and their Society. As if anticipating a broil, and thus attempting to soothe the emotions, the *Literary Gazette*, after giving numerous examples of Collier's emendations and agreeing with Halliwell's criteria, made a special point of reiterating that Halliwell's criticism was offered "in a spirit of friendliness and truth" (10 April 1852, pp. 334-5). At any rate it is not completely surprising that the *Athenaeum* should violently attack the first volume of Halliwell's folio Shakespeare, that Halliwell should feel that Collier, a frequent and favored reviewer and one with an axe to grind, was among the anonymous reviewers, and that Halliwell's immediate response of three pamphlets in 1853 constituted but one volley in a pamphlet war—all this coincidental with the demise of the Shakespeare Society and the sudden interruption of what had been a frank, fruitful, and amicable correspondence between Collier and Halliwell: there appear to be no extant letters between them from 1 May 1853 to 27 December 1856.

Curiosities of Modern Shaksperian Criticism, dated July 1853, was Halliwell's response to the attack on the first volume of his folio Shakespeare in the *Athenaeum* of 2 July 1853 (pp. 796-9). It was immediate, detailed, and far-reaching—responding to twelve "unfair" misrepresentations by the reviewers, as well as elucidating his role in the examination of the Bridgewater House documents and Collier's "misinterpretation" of the Dulwich College Joan Alleyn letter which mentioned Shakespeare. The key figure in all three topics was Collier, and Halliwell seemed convinced that Collier "is generally understood to be one of the *Athenaeum* reviewers!" (p. 20). To Halliwell the attack on his Shakespeare was still another instance of personal animosity and professional competitiveness. He could think of no other motivation. Accordingly, he constantly reiterates his own impartiality and respect for the opinions of others. Once again, he feels himself mistreated, not taken at his full worth, and unjustly abused—like some of the personalities he had treated (Samuel Morland, Simonds D'Ewes), causes he had pursued (the *Letter to Egerton* and the Camden Society), and sensitive "assaulted" authors (Francis

Douce). In this respect his final assertion that he is "personally nearly indifferent to the mere external acknowledgments of criticism ... [i.e. his] consenting to entomb the results of so many years' labour in so small an impression" (p. 30) must be regarded as a kind of rhetorical device to stress how deeply he was involved. The pamphlet is an *apologia* for his professional competence as well. He is at pains to justify his knowledge of Elizabethan "phraseology" and Shakespeare's idiolect. He again rejects the type of emendation which "inclines to violent alterations in the text, in passages that mostly require only a little attention to be perfectly intelligible as they stand in the original" (p. 16). He reiterates his professional care and courtesy in dealing with the "modern forgeries" in the possession of the Earl of Ellesmere (Collier's employer) by quoting *in extenso* from his folio Shakespeare his fair treatment of Collier, admitting with candor that he had believed the documents to be genuine until he had examined them and, in an appended note, adding that the Earl of Ellesmere "most generously" gave him the "amplest permission to express any doubts that may be entertained on the subject." Above all, Halliwell was defending his particular kind of scholarship. For the final charge of the *Athenaeum* reviewer, replicating Peter Cunningham's criticism in his review of the *Life* five years earlier, was intolerable to him: "The man who is now wanted as an editor of Shakespeare, is one who will raise him out of the darkness of antiquarianism into the broad daylight of common sense!" (p. 799). The deep pain it caused Halliwell can be measured by his surrounding his detailed *apologia* with the high moral tone. At the beginning: "Whenever a work possesses valuable information peculiar to itself, there is a certainty that it will be appreciated in time, in opposition to all adverse testimonies" (p. 3). And at the end: "I have a far higher motive than any that could result in the hope of accomplishing a successful refutation of an adverse critic. I cannot but think a public service will be rendered by the exposure of the incompetency and unfairness of a Journal, which, by its own arrogance and subtlety, is calculated to impose on all but those who have paid peculiar attention to the subjects on which it ventures to decide" (pp. 30-1).

The *Athenaeum* responded immediately (13 August 1853, pp. 960-1) and accordingly, not so much with a normal review as with a total rejection of what it regarded as only an "avowed reply" to its review of the folio Shakespeare. There are no details, and no patience, only a harsh repulsion of Halliwell's pamphlet as "one of the rarest displays of egotism that we remember to have seen perpetrated in print," of his "unmitigated puff of his own work," of "exclusive competency in Shakespeare," of his "pretension ... to infallibility as an expounder of disputed texts," and of his inability to "follow"–not to mention accept–"the language of common argument." After rubbing salt, as it were, into each of the very sore points of Halliwell's own defence, the reviewer–once again Hervey–also adopts the high moral tone by denying Halliwell's "insinuation" that the *Athenaeum* "is *lent* to one of the parties in a literary question!" (p. 961): "With a gentleman who can do this we decline further argument." And, stiffly righteous, he concludes, "A higher tone of feeling on his part would have suggested that, of all the others, the hands in question are precisely those into which his book would *not* be placed for review, by those who have the conduct of the *Athenaeum*." His trump–nay, triumphing–card is that the suspected reviewer is not the one Halliwell assumes him to be. Indeed, although Hervey mentions no names, the reviewer turns out to have been John Bruce. But had Halliwell known this, his feelings of persecution would not have been allayed. For in referring to *reviewers* Halliwell makes clear that his sense of conspiracy was always keen. And although at this time he seems to have had fairly cordial relations with Bruce, he could hardly have forgotten the clashes between the Wright faction and that of Bruce and W. J. Thoms.[130] Thus even a favorable comment can be judged as somewhat suspicious, as when the anonymous reviewer in *Blackwood's Edinburgh Magazine* a month later (74 [1853], 303) says nothing of the pamphlet other than stressing the very points made elsewhere: "Mr. Halliwell's competency to deal with the text of our great poet, and with all that concerns him, is, we believe, all but universally acknowledged–the best proof of which is the confidence reposed in him by the subscribers to the magnificent edition now publishing under his auspices; a confidence which, we are convinced, he will not betray by any ill-judged deviations from the authentic readings."

Halliwell's next pamphlet, *Observations on Some of the Manuscript Emendations of the Text of Shakespeare, and Are They Copyright?*, also dated July

---

130. There was some friction towards the end of 1852. Bruce claimed "not to know that I have any such papers" (most likely connected with Bridgewater House) as Halliwell wanted to examine (26 November 1852; LOA 46:26). He then agreed to search for them but Halliwell would need the concurrence of the Council of the Shakespeare Society (1 December 1852; LOA 46:27), finally finding them (22 December 1852; LOA 48:17). On 31 August 1852 (LOA 60:2) Bruce wrote that he could not afford the folio Shakespeare but considered it a "very important" undertaking. On 6 April 1841 (LOA 30:57) Bruce denied having written a review of *Rishanger* in the *Gentleman's Magazine* or any other book of Halliwell's, vowing, "unless I very much change my mind, I shall never do so." In 1846 he savaged Halliwell's *Letters of the Kings of England* in the *Gentleman's Magazine*. See pp. 160-2.

1853, takes up the same theme and stance. Halliwell denies any personal motivation against Collier, even an attack on him or speaking "contemptuously" of his work. In point of fact, however, he hardens his position, having "not at present discovered a single *new* reading ... that will bear the test of examination" (p. 3). To the test of the idiom of language or "common occurrence," he introduces that of "coincidental suggestions" (p. 10), showing that numerous "new" readings in the Perkins Folio had already appeared in editions Collier must have been aware of but which remained unmentioned in his eight-volume edition. Although quick to assert that Collier, working rapidly, might well have overlooked them, Halliwell (not missing an opportunity to demonstrate his courtesy) does imply, however, carelessness (of which he himself had been accused) or, worse, deception on Collier's part. And the question of copyright—Collier's withholding information from his competitors—is thus answered, for Collier cannot claim to own what is not his. At the time, of course, the charge of forgery was not being levelled at Collier. But, whether motivated by personal or professional animus, Halliwell and other prominent Shakespeareans were floating words like "misleading" and "deceiving." The *Athenaeum*'s two-sentence notice (30 July 1853, p. 916) of the work as a "peevish pamphlet," whose judgment "is on a par with its logic," did little to clear the air. And Halliwell's slight, privately issued *Observations on the Shaksperian Forgeries at Bridgewater House; Illustrative of a Facsimile of the Spurious Letter of H. S.*, also in 1853, added little of substance to the argument but doubtless served to darken the cloud hovering above Collier by posing "genuine" against "forgery," "deception" against "truth," for the "whole matter is surrounded by the gravest suspicions and difficulties" (p. 8). And years would pass before the matter was clarified.

+++

• *The Folio Edition of Shakespeare*

When Halliwell announced in 1848 that he planned to spend the next ten years producing an edition of Shakespeare, he little realized that it was to take twenty-four years from the beginning of his "earnest attention" to it in 1840 to the appearance of the final volume in 1865; that when advertising the work in 1852 (envisioning six years for its completion) his estimated twenty volumes would shrink to sixteen, that he would more than once be on the verge of abandoning the undertaking altogether for want of money, nerve, support, or any combination thereof. He had no doubt about his knowledge or capability. Shakespeare was the center of his scholarly universe. There were enough extant and promised editions for him to judge where he could make the most profound impression. In his own editions, reprints, glossaries, and dictionary of early English literature he had collected vast amounts of material for illustration and commentary, so much in fact that he was later able to present the Shakespeare Birthplace Trust with 128 volumes called "Notes upon the Works of Shakespeare," arranged by play—mounted cuttings and handwritten quotations from early books and manuscripts, as well as some critical observations of his own and of others—as "supplementary" to those in his folio edition. In Edward Capell, to whose memory he dedicated the work, he had found a model for textual matters (and recognized another of those maligned figures with whom he was wont to identify). He also had a theory to prove. Its premise was simple: "It is a well-known fact that no literary or artistic work maintains its original value unless the impression is strictly limited." It was the premise restated in his pamphlet *On the Means Adopted to Insure the Rarity of the Privately Printed Works of James O. Halliwell* (1854), which introduced twelve reprints and was to govern his cumulative series of eighty-one reprints published from 1860 to 1864. Accordingly, the edition was limited to 150 copies, each numbered copy with the printer's autograph certificate, and all plates and woodcuts were to be destroyed. The cost was to be two guineas per volume: the whole work, he announced in 1852, was to be completed in six years—"d.v." inserted parenthetically by Halliwell—and the cost to the subscriber would be some £40 (though rising costs might account for a slight increase).

The idea of so limited a subscription was questioned, if not criticized, by some of Halliwell's closest friends and colleagues. On 19 June 1852 (LOA 62:35) Robert Balmanno, writing from New York, suggested that the edition be extended to at least 200 at £5.5 per volume; on 17 August 1852 (LOA 62:31) he urged that the number be at least 250; a few months later he reported that the great majority of subscribers wanted 500 printed (5 November 1852; LOA 62:33). F. G. Tomlins thought 250 copies would be safer than 150 (5 October 1852; LOA 62:18). Thomas Wright, as always, was ready with cunning strategy:

I have been thinking a good deal about your Shakespeare—and I have another plan to suggest to get over your difficulty, which I think will be the safest of all. Print 200, and put the extra 50 copies at 3 guineas—send a circular round to the subscribers, saying that finding with the sub. to 150 copies as originally fixed you would not be able to make the work as perfect as you desired—mention new discoveries of material—you have therefore determined on 200, but for the protection and advantage of the first 150, you have raised the price of all above the 150 first subscribers, whereby the latter will get more for their money than they could have done on the original plan. You will thus get at all events 50 copies at your own disposal, even supposing you get no more than 150 subscribers (23 October 1852; LOA 43:9).

Others found the edition simply too expensive, among them members of the Shakespeare Society–such as Macready, Collier, Cunningham, and Bruce–and did not subscribe. Halliwell, however, was determined not to alter his plan, despite Stevens's admonitory "I fear you will never be able to carry out your vast plan" (9 July 1852; LOA 61:2). Besides, he was not without a measure of idealism, as is evident in his rejection of the "undeserved insult" that his requiring subscriptions to be paid in advance was a "stratagem." Replying to J. H. Fennell, he explained that "a little reflection would have shown you that had money-making been my object I shd have increased the number of copies, but having very distinctly stated in public that the limit wd not be increased under any circumstances, I voluntarily sacrifice all hopes of profit & incur the risk of a severe loss by adhering to the original limit" (30 April 1853; LOA 103:49).

The fulfillment of the plan was to prove even riskier and certainly more arduous than Halliwell could have imagined. But, ever enterprising and ambitious, he could not resist the challenge and set about to produce–"without arrogance," he was careful to stress–the "most copious edition of Shakespeare ever printed, and one of the handsomest and most important series of volumes that could be placed in an English library." Halliwell's management of his folio Shakespeare illustrates the many-sidedness of what may be called his bookmanship. The prospectus, which he also, and cleverly, arranged to be placed in *Notes and Queries* (10 July 1852, p. 47), is a typical mixture of scholarly description and commercial enterprise. Twelve years of preparation behind him and aware of the existence of numerous editions of Shakespeare already or about to appear on the market, Halliwell assures the reader that "there yet remains room for one comprehensive edition which shall answer the requirements of the student and zealous inquirer." It will be up-to-date in annotation and documentation, for "no pains will be spared to render this edition the most complete in every respect that has yet been produced: superseding entirely the Variorum edition of 1821, with the addition of all Shakespearian discoveries of any importance which have been made since that period." Further, the work will be "copiously illustrated by facsimiles and woodcuts, the direction of which has been undertaken by Mr. Fairholt, who has also most kindly promised to assist me in the selection" of historical documents and artifacts, as well as of the monuments at Stratford-upon-Avon and other sites. Among others, Lord Londesborough has made available his collection of English antiquities to strengthen the archaeological illustration. Further details follow, including mention of the price and concluding that "for a comparatively small annual expenditure (about six guineas) [reckoned Halliwell] the subscriber will possess ... what is [not] likely to fall in value. He will possess a work that can never come into the market, but, in its pecuniary relations, will stand somewhat in the position of a proof engraving, only to be possessed by a very limited number." As if this were not enough, Halliwell issued a four-page flyer, "Opinions of the Press on the Design of the Monograph Edition of Shakespeare," citing responses to his announcement in the form of long quotations from the *Art Journal*, the *Athenaeum*, the *Literary Gazette*, and *Sharpe's London Magazine*.

At Avenue Lodge, Brixton Hill, where Halliwell had moved in July of 1846, all his forces were mobilized. Bookshelves and cabinets were the first order of business. Mrs. Halliwell and for a time his sister, Louisa, were put to the task of collating the plays, as well as perusing and as necessary cutting extracts from books for articles and notes. An extensive administrative apparatus was erected: prospectuses had to be conceived, addresses of possible subscribers located, forms printed and circulated to subscribers and for their responses, estimates for the cost of paper, printing, and binding required, permissions for facsimiles to be had and acknowledged, reports on the progress of the edition issued, etc., etc. It was no accident that one of Halliwell's main items of furniture was a small printing press. Bookkeeping was a continuous and arduous task, but Halliwell was a perfect specimen of Victorian diligence, conscience, and accuracy. In an undated note (LOA 85:30) Halliwell scrupulously itemized "My first vol. cost":

Paper	84.0.0
Slips	8.13.0
Fairholt	67.0.0
Travelling Expenses: Stratford, Canterbury, Oxford	31.0.0
Binding	37.10.6
Netherclift	12.5.0
Ashbee	9.16.0
Fisher	3.2.0

```
Brooker .................... 4.10.0
Marriage bond .............. 5.0.0
Drawing of Crown Inn ....... 1.11.6
Carrier .................... 1.3.0
Henry (messages proofs) ........ 2.14
Jewitt (cuts each, for books) .... 8.8.0
Adlard .................... 122.8.6
Sundries say at least .......... 10.0.0
.................... £409.1.6
```

Mrs. Halliwell's diary in 1852 describes how busy they were sending out prospectuses and receiving subscriptions, etc., records punctually how many subscriptions have been received (128 by 29 September, 162 by 14 October, 187 by 22 October, 200 by 26 October), and that "J. has already £1015 pd in advance for the S." (27 October). As if this was not enough, Halliwell kept and sorted practically every letter to and from every subscriber over the entire period. He then had them "1/2 bound in dark calf, strongly mounted" and in 1872 presented them–in eighteen volumes–to the Shakespeare Birthplace Trust (SBT ER 34/1). The concern–including complaints and cancellations, an especially hostile review in the *Athenaeum*, as well as praise and encouragement–continued throughout the production. (Volume 60 [1852-1857] of the Letters of Authors in the Edinburgh collection also contains numerous letters from happy and unhappy subscribers.) And despite occasional discouragement–Mrs. Halliwell's diary records his writing Fairholt that he is thinking of giving up the edition after the Comedies, "making them complete, & adding woodcuts & plates &c in the last volume, & cancelling King John ... [and] of returning the subscribers their money" (30 April 1860); his annoyance with J. E. Adlard's "extremely careless" work on Volume 12 (19 February 1864); the fact that the covers of the Volume 15 have burned "which will partly delay the book coming out" (12 July 1865), among other difficulties–Halliwell did not relax his exacting standards. In 1864, for example, he wrote to his printer J. E. Adlard: "I tell you candidly I intend to aim at a perfection in printing far beyond any attained yet by this generation, & I shall not be satisfied until I can have a book turned out with all the brightness and sharpness of books of the 15th Century ... If I live long enough, & have energy, the books to follow this folio Shakespeare are to beat it into fits as specimens of typography and woodcut printing," concluding with a flattering bit of motivation, "Are you inclined to try to be *the* Aldus of the nineteenth century?" (8 March 1864; LOA 97:28).

The folio Shakespeare was itself a noteworthy specimen. Halliwell chose the folio size, partly as homage to the First Folio, partly because it is most "convenient," its 40 by 29 cm. suiting the "size of the facsimiles, most of which would other wise have to be folded," and partly, to be sure, to convey physically the stature and splendor of the enterprise. Printed on expensive paper and with a generous type size (ca. 20 pt. for text, 14 pt. for citations), the first volume, entered at Stationers Hall on 19 May 1853, weighed fifteen pounds. By contrast Halliwell's preface is brief and to the point. There is hardly a hint of bardolatry in its five pages. The opening is apparently another instance of Halliwell's customary device or tactic of preceding a text with a simple three-or-five-page description or statement of intent rather than with any critical assessment. "Long explanatory prefaces so seldom answer any useful purpose, I am anxious, even at the risk of being thought abrupt, to state the general design of the present work in the fewest words." It would be difficult to object to this view as expanded in at least the first half of the opening paragraph:

The object proposed to be accomplished is to offer,the student an edition of the works of Shakespeare, accompanied by a collection of all the facts and documents respecting their literary history of any importance that have yet been discovered; by copious and discursive annotations on their obsolete phraseology, and obscure allusions, elucidated, wherever requisite, by archaeological engravings; and by illustrative extracts from contemporary works, exhibiting the popular opinions of the time on natural history, science, and philosophy, many of which are adopted, or alluded to, by the great dramatist (iii).

What avows to be a straightforward and objective presentation of extensive data is balanced, in the middle of the paragraph, by a second aim: the investigation and assessment of the authenticity and value of the materials which have been collected by previous editors. In fact, the remaining four pages of the preface reflect Halliwell's engagement in the controversies of the day. He does not hesitate to single out the "skilful fabricators of modern times," and consequently excluding from his work the "celebrated" Bridgewater House manuscripts (iv) and by indirection involving Collier, though not mentioning him by name. He does not hesitate to name Joseph Hunter, "whose acuteness is unquestionable," for having "selected one of his most important philological notes from a work that existed only in the imagination of the inventor" (iv-v). Fabrication and deception extend as well to the "old works made perfect by means of more than one copy" and to "several of the early quartos of Shakespeare's plays, which have been sold of late years, [but] are not really genuine copies" (v). Halliwell goes even further in criticizing several popular editions both for their "censures" of the "elder commentators" and for not acknowledging how "greatly all modern critics are indebted to them" (v). This is a perennial Halliwellian theme, underscored by his dedication of the entire work to the memory of Edward Capell. Finally, generous to those who have helped him, Halliwell names those who have made accessible books and manuscripts, who have been ready with information or have given permission for facsimiles, and promising to restate his obligations at the conclusion of the work.[131] Since his "chief aid has been derived from the free communication of books and manuscripts" (vii), he cannot disguise his "disappointments." In his concluding sentence—clearly more stung than sad—he singles out the Duke of Devonshire and the Prerogative Office for refusing permission for facsimiles of the first quarto of *Hamlet* and Shakespeare's will.

Halliwell's defense of the elder commentators is reflected in the organization of the edition. His adherence to what had become the traditional elements since Rowe is apparent in his opening with a life of Shakespeare. He had already written a life in 1848, and so it is hardly surprising that he should incorporate it into his edition. To a large extent he simply modified his phrasing, although the cosmetic changes are so extensive as to be evidence enough that he did work through the previous version. And, although not much could possibly have occurred or been discovered in the short intervening period between the two works, he did in fact attempt to keep his documentation up to date. He added new records, like Richard Hathaway's will (pp. 91-2); he omitted the inventory of John Richardson (*Life*, pp. 118-19). He deleted material which had been exposed as fabrications, replacing one facsimile in the *Life*—the 1608 letter of Lord Southampton mentioning Shakespeare, one of the spurious Bridgewater House manuscripts[132]—and presented nine new ones. Fairholt provided additional illustrations, more than doubling the number from 75

---

131. A measure of Halliwell's concern is found in the gallant reply of Llewellynn Jewitt to Halliwell's apology for having omitted his name: "You ask me to tell you how you can 'make atonement' for the omission, and I have no objection to doing so by asking you to let me have the pleasure of assisting any of the future volumes in any way in which I can be useful,—the pleasure and gratification I should have at rendering assistance would, believe me, be quite sufficient 'atonement' for you to make" (20 May 1853; LOA 50:28).

132. See pp. 209 and 215.

to 157.[133] He did retain in a prominent position–on the title page in the *Life* and as frontispiece in the edition–the bust of Shakespeare in Holy Trinity Church, Stratford-upon-Avon. This is a confirmation of his view of Shakespeare, a middle-class citizen with middle-class problems and aspirations. It is, of course, what emerges from the "uniformly unspectacular" records and not the works. Halliwell is not a poet or psychologist. But except for those critics who have a personal axe to grind, there are few who would disagree with Schoenbaum's appraisal of Halliwell as "the greatest of the nineteenth-century biographers of Shakespeare in the exacting tradition of factual research which extends from Malone to Chambers."[134]

"The Formation of the Text," the next section, has a somewhat misleading title, for Halliwell pays relatively little attention to the bibliographical foundations or the technical aspects of Shakespeare's text beyond the customary alertness to the claims of the early quartos and the First Folio to textual authority. "For the greater number of plays of Shakespeare," Halliwell states, reflecting the opinion of the day, "the folio edition of 1623 is the first genuine authority; and ... for the others, where copies in quarto are to be found, the degree of critical value is to be ascertained by a careful regard to the circumstances under which the earlier editions appeared, and by a minute examination of the state of the texts" (p. 288). There is little to be argued with in this conservative position. Halliwell is not Greg or McKerrow, nor does he intend to be. His essay is, instead, a development of his philological thesis that Shakespeare, and all early texts for that matter, can only be recognized and thus be authenticated by an understanding of the state of language then and now. The thesis is, once again, that in the time of Shakespeare the "English language had assumed its present form ... that, in fact, the only differences to be traced between the language of Shakespeare and our own consist of peculiarities of diction and phraseology, to which is to be added, in written and printed works, an unsettled orthography" (p. 265). The implications of this thesis affect the nature of the modern edition of Shakespeare. The latter statement, for example, leads to an immediate consequence: Halliwell's preferring a modern-spelling edition to a reprint of early editions, not merely to avoid "unnecessarily embarrass[ing] their perusal by modern readers" but mainly because the old orthography had ceased to "form an integral portion of English grammar" (p. 265).

133. Some of the documents in the *Life* (pp. 335-6) are to be found in the list of illustrations in the edition.
134. *Shakespeare's Lives*, p. 290.

Accordingly, Halliwell concentrates on grammar, discussing and illustrating characteristics "peculiar" to Shakespeare's time. The aim puts him in the main stream of the treatment of Shakespeare's language, in a tradition of grammars which, as in the subtitle of E. A. Abbott's, "attempt to illustrate some of the differences between Elizabethan and modern English." He is also immediate and practical: the outlines guide and restrict the editor in his determination of what is or is not corrupt, as well as reducing the need for countless and repeated glosses and explanations.

The major portion of the essay is thus devoted to grammar. Word order, transpositions, and inversion are discussed (pp. 266-7). Special attention, with abundant examples, is paid to obsolete uses of particles (pp. 268-72), to redundant particles (pp. 273-4), to particles understood (pp. 275-6). After mentioning the need to account for the continual occurrence of ellipsis in Shakespeare and most writers of his day, Halliwell lists and briefly illustrates eighteen other "grammatical idioms," ranging from the "not always correctly used" tenses of relative pronouns (p. 277) to the "proper construction of sentences, involving the use of pronouns and the relative in connexion with each other" (p. 283). He lists thirty (a-z, ab-af) further "peculiar, and, for the most part, less general, modes of construction" (pp. 283-4), conceding that "many of the idioms ... till they are reconciled to the ear by a little practice, appear to be harsh and disagreeable" (p. 284). Halliwell is convinced of their authenticity and their legitimacy in the text. Only in the matter of punctuation, as in that of orthography, is he more flexible, holding that as a general rule the pointing in old editions had no authority and "in fact, the art of correct punctuation was neither practised, nor generally understood, in the time of Shakespeare" (p. 285). Thus he leaves both orthography and punctuation to the judgment of the modern editor to "vary or correct" (p. 284).

These observations serve to support the authority of the First Folio and some of the early quarto editions. They enable Halliwell as well to address the questions arising from Collier's discovery of the Perkins Folio. Admitting that "every old edition is, of course, worthy of careful examination, for it may contain happy corrections of corrupted passages," Halliwell nevertheless asserts, "but, beyond this, none of the later copies are of any value whatever, and should never be cited as *authorities*" (p. 288). To confirm this view, he presents numerous examples from his collation of the first five comedies in the First and Second Folios (pp. 288-94), concluding that the "alterations made in the second folio are for the most part errors in themselves, or corrections of the most obvious inaccuracies" (p. 294). After enumerating further "erroneous and unnecessary alterations and omissions" by the editor of the Second Folio (pp. 295-9), and "additions and insertions ... perhaps more prejudiced to the text than mere alterations" (pp. 299-301), in order to stress the necessity for observing the authority of the First Folio and certain early quartos, as well as to underline the importance of a proper philological frame of reference, Halliwell moves on from an indirect attack on the Perkins Folio through a direct criticism of the authority of the Second Folio to a direct criticism of Collier. For one thing, he asserts, "the question of authority can scarcely here be raised, except to be at once dismissed"; for another, many of the "specious variations" are "identical with later suggestions" (p. 302). Halliwell is diplomatic enough to say that he has "carefully considered" all the "deviations of any importance in Mr. Collier's volume" in the preparation of his own edition. But he is confident enough to assert that Collier, the "editor himself, in some of his supplemental notes, appears to admit their general want of authority, a fact which is incontestably confirmed by parallelisms quoted in the present work" (p. 303). Nor can he resist triumphing:

Enough has now been said to exhibit the principles of criticism, on which the text of this edition of Shakespeare is constructed. Others have acknowledged, in greater or lesser degrees, the truth of most of the positions here sought to be established; but no editor has yet resolved them into a comprehensive philological system, to be carried out in an uniform manner throughout the formation of the entire text. The result is, that in all previous editions, readings are selected, and the ancient text altered, according to the judgment or fancy of the editor having reference only to the particular word or passage; or, at all events, without the assistance which would have been afforded by the adoption of a sound generic theory. The present text will, it is hoped, exhibit that uniformity and truthfulness of character, which should attend the adoption of critical rules formed on the convictions resulting from a long course of reading; and its errors restricted to individual cases, where no philological canons are strictly applicable (p. 303).

Halliwell's regard for the textual authority of the First Folio and some of the early quartos is as well a pronouncement of the literary notion which governed his entire career,[135] even if it meant disagreeing with his close friend Charles Roach Smith, who at the time wrote, "I suspect Shakespeare must not be judged archaeologically. I will be bound he never

135. See, for example, p. 49.

gave propriety of costume or circumstances & their details a thought" (15 December 1853; LOA 53:11). Halliwell's treatment of the plays and their apparatus is, accordingly and not surprisingly, relatively restrained. The introduction to *The Tempest*, for example, proceeds in the standard manner: possible sources, analogues, or prototypes are presented. Shakespeare's reliance on a passage in Montaigne (quoted at length) effects a transition to a discussion of the dating of the play and then to its original production. The earliest notice of the performance on Hallowmas night, 1611, leads in turn to the possible connection of events and places in the play with the maritime expeditions of the period. After elucidating contemporary accounts of travels, strange events and creatures, in order to establish a kind of mythological context, Halliwell proceeds to the stage history of the play to 1807 and closes with brief remarks on the connection between the nature of some of the characters and their costumes.

The play itself is given as a plain text, with notes following each act. The notes show Halliwell's acquaintance with the major editions (which he quotes extensively) and his recognition of the need for glossing unfamiliar words and phrases (which he does by quoting parallel passages from other Shakespearean plays and contemporary early texts). What distinguishes the notes is Halliwell's archaeological bent: his willingness to devote great attention and much space to what in most cases can be considered atmospheric rather than substantive information. And, to be sure, it is difficult for him not to make the fullest use of the material from the storehouse of early English literature he had collected over many years. The display is impressive, although clearly overloaded. The note on *bombard* (Act 2, n. 45), for example, a full folio-page long, is illustrated by quotations from eight other works, as well as one by Shakespeare, and accompanied by a drawing by Fairholt. And, at the other end of the spectrum, Halliwell joins the ranks of editors past and present in glossing the obvious: "All wound with adders" (Act 2, n. 44)–"That is, observes Dr. Johnson, enwrapped by adders *wound* or twisted about me."

The approach remains constant throughout the twelve years which the edition required. Halliwell's particular interest in archaeological research remained dominant, modified only slightly according to the nature of the particular play or poem. As editor, as collector, and as dealer in books, he was conservative and traditionalist. This is not to say that he was totally dependent on tradition, but that he had firm opinions and, given the proper documentation, was firm in advocating them. An examination of his treatment of the plays singly would doubtless reveal a certain unevenness to be expected in any edition of so vast a corpus. Still, the opinions of editors of current variorum editions is not without interest. Recommending only partial collation of Halliwell's *1 Henry 6*, one editor found it "textually almost worthless," since it is heavily reliant on Collier (1842-44). Three others, editors of *As You Like It, The Merchant of Venice*, and *Julius Caesar*, consider Halliwell's text of those plays "extremely independent," "more independent than most 19th-century editions," and showing "considerable independence." All, as well as the editors of *2 Henry 4* and *Titus Andronicus*, recommend full collation.[136]

In the tide of his times—numerous popular and unreliable editions, fabrications and forgeries—stability was to be found in evidence and rational procedure. Halliwell did not hesitate to mention names of contemporaries, to agree or disagree, sometimes convincingly, sometimes not so. But, in all, he believed that his views were derived from or were supported by what he considered hard evidence. Given the luxuriousness of his edition, however, the extravagance of his claims, the exclusiveness of its subscribers, and his own controversial personality, it is not difficult to predict its immediate fate.

It began, even before the publication of the folio edition, in the pamphlet wars and controversies stirred by the discovery of numerous fabrications. Given its overall treatment of Halliwell, the *Athenaeum*'s announcement of the edition on 10 July 1852 (p. 752) closes with a touch of ominous expectation: "The plan is a bold one,–and 'protests .... much.' It will be for Mr. Halliwell to prove himself equal to the occasion." Appearing a year later, on 2 July 1853 (pp. 796-9), the review confirms the suspicion. It puts the work squarely in the midst of the arena, as it were, with an opening short paragraph on Joseph Hunter's reply to the attack on him in Dyce's attack on Collier. From the mildly patronizing tone towards Hunter–his long title "sufficiently explains his pamphlet ... a defence of his old suggestions ... writes altogether in a good spirit"–the review turns to Halliwell with the frowning concern of a parent about to reprove a child for naughty behavior: "For ourselves, we so earnestly desire to encourage every rational attempt to bring Shakespeare criticism and illustration into a more satisfactory condition, that we have from the first been willing to give Mr. Halliwell's attempt not merely a fair and candid, but a kind and deliberate attention,–uninfluenced by any consideration of how far his past labours ... indicate his possession of those qualities" (p. 797). The parent's disappointment is first expressed in sneering benevolence: "His first volume is now before us. We cheerfully

136. Richard Hosley, Richard Knowles, and Ruth McGugan, *Shakespeare Variorum Handbook* (New York, 1971), p. 75.

commend it as a favourable example of modern typography. It is handsomely printed ... and contains a multitude of printed little illustrations ... on stout paper manufactured by Dickinson." The spanking, full and lusty, follows promptly. What else can be expected of one who has, from the beginning, lacked those attributes indispensable for such a task: "competent learning, painstaking carefulness, unimpassioned calmness, and a sound discriminating judgment" (p. 797)? Nothing is spared. The "Life" has only one important alteration of Halliwell's earlier *Life of Shakespeare*; his change of mind regarding the authenticity of the fabricated Ellesmere manuscripts. Otherwise, "we have not been able to find in it anything ["fresh documentary evidence"] of the kind." The "only use" of certain facsimiles is to "enable readers to correct the mistakes in Mr. Halliwell's copies ... both in his former and in his present editions." "A gentleman," scolds the reviewer, "who is very sharp on the blunders of other people should be a little more accurate himself." Halliwell's "Essay on the Formation of the Text" is "perhaps the best of Mr. Halliwell's additions to Shakespeare criticism," but has "slender claims to originality" and fails to acknowledge distinctly his obligations to the 1821 variorum edition and Malone (a particularly stinging rebuke, considering Halliwell's defence of the "elder commentators"). Even more so, the essay is full of grammatical errors, especially of coherence of subject and verb, by Halliwell himself at the very moment he is discussing the same topic in Shakespeare (p. 798). As for *The Tempest*, the introduction contains nothing new, the text differs little from that in the variorum, the antiquarian notes are excessive, the glossarial notes (most derived from the variorum, the "rest ... conceived in its worst spirit") are often dispensable. That the anonymous reviewer, now identified as John Bruce, "sincerely regrets not being able to speak of this book more favourably" (p. 799) is arguable. A year earlier, he had regretted not being able to afford Halliwell's "very important" undertaking (31 August 1852; LOA 60:2). It is clear that Bruce and others have always regarded Halliwell as incorrigible and unredeemable, incapable "above all things [of] attain[ing] greater accuracy and carefulness." Turning the knife, Bruce concludes with what amounts to a thrust–intentional or not–at his own class and profession as antiquary and historian: "such carelessness may go down with an audience of 150,–but would never find favour with the general public. The man who is now wanted as an editor of Shakespeare, is one who will raise him out of the darkness of antiquarianism into the broad daylight of common sense!"

Halliwell was hurt. His wife describes his reaction to the "very nasty article" in her diary entry for 3 July 1853: "It annoys him very much because it is full of untruths & evidently written in spite." His immediate reply, his pamphlet *Curiosities of Modern Shaksperian Criticism,* could not alleviate his anxiety. Attacked was but the first volume of a projected twenty, and he had already to raise the subscription from forty to sixty guineas (so Bruce's doubtless gleeful footnote). The end of the "monster" or "elephant," as it was affectionately called, would take twelve more years. The way was to be long and thorny.

9

Family and Career: 1848-1853

Halliwell could count on his friends to help smooth the way, as they had done before. And in the whirlpool of the suspected forgeries in which Halliwell's pamphlets and folio edition were swirling, they were ever ready with advice and support. Thomas Wright, as always, offered opinions and counsel on how to respond to the *Athenaeum* review: Halliwell should "point out some gross blunders ... which would be understood and appreciated by people in general ... send a copy to all the subscribers, and sell or give away all the rest ... write with great severity, treating the Athenaeum with the utmost scorn and contempt" (Wednesday morning, July 1853; LOA 43:21). Having gone through the proofs of Halliwell's reply, he would avoid the matter of the grammatical errors and "would have nothing but what is strong and telling" (Friday morning, July 1853; LOA 43:22). Some friends offered support by confirming their subscriptions or recommending still others who might subscribe. Others praised the edition: even Panizzi, no ally of Halliwell's, wrote, "I have seen and admired your first vol. of Shakspere which I expect to see very soon spoiled & thumbed by readers" (6 June [1853]; LOA 49:72). Still others complimented Halliwell on his reply: "The reviewer of your first volume will remember your castigation to the day of his death," wrote William Boone, the bookseller to the British Museum (11 August 1853; LOA 54:53). Even those thought to be hostile appeared, diplomatically or tactically or whatever, outwardly at least conciliatory. Peter Cunningham was "more than inclined to be a subscriber," adding humorously that one "defect" of the prospectus was the lack of an "allusion to the thickness of the volumes. Twenty Falstaffs wd not look well nor would twenty Slenders" (9 July 1852; LOA 56:34). Later he rejected Halliwell's contention that he was one of the reviewers (6 August 1853; LOA 56:60). Even Collier, the center of much of the turbulence and himself the editor of a competing edition, although "not rich enough ... to become a subscriber" (11 July 1852; LOA 56:39), said he was "glad ... subscription proceeds so prosperously" (12 September 1852; LOA 60:71) and went so far as to forward a copy of the prospectus of the "Monster" edition to a "very stable friend" who wished to subscribe (4 December 1852; LOA 53:22). There were, in support, even brighter moments, like Wright's reporting, "Isn't Blackwood laying it into [name excised] this time?!!! You will be pleased at what they say about you" (31 August 1853; LOA 42:45). There were, in support, lighter moments, like T. C. Croker's comic "ballad verse" or "May men toe more eye" on Collier in the wake of the Grimaldi satire (August 1853; LOA 47:8).[137] All these responses were predictable, coming over the years from the tight groups around Halliwell and from the larger one composed of those to whom Halliwell had been helpful and courteous but who were not deeply involved in the machinations of the societies or professional rivalries. The greatest support, and offering the most detailed picture of Halliwell himself, came from within the walls of his house at Avenue Lodge, Brixton Hill, Surrey, where he lived from mid 1846 to 1855.

Although the British Museum affair was approaching its climax and Halliwell received a subpoena on 11 June 1846 to appear at the trial, the daily activities of his family seemed undisturbed in their normalcy. Typical is Mrs. Halliwell's diary entry for 25 May 1846: "Lovely day. I corrected 2 proofs of Dict. & wrote to L. Marshall & Miss Ord & worked at Dict. James up at 1/2 p. 5 oc. this morning working at S. I worked & practised & we all walked out after tea." In the days that followed, work and walks continued, the auctioneer came to look at the house, the piano was packed up, as were the glass and the books, Blenheim Palace was visited with the Wrights (who were house guests), strawberries were gathered and (on the day the trial was postponed) raspberries picked. The dropping of the case against Halliwell on 26 June did not interrupt the packing of plate and linen, nor did the moving of the furniture on 21 July prevent Mrs. Halliwell from writing four letters, beginning to read Frederika Bremer's *The President's Daughter*, and walking in the garden with Halliwell and his mother. This busy and yet controlled harmony was remarkable (although for the time perhaps not untypical). When on 23 July 1846 the Halliwells left Islip for a house in Brixton Hill which Mrs. Halliwell "like[d] very much," they did so not only with a sense of relief at the outcome of the British Museum affair and the exhilaration of a new start but also, as Mrs.

137. The title page of this anonymous sixteen-page pamphlet, now attributed to Fairholt, is self-explanatory: *The Grimaldi Shakspere. Notes and Emendations on the Plays of Shakspere, from a Recently-Discovered Annotated Copy by the Late Joseph Grimaldi, Esq. Comedian.* And in black-letter: N.B.–These Notes and Emendations are Copyright, and must not be used by any Editor in any future Edition of Shakspere. The publisher was Halliwell's friend John Russell Smith.

Halliwell's diary continually illustrates, with abounding energy, professional motivation, and domestic content. They were, in short, a happy family.

Avenue Lodge, so Mrs. Halliwell's diary entry for 24 July 1846, had "a drawing room, dining room & study &c. on the ground floor & four bedrooms upstairs with a garden to the road. Windows opening under the verandah." On that, the first day there, in addition to unpacking books and "arrang[ing] our things," they received a visitor from Chelsea who stayed for lunch, and later Mrs. Halliwell continued reading *The President's Daughter.* Within a short time, the household was functioning: bookshelves discussed with the carpenter, furniture arriving, guests coming for tea or dinner, Henrietta Somerset (nicknamed Harry), just three and talking and at four being taught her letters by her mother, the Vauxhall Gardens fireworks viewed, floor cloth, engravings and curtains decorating the dining room, Halliwell arranging the books in his study, the first anniversary of Richard's death marked and the Halliwells coming out of mourning, a nice church found, Halliwell suffering from eye trouble and then a dreadful toothache (which did not prevent him from copying twenty pages of manuscripts), Mrs. Halliwell copying a roll twenty-five feet long. Reading, working, unpacking, decorating, entertaining, theatergoing, sightseeing, shopping, dancing the night away, hearing Harry's lessons, Halliwell's parents joining them in Avenue Lodge, as did Louisa. The months rolled by. On 30 October 1847 Mrs. Halliwell copied six circulars, corrected proofs, and "walked out" with Harry and James; on the next day her second daughter, Charlotte (after Halliwell's mother) Mary (after Mrs. Halliwell's sister) was born. And within a few days she was busy again copying, collating, and attending to all her domestic chores, looking after husband, children, in-laws, and Louisa, who suddenly required leeches, quinine, poppy pills, lancing (Mrs. Halliwell held her head), and poulticing.

The energy of the Halliwells was an important factor of their harmony. They were busy, and their activities were both complementary and supplementary. They worked together and they had their individual pursuits. James and Henrietta worked on projects together, gathered at the piano together, and went on excursions together. James attended his meetings, visited libraries, went to sales at Sotheby's. Henrietta heard Harry's lessons, shopped in town, read current literature in the evening. What bound them, above all, was true and unwavering affection, respect, and concern for the well-being of the entire nuclear family living in Avenue Lodge (including the elder Halliwells who came from Islip to spend half the year there, Louisa, and for a time Sarah Ann, Richard's widow, and her two sons) and in Middle Hill (including Henrietta's sisters, Mary and Kate, Lady Molyneux, her aunt and godmother of Halliwell's first daughter, Henrietta, who took the family name Somerset, and, even though distantly, Mrs. Halliwell's father, the cantankerous Thomas Phillipps, who was never out of her thoughts and with whom she never ceased trying for a reconciliation). The Halliwells shared happy times. Though Halliwell apparently disliked large parties, preferring to stay home and arrange his books (Diary, 20 March 1848) he could always be counted on to join the family: at an evening party given by the elder Halliwells, they danced "till 3 or 4 o'c" (Diary, 11 February 1847); with the Wrights, who were constantly dropping in to spend the day and stay for dinner or over, they "sang & played in the afternoon" (Diary, 1 May 1848). The house was, it seems, always receiving visitors, expected or not. A compact entry for 3 May 1848 in Mrs. Halliwell's diary is illustration enough of the continuous and bustling social atmosphere: "Mrs Wright spent the day here. Mrs Boyce called. Maria Portus also spent the day here. James went to Town after waiting till 4 o'c for Mr. J[ohnson] who came at tea time & missed James. Sarah & Richard [her son] came in the eveng & stayed all night as also Mrs. Wright." The family holidays were special, the events Mrs. Halliwell almost always describes extensively in what is otherwise a memo-like diary, like the trip to Wales in September 1853. The particular charm of the family excursions is perhaps best described by one outside the family. Fairholt in August 1851 (LOA 45:15) replied to an invitation to join them at the seaside in Bognor (where they had taken a house for seven guineas a month) with a poem and an illustration:

> Begging your honor's pardon for my silence!
> And wishing myself with you—many a mile hence!
> I write to say how joyful I should be
> To stroll with you beside 'the roaring sea'
> 'Bathing'—to penetrate the Ocean's Mystery
> Shrimp-eating—just to study Natural History
> Studying mankind 'mong the salt-water blades
> Who've 'everlastin' catching such nice Maids
> Which makes me wish meself a Merman
> If one had fins, and nothing to deter-man!!!!
> No tailors bills to pay—no rag our back's on
> No house or aught that governments lay tax on
> To stop our larking in the briny Sea
> With fish-tailed Nymphs in great felici-tee!!
> Oh that like this 'fond letter' I now write

I could slip to you through the Post this night
I would sing 'Io Paean' like a Lark
Instead of scribbling like an office clerk.
Merely to say I'll try as you propose
To come on Thursday–I'll take care you *knows*
On Monday by the Post *for certain mind*
'Thus good begins but better is behind.'
To send a certain answer as you'll find.

One day of Mrs. Halliwell's description in her diary is perhaps less lyrical but nonetheless atmospherically typical and endearing. On 5 August 1851 she wrote: "Lovely day. I took the children & Meg [Margaret Marsh, a relative] with Mary a long walk on the sands. James joined us. Sent Louisa some seaweeds and wrote to Sarah & fixed next Tuesday for her visit. James bathed. I sat on the shingles & worked my crochet while the children played about. Heard H's music lesson. Corrected 1st proofs of All's Well &c. James corrected pfs of the notes. He & I sat on the beach after dinner. He bathed again & read the paper."

There were also problems. The engagement of Louisa to Samuel Edward Baker (28 July 1848) surprised them all, and happily so. On the next day the elder Mr. Halliwell, James, and Henrietta all wrote to congratulate her. She was delighted. Her wedding on 1 May 1849, as described by Mrs. Halliwell, was interlaced with festivity and sadness:

Poor Mr. H. was very ill and feeble - He was upstairs in his bedroom all the morning. We dressed early Lou in white silk & lace veil & white bouquet looked very nice. Sarah wore a grey brocade dress & white bonnet. I in glacé silk with 5 flowers, white shawl, white lace bonnet & pink wreath. Helen Crookshank, Miss Rogers, & Emily Wood were the bridesmaids. James gave Louisa away (his father being too ill). Her brother, Thomas, married her. All went to Church except Mr & Mrs H. & the children. We sat down to a beautiful breakfast. Mr. H. was present - but there was no speechefying - on account of his illness. After the dejeuner Mr & Mrs E. B. left for Warwick. Mr H. bore the parting very well. The rest of our party with Edwards friends Messrs Weaver, Scott & Coates drove to see the Dulwich Gallery. Returned to coffee & then seperated [*sic*]. Mr H.'s illness cast a gloom over the day.

Mr. Halliwell had not been well for a long time. Halliwell had already taken over some of his tasks, like collecting rents (20 October 1848), and,

an ominous sign, on 3 November 1848 the two men went to Norwood
Cemetery to buy ground for a grave for Mr. Thwaites, a close friend who
had died suddenly. The next spring Mr. Halliwell was seriously ill. On 19
April 1849 he "did not feel at all well & cd scarcely hold his razor this
morning. James went with him to Mr Wade who ordered him to be
cupped which he had done before he came home." Two days later he was
"very weak indeed & had little use in his left side." On 9 May "James
rubbed his fathers legs for him at night - they are cold and stiff." Days of
treatment–leeches mainly–followed, but to no avail. On Sunday, 27 May
1849, Mrs. Halliwell reported:

We were all called up at 4 o'c this morning. Poor Mr H. extremely ill &
breathing with the greatest difficulty. Mrs H., Edwd, I, & the nurse were
there with him all the morning. Dr W. came about 8 but there was no
hope, he came again at 10 o'c & sd he cd not last many hours.
Mortification began & he breathed his last about 1/2 p. 4 in the
afternoon. He did not know any of us. Mrs H. bore up pretty well. We
sent for Sarah who arrived before he died. Edward wrote letters to friends
in the eveng. Mr Lovell called. I saw Mr H. after he was laid out - He has
been a very kind and affectionate father to me. James felt his death most
severely & suffered all day from nervous headache.

The death of Mr. Halliwell at age seventy-two had both an immediate
and a far-reaching effect on Halliwell and his family. Mr. Halliwell is in
some ways a shadowy figure in the story. There are only two letters from
him to, and only one from, his son James among the 15,000 in the
Edinburgh collection and none at all in the Folger collection. But even
one is enough to characterize him as a loving and respected head of the
clan. In a three-page letter of 16 March 1840 (LOA 3:17) written from
Islip to Halliwell in London, he is "gratified" that his "dear Orchard" has
"spent a pleasant evening at the Marquiss' *soirée*," responds to learning that
his son "is going on slowly but surely with [his] Degree examination" with
the "earnest hope ... that it will prove *sure* even to the highest honors, for
I entertain not even a shadow of a doubt as to your capability to do any
thing you aspire to, if it please God to spare your health," asks for and
sends news, hopes for another letter "should you be able to find leisure
from your numerous engagements," and closes, "We are both quite well
& write in best love to you, Richard, Loui, Margaret &c &c. God bless
you My dear Orchard & believe me to be Your affectionate father

Thomas Halliwell."[138] And there was no doubt about his being a self-made man: a linen draper from Chorley in Lancashire, he managed to send two sons to university and a third to a law career. He saw his opportunity in real estate. His house in Islip was modest but in an excellent location, in Rectory Square, in the center of the village. And he was also proprietor of several other properties which he sublet, including two nearby houses and a farm of ninety-seven acres (until recently known as Lower Farm). In London he had properties in Westminster (in the Westminster Abbey muniments alone, there are seventeen boxes of deeds for Halliwell and Marsh), Knightsbridge, and the Strand, in Hook near Kingston-upon-Thames, and in Islip and Charlton-on-Otmoor in Oxfordshire, and elsewhere as well. It was he who bought Avenue Lodge for Halliwell. He became a director of the Westminster Fire Office. He was a good provider, and in his extensive will he scrupulously tailored bequests—property, freeholds, life insurance policies, annuities, stocks, personal effects (including a portrait of himself by Lilly,[139] sure proof of his standing)–to each member of the family, as well as their immediate offspring, including Richard's widow and her two sons. He was prominent enough for his death to be listed in the *Gentleman's Magazine* (n.s. 32 [1849], 104).

He designated his wife and Halliwell as his executors to deal with the considerable estate he had so skilfully and conscientiously accumulated. But his wife was herself ill. On 12 October 1848 she "came home & had leeches on her chest, a slight swelling has appeared on the left side & she had been to Mr Wade." She had never mentioned it before, but that was not the end of it. Her condition worsened slowly but relentlessly. On 25 September 1849 she "had a bad night & her arm was very painful." Opium pills were prescribed. She became much weaker. Although she had always "insisted" upon going to Mr. Wade for treatment, she agreed to be visited by Dr. Septimus Wray, who "ordered hot applications instead of cold" but thought "there is no chance of curing her–it was a dreadful cancer" (7 October 1849). On 29 October she was "quite collected & has

138. In a revealing bit of parental concern Halliwell's brother Thomas wrote Halliwell, "my Father begs me to remind you to write to Cambridge (now that you are not going) about your cap & gown & other things you left" (3 April 1842; LOA 14:21).

139. Although the name is thus spelled in the will, the reference must to one of two portrait painters of the time who spelled their name Lilley: H. Lilley (fl. 1843) or John Lilley (fl. 1832-46). See Christopher Wood, *Dictionary of Victorian Painters* (2nd ed.1978), p. 286.

given orders about her funeral." On 2 November Mrs. Halliwell describes her death with unaccustomed detail:

Dr W. came. Mrs H very bad & had a bad night. James [who was suffering from an attack of nervous diarrhea] took chalk & logwood twice & was rather better in the night & today but still in bed. Ton [the nickname of Thomas] & Lou went out. I stayed at home ... I sat a great part of the day with James & his mother alternately. He got up & went in to her in the morng but was greatly shocked at the change since he saw her. She did not rally today - her body is turning black. She begged us all to go to bed - her last words were to me 'Take care of him' meaning poor James. I left her with Sarah & the nurse about 11 o'c. & went to bed. She never spoke after I left but laid her head gently back & expired about 12 o'c. Nurse called me up in two hours after as I had made her promise, & I went to see my poor mother in law who has been so kind & good to me. I broke it gently to James but he felt it bitterly and it quite upset him again.

The death of his parents brought with it emotional pain and greater responsibilities and worries. Whereas his father had hitherto looked after business matters, had provided his son and family with a house and a certain financial support, and had carefully planned for all after his death, Halliwell suddenly became the sole executor of his parents' estate and had to attend to the task of keeping the properties functioning, paying taxes, collecting rents, supervising the insurance records, paying premiums, and seeing to it that all the beneficiaries, old and young and to come, were correctly treated. Halliwell did not become rich at his father's death, but he accepted the burden of the trusteeship willingly. It involved large sums–in February 1851, for example, he paid £1556.15 for the renewal of the Great Chapel Street property in Westminster; two weeks later he sold a lot for £920–but it was not money he could use for his own needs, which were many. Obviously, the offer of £200 for the Tallis edition was welcome; in 1846 (LOA 28:31) he attempted to sell his early manuscripts to Harvard or the Athenaeum in Boston. In 1850 he was willing to sell his Shakespeare collection to a buyer in the United States, his "only inducement ... is the anxiety to be enabled to have as much funds as I can for my *very* large work which I hope to commence in the autumn" (undated; Folger Y.c.1307[6]). He later offered to sell his "200-300" manuscripts to an interested Bodleian Library (28 February 1852; LOA 49:36). The folio edition of Shakespeare was risky financially, requiring a large outlay even before the subscribers were found and had agreed to pay. Speculation was not unusual. Projects were announced: on 31 July

1850 he told Mrs. Halliwell that he was thinking of printing a folio edition of Shakespeare's plays in forty-five volumes, and a facsimile made of every page in the First Folio. In 1852 he bought the copyright, stereotype plates, and stock of his *Dictionary of Archaic Words* for £350. The strain was great, and it is not surprising that during a walk in the garden on 22 September 1853, so Mrs. Halliwell's diary, he told Sarah he was "fully determined to give up all the Trusteeships[;] she was very sorry as he has done all the business for the family for 4 years for nothing, but his health is not strong enough to continue it - as well as his other literary labours."

There were others burdens as well. Despite Mrs. Hallliwell's appeals and pleadings, there was no peace between the Halliwells and Thomas Phillipps. The struggle was as much financial as emotional. Unhappy with the marriages of his three daughters—Henrietta in 1842, Mary in 1843 to John Walcot, and Kate in 1847 to John Fenwick—affectionately tolerant of his second wife, and rabid in his need for money, Phillipps never ceased in his maligning of the Halliwells and in his attempts to ruin Halliwell. Desperate because he lacked a male heir, he sought ways to deprive Henrietta of her inheritance. Failing, he attempted to extort money from them. In January 1849 (LOA 107:9*), Halliwell mentions that Phillipps proposed that he would accept £50,000 as the price of reconciliation. In an undated note (LOA 212:8), Halliwell defended his supposed "abominable conduct" in not meeting the demand: "When one considers that that is all he asks for his countenance & friendship, what can be said of my conduct in refusing it. Suppose we call it, flagitious?" On 30 January 1852 (so Mrs. Halliwell's diary) a settlement by Phillipps of the "£8000 business" may have satisfied Dr. Samuel Wilson Warneford, a trustee of Mrs. Thomas Phillipps's marriage settlement, but not the Halliwells, who were not even consulted, nor would ever consent. As if this were not enough, Halliwell heard that Phillipps had told Sotheby that the Halliwells had separated (Diary, 26 April 1852). And on 1 October 1853 Mrs Halliwell reported that she had learned her father had had counsel's opinion "about altering the settlement of Middle Hill property so that after [her] death if [she] have no son the estate shall go to Mary's boys to the exclusion of [her] children entirely." This move proved unsuccessful, but it was not to be the end of Phillipps's campaign of ruthless extortion and malicious rumor-mongering.

Litigation, often long-enduring and contentious, was a fact of life for the Halliwells. The elder Halliwell had been involved in numerous law suits. William Lovell, Richard's law partner, was for so many years legal adviser that he was practically a member of the family. Though at this time not critical of Lovell, Halliwell nevertheless, in the midst of all his projects and activities, put his name down in Great Hall, Lincoln's Inn, paid £30.5.6, and was admitted as a student member of the Inn on 7 November 1850. Although he kept up his attendance over the years, he did not go on to be called to the bar, and on 2 November 1858 had his name taken off the books of the Society. The exact circumstances of Halliwell's decision are not clear. It is not very likely that he thought of abandoning his passions for books and Shakespeare. Still, there are hints in his career of options which he must have considered tempting or opportune, especially when his way was bumpy and the load oppressive. In 1842 he confided to Lady Somerset that he was considering entering the Church, "my only object proceeding to my degree" (Phil-Rob c.633:70). In the same year he was thinking of resuming his academic career at Oxford and was being advised that Cambridge would be preferable; he was also inquiring about a job at the Public Record Office. In 1845 he was corresponding with Abraham Hume, who had received an honorary LLD from Glasgow in 1843, about the possibility of receiving an honorary degree (LOA 22:13, 22:14). In 1847 there was a serious offer for him to join William Jerdan on the *Literary Gazette* (LOA 55:35, 55:47). There is no certain answer to the question of whether these were signs of flexibility or restlessness, of adventurousness or dilettantism. Halliwell's following the dissolution of the Historical Society of Science in 1846 with the projection of a new English Theological Society in 1847 (apparently similar to one he had tried and given up in 1841), which in turn did not materialize, or his intention to edit a new Gower series in 1845 or to write a life of Garrick in 1848– no matter what the reason for their not materializing, movement and flux were constant features of Halliwell's career, if not personal traits. His days were crammed and his nights were short. And, of course, there was his book business, the constant pressure of buying and selling. Examples abound. After proving his mother's will, he went to a Puttick and Simpson sale and, buying for Thomas Corser of Manchester, bid gainst Boone, who was buying for Thomas Phillipps (Diary, 1 December 1849). On 11 January 1850 he bought a First Folio for £35. A few weeks later after spending "nearly all day with the tenants in Westminster He bought about 30 lots of Rodd's MSS. at Sothebys at one shilling *p* lot [then] called on the Lovells" (Diary, 4 February 1850). On 30 July 1852, so Mrs. Halliwell's diary, "James went to Town & brought home his 1st folio that he left for Mr. Bedford to bind, it makes a very handsome volume bound in red russia. It was a copy nearly perfect bought by Mr. [George] Bumstead for James & what was wanting was supplied from a copy James bought at Utterson's sale & another copy which he has had for many years." And he sold it to a Mr. Nicholls for

£140 through Russell Smith, to whom he gave £10 (Diary, 29 November 1853). Whether for altruistic or other reasons, Halliwell the busy bookman did not forget to be a benefactor. Over the years and among many instances, the Cambridge University Library received thirty-one works, all but three desiderata (10 June 1848; LOA 9:23), the Chetham Library in Manchester received 3,000 ballads and broadsides (Diary, 16 December 1851), and the British Museum large paper copies of all his printed works (Diary, 8 November 1852).

The stability of a solid and reliable family life somehow smoothed the waves. There was time for pranks in the parlor and for taking the children to Clapham Common to gather chestnuts. And in the midst of what appeared to be the turbulence of his literary career there was, like the eye of a hurricane, one unchanging and imperturbable center: his love of books expressed in his deep devotion to Shakespeare. Having allowed himself ten years to produce a folio edition of Shakespeare, a memorial and something permanent, he set off a flurry of activity. In addition to everything else, he and his family began collating plays, preparing and distributing prospectuses, soliciting and collecting subscriptions. Harry, just ten, "copied a little for him ... & put his pages in order ... to her great delight" (Diary, 4 October 1853). Halliwell himself went to work with hammer and nails on bookshelves and, with his passion for order, had especially built a case of thirty-nine drawers, each to be lettered with the name of a different play of Shakespeare's.

PART THREE

1854-1865

*Fig. 3 Halliwell-Phillipps with his daughters Ellen and Katie in 1862.
By kind permission of his great-granddaughter, Désirée Hancock, née Muntz.*

10

Literary Archaeology
Professional and Personal

By the time the sixteenth and last volume of the folio edition appeared, in 1865, Halliwell was perhaps the most renowned Shakespearean in England and for that matter in the English-speaking world. With the dissolution of the Shakespeare Society in 1853, the balance of power shifted markedly, for the various factions had no central base and the vacuum was filled by individuals. The other leading Shakespeareans were all born in the previous century. Collier, eclipsed by the revelation of his forgeries by 1860 and already in his seventies, had retreated to Maidenhead. By 1865 Knight was seventy-five and had ceased active publishing. Dyce was sixty-seven, and ailing. Halliwell, however, was in his prime, as it were. Thus the curmudgeon Bolton Corney, with whom Halliwell had crossed swords some twenty years earlier, could continue sending corrections to Halliwell's *Shakesperiana* but had to concede, "I feel quite assured that you will take this in good part, and also that the Mr Halliwell of 1860 is more exact than the Mr Halliwell of 1841" (4 April 1860; LOA 73:73). At the completion of the folio edition Halliwell was forty-five years old and showed little sign of slowing down. If anything, his energy increased to meet his expanding horizons. In 1855 he moved to a larger, more agreeable,[140] and more central location, a house in West Brompton, at 6 St Mary's Place, later to be renamed and renumbered 11 Tregunter Road,[141] a London address which he kept until his death in 1889. His family increased: two more daughters were born, Ellen Molyneux on 8 January 1854 and Katherine Elizabeth (Katie) on 9

140. As early as 27 December 1852 (LOA 73:9) Halliwell had written to Hunt that Mrs. Halliwell, was "much better, but is still so delicate I fear we shall be obliged to move altogether to a less bleak neighbourhood."

141. The street was renamed as of 7 August 1863 and renumbered as of 18 October 1867. In a letter to Hepworth Dixon Halliwell explained that he had not moved but would be "pleased ... to offer you some very good port wine" (Saturday, June 1864[?]; Folger Y.c. 1213 [56]).

September 1855. His travels did not diminish, and Stratford-upon-Avon was to become a kind of second home and, in fact, his scholarly and spiritual *Heimat*: he was to buy New Place and other Stratford properties, to help organize and administer a National Shakespeare Fund, and, in reconstituting and supporting Stratford as a national shrine, to have the major role in establishing its memorial library and museum.

The years 1854 to 1865 were perhaps the most fulfilling of his entire career. In addition to the gigantic folio edition, which appeared in sixteen installments, numerous contributions to *Notes and Queries*, the *Athenaeum*, and the *Times*, Halliwell produced some 165 titles in these twelve years. They chart the directions his interests took: Halliwell as bookman reprinting early English texts and, in amassing a library, buying and selling books, manuscripts, and artifacts; Halliwell as author producing volumes on religion, travel, and occasional subjects; Halliwell as Shakespearean producing a monumental edition and representative lithographic facsimiles; and, in a role for which he seemed destined, Halliwell as guiding light, if not guardian angel, of Stratford.

+++

Halliwell's dominant interest in early books and manuscripts accommodated his continuing, albeit diminishing, passion for science and mathematics, his earliest preoccupation. In 1854 he reprinted, as was to be his custom, for private circulation *The Alchemical Testament of John Gybbys*, supplying only five notes and paying tribute to his friend W. H. Black (affectionately known as "Niger"), whose catalogue of the Ashmolean manuscripts he termed "beyond comparison the most excellent of any collection yet published." This slight pamphlet of eight pages is little more than a straightforward inflection of Halliwell's earlier work—e.g. on John Dee and John Claptone—and of course a reminder of his frequent association with the Ashmolean which began when he was a teenager. Another eight-page pamphlet, also privately and generously printed (30 cm.), returns to one of Halliwell's earliest publications, the *Rara Mathematica*, which contained a fragment of the first folio of the manuscript *De Arte Numerandi*. Halliwell does not reprint the four leaves but, in what is perhaps the last exercise of his mathematical skill, sets out to explain the mode of operation of the system presented in the manuscript (Arundel 343) of the twelfth century.

Also subsumed under Halliwell's bookmanship was archaeology, whose focus was not solely on artifacts but obviously on the historical, social, and economic condition of early English society. A longtime "associate" (as the subscribers were called) of the British Archaeological Association, of which he was a member of the Committee for the Congress at Warwick in 1847 and the Council at the 1848 meeting, Halliwell kept up his contributions to the meetings and journal, albeit sparingly and despite the increasingly disturbing internal intrigues and dissension,[142] in a brief comment in 1854 on hornbooks, "the most curious relics of the educational system pursued by our ancestors," and in 1859 submitted an extract from a manuscript relating to the death of King John. In 1854 he published a handsome and substantial volume of transcriptions of "inedited" manuscripts of four *Ancient Inventories of Furniture, Pictures, Tapestry, Plate, &c. Illustrative of the Domestic Manners of the English in the Sixteenth and Seventeenth Centuries* for those "archaeological students who are interested in the history of domestic economy": an inventory of the goods of the Countess of Leicester, 1634-5; of linen, plate, pewter, brass, armour, household goods, maps, books, etc., 1610; inventories made in 1626; and an inventory of the plate, household stuff, pictures, &c., in Kenilworth Castle, taken after the death of Robert Earl of Leycester, 1588. And, also in twenty-five copies, he published *A Brief Notice of the "Mirrour of Government, Both Ecclesiastical and Civil"*, printed in 1658.[143]

Two works of 1860, each privately printed in twenty-six copies, are devoted to the social history of the early seventeenth century. Reprints of rare contemporary tracts, one relates the sensational murders and suicide of Sir John Fites, the other portrays the social condition of the people of Anglesea.[144] Although there is little, if anything, in the way of commentary by Halliwell, the choice of topics is revealing. Aware of its melodramatic character and thus doubtful reliability as "authentic" narratives, Halliwell was nevertheless attracted by their theatricality, his interest in popular dramatic literature reminding him of *The First Part of the Tragicall Raigne of Selimus*. The second, which gives graphic accounts of "vagrants, ale-houses, magistrates people and clergy," while sociologically compelling, was doubtless connected with Halliwell's personal and archaeological

142. In one instance among others Halliwell wrote to Charles Roach Smith that although he was "thoroughly disgusted about the whole matter," he would not wish to withdraw from the Council "out of deference to Mr. P[ettigrew]" (1853; Folger C.b.16[42]).

143. No copy of this work has been located.

144. *A Narrative of the Bloudy Murders Committed by Sir John Fites Alias Fitz, 1605, with an Account of His Suicide at Twickenham; to Which is Added, the Revelation of Two Horrible Murders Done In Lincolnshire, Made Known in 1604* and *A Minute Account of the Social Condition of the People of Anglesea, in the Reign of James the First.*

delight in Wales. Halliwell took his family on a holiday tour of Wales in the autumn of 1859. Out of the experience came in 1859 a transcript of a manuscript owned by Thomas Wright, *An Ancient Survey of Pen Maen Mawr, North Wales*, a communication from Bangor dated 21 October 1859 to the British Archaeological Association describing an ancient British camp at the base of the mountain called Moelycci, and a reprint of *A Short Relation of a Journey Through Wales, Made in the Year 1612, by John Taylor, the Water-Poet*. Most notable was Halliwell's privately printed full-length travel book. *Notes of Family Excursions in North Wales*, remarkable for a number of reasons. Of the vast number of his publications, relatively few are personal as well as professional. Of course the professional works are personal, even passionate, in their own way: out to prove a point, if not contentious then at least determined, devoted to a cause. And they do of course give a picture of Halliwell the professional. Halliwell had more than holiday visits to offer: his collection of works on North Wales was the centerpiece of his sale at Sotheby's on 15 April 1861. But *Notes of Family Excursions*, using the first person singular or plural, addresses the reader as "you," is discursive, informed, friendly, and clearly enamoured by what is seen. The book reveals Halliwell as an occasional writer of some charm, in this instance writing a travel guide for a reader who is not a professional archaeologist or social historian but who wishes to be informed gently and enchanted emphatically. The preface sets the tone and portrays the man. It is worth quoting *in toto*:

What is it all come to? Is it necessary, because I take my family out for a few walks from some of the best known localities in Britain, that I should tell all the world, or by printing fancy that I tell all the world, about them? And the question may well be asked, considering that All the World and his wife go to all these places, and that it is hard if, between them, they cannot pick up for themselves what information is worth having; but they are easy-going, quiet people, who like smooth walking, and so miss a great deal of what is to be seen in the byways. Still, this consideration does not constitute a satisfactory reply. Well, I can only say, as an amiable and celebrated old-clothes' man once observed,–'I'll not answer that; but, say, it is my humour; is it answered?' People now-a-days, at least some people, do not write books for other persons to read, but to amuse themselves with the occupation of writing. It is impossible that we can all expect an audience, seeing that there are now more writers than there are readers.

But again I ask, what is it all to come to? If not for one's own sake, or for that of our friends, or of the public, yet in compassion to our libraries, I would ask the question, and, in the very act of transgressing, entreat all others, were it only for the last consideration, not to sin in this direction. It is fearful to imagine what will be the extent of the British Museum Library two or three centuries hence, if book-making continues at the present rate. The catalogue, instead of as now being comprised within the moderate compass of two thousand folio volumes, will take about a mile of shelf. The reading room will, in proportion, require something like a length of way of ten miles, with a double line of rail for the convenience of readers passing to the various literary stations, conducted by a system of cheap return-tickets. Taking up The Times in 2060, one may read an account of a fearful accident to a party of students proceeding to the Divinity Station on the Reading Room railway, arising from as collision with a book-train. To imagine that anything short of an apparatus of the extent will suffice to the literature of that day, always supposing that the present productive rate is maintained, appears to be visionary.[145]

From this nonsense the reader,–if I have one,–will gather that I have done fishing for an excuse to perpetuate this little volume, but that the bait has been lost, and the hook irretrievably ruined, by a haul of useless weeds, videlicet, the rubbish just shot here (pp. 5-7).

As cicerone and paterfamilias with a family party of eight, Halliwell describes a summer "tramp" on the northern coast of Wales, moving by rail from one locality to the next. There are precise descriptions of towns:

Abergele is the next watering-place to Rhyl. This small town is situated on a gently rising ground three quarters of a mile from the shore. Near the beach is the rising bathing hamlet of Penfarn, this name implying that it was the head of a Roman road. *Pen* is head in Welsh, and the term *farn*, a causeway, is generally connected with traces of a Roman road. It is situated on a dead flat, and with the inconvenience of being compelled to cross the railway line on a level in order to reach the sea. Penfarn at present consists of a few terraces and rows of houses. Fifteen years ago there were only two cottages here (pp. 43-4).

There are descriptions of nature:

Our first excursion from Rhyl is to the village of Dyferth, where the chief attraction was, ought, and may hereafter be, one of the most singular cascades of the kind in the kingdom. The stream that rises at Ffynnon

145. Mrs. Halliwell's diary entry for 9 June 1857 reports that Halliwell visited and was "delighted" with the new reading room of the British Museum.

Asaph, afterwards mentioned, falls here into a perpendicular cylindrical passage in the rock, darkened with moss and ivy; or, rather, it should fall here, but the water is at present chiefly diverted into a neighbouring mine. One of my daughters, though she got laughed at for the apparent bull, not inaptly entered it in her diary as 'a waterfall with no water in it.' And this is literally the case. Instead of a powerful stream rushing over the precipice, the appearance now presents rather that of a dropping-well. It is beautiful, however, even in its desolation of water (pp. 33-4).

There are descriptions of local customs, doubtless of interest to the archaeologist and folklorist:

There was, and perhaps still is, a singular custom on the Sabbath at Holywell, which deserves notice. It is thus pleasantly described by Warner,—Of local customs there is nothing particular, except an unusual mode of summoning the inhabitants to church. This edifice is so situated that when the wind blows from the south or the south-west, the bell cannot be heard in most parts of the town. The parishioners, therefore, allow an annual stipend to a poor man to notify the hour of prayer on Sundays and holidays, which he does in the following singular manner. A leathern strap is suspended round his neck, and a large and heavy bell attached to it, which rests upon a cushion buckled over his knee. Thus accoutred, he traverses the town, jingling his bell (pp. 26-7).

Of a similar character but with a somewhat sharper archaeological focus is Halliwell's *Rambles in Western Cornwall by the Footsteps of the Giants: With Notes on the Celtic Remains of the Land's End District and the Islands of Scilly*, published a year later in 1861 by John Russell Smith, who evidently saw commercial possibilities following the success of the privately published *Notes of Family Excursions in North Wales*. Halliwell may well have avoided the customary picturesque and popular approach because of the recent presentation by "Blyth,"[146] but be that as it may, he produced a charming travelogue for whom one reviewer called the "inquiring visitor," combining history and folk tales, topography and sociology, and extending from disquisitions on libraries to discussions of pies:

146. As pointed out by Frederic George Stephens, the art critic, in his favorable review in the *Athenaeum* (28 December 1861, pp. 879-80). Stephens erroneously referred to Blyth instead of J. T. Blight, Halliwell's illustrator, who produced *A Week at the Land's End* in 1861.

There are few provincial towns of the same size that now excel Penzance in its conveniences for the pursuits of literature and science. The Public Library contains a collection of valuable books, several thousand in number, including a large proportion of standard works and important books of reference. A stranger, properly introduced, can be admitted to the library for three months, with the privilege of borrowing two volumes at a time, on the payment of half-a-guinea. The librarian, Mr. Francis, is in daily attendance, and his anxiety to supply the wants of the reader adds to the comfort of one of the best arranged small libraries in England. Under the same roof is the Institute News Room, where all the leading newspapers are taken in, and to which strangers are admitted for the small sum of half-a-crown for the quarter of a year. Then again in the North Parade is the rich Museum of the Royal Geological Society of Cornwall; and in the dome of the Market-house is the more miscellaneous collection of the Natural History Society, including specimens of nearly everything, from a helmet found at Sebostopol to an ancient British urn. If a person has a taste for anything save eating and drinking, in one or other of these museums something will be found of interest (pp. 27-8).

And if he has a taste for food:

Penzance, and in fact all Cornwall, is famous for its pies. One of the oddest is the star-gazing pie, which is one made of pilchards, the heads of the fish appearing in relief over the crust. Then there is muggety-pie, composed of sheep's entrails, parsley and cream, seasoned with pepper and salt. Duck-pie should be made of ducks unfit to be roasted. At least, it spoils those that are suited to the spit. Cornish pasties are very popular with the working-classes in this neighbourhood, and have been successfully introduced into some parts of Devonshire. They are made of small pieces of beef, and thin slices of potatoe, highly peppered, and enclosed in wrappers of paste. These pasties are eatable when quite hot, but detestable otherwise, excepting to those who like cold potatoe. They are cheap, and, like Sam Weller's muffins, 'werry filling at the price' (pp. 39-40).

Finally, the traveller-archaeologist records another trip in a brief pamphlet published by John Russell Smith in 1863, *Roundabout Notes Chiefly upon the Ancient Circles of Stones in the Isle of Man, from Rough Pencillings Dotted Down in the Summer of 1862.* Not uncritical–"With the celebrated cloven stones of Laxey I was disappointed, believing the cleft in the big stone to be accidental not intentional, and probably occasioned in some

way since the monument was formed" (pp. 8-9)–he is captivated by the
beauty and history around him: "Oh! there are some beautiful spots in the
Isle of Man" (p. 5).

It would be a mistake, in fact, to regard these works simply as
professional or self-indulgent exercises. For there emerges a kind of sense
of the land which accrues to a Halliwell who in searching for records and
artifacts has travelled throughout the country for more than half his life.
Neither pantheistic nor patriotic, neither sentimental nor sensuous,
Halliwell was nevertheless deeply impressed by what he found–and that
was both the outer shell and inner spirit of the country, of which he grew
increasingly proud as his experience and knowledge of it increased. How
else to explain the conclusion of *Rambles*?

The Scilly Isles abound in pretty sea and land views, in fine and grotesque
cliff-scenery, in lovely bays and sea-nooks of every imaginable variety; in
walks whose every turn reveals a new combination of land and water, and
in the less striking, but not less pleasing, rural inland pictures, where ice-
plant covered walls surround gardens in which flowers and plants, that
would perish in the other counties of England, flourish luxuriantly. It
seems strange that a locality possessing so many attractions to the invalid,
who requires a warm genial atmosphere and a placid retirement, should
be, comparatively, so little visited by strangers. But as long as the English
public retain their unfortunate tendency to follow the guidance of the
silliest class–our fashionable people–so long will they furnish votaries to
distant countries, such as Egypt, where the violent alternations of
temperature surrender more than half its patients to certain death; even
so long also will they overlook beautiful spots in their own native land,
not only far more suitable to the invalid, but to all more agreeable, and to
some more interesting (pp. 244-5).

The sentiment is a replication of what Halliwell had said and felt a year
earlier in the opening of *Notes of Family Excursions:*

'Call this a lake?'–observed an Australian friend, while we were standing
on the picturesque little rustic bridge below the inn at Capel Curig;–'call
this a lake?–why, we pass twenty such in a day in our country, and heed
them no more than we should so many ponds.'

It is curious, or, rather, perhaps it is not curious. What I mean is that
it is not curious that at first sight, where grandeur is wanting in scenery,
beauty should not be immediately appreciated; but it is curious that nearly
all of us, especially of those who have seen some of the grander

monuments of the world, should despise the more beautiful allocations of nature when they are upon a somewhat diminutive scale. So say some,–'it is all very well, but Wales will not do after Switzerland.' You might just as well throw Pope behind the fire, because Pope won't do after Shakespeare. Comparisons, as a wise man once said, are odorous. There is really but little to compare, each is so different and so agreeable in its kind. We do not see the grandeur of Switzerland in any part of Wales, it is true; but we see beauty, in its kind, developed in great variety, and of a style yielding perhaps more constant delight than in any part of the Continent. The Vale of the Conway is inferior, as a whole, to the Valley of the Rhine; but it has beauties of its own that would be sought for in vain on the banks of that noble river ... Comparisons are odorous; and North Wales should be studied for itself and by itself (pp. 11-13).

Certain aspects of character emerge in these works. Halliwell is freer and mellower. And they become increasingly pronounced in his professional work, the result (partly at least) of his established reputation and of the tight and loving circle of his family and friends.

+++

"Curiosity" and "rarity" are the terms Halliwell employs to judge and describe the early English works which he dealt with as editor and collector. Shakespeare was the center of his interest, to be sure. But Shakespeare was not simply a person or a writer but an environment consisting of many writers, many documents, and many artifacts. Early English literature was, in other words, a system of interrelated concerns. On the whole, Halliwell focused on popular literature rather than on major figures. If he touched on well known or even major authors–Shakespeare excepted–he did so only insofar as they produced more or less popular works, like prose tales, or offered some limited technical access. Marlowe and Jonson, Spenser and Sidney, Bacon and Milton, appear only sparingly in his *oeuvre*, if at all. With the exception of a three-volume edition of the works of John Marston Halliwell did not produce, in this period or later, anything resembling a standard edition of a major or even minor writer of the early English period–that is, from the fifteenth to the seventeenth centuries.

For some–and from the beginning of his career, as evident in the critical reception of his work–the explanation lay in Halliwell's dilettantism; for others, in his impatience; for still others, in his intellectual incapacity. Be that as it may, Halliwell was a collector and a reprinter;

many of his contemporaries, such as Collier, were also his competitors. And like them, he was not an editor in the modern sense. That he published so many of his works privately, and for subscription, must be a further reason for choosing "curious" and "rare" texts. That he personally preferred comedy to tragedy, prose to verse, humor to solemnity, jests to sermons, must well have contributed to his choices. And his emphasis on popular literature—such as ballads and drolls—is a sign or symptom not merely of a certain temperament but of the archaeologist's attraction to even the smallest artifacts both in themselves and in the socio-historical detail and thus cumulatively the environment which they so intimately portray.

Halliwell's editions in this period are, as before, reprints limited in most cases to twenty-six copies—twenty-five for subscribers, one (normally) for the library of the British Museum under the requirements of the Copyright Act. Between 1854 and 1865 the heaviest concentration is in 1859 and 1860, accounting for some thirty-two publications. All but two of the works by known authors are prose narratives—Thomas Deloney's *The History of John Winchcomb* (1859), Thomas Lodge's *The Margarite of America* (1859), Thomas Dekker's *Decker's Dream* (1860), Robert Greene's *The Notable Discovery of Coney-Catchers' Cozenage* (1859), Nicholas Breton's *The Will of Wit* (1860). All are examples of popular literature and contribute to Halliwell's continuing and cumulative presentation of the manners and morals of the time. All follow the format of the Halliwellian enterprise: a brief two- or four-page preface with an overview of the work and its provenance, a print facsimile of the original title page, and a straightforward reprint of the text. All are usually of the same size (20 or 24 cm.). Along with these physical features, which are economically rational, are Halliwell's habitual recycling of his material: his preface to Deloney's *History of John Winchcomb* is identical with a portion of a paper communicated to the British Archaeological Association and read by James Heywood on 12 September 1859. There is also his custom of paying tribute to friends or authorities, if only to account for his being so brief: his preface to Lodge's *Margarite of America* mentions an "account of Lodge and his works, which was compiled by Mr. David Laing for the Shakespeare Society, [and which] is so accurate, complete, and interesting, it is useless for me to attempt to introduce any novel information on the subject, or to do more than transcribe a short abridgement of it" (v). Recognizable too is Halliwell's indifference towards or disregard for the literary merit of a work, seemingly content with either its rarity alone or perhaps its illustration of particular "old manners and customs." Furthermore, Halliwell was attracted to works of unclear or disputed authorship, as in Greene's *Ghost-haunting Conycatchers* (1860), dubiously ascribed to Greene and Samuel Rowlands, especially as Greene, long a favorite subject, appeared in a cluster of works reprinted in these years. And finally there is Halliwell's response to works with a somewhat complicated textual history (as in *The Will of Wit*) or possessing an unusual feature (such as the woodcut on the title page of *Dekker's Dream*, which contains a genuine portrait of Dekker).

It was not merely the outer environment, so to speak, or his own taste that attracted Halliwell to English popular literature but also the possible connection or allusion to Shakespeare. In reprinting Greene's *Notable Discovery*, for example, he pointed out both the "curiosity" of the work "as a picture of low life in the time of Shakespeare" and "amongst the more curious allusions ... a singular anecdote of Mistress Moll, who may possibly be the person referred to by Shakespeare in *Twelfth Night*, a conjecture not elsewhere noticed" (vi). This focus is especially notable in Halliwell's reprinting of drolls, a subgenre which seems to have met his predilection for drama, comedy, low-life atmosphere, and a vigorous popular tradition emerging from a literary one. The Shakespearean afterlife is represented by *The Droll of the Bouncing Knight* (1860), "constructed" out of *1 Henry 4*, *The Droll of the Grave-Makers* (1860), out of *Hamlet*, and *The Merry Conceited Humours of Bottom the Weaver* (1860), out of *A Midsummer Night's Dream*. *Jenkin of Wales* (1861) is a comic portion of James Shirley's *Love-Tricks*, and *The Doctors of Dull-Head College* (1860) derives from Beaumont and Fletcher's *Monsieur Thomas (Father's Own Son)*. *The Conceited Humours of Simpleton the Smith* (1860), evidently by the actor Robert Cox, was very popular, and was apparently alluded to in Dryden's *Notes and Observations on the Empress of Morocco*. It is not of little interest to note that these volumes suited not merely the scholarly but also the commercial focus of the Halliwell enterprise: they are all small, of uniform size and format, contain the customary brief preface (mainly an indication of source), and are little more than a straightforward reprint of a short text. Moreover, they are all extracted from a single work, *The Wits or, Sport upon Sport*, a miscellany of drolls and playlets, the second edition of which was published by Francis Kirkman in 1672. Halliwell goes so far as to print *in toto* Kirkman's "exceedingly curious" preface to *The Doctors*, for it saves him the trouble of having to explain the "character of the contents of the volume." One further source for Halliwell was *The Theatre of Ingenuity* (1704), from which he extracted two *Shakespearian Drolls* (1859) for his uniform series: *The Mad-Wooing*, out of *The Taming of the Shrew*, and *The Boaster*, out of *1 Henry 4*.

Halliwell could, of course, deal with full-length plays or for that matter complete works of an author. But apart from his folio edition of Shakespeare he did so at this stage of his career as a reprinter of text rather than an editor. In 1856, for what must be regarded as a commercial venture,[147] he contributed to John Russell Smith's Library of Old Authors the three-volume *Works of John Marston*, joining other well-known editors, such as Thomas Wright, S. W. Singer, and William Turnbull. The text is an unembellished reprint in accord with Smith's original concept.[148] The advertised "with notes and some account of his life and writings" is somewhat of an overstatement, since for slightly over 300 pages per volume the notes at the end of each volume are but five, nine, and seven pages long. The preface, an overview of life and writings, is brief and somewhat artificially lengthened by a long quote from Marston's will. The bibliographical description of each of the twelve plays gives in the main only the place and date of publication and at times a summary or a source or an allusion or a modern edition—not original comments but almost always from known works of others. Still, it is worth noting that this was the first modern edition of the works of Marston. And if there was criticism of Halliwell's practice of reprinting "absolutely from the early editions, which were placed in the hands of our printers, who thus had the advantage of following them without the intervention of a transcriber" (I:xxii),[149] then it would have to be for his not producing a diplomatic reprint or for not carefully proofreading the work of the printer. As to the first charge, Thomas Keightley was grateful to have a reprint which gave "people who, like myself, cannot or will not lay out large sums in the purchase of old and scarce books, or spend days in the Museum, an opportunity of seeing how books came out of the hands of the old printers, even when ... the proofs were read by the author, and thus show the absurdity of all that is said about the authority of the folio Shakespeare, and Beaumont and Fletcher, etc."[150] Furthermore, Halliwell did indeed make an effort to point out the obvious substantive misprints in his notes, as well as referring occasionally to variant readings in other editions. And his notes—some 134—while largely glossarial and

147. In a letter to John Russell Smith (in the collection of Arthur Freeman) dated only "Friday morning," Thomas Wright indicated that Halliwell "seems to say he would not like to undertake it for a less consideration than £40 for the whole."

148. Smith asked Halliwell for suggestions and participation in the way of a preface or a few notes for a "series of little volumes called 'Reprints of Old Authors' or The Old Authors of England" he was thinking of starting (30 September 1854; LOA 41:18).

149. See the criticism by W. B. C. in *Notes and Queries* (6 November 1858), 368-9.

150. *Notes and Queries* (27 November 1856), 435-6.

archaeological (and, as in the case of *keel*, I:302-3, self-indulgently more than a page long), are quite in tune with the overall plan of the series and its technical requirements–uniform size and moderate price (two to six shillings per volume)–for a wider public interested in "the study of our older literature."

To his previous editions of early drama for the Shakespeare Society Halliwell issued in 1860 another interlude, *A Pretie New Enterlude ... of the Story of Kyng Daryus*, once again a simple reprint without notes, with a preface (vii), just a few lines long, admitting that its "principal curiosity" is that it is "one of the earliest English religious plays in which the character of the Vice is introduced ... With the exception that Popery is reviled in it, and that Queen Elizabeth is alluded to in the concluding prayer, it is difficult to indicate any particulars worthy of note." What seems to be important is its rarity only, "not more than three perfect copies being known to exist," and that a copy "sold at Rhodes' sale for 28*l*." Of similar motivation is Halliwell's publication in the same year of John Day's comedy *Humour Out of Breath*. In an open letter to *Notes and Queries* he announced a series of reprints of early English popular writers called The Percy Library. He was frank in admitting its limitations: "My leisure will not allow me to add notes, or to do more than give a few preliminary pages of bibliographical notice to each piece." And, as was his custom, he rationalized the limitations: "This is, indeed, all that is really required; for it should be borne in mind that these tracts, however quaint and curious, are less valuable as compositions, than as useful to students for special purposes."[151] Halliwell was evidently anxious to recycle material he had already worked on and in many instances owned. The popular authors named read like an index of the Halliwell enterprise: Greene, Breton, Rich, Lodge, Munday, Churchyard, Dekker, Nashe, Rowlands. The undertaking did not succeed. Instead of a projected five hundred copies for subscribers at "at a small price, a few shillings each," only this volume (albeit the first modern edition) in fifty copies appeared, with a facsimile of the title page of the original but no preface and only five notes (one of which, on "upright shoes," taking more than half the space).

Halliwell's devotion to the theatrical tradition and the stage found further expression in his reprints of early "dialogues," such as *The Wyse Chylde and the Emperor Adrian* and *The Debate and Stryfe between Somer and Wynter*, both in 1860, both from "unique" copies, and both with the

---

151. 28 April 1860, pp. 327-8. The announcement was amplified on 5 May 1860, pp. 346-7. A manuscript version of the announcement is in the Folger Shakespeare Library, C.b.16(111).

standard two-page preface and no critical apparatus—Halliwell reiterating his general editorial stance: "I think it best to follow the errors of the original, even at the risk of incurring the censure of some who will attribute such oversights to the editor."[152] And with an ever-attentive eye he responded to those works, whether in verse or prose, which he thought might contain some connection or allusion to Shakespeare. Some dialogues, like *The Debate*, he could "not help thinking ... suggested to Shakespeare the conclusion of his drama of 'Love's Labour's Lost'" (p. 6). *Fortune's Tennis Ball* (1859), a "curious metrical version of this popular tale [Greene's *Pandosto*], "unnoticed by all bibliographers" and of which no early edition is known, Halliwell reprinted from a unique copy for its connection with the story of *The Winter's Tale*. William Baldwin's *Beware the Cat* (1864)—so rare that Halliwell could find no copy of the first edition of 1551 nor perfect copies of the editions of 1570 and 1584—was less interesting to him for its religious satire than for its "allusions to witches, which are illustrative of the play of Macbeth" (p. 5). Similarly, *Some Account of Tofte's Alba* (1865), as the subtitle makes clear, is "an extremely rare poem, containing the earliest extrinsic notice of Shakespeare's comedy of Love's Labour's Lost." And it is worth noting that Halliwell's interest, as always, is in its rarity as well, for he admits to being acquainted with only three copies, one "formerly belonging to [Thomas] Caldecott, [which] sold at the auction of his library for £4.4s., and resold at Bright's [sale] for £2.11s. [but which] would undoubtedly now produce a very much larger sum." For Halliwell it merits a bibliographical description of the small octavo volume in which are embedded the verses containing the "very curious and interesting allusion to 'Love's Labour's Lost'": "I once did see a play / Ycleped so ... " (p. 18). Furthermore, and for the reasons indicated in the title, Halliwell reprinted in 1865 *Those Songs and Poems from the Excessively Rare First Edition of England's Helicon, 1600, Which Are Connected with the Works of Shakespeare*, containing Shakespeare's "On a day, (alack the day)," which found its way into *The Passionate Pilgrim*, as well as a manuscript list of the poems with the names of the authors.

Halliwell's preoccupation with reprints of early English texts coincided as well with his interest in stage history, as in his *Contemporary Depositions Respecting an Affray at Norwich in the Year 1583 ...* (its short title is *The Players at Norwich A.D. 1583*) with its fragment of the professional life of the actors—among them Tarlton, Bentley, and Singer—and the raucous scuffle and the ensuing death of a gate-crasher resulting in the inquest here reprinted. More scholarly and adventurous were Halliwell's attempts to

152. *Debate*, p. 6.

reproduce theatrical documents by means of lithography, a process Halliwell was early to recognize as a way of achieving authenticity, of conserving valuable documents, and of making them available to a wider public. In 1860 he privately printed a volume containing twenty-two plates of facsimiles of the original entries in the Stationers' Company "having reference to Shakespeare's Plays & Poems," as well as of extracts from *Palladis Tamia* (1598). In the same year and again collaborating with the firm of Ashbee and Dangerfield which executed the facsimiles, Halliwell produced for private circulation in twenty-six copies *The Theatre Plats of Three Old English Dramas:* being "directions written out in a large hand on a sheet of pasteboard, for the use of incoming actors. They were suspended on the walls of the theatre, near the prompter's station, so that each actor might readily know the order of his appearances, and the duties he had to perform" (iii). Noteworthy also is Halliwell's attempt–one of the first of its kind–to photograph old texts. In about 1857 he produced the 1608 quarto of *Richard II* and the 1617 *Famous Victories of Henry the Fifth*. He destroyed the negatives–doubtless to accord with his practice of increasing the rarity and thus the monetary value of the "ten perfect copies" which were preserved. These photographic issues, only two copies of which seem to have survived,[153] are so faded as to be virtually illegible. Still, the effort was a step in the development of the newly emerging process of photolithography which was to supplant the tracing often employed in lithographic reproductions.

Halliwell's extensive reprinting of early popular literature, his effort to make easily available texts otherwise neglected or forgotten, is, in effect, a reflection of his archaeological bent, and his passion for the curious is the antiquarian's delight in the relics of the past through which the past is best understood. For in the main he was dealing with sub-literary texts, anonymous renderings of local and now remote persons and situations, the history and sociology, the science and scatology, of early times. If the source was a unique manuscript or a rare book, so much the better for the special insight and, of course, for the interest of the bookman and collector. Accordingly, Halliwell did not neglect verse, albeit less for its aesthetic as for its sociological revelations and, as the case may be, for its rarity. Such is the case of the "curious" *Scourge of Drunkenness* (1859) with its three poetical dedications, a woodcut on the title page of a child being taught its letters through the medium of a hornbook, and a somewhat

153. The first is in the Folger Shakespeare Library: PR 2820/A22/Copy 1/Sh. Col., and in the Birmingham Public Library: 52786. The second is PR 2812/A24/Copy 1/Sh. Col. and 57345.

complicated bibliographical history. At least Halliwell was honest enough to admit that "with respect to the quality of the verse, the less said the better" (vii). Of similar implication and value are the small collections of mainly anonymous popular verse, both appearing in 1860: *A New and Merrie Prognostication* and *A Treatise of a Galaunt, with The Maryage of the Fayre Pusell*. The former, "suppositiously assigned to Will Summers," jester to Henry VIII, is an example of mock prognostications long in vogue, but for Halliwell mainly of interest for its "singular rarity," including the fact that the original edition is "ornamented, or, as some might say, disfigured, by a series of woodcuts evidently borrowed from some contemporary almanac" (ii-iii) and, possibly, that he thought fit to omit "two or three very coarse lines and words" (iii). The latter is evidently only of interest as a "unique edition printed by Wynkyn de Worde," for the variations of its three editions are "not of great importance" (p. 6), and the little poem, "maryage of the fayre pusell" (pp. 26-9), only for its local allusions. The same motivation was behind Halliwell's various collections of the period. Almost always favoring "inedited" manuscripts he issued in 1855 *Early English Miscellanies, in Prose and Verse* (for the Warton Club) and in 1859 *The Tinker of Turvey, or, Canterbury Tales*. Of even more sociological implication, and still another instance of Halliwell's penchant for folk humor—one of his first reprints was *The Merry Tales of the Wise Men of Gotham* in 1840, another *The Jokes of the Cambridge Coffee-Houses in the Seventeenth Century* in 1841—are his reprints of jest-books: *Conceits, Flashes, and Whimzies* (1860), a simple listing of 287 jests and anecdotes not previously known (one with a reference to Shakespeare[154]) and in 1861 his recently purchased *Sack Full of Newes*, a collection of brief prose "tales," almost always beginning with the tellingly formulaic "There was."

There is a regional dimension in some of Halliwell's reprints as well. His beloved Wales is represented by Humphry Crouch's verse satire against the Welsh, *The Welsh Traveller* (1860), with Halliwell the bookman's remark that the original low price of one penny is testimony to the "curious fact that large, high-priced books of limited impressions, are, in afterages, more common than cheap ephemeral tracts" (p. 6); by the likewise satirical *Humple Remonstrances of Rice op Meredith op Morgan, Shentilman of Wales, With Fery Brave Newe Ballacks, or Songs* (1861), its title reflecting the dialect, and its theme, the patriotic desire for freedom and

154. No. 194 (p. 49): "One asked another what Shakespeares works were worth, all being bound together? He answered not a farthing. Not worth a farthing? Said he, why so? He answered that his plays were worth a great deale of mony, but he never heard that his works were worth any thing at all."

peace; and also by the sober petition entitled *A Viewe of Some Part of Such Publike Wants and Disorders as Are in the Service of God, within Her Majesties Countrie of Wales, Togither with an Humble Petition unto this High Court of Parliament for Their Speedy Redresse* (1861), which Halliwell considered the "one, perhaps, the most important to those who are interested in the religious history of Wales" (viii). Scotland appears in Halliwell's bibliographical description of nine Scottish tales of the late seventeenth century, *Some Account of a Singular and Unique Collection of Early Penny Merriments and Histories, Printed at Glasgow* (1864), all "so far as is known, unique" (it was his own copy), with brief excerpts in verse from such revealing titles as "The Friar and the Boy. Very Detestable, though Unpleasant to All Step-Mothers" (No. iv) and "The History of Adam Bell, Clim of the Clough, and William of Cloudesly, Who Were Three Archers Good Enough, the Best in the North Country" (No. vii). London is represented in *The Ancient Ballad of the Fair Widow of Watling Street and Her Three Daughters* (1860) in which are to be found their tribulations at the hands of her prodigal son and his eventual condemnation by the Star Chamber, and also in the parade of Londoners in the satirical couplets of *An Old Poem on the Mineral Wells at Islington, near London, Describing the Company Who Resorted to Them* (1861), with its sociologically revealing picture of "six hours thus idly thrown away." Finally, popular English history is evident in the yeoman-like patriotism of three sheet ballads, "hitherto unknown to all bibliographers," Thomas Deloney's *Three Old Ballads on the Overthrow of the Spanish Armada* and *The Metrical History of Tom Thumb the Little*, both in 1860.

Much of the satirical material already discussed deals with portraiture, such as the six "grave citizens" employed by the prodigal son in the *Ancient Ballad of the Widow of Watling Street*: Make-shift, Francis Light-finger, Cuthbert Creepe-window, Rowland Rob-man, Jack shameles, and Harry steale-hen; or those who come to take the waters at Islington Wells, among them a "beau bedawb'd with lace, / Conducting in with dam'd grimace, / A tawdry punk in fluttering cloaths, / Whom you must quality suppose" (p. 18), or "A Doctor then with swirling cane, / Well skill'd in each disease and pain ... Next him a young spruce City fop, / Chief of a Linnen-drapers shop, / With a long wig and tilter on, / To make him look like a gentleman." From these portraits it is but a short step to the characters who not only "illustrate the habits and manners of Englishmen"—that is, supply socio-historical data—but must also be considered a kind of preliminary psychological and typological classification. Halliwell was not primarily interested in psychology; his critical tenets rejected introspection. But as archaeologist or one interested in assembling data, his collections must represent as well a psychological orientation, a tendency to view outlines, if not externals, as reality. And if the portraits are overdrawn or even grotesque, they need not necessarily be misrepresentations but are, so the theory of the humours out of which they evolved, comical or tragical, vicious or vain, silly or sage, whimsy or wise, above all recognizable in narrative and in life, and reflecting a heightened social and psychological consciousness. To the gallery of works already discussed Halliwell added three important and entertaining collections of reprints: *Books of Characters, Illustrating the Habits and Manners of Englishmen, from the Reign of James the First to the Restoration* (1857), *The Whimzies; Or a New Cast of Characters* (1859), and *Confused Characters of Conceited Coxcombs, or, a Dish of Traitorous Tyrants* (1860).

+++

Commenting on his newly begun series of reprints, Halliwell wrote to Fairholt on 19 January 1860, "I can fancy you saying the Shakespeare [edition] is enough by itself, but I found a change of pursuit not only *prudent* but *necessary* for the *head.* It is too much to return to one subject all day & day after day" (Folger W.a.81[21/7]). Halliwell's motivation is understandable and, to an extent, typical. For frenetic activity, if not sheer impatience, was from the beginning a professional and even personal characteristic. As a teenager, in the commonplace book he kept at Trinity College in 1836-7, he had copied out the advice of E. D. Clarke as a motto: "I have lived to know that the great secret of human happiness is this—never suffer your energies to stagnate. The old adage of 'too many irons in the fire' conveys an abominable lie. You cannot have too many pokers, tongs, and all—keep them all going." Although the phrase recurs in numerous variations throughout Halliwell's career, and is by no means inaccurate, it would be a mistake to conclude that Halliwell was pursuing different objectives in order to alleviate his chronic headaches or to clear his brain literally or metaphorically. For his devotion to scholarship was constant and not only connected the various roles he played but also gave them added substance and a common direction. His pursuits were roles, each revealing an aspect of a personality which was not disparate but ever indivisible. This is well illustrated in what must be regarded as Halliwell's occasional writing between 1854 and 1865.

Although personal revelations were always to be found in his works—in the way of subjects chosen, critical stances assumed, and hardships acknowledged, not to mention the unabashed use of the first person pronoun—Halliwell found time to formulate a body of writings which seemed to put his personality in the foreground. His role was ever that of conveyor of information, but in these works it is Halliwell the private man rather than the general critic who shapes the information. And it is clear that a "change of pursuit"–the many-irons-in-the-fire attitude–was not to be taken literally. For Halliwell had only one subject, scholarship, which he approached in various ways.

One way was already apparent in the records of his travels to North Wales and Cornwall. The subject is, as always, archaeology, but the pronoun is personal, the atmosphere is familial, and the objective is pleasure. In the direct address to the reader, in the holiday atmosphere, Halliwell not only relaxes into a conversation with the reader about what is seen but, affected by what he experiences and the intimate context he establishes, he himself becomes more expansive and reflective. It is not so much the subject that changes but the tone and the perspective.

"What is it all come to? "is the opening sentence of the preface to *Notes of Family Excursions in North Wales*. It conveys more than the futility of writing or a glancing blow at the abundance of writers or even the tongue-in-cheek admission that Halliwell himself has been seeking an excuse to "perpetuate" the "rubbish just shot here." For one thing the self-styled *paterfamilias* transcends his "family party, eight in number," overcome by the beauty of the landscape and immersed in the depth of historical dimension. For Halliwell the archaeologist re-creates as he recreates. Time is less pressing during a holiday, evoking revery and reflection to emerge from cheerful whimsy and domestic bliss. From the conclusion of the travelogue–"For years and years there will be visitors to Bangor who will never gaze on its beautiful landscape without there flitting by a vision of the pall and the shroud; and the graves near Red Wharf Bay will be the object of sad pilgrimage, tinging with melancholy and gloom excursions from the beautiful city of the Menai" (p. 222)–it is but a short and inevitable step to a lengthy coda, a melancholy Halliwell holding the skull of worldly vanity:

In an obscure corner of the desolate churchyard of Llangelynin, there lay, when we passed by, a human skull exposed to air and weather. Amidst those mountain wilds no one with spade or mattock to give it reinterment, not even a ruddock with charitable bill to cover it with leaves. Yet it is not so many years agone that the occupier of that narrow tenement sighed and laughed, and eat and drank, like you and I. And to be so soon forgotten! Alas that it be so, but it is a rare affection that retains for long the memory of the dead. Happy for him if he, in his day, cultivated favour in that Court where alone forgetfulness never enters (p. 223).

Halliwell becomes Hamlet addressing Horatio and equating the "lonely skull occurring to [his] mind's eye" with the life of a book, his book, which, even if it survives infancy and flourishes for a few years, dies and is "ultimately thrown into a corner, to be completely forgotten by the world as is that solitary skull in the churchyard at Llangelynin" (pp. 224-5). He is also Guildenstern, a young author, being addressed by the skull, whose life and career twenty years earlier were, in litany-like repetitions, "just like me." Although "literature will not fulfil the brightness of its early promise," he warns, his experience leads him to "believe that while very few books will outlive a generation, on the other hand there is hardly one which does not contain one useful fact or the germ of an idea worthy of preservation" (pp. 226-8). So he must write and turn out a little volume "much such a one as this is. It is not the least odds to him if any one reads it or no. The object is attained; the brain is relieved; the headaches are gone." Besides, there is also a "certain benefit to others ... The elder Mr. Weller, moralizing on Death, touchingly observed,–'There's a Providence in it, Sammy; there's a Providence in it, or what 'ud become of the undertakers?' So there is a Providence in the rage for authorship; for, if there were no cacoethes to write, what in the world would become of the printers?" (pp. 230-1).

Given to headaches and depression, Halliwell often resorted to whimsical humor, a Pickwickian stance, in a household of a loving wife and four admiring daughters. It was personal and a nostrum, but it was never divorced from his professional interests. In what was the busiest time of his life, between 1862 and 1864, he wrote a series of light and popular essays for *The Rose, the Shamrock, and the Thistle*, a publication of the Scottish National Institution for Promoting the Employment of Women in the Art of Printing. In May 1862 he produced "A Random Note on the Good Old Times Tending to Show That in Some Respects the Present Days May Be Distinguished as the Better New Times" and in August followed with "Archaeology Run Mad." The first is a sugar-coated reflection on transience and death. His daughters Katie and Ellen, playing around him, will later remember "their dolls, their balls and games, their whoops and their calls, and their favourite nooks ... but not one thought will be given to the episodes of infantine adversity." So "is it with the collective life of the nation. In looking back to the past, those heavy troubles that have made dark and enduring landmarks in our path being excepted, our thoughts are but too apt to strew it in imagination with all the flowers, in forgetfulness of the thorns and obstacles. The good old times!" (p. 3). But *ubi sunt* gives way to the acknowledgment of change: "It is astonishing to note how soon the common things of one year become the antiquities of the next." In the reign of Queen Elizabeth penny books were destroyed daily; "Now-a-days, twenty guineas could be got for a *Tom Thumb* of Shakespeare's time." "Horn-books were in daily use, and were issued in annual thousands until within the last fifty years; yet they are now so rare, that not even a modern specimen of one is to be seen at the Kensington Museum" (p. 7). All is transient; people forget. Two centuries after the death of Richard Tarlton there "was an inn in the suburbs of London, then called the Tarlton, and perhaps there it is still. Men put his picture upon signs, and his image upon tokens. The figure of Tarlton, with his tabor and pipe, was as familiar to the public as that of Queen Elizabeth in her ruff. I should like to know what actor of the present day would be similarly honoured." Halliwell is once again, in altered tone, asserting the importance of his profession as antiquary and author in a personal way—so is his final appeal to be understood: "Ye public, cherish the memory of the few who can harmlessly charm away sadness from the sad, and appreciate well during the time they are with you. They deserve a better fate than is usually accorded to them. In this particular, at least ... we can creditably follow the example of the 'good old times'" (p. 11).

Appearing in August 1862, "Archaeology Run Mad" is almost Dickensian in its spoofing of the doings of various archaeological societies:

If Mr. Toddles, not a member of the learned body, wanted to have a paper on ancient knee-strings, or some equally important subject, read before the society, he went to his friend Mr. Noddles, the Director: 'Excuse my intrusion, Mr. Noddles, but, if you would kindly place reliance on the importance of a discovery I have made respecting the fashion in which garters were worn in the reign of the glorious King William, will you do me the honour to become sponsor for a paper I have written on the subject?' 'My dear Mr. Toddles, you know that, as a general rule, I decline to introduce papers before an opportunity has been afforded for their perusal, but anything from *your* pen,' etc. etc. ... In due time, out comes the paper under the title that to a public not too curious is perplexing in the important question as to whether the essay were written by Toddles or Noddles, for this is its announcement: An enquiry into the origin and antiquity of knee-strings, sometimes called garters, with observations on the method in which they were worn towards the close of the seventeenth century, by Septimus Toddles, Esq., M.N.S., communicated by the Hon. Conspicuous Noddles, F.A.S., M.A.T.S., and the Director of the Society (pp. 1-2).

The essay is as well a gentle reminder of the idiosyncrasies and eccentricities of much archaeological research, a plea for provincial associations to coordinate their activities with the central bodies, and so a justification of the importance of sober archaeological research, including his own, over a "storm made in the teapot, when random conjecture on one side, and pretensions of exaggerated import on the other, are advanced, which lead to an objectionable antiquarian flourish of trumpets" (p. 4).

In 1863 Halliwell contributed ten "Roundabout Letters on Stratford-on-Avon" to *The Rose, the Shamrock, and the Thistle*. Appearing monthly (but for January and November) in the form of letters to the editor–the salutation is "Dear Madam"–they represent Halliwell at his conversationalist best. He plays the role of tourist guide intoxicated with Shakespeare, Shakespeare country, and Shakespeare politics. His approach to the landscape, albeit admiringly enthusiastic, is nevertheless keyed to its relative modesty. "I do not believe that if the Seven Mountains of the Rhine were removed and set down opposite Mr. Hunt's river garden at Stratford, that we should like half so well that beautiful scene ... when, from the terrace of that garden, at early dawn are seen the first rays of the sun on the Avon so softly flowing." Rhapsodic and sentimental are adjectives he employs, but is not prevented from introducing, in another role, his efforts on behalf of Stratford. Commenting on the increase over the years of the value of Shakespeare's birthplace in Henley Street–in fifty years from "something like £250" to £3000–he advertises and slyly celebrates his own efforts and those of his Shakespeare Fund. "So, in our day, some people laughed ... still more at the price which secured Shakespeare's Gardens to the Corporation of Stratford; and they absolutely yelled with floods of ridicule at a scheme which not only proposed the deference to the memory of the poet ... but aimed at the preservation of Anne Hathaway's cottage and Getley's Copyhold." After a mention of the enormous support of such friends of the Fund as Robert Bell and William Euing, and a disquisition on the manner and motivation of giving and non-giving, Halliwell cannot but conclude that "in the case of the Shakespeare Fund, one chiefly of literary sentiment, no person in the world need be at the trouble of framing an excuse for non-subscription."

Sentimental and anecdotal though he may be, Halliwell in Letter No. 2 does succeed in imparting the information and expertise of the literary archaeologist by explaining Shakespeare's relationship with Anne Hathaway. "The fact of Shakespeare, at the age of eighteen, falling over head and ears in love with Anne Hathaway, a lady of twenty-six, is not an occurrence that need be distorted, on no evidence, into a narrative in which fair Anne is represented as inveigling him into an imprudent one." And he can conclude that Shakespeare's "gallipot" was "certainly not Anne Hathaway; neither is it to be discovered in the juice of the grape nor in the eyes of a metropolitan syren [*sic*], who, if we are to listen to the vagaries of Professor Gervinus, stole his love from Mrs. Shakespeare of Stratford." Nor was Shakespeare's gallipot his stealing the deer from Charlecote park, another of Halliwell's favorite subjects. Halliwell's chatty stance does not preclude a solution to which his patient research has led him and from which he was never to waver. "I have the vanity to think that I know pretty well what Shakespeare's gallipot was" is his cheery introduction to what is to be a major and not uncontroversial tenet of his Shakespeare criticism:

What I do believe really was Shakespeare's gallipot consisted in his determination to found a family estate, a determination apparent to any careful examiner of the documents illustrative of his life which have been preserved to our times. With this object in view, he cared more for the pecuniary results of his wonderful dramas than for the preservation of their texts. It is owing to this most unfortunate gallipot, that two-thirds of the plays of Shakespeare have come down to us either in a mutilated, or at least in an unsatisfactory state.

From this conclusion of the second of the Roundabout Letters it is but a short step for "an elderly party like myself," so Halliwell in Letter No. 3, to a meditation on the passage of time: "And must it be that I must meditate on my beautiful Mill-bridge for the last time? For the last time to gaze on Stratford Church—for the last time, to anxiously look for the first view of the Wier Brake rising above the beautiful Avon—for the last time to pause at the Cross-on-the-Hill, and view the charming valley of Stratford." But the foolishness of regretting the passage of time or even the "morbid apprehension of death," however much they "imply a want of trust to that Power to which trust should be implicitly given," cannot prevent Halliwell from mourning the inevitable passing of old Stratford, of a "country split up into brick-field heaps, with hideous railway tracks, and screaming engines,—a bit of smoky Manchester spoiling one of the fairest scenes in Warwickshire." In a kind of Homeric catalogue Halliwell summons up the names of the places and neighborhoods of Stratford, valiantly hoping they will not fade, nor by implication he.

An anecdote about the "wise dispensation which enables so many—always excepting Lord Palmerston—to indulge in the delusion that

they are superior to their neighbours," a theme the essentially retiring and
socially modest Halliwell returned to often, leads him to the conclusion
in Letter No. 4 that the "reason why our great poet is so pre-eminently
noted by his contemporaries as 'the gentle Shakespeare' consisted in a
great measure of his anxiety to avoid giving pain to others ... Shakespeare
was a shrewd man of business, perfectly capable of defending himself
against any one who attempted to overreach or presume, but we may rest
assured that he was more successful than any other man in avoiding hints
of melting-days, and that, with an innate goodness of heart, he was ever
on the alert to soothe, conciliate, and please." Mellow and aging, Halliwell
is undeniably identifying himself with Shakespeare the man. Yet this
connection is not pursued. Instead, in another and well-disguised bit of
autobiographical self-reflection, Halliwell turns on the German critics,
"who write an incredible amount of aesthetic nonsense about
Shakespeare, [and] settle the whole matter by the personal application of
the Sonnets. Very like the dignity of Shakespeare's genius, indeed, to tell
us all about himself in that way! You may depend upon it that he was
never such a goose." Another Halliwell tenet follows: "The deeper
mysteries of Shakespeare's mind passed away to the sound of funereal
music, right round the bell of the Guild Chapel and then away forever, on
the twenty-third day of April one thousand six hundred and sixteen ... Let
us be contented that we know so much of him of the kind and good, so
little of the evil. Let us, above all, rest satisfied with the few direct and
reliable evidences, and not attempt to invest any of his writing with the
interest that would attach to a reflex of his own mind."

In Letter No. 5 the theme is flunkeyism. From what would seem to be
simply a series of anecdotes and observations on a possible
definition–insincere adulation or conventional insincerity being rejected
as synonyms, and respect and independence being preferred as antonyms
of flunkeyism–Halliwell moves to the necessity for social harmony:

If provincial towns are wise, they will cling to self-government as there
[their] dearest, choicest privilege, neither interfering with the aristocracy,
no allowing the aristocracy to interfere with them; both sections of the
community thus preserving that which is the essential necessity of real
friendship–independence.

And typically the message is not abstract but is applied to Halliwell's
personal and professional situation. "Them's my sentiments," he quotes
from a play he has seen:

With these sentiments I have worked what I could work in favour of the town of Stratford; for be it known that more than one person was ready to purchase the gardens of Shakespeare on other conditions, and that the responsibilities incurred by myself arose from the determination that the whole should be under the control of the governing body of the town. A corporation is a local parliament, bearing that relation to a town which the Imperial Parliament does to the nation. Let no town, even in trifling matters, surrender its parliamentary rights. Municipal institutions, I love them, I respect them, and, if in any, in that direction foremost shall for ever lie my flunkeyism.

The remaining letters continue Halliwell's gentle but serious campaign and self-revelation. In Letter No. 6 he defends Stratford of "olden time" against the Philistine destruction of Middle Row; In Letter No. 7 he attacks those who would assume the identity of the Three Tailors of Tooley and with "childish arrogance" criticize Shakespeare, Stratford, and the Shakespeare Fund. In Letter No. 8 he revolves the question of his writing: "Whatever you do, my, friends, be candid. Let us see whether I cannot be so for once, and begin in earnest. Well then, I am a fool to write these Roundabout Letters. Granted! but then, dear gentle readers, are you not bigger fools to read them!" Writing is arduous enough, and Halliwell would prefer not have to meet a deadline, so he asserts in Letter No. 9, "for it is downright cruelty to animals to expect any one to be scribbling anything during the universal holiday of September ... but then, what would become of the *Roundabout Letter?*" And so he delivers a few lines on his "particular weakness," waterfalls. Finally, Halliwell in Letter No. 10 treats once again the importance of subscriptions to the Shakespeare Fund for the formation of a special Shakespearian library and museum in Stratford, his personal ambition and professional aim.

Halliwell's amusingly pointed and self-revealing Roundabout Letters came to an end in 1863. He did produce "A Note on the Story of Bovinian," which appeared in January and was continued in March 1864 in *The Rose, the Shamrock, and the Thistle*; it was a "noting" or a "notice" in the form of a reprint of the introduction or epistle to the reader and chapters xvi to xviii of a "curious old chap-book" printed in 1656. It meets all the requirements of Halliwell's reprints: it has been overlooked by the "most industrious of our bibliographers"; it is "curious" and of "extreme rarity"; it is important within the tradition of folk literature, being a "continuation of one of the best known and most common of all our old story-books"; it is in the much-cherished black-letter, with woodcuts; and, to be sure, it is owned by Halliwell, who "picked it up I don't know where some years ago, and cannot find a notice of any other copy."[155] Since his reprints of such works had not done too well, he had to settle for a note. But Halliwell's penchant for parody and practical jokes in his life and career led him to publish, at his own expense, in December 1865 *A Newel, Which May Turn Out to Be Anything But a Jewel, Suggested by J.O.H.*, in ten copies only, a three-page "modest proposal" for killing fish with a little ball of gunpowder and the assistance of a galvanic battery, which concluded, "why, then, it will only be one of the many instances in which practice shows theory to be liable to error" (p. 9). If the spoof were not as obvious as its targets, the colophon page is headed: "Printed for the Amusement, Delectation, or Disgust, or for a Combination of the three sentiments, of kind and intimate Friends, some of whom will undoubtedly say–'Poor H. is going wild.' Nevertheless, herein lies the safety."

It is unlikely that Halliwell received very much for his contributions to *The Rose, the Shamrock, and the Thistle*, although he could well have used the money. A new and struggling journal, it lasted only three years (1862-65), unable to survive in a hotly competitive market which featured, among others, the *Cornhill Magazine* (founded by Thackeray) and Dickens's *All the Year Round*, the former (according to Wright [Tuesday, July 1861; LOA 75:25]) selling 85,000, the latter's monthly parts 45,000. Very likely its advocacy of women's rights–it called itself *A Journal for the Fair Daughters of Great Britain and Ireland*, printed and published by the Caledonian Press, "The National Institution for Promoting the Employment of Women in the Art of Printing"–was not particularly helpful. And Halliwell had to find time for it in an already crowded schedule. Still, he did so, obviously needing to do so. For he doubtless wished to make his views known to a wider public and to enlist his readers in the campaigns involved in the instituting of Shakespeare memorials in Stratford. In essence, he sought to convince the public and, in so doing, to justify and solidify his own beliefs. His "occasional" writings were meant literally–that is, for the occasion. They were not peripheral but central to the furtherance of his professional activities and the cultivation of his personal inclinations. The same motivation may be found in another body of writings which Halliwell produced "at odd hours," and apparently with great intensity and concentration, for his wife's diary entry for 2 January 1859 notes that he mentioned it "for the first time," of 17 February 1859 that he had finished

---

155. Halliwell wrote on the flyleaf in his copy (now in the British Library): "I believe this tract to be unique. It is not even in the very large collection of quarto chap books in the Pepysian. I sent a comn. of £5.5 for it at Turnbull's sale. It fetched about 26/."

it, "having commenced it on December 16th 1858," and of 26 May 1859 that she was already correcting proofs of a second edition: *An Introduction to the Evidences of Christianity*. Although it seems that Halliwell had indeed "left ... his favourite Shakspeare for the best companion to Shakspeare ... the Bible," so a notice in the *Illustrated London News* (5 November 1859, p. 440), he did so with the same engagement, and not merely as a convinced Christian but also, and importantly, as a scholar anxious to prove the validity of a certain critical methodology, one which, as in the case of his Shakespeare research, relies not so much on the subjective and intuitive as on objective and rational documentation.

The circumstances surrounding the publication are not uninteresting. The first edition, whose preface is dated 28 February 1859, was printed by J. E. Adlard; the impression was "limited to one hundred Copies.–For Presentation Only." The cost was evidently met by the "liberality" of William Atkinson (and there may have been more than one hundred copies printed, one assigning the work to J. O. Halliwell, a second [Folger BT1101.H43] to "A Fellow of the Royal Society"). The immediate aim of the limited private circulation, the preface makes clear, is "with the view of eliciting opinions, from those capable of forming a correct judgment, how far an extended publication may be likely to answer the purpose for which it was written" (iv). In a note to J. B. Davis of 9 April 1859 tipped into the Folger copy, Halliwell writes, "Any suggestions from you would be highly valued, for a new edition will probably be issued soon." Halliwell sent a copy as well to John Bruce, who acknowledged its receipt on 22 April 1859 (LOA 67:66) and included his comments. That Bruce should receive both editions–he acknowledged the second in a letter of 29 November 1859 (LOA 70:45)–may be a further sign of Halliwell's desire to improve his work rather than of Christian fellowship, for he must by then have learned that it was Bruce who had attacked his folio edition of Shakespeare in the *Athenaeum* in 1853.

Atkinson, Halliwell explains in the preface, "had long observed with regret the unnecessary prevalence of rationalism in this country, and was willing, with a kind of partiality, to believe it within the compass of my ability to write a practical treatise that might be to a certain extent efficacious in meeting some of the specious and untenable arguments popularly urged in discussions on the Christian evidences." (The year 1859, it must be remembered, also saw the publication of Charles Darwin's *On the Origin of Species*, the month, November, in which Halliwell's second edition also appeared.) Although admitting that he, as a "layman, who has no pretensions to religious knowledge" (i), Halliwell nevertheless is confident that "with some knowledge of the nature of the arguments" and with his well-practiced reliance on historical evidence, he can add to the "extraordinary weight of the evidence in favour of Christianity" (ii). That evidence, indeed his main contribution to the discussion, was to be found in the "testimonies of independent authors, such as Suetonius, Tacitus, or Celsus, the Epicurean philosopher" (iii). These Halliwell interweaves into his text in a sober fashion, numbering his paragraphs to heighten the sense of neutrality and avoiding in his diction any "spirit of advocacy." For all its apparent disinterestedness, it is equally apparent that Halliwell was interested in more than displaying his knowledge of classical historians. There can be little doubt that he believed what he had written—religion was an important ingredient of his family life; in "A Note on the 'Essays and Reviews',"[156] he spoke out passionately for the "truth of Christianity, and the value of the Scriptures as a Revelation":

We can never compel men of our own efforts to embrace religious faith by the production of any number of testimonies. The very idea of evidence implies a necessity for demonstration, and, in that sense, the study of a proof for Revelation may even be regarded as impious. But reasoning and evidence may be agents in the great work, if they but only induce the study of the volume by which Faith is gained (p. 64).

And there can be no doubt that he believed in the method he had employed. His total engagement is also to be measured not merely by the fact that he had to write in "odd hours" but by the fact that he sought suggestions for improvement and acted upon them. For later in the year he produced a second edition with "many alterations and corrections" which, among other things, involved the changing of the numbering of the paragraphs from sixty-four to seventy-one. The second edition found a publisher, Longman, Green, Longman, and Roberts, after having been praised but declined by Macmillan. The reviews were favorable: The *Critic*, for example, found that it was "stated ... clearly and elegantly";[157] The *Educational Times* praised Halliwell for producing the "primary features of Christian evidence in as plain and intelligible a manner as it is possible";[158] a long and detailed assessment in The *Christian Reformer* noted "blemishes and inaccuracies ... not to disparage the work, but because they are essential to a just criticism. The author's style, illustrations and arguments,

156. *St. James's Magazine*, 1 (1861), 61-4.
157. 13 August 1859, p. 157.
158. August 1860, pp. 181-2.

all deserve approbation."[159] But it is unlikely that the work was a commercial success; nine copies of the first impression were offered in Halliwell's sale at Sotheby's on 15 April 1861, fetching 2s.6d. each; the original price of the second edition was 3s.6d. No matter. For as he wrote to George Livermore he could not "help thinking [the book] might do some good in America ... Profit was not my object in writing it, so if there is an inclination [by a "respectable" publisher in America] to reproduce it, remuneration need not be made a question" (17 November 1860; Folger Y.c.1247[1]). For all the financial complications of his projects and the stringencies of his domestic needs, Halliwell in his central as well as occasional writings placed principle above profit.

159. n.s. XVI (1860), 430-3.

11

The Bookman

Still, as an active bookman Halliwell had to make his wares known. Like other booksellers, but perhaps more discreetly and professionally, he published bibliographical descriptions of works he had acquired with the aim of showing off his collection and selling certain "curious and rare" items. In 1854 he described a unique edition of 1605 of Sidney's *Arcadia*. Following a brief history of previous editions and a three-page quotation of bibliographical details from this fifth edition–enough to satisfy the bibliographer that this edition, unnoticed by Lowndes, was unique–this five-page "short notice" concludes with a nod to the "increasing popularity" of the writings of Sidney and, to be sure, to the unstated but certainly high value of this edition, considering that even the third edition of 1613 fetched "upwards of £8 a few days since, at an auction at Messrs. Sotheby's ... a fine copy, but still the price appeared to be large for a book of constant occurrence" (p. 7). Other privately published sales catalogues followed, containing bibliographical descriptions of early English literature, often with added remarks on prices fetched for similar works at various sales. Also in 1854 came A *Brief Account of Theological Manuscripts in the Library of James O. Halliwell*, with descriptions of five items, including *The Prick of Conscience* and *The Castle of Love*, as well as *Descriptive Notices of Works in a Small Collection of Sydneian Literature in the Library of James O. Halliwell*, again a generously printed account of nine Elizabethan titles, from a 1591 quarto of Sidney's *Astrophel and Stella* ("the text being perfect, but unfortunately the title page, and probably a dedication, is wanting") to Davison's *Poeticall Rhapsody* of 1621 (the volume, "unbound, was sold at Bright's sale for the sum of £2 15s, a moderate price") to three editions of *The Countess of Pembroke's Arcadia* (the first of 1590 "of extreme rarity" and folio editions of 1593 and 1599). In 1855 there followed, in the same format and manner, *Brief Notices of Bibliographical Rarities, in the Library of James Orchard Halliwell*, with descriptions of forty-five items in English or relating to English literature, "upwards of twenty ... believed to be absolutely unique, and eight of which only one other copy of each is known." With his customary *apologia*, Halliwell confesses, "My leisure has not permitted me to insert more than very slight and inadequate descriptions" (v). But for what is to all intents and purposes a sale catalogue, Halliwell's "chief object"–to "select works the titles of which were either not recorded elsewhere, or were clearly inaccessible to the student" (vii)–has been achieved. For the aim of the "present small addition to our bibliographical literature" will be clear "at all events to those few to whom a privately-printed work like the present can with propriety be addressed"(viii). In 1856 he issued *A Catalogue of an Unique Collection of Ancient English Broadside Ballads*, a luxuriously printed work listing 408 black-letter items, with one issue giving prices from 10s. 6d. to £12.12.0–on the average ca. £2 each. And in 1862, in the format of his small reprints, Halliwell privately printed *A Brief List of Some of the Rarer and Most Curious Old-Book Rarities in the Library of J. O. Halliwell*, devoting generously a page per title to what he characterized as "my little Pepysian," containing "more unique books than are to be found in the Capell collection, or in many a college library." Assembled over a period of many years, the seventy works described present a cross-section of sixteenth- and seventeenth-century literature. Those which are considered to be unique range from No 4, *Writing Tables* (1604) to No. 34, Ford's *Honor Triumphant* (1606) and from No. 19, *A Paradox Proving by Reason & Example That Baldness Is Much Better than Bushie Haire* (1579) to No. 24, *Willobie's Avisa* (1635). Among other "great rarities" are No 58, Greene's *Newes Both from Heaven and Hell* (1593), No. 61, Churchyard's *Fortunate Farewell* (1599), and No. 33, Jonson's *Look on Me London* (1613). Halliwell's publication, backed by his personal intercession, was successful: he sold the collection to the British Museum Library in 1862 for £450, despite the strenuous efforts of his father-in-law, Thomas Phillipps, to block the sale. And, as was his custom, he was able to recycle certain items, selling the originals of works he had recently produced as reprints, such as *The Sack Full of News*, *A Narrative of the Bloudy Murders*, *A New and Merrie Prognostication*, and *The Will of Wit*, among others.

The heart of the collection–as of the collector–was Shakespeare. Between 1854 and 1862 Halliwell issued seven privately printed works announcing Shakespearean titles and Shakespeareana in his personal library and, as it came to be called, museum. The first, *A Garland of Shakespeariana*, indicates the extent and scope of his understanding of what is involved in the study of Shakespeare, although there is no prefatory explanation at all. It contains no works by Shakespeare but rather items which must occupy a place in a Shakespearean library. The sixteen items listed range from No. 5) Greene's *Groatsworth of Wit* (1621), for its "earliest undoubted notice of Shakespeare known to exist," to (No. 8) the *Catalogue of Mr. Capell's Shakespeariana* (1779), and from (No. 11) Thomas Park's Copy of Robert Heron's *Letters of Literature* (1785), containing Shakespearean criticism (which "was bought for me at Mr. Dawson Turner's sale, I think for 15s.") to (No. 14) *Cornelium Dolium* (1638), "with the curious frontispiece of the tub, engraved in the folio Shakespeare." The "museum" concept is illustrated in Halliwell's offering of (No. 3) the large original drawing of Herne's Oak by Paul Sandby ("carefully framed and glazed") and (No. 4) the ancient token of the Ship Tavern ("curiously illustrative of a passage in the Two Gentlemen of Verona"). Objects and artifacts, like the drawing–"bought for me at Puttick and Simpson's, with a few modern MS. collections on the oak, for £5."–became standard items of the bookman's trade, as they were for Halliwell the archaeologist. In 1856 Halliwell's *Lyttle Boke Gevinge a True and Brief Accounte of Some Reliques and Curiosities Added of Late to Mr. Halliwell's Collection* was devoted to illustrating Shakespeare. Thirty-three of the thirty-four items included tokens of the Boar's Head and of the White Hart taverns, a large piece of Shakespeare's mulberry tree, a fragment of a drinking-glass found in the cellar of the Boar's Head, and a betrothal ring with the initials W. and A. (with a "reasonable probability of being the betrothal ring of William Shakespeare and Ann Hathaway"). For the sole book in this collection, *The Book of Merry Riddles* (1617), Halliwell paid the bookseller George Bumstead a commission of £20. The more extensive *Brief Hand-List of Books, Manuscripts, &c., Illustrative of the Life and Writings of Shakespeare; Collected between the Years 1842 and 1859, by James O. Halliwell,* privately printed in thirty copies in 1859, simply lists 355 items, leaving adequate space between the entries for "occasional memoranda." Although the information is scarce–mainly title and date–the range is impressive: the Dering manuscript of *Henry the Fourth* (which Halliwell had described for the Shakespeare Society in 1845), no fewer than twenty Shakespeare quartos, a copy of the Second Folio of 1632, numerous dramatic texts of the seventeenth century, even eighteenth- and nineteenth-century works of literature and criticism, "most of [which] have been used, in one way or another, in the compilation of [Halliwell's] folio edition ... towards the illustration of [which he has] never willingly spared whatever of expense or labour" (vii). An even more massive work was Halliwell's *Hand-List of Upwards of a Thousand Volumes of Shakespeariana Added to the Three Previous Collections of a Similar Kind Formed by J. O. Halliwell* (1862), privately printed in twenty-five copies, in which 780 items of the widest variety are given: from Singer's annotated copy of the Second Folio to a 1608 quarto of *King Lear* (purchased of F. S. Ellis for £25), from Thomas Gray's copy of

Shakespeare with manuscript notes, and from a Crab-tree relic bearing the carved head of Shakespeare to a "curious volume from Ireland's Shaksperian Library." Spanning more than three centuries, the range of interest is matched by that of the "pecuniary value": from £63 (presumably for an Aspley Second Folio purchased of Lilly for £31.10s.) to 1s. (for a small china plate with an engraving of the birthplace of Shakespeare before the alterations). And the collection includes, as to be expected, works already reprinted by Halliwell, such as *A Brief Hand-List of the Records Belonging to the Borough of Stratford-on-Avon* (1862) and the photographic facsimile of *Henry V* (1857).

At the core of it all was Shakespeare. In 1857 Halliwell issued in twenty-five copies *Early Editions of Shakespeare*, listing and briefly describing his fourteen "absolutely genuine" quartos: *Hamlet* (1603), *Henry V* (1617), *Richard III* (1598), *2 Henry IV* (Qo 1600), *Sonnets* (1609), *Richard III* (1605), *Pericles* (1608), *King Lear* (1608), *1 Henry IV* (1608), *Romeo and Juliet (1609)*, *1 Henry IV* (1613), *Pericles* (1630), *The First Part of the Life of John Oldcastle* (1600), and *Troilus and Cressida* (1609).[160] In an accompanying prospectus he announced that he "urgently desired, in aid of the large folio edition of Shakespeare now in the course of publication," early editions, offering "no less than £100 ... for a perfect copy of the first edition of 'Titus Andronicus'." In 1860 he expanded the title to include, for the first time, a "complete list of the various early quarto editions of the plays, in which the titles and imprints are given at length." *A Brief Hand-List of the Early Quarto Editions of the Plays of Shakespeare; with Notices of the Old Impressions of the Poems*, also in twenty-five copies, includes as well the four Folio editions. And, in a bit of emphasis and perhaps pride, he reprinted the contents on blue-tinted paper as *A Skeleton Hand-List*, allowing the upper third of a complete verso side for the individual title and imprint, with the rest and facing recto side blank so as to afford room for manuscript notes on the bibliographical peculiarities of each of the ninety-four editions of the plays and poems.

Halliwell's engagement with Shakespeare at this time was not limited to collecting and furnishing a personal library and museum. In addition to his very considerable labor on his folio edition and his enormous involvement with the National Shakespeare Fund and the establishment of a library and museum in Stratford, as well as the reconstruction and

160. In a "Notice to the Seventh Part" of Lowndes's *Bibliographer's Manual of English Literature* dated 28 November 1861, Henry Bohn defended its "extremely moderate" price by comparing it to the work of "a well-known literary antiquarian [who] has recently printed a small number of copies of a dry list of the twenty quarto plays of Shakespeare, which is sold for about half a guinea."

preservation of Stratford as a historical monument if not shrine, Halliwell continued his experimentation with facsimiles of Shakespeare's works. In 1860 he issued, in twenty-six copies, the title page and five further pages of the 1605 quarto of *Hamlet* to show that the typographical variations with the 1604 edition "appear to be of the most trifling description." He also had a hand in 1860 in the facsimile edition of the first (1603) and second quartos of *Hamlet*, the "Devonshire Hamlets," "so arranged that the parallel passages face each other," with a bibliographical preface by Samuel Timmins and priced at 12s.6d. And encouraged by the technical expertise of E. W. Ashbee, he began superintending facsimiles of all the editions of Shakespeare's plays and poems printed before the First Folio of 1623, announcing in a prospectus in the early 1860s that he felt the "inestimable importance to the student of these pieces, and believing that I am the only person in the world who has access to a *complete* series of them." As bookman and of necessity businessman, he placed a great deal of emphasis on the conditions of subscription. As always, these were consistent with his views on the value of strictly controlling the number of copies printed: having neither time nor inclination to "attend" a large subscription at a low price, and "by adhering to the strict limit proposed, any copies unsubscribed for will always realize high prices, and I feel secure as to the risk." Varying only slightly the conditions for other of his works, Halliwell stated that the "impression will be most strictly limited to *thirty-one* copies *only*," each copy to be numbered by him and "attested further *by both artist and binder*." As if this were not explicit enough, Halliwell went even further: "Fifty copies will be struck off on fine paper, out of which the binders will select thirty-one of the best and clearest impressions for binding, after which the remaining nineteen copies will be destroyed, *such destruction being attested in each copy, and every copy being numbered in writing*." And still further: "*permanent* libraries will receive a few, the remainder to subscribers at five guineas each." Commencing in 1861, the series reached forty-eight volumes and was completed in ten years, volume 1–its preface dated 15 November 1871–containing the general title, the preface, a list of contents, and three facsimiles of original variant title pages.

There were financial risks for Halliwell, who had to pay to have the work produced, and there was the strain–administrative as well as financial–of keeping a subscription going. This applied to the continuing folio edition. Nevertheless–or perhaps to bolster the sagging sales of some of his reprints, as he had in offering them "anonymously" in Sotheby's sale in 1861, fetching £415, "better than he expected altogether"[161]–he issued proposals also in 1861 for a "very choice and limited impression of an unique collection of reprints of curious old English books." This time his approach was, on the surface at least, less rigid. The seven-page prospectus began with a dialogue between friends about the pros and cons of reprinting in large or small numbers. The result of the amiable page-and-a-half conversation was predictable: Halliwell's experience had taught him that there were not a sufficient number of persons interested in old English literature to pay for cheap reprints. That is the "practical" answer to the "theoretical" premise, Halliwell is certain, for he had tried the plan of a larger number at a cheaper price with his recent attempt at a "resuscitation" of the Percy Society, and it had failed. Halliwell thus kept to his old plan of selecting works of "great rarity and curiosity": a first series to form a "very curious library of early English literature; a second series to consist of printed catalogues, that is, where rare books may be consulted." New is Halliwell's plan to print fifty-two copies and to send each subscriber two copies, one to be preserved and one "*mutilated in occasional leaves, so that in any case of death or neglect, no more than twenty-five perfect copies could ever come into the market,* one, the twenty-sixth copy being sent to the British Museum under the provisions of the Copyright Act" (p. 5). After guaranteeing to number each copy and promising to follow out the plan fairly, Halliwell attempted to lessen the risk of financial harm to himself (having been the victim of a "serious ... loss from defaulters") by laying down five conditions: subscribers will pay at the rate of three-halfpence per page, two copies costing three-pence per page; subscribers will pay when at least five pounds are due so as to spare Halliwell the "onerous" administrative troubles; subscribers may withdraw at any time, but not criticize the works on the plan; foreign subscribers are to use a London agent; and booksellers may not be used as agents.

It is not clear from the list of eighty-one titles identified by Lowndes as "Halliwell's Reprints of Rare Books" (IV:254-61) which of those dated from 1860 (that is, number 39) belong to the series, for only two works are given as having been printed in fifty-one copies (although there are numerous of a printing of Halliwell's customary twenty-six, with those twenty-five consisting of "occasional leaves" not included). The two are doubtless of the second series and continue Halliwell's practice of the scholarly presentation of catalogues of important collections. They are his own selections of the early English literature of the sixteenth and seventeenth centuries from the printed catalogues of the Malone

161. So Mrs. Halliwell's diary entry for 2 February 1861.

(amounting to 96 pages) and Douce (151 pages) collections in the Bodleian Library for the "use of students who do not care for the modern portion of the library, and who find that a folio volume is inconvenient for constant reference," so the identical prefatory note in both volumes. As to be expected, Halliwell's selection included titles from all disciplines–literature, medicine, history, theology, etc.–and did not exclude such works (in, for example, the Malone collection) as Everard Digby's *Short Introduction for to Learne to Swimme* (1595) or the anonymous *The Mother's Councell, or, Liue within Compasse* (n.d.).

Although he did not announce it as part of the second series, Halliwell's making available of reference tools is illustrated in his *Dictionary of Old English Plays, Existing Either in Print or in Manuscript, from the Earliest Times to the Close of the* Seventeenth *Century* (1860), another title which suited John Russell Smith's offerings. It is essentially a reworking of the fourth edition (1812) of the *Biographica Dramatica* by Stephen Jones, with Halliwell noting "additions for nearly twenty years" and adding "various alterations in the text." Halliwell's task was mainly one of selection since he had to compress three volumes of double columns totalling 1700 pages into his 296. He had experience, having done so with other works. On the whole he was judicious, at times shortening an article (e.g. on *Titus Andronicus*), at times copying it *in toto* (e.g. *Acolastus*), but apparently taking no notice of the errors pointed out in a review of Jones.[162] And he saw fit to add a list of the collected works of dramatic authors (pp. 282-5), including the four Shakespeare folios and the editions of Dyce (1858), Staunton (1858-60), and the first nine volumes (1863-60) of his own continuing edition; collections of old English plays from 1793 to 1848 (pp. 286-90) and miracle plays from 1823 to 1843 (p. 290); and a useful index of authors (pp. 291-6). And despite his enormous workload, Halliwell responded to the appeals of the widow of the recently deceased Leigh Sotheby and agreed as friend and colleague to supervise the printing and organize the subscription of an impression of fifty copies of three quarto volumes at eight guineas per volume of the manuscript of Sotheby's "Bibliographical Dictionary of the Printed Works of English Poets, from the Earliest Period to the Accession of Charles the Second."[163] The remark at the end of the prospectus is very much in the vein of Halliwell: "Of course, by a trifling additional expenditure, a

162. Understandably, to be sure, for the review appeared much earlier, in June 1812, in the *Quarterly Review*, pp. 282-92.

163. An exchange of letters between Halliwell and Julia Sotheby from 1862 to 1866 is to be found in the Edinburgh Letters of Authors.

hundred could be produced for half of this subscription, two hundred copies for a quarter of it, and so on; but a large subscription would be out of our power to manage." The plan did not succeed; the work was never published.

Halliwell, however, was apparently not deterred from producing other reference works for students of Shakespeare and early English literature. In 1864 he published *A Hand-Table of Regnal Years: For the Use of Enquirers into the History of the Shakespeares*, perhaps the first of its kind, so arranged as to "facilitate researches amongst our public records [from Edward IV to Charles II] and render mistakes in the reckoning of dates given by means of those years less likely to occur." A purely utilitarian work from which he could not hope for material gain since only fifteen copies were printed, it is another instance of Halliwell's desire, which began very early in his career in 1839 with his *Few Hints to Novices*, to assist others in the cultivation of research methods and tools. Further examples of Halliwell's providing reference tools stem from his lexicographical interest in early modern English and provincial dialects. Although in 1856 he abandoned a glossary of early English—"I relinquished this work after printing a few sheets, & only two copies of proofs were preserved"—which was obviously connected with his work on Shakespeare, his reworking, as earlier on similar projects, with Thomas Wright of Robert Nares's *Glossary; Or, Collection of Words, Phrases, Names, and Allusions to Customs, Proverbs, &c.* (1859) and his *Selection from an Unpublished Glossary of Provincial Words in Use in Warwickshire in the Early Part of the Present Century* (1865) are manifestations of his Stratford pursuits and of course his edition of Shakespeare, for "some of the explanations curiously illustrate the phraseology of Shakespeare." And it is not surprising that he should make known suggestions regarding the proposals of the Philological Society for a new dictionary of the English language. Signing himself "A Student," he responded in the *Athenaeum* of 1 August 1857 (pp. 976-7) to the "resolutions" of the Dictionary Committee (consisting of R. Chenevix Trench, F. J. Furnivall, and Herbert Coleridge) made on 24 July 1857 (pp. 944-5) by recommending that the "noble" scheme be expedited by printing "occasional [and indexed] volumes of the best portions of the material as they come to hand," from which, when at least 100,000 or more slips had been collected, a "grand alphabetical Dictionary" could be formed.[164] In

164. Halliwell's interest in lexicography never abated. A few years earlier, Longmans informed him that they "were unable to avail ourselves of your offer relative to the forthcoming edition of Johnsons Dictionary" (26 September 1853; LOA 53:56).

a reply of 8 August 1857 (p. 1007) Coleridge rejected the recommendation, feeling that "Student" had "overrated" both the time and technical difficulties necessary to reduce the "mass to a dictionary form." In a letter of 18 August 1857 (LOA 63:16) Coleridge, having surmised that Halliwell was "The Student," indicated that the plan was only for a supplement to the dictionaries of Dr. Johnson and Charles Richardson with which the Philological Society "*hereafter* ... may be enabled to accomplish a national Dictionary, which may be to English what Liddell & Scott is to Greek." Still, for Halliwell's offer of assistance from his library Coleridge was "very much obliged" and asked for the loan of certain volumes. In the same month Furnivall went further. Having been forwarded Halliwell's letter to Coleridge, he asked about the dating of certain early works and, of seminal importance, "with what book should you start your quotations in an English Dictionary?" (Friday, August 1857; LOA 63:27).

Finally, and obviously, Shakespeare was never out of Halliwell's mind. In addition to all the major undertakings–his folio edition, library and museum, Stratford–Halliwell never ceased to produce smaller contributions to the study of the great poet. In "A Note on Some Unpublished Works of William Basse, the Author of the Earliest Elegy on Shakespeare," a paper read on 12 March 1862 before the British Archaeological Association,[165] he uncovered the "first English writer ["hitherto unknown to poetical antiquaries"] who paid an eloquent tribute of respect and affection to our beloved author." Stage history was represented in a reprint in 1865 of *A Copy of a Letter of News Written to Sir Dudley Carleton, at The Hague, in May, 1619*, with its notice of a performance of *Pericles*, leading Halliwell to observe that the "revival of this play at Court in 1619 may possibly have occasioned the publication of the drama in that year, when an edition appeared from the press of Pavier"; and in a reprint also in 1865 of *The Remonstrance of Nathan Field, One of Shakespeare's Company of Actors*, a letter to a Mr. Sutton, preacher at St. Mary Overs., 1616, which "may be thought to be singular [in] that he should be able to write so well in a religious strain, one very rarely used by actors of the time." Among Halliwell's other contributions to the study of Shakespeare's text are a notice in the *Athenaeum* of 21 March 1857 (p. 375) describing his copy of the prose narrative *The Painfull Adventures of Pericles*, which he was to use in his edition of the play, in the meantime listing the early editions in his collection; a reprint in 1865 of his newly discovered

165. And printed in the *Journal of the British Archaeological Association*, 18 (1862), 280-3.

Newes from Virginia (1616) by Richard Rich, its reports of hurricanes and shipwrecks and mention of the Bermoothes suggesting a possible connection with *The Tempest*; a discussion and bibliographical description of Robert Chester's very rare *Love's Martyr*, with lithographic facsimiles therefrom by E. W. Ashbee of Shakespeare's poems "Let the bird of lowdest day" and "Threnos" from *The Phoenix and Turtle*; and with Eliza M. West the privately printed *Shaksperian Parallelisms* (1865) from Sidney's *Arcadia* not merely in *The Tempest* and *A Midsummer Night's Dream* which the full title mentions but also in fifteen other plays spanning Shakespeare's entire career from *Titus Andronicus* and *Love's Labour's Lost* to *Coriolanus* and *Pericles*. Finally, it is noteworthy that Halliwell demonstrated his very personal engagement in the history of Shakespearean textual criticism by issuing in 1861 "only for presentation" and at his own expense *A Few Words in Defence of the Memory of Edward Capell.* Another of Halliwell's tributes to those persecuted, it is first a response to the fact that the "labours of the dead are too often noticed only to be dismissed with severity ... in most cases with unjust severity" (p. 5). But it is not simply the reverence of the past, nor Halliwell's repeated intercession on behalf of those he believed to have been unjustly treated. The issue is one of critical stance, and for Halliwell, Edmond Malone, "so far from being a mere 'laborious commentator on the meaning of words and phrases,' was one of the first to teach us the true principles upon which the metrical and philological system of Shakespeare is constructed" (p. 8). Halliwell is even more emphatic in defence of Capell. In what amounts to an *apologia* for Capell's kind of labor, Halliwell admits that the study of Capell's work requires great patience but finds the rewards considerable. "On the whole," he asserts, "no other critic of any time has yielded so much of practical and useful information" (p. 10). Halliwell regards Capell's homely and learned perseverance as a cardinal virtue. "Capell was not a man of genius; but no man of genius has ever been and ... no such a one can ever be, a successful critic on Shakespeare" (p. 11). For the "eminently practical and dramatic character of Shakespeare's writings ... appears to place them rather with the range of study followed by unimaginative minds, than of the speculations of the philosopher" (p. 12). Following Capell's example, Halliwell is certain that his "own judgment is not to be set up in opposition when it happens that the words of the author are not to be for the present understood." A "*firm belief in the perfection of* [Shakespeare's] *dramatic genius*" (p. 12) is essential for the critic, whose task is to "sit merely at the feet of the teacher, listening to his words, and endeavouring to enter into their meaning" (p. 13). This is not blatant idolatry, however, for Capell took up "every question in a plain, common-sense manner, having due regard to the author's peculiarities." Given Halliwell's respect for the past, his desire to acknowledge his debt to his predecessors, his defence of the unjustly treated, and his *apologia* for a particular critical stance, it is not surprising that Halliwell was to follow this tribute with a dedication of his sixteen-volume folio edition: "I venture, with all humility, to dedicate this work to the memory of the ablest and the most neglected of Shakespearian critics,–EDWARD CAPELL."

The bookman Halliwell was an active participant in the book business, not merely producing books for subscribers but from his days as teenager passionately buying and selling them. His dealings were so numerous and the details often so fragmentary that only an overview is possible. But those details which are clear and indisputable are enough to indicate that even the tip is of an iceberg of very considerable magnitude. Between 1856 and 1863 he had seven sales at Sotheby's, offering some 3530 items which fetched £3911.11.0. Among the 413 items sold on 23 May 1856, "chiefly consisting of the books used for the first five volumes of Mr. Halliwell's folio edition of Shakespeare," were thirty-nine works by or attributed to Shakespeare; among them a First Folio (which was bought by Henry Stevens for £39), a Second Folio (fetching £5.7.6), Capell's copy of the 1608 quarto of *Henry 5* (£8.18.6), a 1600 quarto of *The Merchant of Venice* (£37), a copy of *The Sonnets* of 1609 (£41), and a *Rape of Lucrece* of 1655 (£25.10.0). Among the others, indeed a small but representative library of Shakespeareana and English literature from the sixteenth to the nineteenth century, were Alexander's *Monarchicke Tragedies* (1616), a French translation of Bandello's *Histoires Tragiques* (1603-4), Bright's *Treatise on the Sufficiencies of English Medicines* (1615), twenty-four volumes of emblems printed in The Netherlands between 1573 and 1729, a Latin work by Henry VIII (1537), Knight's *Life of Shakespeare* (1843), Steevens's *Catalogue of Mr. Capell's Shakespeariana* (1779), Armin's *History of the Two Maids of More-Clack* (1609), Beaumont and Fletcher's *Coronation* (1640), Florio's *First Fruites* (1578), Jonson's *Every Man Out of His Humor* (1600), Prynne's *Histriomastix* (1633), *Selimus* (1594), and Meres's *Palladis Tamia* (1598). The sale is mentioned in Mrs. Halliwell's diary entry for 25 May 1856: "On the 23d Mr Stevens came in the evening & told James of the result of the sale of his books at Sothebys on that day. They fetched £706.0.6 being £200 more than expected. There was quite a furore for his books & some things went very high - he gave me 3 gs for a present."

The 988 items sold at Sotheby's on 21-23 May 1857 fetched £1047.6.6, and included such valuable Shakespearean works as 1600 quartos of *2 Henry 4* (fetching £100), of *The True Tragedie of Richarde Duke of Yorke*

(£60), of *Much Ado About Nothing* (£65), and a 1599 quarto of *1 Henry 4* (£75), as well as a wide range of English literary titles, specially works by Shakespeare's contemporaries, such as Fletcher, Ford, Gascoigne, Heywood, Jonson, Kyd, Lyly, and Lodge. Interesting is the extension of Halliwell's collection to embrace artifacts, such as a fragment of Shakespeare's mulberry tree, a cup made of the wood of the mulberry tree, and "the heel of the shoe kicked off by Mrs. Siddons in throwing back her velvet train whilst performing the part of Constance in King John in 1795." A year later, on 14 June 1858, Halliwell sold 328 items fetching £777.19.6, among them a 1609 quarto of *Romeo and Juliet* (£86) and a copy of *The Sonnets* also of 1609 (£154.7.0), as well as works by Heywood, Jonson, Marston, Massinger, Middleton, and the hit of the sale, lot 328, a Shakespeare autograph signature, affixed to the mortgage deed of a house in Blackfriars (dated 11 March 1612/13), which was bought by William Boone for the British Museum Library for the stunning price of £315.

Halliwell's next sale at Sotheby's, on 13 June 1859, was less interesting, 348 items fetching a mere £466.15.6. The highest-priced Shakespeare items were a 1625 quarto of *Richard 2* (£32.10.0) and a 1600 quarto of *The Merchant of Venice* (£21). On 2 February 1861 the sale was more unusual, consisting only of reprints and facsimiles, "the impressions of which were mostly limited to twenty-six or thirty copies." In all there were but twenty-eight separate titles, the multiple copies totalling seven hundred items. The prices were as little as 4s. each (for *Humour Out of Breath*, the first and only offering of the ill-fated Percy Library); only three titles (Breton's *Will of Wit*, Taylor's *Short Relation*, and *Confused Characters of Conceited Coxcombs*) passed £1 each but did not reach £2. Admitting the sale to be "peculiar," the prefatory note, surely written by Halliwell, explained it as being "merely an experiment to ascertain if such bibliographical curiosities can thus be made to meet their expenses without the trouble attendant on subscription lists." Given the meager results of the sale, the answer must have been no. These reprints of 1859 and 1860 were not very successful, nor were the subscriptions, else–considering Halliwell's views on the value of small printings–the works would not have been put up for public sale. The sale brought £415.6.6 and Halliwell's wife's diary entry for 2 September 1861 that the sum was "better than he expected altogether." Even more disappointing were the results of the sale a few months later, on 15 April 1861, consisting of 546 items, including multiple copies of individual reprints (e.g. *Shaksperian Drolls*, and *The Humble Remonstrances of Rice op Meredith op Morgan*) and the entire stock of *Notes of Family Excursions in North Wales* and the handlists of the Douce and Malone collections in the Bodleian Library. Halliwell was evidently clearing out his stock of reprints and minor or obscure works. A prefatory letter to Sotheby and Wilkinson, printed in the sale catalogue and dated March 1861 but unsigned, amounts to both a description of Halliwell's situation and an admission of the failure of his scheme. It also provides an insight into the Byzantine world of book-dealing:

It has become the fashion of late years to accompany catalogues of certain kinds of book-sales with prefatory remarks explanatory of their nature and cause. The plan is not objectionable, provided these are restricted to the statement of a few plain facts; and, indeed, there is an advantage in it, buyers not unfrequently being influenced by the circumstances under which collections, small or large, are brought into the market.

For many years it has been my practice to be constantly purchasing books in number far beyond what I cared to retain, and as constantly accepting your services in disposing of portions of them. In this way, I have acquired a knowledge of an extensive and peculiar class of books that I could not have obtained in any other manner; but I find that the system has been the occasion of so much absurd misapprehensions, it is quite time to abandon it.

If a plan of this kind could yield a profit, I should be the last to care for any fustian gossip; and as for the dignity of the matter, I never could understand the distinction in that way between an author selling a book and a country gentleman making money on the sheep in his park, or one of a still higher rank selling his pigs. But when, as in book-sales of this kind, even extravagant prices obtained for occasional rarities never balance the loss on the miscellanies, added to the expenses of sale, it seems to me that any continuation of a plan which entails other inconveniences also is scarcely advisable.

The present, therefore, will be my last sale of the kind, and indeed of old books of any kind, at all events until the completion of a large work now in progress, when it is possible that I may not care to retain my still unrivalled accumulation of materials on the particular subject.

It may be well to add that all the lots in the present day's sale will be sold strictly without reserve.

I do not add my name. To those who know it, my signature will impart no information; to those who do not, it is of no manner of consequence.

The sale realized only £191.17.0. And despite his avowal Halliwell had another sale at Sotheby's two years later on 21 November 1863. Items 31 to 237A "from the library of a well known collector," fetched £302.1.6, slightly but not significantly better than the previous sale. Containing a considerable number of multiple copies of Halliwell's reprints (e.g. *An Old Poem on the Mineral Wells of Islington* and *The Sack Full of Newes*) and "Duplicate Shakespeariana," its most attractive lot was a collection of chap-books, garlands, and penny merriments, mainly of the eighteenth century, in fifty-four volumes, which was bought by George Bumstead for £37. But for one further sale at Sotheby's in 1870, this was to be Halliwell's last during his lifetime.

It would be a mistake, however, to see it as the sum of Halliwell's dealings. The Sotheby sales, imposing as they may be, represent only a fraction of his activities and, indeed, of the number of books which passed through his hands. For buying and selling was not merely his occupation, it was his passion. Even a superficial glance at his wife's diary during this period alone is revealing: "sold his Shakespeare Museum to the Earl of Warwick for £194" (22 December 1853); "Dr Bandinel has bought a set of his quartos for the Bodleian Lib." (26 January 1854); "Boone the bookseller has offered £500 for James's collection of 4to Shakespeares" (25 February 1854), Halliwell "bought 3 4to Shakespeares" (17 March 1854); "Parker the bookseller will not buy the plates of J's Dicty outright but will give J. £120 for the privilege of printing 500 copies" (28 March 1854); "a very kind letter from Lord Warwick enclosing a cheque for £200 for [Halliwell's] Shakespeare Cabinet" (17 May 1854); Halliwell "went to Mr Loscombe's Sale at Sotheby's & bought some Shakesp. 4tos for £70" (22 June 1854); "bought Shakespeares betrothal ring for £7.15.0" (22 December 1854); bought the "celebrated Boar's Head ... against the British Museum for £25.4.0" (28 February 1855); "James's 4 folios of Shakespeare are at Russell Smith's & to be sold for £125" (2 June 1855); on vacation in Germany "James went out early and hunted for Old books he found an old translation of Shakespeare into German in 21 vols which he did not know of before and bought it" (24 September 1856);[166] sold his collection of Black Letter Ballads to William Euing for £260 (17 January 1857), "Mr. Lilly called & sold James four Shakespeare quartos from Lord Lindsay's Library ... for £107.10.0" (8 April 1857); "James paid [Professor Mommsen] £120 for a lot of tracts amongst them the Shakespeare Sonnets 1609 - which alone cost £84" (13 April 1857); "Lilly bought the

---

166. Despite the rigors of travel, on the next day he wrote to Thomas Wright from Baden-Baden: "It is astonishing there scarcely seems to be *any* old English books of *any* description over here. There are lots of MSS. though not of a class one cares much about. I picked up a rather curious collection of MS. tracts 15 Centy at Frankfurt at a curiosity for 12 shillings but nearly every thing of the kind is monastic theology" (25 September 1856; LOA 281:56).

Henry 4th 4to for £100" (23 May 1857), "James went early to the Museum with his 10 4to editions of Shakespeare's Plays, which he has offered to the Museum for £1000" (18 June 1858); received "a packet of very rare & curious tracts wch he had bought of Mr Payne Collier for £190" (21 January 1861).

These actions were only part of a larger complex which, in addition to his production of catalogues, handlists, inventories, calendars, collections, and the like, included an extensive correspondence with numerous publishers and printers, as well as with prospective subscribers, buyers, and sellers. In the Edinburgh collection alone there are, for example, 278 letters from Thomas Corser to Halliwell testifying to Halliwell's spirited engagement on behalf of Corser, who was putting together a library of Early English poetry, a portion of which is described in *Collectanea Anglo-Poetica* (1860-83). "I can only say," Halliwell wrote, "that it will give me the greatest pleasure at any & all times to execute any commissions for you in my power in London" (18 February 1868; LOA 131:4). And such was the case for others as well, including Henry Huth and the Earl of Warwick.

What is obvious from this brief summary of some of Halliwell's activities as bookman is that large sums of money were involved, and that speculation was an important feature in the dealings. There were considerable risks for one who did not have a large and stable income, and it is not hard to imagine that Halliwell had to do quite a bit of juggling to keep solvent. The way was not easy. He had to take his measure of setbacks, as in his desire to buy a first quarto of *Hamlet* (1603), complete but for the title page. M. W. Rooney, of Dublin, asked £100 for it, Halliwell offered £50, but directed him to Boone, who bought it for £70 and then sold it to Halliwell for £120.[167] In addition to errors in his own judgment, Halliwell had problems with the subscriptions to the folio edition: with subscribers who were late in their payments or were unable to pay and had to be replaced while taking advantage of Halliwell's guarantee to return the payments of those who were not able or willing to continue. And there were often unforeseen problems, as when Thomas Phillipps, not content to ruin Middle Hill for his daughter and son-in-law, attempted to block the payment of £450 by the British Museum for books Halliwell had sold them, asserting that Halliwell had "affixed fictitious prices to them" (so Mrs. Halliwell's diary entry for 23 October 1862).

167. Still, Halliwell was overjoyed to have it, as is illustrated in his note preceding a photographic copy (EUL Hc. 9.6): "In the summer I bought the Hamlet of 1603, I employed a photographer to make a copy of it, not trusting it out of my sight. The apparatus was set up in our little garden at Brompton, & all was done in my presence, no one but myself being allowed to touch the book."

Although Halliwell was able to prove that he had acted correctly, money was indeed a problem in all of his undertakings as bookman. But his passion was intense and unwavering. As he wrote, not untypically, to W. C. Hazlitt to whom he would show books only by appointment, "with my temperament, an unexpected visitor in the morning interferes with my reading, & in the evening I am too fatigued to receive visitors ... excepting of course any one whatever who has something of Shakespearian interest to bring–everything must give way to Shakespeare" (22 January 1868; LOA 152:29).

· 12 ·

The Folio Edition
and the Shilling Shakespeare

The way of the folio edition of Shakespeare was long and thorny. Halliwell's struggle to keep the project going–to find and retain 150 subscribers, to keep the price stable or at least reasonable, to honor his guarantee to refund the money if the work was not completed,[168] to deal with the impatience of the subscribers–is well recorded in his voluminous correspondence and in his wife's diary. He had also to endure the fact that fellow Shakespearean editors could not make full use of his work because of its price. Howard Staunton, his good friend and colleague, was obliged to ask for cancelled sheets of the edition (9 August 1856; LOA 62:13); Thomas Keightley confessed, "You must not be offended to find no reference to your magnificent folios for they have ben totally out of my reach" (August 1866; LOA 115:19). As for himself, in not untypical confessions during this period Halliwell wrote to Charles Roach Smith after completing the fifth volume, "I fear it is killing me what with anxiety & work" (11 February 1856; Folger C.b.16[77]), and to his close friend and collaborator Fairholt some months later:

Scarcely a week passes without fresh calls on my Time. It is very hard work to do such a large book with numerous family cares & connexions & I find the business of life increases with years, so that if I had not worked hard when I was young I *could not* now. The present vol. has been altogether a most arduous one–my materials are so immense, the difficulty has been what to preserve & what to throw out. Only fancy, the notes to *one act alone* of Twelfth Night making *forty-two closely printed folio pages!* after

---

168. A promise he reiterated even to close acquaintances, such as W. P. Hunt. See, for example, 30 October 1852; Folger Y.c.1237(1) and 30 November 1852; Folger Y.c.1237(3). Later, well on with the work and beset with difficulties, he wrote to Hunt: "I am determined not to owe any subscriber anything. The fact weighed on my spirits, & I must get relieved from the responsibility, the only debt I owe" (23 October 1860; Folger Y.c.1237[15]).

my throwing out not only masses of material, but a good many prepared notes. If I had waited a few years more, the accumulation of matter would have been passed [*sic*] any one's management (2 October 1857; Folger C.b.16[87]).

He was, moreover, forthright enough to record his difficulties publicly, as it were. For one thing, he printed progress reports for his subscribers, such as circular letters to volume 8 (29 November 1858; Folger Y.c.1237[12]) and volume 10 (11 October 1861; Folger Y.c.1307[21]). For another, he went so far as to preface his business matters in volumes of the work itself, not shying away from unpleasantries and seeking always to inform and so soothe his subscribers. In a printed "Notice" dated 31 January 1854 accompanying the second volume (of Folger copy 1), he explained that they will "be glad to know that the Editor's *materials* are prepared to quite the end of the work, and that illustrations are being gradually made for the whole, some being already completed even for the last volume." In another, included in the sixth volume (and also in the Folger copy), he advertised and gave the prices for the as yet unsubscribed six India paper copies, explaining that the "graduated scale" of prices—ranging from eighty guineas for the first and second volumes to one hundred for the sixth volume—"appeared to [him] to be the fairest possible way of meeting the heavy expenditure." In a circular of 11 October 1861 (Folger Y.c.1307[20]) relating to volume 10 he discussed the arrangement and thickness of the remaining volumes and asked for subscribers' views as soon as possible. The opening of the preface to the eleventh volume (27 April 1863) is revealing as explanation and *apologia*:

After a much longer interval than usual, the eleventh volume of this edition of Shakespeare makes its appearance. It must be recollected that from the first the entire labour not merely of the work, but of the whole of its business arrangements, have been borne exclusively by myself; for the few notes communicated by others, acknowledged in the proper places, amount but to a few pages in all, and can hardly be regarded in the light of assistance. The incessant working on one work and subject had proved almost too much for my strength, and there have been times when I believed that I should have been compelled to abandon the completion of the task. This feeling has now passed away, and the preparations for the remaining four volumes are in a sufficient state of forwardness to warrant the expectation that they may be produced more rapidly and regularly (vii).

Added to these forms of communication, which constituted a kind of newsletter, Halliwell carried on a running exchange of letters with individuals, even providing printed forms for them to subscribe, pay, and withdraw with ease.

He also had to contend with criticism from without. On 4 September 1858, for example, the *Critic*, normally friendly towards Halliwell, published a letter (p. 551) from "A Subscriber" who "shall be glad to know when it is likely any further issues will take place. It is several months since the seventh volume appeared, and at its present rate of production few of Mr. H's subscribers can expect to live to see it completed." A week later, on 11 September 1858 (p. 555), responding to several complaints, a leader in the *Critic* reviewed the situation and, after acknowledging that Halliwell "has been harassed by family matters and other distractions" and clearly denying that it is "laying to the charge of Mr. Halliwell anything which is at all inconsistent with the most perfect *intention* of good faith," came to the conclusion that "All that we say is, that the whole affair presents the most singular instance of want of business management in the whole history of publishing; and the moral to be drawn from it seems to be this,—that it behoves each one to keep to his trade, authors to their authorship, and publishers to their publishing." Furthermore, as an added difficulty for Halliwell to reach and maintain the desired total of 150 subscribers there were no longer major reviews of the individual volumes as they appeared. This was his own doing, strangely enough but not surprisingly, for he was "much annoyed," he wrote to Hepworth Dixon, that one of his subscribers had written to the *Athenaeum* about a review of the folio Shakespeare, explaining: "I like working on for a few in my own fashion, without reference to the public, & would very much indeed prefer that none of my subscription books should be noticed in print" (5 December 1865; Folger Y.c.1213[63]). Despite his early and perhaps obstinate optimism that, as he wrote to the New York booksellers Evans and Brittan in 1852, he did not need any further subscribers since "I expect, when the London season begins, I shall have at least 250 applications" (12 October 1852; Folger Y.c.1219[1]), he was still offering sets of the work for sale in 1870, five years after the completion of the edition. In a prospectus advertising both the folio edition (eighty guineas for the plain paper and 150 for the India paper set) and the facsimiles of the quartos (five guineas per volume and three hundred for the set) the distribution of plain paper copies of the folio edition reveals twenty-five gaps (and not the twenty Halliwell declares). Halliwell even lists five changes of ownership, and there had been certainly more over the years. And tellingly he found it necessary to

defend his "limitation of impression": "It is the one only possible method
by which the original subscription price can be sustained or exceeded. It
seems to me that subscriptions for a work should not be asked for with
a feeling of indifference to the depreciation of its value at a subsequent
period." Defensively and grumpily, he continued:

It is said that this limitation prevents many a poor student who could use
such works from possessing them; but books of this kind must anyhow
be expensive, and, as a rule, such an one could as little afford ten as eighty
guineas for one publication. Moreover, any one taking a real interest in a
pursuit never grudges the trouble of seeking his information in the various
libraries (p. 21).

For this kind of monumental publication there could be no compromise,
even if it meant ignoring the reasonable plea of his intimate friend Charles
Roach Smith:

The great misfortune is that none of the true *students* of Shakespeare get
any information from your folio edition; or, rather comparatively few; &
with great labour. It is a book *for the rich only*. Thus far it is a paradox.
There would have been no breach of faith with these wealthy worthies to
have allowed six copies of the *Notes* to have been printed off for poor
students, they engaging to burn them, when read & noted, so that the
millionaires should not be seriously wounded in soul or in purse (3 June
1866; LOA 113:7).

     Despite this apparent truculence it cannot be said that Halliwell had
little desire to promote Shakespeare among those who did not have "ten
twenty or 30 thousand a year" with which to fill their private libraries or
support a "real genuine antiquarian work of good merit" (as he wrote to
Charles Roach Smith in another context [12 August 1859; Folger
C.b.16(98)]). True, he felt scholarship was the province of the few, and
only still fewer needed to own the "rare" and "curious" volumes he
reprinted. But when it was a question of establishing a library and
museum in an authentic Stratford for the nation or providing the nation
with a text of Shakespeare, Halliwell was never aloof to, though not
uncritical of, the need for nurturing and improving the cultural status of
the various classes of society. In fact, the interrelationship of these two
popular objectives was seized upon and highlighted in a prospectus issued
by Halliwell in 1863. It is entitled "Shakespeare for the Working Classes"
and begins with a call to the nation:

Unless some steps are at once taken to increase the knowledge of the writings of Shakespeare amongst the great mass of the people, it may well be feared that the announcement of next year's celebration will fall listlessly on the ears of an important and the largest section of the community. However we may like to disown it, to the great public Shakespeare is but a name. Many a working-man will say,–'Well, I should like to read Shakespeare, and know what he has done to merit all this fuss being made about him.' If the works of Shakespeare have exercised a beneficial influence, if the nation really does owe a debt of gratitude to their author, surely that influence and that debt should be participated in by all classes.

To meet the challenge, Halliwell announced that he proposed "to give the entire dramatic works of Shakespeare, in one volume, double columns ... edited with the results of late discoveries, accompanied with a Life of the Poet, and a copious Glossary of obsolete words and phrases. I can include all *in a volume of seven hundred and sixty-eight pages*, and this volume I propose to issue at the price of *one shilling*." To some, this may appear to be still another instance of Halliwell's purportedly seeking profit rather than exercising principle. For he was doubtless aware of the existence and success of Dicks's first-one-volume edition (1861), of which Jaggard reports that "according to a letter in the *Bookseller*, 1st July, 1868, John Dicks sold within a few years nearly a million copies of this shilling edition, which appears to be the highest record of the kind."[169] It is hard to deny the profit motive. Halliwell's correspondence with publishers and friends is full of excited notions of the "enormous success of the work." To John Russell Smith, the "experienced publisher" mentioned in the prospectus, with whom Halliwell had begun negotiations, he asserted, "I firmly believe, if properly managed, the sale will extend to hundreds of thousands. If advertised by bills, it would sell like wildfire in such places as Birmingham" (3 October 1863; LOA 98:25). The enthusiasm of his concluding sentence, after numerous technical details, is noteworthy: "Altogether, if we don't make a book 'to set competition at defiance' I am a Dutchman." Smith, however, was not convinced the scheme could be profitable. After "thinking over the Shakespeare ... till my head aches," he produced a detailed analysis of the costs of production and distribution. His penultimate sentence–"Something may strike *you* to shew how the scheme may be carried out in another way"–was followed by the

169. William Jaggard, *Shakespeare Bibliography* (Stratford-upon-Avon, 1911), p. 535.

unambiguous "*I* give it up" (8 October 1863; LOA 98:23). Halliwell hesitated, his wife's diary entry for 19 October 1863 reporting that he was "thinking of giving up the Shilling Shakespeare & raising the price to 2/6." Yet Halliwell's enthusiasm was unbridled, spurred by his sense of a national responsibility, a conviction of the importance of a cheap edition, an ebullient agreement with "people competent to judge [who] declare [it] will be the publishing marvel of the age." He decided, so the prospectus, "not to abandon the design [but] to execute it at my own risk. [For] I am so convinced of its importance, and at the same time rely so confidently on the public reducing my liability by a large subscription list for copies." Although taking advice from Adlard and indirectly Bohn (18 November 1863; LOA 99:50) on ways of reducing costs, Halliwell was determined to do it his way. The outlines of the Halliwellian enterprise are recognizable, but with certain modifications favoring the author: the printer is once again J. E. Adlard, who, however, this time "has kindly undertaken the business details"; subscriptions are sought, but this time not on an individual basis but "not ... for less than one hundred copies." And, to be sure, still burdened with countless obligations, Halliwell might even be tempted (as was his wont) to recycle material, for his folio Shakespeare was nearing completion, and the annexed specimen lines from Act 4, scenes 6 and 7 of *3 Henry 6* are identical with those of the folio edition (which had just appeared) as printed by the same Adlard. And economically, like so many of his reprints, the Shilling Shakespeare was to be a clear reading text without notes. He was obviously speculating, both patriotically and financially, on the response of his fellow countrymen. He gave up the business part, it is true, but he also arranged a deferred royalty with Adlard–"he gets nothing unless over 50,000 copies are sold," so his wife's diary entry for 31 October 1863)–resembling the one he had negotiated with Smith: "*after* a sale of fifty or sixty thousand ... a halfpenny a copy for every copy sold beyond that number" (3 October 1863; LOA 98:25). And, in his excitement, he may even have lost his perspective, for in his letter to W. O. Hunt his "*profound* secret" was that the "publishing marvel of the age" was "*actually in the press*" (18 November 1863; LOA 89:65).

It was not, however. Or if it was, it was stopped. It is not clear exactly how many subscriptions had been received by this time. Mrs. Halliwell's diary mentions eight hundred by 15 October 1863, which may or may not include the six hundred listed in Halliwell's prospectus (four hundred by William Tite and one hundred each by John Haes and Adlard). Bulwer Lytton subscribed for another hundred on 20 October. In any event, and for whatever reason, the work did not appear. The enterprise did not disappear either. It was put on ice, so to speak, to be picked up again three years later.

The folio edition of Shakespeare, however, was unstoppable. True, Halliwell was often and "very seriously thinking of abandoning the Shakespeare," as he wrote to Fairholt (30 April 1860; Folger W.a.81[22/3]), standing to lose at least £1000 less if he stopped than if he were to continue and offering to pay back advance subscriptions and buy back volumes already printed, perhaps restricting the whole to the Life and Comedies. The eighteen volumes of what was entitled "Shakespeare Folio Papers" that he presented to the Corporation of Stratford-upon-Avon (in the Record Office of the Shakespeare Birthplace Trust as ER34/1) are a detailed record of the tribulations and laboriousness of the undertaking. Scrupulously collected and sorted, "1/2 bound in dark calf, strongly mounted" (so Halliwell's handwritten instructions), they contain letters from subscribers (often arranged by Halliwell according to their subscription number–e.g. 111 = Henry Stevens) on the receipt of and return of individual volumes, on the acceptance or withdrawal of subscription, as well as on all financial transactions, such as checks, receipts, even a bankruptcy statement from an insolvent subscriber. But adversity seems to have spurred him on. Even the advice he had sought of his brother, Thomas, who did "not hesitate to say–stop it! by all means" (3 May 1860; LOA 81:1), did not deter him. Responding to a fire which destroyed his woodcuts and relevant material–some of which did not belong to him and for which there was no insurance–Halliwell wrote to Fairholt: "Now instead of this misfortune stopping the book, I have *fully* made up my mind to use every exertion to get on faster" (23 April 1860; Folger W.a.81[22/1]). Halliwell continued admitting problems: at times not without a certain irony, as in his remarks to Helen Gipps–"The present subscription is four guineas a volume, the last book I will ever do by subscription!, but it was unavoidable in this case, for only fancy a publisher undertaking a work in folio volumes, each volume of three inches in thickness, and *fifteen pounds* in weight!! Whoever subscribes will at all events have a *heavy* book" (25 January 1861; LOA 151:1)–at times in dead earnest, as in the preface to the eleventh volume (quoted above) His wife's diary enumerates further problems. In her diary entry for 19 February 1864 records that Halliwell was "annoyed that Adlard had done this volume [twelve] very badly & had been extremely careless." On 12 July 1865 she reports that, following a fire in Tuckett the bookbinder's workshop in the British Museum, the covers of the fifteenth volume "are burnt which will partly delay the book coming out." But despite all his difficulties, and many more of a personal and professional nature, all the volumes did come out. And, in fact, with a supplementary volume, *An Historical Account of the New Place, Stratford-upon-Avon, the Last Residence of Shakespeare*, presented by Halliwell as a bonus to his subscribers. As a fitting climax he issued a printed invitation, dated 22 December 1865 (LOA 102:45):

The Favour of your Company is requested at an Entertainment at the Bedford Head Hotel, Maiden Lane, Covent Garden, on Saturday evening, December 30th, at Seven o'clock, to celebrate the completion of Mr. J. O. Halliwell's folio Edition of Shakespeare.

A handwritten version of the Bill of Fare is accompanied by Halliwell's comment, "This is a bill of fare of a supper I gave to the workpeople engaged in the printing & binding of my ponderous book. Joseph Lilly was chairman" (LOA 230: 66). The fare is not inappropriate to the occasion:

> Haunches of Mutton
> Sirloins of Beef
> Hams
> Tongues
> Boiled Turkeys
> Roast Turkeys
> Geese
> Giblett & Rump Steak Pies
> Boiled Legs Pork
> Roast Pheasants [written vertically]
> _____
> Vegetables of
> all Kinds in Season
> _____
> Plum Puddings
> _____
> Dress'd Salads
> Cheese &c &c

Halliwell's "health was proposed in flattering terms and *enthusiastically drunk* with 'Musical Honors'," Lilly reported (1 January 1866; LOA 102:51). And the response from the "*truly happy & comfortable*" guests was both an acknowledgment of the past and a look into the future:

Sir

The undersigned, on behalf of the Compositors, Pressmen, & others in the employ of Mr. J. E. Adlard who had the privilege of partaking of your generous fare on Saturday last, desire to express to you their grateful thanks for your very great kindness. The unbounded hospitality displayed by you on this occasion will always be a source of pleasure to dwell upon. They consider it an instance of a most kind & generous feeling towards a body of workmen who have had in their humble way a share in the production of so grand a monument to William Shakespeare, as the noble folio work just completed, which work, it is felt by all, will cast a lustre on yourself as Shakespeare's most learned & talented editor.

Wishing that the new year may bring with it increased happiness to yourself & family

We remain, Sir,
With the very greatest respect
Your obedient Servants,
Thos. Smith,
W. E. Andrews

They would perhaps not be surprised to learn that in addition to everything else Halliwell was already at work on a new enterprise called "Illustrations of the Life of Shakespeare," which presaged his magnum opus, *Outlines of the Life of Shakespeare.*

·13·

Stratford-upon-Avon
Publications, Institutions, Celebrations

About a year before the "entertainment" celebrating the completion of the folio edition, there was another gala evening, this time in Stratford-upon-Avon. Halliwell had gone to Stratford and had written to his wife in a casual manner: "By all means get the apples & a good lot of them—as many as will go in the cupboards—but take care to buy a sort that will keep" (13 October 1864; LOA 221:34). In a response to him—he had signed himself "Y.v.a.h." ("Your very affectionate husband")—she hoped he had "reached your favorite provincial town safely, & are not much fatter yet—*pray* try, and keep within bounds" (20 October 1864; LOA 100:13). This exchange of domestic concern and advice may well reflect the routine of Halliwell's travels as he searched for "illustrations" of the life and times of Shakespeare. On this occasion he was, as was his custom, to visit his good friend and ally in Stratford, William Oakes Hunt, who (succeeding his father) had been Town Clerk from 1818 until 1864[170] and, from 1820 to his death in 1873, Clerk of the Peace (a principal administrative officer for the County of Warwick), to discuss matters concerning the Shakespeare museum. What was not routine was the dinner given by Edward Fordham Flower "for 102 of his friends, townsmen, & county gentry" upon his retirement as mayor on 26 October 1864. The bill of fare was extraordinary: three soups, three fish dishes, five entrées, eleven main courses plus "pheasants, hares, partridges, grouse," a dozen desserts, cheese with sardines, and anchovies and salads.[171] Perhaps even more startling, and telling, was the scene described by Mrs. Halliwell in her diary entry for 27 October 1864: "James's health was drank & the cheering & noise when he rose was tremendous, & was

---

170. He resigned during the controversy over the amalgamation of the Borough and County police force.

171. A copy of the Bill of Fare is in the library of University College London: Ogden 72, No. 10.

repeated soon as it quieted a little, louder than ever & they kept Jamie on his legs for 3 min. or more. He said 'That he was sure if he made a speech, he shd make a fool of himself & thought he had better sit down' which he did." This acclamation was not routine certainly, but neither was it the result of the wine. For it was but one climax in a series of climaxes marking a relation-ship between Halliwell and Stratford which stretched over some forty years, and from its ups and downs emerged what must be regarded as Halliwell's two *magna opera*, his *Outlines of the Life of Shakespeare* and the establishment of the re-created monument to Shakespeare called Stratford-upon-Avon.

This double and inseparable focus was apparent early in Halliwell's career. After the British Museum affair was settled in 1846 Halliwell concentrated more and more on Shakespeare. He began work on his *Life of Shakespeare* (1848), a relatively short work of some 350 pages which, in its archaeological documentation, was a forerunner of his massive *Outlines*, the last edition of which to appear in his lifetime, the seventh in 1887, reached two volumes totalling more than 900 pages. For his scholarly work Halliwell needed Stratford, and in 1847 he began a long and intimate relationship with W. O. Hunt. In the same year,[172] the entire Shakespeare community was electrified by the announcement that "the truly stirring relic of a most glorious period, and of England's immortal bard," Shakespeare's birthplace, was to be sold at auction at twelve o'clock on Thursday, the 16th day of September. Although Halliwell's role in the purchase was relatively modest,[173] it became almost instantly clear—as Halliwell volunteered in the following year to arrange and catalogue the early records of the Stratford Corporation (with the farsighted stipulation that the more important loose documents be bound[174]) and was already

172. See pp. 182-3.

173. It should not be underestimated, however, for he was a recognized capacity. His wife's diary entry for 22 July 1847 records that "James went with the Arch. [British Archaeological Association] Gentlemen to Stratford on Avon to the Meeting held for the consideration of what was to be done with Shakespeares house. James was exceedingly well received on acct of having written so much on Shakespeare & a paper of his 'On the credibility of traditional anecdotes respecting Shakespeare' was read by Mr Pettigrew & immensely cheered & applauded."

174. See, for example, 8 May 1848; Folger Y.c.1236(7). A few days later, having received the agreement of the Corporation, Halliwell repeated his stipulation: "I think that at a very trifling expence the Corporation might put the early documents into a state in which preservation & facility of reference might be advantageously attained" (13 May 1848; Folger Y.c.1236[8]). He did so again on 3 August 1848 (LOA 34:19).

confiding to Hunt that "the project of a good Shakespeare Museum at Stratford quite haunts me" (Wednesday, September 1849; Folger Y.c.1236[11])– that if Halliwell needed Stratford it is not too much to say that Stratford needed Halliwell, as the acclamation at Flower's farewell dinner loudly acknowledged. By 9 November 1848 (Folger Y.c.1236[13]) Halliwell was already of the opinion that the Corporation "should have a large oak cupboard at the end of the guild chamber to hold the volumes when they are bound."

+++

As the *Life of Shakespeare* was inevitably absorbed into the folio edition, so it too required documentation and in turn stimulated further documentation for still another larger work, one which ultimately was to become the storehouse of all the archaeological data necessary for the study of Shakespeare's environment. The discovery, assembling, evaluation, and classification of much of these data became the twenty-six publications Halliwell produced between 1862 and 1865. After one such publication in 1862, there appeared five in 1863, eleven in 1864,[175] and nine in 1865. They are not literary documents or reprints of early popular English literature. As a body they form a section of a descriptive catalogue of the records of the Borough and Corporation of Stratford-up-Avon, especially in the time of Shakespeare and with a certain attention to those documents which are related in one way or another to Shakespeare, his family, and their surroundings.

Quite typical is the first publication of this material, *A Brief Hand-List of the Records Belonging to the Borough of Stratford-on-Avon. Showing Their General Character; With Notes of a Few of the Shakespearian Documents in the Same Collection* (1862). Privately printed in only fifty copies, it is a simple listing of the contents of the documents as arranged in boxes and drawers (as opposed to those bound in volumes). Forty-seven are briefly described, as for example:

VI.

A Large Collection of Documents, chiefly expired leases, respecting estates of the Corporation in the Church and Chapel Street Ward,

175. The total includes a communication to the *Athenaeum* (30 April 1864, pp. 612-13) describing a large folio manuscript volume being exhibited at the Birthplace and containing information about Shakespeare's presence in the King's Company on 15 March 1604.

including Old Town, Chapel Lane, and Scholars Lane or Tinkers Lane. *Second drawer from the top on the left in the same* [i.e. large] *case.*

Both the "rare" and "curious" contents and the careful printing (replete with long *s* and decorative capitals and ornaments) make it logical for it to appear in the list, as number 73, of Halliwell's offering called "Rare Books." Perhaps the most prominent of this series of publications is *A Descriptive Calendar of the Ancient Manuscripts and Records in the Possession of the Corporation of Stratford-upon-Avon; Including Notices of Shakespeare and His Family, and of Several Persons Connected with the Poet* (1863). A stately volume of 475 folio-sized pages and limited to seventy-five copies, it is the result of Halliwell's systematic examination of the records which "bear date from the thirteenth century to the year 1750," making good his assertion that in the previous work "nothing in the way of a Calendar [was] attempted," for "such task would require much patient labour spread over a long period [and] to accomplish it properly, every document must be carefully read, and its contents accurately ascertained." Not unlike Halliwell's other reprints, each section of the transcription is preceded by a brief statement, as, for example, that pertaining to "The Orders of the Town Council":

The order-books of the Town Council of the Borough of Stratford-on-Avon commence in the year 1563, and continue in an uninterrupted series to the present day in folio volumes marked A, B, C, &c. In the first volume the Chamberlains' accounts are mixed up with the minutes of the Council, the first page commencing with the accounts of the poet's father,–'thaccount of John Tayler and John Shakspeyr, chamburlens,' 1563. The books containing the orders made in the first ten years after the charter of Edward the Sixth is missing, and no doubt was so in 1793 when Malone borrowed the Council Books. See his receipt in these books of 28 June, and 2 September, 1793. If I recollect rightly I have traced a leaf of the first book amongst some miscellaneous documents at Stratford, a circumstance which would lead to the belief that the volume had been wasted. These books are of such extreme value and interest, that the following excellent index to their *principal* contents, kindly communicated by W. O. Hunt, esq., will form, with a few additions, an important section of the present volume (p. 66).

As with most of Halliwell's reprints, the transcription preserves the "ancient orthography and bad Latinity," his customary explanation for the "apparent errors" often ascribed to his haste or ignorance. And, as was his custom, he dedicated the work to a worthy supporter, E. F. Flower, "not merely [as] a mark of respect tendered to the Mayor of Stratford, but ... one due ... personally, in acknowledgement of the strong appreciation [he] exhibited throughout of the importance of the undertaking" and included the volume as number 74 of his "Rare Books." From these works, which presented overviews of documentary sources, Halliwell followed two paths. On the first, he expanded his coverage of Stratford and its inhabitants; on the second, he focussed more precisely on the immediate Shakespeare connection. To the first belong his reprints of documents of socio-economic interest: *Extracts from Ancient Subsidy Rolls* (1864) and *A Levy Made in July, 1697, for the Relief of the Poor* (1865)–both limited to ten copies only, fifteen copies of the twenty-five originally printed of the second title destroyed by Halliwell to maintain their value–and "An Inventory of the Furniture, Etc., of a Tavern at Stratford-on-Avon, Taken in the Time of Shakespeare" (1863).[176] Of personal and historical interest from the point of view of individual inhabitants of Stratford: the butchers Nicholas ap Roberts and Griffin ap Roberts (1864) and *The Will of Sir Hugh Clopton, of New Place* (1865)–the first in ten copies only, the second originally in thirty copies of which Halliwell destroyed twenty. And, of a similar number, a demographic climax: *A Nominal Index to J. O. Halliwell's Descriptive Calendar of the Ancient Records of Stratford-on-Avon* (1865), an invaluable census, as it were, in seventy double column pages of all the persons appearing in Halliwell's earlier systematic examination.

Focussing more precisely on Shakespeare and his more immediate heritage and environment, Halliwell privately printed in 1863 an eight-page volume called *Shakespearian Facsimiles* (Rare Books 77) with the help of E. W. Ashbee, a collection of sixteen plates ranging from "Plans of Shottery Meadows" (Plate I) and "Signatures and marks of members of the Hathaway family" (Plate III) to "A list of moneys collected at Stratford in September, 1611" (Plate XV) and "A plan of Stratford-on-Avon, 1802" (Plate XVI). In the following two years he published a number of selections from Stratford records in the form of reprints. From the Council Books of the Corporation extracts "especially with reference to the history of the poet's father" (1864, Rare Books 78); from the parish registers of Holy Trinity Church, in ten copies, "extracts of entries respecting Shakespeare, his family and connexions" (1864); from the vestry book of the church, "notices of the Shakespeare family" (1865). He also produced and published in ten copies each two works relating to

176. In *Collectanea Archaeologica: Communications Made to the British Archaeological Association*, 2:1 (1863), 93-114.

Shakespeare properties: *The Abstract of Title to the House in Henley Street* (1865), "in all probability the only instance in which the pedigree of the birth-place of a great author can be traced uninterruptedly for considerably upwards of two centuries," and *Two Indentures Respecting the Cage* (1865), a house in High Street bought by Thomas Quiney "with a portion of the money" bequeathed by Shakespeare to his daughter, Judith, Quiney's wife.

Halliwell did not restrict himself to town records alone, for his perspective was wide, as well as diachronic and synchronic. He included among his reprints (of normally ten copies each) the works of others who over the years had dealt with Stratford and Shakespeare. One was the Stratford poet John Jordan, who in about 1780 recorded his collected material for a life of Shakespeare and a history of Stratford. In 1864 Halliwell published in ten copies selections under the title *Original Collections on Shakespeare & Stratford-on-Avon.* Although aware that Jordan's writings were "not always truthful," Halliwell nevertheless found them of "considerable value as supplying hints for the true sources of the traditional stories respecting the great dramatist, and containing scraps of local information no where else to be met with." Among the selections were "Stratford-upon-Avon," "The Family of Combe," and "The Family of Shakspear." A year later, in 1865, Halliwell transcribed a manuscript "copied from the original presented by John Jordan to Edmund [Halliwell's customary spelling] Malone ... dated 1826," entitled it *Original Memoirs and Historical Accounts of the Families of Shakespeare and Hart, Deduced from an Early Period, and Continued Down to the Present Year 1790,* and published it in ten copies. This time Halliwell was less diplomatic in his treatment of Jordan: "The literal truth is,–and it is of no use concealing the disagreeable word,–he was dishonest ... If Jordan had been as truthful as Wheler ... his writings would now have been of remarkable value." Still, Halliwell the scholar was intrigued by the prospect of dealing with "literary misrepresentation, and even occasionally ... forgery." For "there are many circumstances connected with the Hart family not to be met with elsewhere ... Jordan often gives useful hints for researches; and there is very little amongst his papers which does not deserve a careful perusal" (vi).

Jordan was of interest to Halliwell not merely for the information about Stratford but also for his connection with Edmond Malone, who had also taken up the task of writing a life of Shakespeare. Halliwell transcribed Malone's correspondence with Jordan in 1864 and published it in ten copies, despite his awareness of Jordan's unreliability. It may well be that one of the attractions for Halliwell, as well as for numerous biographers, lay in the fact that "although it is truly unfortunate that none of his statements are to be depended upon without corroborative evidence; but as he mixed truth with fiction, they are all worthy of careful investigation" (p. 5). Malone appears again in 1864 in Halliwell's edition (in thirty copies, twenty of which he destroyed) of his correspondence starting in 1788 with James Davenport, vicar of Stratford. These letters, of "considerable interest and curiosity," concern sources of inquiry still open to investigation, especially the family of Sir John Bernard as well as other details concerning Shakespeare and Stratford.

Foremost among the Stratfordians who provided Halliwell with material was Robert Bell Wheler (1785-1857), a local who devoted his life to the study of the history and topography of Stratford and had been treasurer, secretary, and solicitor to the Stratford Committee for Shakespeare's Monument in the 1820s as well as a member of the Committee for the purchase of the Birthplace in 1847. In 1863 Halliwell reprinted Wheler's rare small quarto volume of 1824, *An Historical Account of the Birth-Place of Shakespeare*, to be "sold at the poet's birth-place for the benefit of the birth-place fund." The Birthplace was synonymous with the Shakespeare library and museum with which Halliwell was deeply involved, and to which (through the generosity of his sister after his death) Wheler was a major contributor. A short while later, in fact, Halliwell published at his own expense in one hundred copies and not for sale *A Brief Hand-List of Collections Respecting the Life and Works of Shakespeare, and the History and Antiquities of Stratford-upon-Avon, formed by the late Robert Bell Wheler* (Rare Books 76)–114 items of the Wheler Collection arranged chronologically and ranging from the original manuscript of Wheler's *History of Stratford-upon-Avon* (No. 22) and "Mr. Wheler's collections on the Jubilee, containing much curious matter respecting the Garrick Jubilee" (No. 25) to "A large block of the mulberry tree, and a piece of the very wood out of which was made the box presented to Garrick in 1769" (No. 61) to "An oil painting of Stratford, showing the parish church before the wooden spire was taken down in 1764, and also the charnel-house" (No. 64). One of the most interesting items, the first listed, is Wheler's "Collectanea de Stratford," described by Halliwell as a "marvellous example of the results of the unrivalled industry and accuracy of the late Mr. Wheler, in 536 quarto pages, so minutely written, that a transcript in ordinary calligraphy would fill half-a-dozen volumes of a like size, well deserv[ing] to be placed in the fore-front of this little hand-list" (p. 3). In 1865 Halliwell selected and transcribed various items therefrom–letters, proceedings, memoranda, abstracts–adding an occasional comment or brief connecting text, called it *Collectanea Respecting the Birth-Place of*

Shakespeare at Stratford-on-Avon, and published it in ten copies.

+++

Halliwell's involvement in the Birthplace was not distant but immediate. For one thing, he was directly involved in the establishment and furtherance of the Shakespeare library and museum, which was located in rooms of the Birthplace in Henley Street. It is not unlikely that he prepared—or at least had a major role in—such tourist material as A *Brief Guide for Strangers Who Are Visiting Stratford-on-Avon for the First Time or Who Are Staying in the Town for a Few Hours* (1864), as well as an extract therefrom, *A Brief Guide to the Shakespeare Library and Museum, Stratford-on-Avon* (1865).[177] From his engagement for material for his *Life of Shakespeare* in 1847 to his offer to arrange and catalogue the records of the Corporation, Halliwell became inevitably involved in the "business" of the Birthplace. Over the years this included, among other activities: his vision of a "good Shakespeare Museum at Stratford, which "quite haunts me" (Wednesday, September 1848; Folger Y.c.1236[11]); his insistence that the records be bound and stored in a large oak cupboard at the end of the guild chamber (9 November 1848; Folger Y.c.1236[13]); his seeing to it that W. O. Hunt was unanimously elected to the Council of the Shakespeare Society, for "Stratford should be represented in our Society" (27 April 1849; Folger Y.c.1236[16]); his offer to arrange and perhaps catalogue the collection of manuscripts of Captain James Saunders (1774-1830), a member of the Corporation in 1814 and mayor in 1822-3 (27 April 1849; Folger Y.c. 1236[16]); his repeated "thinking that [Hunt] will find a concealed panel in [his] fine old house which will reveal to light a MS. of the Tempest or a bundle of Shakespeare's letters" and his urgent "If such an event did take place I should be too impatient for the railway & wish for the telegraph" (17 July 1849; Folger Y.c.1236[17]); his desire (with Hunt's assistance) to buy a John Shakespeare deed from an acquaintance of Hunt's (26 December 1850; Folger Y.c.1236[20]); his wish to make facsimiles of all the most important documents, even bringing his own lithographer (25 April 1851; Folger Y.c.1236[22]); his continuing interest in purchasing "genuine old" objects, such as the twenty desiderata listed in a letter (12 April 1852; LOA 66:13) to his friend Thomas Crofton Croker (ranging from an antique seal or ring with Lucrece to a Spanish pouch and from a bombard for wine to a sacring-bell), some of which

177. Both were printed by Halliwell favorites: the first by J. E. Adlard, the second by Thomas Richards.

were acquired and later presented to the Shakespeare museum; his receiving the latest news from Hunt, such as the fire at Shottery, Anne Hathaway's cottage escaping damage (26 October 1852; LOA 50:29).

Halliwell's engagement with Stratford increased in intensity as he was drawn more and more into its civic and financial affairs. In a Bill of Complaint filed in Chancery on 16 April 1859–Thomson v. Shakespear–a number of Stratford citizens of the Shakespeare Birthplace Committee brought suit against nephews of John Shakespear for failing to pay a considerable sum (£2500) towards the "protection, preservation, &c." of the Birthplace, as mentioned in the will of their uncle, who died in 1856. Although his name does not appear among the plaintiffs, it is very likely that Halliwell played a significant role in the action. Jaggard, in fact, regards him as the editor of the bill.[178] Be that as it may, there is little doubt about Halliwell's next move, which was spectacular. For all his continuing financial problems with his publications, not to mention his ongoing costly legal struggle with his father-in-law over Middle Hill, Halliwell did not shy away from taking a resolute step. In a letter of 22 October 1861 (LOA 221:24) to his wife he announced, "I have purchased New Place for fourteen hundred pounds," cautioning, "All this need not be babbled out until it appears in the papers at the end of the week." The action was decisive, and involved no small sum, but was not ill considered, for Halliwell had carefully prepared for it. Almost a year earlier, on 27 January 1861 (LOA 104:39), he had written to Hunt:

I see from Adt. that New Place is for sale, & understand from Dr [David] Rice that the price is 3000 guineas, I presume freehold, but he says nothing on that point. If only one house, the price appears exorbitant, considering that after all none of Shakespeare's own residence is preserved. I could not myself entertain the idea of purchase unless it was unquestionably good as a permanent investment, but I have a wealthy friend that might listen to my advice on the subject, & give something for the association of the residence for the poet ... Personally, I am much more inclined to buy Anne Hathaway's cottage, should it ever occur for sale.

In the intervening months he added the purchase of the Great Gardens for some £2000 to his shopping list, for it is clear that the idea was in his mind much earlier. In reprinting his article "The Last Days of Shakespeare" as a separate publication in 1863, Halliwell described it as

178. *Shakespeare Bibliography*, p. 23.

"the first paper in which the poetic and historic interest attached to the Gardens of Shakespeare was brought before the notice of the public. It was written in 1861, long before the purchase of them by public subscription was suggested" (p. 5). And he was convinced that acting as a private person was speedier and more effective than any committee could be, for the threat of real estate speculators was great: his wife's diary entry for 25 October 1861 mentions a Mr. [E. T.] Smith of Cremorne Gardens (a place of popular entertainment by the side of the Thames in Chelsea) being at Stratford "with the intention of purchasing it for a sort of Crystal Palace Gardens"; Halliwell himself in a letter to Hepworth Dixon mentions Smith and a Building Society as "interested parties" (6 November 1861; Folger Y.c.1213[5]). He had in fact anticipated the Corporation, for his wife's diary reports on 19 October 1861 that when Edward Fordham Flower, the mayor of Stratford, called with a "proposal to James for a few to join together & buy the place & let the house—[he] was astonished when he heard the sum J. had already collected." (Thanking Helen Taylor for her contribution on 28 October 1861 [Folger S.b.80(10)], Halliwell reported that £800 had been "in all subscribed out of £1500"; on 13 November 1861 [Folger Y.c.1213(6)] he wrote Hepworth Dixon that £2706 had been subscribed.) To be sure, Halliwell negotiated with the Corporation to take over and administer the property. "Unless I hear that the Corporation decline the responsibility of keeping it up," he wrote to Hunt just a few days before the purchase, "my great object will be to get it into their hands" (16 October 1861; LOA 198:18). Accordingly, he "offered it on his original conditions to the Mayor & Corporation of Stratford-on-Avon, who in conclave yesterday duly received it with acclamation," his wife records in her diary entry for 23 October 1861. And two days later she reports of negotiations for "the remainder of the property wch belonged to Shakespeare includg the Bowling Green &c for £2000 wch James is anxious to buy for the nation & make it a Park," adding, "He was extremely well received by all at Stratford, and his health drank with applause at the Mayor's dinner, wch he however excused himself from attendg. He dislikes everything of the kind" and also when asked whether a testimonial would be "agreeable" to him, he "declined it most decidedly." The Corporation did recognize Halliwell's efforts with an official vote of thanks, expressing "their grateful acknowledgments for the spirited and liberal manner in which he has come forward, impelled by his reverence and admiration for the memory of genius, to rescue and preserve this hallowed spot, consecrated by its associations with all that was mortal of our great Townsman, from further desecration." Mrs. Halliwell was so impressed that she copied the whole tribute into her entry for 28 December 1861.

Lest it appear that Halliwell's actions were motivated mainly by a shrewdness which came from a series of long and tedious legal battles in which he had been engaged ever since the British Museum affair or by a dreamy reverence of the memory of the noble bard, it may be well to refer to feelings expressed in his travel books and his growingly prominent devotion to what may be called his national experience or heritage. It was not so much outright patriotism in the political sense, although he was increasingly outspoken in his opposition, for example, to native works finding a home outside of England.[179] Rather, it was almost pantheistic, a strong sense of a modest and lovely countryside not despoiled by crude modernism or disfigured by thoughtless change. "Birth Place all altered," he wrote to his wife, his "dearest Harry" (24 March 1861; LOA 221:26), "turned into a kind of Camberwell cottage ornée, with garden, font, fragment of Town-cross, Birth Place genuinely preserved, the modernized inn next door completely altered, brick work removed, the old timber work restored–pentices over the Birth Place–gable windows in the roof–Garden to the Guild pits on the site of which a hideous County Police Office instead of the fields little Billy looked at." And a few days later he wrote to Hepworth Dixon, "Stratford with all its cleanliness has not to me the vivid charm it possessed in years gone by when Henley Street with all its squalidness exhibited so much better its great antiquity" (2 April 1861; Folger Y.c.1213[2]). Not surprisingly, Halliwell opposed the railway and the "improvements" which the sharp rise in property values brought with it. Responding to the destruction of the old Middle Row in Bridge Street in 1863, under the direction of Robert Hobbes, Halliwell proclaimed, "If Mr. Hobbes were not one of the most respected and agreeable men in Stratford, he ought, in penance, to be made to stand in front of the market house, looking at the waste he has created and have his ears well lugged for his pains."[180] What else could be expected of a patriot, who was also a reverer of Shakespeare, an antiquary and an archaeologist?

179. In one of numerous instances, and with some prescience, Halliwell wrote to George Livermore, an American antiquary, that he was "interested in ascertaining what classes of old English books have mostly gone to America," and added, "I wish this country was joined to yours by an isthmus. I don't like the treasures of English literature being divided so much as they are getting to be" (17 November 1860; Folger Y.c.1247[1]).

180. Quoted in Nicholas Fogg, *Stratford upon Avon: Portrait of a Town* (Chichester, 1986), p. 157. Halliwell lamented the destruction of Middle Row in his Roundabout Letter, No. 6.

What else but determination and work. "The money must be got, & if necessary degradation overlooked, sooner than have Shakespeare's memory desecrated," Halliwell wrote to Charles Roach Smith. "It won't matter to posterity how it was done, so that it is done" (5 November 1861; Folger W.b.67[54]). And how else but with the mechanism Halliwell was most practiced in–subscriptions. With enormous zest he put new urgency into a National Shakespeare Fund. In October 1861 he launched a fervent fund-raising campaign. There were letters to the *Times* and the *Athenaeum*; the *Illustrated London News*, *Punch*, and the *Era* were mobilized; clubs (such as the Athenaeum) and associations (such as the Archaeological Institute) were approached, national and local committees were reinforced or newly formed; friends and colleagues were buttonholed. As was the custom, Halliwell put his whole family to work. Mrs. Halliwell's diary records that on 11 November 1861 "We began directly after breakfast stamping folding & directing circulars & kept on until noon as hard as we could. James also working ... We have to send off 4000 circulars by Thursday ... I directed 530 envelopes today"; on 12 November: "We were all busy today again. Miss [Eliza] W[est] & I directing envelopes, H[enrietta[& C[harlotte] stamping, E[llen] & K[atie] sorting Circulars, & the servts taking them to post. I copied 605 directions today - left off at 11 o'c. at night"; on 19 December Aunt Margaret [Marsh], a Christmas house guest, "folded circulars in & filled a good sized clothes basket with them, the little ones separated the sheets."

Furthermore, to meet the present urgency of the purchase of New Place Halliwell, in a letter to the *Times* of 15 October 1861 (p. 9), appealed not only to the patriotism of all Englishmen and contributions from the "colonies and from America, notwithstanding the present unhappy differences in the latter country," but, realizing that "smaller sums" would take too long to amass, also immediately to "persons of wealth of his country." Since he estimated that the "fair price" of £1500 was needed, and "there is no time to collect this sum by dribblets," he appealed to fifteen donors to contribute £100 each. Of significance was not only the scheme itself but Halliwell's willingness, should the subscriptions "still be of an inadequate amount," to "advance any sum necessary, not exceeding *400l.*, without interest, for a limited time, hoping and believing that amount, if time were allowed, could be collected in smaller sums." In addition, he made it clear that since "it is right when asking the public for money to say exactly what will be done with it," he proposed to transfer the property to the corporation of Stratford-on-Avon, but "on the express conditions that the public be always freely admitted, and that no erection of any kind be ever permitted in the gardens. This is the grand thing to guard against—to prevent the spot being messed and cockneyfied." The target was widened to include the purchase of the Great Gardens: another £2000 needed. Just a few days later, in a letter to the *Times* of 28 October 1861 (p. 7), Halliwell listed seven donors of £100 each—Henry Huth, G. L. Prendergast, H. R. Sheridan, William Tite, James Parker, Benjamin Webster, and F. W. Cosens—noting that "no fewer than four persons (two in the above list) came forward to say that, in case I did not succeed, they were each of them willing to purchase the estate for public purposes." But since Halliwell considered it "great pity if any one person were allowed to purchase without being subject to conditions previously made in the public interest," he would himself "rather adhere to [his] original proposition, and advance 400*l.*" And to underscore his actions were only in the public interest, Halliwell promised (in the first letter) that "after the sale is over I will duly render an account of my stewardship."

To celebrate the purchase, one of Halliwell's friends composed a "Song to Mr. Halliwell" dated 30 November 1861 (UCL Ogden 72, No. 21), to the "Air: Fare thee well, my own Mary Anne":

> Halliwell, my dear Shakespearian,
>> Halliwell for a time
>> Is the heart of the best
>> Shakespeare lover at rest
> And I am bound unto thee, gentleman.
>
> The Garden of Shakespeare is sacred propertie
>> Halliwell as you know
>> And it ne'er shall be said
>> That they groaned 'neath the tread
> Of the fool or the knave, it shan't be gentleman.
>
> Fare thee well, my bold Shakespearian
>> Fare thee well, for my rhyme
>> Is now at an end
>> May my blessings attend
> Thy footsteps, believe me yours faithfully—Pan.

Three cheers for Mr Halliwell! May his shadow never grow less, and may a thrill of joy pass over his frame, while reading the above parody of Pan's on the subject of his successful Shakespearian gardening operations.

This good-humored tribute—as well as "Shakespeare's Garden: A Lay of Stratford imitated from Macaulay," composed and illustrated by Fairholt (5 December 1861; LOA 208:13-14), and also a sonnet by the Reverend Dr. George Aspinall celebrating the "great Halliwell" (Diary, 16 November 1861)—sets off the surgingly serious efforts of Halliwell, who increased the intensity of the publicity with a series of appeals in the form of flyers, beginning with *A First Appeal to the Public for the Preservation of the Gardens of Shakespeare*, essentially a reprinting of his letter to the *Times* of 15 October, followed by a quick succession of slight variations on the same theme on 31 October and 11, 14, and 30 December 1861. The intensity was needed to accommodate the expansion of the undertaking. Halliwell issued a comprehensive outline of a vast project entitled *The National Shakesperian Fund* on 20 November 1861. In addition to New Place and the Great Gardens, also to be secured were the portion of the Birthplace still in private hands, Anne Hathaway's cottage, the Getley Copyhold Estate opposite New Place, "one or two minor objects of this kind, and, to complete the good work, a Library and Museum, properly endowed," as well as "the calendaring and preservation of those records at Stratford-on-Avon which illustrate the Poet's life." He was straightforward about the financial dimensions: "About £20,000 will be required for the first mentioned objects; and from £30,000 to £40,000 to build and endow the Library and Museum." And he doubtless made use of the momentum to counteract such severe criticism not only of the expense but of the entire enterprise as that of the *Saturday Review* of 30 November 1861, which charged that "Mr. Halliwell's scheme curiously unites the functions of Brahma, Vishnu, and Siva. He is to be the creator of the museum, the preserver of the garden, but, strange to say, the destroyer of the theatre" and concluded, "to us, Shakespeare lives far more in his plays, read and acted, than in the bits of foundation which Mr. Halliwell hopes to expose to the reverence of England and the world" (p. 558).

What was necessary, and is strikingly present in the appeal, was discipline. Fifteen laws of the Fund are listed, covering in the main the financial transactions, from the selection of the design of the buildings (the option given to the first subscriber of £10,000 or upwards) to the bank into which subscriptions are to be paid (Halliwell's account at the Western Branch of the Bank of England, Burlington Gardens). Important, and significant as far as Halliwell's reputation and liability were concerned, are the provisions for auditing among them: "Every person subscribing £100 or upwards to the Fund shall nominate an auditor, and Mr. Halliwell's accounts and vouchers shall be open to examination whenever, and as often as, the auditors so nominated shall appoint." And "A

subscriber of £100 may, if he pleases, appoint himself as an auditor."
There follows an exact plan of the properties and a list extending the
seven who contributed £100 (mentioned earlier) to fifteen–A Lady,
anonymously,[181] Miss Burdett Coutts, James Dugdale, Henry Johnson,
Lord Overstone, the Misses Moore, C. H. Bracebridge, and Charles
Rawlings–with a note that "upwards of £1200 ... were promised in four
days only, viz., between Oct. 31st, and Nov. 3rd." Finally, illustrating the
surge of engagement, Halliwell lists further subscriptions, from an
additional £500 from Miss Burdett Coutts to £100 each from His Royal
Highness the Prince Consort and three others down to £5 from
Alexander Dyce and numerous others. Perhaps indicative of the
excitement generated by the adventure is the comment of John Payne
Collier, who, at age seventy-two, contributed £50 (he had an annual
pension of £100) and remarked: "As Shakespeare, while the race of man
exists, can never be old, so the mere contemplation of anything relating
to him & his works make me feel young again" (20 November 1861;
Folger Y.c.1213[7]). Halliwell's contribution may have been enough to
make him feel old before his time. He collected and retained practically
every financial transaction and bit of correspondence and printed matter
relating to the Fund, had them mounted and bound, and presented them
in twenty-eight volumes (lacking volumes 9, 11, and 26; all but 27 and 28
indexed) as the Shakespeare Fund Papers to the Corporation of Stratford-
on-Avon in 1872 (now in the Record Office of the Shakespeare Birthplace
Trust, ER34/2).

What a Committee for Birmingham report of January 1862 (SBT
ER34/2/14-15) mellifluously described as Halliwell's "labour of love, and
refusing all remuneration direct or indirect" was in reality an immense and
wearying task. What it entailed can be derived by an easy extrapolation
beyond selected illustrations. There are typical letters to Hunt in, for
example, September and October 1862. For one thing, there was "so
much delay & trouble attendant on the working of committees ... [that] I
made up my mind to have nothing to do with them except as independent
auxiliaries" (3 September 1862; LOA 195:6), especially since the money
collected by them has not been subject to his general control. A day later,
in another matter, he wrote, "'It would be considered a greater desecration
to *punch* a way from the Swan into the Birth-Room.' I should *rather* think

181. Most likely, Helen Taylor. In assuring her that her "noble gift shall be duly
acknowledged in the terms you prefer," Halliwell added, "I hope you will kindly
change your mind & allow me to place your name in the honoured list" (28
October 1861; Folger S.b.80[10]).

it would. Why, I should deserve the hardest punch on the head that Ensign Hunt could give me (I doubt if I can put the case stronger) if I had ever thought of such a thing, much less proposed it. My suggestion, a hasty one, had regard to there being a passage already open down stairs & to the belief that there was nothing but some modern partition somewhere upstairs to prevent a passage being made *leading* to the Birth-room. I have nothing whatever to do with the Birth-Place, & have quite enough on my hands with the Shakespeare Fund" (4 September 1862; LOA 198:12). Two weeks later, reacting to some act of his which may have prevented the "Local Committee obtaining subns of large amount, & that [his] withdrawal would carry out the objects," he countered: "When, however, one reflects on the little the Warwickshire gentry did when the Birth Place was bought, a scheme supported by so many high names, I own to having small hopes of them. My own opinion is that for every £5 you get from Warwickshire, I shall get £50 from the public at large, & for one present you get there for the Library or Museum I shall get ten" (20 September 1862; LOA 213:37). Still another matter: "I intend to issue ten thousand prospectusses of the Fund from London in the autumn, which will no doubt bring in some money, though the Cotton famine & American war sadly work against it. The public not individuals must be relied upon" (26 September 1862; LOA 213:30). "Now as to New Place," he wrote to Hunt on 20 October 1862 (LOA 213:23), "Surely nothing can be done at present but pulling down the walls to throw open the bowling green into the rest. There is also a place of convenience in the corner which should be removed. I suppose the materials would pay or more than pay for this, but whether they will or not, I will willingly authorise so much to be done at once if you kindly undertake it." Furthermore he will be going to Stratford to work at least ten hours a day on the records and would like to complete a calendar during the winter of all the records before 1750 (21 November 1862; Folger W.b.90[1]).

To these more or less policy matters must be added the massive contents of the twenty-five extant volumes of the Shakespeare Fund Papers which contain, among other things, printed acknowledgements of receipts of subscriptions and the extensive personal correspondence thereto, records of the payment of land and assessment taxes on the Shakespeare properties, travel expenses, questionnaires asking for opinions regarding access to the gardens and the selection of auditors and their reports, checks deposited and withdrawals made from Halliwell's account at the Western Branch of the Bank of England, drafts of pamphlets (such as "Reasons for Investing the Shakesperian Properties and the Shakespeare Library & Museum in the Mayor and Corporation of

Stratford-upon-Avon," dated August 1862) and of letters to the *Times*, suggestions for the preservation and arrangement of the records, lists of articles sent by Halliwell in packing cases by rail to Hunt, letters to the Stratford Board of Health asking permission to excavate under the pavement in front of New Place, detailed expense accounts, minutes of the Executive Committee, itemized receipts of the National Shakespeare Committee in the Bankers's Pass-book, and literally hundreds of other documents which constitute the central and many-sided role of Halliwell in the history of the Stratford enterprise. And a further folio volume–SBT ER 34/3–is designated "Bills for New Place, including the labour in the Gardens and the receipts to the same" from 1873 to its transfer to the borough of Stratford in 1876 and contains records of transactions involving insurance, taxes, rates, gas, oil, florists, locksmiths, glaziers, carpenters, printers, and a host of others.

Halliwell's massive correspondence with W. O. Hunt in these years is itself a notable record of the farthest reaches of his engagement. In a letter of 9 January 1863 (LOA 84:5) he is concerned with the binding and framing of the Wheler papers, having completed their arrangement and suggesting how best to deal with duplicates. A few days later (4 February 1863; LOA 86:54), having ordered six to be framed, he recommends that some of the remainder "be put under the glass cases, whilst the rest can go in the drawers up stairs," adding that since he does not trust any of the documents with the framer, "They are all inserted in the frames in this house." Nor does Halliwell shy away from the most minute of details: "Do you not think," he continues, "it is absolutely necessary that a table (it *should have at least one drawer to contain memoranda of gifts &c*) should be in the upper room? It will be very inconvenient unless there is a table with inkstand in a library. It need not cost a great deal, & if you agree with me in this, I will willingly pay for it, if you will very kindly order one at once." Furnishing the library was no small matter, for Halliwell was determined that the appearance be dignified as well its use practical. In regard to the Council Chamber, for example, he advised Hunt that "if the oak, every bit of which should be exposed, were oiled or varnished, if the plaister were painted, & if a new floor were made, the room would then assume as much of its ancient character as is now possible" (7 November 1863; LOA 96:25). From Hunt he was informed that "Marshall is getting on with your Book Case and Drawers, it is proposed to insert the Oak from Shakespeare's Barn at the top of the Drawers in the centre in front of the Book Case. Marshall has given a design, with an Inscription ... for your approval" (11 February 1865; LOA 5:47). As well as the inside, the outside of New Place was a concern. The old foundations had to be examined and renewed, and Halliwell helped by paying for the excavations himself (9 February 1863; Folger Y.c.1213[10]), informing Hepworth Dixon (the other honorary secretary) that he had already paid £100). He was even troubled lest "any refuse from New Place or Nash's House, be disposed of, [for] there is the greatest danger of its being repurchased by some speculator, and no matter what rubbish, an advertisement of 'relics from Shakespeare's last residence' would do mischief." Accordingly, he gave precise instructions to Hunt on how to deal with old oak and old brickwork (11 February 1864; LOA 85:50).

Stocking the building was of primary importance. Halliwell was a major contributor to the library and museum, sending an almost continuous succession of parcels of books, manuscripts, pictures, and relics from his own collection, and even five copies of his calendar of the records which he had had printed and bound at his own expense (15 July 1863; LOA 91:12), making the Corporation of Stratford the first in England to have a printed calendar of its records.[182] The Birthplace Trust library accessions book currently lists 508 books contributed by Halliwell; the total is more likely in the thousands if all items are considered.[183] Halliwell was also occupied with donations for the collection, ranging from books and tracts from John Payne Collier (12 February 1863; LOA 84:21)–who hoped that Halliwell "will make all proper arrangements for the custody of the books"–to three sketches from Frederick Goodall (15 July 1863; LOA 91:12). The task was a delicate one: on the one hand, Halliwell had to tempt possible donors; on the other, he had to run the risk of offending them if their gifts were not appropriate. Collier, for example, who was a Trustee of the Birthplace and a major figure in the Shakespeare industry, had books "rejected," among them a hundred

---

182. Characteristically, Halliwell found the idea of reimbursing him "extremely distasteful": "The expenses are of course large," he wrote to Hunt (20 July 1863; LOA 95:30), "the mere printing forming only a part, the paper on which it is printed having cost me £4 a ream, I believe the most expensive printing paper used by any one, & various items swelling up the account to a big sum, but on the other hand there will be over fifty copies for sale, so I shall get a considerable part of the outlay back. As to my time, the work was a hobby, & so I need not be paid for that, & I don't see, if treated as a matter of remuneration, where the money could come from ... If the Corporation really are pleased that the work is accomplished, they will amply repay me by a vote of thanks engrossed & framed like the previous one. I should value that very much, & I should not care to have anything else."

183. On 7 February 1872 (LOA 141:5) alone, at a special meeting the Trustees accepted his gift to the museum of between 200 and 300 volumes.

dramas by Shakespeare's contemporaries, and yet was made to feel that he had not been "affronted" nor had a "right to say a word against their [the Committee's] decisions" (22 July 1865; LOA 109:42). The decisions were, of course, Halliwell's, and he did not hesitate to give utmost priority to authenticity and immediate relevance. In a note to a letter from James Law (7 December 1865; LOA 150:27) offering a portrait of the "immortal bard," Halliwell remarked: "Looked at this portrait, 13 Dec. 1865. Undoubtedly a make up of last century. I did not, however, say so to the owner, or I should have got a punch on the head." Halliwell had to be firm, if need be, with the countless donors who were attracted by the enterprise. Declining an oil painting of Shakespeare offered by Joseph Hill, he wrote that even if the Museum had funds for purchases, he would not be interested, "oil paintings of the Poet having been manufactured by cartloads. My chief weakness is for *old editions* of his works, which *cannot* be forged" (9 December 1865; Folger Y.c.1231[8]).

Custodial concerns were inseparable from managerial ones. Acquisitions, accommodation, and upkeep were essential on a day to day basis, as was a flexible response to the growing or lagging interest in the enterprise. The number of visitors was an important consideration, as was the ability of the town to deal with them. Money was always a problem in itself and within the web of the public and private interests of the Corporation. For all his immaculate attention to the smallest of details, Halliwell never lost sight of the national interest and thus was from the beginning concerned about the stability of the undertaking. His passion for authenticity was matched by his meticulous attention to the development and future of the institutions. Informing Hunt of his having obtained a "valuable copy of the Chandos portrait ... "a fine work of art, worth a considerable sum of money, and a great catch for Stratford," and being "so sure" that he could obtain numerous "things of great value for the Fund," he was nevertheless insecure. "I cannot help feeling anxious that something should be done to put the Museum on a safer footing than it now is ... As things at present stand, I see no guarrantee [*sic*] for the *future* proper surveillance over the contents (6 January 1864; LOA 88:23). Urging Hunt to consult with sympathetic city fathers, like Hobbes and Frederick Kendall, Halliwell realized only too well the need to cultivate the vested interests. His immense rapport with Hunt (and his family), an invaluable asset, enabled him to deal efficiently with everyday matters: Halliwell was never so aloof as not to have to be asked whether croquet might be played in the New Place gardens "on the part Tom Hunt does not use for quoits" (Diary, 27 July 1865). But for middle and long range policy he turned, among others, to Edgar Flower, the mayor, wishing he could "persuade" him to "spend a little money in restoring the Council Chamber and the *most interesting* room beneath," but more importantly urging that "great care should be taken not to alter" and stressing that "anything of the kind must of course originate with [Flower]," whose mayoralty "may be distinguished for great things at Stratford" (13 February 1863; LOA 86:56).

Halliwell had to deal with a host of problems, small and large, even from friends and well-wishers. He did so with determination and diplomacy in order to achieve his ends. He was not put off by his good friend Pettigrew, who "seemed to think it was ridiculous," so Mrs. Halliwell's diary entry for 10 November 1861, "James attempting to get the sum of money he wants, & did not at all encourage his endeavours." When Alexander Dyce "demurred" from contributing to the Fund, "Jas told him that he was determined to have his name, & if he wd not subscribe that he (James) wd put his name down in the papers for £5 & wd pay the money himself - After that Mr D. asked what was the lowest sum he cd give? J. said £5 & as much more as he liked. He gave £5" (Diary, 17 November 1861). In a particularly delicate and weighty situation Halliwell had to deal with Miss Burdett Coutts, one of his most important sponsors, who wished to buy the properties herself or at least guarantee their purchase. "I regret that I cannot assent to Miss Coutts' request to buy the Theatre or any of these properties for herself," he wrote to her agent, W. H. Wills, on 29 October 1861 (SBT ER34/2/13:35), "The refusal of them has been promised to me." For Halliwell the venture was not solely a matter of personal pride but "finding the public beat Shaksperianly well," he continued, "I have set my heart on a national Shakespeare subscription list, the promulgation of which will not only assist these objects, but tend to promote the study & love of Shakespeare throughout the country." In fact, he declared, "I would rather lose it all than not preserve it to the country." Not wishing to alienate Miss Coutts, however, he maintained, "I could never in common honour have allowed any one to pay my own guarantee of £400" and suggested "as to the purchase, therefore, if Miss Coutts will kindly give £100, no more will be required." And not wishing to lose her financial support, he went further, suggesting that she give £1000 to the Fund for future use and concluded (in a postscript):

The lavish generosity of Miss C. in this matter only makes me the more anxious that the public should contribute their proper share. If when all these objects are accomplished, Miss Coutts finds that she has not been called upon for any thing like what she expected, as I earnestly hope may be the case–on a plot of ground not Shakspn but in Stratford would appropriately be placed in the Liby & Museum. The accomplishment of such an object would delight me much, & if my efforts are crowned with the success I desire, I hope that Miss Coutts may be induced to divert what will be saved from her offers in these projects to the furtherance of that design.

This was not the end of the matter. Halliwell had to endure charges of self-interest and even of dishonesty, which he countered in a revealing response to Wills of 6 November 1861 (SBT ER34/2/14:77):

I am convinced that you misunderstand the reason of my extreme sensitivity respecting the guarantee. It is not that I care to secure any credit for the movement. So far from this, I at once & absolutely refused a substantial & honourable testimonial offered me at Stratford. It is that I shrink from dishonestly occupying a position of credit before the public. Almost any disgrace, in my idea, rather than that.
As to the rest, I certainly wish a control over the properties as to the condition as to wch they are to be given over to the Corporation, feeling convinced that hardly any one else has studied the local biography of Shakespeare so minutely, & therefore so capable of forming a judgement on these matters.

Two days later (8 November 1861; SBT ER34/2/14:57) he wrote directly to Miss Coutts and bravely reiterated his position:

Whereas my long & intimate acquaintance with the local biography of Shakespeare renders the poet's memory safer in my hands than it can possibly be in those of any one, however judicious, not having that knowledge, & whereas it will be my duty to attend most carefully to any suggestions you may be so kind as to make, yet if you had had the control, the higher social position in which you stand would have precluded the possibility of my interference in any way with your course, however strongly I might feel on any particular point.

In the end, the matter was resolved. Miss Coutts contributed an additional £500 and remained a strong supporter of the Fund, as well as one of Halliwell's most eager customers.[184] Later, in a memorandum in the first

184. Just a few years later Halliwell exhibited a similar kind of benevolence in dealing with Miss Coutts. Responding to her interest in acquiring the Droeshout

volume of the Shakespeare Fund Papers he presented to the Corporation in 1872 (also LOA 208:33), Halliwell explained the matter thus:

There was some little misunderstanding respecting the second purchase-money of £2,000. I bought the Great Garden on the strength of a telegram authorising the purchase on behalf of a well-known millionaire, in the idea of course that it was to be added to the previous estate & on similar conditions. After I had contracted for the purchase, I was told by the agent that I was expected to continue to receive subscriptions from the public without revealing the nature of the transaction. I declined to solicit subscriptions while under the protection of a secret guarantee, & the matter ended by my receiving £500 and undertaking the risk of £1500 on my own shoulders.

Halliwell had to deal with other "friendly" forces which rushed to celebrate Shakespeare in their way. Even before the purchase, he was asked whether he would agree to be vice-president of a Shakespeare monument committee, with the actor William Charles Macready as president (28 May 1861; LOA 135:37). He declined, later explaining to Hepworth Dixon (in his capacity as editor of the *Athenaeum*) that his scheme, the purchase of the Shakespeare properties, would "do real honour to the memory of Shakespeare, & save us from being inundated by the threatened absurd movements for a monument statue or mausoleum" (6 November 1861; Folger Y.c.1213[5]). That was not the end of it, however. Thomas Wright reported in an undated letter (the year 1863 supplied by Halliwell; LOA 95:46) that the London committee "came on the question of the character of the Monument and its sight (I mean site)–another lot of nonsense. Furnival [*sic*] had seen Ruskin, and Ruskin says we must have a sort of tomb-monument, with a canopy supported by slender pillars, and I suppose W. S. kneeling down and his babbies on each side, and he said the difficulty of finding a sight, or

portrait of Shakespeare he had discovered, Halliwell wrote to her agent W. H. Wills: "I cannot afford to keep expensive rarities, & I could not bring myself to take a profit out of Shakespeare's face to put into my own pocket. This rarity is so unique, & its genuineness so unassailable, that I am convinced it is reasonable at 400 gs., & if Miss B[urdett] C[outts] purchased it at that sum, I should place the excess £315 to the credit of the Shakespeare Library at Stratford, a sum that would enable me to do wonders there in a few months–I believe I could with that sum pretty well complete all the Shaksperiana of the last & present centuries worth having. This is an object I have very much at heart" (8 November 1864; LOA 7:73).

getting a sight, was that no building in London was worthy to stand within sight, of a statue of Shakespeare." His ridicule was matched by Halliwell's. Responding to the growing public support for a monument, he wrote to Hepworth Dixon (17 June 1863; Folger Y.c.1213[15]) that it "is an object which is, firstly, useless, secondly, unnecessary, thirdly, degrading rather than honourable to a genius so mighty, fourthly, one in which a likeness is impracticable, fifthly, one which will most likely result in a monument that will not satisfy the taste of future ages, & so on."[185] Sensibly, he suggested instead a central Shakespeare library and museum at Kensington Museum or Exhibition to satisfy public opinion "going in favour of a Statue because it sees nothing else *in London* tangible." But realistically he admitted that "if public opinion runs strongly in favour of a statue, it is of no use fighting against it," stressing, as always, that "nevertheless a serious responsibility rests on taking a vast Shaksperian sum from the public for such a useless and unnecessary object." But his hopes that public opinion would not be in favor of a statue (19 June 1863; Folger Y.c.1213[16]) were disappointed by the "queer folk here" in Stratford who, having hardly contributed to saving New Place Gardens from the builders, want to erect a memorial in Stratford, although with "the whole place as a monument to him, & some precious memorials of his life yet unpurchased, it seems to me a right-down sin to spend money on a modern monument." In this matter Halliwell could support his opposition since a structure in the gardens, so he wrote to Collier (10 December 1863; LOA 91:23), was "in violation of the terms upon which the money was collected." Collier agreed (11 December 1863; LOA 91:49), but Charles Flower, the mayor of Stratford, did not, although (as Halliwell wrote to Hunt in a letter of 6 January 1864 [LOA 91:43], marked "not sent") he "may talk & bluster till a blue moon appears, but he will never get over the absurdity of his being now the active promoter of the Stratford statue, after having spoken & voted against one." Halliwell went so far as to poll the subscribers to the Fund[186] and received "opinions ... so strongly worded, that anything like unanimous consent, without which it would be impossible to grant the site [the Shakespeare Gardens], is altogether out of the question" (18 December 1863; LOA 91:37). Still, the

185. The letter must have been of special importance to Halliwell, for he made a copy of it for his literary remains–see LOA 93:15.

186. Not exactly neutral, the draft of 7 December 1863 (H-P Coll. 303, inserted between pp. 12 and 13) asked "if the subscribers to the Shakespeare Fund will consent to such an infringement of the original conditions of the Fund," not hesitating to add, "I may be perhaps kindly excused suggesting to difficulties likely to arise should any of the original conditions of the Fund be violated."

pressure was great and Halliwell was compelled to offer at least a hypothetical alternative: the constitution of the Shakespeare Fund could permit a monument to be placed "so that the front of it was not more than sixty feet from the garden wall of the Infirmary." To Hepworth Dixon, Halliwell wrote, "I think it is monstrous to support anything of the kind when money is still wanted for the New Place, Hathaway Cottage &c. I wonder what people would say if we were collecting money for a monument in London, if Shakespeare's house in Southwark were in existence & in private hands?" (24 March 1864; Folger Y.c.1213[48]). In point of fact the Londoners were intensifying their plans for a monument. Ironically enough, as honorary secretary of the National Shakespeare Committee, Halliwell had little choice but to appear to support a Shakespeare memorial (so the flyer of 2 March 1864 [LOA 28:22] appealing for subscriptions), "the erection of a Statue of the Poet in the Green Park, close to Piccadilly ... of Bronze ... placed under an Architectural and Decorated Canopy." And as an added irritant, since it would siphon still more funds from the Shakespeare Fund and Halliwell's objectives, "Any Balance which may remain after providing for the Monument will be devoted to the erection and endowment of a Shakespeare School, in connection with the Dramatic College, for the education of poor Actors' Children." An even more immediate and painful cause of Halliwell's distress was the behavior of the pressure groups in London and in Stratford. As he confided to Hunt, "if I could have foreseen all these disagreements I should have kept clear of the London Committee, not because I think their object erroneous, but because I much dislike squabbles" (28 January 1864; LOA 2:3). As it turned out, it may have been these very squabbles that doomed the project. For James Hain Friswell wrote to Halliwell, "You will believe me when I say I regard the failure of the Shakspeare Statue, which started so well, as a National disgrace; but this disgrace especially attaches itself to certain busybodies who desired to 'manage' every body & could not even 'manage' to be ordinarily polite to gentlemen who had worked as hard & would work much harder than themselves" (25 July 1864; LOA 6:39). Nor could Halliwell draw comfort from Clarence Hopper's news that "the Stratford people seem to have come worse out of their affair than the London Committee with an enormous deficit of 3000£ so they must be sickened with Shakespeare and you with Stratford" (7 September 1864; LOA 7:75). And so it was, Halliwell having to engage not merely agitating individuals but in this case, as in others, to endure the fractious tactics of rival groups.

Perhaps the severest test Halliwell faced was the Tercentenary

Celebration planned for 1864. As early as 30 September 1862 he took a stand: "To say the truth," he wrote to Hunt (LOA 195:23), "I don't take any interest in the Tercentenary matters. I like working quietly in my own fashion, getting out of the way the moment it comes to flags drums dinners &c. Ten to one but what the whole thing will be a piece of tomfoolery, worse if possible than Garrick's, which, in the opinion of all sober people, is the most stupid episode in the life of that eminent man." Still, as honorary secretary of the National Shakespeare Fund and guardian angel, as it were, of the Stratford venture, he had to show at least some accommodation to the tide of the times. He could hardly avoid becoming honorary secretary of the London Tercentenary Committee in 1863. For all his inherent rejection of "distasteful" public displays and desire to "carry out the best objects of the Shakespeare Fund in a quiet manner" (19 March 1863; LOA 95:4), he was swept along by the surge of national sentiment and issued, with Hepworth Dixon, a call for local committees throughout the country to join the National Shakespeare Committee in celebrating Shakespeare's birthday by subscribing either to a monument in London or to a fund for local objects (undated; LOA 1:34).[187] Months later, repeating almost the same phrases to Hunt in characterizing such celebrations–tomfoolery, drums, trumpets, flags, &c.–he could only "hope the coming one will be more creditable" (2 January 1864; LOA 90:39). For it was clear to him that the organizations were overlapping and to a certain extent mutually supportive. Halliwell was even invited, and contributed, to the events of other simultaneous movements, like the Workingmen's Celebration with its "Ceremony of Planting the Shakespeare Oak, the People's Memorial of the Poet, on Primrose Hill, on Saturday, April 23rd, 1864." And not without a measure of teeth-gnashing, for as he confided to Hepworth Dixon in urging him not to have anything to do with the Workingmen's Committee, "I don't believe & never did one single word of the working classes assisting the object. It is all moonshine" (17 May 1864; Folger Y.c.1213[51]).

Halliwell was not being hypocritical, it must be stressed. For if he tended to be silent in public–in reporting the scandalous rejection of Thackeray as vice president of the National Shakespeare Committee at its meeting of 8 December 1863, the *Illustrated Times* described Halliwell as one "who never opens his lips, but forever sits, 'like patience on a monument, smiling at grief'"–he was nevertheless determined in his letters

187. LOA (1:34) is undated, but in a letter of 16 June 1863 (Folger Y.c.1281[10]) Halliwell asks for the insertion of an enclosed paragraph "which has been prepared for the leading provincial journals."

to Hepworth Dixon in London and his friends in Stratford to make the most, if not the best, of what appeared to him to be questionable organizations and events, like Staunton's "Crystal Palace [scheme which] has got to be such a regular Punch & Judy show ... a Shakspearian celebration there would be a fearful blunder" (19 March 1863; LOA 95:4). To achieve the most or the best Halliwell committed himself to hard work for the greater cause, albeit not always duly recognized or appreciated: not only the massive correspondence and massive bookkeeping, but also the massive publicity campaign, appeals for funds and arrangements for fund-raising events like the readings and recitations by Charles Kean and the entertainments of Dillon Croker. And true to his stance Halliwell, who did most of the work, asked to be told what to do, conceding the role of "*directing* secretary" to the more extrovert and "blustery" Hepworth Dixon (23 June 1863; Folger Y.c.1213[18]). "I am an advocate for despotism in these matters," he reiterated months later (2 December 1863; Folger Y.c.1213[34]). Much of what he was doing was onerous. Having sent out a large mailing, for example, he appealed to Hepworth Dixon, "*Pray* [underlined four times] get some one else to send out notices. *I hate* the job *like poison*," underlining the words of his aversion eight times (Tuesday, June 1863; Folger Y.c.1213[53]). But he continued nevertheless, and despite activities which were repugnant to him: countless meetings and countless clashes of interests, leading him to despair that "all the chief good I anticipated from this movement–the spread of Shaksperian reading and sentiment–is already gone by these lamentable squabbles" (22 January 1864; Folger Y.c.1213[44]), not to mention the "confusion & mis-spent money at the late *celebration*" which Collier charged (27 May 1864; LOA 92:6).

There were personal disappointments as well, like the resignation (under "great pressure exerted at Stratford" [11 September 1863; Folger Y.c.1213(32)]) of Charles Flower, his important ally, from the Tercentenary Committee (29 August 1863; LOA 89:7). "I did my best to avert the catastrophe," he wrote to Hepworth Dixon, "but it was of no use."[188] In fact, "I got dreadfully badgered there," he explained, laying bare another difficulty, "for belonging to the London scheme" (11 September 1863; Folger Y.c.1213[32]). Perhaps more upsetting was the announcement of the resignation of the trusty W. O. Hunt because of

---

188. The phrase "no use" must have made an impression. Some months later, after a paid secretary had been decided upon, "Bohn slapped J. on the back today," so Mrs. Halliwell's diary entry for 29 February 1864, "& told him he 'was no use'."

internal difficulties (14 November 1864; LOA 6:59). And in London there was buffeting as well, like the attempt (which failed) of others to arrange for royal patronage or the scrambles of rivals for funds raised. Halliwell was only too aware of the pressures, and he was not defenseless. Despite his belief that "it will be all very pleasant to me if I have no responsibility," he avowed that "I shall be glad to do what I can" (30 June 1863; Folger Y.c.1213[22]). And that meant he could devise plans as well as well as distribute notices. Just a few days later (3 July 1863; Folger Y.c.1213[24]) he presented Hepworth Dixon with a strategic overview and a tactical plan:

Would it not be well in forming the Executive to consider the advisability of including one or two persons likely otherwise to be troublesome? If the Executive consist solely of people drawing one way, the simple fact will stimulate opposition, & encourage the accusation of cliquery. By all means have a *certain majority* of attendant friendly members, so that the grand object in these matters, a vigorous & able despotism, is maintained, but one or two of a possible opposition indoors would conciliate opposition out of doors.
I dread this mob coming in, but I strongly suspect after all they will like to work separately from us. If they do come in, it would be well to think how far it would be in their power to upset the executive formed on Monday, on which day it would be well, would it not, to elect those of your personal friends who are eligible.

But in the end, although he could "dare say I may survive the attacks" in London and Stratford (11 September 1863; Folger Y.c.1213[32], and indeed did so, the various groups continued their ways, more in the spirit of rivalry than harmony.[189] At the mayor's banquet in Stratford on 26 October 1864 Halliwell's "health was drunk & the cheering & noise when he rose was tremendous." But not all the plans had been realized, not those of London or Stratford, the geographical and ideological poles of the efforts on behalf of Shakespeare. Halliwell's headquarters were in

189. It is of course impossible to deal here in a detailed manner with the complexity of the Tercentenary Celebration. There is a full-length contemporary account by the secretary of the Stratford-upon-Avon Committee, Robert E. Hunter, with the explicit title: *Shakespeare and Stratford-upon-Avon, A 'Chronicle of the Time:' Comprising the Salient Facts and Traditions, Biographical, Topographical and Historical, Connected with the Poet and His Birth-Place; Together with a Full Record of the Tercentenary Celebration* (1864). A concise account is given in the monograph by Richard Foulkes, *The Shakespeare Tercentenary of 1864* (London, 1984).

London, his heart in Stratford. But his soul was in his work. He still had
to develop the Shakespeare properties: to acquire some and restore and
preserve all. There were records too that required his attention, and a
library and museum to be firmly established and made functional. And it
cannot be surprising–even if Alexander Dyce's characterization "There is
really no end to your Shakespearian undertakings: they quite astonish me;
and, as you speak positively of your 'madness', I shall not be rude enough
to contradict you" (Tuesday, January 1863; LOA 96:42) were
unknown–that Halliwell should crown the Shakespeare activities and
celebrations of the first half of the decade and the completion of his folio
edition in 1865 with the official announcement in November of a new and
grand work to be printed uniformly with the folio edition, though (so the
prospectus) the volumes will be not quite so thick, "about (certainly not
less than) two inches in thickness [and] far more profusely illustrated with
wood-engravings [and] every effort [made] to excel its predecessor."
"Another big book–of course on Shakespeare," he wrote to Charles
Roach Smith (6 December 1865; Folger C.b.16[131]), "What other author
is worth troubling oneself [*sic*] about?"

It was to be called *Illustrations of the Life of Shakespeare*. Halliwell had
mentioned his plans for a new life of Shakespeare "which I intend to do,"
so he wrote to Hepworth Dixon on 9 February 1862 (Folger
Y.c.1213[10]), "by degrees on a very elaborate scale in folio volumes." And
in the same year he had asked J. T. Blight to make sketches for him at and
near Stratford. In point of fact in 1864 he had already published *An
Historical Account of the New Place, Stratford-upon-Avon, the Last Residence of
Shakespeare*, a luxurious folio-sized volume in which he reprinted "all the
documents possessing any real claims to importance at full length," as well
as parts of others, most "for the first time," and richly illustrated with
contributions by Blight, Fairholt, Ashbee, and Rimbault (vi), about which
Halliwell's Shakespearean colleagues were enthusiastic: Staunton called it
a "very noble looking volume" (10 April 1866; LOA 112:1); Collier
remarked, "All lovers of Shakespeare, that is the whole world where he is
known, are indebted to you" (12 April 1866; LOA 113:36); and Dyce,
reacting to the "magnificent present," was "really astonished at
[Halliwell's] indefatigableness" (14 April 1866; LOA 113:15). Although the
Illustrations was first conceived as a "supplementary volume to the folio
edn & is presented by me [at his own expense] to the subscribers" (24
October 1865; Folger Y.c.1213[62]), it was also a continuation of works
already produced–like his *Life of William Shakespeare* of 1848–and of
actions already accomplished–like the purchase of New Place–as well as
a bridge to what was to occupy him until his death some twenty-five years

later and was to become—despite Halliwell's low-key assertion that his "folio books are merely storehouses for more popular writers" (24 October 1865; Folger Y.c.1213[62])—the consummation of all his Shakespearean efforts, the crowning achievement of his career and life, the *Outlines of the Life of Shakespeare.*

14

Family, Feud, and Friends

Halliwell's tireless activities were matched by those within his family. There was always something going on. The last days of 1853 were no exception. On 16 December Mrs. Halliwell was "ill in the night with shivering & bilious attack." On 20 December Halliwell took his daughter Henrietta Somerset (called Harry) to Mr. Canton to have a tooth out; in the evening she received "another prize for diligent attention to her studies." On 21 December Halliwell was in bed nearly all day with a headache, and Harry heard Charlotte's lessons. On Christmas day, although "at home very quiet all day," Harry had a "terrible toothache"; two days later she had another double tooth extracted. On the last day of the year Mrs. Halliwell's diary records that she "heard C's lessons & worked. James wrote letters upstairs & took the children to slide on the ice at Clapham Common. I walked in the garden as it was a lovely day. Saw Mrs Koch & asked her to lunch here on Tuesday. Mrs Eicke called. I read Miss Pardoe's Louis XIV." A week later, on 7 January 1854: "It poured with rain. J & I corrected pfs. & he looked over accts. I worked & read in the evening. Did not feel very well." The next day: "I was ill all last night & at 1/2 p. 5 this morning James went for Mrs Blunden (the nurse) & afterwards for Dr. Wray. My youngest girl was born at 1/2 to 8 this morng before Dr. Wray got here. She is a very little baby." The other children were "delighted with the new baby," she wrote to Aunt Graves a few days later. Thomas Halliwell, James's older brother, was to be "godpapa" and their friends Mrs. Taynton and Mrs. Koch were to be godmothers. The baby was christened Ellen Molyneux (Mrs. Halliwell's mother's maiden name) on 1 February 1854.

A household of three children meant further familial obligations, which Halliwell willingly shared with his wife, though burdened with business pressures, travel, and scholarly enterprises. There were vaccinations for the children, lessons to be heard, servants to be supervised. Mrs. Halliwell's diary describes a not untypical day, 7 September 1854: "Hot day. Baby better. Gave C. castor oil, but she was poorly all day. She went in garden. Dr W. came he says there are black flags put up in Town in the streets infected with Cholera. Charlotte sd her lessons very well & played wth baby. I worked, read, settled bills, wrote to Lou & Mrs. Walcot after tea. James looked over his correspondence & tore up some letters. Mr. Wright drank tea here." Harry began to keep a diary in June; in August Charlotte "sat beautifully on her donkey tho' it was the first time on a side saddle." Little Ellen had health problems: her arms were inflamed after the vaccination (15 April); she was "poorly" and to improve her appetite Dr. Wray ordered sulphuric acid and gentian (23 September); diagnosed as having the "thrush" (28 September), the baby had her top gums lanced (6 October) and, finding her much "relieved," was fed "roast beef and gravy - port wine & brandy & water, in fact anything we cd possibly get her to take" (7 October).

By January 1855 Harry and Charlotte had begun writing stories and were day boarders at Miss Edwards's school at £25 per annum. "Dear little Ellen," one year old on 8 January, was "good all day" and a few weeks later walked three steps alone. Mrs Halliwell continued her working, nursing, reading, copying, shopping, visiting, writing apparently without effort and without interruption. Halliwell rose every morning at six and worked at his Shakespeare before breakfast, after which he worked, read, copied, visited, travelled, wrote energetically and without interruption. Not only did the children have their illnesses: Halliwell was given to severe headaches, and Mrs. Halliwell had moments of weakness. But this was all routine, as were the numerous visitors who dropped in and stayed for tea or supper or for the night, the string of letters from wife to husband during his travels which kept him abreast of his mail, the children's activities, London news, wished him success with his paper or his dealings, etc. etc. and lovingly signed "Your affectionate wife Henrietta Halliwell." There was bustle in the household and immense harmony. This was a happy and thriving family.

And there was to be more. Avenue Lodge was comfortable, the Kochs and the Eickes were good neighbors and friends, and Dr. Wray was nearby. But the house was perhaps too small. And Mrs. Halliwell, for reasons not too clear, did not feel too well in Brixton Hill. In December of 1854 Dr. Wray was a frequent visitor, and on 27 December 1852 (LOA 79:3) Halliwell wrote to Hunt that "Mrs Halliwell is I am thankful to say much better, but is still so delicate I fear we shall be obliged to move altogether to a less bleak neighbourhood." And so, in addition to everything else, Halliwell, ever the caring and dutiful husband, began house-hunting in 1855. On 26 June he went to Brompton to look for a house. On 28 June he and his wife and two daughters "drove to

Wimbledon Common, but all the houses there were too large, then to Fulham but the place is surrounded with water & damp, then to Sumner Place Brompton. Went over No. 18 wch we liked very well." On 18 July Halliwell called on his neighbors the Eickes and announced that the had taken a house in West Brompton. A few days later they visited the new house at 6 St. Mary's Place and immediately arranged for the chimneys to be swept and the floors scrubbed. Over the next month or so the long move took place: on 3 August Mrs. Halliwell rode in a fly with her best glass and china about six miles across Clapham Common, over Battersea Bridge and up Gilston Road to St Mary's Place; on 6 August Halliwell in a cab "took the remdr of the pictures & glass doors of his bookcase & some other things to Brompton and 9 pots of slips & cuttings of flowers for the Misses Pettigrew ... Mr Franks began painting the new house in the Drawing & Dining rooms, he has engaged to do so for 11d p. yard"; on 9 August a van was sent off, also a fly, and Mr. and Mrs. Halliwell (having had to apply laudanum to her side to assuage her coughing) went off to superintend the unpacking. It was the thirteenth anniversary of their wedding day. The following weeks were enormously hectic, as the packing and unpacking, the renovating and decorating, continued feverishly. On 21 August Mrs. Halliwell reported, "We sleep on the floor" and remarked on 8 September that on the photographs of Halliwell (taken by Dr. Diamond on 5 September) he "looks old & melancholy." And yet it is little wonder, given her absolute energy and control, that she should laconically report that on 9 September she "was taken ill at 1/2 p. 11 & confined at five minutes to 2 o'clock of another fine little girl," again the doctor arriving too late despite Halliwell's frantic efforts. She was christened Katherine Elizabeth on 17 October with Lady Molyneux as godmother. The nuclear family was now complete in the new house.

The move, like the others in Halliwell's life, had a certain symbolic quality. It seemed to suggest a fresh start. And it was, for all intents and purposes, to be the last house Mrs. Halliwell was to know. Not only had the neighborhood changed but the makeup of the household as well. At the same time the Halliwells were moving from Brixton Hill to Brompton, they took it upon themselves to find and furnish a house near Ramsgate for two of their household, Margaret Marsh (a maiden aunt) and Alice Warland (their cook) to whom they were devoted. Thus new servants had to be engaged and tried out, and a nursemaid, and a governess. And as if to characterize the fresh start further, Halliwell made his first trip to the continent. In the last week of October, after a five-hour "dreadfully rough" crossing from Dover to Calais, he visited Lille, Malines, Gent, Antwerp, Rotterdam, Amsterdam, Utrecht, and the Hague, returning on

29 October with, dutiful husband and father, a lace collar, three bracelets and some engravings for his wife, a doll each for Harry and Charlotte, and an "immense box" of toys for Ellen.

But there was, of course, the past to be dealt with in the present. On 27 April 1854 William Lovell sent Halliwell a bill for his services in the British Museum affair of 1845-46: £70.15.2. The sum was considerable, especially at a time when, among other expenses, Halliwell was investing heavily in the production of his folio edition and was concluding an intricate financial transaction to guarantee his wife £8000 in case she died without becoming entitled to the Middle Hill estates, by agreeing to pay £6634 in case she did become entitled.[190] (And if he was collecting rents on his father's property in Westminster and elsewhere, he also had expenditures, paying—so his wife's diary entry for 25 February 1851—£1556.15 for "renewals of Great Chapel St property in Westminster.") A week or so later, on 11 May 1854, he "sent off the copies of his Archaic Dicty wch he had sold to Boone the bookseller for £250 - stereotype plates & all"; and on 15 May 1854 (LOA 60:3) he received £200 from the Earl of Warwick for a "collection" of "articles" and additional expenses. Halliwell was actively and apparently profitably dealing in books and manuscripts, and evidently earning just enough to provide for his family in more than a modest manner, providing there were no large or unexpected demands. Halliwell, it could be said, had no financial problems on a day to day basis; what problems he had (or might have) were middle- or long-range ones. And these were not inconsiderable. Lovell's bill did not so much summon up the trauma of the charge of theft and his exclusion from the library of the British Museum—he had long since established a modus vivendi with the Museum in both scholarly and business matters—as constitute still another painful reminder of his continuous and seemingly never-ending entanglement in legal matters. As Robert Bell, in a kind of choric lament, wrote him, "Is there no end of your terrible law troubles? It is wonderful how you can get through your labors with these anxieties pressing on you. "With all my heart I wish they were ended" (11 December 1856; LOA 41:74). Indeed, Halliwell had to consult many lawyers in his lifetime; his enrollment in Lincoln's Inn is as telling as the note of 10 May 1854 in his wife's diary, the substance of which was to be repeated during his lifetime: "J. went to bed with a bad sick headache caused by worry from business matters." The legal problems were of different kinds and over a long period of time. All were intensely personal.

190. See 24 December 1866; LOA 196:15.

The main battle was with Sir Thomas Phillipps, who never ceased in his campaign against his daughter and son-in-law. In 1855 Mrs. Halliwell accepted an invitation to Middle Hill, trying as always to effect some kind of reconciliation. Halliwell did not object, hoping to assuage his wife's grief and doubtless searching for peace for his family. Instead, Mrs. Halliwell learned that "the consequence was a shameful report ... immediately spread abroad everywhere," so she wrote to her father, "that we had quarrelled, and were going to separate, which report was traced after a great deal of trouble to Middle Hill itself" (16 October 1855; Phil-Rob d.161:31). A week later (23 November 1855; Phil-Rob d.163:33), having traced the report to the bookseller Thomas Rodd, she was still quite willing to believe her father's denial, as well as that he had not written letters against her husband to "influential persons" in Worcester and Gloucester. Since it was her "first duty" to defend her husband, however, she had to face to further insinuations from her father: "I had a letter from Town to day saying H. was going to sell his Shakespear Collections. I understand he is gone abroad & the surmise is that he is run away. Is it true? Are you in difficulties?" Her response was simple and naive: she explained that Halliwell was "taking a pleasure Tour for ten days with a friend through Flanders & Holland where he picked up some curious old Plays." Her naiveté was repeated in almost the same words in another letter a week later when she again hoped her father would help them find and punish the perpetrator of a "long series of falsehoods, and it is particularly important, as anything affecting his credit is very serious," she stressed, "as you probably know he is incurring a great responsibility with his folio Shakespeare, and living near London, with the childrens education and heavy expenses, it is necessary to be careful" (30 November 1855; Phil-Rob d.163:35).

Phillipps's crusade against the Halliwells was as much mercenary—he was constantly being pursued by tradesmen—as megalomaniacal. Since he had no male heir, and the vast Middle Hill estate was destined for his daughter and her husband, he attempted to squeeze concessions from them. Playing the alternative roles of grieving and punishing father, he put enormous pressure on his daughter, charging her with disloyalty and dishonor. Ceaselessly seeking reconciliation, Mrs. Halliwell was caught between father and husband. And it was a measure of her moral strength and love for her husband and children that Phillipps's mistreatment may have broken her heart but not her resolve to stand by her husband. Phillipps tried everything to secure his property. On 2 June 1857 (LOA 229:39), he proposed the following:

There is a mode by which we may be reconciled, if you and your Husband should feel so disposed, & that is, if you both wd agree that your Daughters should marry to my satisfaction[.]

If you both agree, I will leave my printed Library to your eldest Daughter (worth many thousand Pounds) & I would not remove it from Middle Hill, & I would leave her or her Husband a large property of my own, of great importance to the Middle Hill Estate.

I am Yours affectionately

TP

PS. Give my love to my Grand daughters.

This proposal "much surprised and pained" Mrs. Halliwell, who rejected it as not in the interest of herself and her children because, among other reasons, of the "very great injustice [Phillipps was] inflicting by spoiling the property" (18 June 1857; Phil-Rob c.541:92). As early as 1855 she had been informed by her sister Kate and her husband, John Fenwick, that "Papa ... has cut down the beautiful avenue of old Elms from Broadway Church towards the Kitesnest ... The water comes into several of the rooms & he has filled the drawing room with packing cases full of books leaving a narrow passage to walk between them & this is the only room they have to live in every other room being filled" (Diary, 14 September 1855). Indeed, Phillipps, thought "mad" by George Hillyer the solicitor (Diary, 28 May 1857), had been increasing the pressure by threatening to cut down the timber on a vast scale and thus diminish its value as well as its attractiveness. It was no secret to the Halliwells that the Middle Hill estate comprised about 5,000 acres, the rentals brought from £5,000 to £8,000 per annum (Diary, 8 June 1857), and that he intended to cut down "one or two hundred thousand pounds" worth of timber (Diary, 30 May 1857). And so it came, as it had to come, to a Chancery suit, the Halliwells as plaintiffs seeking an injunction restraining Phillipps "from cutting digging up removing selling and disposing of any Timber or timber like trees or saplings forming Avenues or Vistas leading up to the Mansion House called Middle Hill House." The Court's decision was Solomonic: useful timber "for the purpose of shade protection and shelter of cattle" and the like is not to be cut; timber not "impairing the beauty or Park like character of the property" might be. In any event a final decision was postponed until there was an exact specification of which trees were to be cut (14 July 1857; Phil-Rob c.541:90). Reports that the buildings on the estate were "*notoriously* in a shocking condition" by Hunt (8 July 1857; LOA 64:17) and others–another of Phillipps's tactics–were not brought up but were also of concern to the Halliwells. On the surface, the

situation seemed resolved. On 9 November 1857 (Folger C.b.16[88])
Halliwell informed Fairholt that "the Chancery Suit is over, all costs &
everything settled, so that unless something unexpected turns up I may
expect to be easier in mind than I have been for years." He did, however,
indicate financial strain: "I particularly want to avoid drawing more checks
than absolutely necessary until after the turn of the *next* half quarter ... My
expenditure this year has for me exceeded all proportions." And despite
his hopeful expectation the emotional strain was evident. In her diary
entry for 8 June 1856 Mrs. Halliwell reported that "it was so close in
church that James felt faint. He went to Brixton after dinner & called on
[Dr.] Wray as he has had palpitations of the heart. Wray sd it was nervous
irritability & weakness & prescribed quinine & cold water sponging daily."
On 19 April 1856 (Folger W.a.81[17/6]) he had written to Fairholt to
spread the word that he had so much work that he did not want "*any one*"
to visit him "*unless* [underlined three times] they have got hold of some
early edns of Shakespeare, & then even Old Nick himself would be
welcome." A few weeks later: "I *cannot* have any one except by *special
invitation*. Even five minutes interruption is often an intenser nuisance than
I like to say" (5 May 1856; Folger C.b.16[78]). On 19 May 1857 (so Mrs.
Halliwell's diary), before his thirty-eighth birthday, he "bought a new sort
of braces to keep his shoulders back & prevent stooping" (a condition
which worsened, Mrs. Halliwell attributing it to "so much writing while
young" [Diary, 17 March 1860]). And months later: "Scarcely a week
passes without fresh calls on my Time. It is very hard work to do such a
large book with numerous family cares & connexions & I find the
business of life increases with years, so that if I had not worked hard
when young I *could not* now" (2 October 1857; Folger C.b.16[87]).

   The strain was to increase. Phillipps continued his assault on his
daughter's sensibility, avowing that her "heart if left to its own dictation
could not have penned such letters" (4 November 1857; Phil-Rob
c.541:94); that, further, she had not even opened his letters offering
solutions; and in her "running away" she "ran the risk of *killing me* ... When
a daughter runs away from her home does she not disgrace her Parents &
Family & make them the laughing stock of the World?" In criticizing her
father for not having an interest in his grandchildren, in rejecting his offer
worth £50,000, in overstating her need, in instituting a law suit, among the
eight points Phillipps itemizes, his daughter has abused him, has not
displayed the "*natural affection a Parent expects from his Child*" (26 November
1857; Phil-Rob c.541:96). Personal intervention by others was of little
help. In three long letters to their good friend Rosa Taynton, who sought

to mediate,[191] Halliwell explained his position in a sober manner, denying "malice," and affirming his "desire to be treated with fairness & consideration" (4 January 1858; Phil-Rob c.549:219), reiterated his "sincere pleasure" at an agreement in which all could concur (16 January 1858; Phil-Rob c.549:225), and asserted his willingness to "consent to let the past be forgotten, & express regret for any causes of irritation that have occurred" (5 February 1858; Phil-Rob c.549:227).

All the while, Phillipps held to his plan of selling a large quantity of timber, and on 19 March 1858 (Phil-Rob c.663:1) the Court ruled in his favor, the investigating agents having determined that most of the timber was ripe for cutting and eliciting Mrs. Halliwell's diary entry for 20 March 1858:

James heard from Hillyer [his lawyer] that we were beaten in the Timber Suit - Papa having 16 affidavits several of which were to say that his father never intended to keep Middle Hill as a family estate. There was an attack made on me by his solicitors saying I had written & tampered with his tenants - That all Papa wanted the money for was to provide for Mary's children & which I from avariciousness wanted to prevent &c &c all most false. James's solicitors offered to stop all proceedings if Papa would undertake that the money should really go to Mary's children - but his solicitors would not agree to that - Mrs. Taynton's private letters & one of my aunts (I dont know wch aunt) have been shown. Papa has done all he could to ruin us.

He did more. Having already publicly "abused" Halliwell at Sotheby's (Diary, 23 May 1856) and also attacked Halliwell "about the MSS. Affair in Court" and although having been "stopped at it at once" by the Vice Chancellor (so Mrs. Halliwell's diary entry for 3 April 1858), Phillipps energetically advertised the worth of the timber as at least £23,000, almost double the initial estimate of £12,000.[192] And the mention of Mary's children was especially bitter. Two years younger than Mrs. Halliwell, Mary, Phillipps's second daughter, who was married to John Walcot, fell severely ill in 1857. Despite being painfully separated from her sister (and

191. In a touching diary entry for 17 June 1856 Mrs. Halliwell "Sent Henrietta, Charlotte & Ellen with nurse in a cab to Mrs Tayntons 20 Chapel St. Belgrave Sq. & did not tell them who they were to see. Papa & Mary were there with Mrs T. & they were pleased with the children. Papa gave H & C. each a ring & discovered himself to them. They were very pleased & surprised - it was the first time they had ever seen him."

192. Munby, *Family Affairs*, p. 76.

their younger sister, Katharine), Henrietta wrote and visited her. At one point during Mary's illness, Mrs. Halliwell travelled 240 miles in a single day (22 June 1857) to see her. On 30 October both Halliwells visited her. On 25 January 1858 Mrs. Halliwell "had a very bad account of Mary. James ran out instantly for a Cab, & we jumped in without breakfast or any luggage whatever, not even a comb or brush, & went to Paddington." On 29 January "James left a cheque for £10 with Kate for poor Mary–they are poor & pinched for money & Papa & Mr. Walcot do not help them." On 3 February: "Heard from Kate. Mary much better and able to sit at table but they cannot leave their lodgings for lack of funds. I wrote to Kate & James sent another £10 for Mary." And on 6 February he sent John Walcot another £30 so that she could have more comfortable lodgings in Torquay. Mary died on 26 February. Mrs. Halliwell "was close to her when she died ... James did not come to the house–he did not want to do anything that wd bring down Papa's anger on John & so kept away on purpose ... Papa was not there–she hoped he might come–but scarcely expected he would–he has a dislike of scenes of the kind." The Halliwells were not invited to the funeral on 6 March, John Walcot apologizing that "Papa would be averse to it!" But they did go into mourning, Halliwell having gone to Harvey's for his wife to order the mourning. "Papa has not put one of his servants in mourning which grieves me," Mrs. Halliwell wrote on 28 April.

And there was even more business for the lawyers. In a letter dated only 21 July (Folger W.a.81[5/6]) Halliwell informed Fairholt, "Yesterday I heard Sir T. Phillipps had voluntarily addressed the Council of the Royal Society of Literature against me. Only fancy one's wife's Father appealing to a public body gainst her husband. Of course I at once placed the matter in the hands of my Sol[ici][to]rs but it is a great nuisance if I am obliged to appeal to the Courts for protection." Phillipps had written to William Vaux, secretary of the Royal Society of Literature, on 2 June 1858:

On looking over the List of the Royal Society, I was extremely surprised to see the name of James Orchard Halliwell as an Honorary!! Member. As this is the person who has never cleared himself from the suspicion of having stolen MSS from Trinity College I can not understand how the R.S.L. ever admitted him at all, & still less as an *Honorary*! Member. Not only is he suspected of the above, but he has since that, I am informed, attempted to defraud Mr. Boone, the Bookseller, to whom I refer the Society for information.

If therefore the R.S.L. still continue his name on their Books I regret to say I must withdraw my own. I shall be much obliged to you therefore if you will do me the favour to inform me what steps the Society intend to take in this matter that I may be enabled to act accordingly.[193]

In a letter of 27 June 1858 (Phil-Rob d.168:189) to his agent, Phillipps added still another charge, suggesting that he "call on the Secretary of the Camden Society or the Percy Society & enquire if J.O.H. was not nearily [*sic*] or quite expelled from one of them, or from some other, on account of embezzlement of money while he was Treasurer." But for the mention of Boone, the charges were not new and require little in the way of further elucidation. Phillipps kept them and others warm, as it were, throughout his lifetime: in 1863, for example, he was correcting proofs for further use of the infamous anonymous "O Sir Thomas" letter which warned him against Halliwell in 1842.[194] It is not clear what the defrauding of Boone meant. Halliwell paid Boone £120 for the 1603 *Hamlet* he purchased in 1856. In another instance Boone assured Halliwell (1 January 1857; LOA 60:43) that he was "very sorry" as to be thought "so unreasonable as to imagine" he could find any fault with Halliwell, explained that he had made a fair offer for the Shakespeare plays "upon the possibility of ... using some of the leaves to complete other Copies," and wished him "very many happy new years." In still another, Boone's bill of 4 May 1858 (LOA 119:18) for the remaining stock of Halliwell's *Dictionary of Archaic and Provincial Words* and the stereotype plates was addressed to John Russell Smith, and there is no evidence that it was not paid on the stipulated dates of six, nine, and twelve months. In any event, the Council's inclination to expel Halliwell—Vaux, it is interesting to note, had entered British Museum service in 1841—was held in check by formalities which had not been observed and, besides, as Vaux wrote to Phillipps on 10 June 1858:

It was felt, that practically, however guilty J.O.H. might be, the Council really had no grounds whatever on which to move: the case of Trinity College had broken down—the authorities of the British Museum on the faith of this failure had restored to him his licence to read in their library—and no one in the Council had had any knowledge of the nature of the dispute between Mr. Boone & J.O.H.—or in what manner the former had been injured by him, or felt aggrieved at his Conduct.[195]

193. In Munby (*Family Affairs*, pp. 78-82), who reproduces the relevant exchange of letters. Copies of the letters between Vaux and Halliwell's solicitors Hillyer & Fenwick are in LOA 24: flyleaf, 1-4.

194. A copy of the proof with corrections dated 7 August is in the library of the Grolier Club in New York.

195. In Munby, *Family Affairs*, p. 80.

In the end, Phillipps angrily resigned his membership (as he had from the Cambridge Antiquarian Society in 1853) and Halliwell did not bring "an action against the Council for 'malicious publication' of libellous matter," nor was there cause (so Vaux in the same letter to Phillipps of 19 June 1858) for him to "apprehend Mr. Halliwell had better not throw stones."[196] But Phillipps was to remain silent for only a relatively short time.

There were other legal actions to be dealt with. In 1855 Sarah Ann Halliwell, Richard's widow, who had had excellent relations with the Halliwells, filed a bill of complaint for the further support of her two sons, Thomas and Richard (Bisset). They had been provided for in the will of Thomas Halliwell, the family patriarch and their grandfather: each was to receive £20 annually to the age of eight, thereafter £50, the sum for each not exceeding £500; Sarah Ann was to receive £100 annually for as long as she remained unmarried. The Court ruled that a "proper allowance" be made for the two children "out of their respective shares of the personal estate" and for Sarah Ann out of the real estate of Richard Halliwell. Although Halliwell had turned over the management of his father's trusts to his brother, Thomas—which Sarah Ann regretted (Diary, 22 September 1853)—he was still very much involved in family affairs and finances. It is not exactly clear what transpired but the legal proceedings dragged on, the Halliwells evidently of the opinion that Lovell, Richard's partner, was not forthcoming in acknowledging Richard's share of the firm's revenue. There was an obvious strain in the relationship between the Halliwells and Lovell. In her diary entry for 16 February 1857 Mrs. Halliwell mentions that "James went to Hillyers with papers & heard that Mr Lovell abuses James before the Chief Clerk so much that he was obliged to be silenced." Halliwell seems to have lost a suit, for Mrs. Halliwell reports that on 8 August 1857 he "paid part of the money today in Chancery Suit Halliwell v. Halliwell." Halliwell bore no grudge against Sarah Ann or her sons. When he learned of her severe illness on 18 November 1858 he and his wife offered to visit her immediately but were then told she had died the day before, whereupon they wrote to the boys and invited them to come to Brompton. The situation was not uncomplicated, for William Lovell had been appointed their guardian in Sarah Ann's will and their uncles had not even been consulted. The boys answered promptly (22 November 1858; LOA 71:21), addressing only "My dear Aunt," saying they felt "too acutely our Mamma's death to make any visits" and ending, "Will you thank our Uncle for his expressions of

196. In Munby, *Family Affairs*, p. 81.

kindness towards us." Mrs. Halliwell surmised (25 November 1858) it was a "letter evidently dictated by Mr. Lovell," noting also that "they did not write to James at all." It came from Albion House, St John's Wood in London, not very distant from Brompton.

It was a difficult time. On 10 July 1858 Mrs. Halliwell reported that Halliwell "cannot work yet he has been quite unfitted to do anything, and though he has tried several times was obliged to give up" and, a few days later, "he thinks of giving up the editing of the folio Shakespeare after the 8th volume is done, & returning the money to the Subscribers. He finds he has so many interruptions, & is so worried about business, & as the Comedies will be finished in Vol 8, he thinks it the best plan to give it up" (14 July 1858). Even a much-needed family holiday turned from idyllic to "most wretched": while they were in Clevedon in September of 1858 little Katie came down with scarlatina, then in October Ellen, Charlotte, and the nurse as well, and Mrs. Halliwell was diagnosed as having spasmodic asthma. To Fairholt, in a not untypical bit of reflection at this point of his life, he wrote: "What is your opinion of life! I am 38 & find life is not what it was–not the same freshness hope or trust–more inclined to take a business view, & abolish sentiment–& believe in the real affection of very few" (Tuesday, 1858; Folger W.a.81[23/2]).

And that affection came uninterruptedly from his wife and children, his brother, Thomas, and sister, Louisa (Mrs. Samuel Edward Baker) and their children, from members of his household, like Emily Mary West (the governess), from old friends of the family, like Caroline M. Birkenhead (Mrs. Halliwell's former governess) and Rosa Taynton, and neighbors, like the Kochs and the Eickes, and to be sure the closest colleagues and associates who were always dropping in and writing often, like Wright, Fairholt, Pettigrew, Croker, and Charles Roach Smith. Individual personalities and the sense of family which delighted and supported Halliwell are evident in letters he received from his daughters in the late 1850s. Typical is one from Henrietta Somerset dated 28 October 1857 (LOA 63:17) when she was fourteen:

My dear Papa,
That little box does so capitally to keep my money in, I have tied a piece of tape to the key and put it in a little parcel with some other little things. I have not seen Uncle Baker since the day you came. Has Uncle Thomas or any of the boys been to Clevedon. Is it fine at Clevedon now. There is a finger of my cake left now, but the apples are not quite gone yet. One of the girls found on the Kewslake road today a pearl knife a very small one. dinner is just ready now. I left the little portrait of Grace at Aunt

Louisas. The tide is coming in nicely now. Three young ladies are going out to tea. I am going to mend my stockings now, so I have nothing more to say. Believe me to be Yr affectionate Daughter Henrietta S. Halliwell. It is not well written but I am in a hurry.

Another is from the talented Charlotte, almost twelve, writing in a firm hand on 22 June 1859 (LOA 68:39) from Brompton to her father who was visiting the Bakers in Weston-super-Mare:

My dear Papa,
I wish you many happy returns of your birth-day. We went to see the school children have their feast in the field opposite. Do you give Gracy and Ernest sugar every night to quiet them. Miss West's sister came on Wednesday, she is quite well. Do you play with Mr Elwell's boys now, and walk on the Flagstaff every night with Mr Jackson, Aunt Lou and Mr Elwell. I have learnt more than an act of Shakespeare's Midsummer Night Dream. How are old Mr and Mrs Baker, and Miss Weaver. Henrietta, Ellen, Katy, and I send our love and kisses to you. The puns and riddles are going on now, but there are not so many as there were when Aunt Lou was here. Give my love to Aunt Lou and Uncle Baker. I remain Your affectionate daughter, Charlotte Halliwell.

And equally typical is Mrs. Halliwell's description of 28 December 1859:

Wrote to Bedford for candles & sent Christmas number of Illustd News to Eliz. Molyneux. We had a frolic in the eveng. The children & Meg [their aunt, Margaret Marsh] dressed as boys. Meg like Sir H. Dryden. Papa in his white drawers, & nightshirt & my nightcap like an old woman. I put on 6 or 7 dresses & a cap & James's hat & dressed like a Welchwoman, an immense size, there were roars of laughter. Mr Wright here to tea.

For his part, despite all the legal and professional tensions, the constant bad headaches and accompanying fatigue and depression, Halliwell was always the beloved and admired paterfamilias, taking the family on outings and holidays, to the theater and exhibitions, buying them gifts, and in his travels maintaining an unbroken correspondence with each one. And there was always time for his friends—letters and visits and spontaneous nights out at the Gaiety or the Adelphi and dinner at Evans's—and for acts of generosity, concern for their health and well-being, and true sadness at their death. By 1860 Halliwell's "ruling passions" were very clearly defined. For one thing he was an indefatigable worker, obsessed with his pursuits, and an equally dedicated family man, single-minded in his devotion. For another, he was light-hearted, fond of games and practical jokes, puns and farce, and yet equally given to moods of gloom and despair. From his earliest days he was given to playful foolery. "James played off a trick," Mrs. Halliwell reported (Diary, 6 May 1847), "upon the assembled antiquaries by burying a pair of old tweezers in one of the graves [in a Saxon cemetery] & allowing Mr Roach Smith to find it, who declared it to be an Antique at the time of the Saxon's." In the 1860s this disposition did not change. On 14 April 1860 "James heard from Lou who is astonished at the boxes of plate paper James sent her, not havg really believed that there had been a fire at Sutton, or even that James had bought a cottage, she thought it was a hoax, as he is so often playg tricks." On a family holiday in Cornwall he amused himself by trying to catch trout in his open umbrella (Diary, 12 August 1861). "James startled us by coming behind us & shouting - an amusement he is fond of when we dont expect him," his wife records (Diary, 2 April 1862). While on holiday in Wales "James played all sorts of pranks & ran along the dusty sand without his boots behind Mr B[light] to catch him unawares" (Diary, 24 August 1864). On 29 August 1864 Mrs. Halliwell "found them ... throwing stones at a heap they had set up. Tried to make them return with us as it was dinner - but they objected not havg finished the game." And Halliwell could bear embarrassment with good humor: falling "bodily into [a] stream & was covered with mud - new trousers ruined & coat spoilt - he went home roaring with laughter" (Diary, 22 June 1865).

Most characteristic of all perhaps was his devotion to the theater. He was not just present at performances of Shakespeare–he hardly ever missed a performance by Macready or Kean–but he was especially captivated by the music hall, ever a loyal visitor to the Gaiety, the Adelphi, or the Canterbury to lift his spirits, as, for example, when on 19 June 1860 Mrs. Halliwell reported he "was not very well & felt faint & lay down about tea time ... James got better & afterwds he & I went to Strand Theatre to see his favorite piece 'The Miller & his Men'." He had a "rage for theatricals," his wife wrote (30 May 1860; LOA 73:32), despite his brother Thomas's "connecting theatricals ... with a certain *free & easy* kind of society which is not desirable to encourage" (24 May 1860; LOA 73:41). Combining both his theatrical bent and his fondness for pranks, Halliwell pretended to take a part in a performance on 2 June 1860 of the farce of "The Wrong Bottle," presented by the Kemble Amateur Club. He included the bogus program of this "hoax" (Diary, 20 May 1860) among his literary papers (LOA 230:67), along with cuttings on the deaths of music hall comedians and at times short comments. One such, dated 24 May 1860 (LOA 236:31), is both a tribute and a bit of self-revelation:

The death of Albert Smith announced this morning affected me more deeply than I could have imagined that of one who was not even slightly acquainted with me could have done. It was only a few days ago, not a week since, that I took my daughter Charlotte to see his entertainment, & I little thought when he closed the old familiar door at the Egyptian Hall it was the last time I should see him.

I was present on first night of his Mont Blanc, I think in 1852, & have been a frequent visitor since that period, believing him to be unrivalled in the peculiar entertainment he produced. My seat was usually just opposite him in the front row of the area, facing the little box into which he emerged from a narrow door. His Engineer's story was inimitable, & his patter songs I think superior to those of Mathews. But his chief merit was the decided part he took against the conventionalities of the day, which he lashed into with so much humour & tact that even the prejudices of those affected by his goodnatured sarcasms were not greatly offended.

In the same year, 1860, nearing the peak of his career and before his fortieth birthday, Halliwell prepared his will and asked his brother, Thomas, and his lawyer, Arthur Wood, to join in the trusteeship, the latter hoping "it may be long (if ever) ere I am called on to act under it" (14 April 1860; LOA 71:58). The reasons were many, contradictory perhaps, but not divisible. In essence Halliwell–for all his adventurousness and speculation, and for all his love of fun and farce–was sober and straightforward. He knew how to plan and maneuver but preferred to let others take the forefront: that was better done by a Thomas Wright or a Hepworth Dixon, to whom he gladly took a back seat, as it were. In the business of buying and selling books he knew exactly what he wanted and what to pay, but if he wanted something badly enough he did not quibble about price. As he wrote to Hemming & Co.: "It is a rule with me not to make offers for anything of the kind. When a definite offer is made me, I then return the articles or a cheque for the amount immediately. It is the only way to prevent protracted negotiacions which curiosities are rarely worth" (2 March 1864; LOA 97:18). In another and telling instance (and by no means the only one)–certainly unacknowledged by those who criticized his tactics–Mrs. Halliwell reported on 6 April 1862: "Mr Tite M.P. called with a friend & showed James a curious & valuable edition of Shakespeare's Poem 'Lucrece' which has been sent to him by a Country Clergyman, who wants £50 for it. James told Mr T. its value & sd he would give him £150 for it wch surprised Mr T. very much." Halliwell was genuinely moved by the death of Lord Londesborough but was clear enough in separating the man from the class: "I have got a strong idea," he wrote to Fairholt (16 January 1860; Folger W.a.81[21/5]), "he liked his antiquarian friends better than the grand folk. It showed his taste. The aristocracy are such fearful apes." It was advantageous for him to be a member of a gentleman's club; he had belonged to the Garrick Club for a very short time but withdrew, he wrote to Charles Roach Smith (11 September 1862; Folger C.b.16[120]), "not caring to pay six guineas a year for the privilege of dining at a dearer rate than one can at a chop-house. I am not too proud to lunch off a biscuit a bit of cheese & a glass of porter at the bar of a public or to dine for 1/6 at a chop-house."

Halliwell's ambivalence–most obvious in his ceaseless professional activities and his oft-repeated intention to give up literary pursuits–was to increase until he did move to the sidelines, as it were, and sought refuge years later, as Wright advised on 22 September 1860 (LOA 75:5), in "some healthy place not too far from London, where you might live at a moderate rate." However, until the completion of the folio edition and the firm establishment of a library and museum in Stratford-upon-Avon, among other enterprises, there could only be thoughts or threats of withdrawals. For even if Halliwell could restrict his professional activities–which was doubtful–he was unwilling to deny his full attention to family and friends. On the contrary, these–perhaps his busiest professional years–were also the richest domestically. Halliwell's household of four children, three servants, the governess Miss West, not to mention the ceaseless stream of house guests and visitors kept him happily occupied. Accounts of family trips, usually of two or three months annually, to Wales in 1860, to Cornwall in 1861, to the Isle of Man and Wales in 1862, to Stratford and Wales in 1863, to Wales in 1863, to Dawlish in 1865, among others, are fully and delightfully described in Halliwell's two travel books[197] and in detail in Mrs. Halliwell's otherwise generally spare diary. In explaining a two-month delay in answering a letter from George Livermore, Halliwell reveals family harmony:

My habits of life will explain this. From early in October to early in June the following year I work as Johnson used to say like a Turk–through the coldest weather, I am rarely in my study later than 6 o'clock in the morning. From June to the end of September, we ramble about in the dear interesting old nooks of our old country, & during that time

197. See pp. 246-51.

Shakespeare is for the moment thrown aside, & an antiquarian & topographical book takes its place ... These country rambles renovate one with energy that lasts for many months, & I do believe we all do more work than if we were in harness all the year round. They have been the most agreeable days of my life—my Wife botanizing, one daughter hunting after minerals, another sketching, & all being good walkers, not shrinking at hedges or ditches or moors or even bogs, we manage admirably (15 October 1861; Folger Y.c.1247[2]).

On a daily basis there were, of course, the more or less routine events of family life. In mid 1860 one Serjeant Plath was coming once a week to drill the four girls "for expanding chest & limbs." After a long preparation (including lectures and not being allowed to go to the opera in that time) young Henrietta was confirmed on 23 June 1862. In the same year both she and Charlotte were regularly given copying to do, and by the end of 1863 all four girls were copying texts for their father (and like their father the children had a little printing press). Routine did not rule out parental affection and pride, as evident in Mrs. Halliwell's diary entry for 25 March 1862: "After dinner I worked, & gave E. and K. a music lesson - while James slept a short time & then went to work. After tea I played a little & worked while H. read the Queens of Engld. E. & K. put their puzzle of the Kings of Engld together. Katie is very quick, & put them all out in their proper order of succession from William the Conqr to Victoria from memory - she is only 6½ years old." An endearing scene of familial affection and solidarity is described by Mrs. Halliwell. On 23 January 1862 the whole family and the governess Miss West met at the Post Office Savings Bank at Knightsbridge, where "I put in £5 part of my last years earning for work, Miss W. put in £15 Charlotte put in 12/6 from her money box & 6/4 her Papa owed her for work & he put 1/2 to it making a pound for her—Ellen put in 8s/ from her box & James made it up to 10s/. Katie put 3/8 from her box & J. & I made it up to 10s/ also. Each of us had to sign all our names in full three times. Miss W. guided E. & Katies hands." At the beginning of 1864 Katie and Ellen were having dancing lessons. A few months later Charlotte, who had been attending art classes at the South Kensington Museum in 1862, won medals for her drawings and was confirmed.

The three-storey house at 6 St Mary's Place—soon to be renamed and renumbered as 11 Tregunter Road—was as comfortable as Mrs. Halliwell could make it for her family and visitors. Halliwell, however, did not leave it entirely to her. "James," she reported on 1 January 1863, "went to Mr Emery the plumber & consulted with him about having the drains opened in order to discover whether the unpleasant smell in the schoolroom (on a level with the kitchen) proceeded from the rats having made holes in the drains, & so got into the house. It wd be an expensive affair & James thinks he must write to the landlord about it." In her diary entry for 19 March 1863 Mrs. Halliwell describes a hectic night-long chase after a rat. When Mrs. Halliwell, on another occasion, "gave Mr Brake instructions about fitting up venetian blinds &c in the rooms," Halliwell "saw Mr Emery & decided to have the house painted outside at once" (Diary, 20 July 1864). A few days later (27 July 1864), "We have 10 men & boys today - white washing, plastering, carpentering & bell hanging & papering." But for all his domestic involvement and concern, there was one thing about which Halliwell was adamant. "Hunting for some present to give James on Christmas Day ... is a difficult matter," complained Mrs. Halliwell, "as he will not have anything smart or even comfortable - I bought a new set of fire irons - which wd at least be *useful*-he will not have carpet, rug, or matting in his study" (Diary, 18 December 1863). What he would have were drawers for his study: four new ones on 2 July 1864 brought his total to 192. And, of course, as Mrs. Halliwell reports (Diary, 10 February 1863):

James busy settling things in his study-& has a case put there for his own copy of folio Shakespeare. The walls are hung with Pictures. No. 1. Portrait of his father Thos Halliwell, 2. Picture of the Stratford Jubilee given him by Mr Bolton of Shakespeare Hotel-3. Cast in plaster colored of Shakespeare head from Mr Green-4. Portrait of Shakespeare bought of Mrs Burbage of Cambridge. 5. Painting of Shakespeare's Monument from Mr Green. 6. Copy of Vote of Thanks to J.O.H. from Corp. of Stratford-framed and glazed. 7. & 8. Two water color drawings of scenes in Stratford-9. Deed of Settlement of New Place &c made in 1652 with Autograph of Shakespeare's Granddaughter Eliz. Barnard his last lineal descendant on parchmt framed & glazed. 10. An old list in MS on paper-framed & glazed.

Halliwell's concern for his family was not limited to the inhabitants of the house in Brompton. His brother, Thomas, and sister, Louisa, produced nephews and nieces; his brother Richard left two sons. The relationship of these young people to their uncle James was more than casual, deepening as the years passed. In the early 1860s Halliwell was responsive to their needs. From school at Clevedon Reginald Ashley (Regie), his brother Thomas's son, thanking his "dear Uncle James" for a present, wishes he "were here and I could teaze you" (April 1860; LOA

73:64). When his brother, Thomas Frederick (called Freddy), turned to Halliwell to "borrow money for a bill wch he is afraid to show his father for billiards & beer at the College" (Diary, 3 December 1860), Halliwell forwarded the letter to his brother benevolently, as may be deduced from Freddy's letter to him of 15 December 1860 (LOA 71:25) in which he discusses his career plans and concludes with an endearing "P.S. Papa has received your letter and will answer it either tonight or Monday morning. I hope you will excuse this badly written letter, as I have a bad pen, bad paper, and dont know what to say." Another nephew, Richard Bisset Halliwell, the second son of Halliwell's deceased brother Richard, was less awkward and more troublesome. Having run away from his guardian William Lovell and having "written since through a friend sayg it wd be no use trying to trace him, that he shd change his name, dye his hair &c. ... [and] has been heard to say he wd not be kept until he was 21 & wd go to Ceylon" (Diary, 18 December 1860), he was causing great distress in the family. And so Halliwell, responding to the appeals of his brother and sister, placed an advertisement in the *Times*, "about 4 lines sayg that R. B. H. wd be kindly received by any or all of his father's late relatives; for wch he pd 4s/." (Diary, 18 December 1860). Sometime later he "heard from Louisa that his nephew Richd Halliwell has married at the age of 19 Miss Austen aged 17 dau[ghte]r of Mr Austen architect to whom Richard is articled & that it is a runaway match" (Diary, 15 May 1862). Richard Bisset did not go to Ceylon, but later in the same year Freddy fell heavily into debt (even pawning his father's watch for £11) and appeared in the house in Brompton, "in the dumps" with his brother, "dreadfully cut up" and given "an affectionate farewell [and] embracing us all" was determined to leave England (Diary, 4 December 1862). Half a year later, off to New Zealand, he wrote to Uncle James: "I hope and intend to do better in the new country than I have in the old" (31 August 1863; LOA 86:20). These were not the only instances of Uncle James's involvement; there were also to be others, and more cheerful ones too, with members of the expanding Halliwell family.

The circle was even larger than the family, encompassing a considerable number of friends who, like the relatives, often just dropped in unannounced (like Wright, who from his nearby dwelling in Sydney Street, habitually appeared for dessert) and at times stayed on for the night or for days or even months and experienced the uncomplicated hospitality and cheer of the Halliwell family. And from Halliwell himself they could count on generosity and help if needed. Taking an interest in the literary career of Helen Gipps, for example, he wrote a short notice of her first work, the three-volume *World's Furniture* for the *Athenaeum*, albeit careful to point out to the editor, Hepworth Dixon, that although "to me, all fashionable novels are alike detestable. You will readily see that the notice is a strictly honest one, with no unfair leaning to the author" (17 December 1860; Folger Y.c.1213[1]). Congratulating her on the public success of the work (25 January 1861; LOA 151:1) was not the end of his involvement. For Helen Gipps, bitterly separated from her husband, Philip, was invited to stay with the Halliwells, remaining with them from 6 March to 28 May 1861 (she appears as a "visitor" and "authoress of novels" in the 1861 census), during which time the Halliwells almost uninterruptedly attempted to effect some kind of reconciliation by means of countless conversations with her and her husband. Halliwell was able to arrange for her to be allowed to see her children, and after a whirlwind of legal activity–lawyers engaged and judges consulted–was able to settle the affair without court proceedings: "All arranged without Helen's knowledge" (Diary, 18 June 1861) and without "a word of thanks [from others involved] to James, for all his trouble to save the family from disgrace" (Diary, 21 June 1861).

Halliwell did much to help others with their work. In 1863 he advised Sara Price on how best to see her book on fungi published, outlining in a detailed correspondence with her and Lovell Reeve, the publisher, how best to finance the work. In effect, he laid the plan for the size of the volume, the number of illustrations, the role of the subscribers, and added, in a letter to Lovell Reeve, "privately that the authoress has recently lost the greatest part of a nice fortune through the rascality of an agent, & so the money is of consequence to her, a fact which will I am sure induce you to stretch a point as far as possible in her favour" (13 February 1863; LOA 85:65). In 1864 Halliwell vowed to "spare no efforts" in assisting Julia Sotheby, widow of his auctioneer friend S. Leigh Sotheby, in her attempt to publish Sotheby's "valuable bibliographic poetical MS." for which he issued a prospectus in 1861 called "A Bibliographical Dictionary of the Printed Works of English Poets, from the Earliest Period to the Succession of Charles the Second ... To Be Printed from the Author's Manuscript, under the Care of J. O. Halliwell." Halliwell went further than agreeing to edit the work and making suggestions as to the number to be printed and the ways of finding money and subscribers. "I quite agree as to the fifty copies. I do not exactly gather ... if you would like me to take the risk off your hands," he wrote to her on 9 December 1864 (LOA 6:37), "but I am experienced in such matters, & might manage to make both ends meet when you might lose. Of course I cannot at present promise to do so, but if sufficient subscribers were forthcoming, I think I could manage it & relieve you of all trouble & responsibility; that is to say, of course, if this is what you would like." Halliwell's generosity–if not gallantry–is evident, although the project was not realized.

It was also evident in numerous acts of generosity to institutions with which Halliwell had personal and amiable contact. On 10 April 1862 (LOA 68:41) he offered "two or three hundred volumes" to the Public Library in Penzance; on 9 June 1863 (LOA 93:36), 180 old English plays to the Royal Dramatic College. Other recipients included Harvard University (9 February 1864; LOA 97:33), the Birmingham Public Library (2 April 1864; LOA 87:15), not to mention the Shakespeare library and museum in Stratford-upon-Avon and numerous individuals. Characteristic of his spirit is Halliwell's remark to Henry Octavius Coxe, librarian of the Bodleian Library, on a gift he has sent: Halliwell does "not consent to its being received under the Copyright Act. Bodley is most welcome to the vol, & I wish with all my heart that I were rich enough to send it all the books I edit" (15 December 1863; LOA 91:45).

Generosity was evident closer to home as well. In addition to a steady flow of gifts to all members of the Halliwell family, near and far, Halliwell did much for his circle. Within his household he was especially gracious to the governess, Eliza Mary West. On her leaving at the end of 1865 after nearly seven years of service, she was presented with a "gold half-hoop ring set with Turquoises" as a farewell gift, and he printed her notes as *Shaksperian Parallelisms, Chiefly Illustrative of The Tempest and A Midsummer Night's Dream, Collected from Sir Philip Sydney's Arcadia,* and doubtless agreeing to her proposal to consult with him on "something else" she was commencing (19 December 1865; LOA 102:48). She came by quite often after she had left her position as governess and frequently stayed with the family as a houseguest.

Perhaps even more striking was Halliwell's support–along with Wright, J. B. Heath, Hugh W. Diamond, William Chappell, and J. W. K. Eyton, who had also recommended him–of his lithographer Edmund William Ashbee's candidacy for admission into the Society of Antiquaries. Inquiring as to the reasons for his having been rejected, Halliwell was told by John Bruce he could not explain the "cause for the black-balling ... beyond the objection to him as a tradesman," although he conceded that "there are members who have a great apprehension that they may live to see FSA on a shop bill, or in a trade advertisement" (12 January 1861; LOA 71:45). Halliwell was disturbed by this injustice, and comforted and supported Ashbee until he was finally elected on 8 January 1874, having retired from trade. Others could count on Halliwell's support as well when it came to some kind of injustice. He was approached by Richard Sims, who appealed to him as one of the "gentlemen who are known in the literary world," to serve as referee for a vacancy he was applying for in the British Museum. The detailed outline of his having been passed over for promotion from the time of his entering the service some twenty years earlier was bound to strike a responsive chord in Halliwell, especially because of its mention of favoritism (Panizzi's name occurring often), ill-informed Trustees, and "Sir Frederic Madden's opinion ... that all vacancies of this kind in *his* Department ought to be kept for gentlemens sons" (29 April 1862; LOA 80:29). In the case of both Ashbee and Sims, among others, justice meant an honest and independent assessment of individuals by others and of themselves. More and more, Halliwell rejected position and pose. Agreeing to a request that extracts from his works be reprinted, he stipulated, "I earnestly hope that nothing like flattery of my Shakespearian efforts be inserted" (12 December 1863; LOA 84:28). With Henry Brown, a bookseller with literary ambitions, Halliwell had a long and patient correspondence and succeeded in helping him in the publication of *The Sonnets of Shakespeare Solved*. Holding that no publisher would print Brown's manuscript "as a free gift," Halliwell advised him to "try the experiment of maturing" his thoughts, and did not spare hard truths:

As to your attempts at conjectural emendations ... while I am bound to say they are ingenious, they are at the same time absurd in a most preeminent degree. By & bye, with more mature reading & reflection, you might enter on these matters. These truths are unpalatable no doubt, but if you are wise you will reflect & feel that I can have no object but your welfare in stating them. Speakers of unpalatable truths almost always offend, but I think I should be treating you cruelly not to state my views frankly (22 October 1864; LOA 99:38).

Halliwell's concern for the welfare of others was, at this time especially, a measure of his increasing experience and age. Before his forty-fifth birthday he wrote to his wife, "In re Birthday—I don't want to know how very old I am getting" (Wednesday, 1865; LOA 220:1). A year earlier, Frederick Haines agreed to be his literary executor (26 May 1864; LOA 92:8). Around him were constant reminders of age and aging: Dyce was ailing, so much so that Halliwell felt impelled to write to Dr. Bence-Jones, the liver specialist who was treating him (13 May 1861; LOA 79:8). Collier, confessing to have "lost much of my former energy" (9 November 1860; LOA 73:54), was increasingly mentioning having heard the chimes at midnight (as it were) as when he, "an old fashioned fellow, now 73," looked back in 1862 at the twenty-five years of their acquaintance (21 March 1862; LOA 68:40). Most affecting was the lingering and fading health of his merry friend Fairholt, which elicited a continuous flow of letters of encouragement and cheer for more than half a dozen years. In the year before his death Fairholt asked Halliwell and Charles Roach Smith to be his executors (24 January 1865; LOA 5:68); a day later, he wrote, "You were always kind to me, no one could be more so, and God knows I will never forget it" (25 January 1865; LOA 5:3). And so Halliwell took upon himself the sad task of preparing for Fairholt's death. Heartbroken but realistic, he advised Fairholt to be very precise in his will: "It has been a habit with me, derived from my Father, to make such things matters of constant thought—I have made at least a dozen & altered a dozen in my time, altering them according to circumstances. I do think it such a pity for the things we love to get into improper hands" (21 January 1865; Folger W.a.81[37]). In the same year Halliwell's good friend and colleague, Thomas Pettigrew, like Halliwell F.S.A. and F.R.S., as well as vice-president of the British Archaeological Association and editor of its journal, dwindled. "Again & again I have to thank you for your very kind & affectionate attention to me & mine," he wrote to Halliwell (29 May 1865; LOA 109:57), eliciting Halliwell's caring, "You really should not continue that excessive wear & tear of headwork day after day, & week after week. No frame can stand it" (12 July 1865; Folger Y.c.1307[26]). In the autumn of 1865 Halliwell visited the ailing Pettigrew almost daily, on one occasion twice despite the bitter cold. Pettigrew, a widowed father of twelve, died on 23 November 1865, survived by three sons and three daughters. In the same year Halliwell began collecting money to support his longtime companion and colleague, in many ways his mentor, the irrepressible Thomas Wright, who was to lose his mind.

But, for all this, the house in Brompton was hardly ever dark, and always open to one friend and all. On a not untypical Sunday, 8 October 1865, Mrs. Halliwell's diary reads: "Wet early this morning. I went to Church in the morng with Charlotte, Mr B. & Miss W. Mr Burr came to dinner making 10 in Dining room - & five in the kitchen because Mr Thompson & his son dined here. Went to Church in the eveng with C. Alice & Meg - It rained coming home and lightened as well - James heard that Mr P. was much the same. I gave Mr Burr two portraits of Jamie's & one of my own for Mrs B - Mr Croker drank tea here." On the next day, among other things, "Mr Hopper & his little boy came to dinner making eleven of us - Mr Wright came in to dessert wearing his new wig which is just made - he havg had his head shaved." Later Meg, Alice, and Julia

Pettigrew were invited for a stay, and John Elton Halliwell, Thomas's second son on holiday from Magdalen College Oxford, spent almost all of December with the Halliwells. In these years the house and the Halliwells received all.

Only Thomas Phillipps was missing, although he was never out of mind. By chance daughter and father met in 1860, eighteen years after the elopement:

While I was sitting in one of the picture rooms [of the South Kensington Museum] an old grey-headed gentleman passed, looking closely at the pictures about two yards from us & Helen asked if I knew him. I said 'no' twice, but when he turned I recognized Papa directly, & went up to him. He did not know me, but was very polite & asked my name. I said 'Harry'. 'No, is it possible', he said, I replied 'Yes' & he shook my hand warmly, came & sat down for a few minutes & talked & spoke to Larry - he told me he had been ill & just recovered from the gout which was not a complaint to shorten life; he stopped only a few minutes, did not mention James's name, but asked after the other children. I was glad I had seen him - he looked old & thin but very well (Diary, 26 May 1860).

Mrs. Halliwell's emotional surge did not last long, for two weeks later, in responding to her birthday wishes, he "wrote very unkindly & said he did not see the use of our corresponding unless I am desirous of being reconciled by doing all he wishes" (Diary, 11 June 1860). In an apparent rage at being sent a copy of Halliwell's letter to the *Times* asking for support of the National Shakespeare Fund (15 October 1860; Phil-Rob c.632:97), Phillipps wrote in "Dis" before the "Hon." preceding Halliwell's listing of his memberships in numerous societies. Shortly thereafter, Wright commented on a letter from Phillipps, "who seems to be getting queer in the understanding. He directed it to me at *Uriconium*!!! which of course would not be found in the post office directory unless it had been published in the time of the Romans" (4 November 1861; LOA 75:23). Whatever his mental state, Phillipps was relentless in his attempt to wrest Middle Hill from the Halliwells and to discredit Halliwell. In 1862, when the financial pressure on Halliwell was especially intense—he was forced to sell his American stocks at a loss of £600 (Diary, 22 February 1862)—Phillipps proposed still another alternative: a division of the Middle Hill estates in which he was to take Broadway and Manchester "absolutely," Buckland and Laverton "for life," and Halliwell was to take Childswickham "absolutely" (27 May 1862; LOA 4:13). This proposal was promptly refused by Halliwell (2 June 1862; LOA 196:2), as was the proposal that Buckland as well as Childswickham should be his (9 January 1863; LOA 196:2*). On 13 January 1863 Mrs. Halliwell recorded that Halliwell received another letter from William Philips, her father's solicitor, in which "he says–that (James) will probably agree to our taking the Buckland & Laverton estates–Papa retaining all the Broadway estates!! It appears very strange to us that he should propose such a thing, & his object can only be guessed at–namely that he wishes to found another estate with a Philips for possessor of Middle Hill." Further proposals and counter proposals were of no avail, however much the Halliwells were inclined to settle the strenuous and costly affair.

The situation was exacerbated not only by Phillipps's continuing devastation of the house and property but also by his personal vendetta against Halliwell. Parallel to the negotiations, and not having succeeded in discrediting him with the Royal Society, Phillipps attempted to block Halliwell's sale of early chapbooks to the British Museum. Having written to the Lords of the Treasury to stop payment, he wrote as Trustee to the Keeper of Printed Books, John Winter Jones (erroneously addressed as David Jones), on 21 October 1862 that he did "not believe a word of his [Halliwell's] having given 8£ each for them."[198] Subsequent exchanges with Winter Jones and Panizzi, as well as an attack on his fellow Trustees,[199] led only to Phillipps's cancelling his supposed intention of giving his collection to the Museum and his resignation as Trustee. He did, of course, succeed in mentally assaulting Halliwell, who wrote to W. O. Hunt, "I am nearly worn out by his incessant attacks, which at times & for long periods together render me so morbidly gloomy I hardly know what I am about, & distress me occasionally almost beyond endurance." At the same time, however, Halliwell's resolve was strengthened: "His present fury," Halliwell continued, "arises from my not agreeing to his preposterous terms for barring the entail, but as we have enough to live on now, & shall be comfortably off at his death even without Middle Hill, I do not see why we should throw up future prospects for an immediate advantage" (1 November 1862; LOA 190:12). Phillipps's tactics were often contradictory–as Mrs. Halliwell noted, "he is trying to make J. out a swindler at the very time he is trying to persuade him to enter into a family arrangemt about the property" (Diary, 23 October 1862). They continued to be so, and with increasing cruelty.

198. In Munby, *Family Affairs*, p. 83.
199. *Ibid.*, pp. 83-7.

PART FOUR

1866-1878

*Fig. 4 Halliwell-Phillipps in middle age. By kind permission of his
great-grandson, Lt. Col. William Walcot Stewart.*

15

Shakespeare and Satellites

With both the National Shakespeare Fund and the folio edition of Shakespeare behind him, Halliwell continued his engagement with the library and museum at Stratford, with the administration and the accumulation and arrangement of the collections. (This by no means light obligation will be discussed separately.) As far as his scholarly research and activities surrounding his profession of bookman were concerned, Halliwell's energies were undiminished. They were also more concentrated than before. Aside from the various publications connected with the history of Stratford and the impending "illustrations" or, as they were ultimately to be called, "outlines" of the life of Shakespeare, the greater part of his publications dealt with Shakespeare and Halliwell's personal library, which meant, for all intents and purposes, his activity in the book trade. Former favorites, such as the publications of items of early popular literature for their own sake or records of early theatrical history or archaeological subjects, played less of a role.

Publications dealing directly or indirectly with Shakespeare were dominant. Although the edition was finished, there was still a tremendous amount of material left over or to be discovered. In 1872 Halliwell presented the Shakespeare Birthplace in Stratford with 128 volumes, arranged by play, of supplementary notes which had found no place in his edition. Over the years he had cut out significant passages of countless early works, had transcribed others, and, as was his wont, had pasted them in bound volumes for the use of future commentators.[200] They are valuable both in themselves and also—should their sources be identified and classified[201]—as evidence of his reading and of course of the depth and breadth of his library. Most of the extracts were related only indirectly to

---

200. Cutting-and-pasting was the standard practice of the Halliwell enterprise. In preparing the notes to the folio edition, for example, his wife pasted 400 slips for *1 Henry 4* on 11 December 1868 and 400 on the following day.

201. Postgraduate students at the Shakespeare Institute in Stratford have been attempting to identify the sources of notes to selected plays.

Shakespeare in the form of allusions and analogues. As such they fulfilled several functions. In addition to illustrating Shakespeare in the "archaeological" manner, they met Halliwell's taste for early popular literature, being of the "curious and rare" type he so cherished, and, although the days of large series of reprints seemed over, for publishing them privately for subscribers. Reflecting the tide of the times, and of Halliwell's career, they appear only in 1866 and 1867. Two, printed by Thomas Richards in the customary 21 cm. size and limited to ten copies each, were reprints in 1866 of Samuel Nicholson's *Acolastus*, a poem of 1600 of six-line stanzas, and in 1867 of Francis Sabie's *The Fisherman's Tale*, a poem of 1595 in two parts in iambic pentameter. The former contains "plagiarisms" from *The Rape of Lucrece* and *Venus and Adonis* in the main, as well as echoes from *3 Henry 6* and *Hamlet*. The latter, so Halliwell's title page, was "founded on the story used by Shakespeare in the Winters Tale." Four further volumes were in the familiar Chiswick Press imprint and size (15 cm.) and privately printed in copies of ten each: in 1866 the prose *Tale of Tereus and Progne* (from George Pettie's *Petite Palace of Pettie His Pleasure*, 1576), "referred to several times by Shakespeare" (so the title page), mainly in Shakespeare's "recollection" of it in the second act of *Cymbeline*; and in 1867 *The Moorish Marriage*, a prose tale in Spanish (translated by Halliwell's friend F. W. Cosens) of the year 1332 by Don Juan Manuel, "bearing some similarity" to the story of Shakespeare's *Taming of the Shrew*. In the third, *An Attempt to Discover Which Version of the Bible Was That Ordinarily Used by Shakespeare* (1867), Halliwell simply gives twenty-seven parallel passages between the Geneva Bible of 1560 and Shakespeare's plays with the airy explanation, "Although the contents of the following pages may be thought to be more curious than altogether satisfactory in regard to the illustration of the interesting question attempted to be solved, they will, it is thought, tend to the impression that the version of the Bible usually read by Shakespeare was that known as the Genevan" (p. 5). Halliwell goes no further in proof than to offer the fact that it "first appeared in the year 1560" and the not very conclusive observation that it "was the one chiefly read in family circles in this country during the youth of the great dramatist."[202] Similarly, *Some Account of the Popular Belief in Animated Horse-Hairs, Alluded to by Shakespeare in the Play of Antony and Cleopatra* (1.2.192-4), of which twenty-five were printed

202. Halliwell doubtless made use of Thomas Eaton's *Shakespeare and the Bible* (1858), which he owned and evidently sold to the Earl of Warwick, the copy now in the Folger Shakespeare Library. Only two of Halliwell's parallels (Nos. 14 and 20) are not in Eaton, but Halliwell did use a different version of the Bible.

and fifteen destroyed in 1866, gives various accounts from the sixteenth to the nineteenth centuries to show that the "notion that hair of a horse dropped into corrupted waters will turn into a living worm ... is even now not obsolete." In a fifth publication in the familiar Chiswick Press mode, *A Discovery That Shakespeare Wrote One or More Ballads or Poems on the Spanish Armada* (1866), Halliwell uses what is essentially a reprint of the first portion of Henry Chettle's *England's Mourning Garment* (1603) to prove, as "it appears to me," that Shakespeare wrote songs on the subject. His "proof" is hardly evident, not extending beyond the surmise that the Armada is referred to and by the three poets who had written songs or poems on it "to the glory of our *Eliza*," that they were composed long after the dispersion and that "no production of the kind would have been published or known to Chettle as the work of Shakespeare, had not the latter been then in the metropolis" (p. 23). Halliwell's dubious "we may reasonably conclude" is not strengthened by his pious "Let us hope that the song or poem may be discovered," nor by his printing in three pages of the "following extracts [of ballad entries] from the Register of the Stationers' Company taken from transcripts made by Mr. Collier."

More substantial, and of considerable importance, are two reference works finished within months of each other in October and December of 1866. The first, *A Hand-Book Index to the Works of Shakespeare*, stems admittedly from a manuscript compilation accumulated over the years with "many of the explanations ... inserted hastily, without a view to publication." Halliwell's customary "excuse" for publishing hastily notwithstanding, this work of 551 pages is formidable. It is not simply an extract from the concordances of Francis Twiss or Mary Cowden Clarke, which Halliwell deems "invaluable," but in its explanations a commentary and in its expansion under certain headings a thesaurus-like stocktaking of the Shakespearean idiolect. In the first instance, although contexts are not given Halliwell attempts to disambiguate headwords. Thus he explains *course* as "(a) A term at bearbaiting. Macbeth, 268.–(b) A sea term. Tempest.–(c) The course of a horse, or a charge in a passage of arms. King John." *Speed* is explained as "(a) Fate; event of trial. Winter's Tale, 316.–(b) "'Tis good speed," par. wanted for Winter's Tale, 304.–(c) A clownish servant to Valentine. Two Gentlemen of Verona, D.P." Noteworthy is also that Halliwell gives specific references to specific uses by means of page numbers in the Variorum edition of 1821 (whereas Twiss gives only act-scene references without contexts to the Malone edition of 1793, and Cowden Clarke gives act-scene and context but without indicating the edition used) and at times collocations, as under *house*–"Eaten me out of house and home," "An Englishman's house is his castle"–thus producing something resembling a miniature index of familiar quotations or proverbial sayings. Secondly, he expands certain headwords to produce what may be the first inventory of Shakespearean items and concepts. The Contents lists but eight categories, from Actors in Shakespeare's Plays to Proverbs to Sources of Plots to English Localities and London Sites. But there are far more: all the breeds of dogs under *dogs*; all the parts of houses (bay windows, chimneys, hearths, gates, etc.) are listed under *houses*; under *military* are found all the weapons and their parts. Synonymy is attempted in entries for verbs–e.g. *take* or *turn*–and nouns–e.g. *forfeit* or *inversion*. A historical onomasticon of sorts is found in such entries as *Gloster;* a geographical atlas under English localities or London. In short, the lexical and encyclopedic information, while not entirely original, is considerable, far surpassing the information normally found in concordances. That Halliwell should limit the work to fifty copies would be surprising if it were not for his dedication to limited printings.

A few months later (the preface is dated 20 December 1866) he did produce a *Lineal Concordance to the Poems of Shakespeare* (1867).[203] As he had remarked in the preface to the *Index*, the poems were not treated in Twiss or Cowden Clarke. Again using the paginal references to the 1821 variorum edition, "that being the edition above all others invariably found in the library of the Shakespearian student," he produced a somewhat novel arrangement. First, however, it must be pointed out that the poems treated are only those in the 1821 variorum (that is, *A Lover's Complaint* is omitted) and, most important, only adjectives are given and not all proper nouns. Still, Halliwell's contexts, consisting of a complete line of printed text, are semantically adequate to illustrate the lemma, and his incorporating the "indicial" word within the line–identifying it as the first substantive in the line and italicizing it–is grammatically satisfying as well as space-saving. A slightish volume of only 164 pages, it was printed in only ten copies, astoundingly enough,[204] although it apparently achieved

203. In all fairness, it must be acknowledged that this was perhaps more than the customary family production. In her diary entry for 24 March 1868 Mrs. Halliwell writes of "the concordance which I did to the Poems, & which James printed & had bound last year."

204. Admiringly, F. W. Cosens wrote (9 March 1868; LOA 132:28): "You really are one of the most amiable unselfish creatures I ever knew. I am afraid that I should become very irritated at being informed that books out of which I reaped nothing but huge mental labour and no pecuniary profit were too expensive–The Concordance to the Poems is worth its weight in gold and must have cost you no end of labour–but the world is a very decent place and would be much better if

Halliwell's strategy. Reporting to W. P. Hunt (28 March 1868; UCL Ogden MS. Add. 189) on this work and others, he rejoiced:

Mr Windus's copy of my Folio Shakespeare realized £100, but if the subscribers have discretion enough to keep the copies for a few years, this price will I have no doubt be very largely increased. My little serials sold at marvellous prices, most of them double, & some more than three times the original subscription. My Concordance to the Poems, the subscription to which was £2.2.0, sold for £6.7.5, & Bumstead yesterday offered me £10 for a copy urgently wanted, but I have only my own left, & could not sell it at any price.
All this is extremely satisfactory, & shows the wisdom of short limits with these specialities.

There were disappointments, however. The Shilling Shakespeare enterprise, dormant since 1863, was revived in 1866. In mid 1866 Halliwell began an extensive correspondence with J. C. Hotten, who, in response to Halliwell's query as to whether Hotten's project was an "independent idea, or a resuscitation" of Halliwell's of 1863 (18 August 1866; LOA 114:6), answered that the idea had occurred to him some months earlier one morning in bed (24 August 1866; LOA 115:41), and he hoped to sell 100,000 copies (16 August 1866; LOA:7). Halliwell offered to superintend the project and supply the "briefest biography," without remuneration, provided that the design of 1863 was kept and the Globe edition not copied. In the letters which followed, Halliwell attempted to brake Hotten's extravagance with his own pragmatism: "Everything about the book [should] be done in a simple plain commonsense style, with no flummery ... let all rhapsody be avoided," he implored (26 August 1866; LOA 115:35). He was against mentioning various readings in footnotes, sensibly holding that "it would be impossible to tell where to stop." Plays which he felt were not Shakespeare's, such as *1 Henry 6* and *Titus Andronicus*, "should be in *very minute* type in 3 columns," for they are "rubbish." Details of the production process did not escape his attention: it was desirable to have rough proofs, revises, sample pages; nothing should be taken from other editions without permission (4 September 1866; LOA 115:36); the

it were not for a portion of the grumblers who seem dissatisfied with everything and desire literary corporative stores where all the material shall be supplied free gratis for nothing. I scratch my head sometimes and am sadly ashamed of my fellow creatures."

copyright of emendations must be observed. But despite Halliwell's meticulous concern and Hotten's keen tactics (23 September 1866; LOA 114:48) and ever-bubbling optimism–the "commercial horizon brightens," he has "made up [his] mind to proceed at once" (19 January 1867; LOA 122:3), indeed to proceed "with vigour almost immediately" (25 January 1867; LOA 125:33)–the enterprise seemed stalled. Halliwell turned, as always, to Wright for information and learned some months later that Wright had seen Hotten, who "seemed as busy as ever. Lots of things in hand. He seems to go on well," but, cautioning, "I cant help thinking that there are a great deal of speculations now going on among the publishers which will be dead failures" (17 August 1867; LOA 126:18). Halliwell waited, but not having heard from Hotten for "more than a twelvemonth," he rightly concluded that the Shilling Shakespeare had been abandoned or, if not, he could no longer devote his full attention to it. A by no means small measure of his disappointment is evident in the reverberations of an utterance he made at this time in another context: "To say the plain truth, I do not believe that the public at large either know or care anything about the state of the text of Shakespeare or desire to understand the Poet thoroughly" (21 February 1868; LOA 132:6).

The main thrust of Halliwell's energies in this period was concentrated on editions of Shakespeare and, as it developed, on the expansion of his own library. In 1871 Halliwell completed his supervision of the lithographic facsimiles, begun in 1861, of all the early quarto editions of Shakespeare's works published during his lifetime–actually up to the 1622 *Othello*. Executed by Edmund William Ashbee, the forty-eight (originally projected as fifty) volumes must be regarded as a milestone in the history of Shakespeare scholarship since they represent the very first attempt to make all the early quartos available. They were published privately in a printing of fifty, of which Halliwell destroyed nineteen, leaving him his customary thirty copes (plus one for the British Museum Library). They were expensive, priced originally at five guineas per volume. Judging from the number of prospectuses issued over the years, Halliwell may have had trouble disposing of them all. In a further description in his *List of Works Illustrative of the Life and Writings of Shakespeare* (1867), including the names of ninety-five subscribers, Halliwell offered those who subscribed to the entire series at five guineas per volume before 1 August 1866 an additional four volumes gratis. Of the twenty-one titles already printed by 1867 only eleven were marked "Out of print separately." At the Windus sale in 1868 twenty-seven facsimiles fetched a total of £107.3.6, with individual prices ranging from £2.3.0 (for a 1608 *1 Henry 4*) to £6.15.0 (for a 1602 *Henry V*). Even the "threat" in a prospectus of 1871 indicating that on the conclusion of the series the price would be 300 guineas did not seem to inspire purchasers. At the Tite sale (1874) the series fetched £136; at the Ouvry sale (1882) £176. And at the 1889 sale of Halliwell's own library it sold for a mere £55.[205] However, the value of this first-ever venture to students of Shakespeare must have been immeasurable. It was a serious undertaking. And Halliwell devoted most of his preface to the lithographic facsimiles (dated 15 November 1871), which reflected the experience gained from the course of the series since it appeared at the completion, to a discussion of the complexities of older texts. Although the "greatest care has been taken [in the tracing] to ensure accuracy" (p. 6), it is important, he asserted, to recognize that original editions may themselves be unclear (because of bad inking, for example, or battered type) and that printers kept "the text in formes, printing a few copies at a time, and perpetually altering and correcting the text as each impression was required" (p. 7). These truisms could not be taken for granted at the time; even renowned Shakespeareans like Furness had to learn that "all copies of the original editions are not alike." Experience had taught Halliwell that "to assert that, on delicate and minute points, references to the originals are rendered unnecessary [by facsimiles], would be manifestly an exaggeration" (p. 6). Circumspection and conviction led him to conclude:"Not anticipating an absolute freedom from occasional differences of opinion in our interpretation of minute letters and points, but confidently expecting that the more these facsimiles are used by the student, the more it will be conceded that the process we have employed is that the most likely to have ensured practical accuracy" (p. 10).

In 1870 and 1871 Halliwell issued two further lithographic facsimiles of early quartos. One, the 1615 quarto of *Richard II* (Q5), has no preliminaries but it is obviously the work of Ashbee and is identical with No. 45 in the series. A handwritten note by Halliwell–"The only copy printed in this form," i.e. on both sides of the leaf (whereas in the series only the recto side was used)–connects the work with Halliwell but does not explain the circumstances. A Warwick Castle bookplate suggests that Halliwell included it in his sales to the Earl of Warwick, whose library he was instrumental in forming and then in cataloguing. Since it is a unique copy it may very well be that it was made up specially for Warwick and then, the necessary paginal adjustments made, included (Halliwell ever

205. Interestingly, the rival Griggs and Pratorius facsimiles in forty-one volumes (wanting Nos. 17, 37, and 38) supervised by Furnivall fetched only £1.10.0, although it included both copies of the 1604 Hamlet (i.e. with and without the "offensive passages" by Furnivall), two volumes with MS. notes by Halliwell, and free copies of the volumes yet to be published by Quaritch.

given to recycling) as No. 45 in the series. The second is a print facsimile called *A Tragedy of King Richard the Second, Concluding with the Murder of Gloucester at Calais. A Composition Anterior to Shakespeare's Tragedy on the Same Reign, Now First Printed from a Contemporary Manuscript.* Although Halliwell's name does not appear on the title page and there are no preliminaries, it is doubtless his production: it has the familiar format, the customary printer (Thomas Richards), and the recognizable note, "Eleven copies only ... J. O. Halliwell." Moreover, Halliwell described the volume in a communication to the *Athenaeum* (1 April 1871, pp. 401-2), a manuscript bought by the British Museum (Egerton 1994) at the Charlemont library sale at Sotheby's and containing several other early plays, "some of [which] appear to be exceedingly well worthy of publication."

On 4 June 1875 (LOA 197:32) Halliwell was asked by Chatto & Windus whether he "would kindly write a few words of introductory notice" to—so the enclosed squib—"An exact Reproduction of the extremely rare Original [of the First Folio of 1623], in reduced facsimile by a photographic process—thus ensuring the strictest accuracy in every detail." They knew, of course, of "all [his] Shakespearean enterprises" and that he might well respond to their hope that the facsimile "will do some good by bringing the original text of Shakespeare into the hands of Students of every grade." A reputable publisher, Chatto & Windus was investing over £1000 in the venture and asking a price of only 7/6. Halliwell wrote a preface of seven pages, his name evidently so well known as to attract a much-needed large number of purchasers (which it evidently did, since 2985 of the 3000 copies printed were sold by December 1887). The preface itself, while routine, is not without interest. For one thing, Halliwell's presentation is restrained. The authority of the First Folio is asserted: "The value of the First Folio is so unequivocal, that there is no necessity for its wildest partizan to resort to exaggeration" (vii-viii). And his summary of the texts underlying those printed in the Folio indicates his up-to-date command of current editorial scholarship and practice. In fact a brief comparison with standard modern appraisals—for example, W. W. Greg's[206]—shows total or substantial agreement in all cases except for *The Taming of the Shrew* and *2* and *3 Henry 6* (which he considered "first editions," not acknowledging foul papers or manuscript possibilities) and *1 Henry 6* and *Titus Andronicus* (which he believed were not by Shakespeare). Secondly, despite the publisher's assurance that Halliwell "will perceive every word and comma is as distinctly legible as in the best 500£ copy," Halliwell conceded that "by the aid of modern

206. *The Editorial Problem in Shakespeare* (Oxford, 1954), pp. 183-9.

science it is now placed in a conveniently reduced form within the reach
of all," but was sensible and experienced enough to conclude: "It is not
of course pretended that any facsimile of any old book will in all cases of
minute research entirely supersede the necessity of a reference to copies
of the ancient impression, but for all usual practical objects of study this
cheap reproduction will place its owner on a level with the envied
possessors of the far-famed original" (xi). There is no evidence that
Halliwell had anything to do with the reproduction itself, although the
facsimile has come to carry his name, "somewhat misleadingly," as
Charlton Hinman has remarked.[207] Nor should Hinman's strong
reservations about its reliability reflect on Halliwell.[208] And Halliwell
himself even had misgivings about his preface, admitting to C. M. Ingleby
on 5 December 1880 (Folger C.a.11[25]), "that little Preface to Chatto's
photo was written hastily by me at Ilfracombe in the midst of the most
painful domestic anxieties."

Halliwell's Shakespearean enterprise took other forms too. In 1868 he
published two small volumes of "selected notes" on *Antony and Cleopatra*
and *The Tempest*. They were apparently to be the pilot volumes of a series,
as their uniform format and identical prefaces indicate. Although he
confessed in both that he had "abandoned the critical and philological
study of the text of Shakespeare in favour of a more exclusive attention
to the Biography of the Poet and the history of the early English stage"
(p. 5), he admitted that he was left after the completion of his folio edition
with a "large quantity of new materials," which it were a "pity to destroy."
Therefore he decided to print a selection "of what appears most worthy
of preservation"[209] on each play separately, trusting "there will be hardly
a volume in the series, however diminutive, which will not offer

207. "The 'Halliwell-Phillipps Facsimile' of the First Folio of Shakespeare," *SQ*,
5 (1954), 395, n.1.

208. Hinman's objection to the "strange monster"–i.e. its being made up from
various copies of the Folio–cannot be denied, although his rejection of it as "an
anomalous mixture of textual peculiarities such as has never existed in any one
original First Folio" (p. 398) may well, in part, apply to his own synthetic facsimile.

209. So a handwritten prospectus "Selected Notes upon the Plays of Shakespeare," dated March 1868 (UCL Ogden Add. MS. 189). "The impression will be
limited to 50 copies, 25 of which will be reserved for complete sets not to be
subscribed for under £42 a set at the conclusion of the work. But to those who
subscribe to the series now, taking the volumes as they appear, the subscription
will be fifteen shillings a volume. Retaining a copy for myself, & presenting 5 to
public libraries, the subscription-list on these terms will close after 19 names are
received."

information of some little use to a future editor" (p. 6). Only these two
volumes of a projected thirty-six appeared, though there were to be others
resembling them a decade or so later. Generously printed and with paginal
references (like Halliwell's other reference works) to the 1821 variorum
edition so as to reach a wider audience, the selected notes represent all the
areas of commentary, from simple glosses to variant readings, from
sources to allusions, from parallel readings to technical explanations–in
short, all of Halliwell's archaeological and lexicographical accents. Nor is
Halliwell skimpy or rushed. Despite the slimness of the volumes–forty-
one and sixty-two pages, following a preface of two pages respectively–a
single note may range from a short phrase to excerpts several pages long.
There are eighty-six for *Antony* and 120 for *The Tempest*. As might be
expected, most consist of parallels from early English literature of the
sixteenth and seventeenth centuries, not a few from works in Halliwell's
own library. Glosses are often from contemporary dictionaries, such as
Florio (1598 and 1611), Cotgrave (1611), Elyot (1548 and 1559), Huloet
(1572). Quoted are plays and poems, tracts on navigation and husbandry
and religion, on history and witchcraft and geography: a virtual cabinet
library of well-known and obscure works emerges. And of course, there
are echoes from numerous works Halliwell had himself edited or
reprinted: *Westward for Smelts*, *The Will of Wit*, *The Fisherman's Tale*, *Beware
the Cat*, *Love's Martyr*, among others. It is difficult to estimate the value of
what are admittedly leftovers. Much depends on the point of view of an
editor and, to be sure, the dominant editorial bias in any particular period.
It is clear that few editors can afford the luxury of extensive excerpts from
early works; still fewer are disposed to accept the archaeological approach
to literary studies. Although the majority of the notes are original, in the
sense of not having been used before–it should be stressed that it is
Halliwell's method not to repeat notes but to expand them–a comparison
with, say, a modern variorum edition such as of *Antony and Cleopatra*
(1990) reveals that few of these notes have found their way into editions
of Shakespeare. "Curious and rare" were Halliwell's watchwords, and so
his notes appear to remain. That may be one reason why he abandoned
the series for the time and, instead, a few years later presented them in 128
volumes to the Shakespeare Birthplace, where they may be consulted if
not by the "future editors" Halliwell envisioned, then by those engaged in
the study of the varieties of early English literary works and indeed in the
history of scholarship itself.

Halliwell provided a comprehensive outline of his Shakespearean
activities in 1867 with his *List of Works Illustrative of the Life and Writings of
Shakespeare, the History of Stratford-on-Avon, and the Rise and Progress of the*

Early English Drama. It is at once an advertisement of his works past, present, and future, as well as a summary of his own astounding enterprise, the rest of the title page reading, *Printed for Very Limited and Private Circulation at the Expense of J. O. Halliwell. 1850-1866.* Listed under the running head-title *Shakespeariana* are his folio edition, its terms, subscribers and the countries they represent; the "Miscellanies": twenty-five of his reprints; "Books Illustrative of the Life and Works of Shakespeare, the History of Stratford-on-Avon, and the Annals of the Old English Stage": thirty-five titles in an impression limited to ten copies each; "Entire Facsimiles in Small Quarto Volumes, of All the Editions of the Plays of Shakespeare, Which Were Printed before the First Folio of 1623, and of Those Editions of the Poems Which were Printed in Quarto": nos. 1-21 "now ready," nos. 22 to 54 "to be Facsimiled, completing the Series"; and finally the announcement of *Illustrations of the Life and Writings of William Shakespeare*, "Preparing for the Press, by Subscription, and for Subscribers Only, in Folio Volumes, profusely illustrated by Engravings on Wood." And in a telling little "Note" is the ever-fervent collector's wish to purchase early editions of Shakespeare, especially an imperfect copy of the 1598 *Love's Labor's Lost*, and to offer a hundred guineas for "the first three leaves of text in fine condition," although aware that it had been sold at auction in 1826 for two pounds and six shillings.

Halliwell produced this collection of titles not merely to advertise but also, in his preface, to emphasize his objective–"the preservation of a vast quantity of Shakespearian materials, useful to the student and critical reader, which are either too diffuse or too technical to be included in works prepared for the general public" (p. 5)–and to justify his faith in what he described as the "somewhat peculiar mode of circulation," i.e. limiting the number of copies printed. Halliwell did not disguise the fact that he was responding to "urgent applications ... to render these works more accessible" (p. 7); nor did he hide his irritation with "some of that numerous class, who believe they can always regulate the affairs of their neighbours to advantage." His argumentation is personal and economic, a faithful reflection of Halliwell as man and as businessman.[210] Although he "cannot afford to work at these favourite studies without the prospect

210. In November 1865 (UCL Ogden 72, No. 16) he issued a flyer asking to "know with as little delay as possible what support I am likely to receive. Upwards of a thousand pounds have already been expended in the preparation of materials, literary and artistic; and I am anxious to keep the engravers at work, at the same time that I am naturally unwilling to do so until I know that I can proceed with the undertaking."

of remuneration, [being] not sufficiently well off–who is, in these mercenary days?–to despise by any means the pleasing contemplation of substantial profits," he cannot "*personally*" manage larger numbers: "the collation, transmission, and keeping the accounts entail, as it is, a sufficient encroachment on [his] time" (p. 6). To undertake more would involve a house for business and storage, clerks, dozens of ledgers–expenses, he suspects, which "would either swallow up the margin of supposed profit, or reduce it to an insignificant amount" (p. 6). In his economic reasoning, as in his scholarly activities and his personal life, Halliwell's keyword is "practicable." And it served to reinforce his passion to do his things his own way and to take full responsibility for their success or failure. This, despite the fact that he often admitted, "I am so fidgetty in any matter of business, having made so many mistakes in my life" (16 July 1866; Folger C.b.17[11]). Even isolation was not unusual or unwelcome.

By 1 January 1867 Halliwell was able to boast of the Prince of Wales at the head of ninety-five subscribers to his forthcoming *Illustrations of the Life and Writings of William Shakespeare* constituting a veritable who's who and gazetteer of his life and career. Among the inevitable mix of peers and publishers, antiquaries and academics, collectors and clerics, friends and followers, institutions and institutes were the Earl of Warwick, the Duke of Buccleuch and Queensberry, the Duke of Devonshire; John Camden Hotten, John Wilkinson, Messrs. Sampson Low, Son, and Marston, John Russell Smith; Henry Huth, F. W. Cosens, Frederic Ouvry, Benjamin Godfrey Windus, William Euing, Henry Stevens; W. O. Hunt, E. W. Ashbee, Frederick Haines, Thomas Halliwell, Samuel Timmins; the Society of Antiquaries, the Bodleian Library, the Liverpool Free Library, the London Institution, the Library of the Corporation of London, the South Kensington Museum Art Library, the South Kensington Museum Educational Library, the Public Library of Penzance. There were subscribers as well from Germany, the Netherlands, and the United States. Described in detail (pp. 53-69), the project was ambitious: a luxurious series of folio volumes at four guineas each containing a collection of contemporary documents and books enhanced by an "elaborate system of artistic illustration" (including expensive woodcuts), a "creditable ... specimen of English typography," with "neither pains nor expenses" spared "in an attempt to emulate the finest examples of the ancient presses" (Halliwell having earlier won over the printer of his folio Shakespeare, J. E. Adlard, with the challenging, "Are you inclined to try to be *the* Aldus of the nineteenth century?" [8 March 1864 1864; LOA 97:28]). Shakespearean commentary was to be provided, since despite the "dislike in some quarters," Halliwell was always of the opinion that the works of Shakespeare "require and deserve, for their complete interpretation, a larger amount of commentary than do those of any other English writer." Similarly, objects in Shakespeare's Stratford (and London), generally neglected but indispensable, were provided, a great many emanating from Halliwell's and J. T. Blight's long stays, "summer after summer," investigating every nook and corner, Blight having "made for this work the almost incredible number of *six hundred and thirty-two* original sketches of old houses, scenery, and details of archaeological remains in the locality of Stratford and its neighbourhood *alone*." The strictness of the conditions of the subscription–including Halliwell's pledge to limit the number of copies, to deal with the waste, to destroy the woodblocks as the work proceeded–is not surprising, of course: the seriousness of Halliwell's undertakings always directly proportional to the severity of the conditions of subscription, the expansiveness of the vision in tight tension with the restrictiveness of the enterprise. Halliwell was both projector and bookkeeper. His intensity of purpose and awareness of risk are apparent in what seems to be an almost derisive coda to the announcement:

The nature of the work must not be misunderstood. It will not be a mere collection of shreds and patches, but a series of Shakespearian treatises, compiled with great labour, dispersedly arranged, so that, should the work arrive at an early termination, it will still be a perfect book in the sense in which book-buyers use that expression. And so large a support will be required to meet the expenses, perhaps I may be excused indulging the hope that its character of a quaint picture-book (including much which will be illustrative of ancient art) will recommend it to the favour of many who take no special interest in abstruse researches, and even obtain for it a place on the drawing-room table (pp. 68-9).

Motivating all is, to be sure, Halliwell's love of Shakespeare and archaeological research, and it would not be improper to add his fascination with business ventures. Deeper perhaps, and animating all, is his attempt, ever increasing as he grew older, to capture and preserve the past in English literature and life. His appraisal of the sketches and engravings he has collected, "unrivalled in extent and interest," is not literary or artistic but reflective if not almost spiritual:

The value of the sketches, both the old and the modern ones, is immensely enhanced by the alterations so rapidly progressing in Stratford and the neighbourhood. Even during the last year or two, several objects of interest sketched by Mr. Blight have either disappeared, or lost their ancient characteristic features. One cannot mention without emotions of deep regret what was until lately the most charming of the environs of Stratford, the mill-bridge and the weir-brake, a locality traditionally associated with Shakespeare, and one with which he must have been familiar. All the picturesque character of this spot is now for ever ruined by the advent of one of those noxious railways which are destroying the scenery of England, obliterating its rural character, substituting the hideous noise of a screaming whistle for the harmony of birds, and gradually even exiling quiet thoughts. We are passing now into a new order of things, and I have been only just in time to preserve a glimpse of that England which Shakespeare loved (p. 63).

The *Illustrations* did not appear until 1874, despite the imposing initial list of subscribers and Halliwell's undeniable desire. And when the first volume did appear, it was also to be the last. Although lack of funding was a major reason for the delay and the discontinuance, as Halliwell admitted to John Henry Ellis, one of his subscribers (28 April 1870; Folger Y.c.1218), there are others—especially the personal ones—which must be seen in their proper context. For the moment it may be sufficient to observe that whereas Halliwell published twelve separate works in 1866 and thirteen in 1867 (not including the quarto facsimiles), there was a sudden drop in the following ten years: there were no major works, a few very brief reviews, three facsimiles without any apparatus and one without his name, and such-like. In 1869, 1873, 1877, and 1878 there seem, startlingly enough, to have been no publications at all.

Although Halliwell's announcement was welcomed in most quarters, there were others who were suspicious and critical. As always, Halliwell sought publicity, and it was his custom to send his prospectuses to journals and newspapers throughout the country and to collect and mount cuttings. Responses to the *Illustrations* in early 1866 (in H-P Coll 303 in his bequest to the University of Edinburgh), such as those from the *Northampton Mercury*, the *Manchester Examiner*, and the *Birmingham Journal*, were generally cordial and supportive. But the response of the *Reader* (17 February 1866, pp. 179-80) was skeptical at best, its very opening as much a blast against much Shakespeare scholarship as against Halliwell and his project: "Mr. Halliwell announces another Life of Shakespeare. Is he likely to give us any new fact? We are afraid not." Halliwell's 1848 *Life of William Shakespeare* is praised as "one of the best we have," but the prospect of overloading, of opening the floodgates of information which adds little or nothing to what is, or can be, known about the life of Shakespeare can only cause "misgivings." It is obvious that not only are profuse and irrelevant illustrations being attacked but what is also being challenged is the rationale of scholarship that does not terminate with a clear and present result, that does not (so the reviewer) "really wind up Shakespeare's life." This controversy regarding proper scholarship is at one end of the scale. At the other is the upheaval in the personal life of Halliwell caused by the death in 1872 of his father-in-law, Thomas Phillipps, and the tragic accident which befell his beloved wife Henrietta in the same year, as well as his own diminishing powers.

Halliwell refers to "circumstances [that] enforced almost exclusive attention to other matters" in the prefatory note to *A Fragment of Mr. J. O. Halliwell's Illustrations of "The Life of Shakespeare,"* which he issued in 1874 "For Presents Only" (adding a handwritten "Fifty Copies Only"). His purpose was to revive the project by announcing that the book was "at last" in the press (but not failing to acknowledge that "so many interruptions retard its progress that the appearance of the First Part will still perhaps be delayed for a considerable time"); to placate friends and supporters (smilingly hoping "this step will, at all events, relieve the solicitude of my friend, Mr. Furnivall, who is in an alarming state of disquietude lest I should be removed from the scene before the papers are given to the world"); and to celebrate through advanced publication of pages 86-91 of the appendix, "A Collection of Papers relating to Shares and Sharers in the Globe and Blackfriars' Theatres," which he had found in 1870 among the miscellaneous records in the Lord Chamberlain's Office and had communicated in a letter to the *Athenaeum* of 13 August 1870 (p. 212).

Despite Halliwell's apprehension the whole volume was published some months later—the preface dated September 1874, whereas the "Note" in the *Fragment* was dated February 1874—by Longmans, Green & Co, whom Halliwell asked to undertake the publication on commission since (as he wrote them) they "would of course never dream of taking the risk of a work which cannot possibly pay its expenses (14 September 1874; LOA 234:9). The printer was J. E. Adlard and, as promised, the volume was stately in size (36 x 24 cm.), generous in typography (on handmade paper which cost Halliwell "close on £5 a ream"), and impressive in pictorial matter. Described by one prospective buyer as an "oblong quarto," the volume was priced at £2.2.0 (16 December 1874; LOA 110:31). The full title differs slightly but not insignificantly from that announced some seven years earlier: "Illustrations of the Life and Writings of William Shakespeare" becomes *Illustrations of the Life of Shakespeare in a Series of Discursive Essays on a Variety of Subjects Connected with*

the Personal and Literary History of the Great Dramatist. It signals the
confession stated at the opening of the second paragraph of the preface:
"In the absence of some very important discovery the general and intense
desire to penetrate the mystery which surrounds the personal history of
Shakespeare cannot be wholly gratified" (v). And it foreshadows the only
valid approach, the modest admission in the sentence following:
"Something, however, may be accomplished in that direction by a diligent
and critical study of the materials now accessible, especially if care be
taken to avoid the temptation of endeavouring to decipher his inner life
and character through the media of his works." The reference is to the
critical dispute with Furnivall and the work of the German critic Georg
Gottfried Gervinus, who had used verse-tests to divide Shakespeare's
works into three "psychological" periods.[211] Halliwell countered by
providing documents to underline his thesis that although "those works
in which the perfection of art was attained may have been the fruits of
express or cherished literary design, but all his [Shakespeare's] writings
were the products of an intellect which was applied to authorship as the
readiest path to material advancement" (vi). Therefore, he felt, to know
the history of the contemporary stage, the theatrical scene and the
circumstances of production, to know literary styles and the conditions of
authorship, is to approach knowing the author. Asking Ingleby whether
there were any sixteenth-century court rolls containing a reference to the
Tarltons in Ilford, he exclaimed: "*My life is waning, & no day ought now to be
spent without making an effort to find out something about the old actors & the stage*"
(29 May 1873; Folger C.a.23[27]).[212] Documentation is superior, in short,

211. See, for example, pp. 498-502.
212. Halliwell was proud of a poem (LOA 233:65) "written by my daughter
Ellen, when she was very young [she was thirteen], for me to remember the
actors's names by":

Shakespearean Actors

The actors we must now begin,
The letter A, the first is *Armin*;
Then on to B, the second stage
Bonfield, Bryan, and also *Burbage;*
Then the C's we next must tell,
Cooke, Cowley, Crosse, and *Condell;*
E has only one alone,
And that is the actor *Ecclestone;*
E to the letter F doth yield,
There is but one and that is *Field.*

to criticism used to establish the chronological order of his works or, put another way, to "conjectural generic ethical designs" used to establish an author's inner life and character. Only a "critical investigation into the truth or purport of every recorded incident in the personal and literary history of Shakespeare" and "notions of his surroundings" can "bring us nearer to a knowledge of Shakespeare's personality." And at the same time Halliwell was challenging another contemporary proposition. In an extract from a letter to his friend William Elwell (significant because he chose to make it for his collection), he asked for an opinion, for "two or three lines on this point":

The favorite theory of modern philosophical writers on Shakespeare is that there is what they call a moral unity in each play–that is to say, that all the several actions in each play point to & terminate in one moral idea or lesson. Now I am saying in the first volume of my new work that not

Of the letter G there are enough,
Gabriel, Gilburne & Mr *Goughe*;
Then the H's let us see,
They are *Harvey, Heminges, Humphrey*;
There are two K's for us to tell
And their names are *Kemp* & *Knell*.
There is a solitary Letter L.
That is *Lowin* who acted well;
Now to the end we are getting near,
The letter O and that is *Ostler*;
More than one P. Let us hope,
There are two, *Phillips* and *Pope*;
The letter R there is still,
Rice, Robinson and *Rossil*;
The letter S is not alone,
Shank, Sinklow, Sly, & *Swanston*.
We to the letter T have come truly
Tarlton, Tawyer, Taylor, Tooley.
Now I'm glad to say we've done
With actors *Underwood* & *Wilson*.
                    Ellen Molyneux Halliwell
                       Nov. 30th 1871.

Halliwell printed the poem on pp. 26-7 of his *Memoranda, Intended for the Use of Amateurs, Who Are Sufficiently Interested in the Pursuit, to Make Searches in the Public Record Office* (1884).

only had Shakespeare no such settled design to trammel him, but that if he really did work with any such design he would not be the Poet of Nature–not be true to Nature–for we do not find in actual life as a rule that a cycle of incidents evolving from a number of persons are contrived to establish one moral lesson (26 September 1874; LOA 214:25).

Written in what Halliwell described to Longmans as "a sober language without the usual Shaksperian rant," the discursive essays, a number of which were also published separately, treat such topics as "The Two Gentlemen of Verona," which is concerned with sources; "The Old English Religious Drama," dealing with the "quaint pageants" Shakespeare may have witnessed; "Unconnected Shakespeares," on the spelling of the name (a favorite topic of Halliwell's); "Shakespeare's Mulberry-Tree"; "The New Place"; and "Shakespeare's Manuscripts," on the possibility that manuscripts may still be in existence. These brief pieces are followed by an appendix (pp. 81-127) consisting of transcriptions of thirty-one documents which support the assertions made in the essays. They range from: No. I. Contract between Henslowe and Allen, on the one Part, and Peter Street, Carpenter, on the other Part, for the Erection by the latter of the Fortune Theatre near Golden Lane, January 8th, 1599-1600; to No. V. Patent under the Great Seal licensing Fletcher, Shakespeare, and others, to perform Comedies, &c. 19 May, 1603; to No. IX. A Collection of Papers relating to Shares and Sharers in the Globe and Blackfriars' Theatres, 1635; to No. XVI. An Order of the Lords of the Privy Council "for the Restrainte of the imoderate Use and Companye of Playehouses and Players," June 22nd, 1600; to No. XXIX. Will of John Davenant, of Oxford, Vintner, Proved on October 21st, 1622; to No. XXXI. Bill of Complaint brought by John Shakespeare, the Poet's Father, against Lambert in the Court of Queen's Bench, 1589, respecting an Estate at Wilmecote near Stratford-on-Avon. A similar cross-section of topics is evident in the list (p. 128) of sixteen engravings inserted in the text, including No. 1. The Remains of New Place, No. 2. Norden's Survey of London, 1593, No. 6. Facsimile of an Entry of Payment to Shakespeare and others for acting in two Plays before the Queen in 1594, No. 7. Greenwich Palace in the Time of Shakespeare, No. 9. Part of the County of Warwick from a Map published in 1603, No. 13. Piece of Brick Vaulting discovered at New Place, No. 14. Signature of William Bott, and No. 16. Entry of a Payment to Shakespeare for a Load of Stone, 1598.

The reception of the work in the *Athenaeum* is a measure of the seriousness with which it was taken. The review of 12 December 1874 is long (pp. 797-9) and sympathetic. Halliwell's critical stance is outlined and set against that of contemporary German criticism. The essays are patiently analyzed, and the conclusion is not entirely surprising–despite Halliwell's apologetic description to the editor, Hepworth Dixon (15 July 1875; Folger Y.c.1213[78]): "I fear you will find it too matter of fact to suit you. I am not up to the flowery & imaginative":

The industry and erudition displayed in this work are not less remarkable than the clearness with which it is conveyed. A life's labour is implied in the citation of authorities. The work is, indeed, a high result of scholarship, and, when finished, will appear something like a national vindication (p. 799).

The work was not finished, however. It is even doubtful whether its ever-expanding successor, *Outlines of the Life of Shakespeare*, which grew from a first edition of 192 pages in 1881 to a seventh edition of 848 pages in 1887, would have been finished if not interrupted by Halliwell's death in early 1889. For Halliwell had warned in 1867 that he was producing a "series ... dispersedly arranged," each part complete in itself, as it were. This description, formalized in the new title, *Illustrations*, indicates that in 1874 at least Halliwell had not yet come to the end of his researches and, more importantly, could not possibly come to a fixed assessment of them and, for that matter, to a fully realized portrait of Shakespeare. As late as 28 November 1874 (LOA 235:1)–i.e. after the publication of Part One–Halliwell explained to Longmans: "it is impossible for me to state the nos. of Parts my *Illusns* of the Life of Shakespeare may consist of ... My collections are so large in extent, the probability is that the work wch *is* a pet hobby will continue to appear at intervals for several years to come." Yet a few weeks later, on 20 December 1874 (LOA 110:31*), he replied to Edward Adamson, a subscriber to the folio edition:

My original plan was to issue a *subscription book* uniform with my Folio Edn. of Shakespeare, but fortified by change of circumstances I determined never to be again troubled with printing a work by subsn. The one now published by Messrs Longmans is not quite uniform with that work, but no other will appear.

Outlines does not convey the sense of an ending, but rather one of an ultimate aim not fully achievable. A portent of that is discernible in the concluding paragraph of the preface of the *Illustrations*:

It only remains to add that no chronological or other specific order has been attempted in the following pages. The arrangement of the various essays is the fortuitous result of my own convenience or humour, the compilation of this work being in fact merely one of the amusements of the declining years of life. It is followed, as all recreations should be, earnestly and lovingly, but in complete subjection to the vicissitudes of one's own temperament and inclination (viii).

And a more solemn note was struck in Halliwell's regretting to Longmans (28 November 1874; LOA 235:1) that he could not be more explicit in fixing the number of parts: "so much depends on one's health & temperament, & not being a young man I am most anxious not to pledge myself in any way in the slightest degree in the matter." With Hepworth Dixon the tone was heavier: "When the 2nd [Part] will appear I know not. In fact I am getting wearied of literary work & have scarcely touched a book for the last 6 months" (27 June 1875; Folger Y.c.1213[77]). On 25 October 1876 (LOA 238:63) he asked Longmans to withdraw the book from circulation. "Although a good bit of the second Part ... is printed," he explained, "I regret to say that owing to more than one circumstance, but chiefly to a diminishing power for mental labour, I find it imperative on me to discontinue the work." And it is not without some impatience and perhaps frustration that he informed his friend C. M. Ingleby: "Let me assure you that I am not the man to fool my friends by telling them that I mean to give up literary pursuits when I do not. You will never see the 2nd Part of the Illustrations. Although a large portion of it was printed I have had the types broken up" (3 November 1876; Folger C.a.11[6]).[213]

The pressing circumstances he had mentioned and his almost oppressive sense of aging had an effect on the work he produced. To a great extent all his publications, like his interests, were "discursive," although they revolved, at differing distances and speeds, about the central theme of Shakespeare and early English literature. From the beginning of his career Halliwell was always aware of the value of public communication and discussion. He realized the importance of puffs and of reviews, not infrequently writing notices of his own works (albeit anonymously, according to the style of the times); and he was, of course, constantly issuing prospectuses of his projects and advertising his book

213. Halliwell went so far as to print a form letter (allowing him to fill in the day, month, and, after a printed "187," the exact year) with the following text: "As I am relinquishing my Literary and Collecting pursuits, it is but fair to you to mention the circumstance, in order that you may be spared the expense and trouble of sending me your Catalogues. With many thanks for them up to this time ..."

needs. This activity did not diminish as he grew older, became more well known, and had more to do than he could possibly manage. On the contrary, his discoveries impelled him to make them known; his position seemed to require him to take a stand. Between 1841 and 1888 he wrote some twenty-eight letters to the editor of the *Times* on topics ranging from the Corn Laws (13 August 1841, p. 5) to the charnel house of the Stratford church and Shakespeare's grave (30 January 1888, p. 12). Between 1842 and 1878 he wrote some twenty-four signed articles and letters to the *Athenaeum* on a range of Shakespearean and related topics, as well as on his controversy with the British Museum. Between 1849 and 1888 he contributed some seventy-two items on Shakespearean and early English literature to *Notes and Queries*. These are but the most prominent of Halliwell's countless efforts to assert himself in the public arena. And if, as in the case of the anonymous reviews, his name did not appear, his point of view was unmistakable. Among abundant examples are those in the *Athenaeum*, for which Halliwell began to write reviews and submit "gossip" material in the 1860s, much of it solicited by Hepworth Dixon, the editor and fellow secretary of the Shakespeare Tercentenary Committee. In a longish review of S. W. Fullom's *History of William Shakespeare, Player and Poet, with New Facts and Traditions* (25 January 1862, pp. 113-15) Halliwell defended reasonable and credible research: "Literary inquirers with moderate expectations, investigating the history of obscure people of the sixteenth century, are satisfied if they can find once in a way, and after much research, an authentic record respecting them. Mr. Fullom soars far away beyond these humble investigators" (p. 114). In a harshly brief review of Samuel Bailey's *On the Received Text of Shakespeare's Writings and its Improvement* (22 March 1862, p. 394), Halliwell inflected his habitual skepticism of conjectural emendation: "It may be safely laid down as a general rule, that no one is as bad a judge of the value of a conjectural emendation of a presumed error in the text of Shakespeare as the originator of the alteration ... If Mr. Bailey had but reflected upon the possibility of being himself classed with these unfortunates, this volume would perhaps never have been published." Halliwell could be diplomatic as well, describing J. C. M. Bellew's *Shakespeare's Home at New Place* (21 March 1863, pp. 393-4) as a "collection of discursive observations on various facts and traditions respecting Shakespeare, and on families residing within, or in the neighbourhood of the poet's native town," when he himself was at work on his own *Historical Account of the New Place* (1864) and was about to launch his *Illustrations*, itself a *Series of Discursive Essays on a Variety of Subjects*. "We are far from saying that the results of this kind of discursive research may not turn out in one way or other to be useful to a future biographer," Halliwell grants, but the professional in him continues, "but they appear to us to be chiefly materials which might fairly be collected for reference by an earnest man who intended to compile a life of the poet–hardly those which should fill a volume which, according to its title page, is a History of New Place." If convinced, Halliwell could be forthright and enthusiastic. Although aware of its limitations–such as the "inevitable necessity" of "quoting conjectural readings of acknowledged inutility" or attributing some authority to the three later folios (p. 416)–Halliwell, in reviewing the first volume of the Cambridge edition (14 November 1863, pp. 640-2), does not hesitate to say that "it is likely to be, when completed, the most useful one to the scholar and the intelligent reader which has yet appeared." And he is able, along the way and among other things, to outline the problems which face editors–"How the poor editor of two or three centuries hence, when the number of editions deserving consultation will amount, at the least, to three or four thousand, may be able to manage, is a question the consideration of which may happily be postponed"–and to pay tribute to his much-maligned idol, Edward Capell, "whose conjectures are not very happy ones, but whose volumes of 'Notes' have never received the high degree of praise they so well deserve .... [being] by far the most important contribution to Shakespearian literature that appeared in the eighteenth century, although its merits are unfortunately obscured by the manner in which it was written–the 'monstrous gabble,' as Johnson was pleased to call it." Ever open to the curious and rare when solidly researched, Halliwell praised William Kelly's *Notices Illustrative of the Drama ... Extracted from the Chamberlains' Accounts and Other Manuscripts of the Borough of Leicester* (22 July 1865, pp. 110-11) as "one of sterling value, containing a variety of out-of-the-way information not readily met with elsewhere." And considering his conflict with the German scholarship associated with Furnivall and Gervinus, he was open-minded enough to appreciate Albert Cohn's *Shakespeare in Germany in the Sixteenth and Seventeenth Centuries* (25 March 1865, pp. 416-17) as "one of the most interesting and valuable contributions to Shakespearean literature which have ever reached us from Germany" and to encourage the "accomplished author to further efforts in the same direction." Not to be overlooked are Halliwell's even-handedness and generosity, evident in his brief notice of *The Sonnets of Shakespeare Solved* (26 March 1870, p. 420) by Henry Brown, with whom he had patiently corresponded for many years and whose work he had helped publish, he himself paying for the printing of the prospectus and not receiving any mention in the Preliminary Remarks or the Preface:

A story is told of a Yorkshire farmer who, considering one book as good as another for winter reading, brought for this purpose a copy of the old folio edition of Johnson's Dictionary. By the time he arrived at the letter 'h,' he remarked that he could neither make out the plot, nor exactly understand what the author was driving at. We are in a somewhat like predicament after a perusal of Mr. Brown's work on the Sonnets of Shakespeare; but although we cannot say that the great mystery is solved, it is undeniable that the book is written with good feeling, and is evidently the result of much thought and study. It is the first publication also of a self-taught working man, and adverse criticism would be out of place even if deserved. If Mr. Brown has failed in his main object, it must be remembered that other writers of acknowledged eminence have been equally unsuccessful (2 June 1868; LOA 140:23).

Among the other "satellites," works revolving about the central theme, in the period from 1866 to 1878, were those dealing with early English popular literature: *The Booke of Merry Riddles, Together with Proper Questions, and Witty Proverbs, to Make Pleasant Pastime. Now First Reprinted from the Unique Edition Printed at London in the Year 1660* (1866), consisting of seventy-six riddles and solutions preceded by a three-sentence note by Halliwell; *A Collection of Seventy-Nine Black-Letter Ballads and Broadsides, Printed in the Reign of Queen Elizabeth between the Years 1559 and 1597* (1867), on which Halliwell commented, "I did all the notes. Tom Wright all the Introduction";[214] and *Greene's Groats-Worth of Wit, Bought with a Million of Repentaunce* (1870), a simple reprint of the edition of 1596 with no editorial

---

214. So Halliwell's handwritten note on the back of a postcard to Ernest. E. Baker inserted in the Folger copy. Wright provided a twenty-five page introduction, Halliwell added almost fifty pages of notes to the project which was prefaced by the publisher Joseph Lilly. Originally, Halliwell agreed to edit the ballads in the collection of Henry Huth, but did not wish his name to appear. Although Huth did "fancy it will be generally known that you are the Editor ... As far as I am concerned you may be quite sure that any attack on the book will have no effect, but I can understand that it will be disagreeable to you" (7 April 1866; LOA 113:20). Halliwell did finally withdraw as editor (29 March 1867; LOA 123:23), but only after he had put considerable effort into the project, advancing £65.19.0 for woodcuts and transcripts (19 August 1866; LOA 115:13), seeking a "sanction" from Huth for each sheet (22 October 1866; LOA 122:22), and recommending Wright for the introduction (10 May 1867; LOA 121:20)–in short, withdrawing only after the work was practically ready for publication.

information or apparatus.[215] Those works dealing with theater history, another of the "satellites," include two from the Chiswick Press printed for Halliwell in ten copies each: *Papers Respecting Disputes Which Arose from Incidents at the Death-bed of Richard Tarlton. the Actor. in the Year 1588* (1866), a reprint without notes, but with a very brief preface; *Notices of Players Acting at Ludlow*, in twelve pages of 15 cm. without any apparatus at all; *A Collection of Ancient Documents Respecting the Office of Master of the Revels, and Other Papers Relating to the Early English Theatre* (1870), reprinting manuscripts in Latin and English formerly in the Haslewood collection but without Halliwell's name except for his customary numbering of the copy; and, in addition to his mention and reprint of the document on the establishment of the Globe and Blackfriars theaters already referred to,[216] *A Curious Paper, of the Time of Queen Elizabeth, Respecting the Office of the Revels* (1872), no more than a simple print transcription from the Lansdowne manuscript in the British Museum.[217] Not to be overlooked is Halliwell's arrangement of the publication of A. H. Paget's *Shakespeare's Plays: A Chapter of Stage History. An Essay on the Shakespearean Drama* (1875): he paid for the printing of 250 copies and for 500 extra copies to be given to the members of the New Shakspere Society "which would make the book known" (13 April 1875; LOA 74:12). Finally, Halliwell's continuing involvement with the British Archaeological Association—he was elected to the Council in 1868 and vice president in 1876—is evident in three short pieces which appeared in the *Journal* in connection with their meetings in those places named and whose very titles testify as further "satellites" to his interdisciplinary approach: "A Few Notes on the Collection of Early

215. Earlier, Henry Huth had urged Halliwell not to bid against him for the work, assuring him that he could borrow it for as long as he liked (3 April 1869; LOA 163:32). The work has another interesting aspect. In a handwritten draft of a prospectus (dated January 1871) inserted in Folger copy PR2544.G7.1870 As. Col. Copy 2, Halliwell, "unable to spare the time necessary for attending to an ordinary subscription list," proposed "to issue some curious works illustrative of the Life of Shakespeare & the History of the early English Stage amongst *ten* subscribers, each subscriber paying his share (one tenth) of the expences. There is now ready,—*Greene's Groatsworth of Witte* ... produced at a cost of £14-15-0, the expence, therefore, of each copy being £1-9-6 ... To prevent any misapprehension, it may be well to state that I shall of course pay my share for my own copy, & charge nothing for my services when they are required. As a rule, however, the texts will be transcribed & collated by professional copyists."

216. See p. 367.

217. Halliwell identifies it as No. 83, which is not now to be found there in the Lansdowne catalogue.

Editions of Shakespeare in the Library of the Earl of Verulam" (1870), pointing out the most valuable quarto in the Gorhambury collection, an 1608 *King Lear*, which, chiefly formed from corrected sheets, exemplifies the way "corrected and uncorrected sheets were bound up indiscriminately"; "On the Municipal Archives of Dorset" (1872), a listing of interesting manuscripts found by Halliwell in his searches in the corporate towns of Dorset; and "Some Suggestions Respecting a History of Broadway" (1876), listing the chief sources of information for archaeological research and, to be sure, of more than passing interest to Halliwell himself because of the role it played in his own life and, so he concluded, "without ... risking the imputation of indulging in a merely fanciful theory, we may venture to add Broadway to the list of those favoured localities which in all probability were familiar to the great dramatist."

As the years passed, the literary "satellites" at least tended to be briefer and less ambitious perhaps. Later, a good many pieces were provoked by controversies in which, judging from the tone, the personal seemed to outweigh the professional, ego more at stake than enterprise. And an increasing number were concerned with what may be called stocktaking, inventories of Halliwell's collections, much a characteristic of his aging as of his profession.

16

Stratford-upon-Avon
Works, Work, and Worries

Even after the Shakespeare Tercentenary celebration or, more accurately, especially after it, Stratford continued to be at the center of Halliwell's professional life, the focal point of both his Shakespeare scholarship and the living monument of the "great dramatist." As Blight wrote to him, "Stratford without you would not be Stratford. It would be like a green field without a daisy" (25 October 1868; LOA 137:8). There was much to be done: records to be investigated and results to be published, the Shakespeare properties to be expanded and consolidated. The former was relatively straightforward: Halliwell was essentially his own man in deciding what to investigate and publish. The latter was more complicated: Halliwell was but one voice among many in a town of which he, neither native nor resident, was not exempt from the intrigues of cliques and the ambitions of individuals.

The works associated more or less directly with Stratford in the period 1866 to 1878 are relatively few: four in 1866, five in 1867, one each in 1868, 1870, and 1872. This distribution, showing a heavy concentration in the early years, is similar to that in the other areas of his scholarly production and is likely connected with the two climactic events of 1872, the death of Sir Thomas Phillipps and the tragic accident which befell Mrs. Halliwell. All but one of the publications are simple transcriptions of records concerning Stratford; although described as "edited" by Halliwell, they normally contain no editorial apparatus beyond an occasional short "Note" or brief preface and were generally privately "printed for the editor" by Halliwell's favored Whittingham and Wilkins (the Chiswick Press) and limited to ten copies only (in some cases fifteen copies destroyed). Interestingly enough, seven of the twelve do not bear Halliwell's name on the title page but are undeniably his work. If the subject-matter were not enough, then the format and the printer are certainly his hallmarks. That would be the case, for example, with *A Descriptive Account of a Series of Churchwardens' Presentments, Etc. Appertaining to the Parish of Stratford-on-Avon* (1867), with a preface by Clarence Hopper, but whose make-up, printer, subject-matter, and handwritten "Ten Copies Only. Number Four. J.O.H." (in the British Library copy) suggest Halliwell's strong participation. Likewise, in addition to these criteria, Halliwell is present in an appended short note to *An Extract from the Unpublished Diary of the Late Joseph Hunter, F.S.A. Containing an Account of a Visit Made to Stratford-on-Avon in the Year 1824* (1867), or, as in *Selected Extracts from the Ancient Registry of the Causes Tried in the Court of Record at Stratford-upon-Avon in the Time of Shakespeare* (1867), as well as in his handwritten "Edited by J. O. Halliwell," or, as in *The Probate Copy of the Will of Shakespeare Now First Printed from a Manuscript Copy of It Made by the Rev. Joseph Greene ... in the Year 1747* (1872) by his handwritten inscription of copy No. 9 presented to the British Museum.

These reprints of records and documents were more pamphlets than anything else, ranging from as few as three leaves to about sixty pages. They are, of course, contributions not merely to the history and topography of Stratford but also to Halliwell's larger plan of "Illustrations." Mainly extracts, they are not meant to stand by themselves, and some were incorporated into the greater work. The one Stratford publication in this period which was meant to be independent and was somewhat different in orientation from the others was *A Catalogue of the Books, Manuscripts, Works of Art, Antiquities, and Relics, Illustrative of the Life and Works of Shakespeare, and of the History of Stratford-upon-Avon; Which Are Preserved in the Shakespeare Library and Museum in Henley Street* (1868). As the title indicates, it is not so much concerned with "ancient records" as with a contemporary institution. The title page does not give an author. Although the compilation was ascribed by Halliwell to Clarence Hopper, there is good reason to believe with the bibliographers Justin Winsor and William Jaggard that the main hand is Halliwell's: the nature of the contents points to him, as does the role he had undertaken in their acquisition and cataloguing, as well as the fact that the volume was printed by one of Halliwell's favorites, J. E. Adlard, for the Shakespeare Fund, of which Halliwell was honorary secretary. And, to be sure, Halliwell is the author of the prefaces to both the book itself and doubtless the concluding portion on the Shakespeare Fund. The volume is three times longer than any of the other publications and is of more interest as a chronicle of the times and a history of the establishment of the library and museum in Henley Street, the center of the attempt to preserve and propagate the legacy of Shakespeare.

The work is framed by the Shakespeare Fund. The preface lists seven objectives at its inception in October 1861 and remarks that three of the most important of them have been "nearly completed," among them the formation of the "valuable" library and museum. At the other end of the volume, pp. 173-83, devoted to the Shakespeare Fund, are a brief preface outlining the progress made since 1861 and its "main designs at present [which] are to complete the work commenced at New Place and to increase the efficiency of the Library and Museum," followed by a financial statement of money collected (£4188) and expended (£4073.6.5) and the "comparatively small amount (£2000) at present urgently required." The subscribers are listed and the amount subscribed, including also, and separately, those in Paddington, Wrington, Stratford, and Birmingham. The body of the catalogue is not so much a classification as an arrangement according to major contributors or groups thereof (items 1-1076), purchases (items 1077-1132), the New Place (items 1133-1148), and (most likely the work of Halliwell) a chronological index of the printed books, tracts broadsides, etc. from 1556 to 1868 (pp. 165-71). The main individual contributors are Anne Wheler on behalf of her brother, Robert Bell Wheler, who had died in 1857 after a lifetime devoted to the history of his birthplace, Stratford (items 1-286), W. O. Hunt (items 305-397), and Halliwell (items 507-953), as well as a group of various donors accounting for items 954-1076. Valuable for local history is the collection of transcripts and drawings of Captain James Saunders (items 464-506). Wheler's collection is perhaps the most important, especially his autograph manuscripts, such as the "Collectaneas de Stratford," 536 quarto pages of minutely written transcripts. Halliwell's contributions, by far the largest in number, consist almost entirely of printed works of the eighteenth and nineteenth centuries: plays by or adapted from Shakespeare make up the largest group, some works connected with theater history, such of his quarto facsimiles as had reached publication, a few translations, a number of Halliwell's articles, reprints, and editions, a few multi-volume editions of Shakespeare (Theobald's seven-volume of 1733, Rann's six-volume of 1786), and assorted miscellanea, including playbills, autographs, letters, and such-like. Of interest is the last item (No. 953) Halliwell contributed: a large oil painting of Windsor and the Castle, showing the street where Falstaff is said to have been carried down in the buck-basket. Only one of the many "works of art, antiquities, and relics" Halliwell was to bequeath, it serves to indicate the full extent of the collection, which included two large stones from the ruins of New Place, when the building was demolished by the Reverend F. Gastrell (No. 395), the base of the pedestal of the Old Market Cross, which stood at the top of High Street (No. 396), a thin slip of wood from the tree in Windsor Park ... considered to have been the original Herne's Oak (No. 954), the mulberry-tree in the Great Garden (No. 1133), an ancient shovel-board from the Falcon Tavern opposite New Place (No. 1134), an engraving from the Felton portrait of Shakespeare (No. 1138), a photograph of Stratford Church, showing the Chancel (No. 1140), to name but a few. The books Halliwell presented are not impressive, nor are they particularly valuable. Only one, a second edition of 1575 of Ovid's *Metamorphoses* in the translation of Arthur Golding, is contemporary with Shakespeare but is only peripherally of literary relevance and financial interest. Still, together all do exemplify the environment, as it were, of Shakespeare studies, and they do make a statement about Halliwell's activities as bookman and collector and about his library. Furthermore they demonstrate his generosity and engagement.

That engagement was total, and was in evidence not merely in his frequent working visits to Stratford, where his name (so John Pickford on his return from Stratford) "is as familiar as a household word" (4 July 1870; LOA 158:40), but also in the objectives, obligations, and obstacles which are contained in Halliwell's voluminous correspondence with W. O. Hunt and, later, his successors—and which answer Thomas Wright's sarcastic query and appraisal: "Have you got a sweetheart at Stratford? that you make so much noise about it. If not, what *is* the use of the place? ... Stratford is a small town with a little over three thousand, and not a mountain or a rock within sight, and a churchyard that is too watery to be buried in. So dont say any more about it" (15 October 1867; LOA 129:8).

Halliwell did. He was very clear about what he wanted to achieve in Stratford. For one thing, there was the transfer of the New Place estate, which he had purchased in 1861, to the Corporation of Stratford. For more than a dozen years, however, the Corporation declined to accept the responsibility and expense of maintaining the property, leaving Halliwell with the proper care and management of the museum and gardens and their use by the public. On 31 March 1875 (LOA 230:73), aware that he could do so only as long as he had "health & strength" and, as always, aware that "in the event of my decease inconvenient legal complications might arise not only in regard to their future management but even in respect to the question of tenure," Halliwell prepared a circular proposing the only "safe course to be pursued in the matter, namely, to transfer the legal estate to the Corporation vesting its management in the hands of the Trustees of the Birth Place who would then have the control of two properties of an exactly analogous character."[218] He sent copies to twelve

218. "The Trustees," Halliwell added, "consist of the Lord Lieutenant of the County of Warwick, the High Steward, the Mayor & Aldermen & Town Clerk of

"generous subscriber[s]" to the New Place Fund, among them Cosens, Huth, Lady Burdett-Coutts, Lord Overstone, and Lord Northampton—all of whom had from the beginning contributed at least £100 and in most cases more—and to Collier, obviously counting not on his money but on his influence as Trustee (LOA 230:74).[219] A year later, after some further deliberation, Halliwell finally received the engrossment of the conveyance and the deed for his signature (7 April 1876; LOA 225:35). He returned the necessary documents to Robert Hobbes, and the matter was at last resolved. On 13 January 1877 (LOA 240:63) he informed Hobbes that it was a "relief" to him "to hear that the New Place Conveyance Deed had been enrolled in Chancery for the requisite six months, so I presume that now there are not likely to be any legal complications respecting the estate in the event of my decease."

But that was only one of Halliwell's main concerns. Reflecting objectives mentioned in various publications, Halliwell listed in 1872 (18 February 1872; LOA 196:24) five, feeling "that it cannot be many years before, if life be spared, I should be able to accomplish the following objects at Stratford-on-Avon":

1. Purchase the Theatre
2. Refront Nash's house
3. Restore the Guild Chapel
4. Re-ancient the front of the grammar School
5. Buy Anne Hathaway's Cottage.

His "heart ... long ... set on the removal of that unsightly obstruction, the Theatre," W. O. Hunt responded immediately to Halliwell's acting "wisely" in making it the "first and principal object of [his] desire to accomplish" (20 February 1872; LOA 187:9). Although the property had been offered to Halliwell for £1100 years earlier,[220] Hunt believed it could be had for much less and asked for authority to purchase as many shares

Stratford-on-Avon, the Vicar & Head Master of the Grammar School of the same Town, & a few others who are elected."

219. A letter with much the same text, dated 27 February 1875 and addressed to J. J. Nason, the mayor of Stratford, was printed in a newspaper and followed by a statement that, "as the present offer did not entail any expenditure on the part of the Corporation, it was advisable that they should become possessed of the property. (Hear, hear.)."

220. Hunt says in 1842, which (if correct) would mean that Halliwell was already involved at age twenty-two. It is not unlikely that Hunt meant 1862, although William Thompson mentions 1864 (11 April 1873; LOA 117:14).

at a reasonable rate as he could for Halliwell. However, Halliwell immediately and forcefully rejected this approach: "I would not touch a share even with the longest pitchfork, & as for becoming a shareholder in the Stratford Theatre, with all the liabilities, even if Shakespeare & Sir Thomas Phillipps were both of them to come to life again their combined entreaties would fail in inducing me to enter upon so dangerous a path" (23 February 1872; LOA 188:37). Halliwell was assuredly not inclined to start another public fund-raising appeal. But just three days later he announced he was willing to purchase the Theatre and site on Chapel Street out of his own means for a "fair & reasonable sum" if all the company of shareholders concurred in the sale so that he might "obtain a good & perfect title to that property" (23 February 1872; LOA 196:21). A few days later he was "much gratified," he wrote to Hunt, "by the kind terms in which the resolution of the offer of the Theatre for £550 was framed" (4 March 1872; LOA 192:39). At a meeting of the Committee of the Theatre on 1 March 1872 (LOA 135:22) it was unanimously resolved that the property be offered for £550 at the rate of £15 per share; a sample printed response form of agreement for each shareholder was included. The sale completed,[221] work was begun immediately on tearing down the Theatre in order that the site on which it stood, adjacent to New Place and the Gardens, might be used to complete the New Place scheme harmoniously. Halliwell, he later learned, was obliged to pay for the "filling up" as well (4 June 1872; LOA 200:6).

That was not the end of the matter, however. During his mayoralty Edward Gibbs wrote on 4 December 1872 (LOA 169:26):

I entertained with others the notion of a Memorial Theatre, for which we thought the best site would be adjoining 'Shakespeare's Great Garden' extending nearly the whole length of the late Bowling Green and from thence into Sheep St ...
My idea of a Memorial Theatre.–A first class handsome building a beautiful object as seen from 'Shakespeares Great Garden', *to be approved by you*, and prepared internally & externally to receive really artistic embellishment in illustration of '*his*' Immortal Dramas both in Painting &

---

221. Learning that Halliwell had bought the Theatre, Howard Staunton congratulated him on his "spirit and liberality," suggesting smilingly that as "Lord Bountiful you might earn 'an infinite' of *kudos*, and do much to bring folks' minds back again to Shakspeare and the musical glasses, were you to offer publickly a prize, say a copy of your magnificent edition of 'The Bard,' for the best of emendation or explication of half a dozen *inscrutables* which we might pick out" (1 April 1872; LOA 134:23).

Statuary, the Stage to have every appliance for dramatic representation, the Auditorium strictly economized to contain only a sufficient audience to pay &c.

The project was not then realized. Halliwell agreed substantially, suggesting that "the Theatre itself might be tastefully & appropriately decorated, while attached to it, under the same roof, there might be a gallery of Shaksperian art, &, if practicable, a further extension of building to admit of a Free Library" (3 January 1873; LOA 212:20). However, at his "time of life, with numerous other calls on [his] time & purse," he could not join the "scheme." But in February 1875 (LOA 28:32) a Stratford committee, with Charles Flower as secretary pro tem, called for subscriptions for a Shakespeare Memorial Theatre (as a monument to replace the one Flower had for years tried to have erected in Stratford), having been presented by Flower with a two-acre piece of ground on the Bancroft on banks of the Avon, the site of Garrick's pavilion. Donors of £100 and more were to be governors and managers of the property, to elect an Executive Committee, and to frame rules for the general management of the property and fund. Halliwell received the announcement and responded swiftly and cautiously to Flower, evidently attaching great importance to his reply by noting, "Posted the letter of which this is a copy at the pillar box in Tregunter Road, 23 Feby. 1875, at 3.30 P.M. J.O.P.":

It is very gratifying to hear that there is a chance of a respectable theatre being erected at Stratford-on-Avon in the place of the ugly building in Chapel Lane which was a disgrace to the Town.
I need not say that I cordially wish you every success, although my other occupations & engagements will preclude my taking any active part in the promotion of the object. I must decline therefore being one of the Governors of the proposed theatre, but if a donation of fifty guineas[222] will not involve me any liability of any kind or constitute me a shareholder in the proposed undertaking, it will give me the greatest pleasure to subscribe that sum as soon as there appears to be a satisfactory prospect of the scheme being carried out (23 February 1875; LOA 28:32).

222. A favorite sum. Mrs. Halliwell's diary entry for 19 February 1872 records that "James has sent £50 to the Artists benevolent Society, £50 to the Dramatic Fund £50 to the Mark Lemon Fund. £50 to the Artists Orphan Society also £50 to the Drury Lane Theatrical Fund."

To Charles Roach Smith he attributed his position to age and lack of energy as well as time (31 March 1875; Folger Y.c.1281[25]). On donating the fifty guineas, he reiterated his cautious distance, writing to Charles Lowndes, "I give it on the distinct understanding that it is a voluntary subscription & will in no way bind me as a shareholder" (25 May 1875; Folger Y.c.1250). And he did not follow Hobbes's invitation to be his guest on 23 April 1877 "on the occasion of laying the first stone of the Shakespeare Memorial buildings with Masonic honors" (15 April 1877; LOA 238:33). Nor did he attend the Inaugural Festival marking the opening of the Memorial Theatre on 23 April 1879. It is not hard to imagine why. Although there may be the reasons he himself mentioned, he must have been appalled by the tastelessness of the construction. On 15 January 1879 (LOA 241:3) his daughter Katie wrote to her "darling Old Man": "You ought to have come up—if only to see the abominable erection they are pleased here to call a Theatre. I know nothing about it, of course, but it seems to me out of keeping with the river, Church & every thing else."[223] The description was likely to elicit a nodding response from Halliwell, who all along had been criticizing the rapid deterioration of Stratford. Examples are abundant. He had done so in agreeing with Hunt's "I am sorry to say that the character of the old Mill Bridge will be destroyed at a great cost between 400 & 500£—there are to be *Iron* columns at the top of the Piers" (9 July 1867; LOA 129:34). And in commenting on the removal of a sixteenth-century building in Shottery, he reiterated his unbroken lament: "I only hope they have not pulled down any of the dear old cottages. It is a pity they can't leave any place alone nowadays" (17 December 1870; LOA 174:37).

Halliwell's depressive response to the tampering was predictable. As archaeologist and literary historian, if nothing else, his lifelong desire was to preserve or re-create the "dear old cottages" and the world they

---

223. "It is difficult ... to find a word to summarise the mixture of timbered, red-brick, and baronial gewgaw which Messrs. Dodgshun and Unsworth had so triumphantly favoured," remark Ivor Brown and George Fearon (*Amazing Monument: A Short History of the Shakespeare Industry* [London, 1939], pp. 222-3). "We may perhaps put it this way: that in no decade was English Architecture further removed from the taste of to-day than it was in the eighteen-seventies. Experts as well as public opinion then liked its art, to put it vulgarly, 'with knobs on,' and the Governors of the new theatre had to accept their experts' verdict. No doubt they approved of it, too. Subsequent judgment deemed the style of the building feeble, fussy, and better suited to be the residence of a medievally-minded modern German in the Black Forest than an expression of Stratford life and a tribute to its greatest son."

represented. It explains the remaining objectives he had outlined to Hunt: to refront Nash's house, to restore the Guild Chapel, to re-ancient the front of the grammar school, and to buy Anne Hathaway's cottage. On 27 April 1872 (LOA 83:21) Hunt was already preparing the way for the refronting, producing the designs that were presented in 1863, making suggestions, and, pending Halliwell's approval, offering to have William Thompson prepare an updated design and an estimate of the cost. Halliwell was not always directly responsible for the fulfillment of the remaining objectives, but was always approached and had a say. He declined to be on the committee for the restoration of the Guild Chapel, for instance, admitting that he had no knowledge of architecture "& should be quite out of place in any meeting on the subject" (28 September 1875; LOA 189:25). He was willing to subscribe, however, and did succeed in being assured by Richard Valpy French that its Shakespearean character would "in no way" be touched (1 September 1875; LOA 189:24). The purchase of Anne Hathaway's cottage did not occur until 1892, three years after Halliwell's death, but he was intensely involved and carried on negotiations. He applied to the owner of the freehold, Alderman William Thompson, in 1864 in connection with the Shakespeare Fund and again in 1867 (11 April 1867; LOA 117:14), and was informed of the "moderate price" of £3000 (29 May 1867; LOA 117:17). And it is not uninteresting to note that among the Trustees who supported the purchase were Halliwell's close friend Frederick Haines and his nephew and executor Ernest E. Baker.

Halliwell was in the habit of giving lack of time and energy as reason for avoiding certain projects. On 30 October 1871 (LOA 186:23), for example, he offered his resignation as joint honorary secretary of the National Shakespeare Committee: although it was "in many respects an advantage as well as a pleasure ... & nothing but an imperative necessity, arising from an increasing nervous temperament, would induce me to withdraw ... the same which has compelled me to withdraw from all my long-cherished schemes at Stratford excepting the one actually accomplished."[224] This explanation was doubtless true but only partially so. For he was constantly occupied with the everyday problems of the library and museum, hardly ever shunning them. They were many and wide-ranging. On 19 December 1866 (LOA 119:32) he urged Hunt to

---

224. Typically, however, he ventured an opinion, suggesting that a "memorial erected to note the site of the Globe Theatre, would be preferable to a small statue." And, of course, he was ready to "spare no pains to ascertain the exact site of the Theatre."

prevent the "wholesale fabrication of relics," not to sell bits of the master wood of the Birthplace too cheaply and to issue written certificates. On 31 August 1867 (LOA 136:16) Hunt "quite" agreed, in another instance, that "the old Clock would be more appropriately set up in New Place than in the Museum." On Candlemas Day in 1868 (2 February 1868; LOA 132:12) Hunt reported the damage done by stormy winds to the Birthplace garden. There were questions to be answered on the purchase of the Felton Portrait of Shakespeare, on the transporting and placing of the Boydell statuary (26 May 1870; LOA 164:23), and on the best way of removing dirt from the group of Shakespeare sculptures (18 July 1870; LOA 173:2). There were regular reports on the number of visitors to Shakespeare's house and opinions to be given on the Sunday opening of the museum. And, most pressing, there was the nagging problem of fund-raising for the acquisition, management, and maintenance of the Shakespeare properties and their contents–a matter which occupies a very large portion of Halliwell's correspondence with Hunt and other Stratford officials and citizens. It is a chapter in itself, being extraordinarily complex. What can be said with certainty is that it required patience and ingenuity. In one of numerous examples of Halliwell's ingenuity (and generosity), he replied to Henry Sotheran's interest in sixty copies of *An Historical Account of the New Place* by saying he did not want money "into my own pocket" and proposing, "suppose you were to give a donation of £25 to the New Place fund at Stratford-on-Avon. In that case, I will make you a present of the sixty copies, & you would be aiding in a work of public utility & interest" (6 March 1872; LOA 208:3). A few days later (9 March 1872; LOA 206:21) he offered F. W. Cosens a 1598 quarto of *Love's Labor's Lost* in return for a contribution of a hundred guineas to the fund. Seeking to attract visitors and their purses to Stratford, he offered the vicar, George Granville, a mummy, whose "unrolling" in Stratford might produce a "fair sum of money" towards the "insertion of painted windows on the South side of the Chancel of your noble Church" (14 May 1866; LOA 112:16). Granville gladly accepted this novel idea (17 May 1866; LOA 112:49). A year later, however, he needed Halliwell's expert advice on "what shall be done" since he had come to the conclusion that "we should never realize any great sum at the prices you named for admission"; besides, he did not "think my neighbours would appreciate the privilege offered them" (14 March 1867; LOA 123:17).[225] When J. W.

225. Halliwell advised Hunt to put the "immense coffin like the mummy is contained in ... into the hall on one side without interfering with any thing or any one" until sold (15 May 1867; LOA 120:11).

Jarvis sent him a wood carving of Shakespeare's head as a present, Halliwell cleverly asked him for permission to bestow it to the New Place museum as his, Jarvis's, gift (13 April 1873; Folger Y.c.1240[10b]). In a further instance, although the "Standing Rule" of the Stratford museums was that "no portrait of any living person is to be received" (1 May 1873; Folger C.b.17[83]), he could inform Charles Roach Smith that he was able to "break the rules" at the New Place museum and place Smith's medal there (16 June 1873; Folger C.b.17[84]).

There were other skills in evidence. He arranged for readings to be given in Stratford by his friend Charles Roach Smith. And he wrote him, "For a comparatively small assistance, I would engage [Joseph Mayer] should be elected a Trustee of the Birth-Place & be next year made as much of to make up for what I consider the rather small attention paid to his munificent gifts to Liverpool" (20 September 1868; Folger W.a.81[55/1]). He was instrumental in arranging for the annual meeting of the British Archaeological Association to take place in Warwick and Stratford. He was urged by John Collis to purchase certain items for the library and museum at Robert Bell's sale (15 December 1870; LOA 174:34) and was himself always on the lookout for interesting objects, like the double pledging drinking cup he noticed in a curiosity shop and so discovered the identity of the bottom part found in the museum (17 December 1868; LOA 150:2). On 21 January 1867, Mrs. Halliwell's diary reports that their daughter Charlotte "finished a water color draw[in]g of Shakespeare's birthplace before the alterations ... It is to be her contribution to Stratford Museum." And of course his own contributions to the library and museum were steady and considerable. Impressive were not merely books, manuscripts, and objects but also the documents and records illustrating his personal engagement with Shakespeare and Stratford. As was his custom, he had ordered special bindings from J. C. Hotten (25 January 1870; Folger Y.c.1232). On 19 November 1871 (Folger C.b.17[68]) he informed Charles Roach Smith: "The study of the text is too much now for my head & I am going to give my collections & unpublished notes on Shakespeare about 140 bound vols. to Stratford on Avon." Two days later Hunt acknowledged the receipt of twenty-eight volumes of Shakespeare Fund papers for the Corporation (21 November 1871; LOA 187:19). Halliwell was proud of these possessions, which he regarded as private and personal, and well aware of where they should best find a home. "I cannot help thinking," barely disguising his affection for a further bequest, "that the collection, numbering between 2 & 3 hundred volumes, all nicely & mostly tastefully bound, will, in one of Marshall's pretty oak cases, form an agreeable feature in the Museum."

And if the matter, he continued expectantly to Hunt, could be "arranged at once, I could advise you of the exact amount of shelf-room required, & Marshall could set about the case under your directions so as to have everything ready for the transfer by February next at latest" (8 December 1871; LOA 198:38). There followed a printed announcement of a Special Meeting of the Trustees (7 February 1872; LOA 141:5) to be held on 15 February 1872 to accept the donation. And Halliwell's sole condition, underscoring his very personal attachment, was observed: that the gift would not be accessible during his lifetime except with his permission. As always, funding was always an urgent problem. Not untypical is the alarming report given by Thomas Salmon, the custodian of New Place, on 30 March 1876 (LOA 224:28):

As usual at this season of the year, I herewith enclose you the bills for the quarter, and also the No. of Visitors which I am truly *sorry to say*, have been *very very few* and *far between*, numbering only 46 which amounts to £1.3.0 at '6 each, this sum I have paid into the Bank to *New Place Acct.*, and I am *distressed in mind*, to know what is to become of *Willm Shakespeare's* last residence, and *your Arduous labours there*–as for myself I must say it grieves *me* to the *heart*, to have to tell you in plain words, that when the enclosed bills are paid, there will be only a balance in the Bank of £3.15.3 which will look very much like a case of *Insolvency* hanging over my *pet place* without the power of warding it off–pray tell me what can be done? and also pardon me if I have spoken too plainly.[226]

Halliwell's relationship with Stratford was complex. He was passionate in pursuit of his schemes but distant in his attitude towards the town as a whole. He was dismayed by its crude materialism and lack of taste. Although a Trustee of the Birthplace, he could not "bring myself to take any interest in their celebrations one way or the other," he wrote to Charles Roach Smith. "You never would believe me when I told you that there were not half a dozen people at Stratford who really in their hearts care for Shakespeare. You will find it out some day if you live long enough, & that it is quite useless to address the inhabitants on the subject in any way which does not appeal either to eye pocket or ear" (27 January 1869; Folger W.a.82[172]). He complained constantly of their lack of generosity: "I know by personal experience of Stratford of late years," he

226. At the annual meeting of the Trustees on 5 May 1876, on the other hand, it was reported that the number of visitors to the Birthplace, "exclusive of those who have not written their names in the Book," was 9,830.

lamented to Hepworth Dixon, "a very occasional guinea is all with one or two exceptions that can be got–in fact, the expences [sic] at Stratford are now almost entirely borne by sixpenny admissions" (13 July 1871; Folger Y.c.1213[72]). He was ever and militantly opposed to attempts to divert funds from the Birthplace to be used for other, often pet, projects, like the Theatre, suspecting personal profit or prestige as a motive. He was not surprised by the report by Frederick Haines of the "preposterous proposition"–Charles Flowers's attempt to divert funds to the Theatre–made at the meeting of the local Trustees in Stratford, and agreed with his opinion: "this would be a complete breach of trust & in all respects a most unwise and wrong thing to do" (8 May 1878; LOA 271:30). And, as has been demonstrated, Halliwell was a sad witness of Stratford's modernization.

What helped nurture and sustain Halliwell's involvement with Stratford was his personal relationship with several citizens of Stratford, especially W. O. Hunt and his family. Although it was his custom to avoid public occasions whenever possible, especially in Stratford, he wrote often and visited privately often. It was mainly through Hunt that he learned much of the local goings-on, such as the news that "old Flower has had an attack of Paralysis ... he lost his speech" (8 May 1866; LOA 113:37) or that "the Flowers have converted the Old White Lion into a Malthouse, & ... set up ... 3 immense Cowls, which ... put me in mind of the 3 Witches in Macbeth ... and you may probably go farther and imagine they are saying 'All ale, Macbeth'" (14 May 1866; LOA 112:11). It is not too much to say it was from Hunt that he learned all he needed to know about the day-by-day happenings, the plans and possibilities of the development of the New Place "scheme," and of course the intrigues and petty politics of the town. In Hunt he had a true ally and a loyal friend. It was from Harry Hunt, with whom Halliwell was fond of carousing in London, that his father's last days were described. "Dear Friend," he reported, "I am very sorry to have to write & give such a bad account of my dear father ... his lungs are greatly affected & he has refused his food very much lately & last night he was calling out quite loud 'Halliwell Halliwell &c' so he has not forgotten you" (7 March 1873; LOA 200:14).[227] A week later he reported the death of his "dear Kind & good father ... without a struggle, *a most beautiful death*," and concluded, "I do not feel able to write more except to thank you on behalf of the family for your kindness of thinking so often of our dear old good & kind parent" (16 March 1873; LOA

227. Dr. John Collis, the vicar, informed Halliwell that "Poor old Hunt's mind & memory are rapidly going" (12 March 1873; LOA 200:13).

200:41). Halliwell, as was his custom, offered to advise the family on the disposition or sale of Hunt's books. A year later he wrote to Charles Roach Smith that Hunt was "the best & truest friend & ablest correspondent I had at Stratford-on-Avon, which is no longer the same place to me" (18 May 1874; Folger W.a.82[200]).

Stratford may not have been the same, but Halliwell's fate was bound up with it. And although he was loath to attend its public functions, he was not unhappy to receive its honors, even such a one as the joking handwritten "resolution" proposed by Harry Hunt and seconded by Robert Hobbes that "in consequence of the improved state and respectability of appearance of Mr J. O. Halliwell ... [he] be requested to sit for his Portrait to be placed in the North Room" (3 May 1870; LOA 163:22). In the letter in which he outlined his five "objects" to Hunt (18 February 1872; LOA 196:24), Halliwell had added a noteworthy postscript: "If I live to complete the above range of objects, I expect to be offered the Freedom of the Town, which will be a great comfort & advantage, as I should then be free to enter the Town & also free to go out of it." That expectation was not to be fulfilled, however. In a letter of 10 May 1876 (LOA 240:22) George Ade, the lawyer, enclosed a note from A. J. Wood (10 May 1876; LOA 240:21), who was of the opinion that the Municipal Corporation Act precluded the granting of the freedom of the borough, nor could an "honorary freedom" be drawn from it. Ade cited further details but could only conclude, "I am Sorry we are unable to give You any hopes of obtaining the Coveted honor." With obvious tight-lipped disappointment Halliwell added a note: "This letter is in reference to the unanimous wish of the Corporation of Stratford-on-Avon to confer on me the freedom of their borough in May, 1876." Nor was the advice of his friend Frederick Haines, also a Life Trustee, that Halliwell seek further counsel to unravel the complications, very helpful—even less so perhaps was the cold comfort of his saying, "In my opinion the Freedom cannot be bestowed upon you in any satisfactory manner so as to make it worth having" (20 May 1876; LOA 226:36).

After expressing his "relief ... to hear that the New Place Conveyance Deed had been enrolled in Chancery for the requisite six months," and presuming "that now there are not likely to be any legal complications respecting the estate in the event of my decease," Halliwell continued to Robert Hobbes, "With this terminates my Shaksn business at S. O. A. In future I shall not interfere in any sort of way, & shall even sedulously avoid attending the meetings of the Board of Trustees" (13 January 1877; LOA 240:63). And not shying away from problems and tensions, he went on to deliver a direct and dignified review of his Stratford experience:

While thanking you gratefully for all your Kindness & consideration to me during the many years I have had a finger in the fire in these matters at the risk of being accused of too much complacency I cannot resist mentioning to you now, my oldest Stratford friend that on the whole I retire in the belief that I have committed no serious error in my management of New Place. It was all but a necessary result from considering the whole solely in respect to the Shaksn associations, & disregarding altogether the wishes of the Town when those wishes interfered with the preservation of the Shaksn sentiment, I should have incurred at intervals the censure of some of the inhabitants, but the latter infliction is more than, as you would say, 'merged in the inheritance' of the knowledge that to the best of my ability I have fulfilled my duty to that public which entrusted so very large a sum of money to my individual honor.

But that was not the end of it. Stratford was too ingrained in his being for him to "terminate" his Stratford "business." There was more to be done—achievements to be consolidated, the enterprise to be extended, documents to be preserved—before the final and convulsive termination of his Stratford business.

17

Buying, Selling, Collecting

The last days of 1865 were filled with bookdealing. On 10 December (LOA 104:11) Collier announced he would send a list of tracts he might sell; on 12 December (LOA 103:13) Lionel Booth offered a First Folio "at a[n] honorable cost"; on 18 December (LOA 101:14) Halliwell offered Dr. Johann Jakob Horner, librarian of the Town Library of Zürich, £200 for a 1611 quarto of *Hamlet*, a 1609 one of *Romeo and Juliet*, and Wilkins's *Painfull Adventures of Pericles* of 1608; on the same day (LOA 101:11) Halliwell offered Professor Christian Petersen of Hamburg £100 for a 1609 *Pericles* and a 1609 *Faustus*; on 19 December (LOA 102:41) Edward Mostyn informed William Tite that he had found a 1607 *Pericles*, to which Halliwell in a letter to Tite of 1 January 1866 (LOA 102:38) responded that it was well worth £150, a sum which he himself would pay even if it were the 1609 edition. Bookdealing was, of course, nothing unusual for Halliwell. He had begun collecting as a teenager, and his passion increased as the years went by. The British Museum affair, not indirectly connected with his sales at Sotheby's when he was but twenty, did not abate his activities. He had personal sales at Sotheby's in 1856, 1857, 1858, 1859, two in 1861, and 1863; he arranged numerous private publications for subscribers based on a theory of financial value; he was engaged in the buying and selling of objects for the Shakespeare library and museum in Stratford; he was dealing with individuals (like Collier) and institutions (like the British Museum).

From the illustrations drawn from the last days of 1865 a few salient tendencies emerge which form a bridge of sorts from the younger Halliwell, almost unbridled in his desire to expand his activities in as many directions as possible, to a more mature Halliwell, constantly aware of his age and increasing frailty and attempting to temper his passion and circumscribe his horizon. For one thing, the sums mentioned indicate that Halliwell was a "player" of some magnitude and, considering his financial status at the time, not oblivious to the risks involved in speculation. For another, Halliwell was acting on commissions for others and was being sought after for and dispensing opinions and advice. His letter to Tite of 1 January 1866 (LOA 102:38) is a fine illustration of his experience and expertise:

You will do a national service by getting the Pericles of 1607, if such an edition exists, & most certainly £150 would be *most extremely* well laid out upon it. Pray offer that inducement, but if the copies are in fair order, *£150 would not be too much for the volume even if the Pericles is the edition of 1609.* Should the Pericles turn out to be the edition of 1609, you will have, I believe, every play in the volume, in which case, if the copies are perfect, *I myself would give £150 for the entire volume,* so if you thought Lord Mostyn might be tempted, very small risk would be incurred *in any case* by naming that sum. It would be well, however, not to make a positive offer without seeing the volume, for if the best plays are defective, it might not be worth a third.

And thirdly, as far as his own collecting is concerned, there is strong evidence of the limits he was setting for himself. Halliwell had always stressed his interest in old English literature, the core of his literary pursuits. But the focus now becomes more precise. In a testy response to Halliwell of 15 December 1865 (LOA 101:12) Collier complained: "I do not perhaps understand your note of yesterday. If your book-case will only hold works of 'constant reference' you cannot want for it any of the rarities I may have, because they are *not* works of 'constant reference'–quite the reverse." Halliwell never ceased to be interested in rarities; on 5 January 1866 (Folger Y.c.1307[28]) he informed an unidentified dealer of his wish to have "any sale catalogues of curious books," regretting that he would have liked to have a catalogue of the Breadalbane library, "as I have no doubt I should have sent you some large commission." But a few days later (8 January 1866; Folger Y.c.1307[29]) he reiterated his current position–"I buy chiefly *old* English books, black letter or others, printed *before* 1623"–and sharpened his focus: "I buy *Shakespeare quartos* in *any* [underlined six times] sort of condition, & perfect or imperfect."

In the last days of 1865 Halliwell was both reiterating what he had been practising and strongly reinforcing his future position. Authenticity was his keyword. It was not long, in fact, before Halliwell modified his acceptance of imperfect books, even old ones. To the bookdealer J. W. Jarvis he indicated (28 March 1867; Folger Y.c.1240[1b]) that he was not interested in an imperfect copy of any book offered him unless, perhaps, it were printed by Pynson, holding that imperfect books "realize so little at sales that unless people are very rich, no one with a family likes to throw money away by buying them." Imperfect copies are not per se undesirable, he continued. It was a common practice to complete them with loose leaves from deficient copies, as Halliwell had done in taking "his 3 folios of 1st ed. of Shakespeare to Mr Bedford who is to work & bind up one good copy out of them" (Diary, 24 May 1852). Restricting his field of interest still further, Halliwell focussed on the one exception: "imperfect early Shakespeares, respecting which I am rabid." There follows the leitmotif of Halliwell's career: his concentration on Shakespeare alone. His correspondence with Jarvis in this period charts his course. He is interested in a 1713 edition of Milton, only if it had an engraved portrait of Shakespeare, "which is all I want the book for" (22 April 1867; Folger Y.d.5[2b]); although only interested in old English plays and poems, not chronicles and charters, he is "so anxious to get hold of some early Shakespeare quartos" (22 May 1867; Folger Y.d.5[5b]); although thankful for Jarvis's interest in his "hobbies," Halliwell (1 June 1867; Folger Y.c.1240[3b]) once again states his lack of interest in portraits of Shakespeare and stresses his desire for rare printed Shakespeares. Explaining to W. C. Hazlitt that he can show his books only by appointment since "an unexpected visitor ... interferes with my reading," Halliwell added, "excepting of course any one whatever who has something of Shakespearian interest to bring,–everything must give way to Shakespeare" (22 January 1869; LOA 152:29). Likewise, to Jarvis he explained: "Kindly recollect that, except during a few weeks holiday in the summer, I am a *very busy* man, everyday fully occupied, my time being *fully* devoted to Shaksn. researches of *importance*. If any *early* editions of Shakespeare turn up, then I go & leave everything in their favour" (1 April 1870; Folger Y.d.5[11b]). The restrictions became even sharper: from informing R. E. Lonsdale that he no longer collects Shakespeareana printed after 1700 (31 July 1868; Folger Y.c.1248[2]) to reminding Jarvis that he is not interested in anything after 1616 (22 September 1873; Folger Y.d.5[16b]). Even more precise, he advised Joseph Hill (20 March 1873; Folger Y.c.1231[10]) that he was not interested in any Shakespeare folio editions, "however cheap," other than the first, "anymore." And "in regard to the first," he added with utter precision, "I only want a copy of the title-page containing the portrait." It is the exquisiteness of the perfectionist that caused him to pay one hundred guineas for the Droeshout portrait (Diary, 17 May 1864 and 21 December 1866; LOA 122:52) and, treasuring it, to refuse offers for it from, among others, Lady Burdett-Coutts and the British Museum. There was even more zeal in his "dream" of a finding a 1602 quarto of *Hamlet*, of which there is no known copy. "I would go down on my knees for it," he confessed to Charles Roach Smith, "as well as give two hundred guineas for it if necessary. If preserved anywhere, it will be found in one of the closets or lofts of an old county family" (3 October 1867; Folger W.a.81[51/2]). The fantasy never left him. "If a Hamlet of 1602 were to turn up," he wrote to Smith a few years later, "of course I *must* find the money for it" (5 December 1872; Folger C.b.17[75]). And a few months later he told Joseph Hill, "For a perfect copy of the Hamlet of 1602–there was such an edition of sixteen hundred & two, & it will probably turn up some day–I would willingly give five hundred pounds: What I want is something *unique* at a high price, not anything common at a low one" (20 March 1873; Folger Y.c.1231[10b]).

There was more than fantasy in Halliwell's concentration. For he was putting his house in order, as it were, and focussing on the one culminating object of his entire career, documenting the life of Shakespeare. And that had a profound effect on his collecting, his library, and his scholarly production. He would, "if useful ... probably give *fancy* prices" for "old documents about Shakespeare, early *unknown* 4tos before 1616, & old documents about the stage or players," he wrote to Hill (20 March 1873; Folger Y.c.1231[10b]), but not solely for the pride of possession. Professional career and personal life merge in his confession to Charles Roach Smith:

I have still got a good bit of energy left, but between 50 & 60 one must not attempt too much. I have arranged to give at once a large portion of my Shakespeare Library to Stratford-on-Avon. My Shakespeare Quartos, worth about £2.000, I shall sell & invest the money. I shall retain nothing but what I require for the Life of Shakespeare & the History of the Stage during that Life, and these will be my sole object henceforth (26 November 1871; Folger C.b.17[69]).

And a year later he emphasized once again to Smith that he was "*only*" buying books connected with his *Illustrations* (5 December 1872; Folger C.b.17[75]). The watchwords "curious and rare" give way somewhat. Commenting on his library, Halliwell described to Smith (20 April 1870; Folger W.a.82[179] what he had designated to Collier as works of "constant reference": "In my small way admission of a book into my choice library proves that I believe it to contain good matter, not having a single volume but containing useful & good matter."

If there were fewer works to be bought, there were, to be sure, more to be sold or disposed of. Halliwell did this in a number of ways. For one thing, he intensified his selling: in addition to single volumes to individuals, whole bundles or collections to institutions. He had done so earlier, having sold a number of quartos to the British Museum, for example, in 1862 for £450. On 6 August 1866 (LOA 119:38) he dispatched a box containing an "entire collection" already catalogued to William Harrison, of the London Library, who remitted £145.16.6 and thanks for Halliwell's "kind offices" (27 November 1867; LOA 148:7). For another, he resolved to reduce his stock of reprints. His privately printed publications began appearing in booksellers' lists, like Joseph Lilly's offering in 1868 numerous titles he had purchased at the extensive sale of Halliwell reprints in the Windus sale at Sotheby's on 23 March 1868. In a letter marked "Private confidential" (10 February 1872; LOA 188:33) he informed Henry Sotheran that he "should be glad to be relieved of the entire stock of the Shakespeares," wishing "to sell the whole lot to you absolutely at once." In 1870 he turned to Sotheby's again. He had already had six sales there between 1856 and 1863, offering 3530 items which fetched a total of almost £4000. In a seventh, on four days starting 14 March 1870, Halliwell, identified as a "well-known collector," offered almost nine hundred items for sale: the items 416-1269 fetched £716.7.0 (not including several other items not listed under Shakespeare or Shakespeariana). In the sale were not merely reprints of his own publications and his quarto facsimiles but also the four Folio editions–the First fetching £360 and the Third (1664) £200 alone. Significant as far as Halliwell's effort at concentration was concerned are not solely the large number of books but their range. The vast majority are post-seventeenth century, from the major and many minor complete editions of Shakespeare of the eighteenth and nineteenth centuries–Rowe (1709) to Dyce (1864), Ayscough (1784) to the Students's and School Shakespeare (ca. 1851)–to numerous translations in German, French, Latin, Dutch, Swedish of the complete and individual plays and poems; from adaptations to stage versions. Under Shakespeariana (items 631-1269) are to be found the most and the least important critical works, mainly of the nineteenth century and in various languages, ranging from Malone's *Life of Shakespeare* (1821) and Gervinus's *Shakespeare* in four volumes (1849-1850) to Alexander Campbell's *Beauties of Shakespeare* (1804) to Karl Otto Hagena's *Shakespeare-Studien auf dem Oldenburgischen Gymnasium* (1847). "The most complete collection," so the title page of the sale catalogue, "of Shakspeariana, English and Foreign, ever brought together, nearly all in choice bindings, and mostly uncut."–a considerable private library, all of it, but like the other such Halliwell had disposed of, occupying physical space rather than contributing to his grand design. It was Halliwell's last sale at Sotheby's during his lifetime.

There were other ways of focussing the collection. In the period from 1866 to 1878 Halliwell intensified his donations to institutions. Harvard University was once again a recipient, this time of twenty-one books and manuscripts, all but four of the sixteenth and seventeenth centuries (20 April 1866; LOA 28:26), as was the British Museum (e.g. 16 March 1868; LOA 140:29 and 18 April 1871; LOA 165:36). There may well have been other motives in play, like establishing or cementing good relations or using good business sense. In the bequest to the British Museum, for example, Halliwell was loath to supply a selection from the series of quarto facsimiles; "If, however, the Museum subscribes to the whole series (omitting of course the two vols. ... already in the library," Halliwell wrote to Thomas Watts, "I shall be happy to present twenty volumes of the series in acknowledgement of the assistance derived in the work from the Museum originals" (16 March 1868; LOA 140:29). There can be little doubt, nevertheless, of Halliwell's generosity, which can never be overestimated. It was spectacularly evident in his bequest to the Penzance Public Library, which in its catalogue of 1874 listed 1616 titles (many multi-volumed) in its "Halliwell Compartment" (pp. 244-320) and another 421 in the Supplement (pp. 320a-332).[228] Halliwell had been much taken with Penzance, as is evident in his *Rambles in Western Cornwall* (1861); it was also the home of his illustrator J. T. Blight. He increased his donations over the years, having originally offered three hundred volumes in 1862; in 1880 a *Catalogue of the Books in the Halliwell Compartment ... Part II* listed a further 832 titles, with the Committee's thanks for Halliwell's "great and long-continued kindness." The collection is vast in scope and offers a cross-section of Halliwell's interests during his entire career. Its core is literary, with a strong emphasis on plays in editions of the seventeenth and eighteenth centuries: Shakespeare is represented by a Fourth Folio, numerous later editions of individual plays,[229] as well as multi-volume complete editions from Rowe (1709) and Hanmer (1745) to Hudson (1852), Halliwell's own works, many critical works and translations, and the publications of the New Shakspere Society, among others. In addition to numerous single titles, Early English literature is found in the publications of the Early English Text Society; the full range of English non-dramatic literature in the volumes of the English Poets; English history in the publications of the Camden Society. Religion is

228. A cutting Halliwell included in his Letters of Authors (1880; LOA 265:52) reads: "The total of his gifts has reached three thousand separate works."

229. In May 1964 at a sale at Sotheby's the University of Edinburgh Library bought for £21,000 over six hundred items–mainly seventeenth-century plays–from Halliwell's bequest to the Penzance Library.

strongly represented, as are lexicography, dialectology, and topography. There is much foreign and classical literature. And mathematics and medicine are not omitted. Striking but not surprising are forty-five catalogues of private and institutional libraries, art collections, sales, and exhibitions. And to his own works on various subjects Halliwell added those of his friends: sixteen works and four volumes of "Archaeological Papers" by T. J. Pettigrew, ten by Thomas Wright, two by Charles Roach Smith and F. W. Fairholt being the most prominent. The bequest was, in short, as intensely personal as it was immensely bountiful.

There was other material to be unloaded: manuscripts, documents, records. Dulwich College was a recipient (29 July 1869; LOA 146:27 and 2 June 1874; LOA 116:13), as was Barnstaple, which accepted Halliwell's offer to pay for the arranging and binding of some of the old documents in the possession of the town council (14 December 1875; LOA 232:65). The massive amount of material—literally hundreds of volumes of accounts and the like—Halliwell bequeathed to Stratford seemed to have no end. On 25 November 1869 Mrs. Halliwell's diary reports (stressing through underlining) an important decision: "*James called me into his study today & told me he had made a Codicil to his Will & that he wished everything in his study to be given to Edinburgh University Library - James signed the Codicil yesterday Nov. 24th.*" The decision was striking and not uncomplicated, reflecting numerous aspects of his personal and professional life. Halliwell was understandably proud of his collection, which represented all he had striven for and accomplished and, as it developed, he was to do. He was anxious to keep large parts of it together, always requiring as a condition, such as in his bequest to Penzance, that each one be kept in a separate compartment and catalogue. Halliwell was obviously concerned that the collection be properly designated and accommodated. He was much interested, for example, in the fate of the Dyce collection. Dyce died in May of 1869, and on 16 June 1869 (LOA 151:10) in response to a query from Halliwell, William Macray wrote from Oxford: "We always had an idea that Mr Dyce contemplated leaving his books to the Bodleian. As he has not done so, it is satisfactory to hear from you that there is not very much in his Library that we do not already possess" (16 June 1869; LOA 151:10). And on 6 January 1870 (LOA 157:32) Alan Cole mentioned the "many changes" the South Kensington Museum had to make to accommodate Dyce's library. His letter was not addressed to Halliwell but to Emily Newcomb (Mrs. Halliwell's cousin); that it was included in his collection is evidence enough of his desire to have his own bequest properly housed and reputed.

It would be an overstatement to say that Halliwell turned to Scotland as a last resort. But the major libraries in England could not be considered, for the collection was for the British Museum, Oxford, or Cambridge either not important enough to warrant the special attention he required or for reasons of previous conflicts or current tensions undesirable or unacceptable. Other institutions were considered. The South Kensington Museum had already indicated, when Halliwell offered to lend his collection of early editions of Shakespeare, that "it would appear to be more suitable for the British Museum" (7 January 1861; LOA 71:33). The Chetham Library in Manchester and the Shakespeare library in Stratford had already been recipients of large bequests. Penzance seemed to be the only town in England that enchanted Halliwell enough–it had also impressed him with its new museum buildings (18 September 1867; Folger Y.c.1213[65])–for him to endow it with a considerable library. He had his own thoughts about a modern research library in London. Rejecting a memorial statue of Shakespeare, he suggested instead a central Shakespeare library and museum in London. What was wanted in literature, he had written to Hepworth Dixon (17 June 1863; Folger Y.c.1213[15]), "were special libraries & collections to supply the place of that *impossibility*, a classed catalogue of the British Museum," as well as duplicate copies and facsimiles of various copies, "which they would of course never have at the British Museum," and concluding, "I do not think I am much given to brag, but give me *ample means* & I would engage even now to bring together a Shakespeare Library that should beat the B. Museum collections into fits." But he was aware that this idea, however attractive, was perhaps more wishful thinking than a viable design. Besides, Scotland had very attractive features. For one thing, it had old and renowned universities and a long tradition of scholarly enterprise. For another, although it was not one of the places he had visited on business or pleasure–in fact, he seems never to have been in Scotland before–he had valuable contacts there. One was William Euing of Glasgow, with whom Halliwell had corresponded since the mid 1840s and to whom he had sold a vast collection of broadside ballads in 1867 for £260. Euing advised him about leaving the collection to the University of Glasgow (15 November 1869; LOA 76:33). Another was David Laing, librarian of the Signet Library in Edinburgh, with whom Halliwell shared many scholarly interests since the mid 1840s and to whom Halliwell was indebted for the loan of a quarto of *Titus Andronicus* (to complete his facsimile series), an act which "I shall remember most gratefully as long as I live" (15 December 1865; EUL La.IV.17). In a correspondence parallel with that to Euing, Laing advised against the Advocates Library in Edinburgh, largely because it was "under the control of Curators elected annually & having full power to pass stringent rules refusing access to the books to any except Members" (15 November 1869; LOA 169:16). He recommended the University of Edinburgh and "having seen so much good & bad management of Public Libraries," suggested that Halliwell "stipulate, that a separate Catalogue of the Collection be prepared & printed within a given period." A further letter (marked "Private") from Laing underlined his preference for Edinburgh (his own university) since Glasgow "has a grand building in progress—but so far as Literature is concerned it is like a Liverpool compared with Oxford" (25 November 1869; LOA 135:35). Halliwell accepted Laing's advice about the site and the catalogue, as well as his suggestions, as incorporated in his letter to the Principal of the university (17 February 1872; LOA 187:22), that the "collection remain always separate & distinct from any other ... [and] That no book be lent or taken out of the library." And in seeking Laing's advice in the first place, Halliwell alluded to perhaps the dominant reason for considering Scotland: "Several important & readily accessible Shakespeare collections existing in this country, while I do not know if a single one in Scotland" (19 November 1869; EUL La.IV.17).

In the same letter Halliwell described his collection:

The whole is exclusively Shaksperian. The library is small, all of it being contained in two large & two small bookcases, but it is choice & select, no rubbish, & every book nicely bound, many by Bedford, 29 quarto Shakespeares &c. The engravings & drawings are the largest collection of the kind ever formed, & these latter with my own MS. collections are contained in about two hundred shallow drawers.

He also included a copy of the codicil of his will with a more expanded inventory, evidently taking into account items to follow in the course of his life:

To the University of Edinburgh I bequeath all my printed books manuscripts engravings drawings maps plans electrotypes wood blocks facsimiles and photographs which are kept and preserved in my dwelling house in Tregunter Road aforesaid and which include my unpublished notes on Shakespeare bound in One hundred and twenty eight volumes my literary correspondence bound in One hundred and forty or more volumes my folio Shakespeare papers and the papers relating to the Shakespeare fund my large collection of drawings engravings photographs &c. illustrative of the life of Shakespeare and Stratford on Avon And all my other literary collections and papers of what nature or kind soever which shall be in and about my said dwelling house at the time of my decease.

Halliwell's referring to his library as "small but choice" is somewhat of an understatement. In the actual number of individual works it may indeed be small, totalling some 1200. And to a certain extent it is choice in the sense of being a selection of Shakespearean literature; like the others which he had assembled and bequeathed, it is a compact standard library for scholars and students. Like the others, it consists of the major editions of Shakespeare, Halliwell's own works, critical works, facsimiles, all mainly of the eighteenth and nineteenth centuries. In addition there are the publications of the Shakespeare Society and the Camden Society, among other such, as well as a smattering of works by such friends as Henry Holl, Samuel Neil, C. M. Ingleby, and Thomas Wright. "Rare" printed works are relatively few and imperfect–such as a fragment on Desdemona from Cinthio's *Novelle* (1593), *Laugh and Lie Down; or the Worldes Folly*, attributed to Tourneur (1605), Lodge's *Euphues Golden Legacie* (1612), and six Dutch plays on Shakespearean themes (1618-42). What can be classified as truly rare, if only because they are unique, are 404 specially bound volumes which record the activities of the scholar and bookman working with his sleeves rolled up, as it were. First and foremost are the first three hundred volumes, which contain some 15,000 letters mainly to Halliwell over his entire career and, of course, treat all his private and professional concerns. Volumes 327-330, the four-volume manuscript of the diary of Mrs. Halliwell, provide almost a narrative version of the letters and amount to a small but important picture of the life of the family as well as a not uninteresting socio-cultural glimpse into the times. These items alone would merit Halliwell's sought-after "rare and curious." But there are more, such as Volumes 331-338 with headings entitled London, British Museum, State Papers, Oxford, Provincial Researches, Private Collections, Printed-Book Researches, and Wills; Volume 340, Collections on Shakespeare's Crab-Tree; Volume 349, Collections on R. Burbage, Shakespeare's Friend and Theatrical Chief; Volumes 360-364, Notes for Provincial Researches for the Life of Shakespeare and the History of the Stage, arranged according to places visited–e.g. Coventry, Chelmsford, Warwick, etc.; Volume 368, Provincial Wills Likely to Be Useful to Shakespearean Students; Volume 397, Memoranda on Old Maps and Plans of London.

To these ways of reducing his stock of works no longer required for his enterprise or for which he had no room–he had purchased a cottage in Sutton in 1860 to store part of his library and had made use of the Pantechnicon[230]–must be added Halliwell's abandoning of widespread private printings for subscribers and his repeated desire to keep his library directly relevant to his special needs and, like those collections of some magnitude he had sold or bequeathed, to be kept intact, to remain a distinct unit or if sold to be so only as a unit, his will being explicit on this point. But all these limitations on his library did not mean Halliwell withdrew from the business of bookdealing. He was too zealous a lover of books and too intrigued by dealing to stop completely or even partially, despite the decline of his energy, his relentless sense of growing old, the stringencies of the market, and the personal crisis in the 1870s arising from his wife's tragic accident and the mounting responsibilities which came of his inheritance of the Middle Hill estates. Not untypical of his passion was his request of the bookdealer James Coleman that he be informed of certain suitable books before they were to be catalogued, even if that meant paying more for them (21 February 1868; Folger Y.c.1206[3]). Furthermore, although by this time he did not attend all the important sales, he made a point of being kept informed of their results, as, for example, when George Bumstead reported on the Smith sale in three consecutive letters–i.e. immediately after each day of the sale–on 29 July 1867 (LOA 127:14), 31 July 1867 (LOA 126:4), and 2 August 1867 (LOA 126:25). From these letters emerge significant features of Halliwell's business character. For one thing, he engaged Bumstead (and others) on a commission basis, thus assuring a certain tactical advantage if his identity could be concealed. This in turn involved not merely the receiving of information from his agent but a closely coordinated operating plan beyond the simple but not necessarily favored one of procuring objects at the lowest possible price. In reporting the results of "this day's Sale" (31 July 1867; LOA 126:4), Bumstead illustrates that close and immediate coordination: "Alfred bid up to £37 for lot 7234 Sidney & I thought I should have got it for the next bid but Mr Ellis took up the bidding & bought it for Lilly for £66. I will bid up to £20 for no 7684 *tomorrow* Taylor the water Poet's works, but if you wish to bid more perhaps you can *Telegraph.*" In a following letter of 2 August (LOA 126:25) he reports on having collated all the lots and found "Taylor 7684" had a "trifling defect in the corner of one leaf," but did not think it would be "*well to*

230. To his dismay the cottage burned down a short while later. And he was concerned about the dampness in the Pantechnicon (24 September 1870; LOA 170:16), not to mention the fire there in early 1874 (28 February 1874; Folger Y.d.5[22b]).

return it on this acct." After outlining the bidding plan and a necessary account of some gossip surrounding the sale–when Mrs. Smith was satisfied with the prices: "if she liked Money," Lilly had commented, "she ought to be thankful"–Bumstead records that "up to the present time" the amount he had purchased for Halliwell was £920.2.6. It should be obvious then that Halliwell was careful about what he was to buy, that he was buying choice items, and that he was willing to spend a great deal of money to get what he wanted. The gossip surrounding this sale also provided a definitive statement from Halliwell on his purchasing policy and, by an easy extension, on his financial dealings in general. Bumstead reported on 29 July that "Mr. [W. C.] Hazlitt wanted to know this morning if you had an Estate coming to you"–another instance of Bumstead's coordinating "I will give you daily advice of what I am doing for you." Halliwell had written an indignant letter of clarification to Joseph Lilly:

I am excessively perplexed in the attempt to discover a reason for the minute interrogatories you made of me on Saturday respecting my purchases at Mrs. Smith's sale. As far as I can gather from you, dire offence would be given if I have bought these books on commission, or to sell again at a profit, the very idea of the latter contingency appearing to put you into a state of excitement.
Now I am not so indifferent to the value of money as not to be charmed by the visions of profit, but on the present occasion it may relieve your anxiety to be informed that I have not purchased a single lot at Mrs Smith's or any other sale, on commission. Every thing I have bought has been for myself & paid for with my own money, & though it may be just possible that two or three lots might resell at a profit, others will assuredly entail a loss, & I feel sure that the trade generally will know that it is extremely improbable that I shall ever in the aggregate get the £723 already expended back again (22 July 1867; LOA 127:27).

Halliwell was a determined and professional buyer and seller. But he was not unaware of the image he may have been conveying or indeed of the trap bookdealing was. In a letter to John Wilkinson in which he asked who had bought the Steevens reprint of the Shakespeare quartos at Nichols's sale and for what price (18 April 1870; Folger Y.c.1298[2]) Halliwell, in self-mockery, predicts Wilkinson's response: "'There's that fellow Halliwell at it again–give him an inch & he will take an 'ell [of a lot!!]–if I don't mind what I am about, I shall have nothing to do but run after his nonsense–I must give 'im the straight tip.' If you do say this, please in justice add that you have brought it all on yourself by your kind offers. You are not the first person who has made a rod for his own back. I have many a time."[231] And he was not without error. There had been a prominent misjudgment in the case of the 1603 quarto of *Hamlet* offered him in 1856 by M. W. Rooney: Rooney had asked £100; Halliwell offered £50 and referred him to William Boone; Boone bought it for £70 and then sold it to Halliwell for £120.[232] There were countless other instances and the consequences were best summarized by Halliwell himself in a letter to Lilly of 30 September 1868 (LOA 140:12): "But for a few lucky chances, the loss on my purchases taken in the aggregate would have been enormous. As, however, I find my system of buying for reading & then selling has been misinterpreted by the trade, I have resolved not to purchase anything not very urgently wanted, so that in future if I buy half a dozen old books in a year I shall be astonished. I certainly have not bought one for some months." Of course, Halliwell did continue buying, sometimes putting down "such thumping sums" that Bumstead, feeling that Halliwell was paying too high commissions, suggested altering the usual system of book-sale commissions "to advantage" (6 March 1869; LOA 149:31 and 8 March 1869; LOA 149:21). At any event Halliwell kept his passion under control and was a well-informed trader, as an unbroken chain of letters on prices and outlooks indicates. He was, on the whole, a cautious one, practising and requiring meticulous accounting and acting with a good measure of candor and integrity.[233] Of numerous examples perhaps a characteristic one may suffice here: his response to the offer by Clement Swanston of the four Shakespeare Folios for £350. In one of

231. In a similar instance of self-mockery Halliwell informed his dealer James Coleman (8 July 1886; Folger Y.c.1206[57]) that although a certain inventory was not dated before 1616, he thought it "very curious & reasonable at the price–in fact if I were you I should try it on at just double the price–but if you did that, kindly make up your mind *absolutely* that you will not blow me up if it does not sell, saying thus to yourself,–'I wish that old goose Halliwell-Phillipps would mind his own business instead of giving me stupid advice–if it hadn't been for him I should have got easily 50/ for the roll, & now I shan't sell at all–it never oh never will roll away', & so on."

232. Rooney's version of the transaction is in his letter to the *Athenaeum* of 27 September 1856, p. 1191.

233. Although given to lending and borrowing quite freely, he was basically wary. His advice to J. W. Jarvis is characteristic: "If I were you, I should be very careful in borrowing anything of the kind. I always decline the loan of curiosities of any description. In case of loss or accident, an ignorant owner might fancy himself entitled to some absurd compensation" (6 December 1872; Folger Y.c.1240[9b]).

two letters to Swanston (who sent three) Halliwell minced no words:

The three later folios are such desperate copies, It is my conviction that £20 would be the outside sum they would realize. At all events, if I bought the four volumes, I would cheerfully guarantee to send those three to Messrs Sotheby's, & if they fetched more, to pay over to the vendor any nett [*sic*] sum beyond £20 realized by me from the sale–not accepting of course any risk of damage or loss at Messrs. Sotheby's.
The copy of the first folio is the only one of the four of larger value, but I am sure that every experienced person will agree with me in saying that the want of two leaves or their supply by facsimile would be commercially fatal, & would hinder any extravagant sum being got either by auction or by private contract.
If I purchased this imperfect copy I should sell the one I bought at the Smith sale for £410, taking my chance of making the former complete by waiting my time. At the present moment, a copy containing the originals of the two leaves could not, I fancy, be obtained under £100 if for that; but by waiting, one might possibly be got for something considerably less (18 December 1867; LOA 124:13).

Halliwell developed his proposal further. Saying that £300 would be the lowest price he would consider for the First Folio, Swanston declined Halliwell's scheme as "too complicated" (20 December 1867; LOA 128:15). That he did is, however, a confirmation of sorts of Halliwell's conscientious expertise.

As dealer, collector, and scholar, Halliwell was in the habit of thinking in terms of libraries or collections, just as he tended to conceive of private publications not as single volumes but as parts of a series since that made good business sense. In his concentration on materials illustrative of the life and writings of Shakespeare, Halliwell sought specific titles, as in his circular *To Second-Hand Book Sellers* (January 1867) in which he listed thirty-three works sought as well as any early separate editions of Shakespeare's plays or poems "in any sort of condition" or *To Booksellers and Others* (1874)–typical of many such[234]–in which he offered large sums for certain works, such as £200 for "the old English romance of Hamblet or Hamlet published several times in the sixteenth century" or for a first edition (1592) of Greene's *Groatsworth of Witte*. But in circulars he always stated his requirements within a larger but circumscribed frame: "as a rule, anything

234. He reproduced this one with a single addition in *The Bookseller* of 4 April 1876, p. 385.

dated after the year 1616 is of no use to me." It is little wonder then that he produced catalogues. He provided them for clients, such as Harrison and Warwick. He urged others to do so, as in his advice to John Fenwick on how to bring in money for the Thirlestaine House library: "Most likely thing to bring in a pot of money would be a Catalogue of the Manuscripts," adding with business acumen, "& *you yourself should make one*, or else all the profits would have to be paid to a compiler" and encouraging him by advising that he use existing catalogues out of which manuscripts were bought so "all that it would require would be a *judicious* pair of scissors and a little first-rate paste!" (28 March 1872; Phil-Rob e.478:64).

The effect of this mode of thought on his own publications was obvious. In 1866 Halliwell issued in fifty copies *A Descriptive Catalogue of a Collection of Shakespeareana; Consisting of Manuscripts, Books, and Relics, Illustrative of the Life and Writings of Shakespeare, in the Library of William Harrison*, in which he briefly described the "remarkable series of the original forgeries and papers of [W. H.] Ireland" among numerous other items, including later Shakespeare quartos, relics, and "several articles ... of a high degree of rarity," such as *Willobie's Avisa* (1605) and *Shakespeare's Jests* (1769). Privately printed and often noted "for presents only" or "a few extra copies struck off for distribution amongst my friends," this type of work enabled him as well to publicize his own collection. In the period from 1867 to 1876 there appeared six such catalogues, ranging from the slight *Handlist of a Curious and Interesting Collection of Early Editions of the Works of Shakespeare* (1867), a description in fifteen pages of sixteen items, to *A Catalogue of a Small Portion of the Engravings and Drawings Illustrative of the Life of Shakespeare*, in which 382 items are proudly described as a "list of a small portion,–a very small portion,–of the largest collection of engravings and drawings illustrative of the Life of Shakespeare which has ever been formed," to *A Catalogue of the Warehouse Library of J. O. Halliwell-Phillipps* (1876), a 108-page listing of "books read, and books collected for reading, during the last few years ... deposited at the Pantechnicon ... compiled merely to guard myself against the purchase of duplicates" (v). Some 4000 titles of the seventeenth and eighteenth centuries make it a noteworthy collection of literary, theatrical, and historical Shakespeareana. More intimately, Halliwell had printed privately (by J. E. Adlard, his favorite) inventories not merely of the works and notes owned but where they were located in his house at 11 Tregunter Road. One such was *A List of the Contents of the Drawers in my Study, and in two other Rooms* (1870). Another was *A Brief Hand-List of the Selected Parcels in the Shakespearean and Dramatic Collections* (1876), with such headings as "Parcels in the Largest Safe,"

"Parcels in Play Safe," and "Parcels in Compartment A [through] I." A third was *A Catalogue of the Shakespeare-Study Books in the Immediate Library* (1876), with titles arranged according to play or topic (e.g. bibliography, law, history of the stage) followed by the location (e.g. study, map room, in parcel) in his house.

These large catalogues dominated his overall publications in 1876, dwarfing two others, a brief article in the *Journal of the British Archaeological Association*[235] (stemming from a talk at their annual meeting) and the short introduction to the Chatto and Windus facsimile of the First Folio. From the clarity of objective and the sheer number of titles it is not difficult to pronounce Halliwell the major Shakespearean of his day. And since around this time Halliwell prepared, among other things, a handwritten "Alphabetical List of Second-Hand Booksellers" (Folger Ma.287) containing "nearly 1000 British [and Irish] booksellers" with their current addresses to whom he sent "my circular," it is likewise not difficult to pronounce Halliwell a major "player" in the book trade. He was dealing with large sums of money: he had after all paid £430 for a copy of the First Folio, having sent a commission of £500 (Diary, 17 July 1867). Bumstead had purchased £920.2.6 for him at the Smith sale; his wife's diary entry for 22 January 1872 mentions that he had spent £5000 producing the quarto facsimiles.[236] And he had clients who sought his advice. One such was Thomas Corser, the antiquary and collector of the noteworthy "Collectanea Anglo-Poetica" (1860-1880), with whom Halliwell entertained a long and voluminous correspondence from 1844 to 1875 (the year before Corser's death): there are 278 letters from Corser to Halliwell in the Edinburgh collection, so many that Halliwell devoted a number of the three hundred volumes exclusively to Corser's letters. Corser was a passionate collector, as strikingly evidenced in his long, closely written, and detailed letters, many written when illness had confined him to his room. Corser asked for Halliwell's assistance, to which Halliwell responded that "it will give me the greatest pleasure at any & all times to execute any commissions for you in my power in London" and continued with a description of his visit to Puttick's and Christie's ("Of course I did not breathe your name") in which he set out to help Corser determine the most suitable "place of sale" for Corser's collection, and, adding characteristically, that he was "somewhat alarm[ed] to hear

235. "Some Suggestions Respecting a History of Broadway," 32 (1876), 431-4.
236. He may well have spent more, for after completing only twenty-six of the planned fifty-four facsimiles, he told Charles Roach Smith that the cost would be "over five thousand pounds" (5 July 1867; Folger C.b.17[29]).

you speak of selling it piecemeal, as I cannot help thinking that such a very important library should have an entire 800 volume catalogue devoted to itself, not only as more effective in every point of view, but as constituting a monument, if at all properly executed, of your life's labour of love" (18 February 1868; LOA 131:4). Equally characteristic was Halliwell's conclusion: "You puzzle me about naming my 'appointment', not being anxious for anything of the kind, unless it were that all but obsolete commodity, a sinecure, a good salary & nothing to do. At present I am & likely to be with plenty of leisure, & delighted at the opportunity of offering my little services to a kind old friend like yourself."

There was mutual benefit involved. For all his caution Halliwell could not resist the lure of important acquisitions. Marking his letter of 24 June 1868 (LOA 150:1) "private" and asking that "the matter be kept a profound secret," Halliwell approached Corser with particulars relating to his purchasing at Corser's sale. At Mrs. Smith's sale he was "compelled to buy & to bid extravagantly" since the "sale realized upwards of £1000 or more beyond what it would otherwise have done." Anxious nevertheless to take part in Corser's sale, Halliwell proposed "handing some property over" to Corser for a credit of £1200 at his sale, Halliwell "of course forfeiting any balance if [he did not] buy up to that sum." In still another financial move in the same year Halliwell proposed (12 November 1869; LOA 188:27) that F. W. Cosens pay him for seven Shakespeare quartos, the Third and Fourth Folios, and forty volumes of later Shakespeare quartos not "now in cash" but by granting him "an annuity of Thirty-Two Pounds Twelve Shillings payable during the life of Sir Thos. Phillipps ... the first payment ... to be made on July 3rd, 1870. Upon the death of Sir Thomas, the arrears of annuity to the time of such event having been paid, the books are of course yours without any further payment of any kind." Cosens agreed. In another transaction in 1869 Halliwell again illustrates the transparent and honest way he conducted his business. on 4 November 1869 (Folger Y.c.1263[1]) he offered Frederic Ouvry, president of the Society of Antiquaries, his copy of the First Folio: "I intend parting with the fine copy I bought at the Smith sale for £410, & as usual losing considerably when a sale is precipitated." At £350 "it is a dead bargain," he commented, "& is certainly preferable to Lord Charlemont's, which sold for £455." It was a "perfect copy ... sound & genuine," Halliwell informed Ouvry on 8 November 1869 (Freeman Collection), not disguising the fact that there were "a few small holes in the body of the book, caused ... by Iron-moulds." He even offered to substitute leaves from his six imperfect copies, although concerned enough to counsel that "it would be a pity to do so, the defects being insignificant, & the operation one which would impair the integrity of the volume." Ouvry bought the copy and received the thirteen extra leaves as well (16 November 1869; LOA 142:121). And a short while later he received the same kind of precise information–including a comparison with other existing copies–regarding Halliwell's copy of the 1616 *Lucrece* (28 April 1870; Folger Y.c.1263[2]).

Whether he was himself buying or selling or not, Halliwell was generous with information and advice to friends. He was thanked by Corser's son for his "kind offer of assistance" in the disposal of his father's library (3 December 1867; LOA 124:16). On 29 June 1868 (LOA 138:33) Clarence Hopper's widow, concerned about the future welfare of his children, asked Halliwell, her "dear Husbands most particular and best friend," for advice, having written a few days earlier (22 June 1868; LOA 140:22), "the Books and Papers I must leave entirely to Mr Halliwell's better judgement." Having received a concrete offer of £18.0.0 for some books, she asked him to tell her "what to do about it" (11 August 1868; LOA 147:3).[237] On 15 September 1873 (LOA 32:2) Lady Tite thanked Halliwell for offering to help with arrangements for the sale of her husband's library, John Wilkinson, the auctioneer, adding his thanks to Halliwell's "continuing" assistance in the Tite sale (26 October 1873; LOA 143:3).[238] And in another instance following Halliwell's offer of help, Ida Hunt, daughter of his great friend in Stratford, specified the advice she needed in the disposal of her father's collection (24 November 1873; LOA 110:24).

It is not entirely coincidental that Halliwell should be offering his assistance to the families of dear friends who had recently died. He was himself a family man and one acutely aware of his increasing age and declining health. His professional life cannot be disengaged from his private life. How else to explain his dramatic utterances in 1876? In a letter of 23 February 1876 (LOA 226:21) to Frederick Locker he reviewed his career as book collector:

For many years I collected *every copy* of every old quarto edition I could lay my hands on and spare the money for. Unfortunately pecuniary exigencies, or rather in most cases pecuniary advisabilities, led me to sell not only duplicates but several which were not duplicates. Never the less

237. In early 1870 Halliwell prepared a circular seeking funds to continue the £10 per year which the recently deceased John Bruce had been paying towards the education of Hopper's youngest child (26 February 1870; LOA 155:16).

238. With characteristic discretion Halliwell requested Sotheby not to sell some of his personal letters to Tite (20 February 1874; LOA 32:3).

at the time of my father-in-law's death in 1872 I had nearly fifty quartos dated before the Restoration, and having then determined to abandon the critical study of the text and adhere exclusively to that of the life in connexion with the history of the stage, I presented my collection together with the larger portion of my Shakespearian Library to the University of Edinburgh. It now forms the only Shakespearian Library in Scotland.

At the same date I also came to the resolution never to sell a book to any one, nor have I done so since. This rule is inflexible and I regret therefore that I cannot meet your wishes by parting with any sole remaining quarto, but if anything turned up of great importance to me in my researches I might be induced to make an exchange.

Later that year he reinforced his determination in angrily answering what must have been his friend Ingleby's questioning his decision:

Let me assure you that I am not the man to fool my friends by telling them that I mean to give up literary pursuits when I do not. You will never see the 2nd Part of the Illustrations. Although a large portion of it was printed I have had the types broken up (3 November 1876; Folger C.a.11[6]).

A month later he rejected his close friend Croker's attempt to coax him out of his resolution:

You do not seem to be aware that in insinuating I bought the Paganini letter lately at Puttick's you practically accuse me of being a disreputable liar, as I should be if I had done so after assuring you I had finally abandoned the absurd folly of collecting (6 December 1876; Folger Y.c.1211[95]).

What he had, he was holding on to; he was no longer giving of his collection. As he wrote to William Atkinson, his longtime friend:

All that I have now remaining in the literary way is a very important Shaksperian Library at Tregunter Road, including rarities that no money could now purchase. This library will stay intact where it is until some one will buy it in the lump for three thousand pounds. It is sure to go at that price sooner or later, & it is not as if I were pressed for the money (19 January 1877; LOA 240:39).

Halliwell was clearly practising concentration.[239] And concentration meant retrenchment and withdrawal into the world of his library. There was wonderment among his friends and acquaintances. Norman Maccoll attempted to humor him: "Wonders will never cease," he wrote (23 February 1877; LOA 242:68). "You have abandoned Shakespeare, you have forsworn Music Halls & now you are going to sell the remainder of your estates. What next? We shall hear of your putting on a dress coat." Halliwell's expanded answer, in almost phoenix-like terms, may be found in a letter of 1 May 1877 (Folger C.b.17[105]) to Charles Roach Smith. "Poor old Tom [Wright] is as you say dead among the living. Add to *dead* the words *to literature* & the phrase would apply to me. I have finally abandoned literary pursuits in every way, busying myself on a plot of land of 13 acres ... finding more than plenty of occupation with my plants birds & trees." Not to be ignored, however, is Halliwell's affecting invitation to Smith to visit him: "Do—do—do."

239. Earlier, it should be mentioned, he had begun disposing of his properties too. In 1871 he offered a house in Holywell Street for £100 to Fred Haines (1 May 1871; LOA 181:8); on 9 November 1871 (LOA 209:18) George Godwin offered him £69 for the freehold. On 14 July 1870 (EUL E.97.13) Halliwell wrote to Walter Williams: "I do not intend parting with the Rifleman Public House, but I intend selling my leaseholds in Struton [*sic*] Ground & another in Great Chapel Street. If you are inclined to negociate perhaps you will drop me a line."

18

Middle Hill: After Thomas Phillipps

But between 11 Tregunter Road, West Brompton, and Hollingbury Copse, near Brighton, there was Middle Hill. And the troubles with Thomas Phillipps. In 1864 Phillipps had left Middle Hill for Thirlestaine House, Cheltenham. "Between 10 July 1863 and 18 March 1864 one hundred and three waggonloads of books were transported, drawn by a total of two hundred and thirty horses and escorted by one hundred and sixty men. This, however, was by no means all."[240] Thirlestaine House was so bulging with books that, so his sister, Louisa, reported to Halliwell (25 March 1872; LOA 206:36), Phillipps wrote to Dr. Pring that he was "sorry he could n't offer him a bed as all the bed rooms were full of books." Middle Hill was left to rot. Mrs. Halliwell's diary entry for 13 December 1866 records that Aunt Molyneux said, "A black cat is now the only inhabitant of Middle Hill & that the ivy is creeping into the Drawing room." In February 1870 (LOA 191:18) Harry Hunt described "a more dep[l]orable sight of a house I never beheld":

the roof stripped of tiles, rafters giving way, which we could see from some distance off–we got through by the front door where formerly there was a window but not a shadow of one left–we could see through the house from the front hall to the skies, & the cielings [*sic*] were hanging in fact so dangerous, I was glad to get out–the drawing room was full of water, & several other rooms, there was hardly a pane of glass whole , *in the whole house.*

On 22 October 1872 (LOA 212:30) Louisa described her returning home "safely from the perils of Middle Hill":

Talk of the Rigi & Mauvais Pas–they are nothing to the dangers happily escaped to day. What with holes in the floors through which you may fall

---

240. A. N. L. Munby, *The Formation of the Phillipps Library from 1841 to 1872* (Cambridge, 1956), p. 133.

to depths unknown, & rotten rafters overhead which may fall & overwhelm the unwary travellers at any moment. Oh! Give me the known slipperyness [*sic*] of the Mer de Glace & the iron rail of the Mauvais Pas!

But that was not the main trouble in 1866–Phillipps was. He attempted (unsuccessfully) to have the lead stripped from the roof and to sell the stoves, pipes, and gutters.[241] Deserted, the house was victimized by vandals, who unwittingly accomplished some of his objectives. Always in need of money, he responded to a proposal by the Halliwells that they receive the estates "in fee subject to [his] life interest," and, "in addition to the charges already in the Estate [he] should have the right to charge the same with the payment at his death of the sum of £50,000." That was on 12 March 1862. Over the next few years the proposal went back and forth between the parties and their lawyers, with the customary conferences and legalisms and delays coolly outlined in George Ade's bill to Halliwell (17 February 1867; LOA 230:56) for £27.0.10 "In Re Sir Thomas Phillips [*sic*]." Negotiations picked up and accelerated in June 1866. Halliwell asked for the opinion of W. O. Hunt, who responded that "he should accept the proposition," reckoning that the rental "in round numbers £7000 ... at 30 years purchase, would realise £210,000–deduct £50,000 and you have £160,000 worth of the property, besides the Timber, which I suppose is of some considerable value" (June 1866; LOA 147:10). George Ade, Halliwell's lawyer, felt that £50,000 was "too much to charge the estates with but [ever the lawyer] you are the best judge of what you are willing to Sacrifice for Rendering from Reversion a Certainty" (13 June 1866; LOA 196:7). Phillipps, through his lawyer, Arthur Walker, signified that he would "require interest [at 4 per Cent for three years] to be paid on the £50,000 from the day of his decease until the principal be paid" (2 July 1866; LOA 196:3). To emphasize the point, Walker sent an extract of a letter he had received from Phillipps which indicated that "there are above 700 more Elm trees fit to cut on my entailed estates. Now if Mrs Halliwell will finish the 50,000 settlement this month" (5 December 1866; LOA 196:13). On 15 December 1866 (LOA 196:37) Phillipps wrote to "Dear Harriet" saying he was "glad to find you are promoting a reconciliation between us by placing a Sum at my disposal, in case you come into possession of the Estates ... I am advised to cut down near 1000 more Elm Trees, but if this arrangement between us can take place *soon*, I will not cut them down. I am Dear Harriet Your willing reconciler T. Phillipps." Mrs. Halliwell answered promptly and

241. See Munby, *Family Affairs*, pp. 94-5.

courteously that she would "cheerfully join in anything that may be arranged by yourself and Mr Halliwell" but it was in her power only to act in "joint appointment" with her husband, who had decided to have a minute survey made of the estates in order to determine their exact value. Displeased that the value should be questioned, Phillipps retorted: "if the Estates are to be valued, before the affair is decided, I am sorry to say I shall be obliged to sell the Trees I spoke of, as it will be a month or more before they could be valued" (20 December 1866; LOA 208:39). Not surprisingly, the negotiations broke down, Walker "assum[ing] that it is your Clients wish to abandon" them unless the matter was continued "within a week from to day" (19 January 1867; LOA 196:12).

In another attempt to assure his wife's security should he predecease her, Halliwell approached Owen Walcot, Phillipps's grandson and his nephew. Since the £50,000 required, Halliwell wrote (25 September 1867; LOA 74:15), was "disproportionate to the risk of your aunt in her 48th year dying before Sir Thomas in his 76th year," he proposed–in this merely "suggestive" letter–to give Owen a charge of £10,000 on the reversion and if he "like the idea," advised him to seek the sanction of a legal (underlined by Halliwell) adviser. Halliwell underscored the importance of the letter by adding a note: "The above is a copy of my letter to Owen posted by me at Tregunter Road pillar-box at 11 a.m. on 25 Sept. 1867." Owen's lawyer, William Salt, suggested £20,000 (22 October 1867; LOA 74:5), a charge which Halliwell rejected (25 October 1867; LOA 74:30), enclosing as support an opinion of Frederick Hendriks, Actuary to the Liverpool & London & Globe Insurance Company (24 October 1867; LOA 230:68). An appeal to John Walcot, Owen's father (15 November 1867; LOA 74:9), did not further the matter. But negotiations continued and on 17 April 1868 Mrs. Halliwell's diary reported that "James & I & Owen drove in a cab to Mr Ades office & went up to his room where he read aloud & explained to Owen Walcot the deed which has been drawn up between James, Owen & myself in which J. & I agree to give Owen Walcot £10,000 if *we* succeed to the Middle Hill property & he agrees to give James £50,000, if I die before Papa as then Owen wd succeed to the Estates."

But that was not the end of it, for it gave way to another and linked matter. A year later, on 1 January 1869, Mrs. Halliwell's diary reported , "Last night Owen [Walcot] spoke to James & asked his consent for his marriage with Charlotte ... James consented - he is very pleased with the match." The first cousins became engaged, and the question of the marriage settlement arose. Since Phillipps seems to have given young Walcot advice as to "marry one of the Halliwells," it is not unlikely that

Phillipps was thinking ahead of what might be in the next generation.[242] Louisa may well have been on the same track in writing to Halliwell, "But why in the world is he [Phillipps] so anxious for the marriage to take place? What is it to him? for of course he would not trouble about it in any way unless he would be in some manner benefitted by it" (13 April 1869; LOA 144:10). And it is just as likely that Halliwell was thinking the same. At any rate, on 23 February 1869 (Phil-Rob c.601:54) the same William Salt, acting for John Walcot, notified Phillipps of Halliwell's proposal for the marriage settlement: £300 per year during Phillipps's lifetime and £10,000 afterwards, with the proviso that Walcot give up "the possibility of enjoying the Middle Hill estate." Salt was quick to conclude that Halliwell was "purchasing Mr. Owen Walcots interests without giving his daughters anything" and suggested that with Phillipps's "support and concurrence" a resettlement might be secured. The proposal—corrected by Salt to £15,000 after Phillipps's death—was declined by John Walcot, so Salt informed Phillipps (2 April 1869; Phil-Rob c.601:56). Salt thought his counterproposal—a resettlement "on the basis of a *certain* life interest for Mr. Halliwell and reasonable provision for his other daughters but the estate to go to Mr. Owen Walcot & his future wife in strict settlement"— might be unacceptable, considering the financial circumstances of the Walcots, because it would not provide any present income for Owen. In a letter to Halliwell, Ade reported that he had informed Salt (15 April 1869; LOA 158:12) that "any arrangement for limiting Mr. Halliwells interest in the estates for life only," now or in the future, "will be futile."

Owen was advised to request more. And Halliwell patiently reminded him that Charlotte would receive £100 a year, "the same sum [he could not resist the irony] which your Father's 'guide, philosopher, and friend'," Sir Thomas Phillipps, promised to allow *his* second daughter on her marriage" and that, as far as the valuation was concerned, "our reversion increases in value every day, your's [*sic*] decrease at a far more rapid pace" (5 July 1869; LOA 74:36). On 9 July 1869, so Mrs. Halliwell's diary, "James saw Mr Ade today & made a proposal to the Walcots - offering to allow Owen & Charlotte 300 p. ann. during Papa's life - £800 p. ann. during our joint lives £20,000 [text stops]." Negotiations continued, however, over the next months.[243] The settlement was finally agreed and signed on 11 December 1869, just three days before the wedding. It is a

242. See Munby, *Family Affairs*, p. 97.

243. Phil-Rob e.418: 89-92, for example, contains an opinion (dated 5 October 1869) on possible alterations of the settlement by the barrister Charles Davidson and, in a letter to John Walcot of 8 October 1869, William Salt's comments on that opinion.

longish and legalistic document which, in essence, concludes that Owen is to give Halliwell £40,000 if Mrs. Halliwell predeceases her father and he inherits the Middle Hill property and alternately is to receive £20,000, and Charlotte is to receive £300 per year during Phillipps's lifetime.[244]

The marriage took place on 14 December 1869. The settlement of the Middle Hill estates, of which the interminable marriage settlement was only a small part, was only to be effected two years later when on 6 February 1872 Phillipps died. To bridge the course of the stalled negotiations between the marriage and the death a letter of 21 March 1871 (LOA 220:40) from Halliwell to his wife will suffice:

I am fully persuaded Sir Thos. will never leave his family a penny, & that any trouble taken with that view (& no trouble could be taken with any other, for affection is out of this question) will be thrown away, but *as* they have commenced an acquaintanceship *inclusive* of Charlotte, I think *both* Owen & Charlotte would be foolish not to humour him as far as they conveniently can, & I shall be only too well pleased if they ever get anything out of the old saucepan, as Owen calls him. But what is the most surprising thing to me that let Sir Thos. bully & oppress as he likes, yet with most people at any time he has only got to say a civil word or two with the wonderful tact he can display that way whenever he has a purpose to serve, & he gets confided in at once. Now here is John Walcot. Sir Thos. by the unprincipled cheat of withdrawing his miserable allowance of £100 a year shortened poor Mary's life by rendering a severe struggle for living necessary. One would have thought this had been enough, but Sir Thos. regularly *did* him a second time by promises (of course never fulfilled) about the £8000 settlement; & yet notwithstanding this, when Charlotte's sett[lemen]ts were in progress he wanted to involve me into entering into his belief in Sir Thos's promises about the estates, speaking of Sir T. as a good fellow, &c. &c. I certainly do hope that none of us may ever be idiots enough to be gammoned by his nonsense & ... no compromise is now possible between Sir Thos. & myself.

The news of her father's death was not unexpected, but its arrival to Mrs. Halliwell was blunt: "My dearest Harry," wrote her sister Kate, "Poor Papa died today. I have only a moment to write" (LOA 228:7). The note appended to it by Halliwell is intriguing: "This announcement of Sir Thomas's death reached us at Weston-super-Mare on February 7th 1872,

244. The document is to be found in the Worcestershire Record Office: BA 8647.

a day never to be forgotten: I rushed up to Town & before the day was over had given my Solicitor instructions for the preparation of the disentailing deed." On 10 February 1872 an obituary, written and finished by Halliwell on 8 February (so his wife's diary entry), appeared in the *Athenaeum* (p. 178). Its opening trumpet–"We have to announce the decease of the greatest book collector of modern times"–gave way to a straightforward and factual report, much in the manner of the day. There was no mention of his person or personality except that he was "not only a fine scholar, but he was one of the most learned men of his age." The only character trait noted was the "ruling passion of a long life–the accumulation of ancient manuscripts." The only connection to Halliwell was extremely indirect, to be recognized perhaps by insiders: "As he died without male issue the estates devolve on his eldest daughter, and the title becomes extinct." It is difficult to interpret Halliwell's exact motivation, perhaps it is pointless to try. Halliwell was too much of a gentleman to be hypocritical, and yet he would doubtless observe the code: *de mortuis nihil nisi bonum*. Be that as it may, the obituary and the event stimulated various ironies. Unaware that the despised Halliwell was the author, Frederic Madden attacked its praise of Phillipps's scholarship and learning as the "acme of absurdity." Hearing of Phillipps's desperate condition but unaware of his will, Staunton wrote, "I sincerely trust Sir T. P.'s magnificent library will not be dispersed, *but will be yours*" (4 February 1872; LOA 188:1). Letters to Halliwell after the death wavered between condolence and congratulation. The faithful Ashbee was one of the first to write: "I cannot do otherwise than congratulate you ... although it may sound somewhat unchristianlike to do so. But I am sure you will appreciate my feeling; for I can assure you that in any occasion of grief to yourself or family no one would sympathize more truly with you than myself" (12 February 1872; LOA 191:14). Halliwell's longtime friend Henry Stevens, after contributing his "share of condolences," continued: "But notwithstanding all my regrets, I must confess that my congratulations & hearty joy in your new accessions are such as, I trust, will excuse their being mentioned in the same note" (17 February 1872; LOA 188:12). Staunton was less diplomatic: "I hope you are as well as can be expected under the terrible implication of an access of wealth. It must be trying, but I should fancy not insupportable" (13 March 1872; LOA 194:16). William Sawyer was enthusiastic. Congratulating Halliwell on his "good fortune," he exhilarated: "May you live long to enjoy the happiness of making others happy!" (17 February 1872; LOA 187:21). And, as for those, like Furnivall, who were unaware of Phillipps's banning the Halliwells from even entering the building in which his library was housed, there was the irony of their turning to Halliwell for access to the collection.

Whatever the exact nature of Halliwell's state of mind at the death of his father-in-law–to which must be added his reaction to the death of his wife's beloved father–there was no joy in it. Relief, to be sure, but no triumph, after literally thirty years of bitter personal and legal strife and frustration. The atmosphere is movingly portrayed in the letter of condolence sent by Caroline Birkenhead, who had been Mrs. Halliwell's own governess in the Phillipps household and remained a loyal friend of the Halliwell family:

And so it is thirty years ago[245] since first you saw her who has been your good devoted & loving wife these many years–long may you yet be spared to each other and enjoy without anxiety the life bestowed on you in this world ... The thought of your altered position often comes to my mind with extreme satisfaction. Sir T. P. lived a long life–He must have spent during that time *nearly* half a million of money! Much to no purpose whatever–while his children were entirely unheeded.–It is a fearful responsibility (21 February 1872; LOA 187:8).

Halliwell was only too well aware of the fearful responsibility that lay before him. He was not a stranger to responsibility: he had struggled for years to secure the future for his wife and children. Unlike Phillipps, he never neglected his loved ones, nor sacrificed them to his own career and ambition. "Prudence," he wrote to Charles Roach Smith, "has compelled me to sell off so many early Shakespeares," though proudly asserting, " I have still one of the largest collections in the world!!" (15 December 1866; Folger W.a.81[51/1]). And so, even as he was receiving letters of condolence, he was already taking on the burden and not the wealth of the Middle Hill estates. To his friend in Stratford, W. O. Hunt, he wrote, "Although immense sums will be required to be laid out on the Middlehill estates, yet as we intend to live quietly, & put the labourers' cottages into nice order instead of erecting a new mansion &c." (18 February 1872; LOA 196:24), he felt he could accomplish his aims at Stratford. On the next day (19 February 1872; LOA 32:29) he was sent a letter from Isaac Averill, "an old resident in Broadway and taking an interest in the welfare of the Parish," who urged "some steps [be] taken as soon as possible to prevent the lawless from running uncontrolled over Middle Hill & doing

245. Phillipps died almost thirty years to the day after Halliwell's first visit to Middle Hill on 22 February 1842.

great damage, daily, to your property. Sir Thomas Phillipps"–Averill made a point of mentioning the willful neglect–"would not prosecute any person found doing damage to the property, therefore the police authorities were silenced." Halliwell must have responded immediately to Averill's suggestion that "a few notices [be] at once posted round the House and buildings cautioning the public from trespassing & threatening punishment," judging from his sister Louisa's wry comment: "I received your placard & think you very mad–'What a severe landlord' your tenantry will exclaim on reading your first appearance amongst them in print" (24 February 1872; LOA 187:7). And it is assuredly with a sense of urgent duty rather than simple possessiveness that Halliwell immediately took up the challenge, writing to Ade that the "disentailing deed, the new settlement & the new Will, should ... be executed simultaneously." More specifically, the "old Voluntary Settlement ... was constructed solely with the view of protecting Mrs Halliwell from injurious advice in the event of my predeceasing her during the lifetime of Sir Thomas, a danger now past. Subject to a thousand a year to Mrs Halliwell for her separate use, & to fair money charges in favor of our children, I must have uncontrolled possession. It is the only course by which I shall be enabled to manage the estates usefully." And he did not underestimate the effort required: "Any further limitation of my power would add indefinitely to the serious difficulties which must, even under the most favorable circumstances, surround my path" (28 February 1872; LOA 233:11). A certain exhilaration was also apparent in the face of the new challenge. Responding with thanks for the gift of a basket of game (which Halliwell had sent to many friends by way of celebrating), Miss Birkenhead excitedly offered a "little suggestion in good part tho' I dare say you wont act upon it":

When you do up Middle Hill–the House, I mean of course–and before you come to the papering of the rooms which can each one be measured for the quantity. Let me recommend you to Mr Whites 8 Holborn Bars corner of Castle Street opposite Furnivals Inn–They have papers of all kinds, French–Gold papers–Bed room papers–& for attics *sent in there* to be *sold* by *auction* or *privately*–Marble Chimney pieces of all prices some very handsome & others plainer–And with a good Choice; the things are *much cheaper* than if you were to go to the manufacturers. Admiral Giffard bought all his papers & chimney pieces there for his new house now building near Bletchingley–& Mr John Giffard also for his very handsome house at Westfield where I was staying (25 February 1872; LOA 187:26).

The Halliwells never inhabited Middle Hill, however. They were well received on a their visit of 14 June 1872: "As soon as we reached Buckland," Mrs. Halliwell reported, "the Church bells rang a merry peal & all the mean women & children greeted us & threw up their handkfs & sun bonnets ... We had a great deal of bowing to do & many of the people seemed very pleased. After we got back to Broadway we packed up & slept there having had a most delightful day." But in 1872, as later, the shadow of responsibility for the estates and the tenants was heavy. At the end of the year Halliwell wrote to Charles Roach Smith, in commenting on a prospectus he had received, "In two or three years I hope, if life & health be spared, to subscribe for everything meritorious of the kind, whether I take an interest in it or no, but at present I am overwhelmed by the extent of dilapidated farm buildings & the necessity of building about two hundred new cottages!" (5 December 1872; Folger C.b.17[75]). And a week later (13 December 1872; Folger C.b.17[77]) he reiterated his concern: he would like to give each of thirty farm-tenants a copy of William Bland's *Principles of Agriculture*, "but I am most anxious about the labourers & their having good cottages & gardens, & I cannot afford to get on in that way as rapidly as I could wish."

Halliwell's vision was not merely familial, patriarchal, economic, and philanthropic. There was an intensely personal dimension to it as well. For one thing, there was the attraction of the land and a more relaxed life, apparent in his invitation to F. W. Cosens to visit him in Middle Hill "when we are living in farmer style, as we hope to do in a year or two" (31 July 1873; Folger Y.c.1209[1]. For another thing, Thomas Phillipps, the owner of the Middle Hill estates, had been a baronet. Despite his advocacy of simplicity and his rejection of class, Halliwell must have been intrigued by the prospect, as he was of other honors. As early as 18 March 1868 (BL Add. MS. 44414, f.169), in sending William Gladstone, First Lord of Her Majesty's Treasury, a copy of his facsimile of the 1604 *Hamlet*–for which "very interesting Volume" he was thanked promptly (21 March 1868; LOA 132:29)–Halliwell broached the subject, cautiously and indirectly:

At the risk of being considered too sensitive, perhaps you will kindly not take it in ill part if I add that I would not send even such trifling testimonies of respect to one who, if life & health be granted, must occupy so exalted a position, were it not that there is not humanly speaking no possibility of my even becoming a candidate for any sort of situation or pension from any Government.[246]

On 27 April 1868 (LOA 131:25) he wrote to the Chancellor of the Exchequer to say that a tax on armorial bearings was too high, holding that if it were lower all would pay. Whatever the outcome, on 11 January 1870 Mrs. Halliwell "walked ... to the Post Office & paid a guinea for James's license for Armorial bearings." On 3 March 1872 (BL Add. MS. 44433, f.309), in a letter to Gladstone marked "Confidential," Halliwell was diplomatic but direct. Referring to the Middle Hill estates, he indicated that he received a "rental of considerably over seven thousand a year," and that "certainly a sufficient number of precedents ... lead to the conclusion that when the estates are of fully sufficient magnitude to properly support the title, the baronetcy is renewed on application." Halliwell was careful enough to ask for Gladstone's "views" before making application. But Gladstone's handwritten comment (on the verso f.310) on the renewal of the baronetcy was not promising: "ack[nowledge] & regret to say I am not as at present informed able to regard what he describes as a renewal in any other light than as a new creation M[ar]c[h] 15." This must have been a deep disappointment after the heady encouragement of Miss Birkenhead, who expected that "by & bye the Queen will ... confer the Baronetage on you with the name (12 February 1872; LOA 187:12*), and of Charles Roach Smith: "Tell me, (privately), if the Baronetcy has been, or will be, given to you. Also, if any of your friends, (supposing it necessary), have taken any steps to secure it for you" (10 March 1872; LOA 206:11). Halliwell had perhaps already prepared himself before receiving word from Gladstone, for in the conclusion of the obituary of Phillipps in the *Athenaeum* he had written, "the title becomes extinct." And perhaps even before hearing from Gladstone–the letter is not in his surviving out-letterbook for the period–he had devised a way of dealing with the disappointment. On 12 April 1872 (Folger W.a.82[194/1]) he answered Charles Roach Smith:

With respect to the Baronetcy, the title is sometimes but not always renewed in these cases, & I have small if any chance of its being given to me. As you well know, honors of this kind are in this country conferred on 'fat & greasy citizens,' not on a hard working literary student even in the rare case, as in this, when there is sufficient wealth to justify the grant.

246. A year earlier (25 January 1867; Folger C.b.17[27]), asserting his pride, Halliwell indignantly denied that he was on the Civil Pension List: "Except I were in absolute want, I would never apply either by myself or through my friends."

But although the title would be in some degree agreeable, it is not so much so to me as [to] be in the least worth a struggle. Too old for society and a mere bookworm, its utility would not be great; but it seems a pity that the rewards of literary work should in England be so mean. Neither you nor I must expect to reap any worldly material benefits. It is well for us that there is a recompence of far greater value.[247]

And two weeks later, the Jaques-like melancholy had hardened. In expressing his "thankfulness" to Samuel Neil that "no article recommending me for L.L.D. [for his bequest to Edinburgh University] or any other honor has been printed," Halliwell made it clear that "Any thing of the kind would be *very most* distasteful in the highest degree to me" (27 April 1872; LOA 192:32).

Intimately connected with the baronetcy–and all titles for that matter–was Halliwell's position regarding the name "Phillipps." Although he was perhaps not as bellicose or malicious towards Phillipps as Phillipps was towards him, Halliwell–despite going along with various attempts at reconciliation stimulated by his wife–had given up on his father-in-law, to say the least. Even the name was abhorrent to him. On 20 April 1870 (Folger W.a.82[179]) he wrote to Charles Roach Smith: "My poor Father [in-law] strictly prohibited his name bing alluded to in our house, & I follow out his wishes now to the best of my powers, the very mention of his name creating with me a cold shudder, & I must beg my friends, unless they desire to annoy me, to abstain form any allusion to him to me *either* by word of mouth or by letter." Yet disregarding the advice of his friend and legal adviser, Arthur Wood, to think before changing his name on the death of Phillipps (10 February 1872; LOA 204:23), Halliwell a few days later wrote to Ade that "the change of name being I always heard his chief desire the name should be preserved–it is only right to follow out the old man's wishes so far as we can" (17 February 1872; LOA 212:9). Halliwell was referring to "old Phillipps," his father-in-law's father, and not to his father-in-law, whose will was proved four months later, on 19 June 1872. In that will, Phillipps followed his father's formula: the beneficiaries were to "use assume and take upon themselves respectively the Surname of Phillipps," as in his bequest to Owen Walcot, and "his heirs in tail male on condition that he take the said name of Phillipps and transmit the said name to his sons." The response of Halliwell's sister,

247. It is interesting to note that LOA 197:30 is a handwritten listing entitled "Burkes Peerage & Bar[one]tage 1872" of names (with page numbers) under the headings Primary, Secondary, and Tertiary.

Louisa, to the proposed adoption of the name was immediate and characteristically direct: "How disgusting is it that 'poor Halliwell' is to pass into oblivion & musty old Phillipps take his place" (18 February 1872; LOA 188:21). Nevertheless on 29 February 1872 a royal licence was issued granting "Mr. James Orchard Halliwell and Henrietta Elizabeth Molyneux his wife Licence that they may take the surname of Phillipps only and that he may bear the Arms of Phillipps and that such surnames and Arms of Phillipps may be used by their issue." In response Louisa modified her resistance goodnaturedly: "No, I don't like your subscribing yourself *Phillipps* at all, however one must put up with it & taking all in all, Chickens for breakfast. Champagne in tumblers. figs ad lib–why I am almost inclined to think Phillipps beats Halliwell" (14 March 1872; LOA 194:11). Halliwell was not entirely comfortable with signing himself J. O. Phillipps, but as he explained to Charles Roach Smith a few days later he was "compelled to drop my old name altogether. I don't like it, but it can't be helped," and signed, "Yours ever & with deep gratitude for years of true sympathy from you when I so sorely needed it J. O. Phillipps," adding a postscript: "*Three P.'s*. A hint for one to mind my *Q.'s*" (25 March 1872; Folger C.b.17[71]). Eight months later he wrote again: "Thank you for adhering to my old name–I wish all my friends did so. Although legally called Phillipps, I mean to retain my Father's name in my new work & in all literary matters" (14 October 1872; Folger C.b.17[73]). "Halliwell" which had been replaced by "Phillipps" became "Halliwell-Phillipps" (officially on 23 May 1879). That apparently reconciling compound, however, reflected the ambivalence, if not tension, within Halliwell. Like his sister, he was loyal to his heritage: his father had worked his way from Chorley to London, had accumulated a notable income, and had generously and affectionately supported a large family. Halliwell's munificent bequest to the Chetham Library in Manchester, among other gestures and tributes, was his acknowledgement of his father's roots: "my Father was a native of Lancashire & ... it was his particular wish that our name should be associated in some way with the literary history of the County" (25 February 1881; LOA 256:15). And, as was his wont, Halliwell made much of his dislike of ceremony, affectation, and "flunkeyism," as well as his preference for simple food: "cold mutton at 5 & port after" was typical fare in an invitation to Croker to "drop in just as it may happen to suit" (16 March 1872; Folger Y.c.1211[14b]); "no dress suit nor any gammon of that kind" was another condition (19 June 1872; Folger Y.c.1211[15]). On the other hand, Halliwell was always ambitious, and the attraction of wealth and social prestige was undeniable. They promised freedom to fulfill his strivings and achieve recognition. And it must not be overlooked that in marrying him Mrs. Halliwell had come down considerably, she who, in the company of her father, had been visiting great houses, had been presented to the Queen, and had danced with Prince Louis Napoleon Bonaparte. Although she did not make demands upon him, and was a faithful and loving wife, her very loyalty to her husband must surely have kindled his desire, in one way or another, to do the best he could to keep alive what she had had from her mother's line (Phillipps, by contrast, was a parvenu, having received his baronetcy in 1821 through the influence of his wife's father, Major General Thomas Molyneux).

Inflections of the particular ambivalence and tension which references to title and name carried continued over the years. The change of name, for example, was almost a standard feature of Collier's letters. In his age and relative isolation Collier found it difficult to adjust: "I do not like your total desertion of your old *well*-known name," he wrote atop his letter of 2 December 1873 (LOA 77:29). "You ought not to suppress the name by which you have been so long & so well known," following his salutation of "Dear H. Phillipps" (3 April 1875; LOA 158:9), and a few days earlier, "I do not like to lose the Halliwell. May you not be called J. O. Halliwell Phillipps?" (9 April 1875; LOA 158:36). Six months later his salutation was "My dear old friend," with an explanation: "Excuse it, if you do not like it, as I could hardly get your two or three names (and the *Halliwell* I could not consent to omit) into the line" (24 October 1875; LOA 219:38). Finally, assured that his wish had been observed he was "glad you do not give up, nor mean to give up, the name of Halliwell" (2 April 1876; LOA 222:19). By the mid 1870s Halliwell was determined to be known by the double name: "I like the name of Halliwell-Phillipps & wish people wd use it," he wrote to Charles Roach Smith (9 October 1874; Folger C.b.17[93]), "but," he continued, aware of the split in his identity, "my legal name by my Wife's grandfather's will is Phillipps singly & so I am obliged to sign myself." And so he did sign himself, and so he did urge his friend Croker to be "*sure*" to introduce him at a forthcoming social occasion as "Mr. Halliwell-Phillipps" (6 June 1876; Folger Y.c.1211[85]). And that *Mr.*, though perhaps insignificant in this context, does summon up connections with Halliwell's ambivalence towards titles and honors. He was surely amused by George Wright's salutation "My dear 'Baron Buckland'" (24 February 1875; LOA 106:3), for they were regularly addressing each other as "Dear Sir James" and "Dear Sir George": "A most ridiculous piece of folly, George Wright and I styling each other respectively Sir James & Sir George. However, it tells sometimes in extra civility at Hotels! So much for the absurdity of English flunkeyism! J. O.

H. P.," he added to a letter he had received from Wright (5 May 1876; LOA 225:27*). But this kind of rationalization does not necessarily undo the knot of ambivalence, as is apparent in his reflection on the title of Baronet:

Even 2 certainly 3 years ago [it] would have had charms for me, but it had not now, & indeed I would not accept it as it might involve the necessity of settlements in due favor of one child. My notions & aspirations have undergone great changes during the last two years–I like to be among my old books & my old friends & not to be bothered by forms & ceremonies. A Knighthood might be useful at Broadway to distinguish one from the heap of other Phillipps's there–& if Disraeli knew the number of broad acres there he wd probably recommend it–but personally I do not mean to trouble about it (3 December 1874; Folger C.b.17[94]).

Title or no, Halliwell did distinguish himself from the other Phillippses at Broadway, if not from Charles or John or George Phillipps (who were named in Phillipps's will) then certainly from Thomas Phillipps, his father-in-law. That the property was left in a "dreadful state," as Thomas Hunt reported, he had heard from "many sources" in attending the funeral (13 February 1872; LOA 204:20). On this there was universal agreement. But the descriptions are usually restricted to the house at Middle Hill. The villages of Childswickham, Laverton, and Buckland also came to Halliwell and were not unproblematic. Right off, in 1874, he sold Childswickam to William Atkinson for £70,000 (minus expenses), doubtless to undertake the much-needed repairs on the vast estates, generally only passingly mentioned, at best, as when Halliwell informed Jarvis that he was going to be at Broadway for a week seeing to the repairs of the farm buildings (3 June 1873; Folger Y.d.5[13b]) or that he will probably spend part of the following year at Middle Hill (9 August 1873; Folger W.a.82[197]). To understand the situation it is necessary to describe the actual state, say, of the Laverton cottages which Phillipps's father had surveyed soon after he had bought the estate from Lord Viscount Weymouth in 1799:

They were very overcrowded. One cottage had 18 people in it, three families with 11 children between them and 'a very poor' old widow. Another cottage had 14, two families and seven children, two widows and a daughter; a third had 12, two families, seven children and another 'very poor' old widow. These were perhaps former farmhouses with two or three rooms downstairs. Altogether 16 cottages contained 95 people, and only one widow lived alone; there were 10 old people amongst the population ... Phillipps was worried when he bought the estate that there were not enough trees growing to repair the houses. Major building was not undertaken until after the death of Sir Thomas Phillipps in 1872.[248]

It was undertaken by Halliwell: "within four years he had built eight pairs of cottages in Laverton, a row of four in Buckland Fields and a pair in Buckland, all built of stone but with Welsh slate roofs, and all carrying an engraved stone with his initials, J.O.P. and the date, 1875 or 1876."[249] It was obviously a task which involved a heightened sense of responsibility, an enormous amount of energy, and a considerable financial investment. Halliwell was fully aware of what lay before him. In addition to wanting to begin renovating Middle Hill, which is "still unhabitable," he wrote to Charles Roach Smith (24 January 1874; Folger Y.c.1281[17]), he was, with characteristic prudence and determination, nevertheless "anxious not to be hasty, such large sums being necessary for the repairs of farm b[uildin]gs & cottages & drainage & water supply–I am bent, if I live, on getting things into good order, but it is very uphill work for a time." But although "in a tempest of haste," he informed Smith, "I am as busy as a bee in cottage building" (20 April 1876; Folger C.b.17[97]). And he was busy not merely with the value of his property but with the welfare of the community, with their quality of life. "If I live two or three years [I] shall be able to make our two villages the very perfections of sanitary arrangements, an object very near to my heart. This is, to our ideas, more important than hastening to rebuild Middlehill," he was proud to announce to Smith (8 May 1874; Folger C.b.17[91]). From John Hartley of the Childswickham Vicarage, Broadway, he received thanks for his "kind donation for the non-insured sufferers from the fire in this place" (12 January 1874; LOA 69:11). From Charles Caffin of the Broadway Vicarage he received thanks for his "generous offer of a piece of land for the enlargement of our Churchyard" (10 April 1875; LOA 74:2), Halliwell having responded to the request within a week. In 1877 he advertised for a "zealous Clergyman of moderate views" for the vacancy in the Rectory of Buckland (LOA 239:38), writing personally as well to the Bishop of Gloucester and Bristol and, sensitively, mentioning that "an extreme High Churchman would not suit the inhabitants" (23 March 1877; LOA 238:17). It should be obvious that Halliwell did not, could not, forget Hunt's description of Phillipps's funeral: "It seems to have been attended by a large concourse of people but none of the Tenantcy were present–

---

248. Anthea Jones, *The Cotswolds* (Chichester, 1994), p. 197.
249. *Ibid.*

nor was the Vicar here invited" (13 February 1872; LOA 204:20).[250]

But Halliwell was beset with problems. In advertising for a vicar, he did not disguise the fact that although the Rectory House was "very attractive in appearance," the buildings and cottages of the Glebe Farm, offered in lieu of tithes, were in a "dilapidated state, and would require a considerable outlay" beyond the large amount (£1700 alone for the draining) already expended. "Such being the case," Halliwell concluded, "the Patron is desirous of appointing a Clergyman of some means who would be in a position to undertake the responsibilities." The repair and upkeep of the vast estates presented a financial burden which Halliwell, for all his idealism, was finding unbearable. It is little wonder that he was moved to sell the Childswickham estate and village (some 1856 acres) to William Atkinson. After some delay the sale was completed on 18 March 1874, the agreed price of £70,000 reduced to £69,803.4.0 a certain land tax and lease were deducted.[251] This very considerable sum—equivalent today to some £3,360,000—as well as the rental Halliwell was drawing from the other properties, was not the end, however. On 19 January 1877 (LOA 240:39) he informed Atkinson that he was making "strenuous efforts to sell the Middle Hill Estates" and alerted his friend to the fact that "whoever buys them would probably wish to purchase Childswickham, a most important adjunct to Buckland & Laverton." And there were personal and familial pressures as well. "I not only want before I die to settle my children on a firm basis," he confided to Charles Roach Smith (31 May 1877; Folger C.b.17[106]), "but also to enjoy a good income myself. At present I have spent & shall have to spend the largest portion in new cottages & repairs. So long as I hold the estates I shall be comparatively poor. When I sell them I shall *with my tastes and habits* be rich ... It is so difficult to leave land by Will amongst 4 children to at all work well." Mounting worries led him to ask Smith to put an ad announcing the sale in a London journal (4 October 1877; Folger W.a.82[211]); three months later (11 January 1878; Folger C.b.17[109]) he reported, "My spirits will be at zero until I sell the Estates & get rid of the necessary heavy expenditure upon them which now presses upon me so severely."

250. John Fenwick's account of the funeral (13 February 1872; LOA 208:8) is slightly different: "No tenants except the 4 Phillipps [*sic*] were specially invited but I daresay many were among the crowd." It is hard to deny, however, that Phillipps had changed drastically over the years. On 30 March 1839, so Mrs. Halliwell's diary, he invited twenty-five tenants to dinner, again on 13 April 1839, and forty on 3 January 1840.

251. Details are found in a Memorandum on the Purchase of Childswickham 1874 in the Gloucestershire Record Office: D540E70.

By 4 June 1878 (Folger C.b.17[114]) he was preparing for the auction of the estates, having decided not to advertise in any Gloucestershire or Worcestershire papers (16 June 1878; Folger Y.c.1197[2]). The mansion house at Middle Hill and the manors of Buckland and Laverton, some 2782 acres yielding a rental of £4400 per year, were offered at auction on 19 July 1878. But the properties were brought in, there being no bidder up to the amounts required. In the following month, however, Edgar Flower, son of Edward Fordham Flower and brother of Charles Flower of Stratford, bought Middle Hill from Halliwell directly for £80,000, and a few months later Buckland and Laverton were bought by the law firm of New, Prance, and Garrard of Evesham for £50,000.[252] What would today be valued at about £6,500,000 brought only partial relief to Halliwell. So overwhelmed with business "complications" and domestic urgencies, he informed Smith (26 August 1878; Folger C.b.17[116]) that he had no time to write letters. Long dwindling after an accident just a few months after the death of her father in 1872, his wife was dying.

252. There seems to be no extant documentation of the purchases in the Gloucestershire and Worcestershire record offices. The information given is derived from newspapers reports of a suit against Halliwell brought in March 1881 by the auctioneers Glasier and Sons of Covent Garden seeking a commission of £1300 instead of the £50 for expenses they had received when the auction was brought in. The judge ordered a nonsuit, not accepting their claim that it was the custom of the trade that the commission should be paid on the amount realized for the property sold within a reasonable time after the auction. While agreeing on the outlines, the unidentified newspaper cuttings–LOA 259:64, 266:5, 282:2–are not consistent on the total sum: £113,000 is mentioned, as is a commission of £1100. But the agreement called for a commission of one percent of the total, and therefore £130,000 seems appropriate, as in the cutting attached to Folger C.a.11(32).

19

Three Weddings and Many Funerals

Halliwell did not bask in the glow of his literary fame. On the contrary, in 1866 he continued his withdrawal from anything resembling a spotlight. He avoided public appearances with greater frequency, and was unable and unwilling to speak in public. He was ready to help in the organizing of a Shakespeare soirée but was insistent that the help "does not include my giving a discourse upon the relics, as I cannot talk in public *at all*" (24 January 1866; Folger Y.c.1307[30]). A few months later (3 May 1866; Folger W.a.81[47]) he informed Charles Roach Smith: "1. I can't speak in public *at all*. 2. I dislike all public dinners, especially Shaksperian ones." In a subsequent letter (30 November 1866; Folger C.b.17[21]), he confirmed his stance by prefacing his signature with "so says your plainspoken & no doubt therefore unpopular friend." That position was reinforced by his almost constitutional emphasis on simplicity: his "beau ideal of an enjoyable meal, some good bread & cheese & ale at a rural alehouse, which in its way is better than any champagne feast" (8 August 1866; Folger C.b.17[14]); his being "better pleased with a bit of cold meat & pickles than with a cart-load of delicacies" (20 October 1866; Folger C.b.17[19]); his not caring "a button where I sleep if there are no bugs" (17 May 1866; Folger C.b.17[9]); even his "almost preternatural dislike to gadding about in the winter months, & I do not even stir out in London after dusk in the Winter above once in 3 months, & not that if I can help it" (15 December 1866; Folger W.a.81[51/1]). He often went so far as to degrade his position and self. After asking that his name be withdrawn from the Pettigrew Memorial Fund Committee, he assured Wright, "You will get on much better without one who is a mere creature of the study & quite unfitted for any sort of public business" (18 January 1867; LOA 121:39). Nor did he care whether or not his name appeared in the Mark Anthony Lower testimonial: "or put down Jack Ketch if you like," he suggested to Charles Roach Smith, "but it will certainly not be wise anyhow to put such small fry as myself near the top of the list" (22 January 1867; Folger C.b.17[26]). George Wright was certainly not off the mark in referring to Halliwell's "retiring and Hermit-like habits" (23 January 1867; LOA 123:12). But he was not exactly accurate either, for there is sufficient evidence that, despite his protests, Halliwell did not disregard Thomas Wright's advice: "Dont give up literature–it is the best thing in the world, even though you do some times get a little hard-worked" (3 October 1868; LOA 137:29). For Halliwell was, *nolens volens*, active in committees, did accept testimonials (despite his proud assertion that he "refused a very handsome one of plate that was started for me at Stratford" [12 January 1867; Folger C.b.17(23)]), and–though he reiterated that he had no time for letters–even drafted a note on "remodelling" the *Times* by altering its format and type so as to accommodate more advertising and thus meet the challenge of its "penny rivals" (September 1866; LOA 114:44*). Furthermore that he did enjoy a night out is beyond question. To a letter from H. O. Hunt of 21 May 1871 (LOA 178:5) Halliwell added: "22 May 1871. Met at the Exhibition of the Royal Academy. Dined at the Tavistock (Salmon, Saddle of mutton, & lobster salad). Then went to the Canterbury & Gatti music-halls, winding up at Evans until a little after midnight." In a note of 13 January 1871 (LOA 171:23*) he "had some oysters at Rule's, Maiden Lane, Covent Garden, one of the few really old fashioned shops of London." He was doubtless pleased to be asked by Robert Cowtan to sit for a photo in his collection of "Men I have known at the British Museum" (27 May 1868; LOA 143:28), as he had been by Lovell Reeve for his *Portraits of Men of Eminence* (21 April 1863; LOA 133:11) and was to be for Henry Barraud's of the Fellows of the Royal Society (19 September 1870; LOA 170:8)–and this despite the fact that he had no illusions about his appearance, writing to Henry Ellacombe: "I have no photos of my ugly mug, or would send you one with pleasure but the fashion of beard-wearing renders all who indulge in it like each other, & Bishop Corbet could address me as he once did a person at Abingdon–'I say, you fellow behind the beard!'" (25 January 1871; Folger Y.c.1217).[253]

It is not likely that false modesty or even hypocrisy might account for this behavior. Contradictions within his personality would seem more likely an explanation. Halliwell was prudent and yet a risk-taker, he was conservative and yet a prankster. "I like occasionally good living with literary work," he reminded Charles Roach Smith, and did not "think it

253. Halliwell must have turned down Cowtan, for his photo does not appear in Cowtan's album (BM 210*b.11). As for Barraud, Halliwell wrote to Charles Roach Smith: "I have such an intense objection to having my ugly mug perpetuated & do not even sit for the picture of the Fellows of the R.S. now in progress" (18 June 1877; Folger Y.c.1281[30]).

necessary to despise a 'champagne lunch' while roving about antiquities" (10 October 1868; Folger C.b.17[47]). He might have doubts about societies and clubs but could annotate his name on a listing of 30 November 1865 of the Fellows of the Royal Society thus, "*The youngest F.R.S. ever elected!* Aetat. 18 at the time. Cleverer then than now!" and preserve it (SBT ER 25/3/10/1). Be that as it may, there were also substantial reasons for his withdrawal. He was "*tormented* by an union of business (which I *detest*) & own literary work (which I like). The two together make a fiendish compound" (17 May 1866; Folger C.b.17[9]). His involvement in business, in the bookkeeping of his subscriptions and of his Stratford scheme was continuous and unrelenting and enervating. As a self-styled "creature of the study" he required peace to contribute to what he envisioned not solely—or even—as personal fulfillment but as a lasting monument. In a number of passionate letters to Charles Roach Smith he made his position clear. Referring to Smith's reading performances and reacting to a sarcastic suggestion that he, Halliwell, could attract large audiences if he read Shakespeare standing on his head, he remarked to Smith (11 September 1866; Folger C.b.17[17]): "It is well he said 'on my head', as I should never attract an audience on my feet, & am half inclined to envy your powers were it not that one recalls the wish for contemporary applause when a simple absolute correction of the text will add for ages in a small degree to the happiness of man, whereas readings are evanescent." It was not that he was against acting—he was after all a passionate theatergoer and his aim as theater historian was to unearth and make evident the exact theatrical conditions under which Shakespeare worked and developed. Travelling through the country in search of dramatic records he was, although a Londoner, not unaware of local theatrical traditions and practices. It was thus his professional as well as his personal conviction which led him to declare:

I dare say you fancy I am somewhat lukewarm about your Shaksperian Readings, so may as well say out that I for one have a very strong opinion that any such efforts are not only great mistakes but injurious, because they tend greatly to interfere with the progress of local theatricals. Unless people can learn to act in the Provinces, in short can go to an acting school, there will be no more Garricks or Kembles. Persons able to read Shakespeare with action ought to combine with others to act, & not pander to the wretched fanaticism which considers Readings or Dramatic monologues proper, but the acting of a play a sure road to Hell. I hate & detest this contemptible hypocrisy, & always deeply regret when I see men of real ability & reputation truckle, however unconsciously, to it (30 November 1868; Folger W.a.81[61/2]).

He may have considered himself "such a mere bookworm & so utterly unfitted for Society [that] I have a great disinclination to bestow my tediousness anywhere," but in the same letter to C. M. Ingleby his "curiosity" was "quite excite[d]" by the Tite-Furnivall row and he was "dying to hear about it" (31 January 1871; Folger C.a.23[26]).

There was, however, no ambivalence about his feelings towards his friends and family. They occupied him fully and passionately, even as he was protesting the contrary, as in his warning Charles Roach Smith to "be quiet at home instead of going on such a wild goose chace [to Rome] & perhaps get ill & die at that wretchedly stinking & unwholesome place," and concluding, "What a bother I do have with my friends to induce them to be rational!" (28 August 1869; Folger C.b.17[54]). In the few years between 1866 and 1872 Halliwell's correspondence contains a procession of deaths and condolences, a passing parade of figures who had played major or minor roles in his career: a long letter to the widow of Charles Kean, with a tribute to the "value & dignity" Kean's "representations" gave to the stage, and to Mrs. Kean personally, "Your domestic loss is so severe & irreparable, it wd appear a mockery to add any ordinary words of condolence" (14 February 1868; Folger Y.c.1246); a note shortly before the death of Alexander Dyce on 15 May 1869: "Called at Rev. A. Dyce's. Poor fellow, I fear that I shall never see him again" (26 March 1869; LOA 149:5*) after an exchange of letters in which Dyce charted the course of his illness, Halliwell having, as early as 13 May 1861 (LOA 79:8), contacted Henry Bence Jones, Dyce's physician; a note attached to the death notice of John Wilkins, "the most tasteful printer I ever met with" (22 November 1869; LOA 157:37); a note referring to a memorial he had placed to the memory of "poor old [Samuel] Gwinnett, a genuine Shaksperian enthusiast–so long Secy. of the Royal Shaksn Club of Stratford-on-Avon" (2 February 1870; LOA 155:5); a sympathetic portrait of "Poor old John Timbs, aged near 70, author of Curiosities of London" (4 April 1870; LOA 153:14*); a note on 15 June 1870 (LOA 162:34*): "Went to Westminster Abbey at noon. The grave of Charles Dickens had been filled up, & two workmen were busily engaged in laying the flag-stones. There was an artist engaged in sketching the corner in which he is laid, & about fifty spectators looking reverentially & sadly at the spot"–this followed by a characteristic remark to Charles Roach Smith, "If Dickens expressed a wish to be buried near Rochester, I think his family have acted weakly in giving way to the snobbish outcry of a few for

Westminster Abbey" (17 June 1870; LOA 162:40); a mention of the death of Bolton Corney, a nemesis and colleague (2 September 1870; Folger Y.c.1298[4]), of Joseph Lilly, "the last of the old generation of booksellers" (4 November 1870; LOA 174:25), of Paul Bedford, who "was I fancy greatest in the burlesque of Norma–no grand part, but it suited his peculiar style of humour" (13 January 1871; LOA 171:23*), of William Lovell, earlier his lawyer and friend of the family (5 August 1871; LOA 175:32). And there were the deaths of many others too, such as the cherished Clarence Hopper in 1868 and the faithful family doctor, Septimus Wray.

Of even greater concern was the condition of Fairholt, his longtime friend and collaborator, whose health had been declining over a period of years. A constant flow of letters to Charles Roach Smith in 1866 describes the course of Halliwell's anxiety. He "seems to me to be very very ill. He scarcely speaks ... though undoubtedly talent is common enough peculiar knowledge & the art of applying it usefully are not to be replaced, & if we lose our friend, very much will be lost with him. I look in every day but do not stay above a minute or two. He evidently can't stand it" (12 March 1866; Folger C.b.17[1]). Fairholt died on 4 April. Though himself ill, out of bed again but "very very shaky" (5 April 1866; Folger C.b.17[4], Halliwell is kept informed of the funeral arrangements, does "feel & shall feel the loss of poor dear Fairholt very acutely," and reminisces about rambles with Fairholt. To David Laing (18 April 1868; EUL La.IV.17) he laments: "Poor Fairholt is perhaps a greater loss to me than to any one, as we have been near neighbours for over ten years, & since 1855 during the greater part of every year constantly together. I feel his loss bitterly." As executor with Charles Roach Smith of Fairholt's estate he immediately analyzes the legal consequences of the will, indicating which bequests should be "separately calendared & valued" (9 April 1866; Folger W.a.81[46]); organizes for "our poor friend a niche of Memorial at Stratford-on-Avon" (25 April 1866; Folger C.b.17[5]); is asked to assist Smith in writing the inscription for Fairholt's tombstone (30 June 1866; LOA 111:25); gives specific instructions thereto:

The inscription cannot be too simple. I should say merely to give his name date of birth & death, in memoriam, but pray have something durable & *flat* on the earth. I put over my parents a *flat slab* of *granite*, which will last humanly speaking for ever, & requires no repairs. Pray don't insult his memory, by those hideous head & foot-stones" (3 July 1866; Folger W.a.81[49/1]).

He reflects with Smith "how apt we are to think any one may be more likely to die than ourselves–but the safe plan is to have all one's affairs ready for such an event" (29 July 1866; Folger W.a.81[50]); he agrees to offer a suggestion for an inscription for the brass intended for Fairholt at Stratford (7 June 1867; LOA 123:30). Almost two years later he is pleased that Smith is doing a life of Fairholt, adding as a postscript, "I cannot tell you how I miss poor Fairholt" (20 January 1868; Folger C.b.17[35]); and he offers to write a "short account of our little tour together to Amsterdam &c." for Smith's "larger life of him, which I hope soon you will set about in real earnest" (17 March 1868; Folger Y.c.1281[12]).

Halliwell's other artistic collaborator was also a constant cause for concern, but of a different quality. John Thomas Blight, whom he had engaged to do drawings for the *Illustrations*, among other things, and whom he had supported for election to the Society of Antiquaries, was an eccentric from Penzance. After accompanying Halliwell for long periods in Stratford and even spending two months as his house guest at 11 Tregunter Road–"a visit altogether to my own advantage," he thanked his host (31 July 1866; LOA 111:46)–Blight became increasingly troubled. "I am not fitted for this life," he wrote from Penzance (3 June 1868; LOA 134:19). "I have been shut up most of my days with what have seemed to me to be vulgarity and narrow-mindedness–& worse–I have an ethereal world of my own which will not blend with this ... A Life Lost–These last three words shall be the title of my Novel. I hate Art. I detest everything connected with what I used to love so much." A barrage of letters in various sizes and colors followed, Blight demanding, "I want money and I want to get away from the disagreeable people among whom I live here" (13 September 1870; LOA 166:22). The tone became surly and bellicose, forcing Halliwell to turn from patient explanations of his own proper behavior in dealing with Blight to a troubled rejection of his "excessive impertinence" (10 October 1870; LOA 166:20). This letter of Halliwell's, "seen by mere accident" by Blight's father, "grieved" him so much that he apologized for his son's "offensive words," which he attributed "solely, to the sad and melancholy affliction," a "very severe illness, which affected his intellect," in December 1868 (12 October 1870; LOA 166:17). Months later, his mind weakening still further, Blight wrote on 19 May 1871 (LOA 181:36):

I direct your attention to the 6th page of the Royal Charter of The Society of Antiquaries of London by which you may understand we may claim our rights in this world, we may 'take' any lands, tenements, and hereditaments whatsoever, not exceeding the yearly value of One

Thousand Pounds in the whole,' by this we may do much good.
I wish you would come here and assist me to secure my wife Evelyna D.
Kidwell because I am greatly opposed here in that respect, in fact I am
publicly insulted, and although I have had no answer to my letters to you
this year I am sure you will yet come down with me on my enemies and
ignorant persecutors. There is no time to be lost, you are also publicly
insulted in this town but not by me.

Not long after, John Kinsman, of the Penzance Public Library, informed
Halliwell: "Poor Blight, I fear his mind is hopelessly gone. You know I
presume he has been in the asylum for 2 or 3 months. Several Gentlemen
subscribe a shilling a week for a limited time towards his maintenance as
his parents have no means" (25 August 1871; LOA 177:38). And then
again, "Poor Blight! I understand the Asylum Authorities have no hope
that his mind well ever be better" (1 November 1871; LOA 185:39).
Halliwell could not have been unaffected by the fate of "poor Blight" with
whom he had had a long and profitable relationship and from whom he
had received 248 letters alone in the Edinburgh collection.
    And there is little to match the exquisite sensitivity and sober
practicality of his wrestling with the sufferings of his ailing and needy
companion Thomas Wright. Marking his letter of 12 January 1875 (Folger
Y.c.1211[63]) to Croker "Private" and also "Strictly Private," he confessed:

The more I ponder over poor old Tom the more difficult the question
appears. To take the things out of pawn merely means their being again
pawned at once again by Madame [Wright's French wife], for of course I
could not retain the articles. I am persuaded that any cash wd not add to
his comfort, though it might to Madame's, who must eventually settle the
question of his debts in her own fashion. I dread coming to London—he
will be coming to Tregunter & getting worse. Any amount of game or
delicacies that I know he fancies I shall of course gladly send, so there is
a chance of his being comforted by such things—though even they may be
sold. I have written to ask him what wine the Doctor recommends, on the
plea that I could send him better than he could buy in the neighbourhood.
You must guide me as to any amount of creature comforts for him. I
suspect it would only affront them, as it did years ago, to suggest a smaller
house. Madame stops the way in any thing. As to the proposed
testimonial, I should not at all like to trust my own judgment in the
matter, but I should be guided at once by the opinion of Mr George
Godwin, who has got about as sound a judgment as any one I know, but
you should state to him fairly the difficulties of the position. Tom is not

fit to be trusted in his present state with a large sum of money, & if Madame had it, the chances are that it wd nearly all go to France as much of some other big sums have. I am persuaded in my own mind that a sum of money wd not add to his comfort, & that is all you & I really care for. What becomes of the 'fair one' I don't care a rush.

There were other blows to be absorbed. Mrs. Halliwell was forced to explain to her father that "some one must have made up their mind to play off a hoax upon you, for it is very certain that none of *my* children show the slightest tendency to being *half-witted*"–Phillipps had referred to the eldest, Henrietta Somerset. And to his charge that the "second is afflicted with a Spinal Complaint," she answered: "though Charlotte has had a weak spine I am very thankful to say the mischief is stopped, and she is better" (1 November 1867; Phil-Rob b.169:83).[254] Mrs. Halliwell was still unable to detect her father's maliciousness, even though he attributed their condition to providence: the consequence of her refusal to effect a reconciliation on his terms "will be that you will fall under the Curse destined for all disobedient Children 'unto the 2nd & 3rd Generation'. I understand the Curse has already commenced."[255] There was also providence of a sort–a "providential escape"–when Mrs. Halliwell had "pasted 400 slips for James on 1.H.4 - & had just arranged them on his oak bookcase under weights to press when Julia Pettigrew came in & stopped to chat - all at once we heard a great noise & I rushed up to find a large [piece?] in the ceiling in James's study had fallen just over the bookcase & exactly where I had been" (Diary, 11 December 1868). The event must have sensational, if not traumatic, for on the very next day (12 December 1868; LOA 148:18) Dyce wrote to "congratulate you & yours on your escape from injury by the falling in of the cieling [*sic*]," he himself having escaped from a blown-down chimney which might have crushed him "to mummy." And on 15 December 1868 (LOA 147:16) Thomas Halliwell asked for details of the "bad" accident, thankful that Henrietta was not hurt; Halliwell himself was so concerned that this and the other ceilings were "so dangerous I am having them all redone, & the only place I have to write in is my dressing-room–& not able to get at a single book or paper" (13 January 1869; Folger C.b.17[48]). Just a few days earlier, on 8 January 1869 Mrs. Halliwell reported another "bad accident": "In going

254. In a letter to Collier (18 September 1867; Freeman Collection) Halliwell explained that "on a long round of country visits of 2 months" one of his daughters "exerted herself too much, & I fear something wrong with the spine in consequence."

255. In Munby, *Family Affairs*, p. 78.

to the Glass cupboard when I opened it a chair fell from the top on to my head & cut it on the top just under my hair ... James was very frightened - My head bled fast & I had it sponged with cold water & then went quietly to bed–Owen & Loui were up. The servants were very frightened." And further there was G. M. Hills's report (20 September 1870; LOA 170:15) that Thomas Wright, Halliwell's dear old friend and collaborator of over thirty years, was "as helpless as a child ... quite broken & lost," his health deteriorating drastically. Both the providential escape and the condition of Wright, although for the moment only worrying, were foreboding.

With such emotional burdens, as well as the legal, business, and scholarly demands, it is little wonder that Halliwell's amazing–even manic–energy and congenital sense of order and system were accompanied by what may well have lain behind and kindled his attempts at withdrawal: depression. On 23 March 1871 (LOA 178:38) William Salter Herrick, a young artist whose acquaintance Halliwell had made when purchasing his portrait of Portia, touched on a subject of mutual concern:

Yours must indeed be a malignant one.–When I think of your home, and the kindness and simplicity that marks it, it makes me very sad to think there should ever be a shaddow [sic], and how much more–so heavy a one. One thing however I feel I can do–now I know how you must seek to remedy it, i.e. storing the most absurd things I come across for a next chat.

"Really & sincerely ... grateful" for the letter, Halliwell recognized the pattern of theater and Evans's, and replied a few days later: "One must think how much there is (with ourselves & most of us) to be thankful for, & as for trouble, if it does not come in one way it will in another, though there are peculiar sorts harder with some temperaments to tolerate" (31 March 1871; Folger Y.c.1230). In a further letter of 22 April 1871 (22 April 1871; LOA 178:40) a bond is forged: shadows, theater, after-theater dinner–a Halliwellian ritual:

A friend used to say to me one half our lives we are hunted by shaddows [sic]–the other–the shaddows hunt us–one of these has been very busy with me lately, so I looked out last night for something to help me shake him off and unluckily drifted into the Adelphi Theatre–i e, from the frying pan into the fire–The first act finished with a murder–2nd a woman to be hung 3rd a death struggle and a man pitched out of window–I sighed for 'Evans's' all the time, and came home–*sold*.

And the undeniable gloom surrounding the death of Thomas Phillipps could not be lifted even by the cajoling consolation of trusty and crusty Miss Birkenhead, who in a letter of February 1872 (LOA 187:36) headed "Wholesome Advice for the 'Book of Fidgets'," counselled:

A friend of mine lost her husband two or three years ago—he had not been a good man in any sense of the word—She has since become a Roman Catholic; for the reason as she asserts—that she may pray for his 'Soul in Purgatory' but it wont do—so take warning—& dont trouble yourself at all about such a useless business—You 'll have enough to do of Worldly business for some time to come! I always hoped to see the day when your good dear little Wife & you would have your own ... It is not likely that I can be of use to you in any way—but you have only to let me know it. I cannot condole with you, except for the many worries & vexations you have endured for years past!!

Nor was he relieved by the friendly bullying of Edward Roberts: "You are as useless as ever I see but you ought'nt [*sic*] to be. You will come to the presidents dinner notwithstanding for it will *not* be tail coats & you will not have to speak except to your neighbours & we will put you at the bottom of the table next Geo Wright if you like" (19 June 1872; LOA 210:5).

But there was nothing shadowy about Halliwell's admission to Charles Roach Smith (26 November 1871; Folger C.b.17[69], "I am nervous sensitive and worried by the least thing, & l am very grateful for words of sympathy like you so often give." And in the same letter, anxious about Wright's health, arranging to give away or sell the larger portion of his Shakespeare library, and intending to spend half a year in the country, he reveals his inner struggle by reporting that his wife and children "are all as jolly as Sandboys." He had recently grown a beard: in a few years he was to comment on the vanity of Louisa's husband "trying to make himself look young": "Why doesn't he grow a greybeard like me & own himself to be an old 'un" (27 October 1878; Folger Y.c.1187[2]). He was intensifying his need for arranging and ordering his collection: thanking Charles Roach Smith for another copy of his *Remarks on Shakespeare*, he explained, "You will wonder what the deuce I want with another. One copy goes into my New Place drawer for the sake of the gardening, the 2nd I have cut up for other drawers, e.g. your remarks on the Charlecote story for my Charlecote drawer &c., & now I want a third to bind up into my permanent library" (22 March 1869; Folger Y.c1281[13]). And yet his wife reported on his fifty-first birthday (21 June 1871): "Thank God he is in very good health both in body & mind."

Mrs. Halliwell was not unaware of her husband's problems. Her diary records them faithfully, without pathos, for all their married life. It may be her diary but its focus is Halliwell, and all the satellites revolve about him. Henrietta Halliwell was a loyal and loving helpmate; she accepted her role and fulfilled it wholeheartedly. Like her husband's, her duty was to her family. And though she had no illusions about the difficulties they faced—as daughter of Thomas Phillipps she was directly involved in most of them—it fell to her to support her husband, to educate the children, and overall to demonstrate stability and exude cheerfulness. Her diary was, after all, not so much a private one—Halliwell had even helped copy parts of it and included some of it in his literary legacy[256]—as an informal history of the family. Although it depicted unhappy as well as happy events, it never criticized the members of the family, nuclear or distant. Almost selflessly and always cheerfully Mrs. Halliwell loved her husband, worked on his projects—collating, copying, pasting, and whatever—wrote him numerous letters when he was away (on 22 March 1871 she wrote him three!), and nurtured and protected her children. Her house was a reflection of that love, protectiveness, and good cheer.

The years between 1866 and 1872 were for Halliwell a period of great stress. 11 Tregunter Road was bustling with activity. Despite Halliwell's attempts at withdrawal, the door was always open to a host of neighbors, visitors, and guests. "Come in pudding time," Halliwell urged Charles Roach Smith, "There are provisions out here at 1.30 & again at 5.30" (12 January 1867; Folger C.b.17[23]). And inviting Croker, "No dress coats nor any gammon of that kind" (19 June 1872; Folger Y.c.1211[15]). Even holiday homes were included. From Worthing Halliwell invited John Wilkinson and his wife: "We have a bedroom a hearty welcome & pretty country around, & you shall smoke as much as you please, or indulge in any other vice that may be agreeable" (28 July 1870; Folger Y.c.1298[3)]. And Halliwell's guests could expect high spirits and good fun. On his return from the United States, Henry Stevens looked forward to a visit: "I am dying to hear & see some of those dear dry old jokes you have been pickling since our absence in America. I shall expect to find them crisp & crunchy" (26 June 1871; LOA 178:22). One such joke may have been Halliwell's modest proposal of 6 June 1871 (LOA 187:32):

256. LOA 240:29, for example, contains "Extracts from my Wife's Diary in 1842," with the remark: "My Wife kept 2 diaries at this time, one brief, the other longer."

A new variety of butcher's food is more required by the public than perhaps anything else. My ideas is that donkeys, clean-feeding animals, properly fatted for the butcher, would supply a kind of food no doubt as good as beef or mutton, probably superior, & certainly a variety. People at first will of course say that those who eat them will be cannibals, but all new ideas are ridiculed at first.

To which Owen Walcot, his son-in-law, added: "I hereby undertake on the part of Charlotte & myself that neither if us will divulge the enclosed secret without J.O.H.'s written permission." The members of the family, it is clear, enjoyed the jokes and contributed their own. A petition to Halliwell signed with their full names by all four daughters and Owen on 15 June 1871 (LOA 181:18) urged the following:

We the undersigned pray and beseech thee, the respected sire of this family to allow Miss Ellen & Miss Katie Halliwell to go over to Haven Street with Owen & Charlotte Walcot this night and sleep there, and to be brought back by the honoured mum & thyself to-morrow, for it occurs to us that one carriage will not carry four and all the meat-pies & delicacies you intend to bring.

The children were delightful. In 1866 Henrietta was twenty-three, Charlotte nineteen, Ellen twelve, and Katie eleven. They all wrote often and charmingly to their "Dear Papa," "My dear Papa," "My dear Pa," "Dear Parsey," and later "Dear Old Man." The youngest–affectionately known as Giant 1 and Giant 2–were especially endearing, as in two letters written from Worthing to their absent father on 27 August 1870. From Ellen (LOA 166:8) a poem:

> My dearest Papa,
> Thank you for your verse
> I'll write another
> Which will be a little worse.
> My dearest Papa
>
> Your 'giants' want you back
> For our morning walk
> With you, we lack.
>
> My dearest Papa,
> We are going to the station

To meet Willie Pettigrew
And Lady Dillon.

My dearest Papa
When will you come
To your Worthing Villa
Baking in the sun.
My dearest Papa
How is Jack Pudding
In omnibusses & cabs
About London scudding?

My dearest Papa
Come back to the seas
Then you will cease
Perhaps, to cough & sneeze.

My dearest Papa
Give my best love
To Jack-Pud & Aunty
And Alice & yourself
And now I must finish
For very soon
Mammy & the Giants
Are going to the town,
And then in the sea
Perhaps we shall go
To dip ourselves in
From head to toe.

And from Katie (LOA 166:9):

My own dearest Parsey,
Thank you very much for your verse. I would write only Mamma writes
so often that there is nothing to say. We both ache from running about
yesterday so much with little Parker & the Wrights; the little Swinburnes
were here too. The Wrights go away to-day ["morrow" crossed out]. I
hope your cold is better & that you will come home on Monday we all
want you. Give my best love to Alice & Aunty & Jacky & yourself.
                                                    I remain
                              Your affectionate child, Mrs Kackleberry.

The two eldest wrote newsy and affectionate letters, especially Charlotte when she congratulated her "dearest Parsey" on his fiftieth birthday, "which I hope you will not spend poring over your dusty old books (no offence to their reverence) but in the bosom of your family with one wee little thought of your Barley" (20 June 1870; LOA 162:7).

Newly married, she was Mrs. Owen C. Walcot. Charlotte and Owen, the son of Henrietta's sister Mary, were first cousins, grandchildren of Thomas Phillipps. They had known each other for years. On a Halliwell trip to Ludlow, not far from Bitterley where the Walcots lived, Owen Walcot (so Mrs. Halliwell's diary entry for 26 June 1861) makes an early appearance: "Mary's eldest boy came to breakfast with us but left at 9 o'c. he is at Grammar School & the examinations are now going on. He is a quiet fair boy, like his father & is to go into the Army." Thereafter Owen was a regular visitor to 11 Tregunter Road, attending church with the Halliwells and taking part in their walks on his trips to London from Oxford, where he was at college. He was in the habit of coming in late. On 8 August 1868 "he returned at 12-30 this morning a.m. James & I were both fast asleep–J. having gone to bed in his clothes before 10 to have a nap, & then awake to let Owen in–but Owen after ringing the door-bell 4 times, wrote a few lines to say he cd not make us hear, & wd return to Charing X Hotel to sleep–He came in this afternoon." Owen, was not, however, a loner, for Halliwell took to his nephew famously and the two shared not only the convivialities of family life but also the pleasures of London's night life. "At 2-45 a.m. this morning," Mrs. Halliwell's diary entry for 31 July 1868 reports, "I awoke & heard a noise & found it was James & Owen returned & they cd not get in with the latch key - I went down & let them in - & they went into the kitchen & got some supper - They had been to Canterbury Hall, Alhambra &c. They left again at 3 a.m. & walked to Billingsgate & saw the fish unloaded, then to Covent Garden to see what was doing there, they had some coffee - & then walked to the Serpentine to see a swimming match wch did not come off - They returned home about 8 o'clk." Owen was a happy companion for Halliwell, an easy-going, undemanding young man who enjoyed cricket and had a passion for billiards, who sang along with the family in the evening, and, as he did on 25 August 1868, "amused himself with standing on his head on the lawn for his uncles amusement." Halliwell was very fond of him and concerned for his welfare, as when he learned that Phillipps had "refuse[d] to help John [Walcot] as he promised when Owen was to go to college" (Diary, 10 November 1864), and occasionally sent money to Walcot and was in the habit of giving Owen a sovereign now and again.

Owen was not a particularly good student. From St. Edmund Hall, Oxford, he wrote to his "Dear Old Squire": "Away from you I am as melancholy as a sick rat and to my utter dismay there is only a month before the exam. I must do all I know, but then you know, so fearfully clever" (18 October 1868; LOA 147:9). Mrs. Halliwell's diary records on 5 December 1868: "James heard from Owen that he has again been plucked havg failed in Divinity - We were all very sorry to hear it but quite expected it." Halliwell was disappointed but nevertheless "wrote & asked him to come to us as soon as he liked." And when Owen "wrote in pencil saying he is laid up with violent cold, shivering & sore throat & that his doctor will not let him go up to his exam[,] James decided directly to go to Oxford & see him & set off at 10 a.m. intending to take a return ticket for two days but sd if he cd return tonight he wd telegraph to me" (Diary, 20 May 1869). He did return the next night after 11, having given the "scout a sovereign ... to look after Owen." But the next morning Mrs. Halliwell "put fresh shirts &c into James's carpet bag - he had a hasty breakfast & started off before ten o'c. to go down to Oxford again to Owen although the Doctor said there was no necessity for him to do so - but Jamie is very fond of Owen & was fidgety about him" (Diary, 22 May 1869), and rightly so, for Owen had scarlet fever.

All the while, the marriage settlement was being negotiated. On 31 October 1868, Charlotte's twenty-first birthday, among numerous gifts and nine letters of congratulations, Owen gave her a "gold guard ring letters a.i.e [i.e. *aei*, Greek for "forever"] enamelled in colors" and on 31 December had asked for and received Halliwell's consent to marry Charlotte, having "spoken to her several days since & she accepted him." All the family was pleased and an early marriage planned, Owen having written (so the diary entry for 27 January 1869) "that he was so delighted to hear they (O. & C.) were to be 'spliced' so soon, that he was obliged to run round & round the table." Mrs. Halliwell began the preparations, working "all day for C.'s trousseau" (Diary, 10 March 1869), "at Charlotte's linen" (Diary, 19 March 1869), and "at Charlotte's clothes" (Diary, 13 May 1869). But the negotiations bogged down, not the least because of the intercession of Phillipps. Among other things, Owen informed Charlotte (so Mrs. Halliwell's diary entry for 18 April 1869) "that Papa means Owen & C. to live at a house of his in Brockhampton nr Middle Hill, & he has given the present tenant notice to quit - Neither O. nor C. like the idea - We have not been consulted in the matter but James says he will not agree to it." And, of course, the lawyers were at work. Mrs. Halliwell wrote to Owen "& told him the proposal to postpone his marriage was originated by Mr Salt who seems to think that something may turn up in a years time - wch I said to Owen meant in plain English the death of one or other of the parties interested - & which I thought horrible to rely upon" (Diary, 13 May 1869). The atmosphere of mistrust is evident in Charlotte's informing her "dear Parsey," "I am very careful about Owen's letters and burn them after reading them two or three times. I have bothered him so often to be careful that it will lose its effect if I say much more" (2 June 1869; LOA 150:42).

When the wedding was finally settled, Halliwell was exhilarated and yet sad. At first, he concocted a lavish plan: "Henrietta & Charlotte shd go to Sydenham & have lodgings for a fortnight & reside there & be married at S. Church as soon as the settlemts are ready to be signed & the weddg breakfast for as many friends as we like is to be in the Crystal Palace" (Diary, 16 November 1869). A few days later Mrs. Halliwell reported, "Jas talked with us about the marriage [-] he has arranged to have the Weddg breakfast at 1 £ p. head in the Coffee room of Gt Western Hotel Paddington & has taken rooms for Henrietta & C. & Alice & Meg for a fortnight as C. must reside there - Poor dear Jamie he cannot bear that she should leave from her own home & he feels it terribly" (Diary, 21 November 1869). It was Mrs. Halliwell's fiftieth birthday; "the dear girls all gave [her] little presents." The excitement was almost too much with everything happening at once. On the next day "James got up very early, & called Owen & asked him to get up & go out with him as he cd not bear to breakfast at home - he was quite overcome & Owen consoled him as well as he could ... Charlotte cried early this morning but went away in good spirits at 5 p.m. I finished packing her boxes ... Heard from Mr Herr the tailor - Charlotte wrote out a list of 72 people to be asked" (Diary, 22 November 1869). On the following day (so the diary entry for 23 November 1869) "James returned home last night at 12 o'clk. he dined at the Clarendon & went to see Toodles at the Theatre afterwds - Owen & I waited up for him - he was much agitated & upset - but recovered himself & went to bed quietly but was up very early this morning." On the next day he made a codicil to his will, leaving everything in his study to the library of Edinburgh University. On 3 December 1869 Mrs. Halliwell bought notepaper for the invitations; Halliwell and Charlotte went to "Veitch's nursery to enquire about bride and bridesmaids bouquets"; Emily Newcomb wrote out a form of invitation "wch James slightly altered & I adopted." On 6 December 1869, ninety-six invitations to relations and friends were sent off: the wedding ceremony to take place on 14 December at 11.15 at All Saints Church, Norfolk Square; the

wedding breakfast at the Great Western Hotel Paddington at 12.30.[257]
Proudly, Halliwell informed Charles Roach Smith: "It is not an usual
wedding party, but includes without exception every old literary friend I
have from 1838. There will be present nearly 20 members of the Society
of Antiquaries" (13 December 1869; Folger C.b.17[60]). The array of
wedding gifts arrived: from Louisa's "very elegant" "frosted silver centre
piece for dinner table" to a pincushion from Ann Badman, her
housemaid.

The wedding itself occupies one of the longest entries in Mrs.
Halliwell's diary:

A very lovely day & mild - We were all up very early & got breakfast over
- James went off directly after breakfast to Town about a plan of the
Tables - & returned before eleven o'clk to fill in the names - The
bridesmaids were as follows with the Bridegroom's friends - Henrietta
Halliwell & Mr Gilbert Moor, Ellen Halliwell & Mr Arthur Koch Katie
Halliwell & Eric Walcot, Owens sister Kate & Mr Mason, Loui & Mr
Hogg. There were four carriages with two grey horses in each - I went in
the first with John Walcot & Mr Wright to the Hotel & saw Charlotte
who was already quite dressed in white silk - Wreath of Oleanders &
orange blossom & Tulle veil waiting for her father She looked very pale
but very pretty - I left her & with Kate & John Fenwick drove to the
Church of All Saints Norfolk Sqre A man was waiting in the side aisle
with our bouquets & presented me with mine & I then passed between
the bridesmaids to the Communion table having first met Owen & his
friends in the Vestry - Charlotte soon arrived with James who was very
nervous - John Fenwick & I stood next to Owen & Kate Fenwick & Mr
Wright on the right hand side of the rails - Owen & Charlotte in the
middle & James & Reginald next to the Bride - John Walcot commenced
the service & married them & Thomas Halliwell who read very
impressively finished it, dear Charlotte behaved beautifully she spoke
every word after John clearly & distinctly & was heard all over the Church
- Owen was more nervous but he got through it well - The Church was
not crowded but a great many of our friends were in the pews. As we
walked up a hymn was played, & when the service concluded the Wedding
March was played as we walked to the Vestry - C. & O. signed first then

257. Halliwell devoted Volume 156 of the Letters of Authors to responses to the
invitation. The index is entitled "Charlotte's Marriage." Among those who wrote
that they could not attend were Collier, Sir Henry Dryden, Charles Flower, Smith,
Staunton, and Samuel Timmins. Phillipps did not attend, of course, but gave his
permission for his daughter, Kate Fenwick, to do so.

Henrietta & Kate as the principal bridesmaids - the favors were pinned on & we returned to the hotel entering by the private entrance at the entrance of which scarlet cloth was laid down - We all assembled in the Reception rooms & our friends soon came in fast James went at once to the large Coffee room to see that the cards with the names on were in their right places & the carte & plan of the tables placed for every one. The breakfast was ready at 1 o'clk. We were more than an hour in the reception room before every one arrived - & Charlotte & I & the bridesmaids talked to our friends & introduced them to each other seventy five people came - The ladies dressed very handsomely, several in Honiton lace shawls & Indian shawls, & handsome jewelry - John Walcot led me into breakfast & seated me at the head of the cross table - James took Kate Fenwick who sat on his right hand at the bottom of the table, there were 36 at the cross table including the bride & bridegroom & their party - the rest of the company were at the long tables which stretched the whole length of the great Coffee room a very handsome apartment supported by marble pillars - While the guests were walking in & seating themselves the band played the Wedding March beautifully - They stopped while John Walcot said grace at the commencement & also when Thomas Halliwell returned thanks at the conclusion After ices & sweets came round - Mr Gordon Hills rose to propose the health of the Bride & Bridegroom & soon after a waiter came & asked me for smelling salts, I had none, & in a few minutes I was summoned to poor Charlotte who was quite upset with the heat fatigue & excitement & was nearly fainting We had the window opened I bathed her face in water & she recovered a little & was able to put the knife into the cake & draw a line across it & sit down again - Mr G. Hills's speech had been stopped but Mr Mason returned thanks in a good speech & then Mr George Godwin proposed the health of the Brides parents, & made an excellent & very kind speech praising dear Jamie whom he had known for so many years - This rather upset me & after Charlotte had risen & bowed very gracefully to the company we left the room - Owen took her out & Blanche Newcomb & I got up two flights of stairs to her bedroom with great difficulty - & sat her in a chair & undressed her - She threw herself on the bed & rolled about saying she did not know any of us, shuddering & saying we looked like dressed up Dolls - she did not know me at all & asked for something of Owens to look at - They brought her dressg case & she was a little quieter We cleared the room of friends & after about an hour I dressed her in her travelling dress & Owen took her down to the Station - Thomas & I following to see her off - before the train left she was quite herself again as soon as she was in the open air. All our friends quietly departed not wishing to stop after Charlottes illness & about 5 o'clk we were all leaving for home. Everything went off beautifully - The music was very good - It was all furnished by Cramer & Beale & cost 8 guineas - There was a piano & Brass band - & dances & galops were played - I came home with John & Kate Fenwick & Blanche. James with Miss West - The girls in the other carriages. At dinner we had John Walcot, May, Kate, Loui, Edith & Eric Walcot - Regi & Miss Barker - Thomas & ourselves & Miss West making sixteen.

The breakfast menu (LOA 169:29) was splendidly all in French: Potage, Entrées, Grosses Pièces (20), Entrées Chaud Froid (4), Salads (4), Entrements (28), and Les Glaces (2). And very special for one who could not or would not make public speeches, was Halliwell's sincere and modest speech (LOA 76:8):

In anticipation of a toast which is inevitable on these occasions–that of the Bride's parents–I have written these few lines to ask to be kindly excused from the duty of an oral acknowledgement. Under ordinary circumstances, an attempt on my part to make a speech, & an endeavour to fly over the moon, would be attended by results about equally satisfactory. At the present moment it is simply impossible. Had it been otherwise, I should have desired to express a hope that my daughter's married life may be as happy as that of our own. If it is, & the now young couple successfully claim in after life as many flitches as we are entitled to, all that I have got to say is that bacon will become very scarce in Dunmow. I should also have wished to observe how gratifying it must be to my daughter to be surrounded by her well-wishers & that her marriage should be honoured by the presence of so many who are distinguished in the various branches of literature; & lastly, how very great a pleasure has been conferred upon Mrs Halliwell & myself by the attendance of so large a number of old & valued friends.

Halliwell was called upon to make another speech, for a year later, on 29 December 1870, his eldest daughter, Henrietta (affectionately, Larry), married Frederic C. N. Hall, a lieutenant in the Royal Navy. Like Owen, Freddy had known the family for a number of years, though not a long as Owen. On 9 December 1867 Mrs. Halliwell reported that "Mr Frederic Hall Lieut. R.N. arrived from his fathers house Shirenewton Rectory Monmouthshire, to dinner he is Revd C. Hall's eldest son." The two young people struck it off. The next day (so the diary) "Henrietta May [Walcot, Owen's sister] & Mr Hall spent 3 hours at Museum, then went to Trafalgar Sq. & lost their way going there, then walked to Westmr Abbey, then through Eaton Sqre–lost their way a second time & did not get home till nearly 5 o'c tired & wet through to the thaw–We had expected them back to lunch. In the evening they went to the Newcombs & danced until 11 p.m. ... They came home pleased with their evening." Their relationship was not as complicated as that of Charlotte and Owen: they were not first cousins, there was no Thomas Phillipps to worry about. Freddy was happily welcomed into the family—the astute Louisa wrote, "I am glad you like F. & have no doubt you will continue to do so as a son-in-law–a good steady youth & not too young" (9 February 1870; LOA 155:6). Like Owen, Freddy went to church with them and joined them in their music, walks and excursions. Henrietta, who had had various bouts of gloom during her younger sister's courtship and immediately thereafter, perked up. On 27 January 1870 "Mr F. Hall R.N. arrived to lunch–James asked him to stay dinner & in the afternoon he & H. went to Ken. Museum." As if animated by Charlotte's wedding, things moved quickly and smoothly. On 7 February 1870 Mrs. Halliwell's diary reads: "This evening Freddy Hall asked Henrietta to be his wife & she accepted him - he is the eldest son of the Revd Charles Hall brother of the late Lord Lanover & a Lieut in the Navy & 26 years of age - H. is the same age. James & I approve of the match, he is clever, steady & very obliging - Ellen & Katie are very amused - his ship is the Troopship Serapis." Two days later Freddy gave Henrietta a gold ring with three pearls for an engagement ring, and Thomas Halliwell wrote to congratulate her. On 12 May 1870 (LOA 163:12) Henrietta wrote coyly to her "dearest Papa": "Now won't you be surprised when I tell you I have a visitor in the shape of Rev. C. R. Hall, he has be[en] staying here since Monday ... Fred told me his father was coming up to Town ... so I thought it would but be polite to offer him a bed."

It is not necessary to rehearse the details of their courtship in 1870 or the natural excitement in the Halliwell household. All happy families are happy in the same way, so the axiom: there were joyous excursions, balls, walks, dinners. For Halliwell the activity was a cause for exuberance, a respite from the increasing tediousness of his professional obligations and legal complications and a confirmation of the high value he placed on a harmonious family. His spirits raised, he once again threw himself into the wedding arrangements–in the very midst of which, on 23 December 1870, Charlotte "was confined of a dead son." The Halliwells had spent the last days with her, then returned to London in weather that matched their mood. While they were waiting for the London train on Christmas day, Mrs. Halliwell reported, "It was bitterly cold & the countrymen's beards

& hair were covered with icicles & the boys hair also - The poor young calves were trying to lick up water from the ice - We got hot water tins at Worcester, & came on to London all day without anything to eat or drink except a little breakfast." After the "bitter cold frost & snow" and the "water frozen & pipes stopped," 29 December 1870 was a "clear day & the sun as it rose shined beautifully." It was Henrietta's wedding day.

We got up very early & got breakfast over & then the bridesmaids dressed & so did Louisa Grace, & Ernest Baker - James keeping up very well - The carriages came at 10 o'clk - Five carriages with 2 white horses in each. The 1st carriage took Mr & Mrs Hall myself & Edward Baker - the other carriages contained 6 bridesmaids, Mrs Baker, Mrs McDonnell - Reginald & Fanny Barker, Ernest & Willie Pettigrew, Mr Wright & Croker & lastly James & Henrietta - Got to Holy Trinity Church, Brompton soon after 11 o'clk - Arthur Koch arrived in time as groomsmen - We took our bouquets as we entered the Church - & the ceremony soon commenced Fred was there before the bride - She went through the marriage ceremony quietly & answered very clearly & so did Fred - Henrietta wore a plain gro[s]grain white silk dress - trimmed with white fringe - Orange blossoms & myrtle were in her wreath, & a plain tulle veil on her head - she looked very nice - Thomas Halliwell married her assisted by Revd Charles Hall the bridegroom's father When it was over the two principal bridesmaids went to sign the register - & then we got into the carriages and drove through the park to Paddington Hotel & went into the reception room while the friends arrived to breakfast - At the Cross Table in the large Coffee room were Lieut & Mrs F.C.N. Hall the bride & groom Revd Herbert Hall & Miss Halliwell (Ellen) Mr Kensington & Miss G. Hall, Mr Arthur Koch & Miss Eva Hall, Mr Fitz Newcomb & Miss Baker, Mr Ernest Baker & Miss K. Halliwell Mr Pettigrew & Miss M. Baker, bridesmaids & groomsmen Revd C.R. Hall & Mrs Halliwell, Revd T. Halliwell & Mrs Bryant, Mr Planché (Somerset Herald) & Mrs Baker, Mr Wright & Mrs Newcomb, Mr Hepworth Dixon & Mrs Haines, Captain Budworth & Mrs Molyneux, Mr A. Wood and Lady Dillon, Mr J.O. Halliwell & Mrs Hall At the side tables were seated - Revd Claude Parez & Miss Newcomb, Mr Walcot & Miss Weaver, Captain Somerset & Miss Herrick - Mr Herrick & Miss Molyneux, Mr Hills & Miss Wood, Mr R. Halliwell & Miss Barker, Revd Edward Elton & Miss Emma Molyneux - Mr F. Haines & Mrs MacDonnell, Mr D. Croker & Mrs Hills, Mr Wilkinson & Miss Pettigrew, Mrs Robinson & Mr Shaw, Mr Ade & Mrs Wood, Mr Parker & Miss Birkenhead, Mr Baker & Miss Tovey, Miss Emma Molyneux, Mr Robinson & Miss Robinson, Miss Edith Newcomb

& Revd J.E. Halliwell, 63 in all.[258] The band played [Newspaper cutting reporting the marriage pasted in here] during breakfast beautifully After breakfast Henrietta & Fred changed their dresses & went down to say good bye to our friends & thirty of us including myself & the bridesmaids & groomsmen went down to the platform & saw them off for Reading where they are to sleep - As the train left the groomsmen cheered which was heartily taken up by the porters - When they left both were in excellent spirits - We returned home about 5 p.m. had tea changed our dresses for the theatre and at 6 p.m. an omnibus which James had hired drove up - our party got in & drove to the Halls in Thistle Grove where we picked them up 14 in the omnibus - James followed in a cab with Croker & Mr Pettigrew & Ernest - Herbert Hall & Owen joined us in the dress circle a party of 20 - to see the Sleeping Beauty - When we got home we supped James & the rest stopped to sup at Evans's.

Once again Halliwell rose to the occasion:

Being one of those unfortunates who are incapable of making any sort of speech, even of the briefest & slightest description, perhaps these few written lines may be accepted in response to the inevitable toast of the Bride's parents. I have to return the best thanks of Mrs Halliwell & myself to you all for so kindly coming, in this inclement weather, not a few from long distances—to personally wish my Daughter happiness in her new career, and to congratulate us on the acquisition of a son-in-law in every way calculated to ensnare that happiness. Living a quiet & retired life, it is only on an occasion like the present that we have the opportunity of assembling together some of our old friends. The few acquaintances of recent years, who honour us with their presence today, will we hope in time allow us to include them in that list, as we are anxious to avoid the folly of the Princess Badroulboudour in being tempted to exchange old lamps for new.

And once again he was lavish, paying the bill (30 December 1870; LOA 172:36) of £68.15.0 from the Great Western Royal Hotel for 62 Breakfasts 21/ ea = 65.2.0; Extra Sherry & Cigars 13s.; Coachman 14s.;

258. Underlining is in the original. Halliwell devoted Volume 172 of the Letters of Authors to responses to the invitation. The index is entitled "Larry's Marriage." Among those who wrote that they could not attend because of age, weather, or distance were Charles Flower and Frederick Kendall (both of Stratford), Sir William Tite, and John Wilkinson.

Musicians Lunches (twice) £1.8.0; Sherry for ditto 18s.

Writing to John Wilkinson a few months before Henrietta's wedding, Halliwell once again delineated his way of life: "You will scarcely believe it possible, but they [Charlotte and Owen], along with *my* [underlined three times] Wife & eldest daughter, & the latter's intended (coming up from Portsmouth on purpose) are going out tonight to a ball! What demon had enticed them to the folly I know not. I stay quietly at home reading my newspaper, tempering the news with a bottle of claret, belonging to the choice but small company of really sensible persons" (2 September 1870; Folger Y.c.1298[4]). Even if the excitement of the two weddings within a year were not taken into account, Halliwell's actual doings would be enough to establish what was the reality of his existence, to confirm in this period as in all periods of his life, the conclusions–elegantly varied but in essence emphatic–of many of his letters: in a "*whirlwind* of occupation" (27 December 1872; Folger C.b.17[78]), "In delirious haste" (12 June 1873; Folger 1211[36], "In a tempest of haste" (20 April 1876; Folger C.b.17[97]), "In desperate whirlwind of haste" (26 July 1876; Folger C.b.17[101]), "In electric & fiery haste" (29 September 1877; Folger Y.c.1211[112]) being just a few of them. He was uninterruptedly busy with his professional and legal concerns, which had him going into town to lawyers and record offices and out of town to Stratford and, "for the purpose of examining the archives of various towns in search for notices of plays & players," on just one occasion "taking a little tour" of archives in such places as Lyme Regis, Bridport, Dorchester, and Weymouth (29 July 1871; Folger Y.c.1213[75]). And there were, of course, his nights out on the town. To a letter from H. O. Hunt (16 July 1871; LOA 175:14) Halliwell added: "*Tuesday.* We dined at the Trafalgar at Greenwich, adjourned to the Alhambra & concluded at the Tavistock. *Wednesday.* We dined at the Tavistock, adjourned to the Holborn Amphitheatre to see Lulu, the wonderful lady acrobat, followed by a visit to the Holborn Assembly Rooms, concluding at the Tavistock with the inevitable whiskey & seltzer. Both days very festive."

If this were not enough. Halliwell was fully engaged with his family and relations. Four daughters received his best attention. When he was not travelling, there was work together, there were days for trips and shopping, evenings with songs and games, and there were always a month or two of family holidays by the sea. And when he as away, there was a voluminous correspondence full of news and novelties. Mrs. Halliwell kept him apprised of business letters and her domestic deeds and needs, such as hiring a cook or needing money, and social activities, such as playing croquet with their neighbors. In a not untypical letter of 7 May 1868 (LOA 131:10) to her "dearest Jamie," she included a copy of a letter he had received, summarized four others, reported that she had sent off catalogues, that the children had visited the Palace and Park and fed the deer, that she had dined with the Wests and their children, paid the bills, needed more money, as well as having given him family news and asked for his. The married daughters wrote often, happy with the husbands but with problems for "dearest Parsey" to listen to or help with. Taking him up on his offer, Charlotte informed him that "I should be happier if I could pay the Chemist's bill which is over £4 before running up another bill–the Christmas bills do rather swamp us & I should be glad of a few pounds just now in case your grandchild arrives alive & kicking on the scene" (1 February 1872; LOA 209:8). But on 28 February 1872 a telegram arrived, so Mrs. Halliwell's diary, "saying that Charlotte has been confined of a dead girl." And on 15 March 1872 (LOA 206:16) Charlotte, "getting on perfectly well," painfully and bravely concluded, "I don't know what you will say to me, losing all your little grandchildren like this–but I must do my utmost to get quite strong & well before any more come."[259] Henrietta also wrote, a long six-page letter on one occasion, describing Freddy's activities–he had joined the H.M.S. Invincible–and the dreariness of living in Hull. Ellen and Katie were, to be sure, steady and enthusiastic correspondents.

To these came a considerable number of letters from a sizable group of nieces and nephews. On 4 February 1867 (LOA 122:13) Halliwell received one of the typical letters from Louisa's daughter, Mildred Baker, to her "dear Uncle Jim":

Thank you very much for he book you sent me. I like it very much. If you can say Smith's smashed 20 times without a blunder I will give you a penny. We had a half holiday to day because it was Miss Smith's birthday and we played games with the boarders we had such fun. We played hissing and clapping and dolls. Erny has gone to school. We are going to have a party at Miss Smiths on friday. We are going to have a half holiday on friday and saturday and a whole one on Wednesday. We have six coos now Mama has cured the cats from eating them up. I think you will have 20 loaves soon.

Good bye best love to all your affectn niece. M H Baker.

259. Charlotte gave birth to a boy on 31 March 1873, but had another miscarriage on 17 January 1874 and still another was feared on 14 May 1874, her fifth pregnancy since her marriage in 1869.

A week later (12 February 1867; LOA 120:15) Louisa's son Ernest wrote to "Dear Uncle Jim":

Thank you very much for the five shillings you sent me I have got it changed. It has been very wet here lately One of the college boys stole thirty six racket ball and three dozen other balls and tried to steal a paintbox out of the drawing room but he was seen trying to take it Mr Barry the head master of the college asked him which he would rather be expelled or to let the praefects do what they like with him he chose the latter he had a good caning from the head master and from the head boy of the college direckly after he had had the caning his mother came in and kissed him and patted him on the back Well's and Skipton two of our old boys have got a scolarship at the college of twenty five pounds a year jolly for them I hope you are all quite well best love to all

I remain
Yours affectionately
E E Baker

Complementing the child's scrawl from Algernon Baker (1 March 1869; LOA 144:21), his sister Grace wrote to her "dear Uncle, J. O." on the same day (LOA 149:24): "Thank you very very very very much indeed indeed indeed indeed for the delightful charming excellent super excellent astonishing gift of a hamper." To which Mildred added her thanks for the hamper (LOA 149:24*) and continued, "It is a great pity you did not send it while Erny was at home and then it would have saved you all that fuss of writing to me every day and saved you some pence. Thank you all the same. Good-bye." From John Elton Halliwell, Thomas's son, there were letters from Oxford thanking him for gifts, giving him information about certain antiquities, and (from his proud father) news that he had had a first and been ordained deacon and later had received a Divinity Scholarship. From another of his brother's sons, Thomas Frederick, Halliwell received word on how he was "getting on" in New Zealand, having evidently settled down after sowing his wild oats at home. There was even word about Richard Bisset, Halliwell's brother Richard's wayward son: a letter from Sarah Chard, his grandmother, asking for money to help support Richard, who had "lost all he possessed in the World," having, among other misdeeds, "Borrowed Money on some valuable things among them his Fathers ring" (4 June 1872; LOA 210:14). These letters reflect Halliwell's kind concern and affectionate engagement; from their number alone it can be inferred that they were always forthcoming and unforced. It is also important to stress that Halliwell took time for his nieces and nephews as he did for his own children. One such instance may stand for many others. In 1863 May Walcot was badly burned when the sleeve of her dress caught fire from a candle in her bedroom. There were fears that if she did recover she would never be able to use her arms again. On 31 October 1867 she was invited to Tregunter Road and stayed until 8 February 1868, during which time she was one of Halliwell's girls, as it were. He treated her lovingly and compassionately. On Christmas Eve day in 1867 Mrs. Halliwell's diary entry reads: "James had a fly & we took May W. & Katie to Canton (the dentist) - K. had a piece of tooth extracted & May had her teeth wch were decayed [from the acids used in the medicines when she was burned] cut off - a cast taken of her mouth & 4 new teeth put in - the pain of cutting & filing was very great - We went to Aley at Knightsbridge & James sent from there a handsome basket of game to Mr Geo. Ade - From De Castro in Piccadilly he sent a box of biscuits sweets &c to Louisa. He paid Ward the Winemerct - we went to Covent Garden & bought oranges & pears for tomorrow - called on Miss Birkhd & had beer & biscuits. Went to Rippon & Burton too - At Grant & Gasks James made May a present of an embroidered white muslin dress for which he paid a guinea (she was very pleased)."

To Halliwell's domestic routine there were relatively minor disturbances: the ceilings falling in, the house redecorated, Mrs. Halliwell's vaccinated against smallpox, the servants disciplined, and the like. To Mrs. Halliwell's household accidents came one which caused much concern. She described it in her diary entry for 15 July 1872 thus:

Fine day - walked out with Jamie & the girls. The girls went to the Town before breakfast In the afternoon went for a ride with Ellen, Katie Owen & Mr Hart the riding master - I rode a high Chestnut horse which I had ridden before it was a good one for trotting & cantering - Eric Walcot was also one of the party - We went along the parade & passed Charlotte who was on the balcony at Argyle House where the Walcots were lodging - we rode off to Offington & home by Tarring but unfortunately just as we got to Tarring a bird flew out of the hedge & frightened my horse and it bolted with me & in the village as I was turning a corner a large cart with brushes was in the way & not having room to pass at the rate the horse was going, it slipped down on its hind legs & threw me into the road; Two kind women picked me up & took me into a cottage & we sent for Dr Worthington who took me & Ellen home in a fly - My forehead had three deep cuts & one on my nose, both my eyes became perfectly black my face was very much swollen & bruised both my hand black & my left

thumb dislocated & my right leg & knee fearfully bruised. Dr
Worthington came again in the evening Ellen went in the evening with
Owen & Eric to tell Charlotte of the accident.

Mrs. Halliwell's report was remarkably calm and controlled, but the family
was alarmed. Thomas Halliwell wrote on 19 July 1872 (LOA 199:8): "truly
sorry–very pleased to hear an improving account this morning & shall be
very anxious to hear of further progress & I hope *rapid* recovery." Others
wrote as well, and Halliwell assured Croker that his wife was "rapidly
recovering" from the shock (23 July 1872; Folger Y.c.1211[16]). But some
weeks later he was more cautious: "My Missus is going on very favorably,
but I fear it may be many months before her system entirely recovers
from the shock" (16 August 1872; Folger Y.c.1211[18]). Life would never
be the same for the Halliwells.

Outwardly of course it was business as usual: Stratford, Middle Hill,
Shakespeare all called and Halliwell responded exhaustively and
exhaustingly. His reaction to the requests and then demands of Furnivall
and his New Shakspere Society, as well as his continuing relations with
other Shakespearean editors, including three Americans, was unabated.
Despite his avowed "I am on the retired list of Literary Hacks & don't
answer no literary questions nor no nothing" (2 June 1878; Folger
Y.c.1211[121])–indeed his adamant, "I have done entirely with literary
work & *hate it* [underlined six times]" (13 June 1878; Folger
C.b.17[115])–he entertained a vast literary correspondence; persisted in
negotiations for a Shilling Shakespeare; searched for dramatic and
theatrical records in Barnstaple, Worcester, Reading, Chester, Colchester,
Tiveton, Gloucester, among other places; was elected a member of the
Council of the Camden Society in 1874 and 1876 and vice president of the
British Archaeological Associations in 1876; continued for a number of
years as an informal adviser to Maccoll of the *Athenaeum*,[260] pursued his
bookdealings despite his "resolution" in 1876 that, as in 1872, "never to
sell a book to any one" (23 February 1876; LOA 226:21). In short, despite
his considerable reservations, he had to admit to Charles Roach Smith:
"Here I am pegging away like an old fool as if my living depended on it.
However, I should take to drink if I didn't" (11 March 1876; Folger
C.b.17[96]).

260. This, although he protested to Ingleby that, aside from giving an opinion
on whether "some conjectural emendations were new or admissible & that is
positively all," he was never asked "directly or indirectly in any way respecting its
Shakespearean management or reviews of any kind" (24 February 1876; LOA
226:18).

But Mrs. Halliwell needed special attention and a change of scene. "My Missus is going on nicely & *slowly* recovering her general health," Halliwell informed Croker. "But the Doctors strongly recommend a long dose of quiet, & fear any great length of stay in London will not at present at least be prudent" (3 November 1872; Folger Y.c.1211[20b]). In a way the enforced rustication was not unwelcome to Halliwell. who had long sought retreat. He admired Charles Roach Smith's "living plainly & without ceremony," asserting that he and his wife "live as quietly as ever, & dislike new faces" (6 October 1872; Folger C.b.17[72]), "are both of us disliking more & more anything but the old English farmhouse style," and that he was looking out for a permanent "sea-side residence" (3 December 1872; Folger C.b.17[74]). And a week later from Worthing: "It is chiefly when in the country that I have time for reading, & have certainly read a wonderful lot of old books in morning in bed the few months we have been here"–and then the almost automatic connection, "Yes, we are all aging; you & I have good health, a blessing worth millions of Sovereigns or millions of acres" (13 December 1872; Folger C.b.17[77]). Mrs. Halliwell's condition required more than the simple life, however. "You seeing her for a few minutes," Halliwell explained to Croker, "have no idea of the *extreme quietude* & absolute freedom from any sort of excitement now for a long time *necessary* [underlined three times]" (6 January 1873; Folger Y.c.1211[26]). For Halliwell there could only be strain: "the old, old story–increasing years, decreasing powers of work, & more & more to do. The cry is still, they come! By *they*, I mean all the terrors of business, queries &c. &c. &c." (8 May 1874; Folger C.b.17[91]). And the litany, increasing in frequency and intensity, of his "rule of avoiding large parties of any kind" (16 June 1873; Folger Y.d.5[15b]); his "being unable to make any sort of speech or address of even the slightest kind. I should break down to a dead certainty at the second sentence" (8 February 1876; LOA 226:15); his persistent unwillingness or inability over many years to appear in Edinburgh to receive an honorary degree, despite assurances that all would be held as simple as possible and no speech would be required; and his growing concern about his health and age, forcing him "to live on rule, taking scarcely any drink but dry old champagne ... In plain words I am not getting younger" (8 December 1875; Folger Y.c.1211[79]).

There was something traumatic in the comment Halliwell added to a letter of 9 December 1875 (LOA 232:26) from Freddy Hall: "P.S. is a reference to a little mad freak of mine one evening in Novr 1875, when I took the chair for about 1/4 of an hour at the Oxford Music Hall at Brighton & got loudly cheered for making a fool of myself!" The apparently lighthearted response to Freddy's frivolous suggestion that, "with a little practice" Halliwell might qualify for the Metropolitan or the Alhambra, barely disguises an increasingly heavy-hearted disposition. What is noteworthy in this period, when his wife was mentally decaying, is the transition in Halliwell from physical weakness–headaches, lumbago, and the like–to mental strain and weakness. He was no stranger to depression; George Wright was ready with encouragement, "You must really rouse yourself in *every possible way* or we shall be having you getting in such low spirits, that life with its many attractions, will be as *nothing* to you, and that must–ought–*never* happen rest assured!" (15 July 1876; LOA 227:12). And again on 19 February 1877 (LOA 242:78): "How sorry I am to hear of your continued indisposition, and the necessity of seeing your Doctor again ... If kindly thoughts and frequent good wishes would restore you to yourself, you would not be long ill or tormented by such troubles as at times, you have to fight against, and which I feel certain like your bodily ailments, are to be got rid of by pluck and a less excitable sensitive nature, as yours has of late become." But his condition had become clinical. He was unwell, "an upset of the nervous system," he admitted to Croker (12 August 1875; Folger Y.c.1211[73]). "Though I have stomach health," he confessed to "dear Old Cro" in referring to Croker's stomach disorder, "there is no use in concealing the fact that I am very bad *indeed* [underlined four times] in nerve power [inserting] more than you can fancy" (31 October 1875; Folger Y.c.1211[78]). To Ingleby he complained: "My nerves are in such a queer state & I avoid at present any sort of literary work or even light reading. So long as there is fine weather it is all very well–but the dark days of winter?? Tell me the remedy" (17 September 1876; Folger C.a.11[5]). To F. G. Fleay he explained, "*My power of enduring head work is so impaired I have definitively abandoned all literary pursuits*" (8 December 1876; Folger Y.c.1222[7]). "You have no idea of the disinclination I have to the simplest kind of mental labour, even to letter writing," he admitted to Charles Roach Smith, compared with which "one of my annual attacks of lumbago [is] nothing at all serious (11 January 1878; Folger C.b.17[109]).

"Sandwich has the melancholy thought of Fairholt and Rolfe. It [does] not seem so long since that we were all there together. Add a similar period to the present time & we shall both of us be in our graves," he had said a few years earlier to Charles Roach Smith (11 September 1873; Folger C.b.17[87]). Four years later: "Oh the days that we have seen!! [inserting] Never to recur," he reminisced. "For though I have so much to be thankful for, the real zest & joy of life are gone from me for ever" (10 September 1877; Folger Y.c.1211[111]). All around him friends were dying: Hunt, Staunton, Dyce, Tite, Black, Wright. Others of the good old days would follow soon: Collier, Planché, Thoms, Chappell, Stevens. It is not surprising that Halliwell should no longer recall Louisa's comic scolding, "Alhambra & Cremorne are all very shocking–& *you* ought to know better at 63" when he was only fifty (25 August 1870; LOA 166:14) and note of one of his favorite places on 13 October 1878 (LOA 233:20*): "Visited Cremorne today. The only remnants left were a few statues looking so miserable amidst scattered debris, & occasional trees." A month later (25 November 1878; Folger C.a.11[13]) he thanked Ingleby for his "great kindness in re the Athenaeum Club," but declined wearily: "There was a time & not long since that I should have jumped at the prospect. I really feel now so lost to all kinds of ambition that, in all probability, were I elected tomorrow I should decline to pay the fees for the privilege of entering a house at the most 2 or 3 times a year."

This was only part of the story, however. For one so gloomily old could also be youthfully jolly. "I had quite a party on Tuesday," he wrote to his "dearest Harry" (6 August 1874; LOA 220:29), "Tom Wright, Ripe, Croker, Percy Farren, & Harry Hunt, after which all of us (excepting old Tom) adjourned to Cremorne, the oldest of the latter party (that is I) being as usual on such occasions the most festive!" A note of 23 April 1875 (LOA 217:26*) emphasizes his "jollity": "Gave a merry dinner party, present, George Wright, Fred. Haines, Chas. Flower of Stratford, J. R. Planché, Dillon Croker, H. Stevens, F. J. Furnivall, Fred. Hall, Dr. Worthington, Myself. Did not separate until 1/4 to 1 a.m. Planché, in his 80th year, the wittiest & merriest of the party!" A social being, he was hearty in his hospitality: "Can't offer beds, but have lots of grub at any hour with welcome" (18 August 1874; Folger Y.c.1211[55]); "A spare bed & a most hearty welcome, with no end of smoking liberty" (14 July 1875; Folger Y.c.1281[26]); "look in at grubbing time" (20 November 1877; Folger Y.c.1211[115]). And along with his invitations was irrepressible "jollity" in the form of playful jokes and puns: asking Croker to arrange to come to dinner with Wright, "sieve view play" (23 January 1873; Folger Y.c.1211[28]); "Why do people shrink from winding up your clock?" he asked Croker, "Give it up? Because sensible folk never if they can help it touch a Croker-dial (Crocodile)!!!!!" (14 February 1873; Folger Y.c.1211[29]); "Do come & dine with me tomorrow (Saturday) at *6 Pee Em Sharp*" (2 January 1874; Folger Y.c.1211[46]; inviting Croker to dinner where he will have "some piscatorial corpses" (18 April 1874; Folger Y.c.1211[34]); "Trusting to have the felicity of hearing from you with all the noose" (27 July 1876; Folger Y.c.1211[88]).

Whether Halliwell's invitations were coming from Worthing or Ryde or Brighton or Ramsgate or the Isle of Wight, his favorite place of entertainment was 11 Tregunter Road, his home, where alterations were going on unceasingly; 1869 and 1872 saw major renovation and decoration. There were structural improvements and interior embellishments. "James set the men to work on the Drawg & Dining rooms today—he chose a green paper for his study & then went to London with Owen to Hartley's and bought a marble mantle piece to replace the composition one in the study he also bought a marble fender which is a style much coming into fashion" (Diary, 5 January 1869). On 17 February 1869 "Trollopes men in the study Emerys men in the bedrooms - Brakes men put up the ceiling in upper passage - & Staples laid gas pipes in the Drawing room - & Marsh began altering the garden." On 1 April 1869 Halliwell went to Dent's and "bought a 10 guinea clock for his study. "The rooms ... look very well now," Mrs. Halliwell reported on 10 May 1869, showing them to the admiring Lady Dillon:

The Din[in]g Room has green paper & gold stars & mouldings - with engravings on the walls & 3 bronze Gas burners. The Draw[in]g room pale blue grey paper & gold stars - gilt mouldings to ceiling & door & shutters - Blue reps furniture. Ormolu Gas burners two on mantle piece & 2 over pianoforte oil paintings on the walls as well as water colors - Rosewood furniture.

Halliwell was very proud of his house and possessions: "This house has been practically rebuilt—I think *for its size* it is now one of the nicest in London—no expense has been spared in rendering it nice in substantial comfort and decoration," he wrote to Jarvis (27 January 1875; Folger Y.d.5[33b]). He even went so far as to allow a guest to smoke a cigar in the study, "the first time he ever allowed one to be smoked *in* the house," the astonished Mrs. Halliwell noted (Diary, 2 May 1869). For all his loss of "zest," he was very much involved in the furnishing and decoration of the whole house and not just his study. "I think I shall be able to manage everything by midday tomorrow," he assured his "dearest Harry," "& arrange for having all the furniture out. I will direct about the wardrobe to Charlotte. There will be a rare mess in the house, two inner walls must be rebuilt or else the stair-case will come bodily down sooner or later" (6 August 1874; LOA 220:29). Tours in North Wales and Lancashire with Fred Hall (19 November 1873; Folger C.b.17[90]) were "pleasant," as were "rambling in Somerset & Devon" (15 November 1874; Folger Y.c.1211[60]) and, as always, bathing in the sea. But 11 Tregunter Road was where his study was, his labelled drawers and specially built bookcases, his collection—his work. It was, above all, home and family.

The family was a constant source of assistance and comfort. The young nephews and nieces, now older, remained faithfully affectionate. Grace Baker wrote to thank Halliwell for the jacket—"a real beauty, worthy of its owner"—he had sent for her twenty-second birthday and, in the custom of easy family intimacies, closed: "I won't send any loves or affections for I know you can't abide 'em so to be curt Good By Your 22. niece Grace Baker" (28 October 1874; LOA 182:10). From Regie Halliwell came reports of work he had been doing for his "Dear Uncle James": scanning the *London Chronicle*, enclosing two items that might be of interest, and continuing his search for Shakespearean "scraps" (24 December 1874; LOA 116:11). From the wayward Richard Bisset Halliwell came word that he had "put away childish things" (15 March 1876; LOA 141:37). To "Dear Erny," his nephew Ernest Baker, Halliwell sent thanks for his dealing with his post (25 October 1877; Folger Y.c.1187[1]), and Ernest, knowing one of his uncle's passions, sent his report of the actor Charles Mathews in *My Awful Dad* (14 December 1877; LOA 241:63): that Mathews was getting too old and "ought to have been at home by the fire in his slippers instead of on a stage deceiving himself ... into believing that he was a boy of fifty."[261]

His own children were constant correspondents. Katie, his youngest and favorite, pertly informed her "dearest Old Man" that the church in Saintbury was "the kind of church to suit you as there was no sermon because there was a christening & at ordinary times Mr Simons only preaches about 10 minutes" (17 May 1875; LOA 201:19). Henrietta, signing "Yr loving Child Larry Hall," was delighted with the "*image* of you & thank you very much for it dearest old Pa, it's just like you look when I ask for something out of your study which of course you don't want to get rid of, & you put yr hand in that most elegant of positions & say 'not for yo'!" (25 September 1876; LOA 240:51). And from Katie came a happy account of the marriage on 6 September 1876 of Ellen to her first cousin Francis (called Frank) Lowry Graves, a captain in the Royal Army:

It was a pretty jolly little wedding & I think everyone enjoyed themselves. And the people on the way to Ellesmere made arches etc & threw rice, fired guns etc. There were lots of speeches at the breakfast, but not set

261. This was Halliwell's opinion too on 27 May 1873 (LOA 202:3*), but on 22 April 1876 (LOA 228:9*) he noted that "A few years ago I thought clearly that he was rapidly failing altogether. Now acting at his advanced age with all the spirit & vivacity of youth."

ones–everyone kept jumping up, like Jacks in the box, proposing each other's healths ... In the afternoon most of the men went to old Mr. Hodgson's to play Billiards & eight of us went for a long walk, by the River Dee. Aunt Kate drove out with Mamma & Puss & Larry stayed at home. There were 18 speeches–we have just counted them up. The breakfast was so very pretty & people sent such lots of flowers & fruit & offered carriages & footmen. We need only have had one hired Carriage. George Graves gave Ellen a splendid gold bracelet with an E. & scroll in diamonds. Uncle Walcot gave her a very nice photograph album–Aunt Kate–an awfully jolly jewel case. Emily Cleland. (a fan). The Newcombs–an ornament and a paper knife. And Mr Molyneux's son, who was a groomsman, gave them a lovely Case of fish knives & forks–& they have done wonderfully well. Frank sent her a lovely bouquet from London–he got it at Wills' and ours came from Shrewsbury. I hope I have not tired my dear man with this account (9 September 1876; LOA 240:33).

It is not clear why Halliwell did not attend the wedding, but after what may have been some initial difficulty with his future son-in-law,[262] he gave his consent to the marriage (10 July 1876; LOA 233:23) and granted his daughter an annuity of £200 on 1 September 1876. Two days after the wedding (8 September 1876; LOA 228:32) Ellen, signing "Your loving child," wrote from Carlisle on her way to Edinburgh on her honeymoon, and Frank added a touching note from "Your most attached son":

We had a beautiful day for our wedding & I hope that the sunshine that then smiled on us may shine on us for the remainder of our lives. Ellen seems very happy. I hope I may always continue to make her so. We have enjoyed our trip so far & I feel happier than I ever felt in my life, & I hope when you see us both again that any regrets you may have felt in giving her to me will be entirely forgotten.

It was Charlotte most of all who informed Halliwell of the sad condition of "Mamma," who was staying with her, "is very well & quite happy & contented ... She has quite left off falling to sleep in the day as she did in London, & sleeps well at night & never wants her

262. From a letter from Graves of 22 October 1875 (LOA 241:73) it is apparent that Graves had agreed to Halliwell's "conditions which under the circumstances I cannot consider too hard. The deductions from my income for professional expences, should I obtain an appointment at Woolwich I believe would be trifling."

medicine–She drinks nothing stronger than hock & cider–and does not seem to care about anything else or miss it" (31 May 1875; LOA 227:26). A year later (9 August 1876; LOA 227:34) a letter to "My dearest Father" from "Ever yr afftte child Charlotte Walcot" attempts cheer but offers little hope:

Mamma was delighted with her letter & the fan this morning & says I am to thank you very much for them. She is very well & quite happy I am sure, the carriage is a grand thing the drives take up the afternoon & she never seems to tire–she is also fond of the garden & the various animals in the farm yard–She is *quite* able to read her letters & to understand them I find. I will see that She always has some silver in her purse, for she does not at all like to be without any, though there is little opportunity of spending any here, however she does not seem at all to care about the bustle of towing & shopping.

Mrs. Halliwell's own writing tells her story more eloquently. On 15 June 1875 (LOA 228:38) Charlotte notified her father that Mamma "wants you to order her a new diary, as she has only two or three pages of the old one left." That diary, a four-volume closely written daily family chronicle covering the period from 1837 to 1875, began to change. In 1870 the handwriting is larger, and the entries have less content and detail. Mrs. Halliwell's main occupation besides walking seems to be sewing and working at quilts for the poor. By 1875 signs of incoherence are apparent: lack of punctuation and fuzzy spelling and grammar. The entries are skimpier and the unsteady hand is unable to maintain the line. Days were skipped or in the wrong order. The entry for 12 April 1875 is not untypical:

I wrotte to Papa this morning and then went out for a walk in the Havenstreet woods In the afternoon and after to lunch Little Johnny also wemt with me Johnny and then came hom after Lunch I read the dreadful wreck at Scilly Charlotte and I arranged the flowers in the glasses Charlotte went down to Mrs Stockdale as she is does not know ho know how to do it This morning I went down to the Woods and came back with a basket of primroses and I was walking two hours 2 hours and a half I also walked for two hours with Johnny and Martha Mr Stockdal camen to afternoon.

The last entries, in a struggling script slanting sharply upwards, were on 7 and 8 July 1875:

Wednesday 7th I had a carriage to St Helens and came back through Ryde in the evening I walked to the common gate with Charlotte to meet Owen Thurstay 8 Owen went to Brighton to play a cricket match I I wrote to Maria Carter

There was obviously little need for the new volume her "attached husband" was fond of presenting her. In a letter to her "dearest Jamie" written just a few days after the request (21 June 1875; LOA 228:31) her fragility of mind is evident in the wavering lineation, dropped letters, uncrossed t's and undotted i's, and failing punctuation:

I am longing to see you aan my dear Girls it seem a lontime withou seeming any of you Now I must congratulate upon yoir Birthday Some and as some people hav just called and Charlotte is out I reailly must go and send fo And with my best love to you all Believe me your your affectionale Wife

Henrietta Phullipps

Almost a year later, a letter Halliwell received three months earlier began "My dear Papa"–"Papa" then crossed out and replaced by "Jamie." The hand was not hers, as the postscript by Fred Hall makes clear: "She was very anxious to write herself but could not manage it, so I took the heads of what she wanted to say, & wrote it, which has pleased her, & she says she is Very happy" (6 May 1876; LOA 224:6). The many doctors she had seen over the years had been unable to check the decline, and so the opinion of W. H. Nicholls (25 September 1876; LOA 243:47) was neither new nor unexpected: "I feel confident that her health, mental & bodily, will gradually fail. I would suggest that Mrs Phillipps should lead as regular and quiet a life as possible, at the same time I do not think for her own sake it will be wise to reside with you and I fear the continual strain upon your nervous system will in the end prove injurious to your health."

It is little wonder that Halliwell began, with even greater determination than before, to restrict his activities. He declined attending a meeting of the British Archaeological Association in Cornwall: "One is, however, compelled at intervals to make rules of life & it was not without long thought, when I found myself getting a little into the swing of going out, that I came to the determination never again to join large parties of any kind. They don't suit me & I don't suit them" (6 August 1876; LOA 228:41). He no longer mentioned his earlier idea (27 June 1875; Folger Y.c.1213[77]) of standing for Parliament. He intensified his "getting to the end of an attentive reading of my correspondence destroying everything that could possibly annoy any one" (19 April 1875; Folger Y.c.1211[67]). He reaffirmed his decision to give up "literary pursuits," despite the pleas of Ingleby (4 October 1876; LOA 240:31) and George Wright (18 October 1876; LOA 233:1). He seemed intent on following Haines's advice that he lead a life of "quiet resignation" (18 October 1876; LOA 233:70).

In 1877 and 1878 he published nothing. But he was not inactive. He travelled in search of literary and dramatic records, holidayed in Wales and Ramsgate and Brighton, visited his daughters. He kept up with his closest friends, wrote frequently to his favorites, Dillon Croker, Charles Roach Smith, and George Wright. He continued sending gifts of manuscripts (e.g. an "old map" to Eton College) and books (six boxes to the Brighton Free Library and Museum). He provided monthly checks of £50 for the ailing Thomas Wright, signed a memorial from the Camden Society for the family of Edward Rimbault. He was distraught on hearing from Croker (24 December 1877; LOA 238:23) that "Our poor friend ["Tom Wright, M.A." added by Halliwell] died last evening at 11 o'clock." Most significantly perhaps, as he intensified his efforts to sell the Middle Hill estates, he began in 1876 negotiations for the purchase of land near Brighton, having been informed that the "*Lowest* amount per Acre is £350" (8 June 1876; LOA 232:42). He pressed hard, complaining to Lady Ogle, the owner, of "such singular dilatoriness, & such a complete & uncourteous disregard to my convenience ... [that] I shall not buy the land unless the purchase can be completed in time for me to fence in & plant during the present autumn" (17 October 1876; LOA 238:21). An even more strident complaint of 31 October 1876 (LOA 236:63)–"I cannot & I will not submit to further delays"–and Halliwell could announce to Fleay that he had purchased twelve acres [for only £250 per acre, he added proudly] near Brighton, was to build a house there and keep 11 Tregunter Road, "so for the rest of my life I shall be a kind of pendulum between London & Brighton–a *pretty* long swing" (8 December 1876; Folger Y.c.1222[7]). Regie, his ever loyal nephew and now a lawyer, supervised the fencing and policing of the property (4 February 1877; LOA 239:63). Halliwell's good friend John Robinson, the architect who had examined the details of the structure of the Shakespeare properties in Stratford for him in 1874, submitted a plan for the erection of a temporary building at Patcham, which was then taken on by the firm of George Lynn & Sons, Brighton, for an estimate of £1475.0.0 (16 April 1877; LOA 230:94). The next few months were filled with reports of the progress of the "workpeople" on the building site: since the bungalow is not yet finished, Halliwell is "having some wooden huts erected for temporary use–a sort of *hutt*entot village–great fun" (18 June 1877; Folger Y.c.1281[30]). By 4 October 1877 (Folger W.a.82[211]) his new address and letterhead was Ditchling Copse, Ditchling Rise, Brighton. But since so many letters seemed to him to have gone astray, he changed his address to Hollingbury Copse, Brighton (31 October 1877; Folger 1211[113]) and, with pleased humor at its provincialism, sent a card to Jarvis reading: "Pardonnez Moi! But *do* men of business put Brighton, *Sussex*, when there is no other post-town of the same name in the 3 kingdoms. Please in future add, England Europe near Africa!" (22 January 1878; Folger Y.d.396[2/3]). By 1 March 1878 (Folger C.a.11[10]) he could invite Ingleby but could not offer him a bed since he had the workmen "in"; in a postscript, however, he added, "My daughter would be delighted to give your daughter a bed. In a wooden bungalow like this all the ladies' bedrooms are together & kept for ladies only. The gentlemen's quarters are not yet ready." In Hollingbury Copse he was taking on a new way of life: "I am up now between 6 and 7, but then I go to bed about 9 p.m. requiring, in common with all idiots, a vast amount of sleep ... my head is full of ruralities not of books & literature" (17 March 1878; Folger C.b.17[111]). Gardening became a passion and "Birds–birds–beautiful birds! My great hobby now. I have got 2 ponds already for them" (10 April 1878; Folger C.b.17[113]).

He invited and expected many guests, to be sure. But he could not expect Mrs. Halliwell: she had never returned to live at Middle Hill, she would never see Hollingbury Copse. On 20 August 1878 (LOA 243:78) her physician, J. W. Roe, recommended that she be put under the care of Dr. Stephen Tayleur Gwynn of Whitchurch, Shropshire. On 4 September 1878 (LOA 243:76) he informed Halliwell that "her mental state is unaltered and her removal, if decided upon, may take place whenever you think fit" and recommended Dr. Gwynn as a "thoroughly human and ... conscientious man." Dr. Gwynn's letter of 7 September 1878 (LOA 243:5) outlined the cost (including a suite of rooms and the required two attendants) at ten guineas a week. A few days later (11 September 1878; LOA 243:55) Halliwell asked his nephew Regie to look over Dr. Gwynn's establishment, and within a week noted that Regie found "everything satisfactory." On 21 September 1878 she arrived, having borne her journey "well & ... is now as comfortable as circumstances will permit" (22 September 1878; LOA 243:13). On 12 October 1878 (LOA 243:14) Dr. Gwynn reported a "decided improvement" in her condition to Captain Walcot: she was taking her usual walk, she called a dog and patted him on the head. A few days later (16 October 1878; LOA 243:57) he wrote that "she is sufficiently quiet now to be able to go out without attracting observation." Nevertheless it was clear to all that, after more than six years of decline, her end was nearing.

The preparations began, painfully, with the dividing up of her valuables. "Dear Barley," Halliwell wrote to Charlotte on 24 October 1878 (LOA 243:39), "Katie certainly should have the gold watch ... As to the other things, I shall be glad if you & Larry will arrange about them." In a note, he added: "The only article I retained for myself was the miniature of my dear mother." Writing from Ellesmere, Henrietta listed her wishes, among them the "bracelet with two turquoises & a carbuncle in the middle. The ring with 3 little diamonds in it. The ring with a snake's head. The glass locket with hair in it. The cairngorm brooch and the ivory fan that belonged to her mother." Charlotte, she continued, will also send a list of the distributed items to Halliwell, following his wish. On 21 December 1878 (LOA 243:32) came Dr. Gwynn's report that "Mrs Phillipps is in some respects much better in others I am sorry to say there is little or no improvement." The details were not encouraging:

She is now almost quiet and only occasionally screams out. She would however very soon become noisy again were not the greatest care taken to keep her perfectly quiet. Last week I thought she was about to cause trouble in that respect. For two days she was excited & restless & much more noisy than usual but by timely attention was soothed down and she is now much as usual again—Her mental condition is not improved and I am afraid there is very little to be hoped for on that point [–] occasionally she rouses and notices things & persons around her but soon relapses into a state of passive quietude.

Halliwell seemed resigned and subdued, the tension evident perhaps in his wish to have a list of the "trinkets" to be divided and that they be carefully packed and registered if sent by post. His passion for order was pronounced, and this was but another instance of it. But somehow the impending death of his wife was consistent with his own desire for withdrawal, thinning out his possessions, and retaining only his core collection. At the moment he was preparing for the auction of the Middle Hill estates, he was going though Thomas Wright's letters to him, "a waggon load," he wrote to Charles Roach Smith, "& was compelled to destroy nearly all, hardly one being free from disparaging remarks on some one or other" (4 June 1878; Folger C.b.17[114]). The action is reconciliatory and peace-seeking, and is accompanied by Halliwell's request that Smith not mention any quarrels in his planned memoir of Wright: "*It is mischievous, & may result in recriminations prejudicial to memories.*

We are both of us quite enough near the grave to render it as well to do our best to hush up all quarrels of every description." He was, in other words, inclined to settle accounts and amicably, as he had done earlier, on 5 April 1876, in remitting £8.8.0 to the Society of Antiquaries on behalf of Wright so that, because his condition prevented the continuance of his membership, Wright would not be considered a defaulter.

But there was a world outside. An erupting public quarrel with F. J. Furnivall and troubling controversy with Stratford, among other events, were to intrude on Halliwell's retreat and his mourning.

PART FIVE

1879-1889

Fig. 5   Halliwell-Phillipps as a tramp in Hollingbury Copse shortly before his death. By kind permission of S.C.M. Hawthorne, the great-great-granddaughter of Halliwell's brother Thomas.

20

The Retired Old Lunatic

"Mourning" must be more precisely defined, however. His "dearest Harry," Henrietta Halliwell-Phillipps, died on 25 March 1879, in Whitchurch, Salop, at the age of fifty-nine. The official cause of death was influenza (five days) and bronchopneumonia (three days);[263] no mention is made of the years of diminishing mental powers and mental shocks she endured, nor of seven years of deep and patient suffering by Halliwell and the whole family as they witnessed the wasting away of their once remarkably active, supportive, and selfless wife and mother. Some details exist. Her condition towards the end is described by Eliza Gwynn, the attending physician's wife, in an undated letter (LOA 243:7) to Charlotte:

Thank you for sending the Cap for Mrs Phillipps. I am glad to say that she continues quite as well as when Julia was here. She drives out most days, & seems to enjoy it very much. The foot warmer & fur rug keep her beautifully warm,& she is sometimes out for two hours in the afternoon. The Brougham is a very comfortable one, & the man who drives it is most careful & thoroughly to be depended on. Mrs Phillipps moves about quite briskly, & generally walks on our tennis lawn for an hour before dinner. We still have considerable difficulty in getting her to take solid food, especially at dinner, but with patience & perseverance, the nurse generally manages to get it taken. We keep Mrs Phillipps entirely free from excitement & she is consequently much quieter, altho' she still shouts a little at times. We shall be pleased to see you whenever you like to come to Whitchurch.

On 24 March 1879 (LOA 243:64), the day before her death, John Withington Roe, a consulting physician, described what may be her last moments:

---

263. There is a certain irony in the fact that a correction of a clerical error in the names was necessary–"Halliwell" was crossed out and replaced by "Phillipps."

She was extremely ill and in imminent danger from Bronchitis, her chest was loaded with phlegm which she was unable to expectorate and in this the danger to her life mainly consists as the necessary blood changes cannot take place in lungs so charged with mucus. Of course her mental state tells greatly against her under these circumstances as the inclination to spit up is disregarded & the relief she would thus obtain is not afforded. Dr Gwynn or his son have been with her almost constantly night and day administering remedies & sustenance. She is in a water bed to prevent sores forming, and I am well assured that nothing is spared that offers any hope of relief. Her breathing is very difficult and unless some speedy change occurs, her state must be hopeless. She recognizes no one and if I may venture to advise in such a matter I would urge that you should not visit her. For you to see her would do no possible good to her and yourself almost certain harm.

In his payment of the doctor's fees Halliwell was reserved and generous. "Although I am satisfied that no charges beyond two guineas could be legally sustained," he wrote to Dr. Gwynn, "yet I have great pleasure in enclosing fourty [*sic*] guineas in acknowledgement of the tender care taken by Mrs Gwynn & yourself in the treatment of my poor wife, a care spoken of in the highest terms by my daughter & others" (5 May 1879; LOA 243:45).

As ever, he itemized the account:

My Cheque therefore is—	
Your fee	42.0.0
Carriage hire	0.7.6
Certificates	15.6
	£43.3.0

This reckoning must be regarded as a form of mourning, just as the division of her dearest possessions among the children must be seen as a desire to cherish a memento more precious than the thing itself. And the crisp care with which it was done is to be construed not as an act of calculation but of respect. Halliwell's retaining only one article, the miniature of his mother, was certainly an unselfish gesture in behalf of his children and a desire to have only that personal token of what was close to him. The gesture is the essence of familial solidarity and continuity—as are the performance of the burial ceremony on 29 March 1879 in the neighboring West Brompton cemetery by his brother, the Reverend

Thomas Halliwell, and in its own way the flat stone on the ground, the type Halliwell had chosen for his parents and recommended for his dear friend Fairholt, "something durable ... a *flat slab* of *granite*, which will last humanly speaking for ever" (3 July 1866; Folger W.a.81[49/1]). The latter serves to amplify feelingly the traditional inscription on her gravestone: "In Memory of Henrietta Elizabeth Molyneux for more than thirty years the devoted wife of J. O. Halliwell-Phillipps, F.R.S. of Tregunter Road, Brompton." And, considering Halliwell's characteristic reserve, the verses which follow must be understood as a genuine expression of emotional impact beyond their commonplace content:

> Indefective wife and mother
> Death ere thou hast slain another
> Gentler or more kind than she
> Time shall throw a dart at thee.

That depth of feeling is found, as well, in Halliwell's simple and restrained tribute in a letter to his most intimate friend, Dillon Croker: "My poor Wife had been so very long practically lost to me & there was relief that her painful life & hopeless stare had come to a close but I have felt the loss more under the circumstances than I anticipated—she was so exceptionally kind & gentle & good in every way." Its intensity is emphasized in his self-control: "The funeral took place on Saturday at Brompton, near where we lived so many years. I may mention that the following was absolutely restricted to members of the family. Had there been any exceptions I should have asked you above all our friends" (31 March 1879; Folger Y.c.1211[128]). The sadness was resonated in the numerous letters of condolence from near and far which Halliwell collected in Volume 243 of his Letters of Authors.

But how can mourning be compatible with the fact that barely three months later, on 19 June 1879, Halliwell, in his local church, St Mary's in West Brompton, married Mary Rice Hobbes? How, in fact, can the marriage of the fifty-seven-year-old "widower and gentleman" (so the marriage licence designations) to the twenty-seven-year-old "spinster" be explained? Mary Rice Hobbes was only two and three years older than Ellen and Katie, and nine and five younger than Henrietta and Charlotte, Halliwell's daughters. All were married but Katie, who lived with her father in Hollingbury Copse. The daughters had moved away, as would Katie just a few years later. Rustication was one thing, loneliness was another. For all intents and purposes Halliwell had no effective helpmate for half a dozen years after his wife's accident, despite the efforts of his daughters. The role she played was vital to his well-being and work, not to mention the burdensome business of Middle Hill with which she was so intimately connected.

The death of Henrietta added immeasurably to Halliwell's already pronounced sense of aging and of losing his strength and so disrupting his professional aims. On the same day that he wrote to Croker, he wrote to Fleay, who had advised him against overwork: "At my age I am hardly likely to return to that. It is just possible that I may put my voluminous collections into order some day, & that will be all. If I die without doing this, they will all go into the waste basket, being written on innumerable slips & unusable by anyone but myself" (31 March 1879; Folger Y.c.1222[9]). The fear of debilitating age and its accompanying lack of fulfillment is a perennial theme of the last decade of Halliwell's life. Receiving a copy of the *Spelling Reformer* from Fleay, he replied that he was "far too old to go in now for a new spell at spelling" (18 September 1880; Folger Y.c.1222[12]). After complimenting Charles Roach Smith on his *Rural Life*, he confessed: "Alack & alas! I have no reading time for Social Notes of modern times. I am old, & every moment of reading time I have now is for Nash Greene &c. 1587 to 1616. So you observe I am still at the old game" (16 January 1881; Folger C.b.17[126]). Later that year he repeated his lament to Henry Wheatley: "Alack & alas! I am in my second year above 60 and if I live do not intend to have literary hobbies after 70, so I am obliged to husband what little strength remains if I would put in any order my Shakespeare discoveries, greatly increased this year" (3 August 1881; Folger Y.c.1297[1]). Inviting Kate and John Fenwick to Hollingbury Copse, he hoped they "will understand I feel old & worn, but not *too* much so to give you both a *most* cordial welcome if you think the air of Brighton downs will be beneficial" (19 September 1882; Phil-Rob c.487:96). The urgency to continue was accompanied by a certain resignation, which took the form of not accepting new challenges and conceding that it should be left to others to do. To A. H. Bullen he wrote:

It is very kind indeed of you to say that you will communicate to me any Shakespearean discovery you may make, but my hands are so full, & it would be so uncertain when I could make any use of anything of the kind, I do hope, that, instead of carrying out that idea, you will at once communicate it to the Athenaeum. The old must give place to the young (20 April 1883; LOA 258:26).

He may have been grateful for anything sent to him, "*provided it is not to be returned*" (24 January 1881; Folger Y.c.1240[21b]).

Aging was not an abstraction, for it was evident in both a general weakness and in specific illnesses. They were not life-threatening but certainly enervating. "No thanks at all for the tract on Public Libraries," he wrote to Charles Roach Smith, "which is printed in a scandalous [uncial] type my eyes won't stand" (23 April 1879; Folger C.b.17[117]). "You amaze me by your physical energy," he praised him admiringly (11 March 1882; Folger C.b.17[133]), "I work hard in my study, but am no more capable of doing your work than of flying over the *moon &* [underlined four times] the planets!" "I am destitute of all conversational powers,–a mere creature of the study," he confessed to (Walter) Theodore Watts-Dunton (5 September 1882; Folger Y.d.329[13]). Halliwell could not disagree with George Wright's complaining about his loss of memory, admitting to Ingleby, "Do what I can I cannot recollect either plots or passages and have to look up every thing almost every time I want it" (2 March 1883; Folger C.a.11[53]). And there were the constantly recurring headaches that had plagued him over the years (2 March 1884; Folger C.a.11[80]). Commiserating with Ingleby's rupture, Halliwell reported: "I am obliged to be bandaged up similarly (for hydrocele not for rupture) & found it insufferable at first, but after *various alterations* & going to a first-class surgical instrument maker (Weiss in the Strand) I can now walk as well with it as without it" (20 October 1883; Folger C.a.11[70]). Commenting on Ingleby's health and his own, he philosophized cheerfully: "What a life of ups and downs this is! And anyhow there are always the Downs here!" (28 May 1885; Folger C.a.11[106]). A similar kind of merry desperation is evident in Halliwell's response to an attack of gout: "the first time in my life I have ever felt that I belonged to the fashionable world!!". (27 November 1885; Folger C.a.11[109]). Two months later he called it a "most *goutrageous* nuisance" (24 January 1886; Folger Y.d.5[69b]). His anxiety about Ingleby's health led Halliwell to mention having just had a "severe attack of muscular rheumatism" (26 July 1886; Folger C.a.15[5]), which, despite the good derived from his having been "ordered away for change ... has left traces not easily to be obliterated" (16 September 1886; Folger C.a.15[7]). Apologizing to Wheatley for not having written, he explained:

I wish I had written, but having to lay down all day in a horizontal position & my papers & everything in dire confusion, I only write by stealth. I had a desperate bad journey on Monday yesterday week but doctor gave some new remedies & he gives hopes in 2 or 3 days of my being able to get out for a little while. Very well in general health, it is the painful & tedious local complaint that is so worrying. However, the pain now is only intermittent (26 June 1888; Folger Y.c.1297[9]).

"I can walk eat drink & sleep like a pig," he confessed a few months later, "but am not up yet to study work" (10 October 1888; Folger Y.c.1297[13]). And in a majestic understatement a month before his death, he reported in a postscript to Jarvis and Son, "My health is not first-class & I fear my strength is waning" (1 December 1888; Folger Y.c.1241[15]).

Shrouding all was Halliwell's chronic "depression of spirits" (27 December 1879; Folger C.a.11[16]). "I can only write by fits & starts," he apologized, "to keep at all without being mentally fatigued. I am obliged to spend a great deal in the open air" (16 February 1880; Folger Y.c.1307[34]). His "mental strength is so obviously failing," he confided to Ingleby, "I appear almost to see paralysis looming ahead" (1 October 1880; Folger C.a.11[22]). He admired Charles Roach Smith–"You are always so terse & cheerful, you make one in good spirits in spite of myself"–if only to demean himself: "I am foolishly in the constant habit of looking at the gloomiest view of things" (16 October 1880; Folger C.b.17[123]). "Don't mention Death," he implored Ingleby, "& its late victims. One never knows whose turn is next. My own brain & nerves are very very weak" (22 March 1881; Folger C.a.11[32]).[264] Ever self-critical, he confessed to Croker: "I am so terribly subject to fits of depression that, although I try to conceal them, I know that they make me appear sometimes brusque & inconsiderate" (15 November 1881; Folger Y.c.1211[152]). Hamlet-like, he characterized Charles Roach Smith as a man of action, "fitted for the world's strife," as opposed to himself: "I [am] a poor creature solely of the study, increasing I fear every day in nervousness." His desire to conceal his depression and nervousness was followed by an urge to escape: "I can come out when *thoroughly* provoked, as in the case of Furnivall. But the latter business has shaken me, & I crave for quiet, if I can get it!" (20 February 1883; Folger W.a.82[221]). In one of his "impossible-to-study moods ... the least brainwork makes me irritable & depressed–*though I carefully refrain from saying anything about it here,*"

264. Never one to overlook the practical, Halliwell admitted in the same letter, "I do not know what I should have done if I had not been thoroughly cheered by winning a suit I had obstinately set my heart on, the week before last." He was referring to the nonsuiting of an attempt to collect £1300 by Glasier & Sons as a commission for their part in the failed auction sale of the Middle Hill estates. Since the actual sale took place later, and was private, Halliwell paid only £50. "I had to print a folio volume of correspondence!! Think of that, Master Ford, I believe I rendered a public service in resisting the claim," he exulted. See p. 428-9.

he confided to Ingleby in a letter marked "*Private*" (2 August 1883; Folger C.a.11[64]). His increasing lack of self-esteem is evident in his attitude towards being photographed. Whereas he had always made light of it, he now developed "an intense aversion to being photoed or portraited & never keep such a thing" (4 November 1884; Folger Y.c.1208[8]). Because of his depression he was "practically confined to the house & copse" (11 April 1885; Folger C.a.11[102]). Suffering from "something very like nervous exhaustion," he was compelled to wind up the fifth edition of his *Outlines* very hurriedly, hardly able to copy out the laboriously compiled index (19 June 1885; Folger C.a.11[107]). A year later he described his state to Appleton Morgan as a "break-down" and, "fearing" he might have another such attack, devoted himself to the sixth edition, and, having done so, "returned to the world that I have for months been out of" (3 June 1886; Folger Y.c.1257[1]). The effect on his work became increasingly burdensome and ultimately devastating: "Having already more to do than my strength will bear I am compelled to avoid most inflexibly everything in the nature of literary correspondence that can entail the necessity of smallest expenditure of time in references or research" (4 April 1887; Folger W.b.90[75]). Although not "laid up," Halliwell confessed, "the matter is ... an inward depression & a mental disability for the faintest kind of exertion in the way of study. I seem to have an invincible repugnance to study—can't do it" (13 September 1888; Folger Y.c.1297[11]). This was three months before his death.

And Halliwell was confronted daily by the terror of losing control. To his failing memory came his inability to order his material: "All my own notes are on tens of thousands of unsorted slips in 8 large drawers, impossible of reference," he explained to Ingleby (22 December 1883; Folger C.a.11[76]). His papers, he was forced to admit to Fleay, "are in such confusion I cannot give the reference" (3 October 1884; Folger Y.c.1222[16]). For one so given to order, it was frustrating for him to admit he could not remember and his "notes are inaccessible ... being amongst thousands of unsorted papers & all written on slips" (15 January 1885; Folger C.a.11[97]). And then there were the ghosts. "What recollections do your interesting note on Sandwich bring, "he confessed to Charles Roach Smith, "Rolfe, Fairholt, Tom Wright &c. now all dust! I am taking advantage of a little spurt of restoration of mentally working health to do a little more work before I join them" (16 November 1880; Folger C.b.17[124]). Certainly Howard Staunton, pursued by blue devils, and Wright's senility, must have come to mind in Halliwell's hallucinatory desire to "sign one [a petition] against *mental* vivisection. I doubt if a mouse with its small brain could endure as much torture as I did, with my preternaturally sensitive nature" (28 February 1883; Folger C.a.11[52]. And then there were the deaths in this decade of good old friends and faithful correspondents: Planché ("released from his terrible sufferings–poor dear old fellow" [1 June 1880; Folger C.b.17(119)])–William Sawyer (poor dear old Sawyer" [4 November 1882; Folger Y.c.1211(163)]), Henry Holl ("delirious & recovery all but impossible" [20 November 1884; Folger C.a.11(90)]), Ingleby ("He died on the 26 Sept. Alas!" noted Halliwell on the last of Ingleby's letters to him of 17 September 1886 [LOA 296:55]). Grotesquely, Halliwell was informed by the ever-loyal E. W. Ashbee that "On Tuesday last a friend writing to me from London informed me that he had just seen in the 'Citizen' newspaper an announcement of your death at Brighton on the previous Tuesday." Halliwell could not help but be touched by Ashbee's "Finding this morning that the 'Athenaeum' did not mention the sad event, I felt that I must go up to town and make some enquiries respecting its truth. It was with intense satisfaction that I then learned the report was a false one, and that you are alive and in your usual health" (7 March 1885; LOA 289:63). Touched perhaps, but whether he was comforted is another matter. Or he might share the merry moroseness of a cutting from the *Brighton Herald* of 28 February 1885, which he included among his literary papers (LOA 299:53*):

Confusion Worse Confounded—As an ingenious local paper, the *Sussex Daily Post*, having erroneously announced on Wednesday the sudden death of Mr J. O. Halliwell-Phillipps, the well-known Shakespearean authority, on being assured that the gentleman had not yet 'shuffled off this mortal coil,' hastened next day to correct the misstatement in those felicitous terms that are a feature of that journal. After explaining how the report was obtained, the writer exclaimed, 'But, alas, it was false!' Whether this ostentatious grief was caused by Mr Halliwell-Phillipps declining to quit this world in order to maintain the *Daily Post's* character for veracity does not appear.

In any event the description of Halliwell's physical condition and mental state may help explain his apparently sudden marriage, his disposition, and his scholarly stance. Hollingbury Copse, secluded and uncomplicated, was doubtless an attempt to escape from an increasingly complex and even hostile world. It was extremely personal. Impressed by a "'transformation-scene' effected at Hollingbury Copse, which, as is well known, was in the past the most unkempt and neglected copse perhaps in the neighbourhood of Brighton," the *Brighton Herald* on 2 October 1880 quoted a "graphic description" by the London correspondent of the *Dover*

Standard which Halliwell kept in his literary papers LOA 265:57):

The owner and occupier has been his own architect, and he has built the kind of place he thought he would like, on a site, which, in itself is a kind of paradise. Indeed, I was reminded of Morris and his opening stanza ... Well, this house I was telling you of (if it can be called a house) stands on a hill. From one window you can see the bleak hills stretching out for miles; from another you can look on to the Channel; and from a third you look into the green mazes of a beautiful copse with clear water breaking and brawling over stones, and slipping and singing between ferns and the roots of old trees ... This residence is entirely built of wood. The floors are wood; the walls are bare polished wood; and the roofs are bare polished wood. And very rich a picture looks on such a wall, and very bright and dainty is a dinner under such a roof. Let me tell you that this residence is built in compartments or what would be called chapels, the chapels being connected with another by corridors. There is a dining-room chapel, and breakfast-room chapel, and a tea-room chapel, and a library chapel, a study chapel, &c., and each has its own particular charm of shape or situation. But I had a sad experience with this word chapel. Our host over luncheon said the room might look like a chapel but it did not make a chap ill.[265]

Suiting Bullen's designation of Halliwell as the "Hermit of Hollingbury Copse" (29 June 1882; LOA 262:69), it was also very remote. Inviting Henry Wheatley to stay for the night, Halliwell was sure to enclose a "sketch-plan of our out-of-the-way locality" and added, "we are very unceremonious people. I have not had for years an evening coat, nor do I appear in a low dress!" (4 October 1881; Folger Y.c.1297[2]). Its problems were relatively trivial: what best to plant under trees (10

265. The sale bill of 6 June 1889 describes the "picturesque and commodious bungalow residence" covering thirteen acres and "commanding a magnificent prospect over a grand reach of country and the sea beyond ... entirely enclosed by a substantial oak pale fence" as a connected group one-storied buildings: the residence consisting of a lobby, entrance hall, drawing room, dining room; private apartments (morning room, bedroom and boudoir, study with adjoining dressing room and bathroom); the visitors' annexe (two bedrooms, smoking room, bachelor's bedroom); domestic offices (servants's apartment, kitchen, pantry, scullery, various cellars, etc.); and "well removed from the house," the stabling, laundry, and the lodge. The grounds are embellished with walks, woods, pools, streams, mimic waterfalls, plantation, shrubbery and a rosary arcade some 350 ft. long.

September 1880; Folger C.a.11[21]), how to deal with the death of two moorhens and the disappearance of others (28 May 1885; Folger C.a.11[106]). Its foil, Middle Hill, was large and unwieldy. Selling it was more than a financial consideration; it was a shedding of a heavy responsibility and a burdensome past. Receiving £7000 a year in interest was infinitely preferable to a huge and risky investment. Passive security was deemed superior to active engagement.

Halliwell's penchant towards withdrawal–his chronic shyness giving way to deep depression–led him to reject earlier aspirations and aims. "My great anxiety has been for years to read every *popular* tract of Shakespeare's time, but at my present age," he confided to Frederick Powell, "it will be as much as I can do to work up my own collected materials so that it is only on rare occasions that I can treat myself to searching after new ones" (15 November 1884; Folger Y.c.1270). No longer interested in a baronetcy, he confessed to Bumstead: "In early life I no doubt should have liked it, but now I should not accept anything of the kind if it were offered, & *not only that but I have a great dislike to a title of any kind*" (9 February 1886; Folger W.b.84[13]). Even the honorary doctor of laws he received from the University of Edinburgh did not deter him form cautioning John Leaver, secretary of the Shakespeare Birthplace Trust, "I don't want to be Doctored until I am ill" (9 May 1884; LOA 292:54*). More striking perhaps was Halliwell's attitude towards "rows." Personally and professionally he was for most of his adult life the center of controversy and conflict, which he countered directly and unflinchingly. In the last decade of his life they continued. But in his withdrawal Halliwell became more and more disposed to avoiding them. "Even if your notion had been correct," he explained to Charles Roach Smith, "it would have worried me very much if my name had been introduced into *any* sort of complaint or 'row'. *Please to recollect that I have neither your spirit nor your nerve*" (29 January 1883; Folger W.a.82[220]). Incorrigible, Smith used Halliwell's name in his complaints against the town clerk of Rochester, eliciting a response from Halliwell: "Now he will look upon me as antagonistic. Oh my–the 'evils that 'rows' bring live after them–*the good is never interred with their bones–because it was never there!*'" [underlined in red] 6 May 1883; Folger C.b.17[140]). A day later, referring to the "mischief that is done by relying on verbalities," he continued, "There am I, with the now great object of my life to keep even out not only of 'rows' but even of acrimonious discussion, *compelled* to *fight* on behalf of a friend. But I tell you–*& I feel it*–that such matters as the enclosed *shake me*, & if much of the kind goes on will compel me to leave my darling studies" (7 May 1883; Folger C.b.17[141]). It is little wonder that one source called him "the most pacific of living Shakespeareans" (1 January 1884; Folger C.b.17[145]).

To the explicit avoidance of rows may be added the more subtle but no less pervasive insecurity evident in Halliwell's increasing desire to be corrected (and doubtless too an extension of his passion for order and neatness[266]). "You can hardly do me a greater favour than telling me of my blunders," he wrote to Ingleby (11 August 1882; Folger C.a.11[43]). A week later he stressed his gratitude to Ingleby for pointing out any "oversights or bad logic or obscure composition, or telling me plainly when you think I am wrong" (20 August 1882; Folger C.a.11[44]). Two years later he confessed he was not "such an old noodle as to dislike owning to error" (29 October 1884; Folger C.a.11[89]). Although Halliwell's explanation–"My leading anxiety & care is to be accurate, no matter how my own views are upset"–is credible, of course, the frequency of such requests for correction and his "anxiety" about accuracy cannot be overlooked in an evaluation of his overall disposition. He was not only anxious about accuracy, in fact, but about critical response. Certain that Ingleby's edition of *Cymbeline* will be his "best authority for the criticism on the text of the play–it cannot be otherwise after the time you have spent upon it"–Halliwell nevertheless had "very little doubts that others who have spent no time at all will be ready to *say* they demolish everything you say. What a thing it is to be so geniussical as to be able to decide in one minute on questions that life-students think it necessary to devote weeks!" (19 March 1886; Folger C.a.15[2]). It cannot be surprising that withdrawal contributed immeasurably to Halliwell's otherwise gracious "The old must give place to the young" (20 April 1883; LOA 258:26) and "I am anxious for younger men to have their innings" (4 April 1887; Folger W.b.90[75]). Halliwell's most comprehensive statement of withdrawal, if not of dissolution of self, is found in his hope that Charles Roach Smith will not include a biography of him in his next volume:

Had I been uniformly steady, like you have been, it would have been a different matter, but it would be a pity to introduce the public to my debts, & follies & squabbles of early life, & without these a biographical sketch would be unfairly & improperly onesided, like things done in the

266. In one of many telling instances Halliwell's sister, Louisa, replied with characteristic bluntness to his criticism of the paper she had used in her correspondence: "Now if this paper does not suit you I don't know what will, the fact is you are getting so fastidious there is no knowing how to please you. I hope your Cambridge foppish days are not returning but upon my word I am very much afraid about it" (18 January 1868; LOA 128:40).

got up biographies. So kindly instead of a biographical sketch give me only incidental notices, there's a dear old boy (23 September 1883; Folger C.b.17[142]).

All things considered, it would not seem far-fetched to attribute Halliwell's second marriage to his urge towards withdrawal, if not to his systemic depression. His comfortable and stable domestic tranquillity was abruptly interrupted in 1872 and diminished as rapidly as his wife's mental health. 11 Tregunter Road existed, and the flow of friends and relatives continued for a while. But three daughters were married, had moved away, and had their own cares. For all her affection Katie, who remained, was not her mother. What was missing, of course, was the kind of household management that so arranges and orders affairs as to enable Halliwell to spend the day in his study and have friends to dinner or tea, packs his case and informs him of his post while he is away. In short, what Halliwell needed was a domestic environment organized caringly and lovingly around him. Little is known of Mary Rice Hobbes. She kept no diary, and there seem to be no letters to or from her. The relatively few pertinent utterances in Halliwell's correspondence tend to see her not for herself but mainly in terms of those qualities she possessed which the aging, retiring, and lonesome Halliwell most needed. For one thing, Mary Rice Hobbes had a Stratford background and may have well met Halliwell as a young child. Her father was William James Hobbes, a solicitor, and brother of Robert Hiorne Hobbes (the city father with whom Halliwell has had much to do in connection with the Tercentenary Celebration and the conveyance of the Shakespeare properties). Hobbes had financial problems and left Stratford for London and a new life and wife. His first wife, Ann, moved to Brighton, where a "Miss Hobbes" is referred to by Halliwell as a "neighbour" in Brighton who is looking for respectable lodgers (8 November 1880; Folger Y.c.1305[2]) and who was pleased to be invited by Jarvis (4 August 1884; Folger Y.d.5[60b]). The relationship of Halliwell to the Hobbes family in Brighton was firm and warm before the marriage. On 20 December 1877 (LOA 238:83) Marion Hobbes, in the naming of her baby, informed Halliwell that "Herbert Halliwell Hobbes sounds better *HHH*." More significant is the information given by Henry Holl a few days earlier (16 December 1877; LOA 237:68). After asking how "Miss Kate" and "Miss Hobbes" are, he continues: "I was seriously ill used and should have been half, or wholly, starved if Miss Hobbes had not taken compassion on me, and insisted on carving on purpose to cut me the tit bits. Give my love to her." Although it is not clear to which "Miss Hobbes" Holl was referring, it is not unreasonable to assume that Mary Rice Hobbes would have to possess those qualities which Halliwell must have sorely needed: stability and good sense and good cheer. And it may be worth mentioning that the only physical description of her that seems to have survived, that by Samuel Timmins, reveals a notable resemblance to Henrietta: "a pretty quiet, graceful little lady, of say 25 or 26, with dark lustrous eyes, a pleasant, modest manner, and just a trifle of delicate health on rather a pale face."[267]

As to be expected, the relationship had none of the initial melodramatic aspects that marked Halliwell's elopement with Henrietta after having seen her but three or four times and the ensuing revenge of a raging father that continued for the rest of his life. But it was apparently not without a certain suddenness, if not tension. Writing on "Ye longest Daye" (21 June) of 1879 (LOA 265:28), Halliwell's jovial close friend and prolific correspondent, George Wright, registered his astonishment: "What a sly dog you are, *never* to have told me a word about your new Marriage ... Who is she?" Ellen was also surprised at the news from her "dearest Old Man"–"I didn't expect anything of the sort would happen so soon"–but was supportive of her father in what might have been his embarrassment or anxiety: "Perhaps as you say there will be a hubbub but I do not see that anybody has a right to interfere with whom you choose to marry. You must know best what will make you happy and I only wish you both every possible happiness & that you will be very comfortable and enjoy yourself on your travels and when you come back to Copsey" (21 June 1879; LOA 253:3). The letters of congratulation which followed were all heartfelt. Two written on 17 July 1879 demonstrate the wide range of emotional approval. One was from the ebullient F. J. Furnivall (LOA 246:1):

Well done you! I *do* congratulate you heartily on the double event, 1. Your marriage, & 2. your return to your old work. Marriage was of course a necessity for you. A man of your temperament, having had so many years of married life, could not have gone on in singleness, with no companion for failing days when they come, & no sharer of daily pleasures & troubles. You 've done the wisest thing I 've known you to do. But who's the lady? Miss Hobbs, the pretty cook, or some one unknown to me? Whoever it is, my congratulations to her, & many happy days to you both!

The other (LOA 248:9), more reflective, was from the ever-faithful old

267. Quoted by Joseph Crosby, *Shakespeariana*, 1 (1884), 227.

friend, Caroline Birkenhead, who had been Henrietta's governess more than forty years earlier:

When my surprise abated I thought 'Well poor man he wants some one to love, & some one to love him & keep him out of mischief—You were happy with your first dear good little wife and if you are equally fortunate with your second edition & there is no reason to anticipate otherwise you will have more domestic comfort than falls to the lot of many men—I am sure men are much better off—& in general live longer when they have a good wife to take care of them in their declining years, and XI years hence when you reach the age LXX you will begin to feel that you especially require some one to think for—& take care of you—I wish you and your young wife all happiness.

Both—indeed all who express an opinion—agree that Halliwell's decision was the right one for him; all emphasize his need for a caring and comforting companion. Notwithstanding the sudden decision to marry and the impulsive honeymoon trip north through York and Durham and on to Scotland, it was clear to all, as to Halliwell himself, what he was looking for.

If stability or a refuge from depression or whatever was not in Halliwell's mind, it was certainly so in his deeds. On 18 June 1879, a day before the marriage, he agreed a marriage settlement assuring his wife an annuity of £2000. For her part Polly or Pollie, as she came to be called by members of the family, seems to have willingly performed the duties of companion and, as need be, nurse with patience and good spirits. She accepted and doubtless promoted the discipline his physical and mental condition required. There was order in his diet. "I eat very little meat, drink neither beer nor spirits (the latter I can't digest at all) & only a little light claret—so you see all my jolly days are over. Time was when I could drink any amount & be apparently none the worse for it," he informed James Coleman (4 January 1883; Folger Y.c.1206[30]. She seems to have been undemanding intellectually. There is a reference to her having an album (in which Maccoll promised to write [1881; LOA 281:3]), and Halliwell did present her with a copy of Swinburne's *Songs of the Springtimes* with the respectful inscription "M. R. Halliwell-Phillipps The gift of J. O. H-P. 22 March 1881." There is no evidence that she helped him with his scholarly work or even copied letters for him. There seem to be no letters between them. Her nature can only be deduced, as from Halliwell's thanking Jarvis for "those beautiful ferns, with pinks for little Missus" (11 October 1880; Folger Y.d.5[44b]) or from her receiving a book on chickens from Croker (8 December 1881; Folger Y.c.1211[153]) or from Henry Holl's "Make my kindest remembrance to Mrs Phillipps, who will of course feel rather dull now that the *Favorite* [Katie married her first cousin John C. Walcot on 25 April 1883] has gone" (4 December 1883; LOA 271:40). She must certainly have been a cheerful hostess, matching Henry Stevens's "Our love to the Missis, her little pet bird & her big pet hyphen" (27 August 1884; LOA 282:66). In a letter to Ingleby describing his visit to the Copse, Guido Schmitt reported: "I was made to feel at home at once by kind Mr. & Mrs. Philipps [*sic*], & stayed to dinner at 6.30. The canary hopped from finger to finger of the 6 persons dining (or rather this was at luncheon time) but at the time I thought a volume in praise of Mrs. Philipps entitled 'The Canary'; into addition of the many effects you see and feel in houses, where there is a warmhearted woman" (14 October 1884; Folger Y.d.1[86a]). In his obituary of 12 January 1889 (p. 59) the *Athenaeum* reported that he "was fortunate enough to find a second wife whose main pleasure it was to care for his comfort and welcome his friends." And she doubtless made a home of the somewhat eccentric and sprawling rustic wigwam. Over the years the letters from members of the family, be they from Katie–"Give my best love to Pollie, she *has* been so good all through my engagement and yesterday & today" (25 April 1883; LOA 263:55)–or a nephew or a grandchild, are consistently affectionate towards Polly. Perhaps the most telling description of the life of the Halliwells in Hollingbury Copse was made by John Vincent, Halliwell's Record Office copyist, after a visit: "You presented to me a most delightful picture of an English home, where reign domestic love and peace" (6 August 1885; LOA 295:57). And if this tribute seems too courteously formal, then there is always the atmospheric rendition which appeared in the newspaper cutting Halliwell kept (LOA 260:67) and commented upon as "a foolish hoax of one of my nephews, 1881":

It may not be generally known that when the Prince of Wales visited this town, he called at Hollingbury Copse, the residence of J. [hand-corrected from printed T.] O. Halliwell-Phillipps, Esq., the celebrated Shakespearian critic. His Royal Highness, it is said, was delighted with the quaintness of the wood and iron houses, and was surprised at their internal comfort; the Copse with its brawling stream, shady walks, moss grown retreats, fish ponds, and luxuriant growth of shrubs, enchanted him. The genial scholar was surprised by the Prince as he was walking in his grounds with his *fidus achates*, Sir George Wright, wearing an old battered hat in which he delights; this circumstance afterwards gave rise to many a sparkling joke when a bottle of the justly celebrated old brown sherry from the Hollingbury cellars, was cracked.

For Halliwell it was a simple case of finding someone to help him overcome his loneliness and depression, someone to shelter him emotionally the way Hollingbury Copse could do so topographically. Marriage offered him not just refuge but some refreshment. To Dillon Croker he described his second wife as "one I believe as amiable as my first," adding gallantly, "she could not be more so" (26 July 1879; Folger Y.c.1211[130]). His tone was bright as he scolded Jarvis for not having contacted him: "Here have I been marrying a young wife, touring to Scotland, peeping out for you in all your old haunts at Newcastle &c. &c. &c. No go. I suppose I must go to Jones's Glyptyc to find you!" (19 August 1879; Folger Y.d.5[40b]). Invitations to friends to visit became frequent and enthusiastic: "Come! Come!! Come!!!" Halliwell urged Croker, mentioning that his "little wife" would welcome him too (11 August 1880; Folger Y.c.1211[142]). Preferring to talk rather than write about Charles Roach Smith's views on *Hamlet*, Halliwell prepared for his visit: "I will set a hundred navvies at work to level up Hollingbury Camp, so that your thoughts may be *solely* Hamletly turned. So come! come!! come!!!" (16 March 1881; Folger C.b.17[130]). The old cheer was evident once again in another invitation to "Dear Cro": "The drama of the Joint of Meat will be generally preceded by the divertisement of the Fish of the Sea, the entire company appearing in both pieces" (3 March 1881; Folger Y.c.1211[146]). The impact of his new wife was great. "Busy as A B" with house alterations, he divulged his plans to his nephew Ernest Baker: "I shall have only two residences, for after having made all the preparations to fit up the Grange at Broadway for an occasional residence, I have changed my mind–the first time I ever did such a scandalous thing!" (19 August 1879; Folger Y.c.1187[3]). And if the marriage settlement was one way of preparing for the future, so was his preparation of a new will–"all left as simple & I think as equitably as possible" (23 October 1879; Folger Y.c.1211[135]).

Halliwell's surge of optimism cannot be wholly attributed to his new "little wife," nor to the manic side, as it were, of his chronic depression. For all his need for simplification and its accompanying withdrawal, for all his obsession with fatigue and aging, he was above all possessed by a determination to see things through, to order his unsorted slips, to bring his work to the promised end. "I am old," he may have confessed to Charles Roach Smith, but "you observe I am still at the old game" (16

January 1881; Folger C.b.17[126]). "It frightens me to arrange my immense materials as rapidly as possible & I am doing what I have not done for years, pegging away in my dog days," he informed Smith (14 July 1880; Folger C.b.17[120]). "Recollect," he remarked to Ingleby, "that slightly creaky people as a rule live the longest," and his advice might apply to himself as well: "the exercise of your vigorous & logical intellect will in itself tend to prolong life" (14 January 1882; Folger C.a.11[38]).

Halliwell's determination was evident in and reinforced by his humor: his often repeated mock lament "Alack & alas"; his devotion to funny anecdotes ("Some years ago I met at Worthing a very deaf old lady on a very rough day. I shook hands & said, *How are you?* I have an idea she imagined I was alluding to the weather, for she replied, 'very wet & windy!'" [27 July 1881; Folger Y.d.396(2/15)]), his gleeful rendition of Jarvis's comic stammering ("When*ever* are w-e-e-e t-o-o-o-o s-e-e-e-e-y o-o-o-u a-a-g-g-a-a-i-i-i-n?" (2 November 1882; Folger Y.d.5[46b]); his desire for a "letter of noose" (9 May 1882; Folger Y.c.1211[156]). And Halliwell's coy invitation to Wheatley, "all sensible people come occasionally to Brighton" (3 August 1881; Folger Y.c.1297[1]), was not an oblique way of saying he was lonely but rather that he thrived in the company of friends, and though he lived "so out of the world" he would "gratefully" receive "any intimation ... of the present state of Shakespearedom" (13 December 1881; Folger C.a.11[37]). To the friends who came must be added the fellow Shakespeareans and other colleagues who made the pilgrimage to Hollingbury Copse. The Americans were especially anxious to pay homage to Halliwell: Furness and Appleton Morgan were among them. Furness sent quaint Indian gifts and buffalo haunches; through Appleton Morgan Halliwell became in 1885 the first honorary member of the Shakespeare Society of New York. William Thomas of the *Daily News* was invited by Halliwell to join members of the Archaeological Association to lunch in his house and then to inspect his "chief Shakespearean treasures" (18 August 1885; Folger Y.c.1289[2]); Joseph Hill of Birmingham was also invited, for the "chief pleasure of having rarities is to show them to those who *really* appreciate them" (19 September 1885; Folger S.b.128[15]). To celebrate the occasion Halliwell proudly issued in two editions *Brief Notices of a Small Number of the Shakespeare Rarities That Are Preserved in the Rustic Wigwam at Hollingbury Copse, Near Brighton* "for use of the members ... on the occasion of their visit ... Saturday, August 22nd, 1885." By this time Halliwell inhabited not only a veritable small museum of rarities but had also constructed a kind of Shakespeare theme park for the benefit of his visitors and the satisfaction of his obsession with Shakespeare. William Rendle's description of the "bed, board, and welcome to boot" of one of his "best most liberal of literary friends" is all-revealing:

Here is a card from Hollingbury Copse in 1886 promising
    Bed.
    Claret.
    Books.
    MSS.
    Records.
    Wood blocks.
    And a welcome.
I went, and could go at will up and down the rambling lanes and curious corners of the one-storied, extensive retreat on the Sussex hills by the sea, the long passages named, the names put up at the corners by friendly wits, George Wright and Henry Stevens, I fancy. There are Wolsey's Walk, Milford Haven, Yorick's Rise, and Falstaff's Avenue. My apartments were in Jaques' Retreat, at the end of Dogberrie Lane; and in the anteroom were a library chair, pens, ink, paper, and blotting-paper, and through the window came ozone and views over the hills. Over the entrance portico, welcome met you in downright Shakespearean black letter: 'Come hither, come hither, come hither. Here shall you see no enemie, but winter and rough weather.' There is the welcome, and within are pleasant sights. Over one mantelpiece is Portia; over another the great lady in whom Imogen still lives, and treasures without end, some well-nigh priceless.[268]

And to the pride of home and possessions there was, as always, the affirming thrust of Halliwell's donations to institutions in Britain and Ireland and as distant as the United States, Canada, and New Zealand (not to mention a loan of £1000 to the London Library (1 July 1879; Folger Y.c.1229[2]) and of his active engagement on behalf of those in need of comfort and help: his petition to Gladstone for a pension for the daughter of his deceased friend Planché, the "eminent dramatist and heraldic scholar" (17 June 1880; LOA 257:59); his role in the success of a pension of £100 per annum for the widow of Thomas Wright (16 January 1881; Folger C.b.17[126]); his support of the beleaguered lithographer William Griggs (19 February 1881; LOA 246:2); his testimonial on behalf of Edward Arber's application for the Professorship of English Literature at

---

268. William Rendle, "Reminiscences and Remarks," *The Antiquary* (May-June 1888), p. 10. The portrait of Portia by the artist William Salter Herrick was willed by Halliwell to his daughter Henrietta Somerset Hall, but it (as well as that of Imogen) cannot be located.

Birmingham (12 April 1881; Folger W.b.83[75]); his comforting words to the publicly maligned George Bumstead (8 March 1882; LOA 259:1); his assistance in the circulation of Georgina F. Jackson's *The Shropshire Word-Book* ("The poor lady is such a fearful sufferer she cannot see to it herself" [31 May 1882; Folger Y.c.1281(33)]); his eloquent defense of Collier against the charge of being "defaulter" for not having paid his dues to the Society of Antiquaries (10 April 1883; LOA 263:51); his liberal contribution to the Lunatic Appeal Fund for an annuity to provide for the confined J. T. Blight, his old illustrator (28 June 1883; LOA 261:67); his offer, as was his wont, to help Collier's daughter Emma (17 November 1883; LOA 278:25) and Ingleby's Rose (10 October 1886; LOA 295:40) to assess and counsel them on the libraries of their deceased fathers. Perhaps even more illustrative of his engagement and perhaps even more touching than his concern for the health of Charles Roach Smith after an operation—"I now do most fervently hope, dear old boy, that you will not require such another ordeal, & that every fragment of the disease has been removed" (10 August 1882; Folger C.b.17[137])—or his searching for a job for his niece, the daughter of his wife's sister, Florence (25 March 1883; Folger Y.c.1211[168]), was his rediscovery of Samuel Charles, his old Cambridge chum, to whom he had dedicated the first edition of *The Early History of Freemasonry in England* in 1840. The once breezy and buoyant Charles, who had kept Halliwell informed of all the relevant Cambridge gossip and happenings. "It is very kind of you to remember an old acquaintance who has fallen into poor circumstances at the end of his life," Charles wrote on 7 February 1885 (LOA 287:55), "I wish I could do something for you here to show that I am grateful for the aid you send me." And Halliwell continued to employ him to do collations, transcriptions, and research in the British Museum, the South Kensington Museum, and elsewhere in London. Halliwell's response was evidently emotional and beyond his generous payments, judging from such comments of Charles's as: "How long it seems since you kindly introduced me to Sir Henry Ellis, who gave me my first ticket!" (22 April 1885; LOA 285:4) and "I feel myself at seventy two getting further and further from the power of taking clerical duty, and know that my occupation is gone" (18 October 1886; LOA 295:75).

Halliwell's concern for others and his generosity were not new. But within the shelter of Hollingbury Copse they helped to modify his melancholy into a certain mellowness. He might lament the passing of the gold old times and friends, but he was now able to come to terms with it, albeit with some rose-coloring. Responding to the notice taken of him, "an old bookworm," in being named the first honorary member of the

Shakespeare Society of New York, he reminisced in a "Communication" of 14 November 1885 to Appleton Morgan.[269] Looking back to the founding of the first Shakespeare Society in 1840, he remembered–or reconstructed–a time when it was "possible for Shakespearean research and criticism to be amicably and temperately conducted ... [with] kind feelings and good humor ... [without] offensive dogmatism and insolent criticism." His gentle portraits of some of the leading figures–Collier, Tomlins, Cunningham, Dyce–are touching. Given as advice to the Americans, Halliwell's celebration of the past was certainly an attempt to confirm his own course then and now. It was also a sign of his inner resolve and sturdy identity.

Bullen's characterization of Halliwell as the Hermit of Hollingbury Copse is also telling, but Halliwell himself had a perhaps more accurate designation. Six months before his death he referred to himself as the "retired old lunatic." His age and his beard, his provincial household and life style, his almost monomaniacal devotion to his research and his unfailing humor had made of him a local character. He loved the land, and it doubtless nourished his energy and dynamism. For despite his failing health and increasing gloominess, despite his repeated attempts at avoiding "rows," he did not shy away from the important matters. Indeed, he met them head on. And, in doing so, he defined himself even more clearly than in his many acts of kindness and concern which he consistently practised. The emergent personality of the last decade of his life could be comic, as in his mock-heroic letter to J. G. Bishop, the editor of the local *Brighton Herald*:

Tarts & cheese cakes!, as Sancho Panza says–but because I send you a scrap from an old book there is no pressing reason for communicating the interesting fact to the people of Sussex. Moreover, publicities with a queer recluse like myself, who disdains conventionalities & has a fancy for doing as he likes without caring a button for public opinion, may result some day in a paragraph in the Herald something like the following –'Many of our thirsty readers may like to know where a glass of really good ale is to be got. We think that we can enlighten them. Mr. H.-P., so well known as a Shakespearean critic, is further distinguished as a first-class judge of old ale, & we mention that he is to be seen imbibing it, nearly every day in the week, in the snug little tap-room of the Cow & Snuffers. A word to the wise is sufficient' (28 October 1882; LOA

269. In *Papers of the New York Shakespeare Society*, No. 5 (1886), 25-9, and reprinted in *Shakespeariana*, 7 (1890), 24-6.

263:24).

It could be stern, as in his letter (of 3 August 1882) headed "A Protest" to the editor of the *Sussex Daily News* published on 4 August 1882 (LOA 261:8*):

At the risk of making a personal notice of too much importance, I must ask your permission to contradict a statement you have taken to-day from the *Whitehall Review*, to the effect that I am one of those who have joined the Church of Rome, no step of the kind on my part having been even remotely contemplated.

Halliwell's true character is glaringly evident in the two great tests of his last years: his turbulently sad quarrel with F. J. Furnivall and his painfully disappointing split with Stratford-upon-Avon.

21

My Nearest and Dearest Enemy

Hamlet-like, Halliwell preferred to see himself not as a man of action "fitted for the world's strife" like Charles Roach Smith, but as a "poor creature *solely of the study.*" But like Hamlet he could "come out when *thoroughly* provoked, as in the case of Furnivall" (20 February 1883; Folger W.a.82[221]). He was admittedly "shaken" by the "business" and "crave[d] for quiet." And well he was and might be, for the encounter with Furnivall was long, very personal, and professionally blistering.

The correspondence between Frederick James Furnivall and Halliwell in the Edinburgh collection consists of ninety-four letters from Furnivall, twenty-six from Halliwell directly to Furnivall and fourteen in which he is mentioned, and as part of a larger context the whole of Volume 247, forty-four letters which Halliwell collected and described as "relating to Furnivall's attack on me."[270] Doubtless because of Furnivall's insistently vigorous personality, as well as crucial issues in the nature and direction of Shakespeare scholarship, the exchange is perhaps the liveliest and most penetrating of the whole collection. Most noteworthy is the fact that Halliwell saw fit to have copied so many of his own letters to Furnivall, thus establishing a rapid-fire give-and-take atmosphere not otherwise to be found. Of the sixty-five letters written by Halliwell between 1872 and 1879, the period which covers their exchange in the Edinburgh collection, forty-one deal directly or indirectly with Furnivall. The letters from Furnivall to Halliwell span the period from 1857 to 1879. And that was not the end of it, for the controversy, never quiescent, erupted

---

270. Included in the count of ninety-four are two ghosts: letters from Furnivall listed in Halliwell's handwritten index to Volumes 234 and 256 but not found in those volumes. In one interesting instance, LOA 256:70 is indexed as LOA 256:39, according to Halliwell's handwritten "My letter about the Dedication." Since he saw to the binding of the volumes, and the numbering of the individual letters was added by a later hand, Halliwell must have changed the order for some reason or other. It is impossible to say whether the deletion of letters 37 and 38 is related.

climactically in the early 1880s and lingered painfully to the end of Halliwell's life.

These dates 1857 to 1879 are not without significance. The thirteen letters from Furnivall between 1857 and 1870–which imply responses from Halliwell not found in the Edinburgh collection–reflect one important aspect of the entire correspondence: Furnivall's reporting on or, in the main, requesting information and assistance for projects on which he was working. Direct in approach and cordial in tone, they indicate a relationship between friendly professionals with similar interests. They also begin to give an outline of the energetic, many-sided career of Furnivall. Thus in his earliest letter (Friday, August 1857; LOA 63:27) the thirty-two-year-old Furnivall was asking dating questions of Halliwell in connection with his "Dictionary-scheme" with Herbert Coleridge, which was adopted somewhat later by the Philological Society, of which he became honorary secretary in 1853. (Although Furnivall became editor in 1862 on the death of Coleridge, he continued collecting material even after the project was taken over by James Murray in 1876 and named *The New English Dictionary*.) Furnivall in the 1850s and 1860s–in fact throughout his life–was committed to the revival and reprinting of early English literature, like Halliwell, Collier, and others. In his early letters to Halliwell he asked for information about the Hampole MS. in Eton (10 July 1866; LOA 111:8), for the location of the Porkington MS. (13 December 1866; LOA 122:16), and for aid in getting access to the Osterley Park collection (29 April 1868; LOA 136:31). Not surprisingly, Halliwell's first three letters to Furnivall contained an offer of help with the MSS. of the Thirlstaine House library (11 March 1872; LOA 208:22), an admission that he has no influence in "gaining [Furnivall] access" to the collection (18 March 1872; LOA 194:19), and information about the Hoccleve MS. which might be gathered from Sir Thomas Phillipps's own printed catalogue of his books. Unable to give "replies to any questions about the Thirlstane House Library" because of his strained relations with his father-in-law, Halliwell nevertheless referred Furnivall–with a personal and confidential touch based on a by then fifteen-year-old acquaintance and belying the rather formal salutation "My dear Sir"–to John Fenwick, Phillipps's son-in-law, "begging" him, "however, kindly not to mention my name; for although we are on friendly terms with the present owners of the library [the Fenwicks], yet considering the silly clause in Sir Thomas's will [forbidding Halliwell and his wife, as well as all Roman Catholics, from entering the house], Mrs Phillipps & myself do not consider that it would be decorous in either of us to introduce *anyone*, or to make any literary enquiries respecting the books" (2 April 1872; LOA 206:24).

Other letters from Furnivall in this early period concern his editing (with J. W. Hales) of *Bishop Percy's Folio Manuscript: Ballads and Romances*, 1867: he informed Halliwell that he needed a cast of the woodcuts for the ballads (20 November 1866; LOA 118:20); that the "Copier is at p. 280 of the Percy MS., & I have about £300 [in subscriptions] promised" (13 December 1866; LOA 122:16); that he needed several more ballads (18 March 1867; LOA 118:24); and the like. The quest for information, opinion, and assistance in his dealing with early texts persisted throughout Furnivall's correspondence: be it a question about the Captain Cox tract (12 August 1870; LOA 173:13), which he edited for the Ballad Society in 1871; be it his assertion that he had seen the "only English copy of Chaucer's *Mother of God*" (2 April 1873; LOA 215:41), doubtless in connection with his Chaucer Society in 1868 and his issuing of the poem in *A Parallel-Text Edition of Chaucer's Minor Poems* (LVII, Parts II:6, 1878); be it his being sure that he "can trace Chaucer's progress, watch his changes & development as also his decline" and, urging Halliwell to do a similar "critical examination of Shakespeare's genius, showing his increase in power, the growth in choice & treatment of subject, the change from complete line to broken line (like Bathurst), the characteristics of his 3 Periods–if 3 be the right number–&c" (27 August 1873; LOA 215:35); be it his asking for a loan of a copy of Francis Meres's *Palladis Tamia* for a reprint, guaranteeing "freedom from damage" (11 December 1873; LOA 215:44); be it his admission of knowing nothing about draining (12 October 1874; LOA 215:8); be it his (repeated) request for the Norden plates of the views of London and Westminster (20 November 1875; LOA 197:7, 22 November 1875; LOA 197:16, etc.); be it his request and then thanks for the loan of a copy of Norden's map of Westminster for his edition of William Harrison's *Description of England* (1877-81) (1 November 1878; LOA 239:26, 6 November 1878; LOA 239:27); be it his desire to see Halliwell's printed collection dealing with actors (2 January 1879; LOA 239:21).

Furnivall's quest for information and opinion extended to Shakespeare, intimately bound up with his announcement of the formation of the New Shakspere Society in 1873, a turning-point in the development of Shakespeare studies and in the relationship between Furnivall and Halliwell. Not unusual is the continuation of individual questions on particular projects on which each of them was working. Furnivall looked to Halliwell for opinions: "Why shouldn't John S. be Wm's eldest brother, born before the Stratford register begins?" (10 March 1874; LOA 215:48); "Have you ever workt *Edw. III* carefully? [Richard] Simpson, [Frederick Gard] Fleay, & I say that only E.'s lovemaking to the Countess of

Salisbury is Sh.'s. Collier says the whole Play is. That's absurd" (4 April 1874; LOA 130:7); "Have you ever gone into the *Sonnets* questions? The thing I find hardest in them is the change of tone in the middle ones from earnestness to absolute trifling & playing with the subject" (2 January 1879; LOA 239:21); "I think that Oberon's last speech looks like an aim at something beyond the play as well as in it, & that the suggestions & *acting* of the *M.N.Dr.* were for an Elizabethan marriage–possibly a triple one" (18 October 1879; LOA 244:6). Furnivall was acute enough to know that, as far as Shakespeare was concerned, he had in Halliwell a captive audience and respondent. "It's all very well," he confidently asserted late in their correspondence, "saying that you want to keep off Shakspere, but he's more part of your real *life* than anything else, & you know it" (6 November 1878; LOA 239:27).

Furnivall was always interested in Halliwell's undertakings and encouraged them. He urged him to publish his "Documents at once" (12 February 1874; LOA 223:40); to "send us a dozen of your titbits, & see whether we won't put 'em in type soon" (2 November 1874; LOA 216:23); not to "get irritated then. Damn me as much as you like. Relieve your mind thus, & then just print your book as fast as you can, & set all our mistakes of fact straight" (5 May 1879; LOA 251:77); to be persuaded to "do a permanent & handy Shakspere book–none of your 25 copies or folios,–but '*The Documents of Shakspere's Life*': *all* the authentic Documents, with any slight comment needed, but nothing else" (14 September 1879; LOA 244:5). Halliwell was a responsive correspondent. Although busy–"I do not see my way clear to a gossip just at present"–he was nevertheless trying to buy a copy of Meres "at any fair price ... and make The [New Shakspere] Society a present of it" (9 January 1874; LOA 32:7). "Tell me what extracts you want," was his offer, "from any of my copies of North's Plutarch & you shall have them" (19 June 1874; LOA 116:35). Further, he revealed that "a copy of the 1592 edition of Greene's Groatsworth of Wit [is] in the library of Sir John Fenn" (26 November 1878; LOA 233:3). He offered advice on research: "I know no one else whose studies would enable him to search the Record Office for the fact you want with any fair chance of success. There are of course many record students far more accomplished than myself but none with the very long training on the one particular subject, without which a result is not to be expected" (12 March 1879; LOA 250:17).

Interspersed with, if not enveloped in, these professional inquiries and responses are personal and domestic details and phrasings which are lively and vigorous, going beyond the customary casual salutations of "Dear Furnivall" or "Dear F" and "Dear Halliwell" or "Dear H" or the closings

"Yrs. ever" or simply "Yours" or "Yrs." In stressing the need for careful and systematic researching–"The discovery of a new fact about S. is of as much use to a Shaksn reputation as the finding out of a new planet is to an astronomical one"–Halliwell could not resist what may be a twitting reference to Furnivall's journalistic activities: "If I mistake not, I know of a certain gentleman whose Chaucerian reputation has been greatly increased by his name being seen in newspapers every week in connexion with Chaucerian discoveries" (16 February 1874; LOA 32:13). In turning down a request from Furnivall, he retorted: "According to your peculiar theory I shall be a wretched doginthemanger old hoss if I do not offer these collections to you merely because you have elected to write on the same subject. It is a funny notion if I state your views correctly. Do enlighten me, there's a good fellow" (8 April 1876; LOA 228:21).

For his part Furnivall was even more open and revealing and personal. Having visited Stratford, he "*must* write to say that if some giant avenger hasn't wrung your neck, you really are a good fellow for clearing that New Place & keeping it all in such nice order. I forgive you all your sins for this, & say 'Bless you, my child'!" (6 July 1874; LOA 215:13). He was "glad" Halliwell had "got hold of something good. You deserve it; tho' you are such a wicked old codger" (4 April 1874; LOA 130:7). His acceptance of one of the many invitations from Halliwell is typical of the man and the relationship: "I hope to turn up on the 19th–'Sunday, April 20th', you say, but my almanac has it 19. It's not a Working Men's Reading night; & so, if I shouldn't put you out, I'll come later, say between 5 & 6, & have a bit of cold beef at your dinner. 'Like the fellow's impudence', you'll say, 'asks himself to dinner, as he asks for my Shakspere finds.' I wish you lived near Regent's Park" (4 April 1874; LOA 130:7).

Furnivall's numerous commitments–"a set of 8 lectures" for the "Oxford Ladies on Anglo-Saxon & Early English up to Chaucer's time" (12 October 1874; LOA 215:8), a lecture "on Elizabethan Literature (of which I know nothing ...), edit Shakspere (of whom you'll say I know less), and finish off Robt of Brunne [*Handlying Sinne*], & Chaucer's Canterbury Tales," as well as "writing a Chaucer Review ... & [having] a Shaksp. Lecture (gratis)" for the Sunday Shakespeare Society (16 December 1874; LOA 215:25), and the like–did not prevent him from being personally involved in Halliwell's family circle. His letters are full of references to Halliwell's household and especially his daughters. "I've no doubt you'll enjoy the party no end," he wrote on one occasion. "It must be pleasant to you to see your girls & their friends amusing themselves, tho' the upset of the house before & after *is* a bore" (5 January 1874; LOA 215:9). He was "glad to hear that the girls are enjoying themselves. They saw too few young folk in town–were like colts in a stable. Hope they'll get nice husbands, who'll love 'em & make 'em happy" (24 September 1874; LOA 215:4). Ellen was his favorite. On a visit to Stratford he mentioned: "By the way, there's a little thorobred chestnut at the Golden Lion which is just the thing to carry Ellen. *Very* quiet & temperate she is. 5 years old. Taylor asks 70 for her, but 'd take 60, I should think. She goes well in harness. Mind you tell Ellen" (7 July 1874; LOA 215:7). There is little need to look for an explanation in the fact that Furnivall's own daughter, Ena, had died in infancy in 1866. The attraction of youth is enough of a reason, as Furnivall explained later in the year, when he lamented that he was unable to join Halliwell on the Isle of Wight: "Would that I could thus renew my youth! But alas I *must* stay in London for the present. Had I a sound right ancle [*sic*], instead of a sprung-sinewed one, I should enjoy heartily a waltz with Your girls–the deux-temps was a weakness of mine–but now, disabled, I must be content to fancy them whirld round by elegant Wightans who whisper all sorts of pretty things to 'em" (16 December 1874; LOA 215:25).

Striking are the openings of the letters: most often, immediate and colloquial, spirited and spunky. From Furnivall: "You don't misunderstand my chaff, I'm sure. You poke me under the ribs, & I give you a stir in return" (17 December 1873; LOA 215:43); "Really you 're too provoking. Here's a good punch in the eye for you" (7 July 1874; LOA 215:7); "What is coming to you in your old age? Breaking out into Verses & Dances!" (16 December 1874; LOA 215:25); "Don't be savage" (26 October 1875; LOA 218:33); "You mistake. I'm not half such a 'mean customer' as you are" (22 November 1875; LOA 197:16); "What perverse inferences you draw!" (12 May 1879; LOA 244:4). Even Halliwell, normally formal and correct, was drawn to counter in his own fashion: "Pardon me!–but I really am at a loss to understand what I have said or written to warrant the insinuation that I am 'touchy'" (10 December 1873; LOA 77:4); "You deserve to have your ears well pulled for making false accusations" (10 April 1874; LOA 116:19); "All right, old boy! I see now we are at one on the Gervinus question" (13 January 1875; LOA 248:50); "Do I understand you rightly? Take this question" (8 April 1876; LOA 228:21); "I am not disposed to desert my birds & trees for dusty parchments" (12 March 1879; LOA 250:17).

These characteristic openings are playful and muscular. They reflect a powerful and yet strenuous bond. Both men were energetic; both were prolific doers. And if Furnivall was the more extrovert, a restless organizer and reformer with a highly developed sense of social action, and if Halliwell was the more introvert, by the 1870s apparently content with solitary and patient researches in record offices and the often anonymous and secretive dealings of the book trade–yet the two men met and mingled in what was the focal point of their personal and professional lives: archaeological philology and especially Shakespeare. In 1873 Furnivall announced the formation of the New Shakspere Society. Just a bit too young to have played an important role in the first Shakespeare Society, which began in 1840, he set about with the amazing zeal that motored all his literary and social activities not merely to re-establish credible Shakespeare studies but indeed both to reform and to re-form them. In doing so, he took on the older establishment–Collier, Staunton, Halliwell, and others–and he took them head on. He was almost fifty, to be sure, and not far behind in years from, say, Halliwell. But, as was his wont, he was determined to change things to his taste. The year 1873 was a watershed in Shakespeare studies. For Furnivall and Halliwell it was the beginning of a relationship which grew in intensity and passion as the 1870s proceeded, reached a climax toward the end of the decade, and then exploded and disintegrated. The two men, who had been so entangled, were torn apart, painfully and with recriminations. The New Shakspere Society ceased to exist a few years later.

The story of the New Shakspere Society is too well known to require much in the way of re-telling here.[271] In outline, Furnivall irritated many important personalities–among them Howard Staunton and Halliwell–by naming them vice presidents without their knowledge or approval. Further, he exalted a "new" and "higher" criticism, based mainly in statistical and metrical studies, which sought to establish a fixed chronology of the Shakespearean corpus and therefrom to discover the mind of the poet at various stages of his career. There crystallized a conflict between two essentially irreconcilable points of view: one, embodied in the *Shakespeare Commentaries* of Georg Gottfried Gervinus and championed by Furnivall, who first supplied an introduction to the English translation in 1874; the other, by Algernon Swinburne in his *Study of Shakespeare* of 1880, which was fatefully dedicated to Halliwell. Charges of abuse and mud-slinging, of vile and obscene language, were levelled against Furnivall from many sides: the so-called Pigsbrook affair erupted into a pamphleting war and a public scandal and led to the demise of the New Shakspere Society.

The amazing thing is that in the turbulence from 1873 to the end of the decade the bond between Furnivall and Halliwell seems not merely to

271. For a concise summary of the Pigsbrook affair, see William Benzie, *Dr. F. J. Furnivall: Victorian Scholar Adventurer* (Norman, Oklahoma, 1983), pp. 197-209.

have survived but to have been strengthened, as it were, through exercise and tension. The domestic touches–invitations, dinners, greetings to family members, mutual visits–continued, of course. But something approaching confrontation, the pressure to justify one's position, and the mutual admiration–often apparent, sometimes just below the surface–of person and accomplishment: all tended to invigorate and perpetuate a relationship which was not static but marked by the kind of camaraderie that only mighty opposites might share.

The importance of confrontation may be measured not merely by the number of letters written, nor merely by their frequency within short periods: Furnivall, for example, dashed off letters to Halliwell on 4, 7, 9, 11, 15, and 17 December 1873; Halliwell retaliated on 8, 10, and 16 December 1873. What is even more striking, and indicative of the significance (if not the passion) Halliwell attributed to the exchange, is the fact that he had so many copies made of his letters to Furnivall–more than to any other correspondent in the Edinburgh collection. The result is a vivid record of their interaction, instead of the one-sided picture which a massive collection of letters addressed only to Halliwell presents. A few examples are worth quoting *in toto*, as they touch on crucial matters and reveal personality.

For one thing, there was Furnivall's peremptory naming of Halliwell as a vice president of the New Shakspere Society:

Relying on what Staunton said, & on your uniform kindness to me, & your devotion to Shakspere, I've put you down on the enclosed, & now ask you to let your name stand. Always try [truly] yrs F.J.F. Can you get me any good names? (4 December 1873; LOA 215:45). I'm very sorry that you won't be on our Committee. But I shall put you down as a Vice-President whether you will or not. *That* you must be content to endure. About Gervinus I can't agree. The spirit of the man is deep & noble. Some bosh, & much Germanism, I admit. But where else 'll you match that book as a whole? Very glad to hear about *Impacient Povertie*; & I *shall be* very glad to have a Shakspere fight with you, & let you knock all the knowledge you can into me (7 December 1873; LOA 215:46). All right. I take your name off, tho' no one but I is responsible to the Prosp[ectu]s written in the 1st person, & signed by myself. Shakspereans are touchier folk than I fancied. Our friend A[lgernon]. S[winburne]. is a regular powder barrel. Please tell me the bits in the Prosps that you specially object to (9 December 1873; LOA 69:20).

Halliwell did not hesitate to reply:

Pardon me!–but I really am at a loss to understand what I have said or written to warrant the insinuation that I am 'touchy'. If I were not afraid of being considered impertinent, I should decidedly say, judging from the tone of your last note, that the boot is on the other leg. A person cannot be touchy unless he is offended or displeased at something unne[ce]ssarily. Now I am neither in the slightest degree offended nor displeased at any portion of your prospectus, nor can I imagine how any one can be. What I did say, & what I now repeat, is that no one can honestly join a Committee of a Society when he does not agree with the sentiments contained in the Prospectus upon which that Society is proposed to be founded. 'Dat is all, my Lort,' as one of the Lichborne Witnesses observes (10 December 1873; LOA 77:4).

Unruffled, Furnivall responded on the next day:

I forget what I said about touchiness; but whatever it was, it was meant more for our friend Staunton than for you. And indeed I oughtn't have meant it at all for you, seeing that you said you 'd have a long Shakspere chat & fight with me, which is just what I want; because I'm only a learner–tho' one on the right method, I hope.–And I hope you 'll give me lots of information & good advice. Also, can & will you lend me a *Meres* to reprint? We can guarantee freedom from damage. Further, will you suggest any other books for reprinting? I think of starting with Meres, the Digby MS Mysteries, & Harrison's England. In critical work, probably a translation of [Gustav] Rümelin's book [most likely, *Shakespeares Individualität und Bildungsgang*, 1874], besides such Papers as we can get. Won't you write us a Paper? Sincly yrs F.J.F. I wish you 'd tell me the bits in my Prosps that you don't like. I've altered 2 bits: changed *wooden* on p. 1, & inserted a clause on p. 2 (11 December 1873; LOA 215:44).

And again:

You 've exactly described the position. We'll chaff & pitch with one another no end, & then eat a bit of mutton together, or drink a cup of tea, for, as a tee-totaller of 32 years standing, I can't drink your bowl of punch. But in aesthetics, if we don't 'bust you all round the town, my chicken,' or knock you into a cockt hat, all the lot of you old fellows, my name's not F.J.F. 'Come on!' as soon as you like. Now just look at this last letter of yours–cocksure as if you 'd been at Shakspere's elbow: 'not a dozen lines left' &c.–pure gammon, my dear Sir. '*Must* have been written after the T.G. of N.' You really have your A.B.C. to learn. You most estimable chaps & faithful workers haven't a fixt principle or a canon of criticism among you. And yet you 're as sure that you know all about it as if you 'd been S.'s amanuenses. I'm ashamed of you! (15 December 1873; LOA 215:36).

Halliwell was quick to retort on the next day:

Go on & prosper, my dear Boy! So that you don't put me upon Shakespeare Committees, of which I have had quite a sickener, so far as I am concerned you shall have it all your own way with your aesthetics & your canons. In the mean while nothing remains for a harmless drudge like myself but to go on collecting facts, which I only hope won't interfere with your canons, or perchance you 'll be giving me a topper over the brain basket. You astonish me with the intelligence that you have been a teetotaler 32 years, but I am more amazed at the fact that you 're alive to tell the tale. Do take a glass of stout of a day, there's a good fellow, or you 'll go into the elm before your time & no mistake. Yrs. ever J. O. Phillipps P.S. Your notes are so sharp & neat I wish to goodness you 'd write on better paper, so that one can preserve 'em better (16 December 1873; LOA 69:41).

Furnivall then ended this bout with an immediate reply on the next day:

You don't misunderstand my chaff, I'm sure. You poke me under the ribs, & I give you a stir in return: But don't think that I for a moment undervalue the great worth of the work you 've done for Shakspere, or that I haven't deep respect for the devotion you 've shown to him & his fame. No more faithful follower has he ever had than you. But as you 've exhausted your line—or will have when your new book is out—I want to work in another line, not yet rightly taken up in England, as I think. There are a good many roads to Stratford, & we 'll wish one another a pleasant journey along our different ones (17 December 1873; LOA 215:43).

There was also the crucial matter of the direction of Shakespeare studies. Although already touched upon in the previous exchange, it was gone into in more detail early the next year, focussing more specifically on the discovering of Shakespeare's mind by determining, statistically, the chronology of the plays. Central is the German influence, especially of Gervinus, on Furnivall. Two clashes of personalities and issues are noteworthy. One heated up in the midst of a letter from Halliwell in the spring of 1874:

You say I do not deserve hanging but merely torturing. Am sorry to observe that you merit both. A nice dance you led me last night! for it was all owing to you that I spent the evening in the perusal of some of Gervinus. The case is far worse than I had thought. Any clever London newspaper-leader writer could do the whole thing far better, & with less palpable error, for I do not believe that any Englishman would fall into such direful blunders, blunders that a superficial reader–the individual who is generally spoken as 'the general reader'–may well pass over unnoticed, the writer's consummate arrogance enabling him to tinsel his work with the appearance of the profoundest critical knowledge (24 March 1874; LOA 69:4).

Stung, Furnivall retorted on the same day:

I *like* your impudence about Gervinus. You just write, on any one play, a comment that shows half the thought, & breadth of scholarship, that his comment on the same Play does. Try it, & see what you make of it. Clever London newspaper leader writer, be bothered! Such men have no insides. G. has. But as to the blunders of fact, such Gervinus may make, does, no doubt. You just put me down a list of all you 've noticed, & they shall be corrected in the cheap edition now reprinting. That will be helping, instead of grumbling only. I certainly hope we shall get a book on Shakspere within 3 or 4 years, that shall be *closer*, & more definite in criticism than Gervinus is, but, if my judgment is worth anything, G. is the best book now on Shakspere as a whole, & will *always* have value, whatever books follow it. If you can show its shallowness, write a Paper on it for N.Sh. Soc. & we 'll give in if we can't defend him against you. I hope you 'll send me your Letter on the Roman Plays [272] by Friday. Thanks for dates &c. Yours F.J.F. Correct any slips in enclosed, please (24 March 1874; LOA 215:31).

The wrangling about Gervinus and what he stood for continued,

272. Halliwell's "Hint on the Date of Coriolanus and Possibly Other Roman Plays," *Transactions of the New Shakspere Society*, pp. 367-70, was read by Furnivall at the seventh meeting on 26 June 1874. He reported immediately: "Your 'Hint' was very well received at the New Shakpere Society last night. No one had a word to say against it, but all felt that a new & very valuable bit of evidence had been brought forward by you. Your modest way of putting it was also felt as a most favourable contrast to [name deleted by Halliwell] ignorant dogmatism ... A cordial vote of thanks was passt to you for your *Hint*. May you give us some more of 'em" (27 June 1874; LOA 215:10).

always a constant source of irritation and yet alliance between the two men. Halliwell could answer Furnivall's request for information about the whereabouts of a copy of the 1592 edition of Greene's *Groatsworth of Wit* and in the same letter attack German critics and expose his own divided self: "Now considering how much I dislike the platform on which that Society was founded, & its Wicked pandering to the ridiculous vanity of the still more ridiculous German critics, you will own that I am correct in describing myself as your preternaturally good-natured friend" (26 November 1878; LOA 233:3). It was not the only stress point. Despite the exchanges of information and the lending of texts, there were barriers resulting not solely from ethical principle[273] or ideological differences but from professional rivalry. A typical instance was the question of copyright, a constant theme in the careers of Halliwell and his friends. The matter became acute when Furnivall asked Halliwell to send him his Norden's plates for use in his edition of William Harrison's *Description of England*. An interlude in late 1875 shows the growing intensity of the irreconcilable. Halliwell began:

Most assuredly I shall not allow any one the use of either blocks or casts of my engravings, & if a copy is made of a single one of them I shall at once apply for an injunction against the publisher or printer. Even in the case of mere facsimiles it will generally be easy to ascertain if mine or other copies are used in a reproduction. It is my intention to protect the Copyright of my new work to the utmost extent the law will allow, & I shall spare no expense in doing so. Considering that I intensely disliked,

273. An interesting and amusing example is Halliwell's comment on one of Furnivall's Socialist undertakings:

There are different views held as to the best methods of befriending the working man. It may be a good & innocent thing in itself to throw museums & picture galleries open on Sundays, but I am one of the many who believe that if this thin edge of the wedge once gets in it will ultimately lead to the downfall of that great palladium of one day in seven for rest, the worst thing for the working classes that could be imagined & equally bad for every one else. Stratford-on-Avon appears to be the oddest place in the world for the National Sunday League to select for a Sunday excursion. Every place of Shaksperian interest is closed on that day excepting the Church. The excursionists may of course attend the service if they please, but they will not be able to examine the Church afterwards or inspect its numerous objects of interest. If you wind up with a Shaksperian address, you will have to deliver it in one of the streets & perhaps get locked up for obstructing the Queen's Highway. Never mind—I'll bail you out (19 June 1874; LOA 116:35).

as you well know, the spirit in which the New Shakspere Society was instituted, it strikes me that I have treated it kindly & even liberally from the first, certainly always recommending persons to join it whenever I had a chance; but I do not intend to allow that Society to appropriate my plans & labours with impunity (19 November 1875; LOA 222:14).

Furnivall did not flinch, replying the next day:

The noble savage in his war-paint–& registering his letter, too! Now don't be angry–drink a bottle of claret, & feel amiable towards all mankind. There's more than 1 map of Shakspere's London in the world: & I shall do what you did: find out that which suits me best, & have it copied. But if in your book you want A. Boorde's Englishmen [Andrew Borde, *The Fyrst Boke of the Introduction of Knowledge*, edited by Furnivall for the Early English Text Society (Extra Series, No. X) in 1870] to illustrate what Sh. says of fashion, Harrison's rogues [*The Rogues and Vagabonds of Shakespeare's Youth* was edited in a somewhat different makeup by Furnivall and Edward Viles in 1869 for the Early English Text Society (Extra Series, No. IX) and reprinted with added illustrations for the New Shakspere Society in 1880], or any other cut we 've got, you 're as welcome to it as the day. Certainly you 've treated us well hitherto. Why not go on doing so? But you, like the rest of men, have got 2 sides to your character; & now you 're showing your bad one (20 November 1875; LOA 197:7).

Furnivall's cajoling and in his next letter mock scolding–"Confound you, you old curmudgeon, we 'll have the Map, whether you like it or not" (22 November 1875; LOA 197:16)–seem to have had the effect of increasing Halliwell's indignation:

Having either mislaid or destroyed your last note, I have only my recollection to depend upon in answering it, so if I am misinterpreting you in any way in this I must ask you kindly to excuse me. The registering of my previous letter as of this arose from my anxiety that they should not miscarry & you, by any possibility hereafter taken in any way by surprise, it being my determination to protect the copyright of my new work & of every engraving in it to the utmost extent the law will permit. If I can prove that a single one of my engravings has been used in any reproduction, & under the new Act I believe interrogatories are sanctioned, I will at once apply for an injunction. A little reflection will show that, apart from this being in harmony with my own feelings in the matter, it is my duty to take this action. My book is an expensive one, &

purchasers might reasonably complain if I sanctioned the reproduction of any part of it in other quarters. It happens that two London collectors have to my knowledge bought the work for the sake of the London plans & views alone. It will I think be generally conceded that any attempt, after this statement, to appropriate my designs would be an act of intense discourtesy. Although very willing as I have shown to assist the New Shakspere Society in my humble way in any direction which will not clash with the design of my own book, you know very well that I am working altogether independently of the Society & have no more idea of pirating its labours that [*sic*] allowing it to appropriate mine. Subject to these reservations, I have every good wish for the Society as well as a most friendly regard for your own talents & zeal, however greatly I differ from you on various important Shaksn. topics (26 November 1875; LOA 223:30).

It is difficult to measure the exact temperature of these exchanges. They continued, with varying intensity, throughout the 1870s. Whether arguing or placating, protesting or jesting, as they intermingled the personal and the professional, the two men were drawn together or, perhaps, found it impossible to separate. In the midst of their various disputes, Halliwell could invite Furnivall to dine with him and his family. Furnivall could say, after being turned down in his request for the Norden plates, "Thanks for your kind invitation. But on the whole I 've come to the conclusion that we do better at arm's length, each grinding away at his own tools." He could plead being personally disappointed: "When I come to you as a personal friend, & ask for a thing that I think any friend 'ud give me for a public work—as in the instances of that plate,— & New Place Sunday, & you refuse, I kick. Hence if we keep apart, I shan't ask things of you as a friend, but shall get 'em for myself when I want 'em, & also think pleasantly of you pioneering away." And then, with a showy sigh, he can conclude: "So, take kindest remembrances to your girls: their faces come smilingly across me now & again" (18 July 1876; LOA 197:33). After vowing not to ask again "after the lesson you gave me about the Norden plates" (26 August 1876; LOA 236:13), he did indeed ask for a loan of Norden's original map of Westminster (1 November 1878; LOA 239:26) and, when his request was finally granted, responded: "It's *immensely* kind of you to lend me such a nice copy of Norden's Map, & I'll behave divinely—for a week at least—in consequence" (6 November 1878; LOA 239:27). In the spring of 1879 Halliwell "should most likely wish to subscribe" to Furnivall's Shakespeare facsimile series "or anything else *Shaksperian*," for "there is good entertainment to be got out of the new

school, & if it excels the old one in other matters as much as it does in
consummate cheek, such grey-headed fogies as myself had better
skedaddle" (13 May 1879; LOA 256:62). Even in late 1879 Furnivall could
balance genuine gratitude and prankish delight by informing Halliwell that
"our Meeting tonight passt you a vote of thanks for your *M.N.Dr.* paper
[*Memoranda on the Midsummer Night's Dream, A.D. 1879 and A.D.* 1855], &
your gift of 25 copies to us; but in the Meeting of 30, there was not one
person who agreed with you" (17 October 1879; LOA 244:8).[274] He could
irritate Halliwell by boasting, "We New folk believe our main positions
impregnable; at any rate, we 're game to answer every challenger," and
then as a final touch conclude, "Kindest regards to your wife" (30
October 1879; LOA 268:21). He could respond sympathetically and
enthusiastically to Halliwell's second marriage.[275] And yet he could at the
same time be embroiled in his war with Swinburne. Halliwell, in fact,
included in the Edinburgh collection a printing of Furnivall's "Mr.
Swinburne's 'Flat Burglary' on Shakspere. Two letters from the 'Spectator'
of September 6th & 13th, 1879" with handwritten comments by Furnivall
(LOA 283:42). And yet at the same time he could write to Ingleby: "I am
greatly in hopes of getting Furnivall down her for a spell in Septr. I am
certain he is working too hard, & having injured myself in that way have
a fellow feeling in the matter" (13 August 1879; Folger C.a.11[14]).

   But the elasticity of the relationship stiffened and snapped a short time
later. Whether the break was caused by the accumulation of years of strain
or whether it was solely the result of the dedication to Halliwell by
Swinburne of his *Study of Shakespeare* and Furnivall's feelings of personal
betrayal, it is hard to say. But the latter is most likely. In the early autumn
of 1879 Furnivall announced a visit to Hollingbury Copse in order to
"persuade" Halliwell to "do a permanent & handy Shakspere book–none
of your 25 copies or folios,–but *The Documents of Shakspere's Life*'" (14
September 1879; LOA 244:5). On 8 October 1879 (LOA 246:8) he wrote
to say how much he enjoyed the visit, which (Halliwell later informed
Ingleby) had lasted "the whole of three weeks" (19 March 1881; Folger
C.a.11[31]). A few days later he was commenting on their differing
opinions on the merits of *Love's Labor's Lost* and *A Midsummer Night's
Dream* (15 October 1879; LOA 245:7). And on the next day, "thinking
over [his] letter of last night," Furnivall did "take it very kindly that you of
the Old Socy should hold out the hand of friendship to us of the New,

---

274. It is interesting to compare the reception of an earlier paper by Halliwell.
See n. 272.

275. See p. 483.

tho' you *do* think our notions awful nonsense, & damn our German friends. 'May difference of opinion never alter friendship,' as the old toast says. We shall go on chaffing one another to the end, I dare say" (16 October 1879; LOA 244:7).

The chaffing did go on, but the end was sooner than both had expected. Furnivall began quietly enough:

During a famous 15-mile walk that my wife & boy & I took with some friends today on the Epsom Downs, I heard, with some surprise, that Swinburne's new book on Shakspere was dedicated to you–& by your leave, as I suppose. If this is so, I hope you did not know what the book was to contain. But the contents are advertised & among them are S.'s paper on Edw. III, & that parody on a meeting of our New Sh. Socy, which appeared in the *Examiner* [1 April 1876, pp. 381-3[276]], both containing as bitter & personal insults to that Socy, in general & me in particular, as S. can write. Every one who reads Shakspere criticism knows the contents & purpose of both articles; & if you deliberately sanction the dedication of the Reprints of them to yourself, you sanction contents & purpose, & go out of your way to approve & adopt a deliberate insult to a body of gentlemen & ladies, of whom some at least have hitherto considered themselves friends of yours. It is not easy for me to believe that you wish to do this. But having heard of the matter, I will not lose a post without bringing it under your notice, leaving you to take such action on it as you see fit (2 November 1879; LOA 245:5*).

Halliwell's immediate response was brief and chilly.

You surely are under some singular misapprehension respecting the significance of dedications, I never heard before of the dedicatee of a book sharing in the remotest degree in either the honours or responsibilities of its contents, nor can I believe that the members of the New Shakspere Society, to which, notwithstanding my aversion to its platform, I am most friendly disposed, can on reflection entertain such an unprecedented notion (4 November 1879; LOA 251:79).

Furnivall's prompt reply is his last in the Edinburgh collection:

276. In the Appendix of *A Study of Shakespeare* as "Note on the Historical Play of King Edward III," pp. 231-75, and "Report of the Proceedings on the First Anniversary Session of the Newest Shakespeare Society," pp. 276-309. Especially pointed are n. 3 on pp. 264-5 and the Note on p. 275.

Your note surprises me. The well-known rule about Dedications is, that the purport of the book is stated to the Dedicatee, & an offer made to lay its contents before him, if he wishes to see it. This is of course what [Thomas Alfred] Spalding did, when asking Browning to accept dedication of his book on *Elizabethan Demonology* [1880]. It is also well known that the acceptance of a Dedication implies sympathy with the author's object. *A fortiori* is this the case when a book is avowedly a partisan one, & *a fortissimo* when a large part of it has been published before, & is known to be an insolent attack on a particular set of gentlemen & ladies. In the present case, you & every one know that that little drunken cad Swinburne has written 4 articles with the express purpose of ridiculing & insulting the ladies & men of my Society, & myself; & yet you want to say that your acceptance of the Dedication of the reprint of these articles does not imply any sympathy with their object, or responsibility for them! The thing is too patently absurd for argument. I do say emphatically, that I shall take the appearance of your name as dedicatee of Swinburne's book as an intentional sharing of the repetition of the insults against my friends & me that the articles contained, & as stopping all intercourse for the future between us. The present is a special case—that of a known reviler of Gladstone, reprinting 4 insulting articles against him, & John Bright accepting the Dedication of them, & then saying that he was in no way responsible for the book. Bright would sooner cut his hand & tongue off than do such a thing (5 November 1879; LOA 246:4).

Whereas Furnivall's distress is apparent in his repetitiveness, Halliwell's is obvious in the cold brevity of what is his last communication to Furnivall in the Edinburgh collection:

Your experience of dedications entirely differs from mine, & you must allow me to retain my opinion that the Dedicatee is in no way responsible for the contents of the author's works. Indeed, were it otherwise, no person in his senses would accept a dedication. If people are foolish enough to think that I endorse all that Mr Swinburne says, merely because the book is dedicated to me, I really can't help it (8 November 1879; LOA 256:70).

This is the end of the correspondence between the two men in the Edinburgh collection. The final and not very admirable quibbling is perhaps an indication of how painful the situation was. But that was not the end of the matter. Halliwell saw fit to write and receive scores of letters—forty-five alone, the whole of Volume 247 in the Edinburgh collection, which "relate entirely to Furnivall's attack on me," as he commented in his handwritten index: a collection which can only be regarded as an abiding testimony to his deep disappointment and distress.[277]

Although no more letters appear to have passed between Halliwell and Furnivall in the 1880s, the uproar which did take place was far greater than anything earlier. The matter became public as more and more individuals were obliged to declare their position. At stake were the state of English literature and criticism, the mission and organization of a society dedicated to Shakespeare Studies, professional rivalries, individual reputations, and personal pride. Earlier, Halliwell could balance opposing extremes in his relations with Furnivall: "As to Furnivall," so was his typical point of view in a letter to Ingleby, "he is disappointed rather than angry with me because (although I fully admit his Socy. has done some very good work) I will not bow down before its ridiculous pretensions or in any way encourage that very childish manifesto–the 'Founder's Prospectus.' But personally I like Furnivall very much, & no one appreciates his great talent & pure motives more than [I]" (30 October 1875; Folger C.a.11[3]). But Furnivall's assaults became so intense and unrestricted that Halliwell was forced to take sides, seek allies, or, perhaps more accurately, the abuse touched so many people that they rallied behind Halliwell, who *nolens volens* became their spokesman against not so much the principles of the New Shakspere Society as against its "Champion" (as W. A. Wright referred to Furnivall). Literally hundreds of letters in Halliwell's correspondence deal in one way or another with Furnivall. Mentions of Furnivall in Halliwell's own letters between 1879 and 1889 exceed all others in the Folger collection. But the conflict was not limited to private correspondence; it was fought out in print as well.

Halliwell, it must be admitted, was not a very willing combatant, as his numerous utterances regarding "rows" testify. Even in the midst of his involvement in the controversy, he did not disguise his resistance or hesitation to being involved. To (Walter) Theodore Watts-Dunton, Swinburne's adviser and intimate friend, he wrote: "I cannot shake off a preternatural disinclination to do anything I ought to do–unstrung & unfit for anything ... How very gratified I was at your kind invite to meet Mr Swinburne & yourself–it will be an immense treat to meet you both, only

277. In the Folger Shakespeare Library collection, mentions of Furnivall in Halliwell's letters are among the three most frequent (along with those of his collaborator, F. W. Fairholt, and his longtime friend, Thomas Wright). From 1879 to 1888 they exceed all others by far.

kindly excuse my warning that you two will have to do all the talking" (5 September 1882; Folger Y.d.329[13]). To be sure, Halliwell was very upset by Furnivall's high-handed and autocratic mode of imposing his will on the New Shakspere Society and his peremptory naming of vice presidents without their permission or even knowledge, causing many to resign. But then again Halliwell was a hardly visible member of the Society, nor intended to be one. And, of course, no stranger to Furnivall's methods and personality, he could not in the beginning at least have been surprised or even very upset. He could not accept the principles or the direction of the research being sponsored and promoted by Furnivall. He had already rejected not only Gervinus and German criticism but had also distanced himself from the statistical and positivistic efforts of English colleagues. But he could at least live with or alongside them, finding a place in his life for those with whom he disagreed. Thus he could send Fleay a copy of the first part of his life of Shakespeare and point out, "I do not expect you will agree in my estimate of the metre test for the chronology–but anyhow I am sure that we shall always agree to differ pleasantly" (12 October 1874; Folger Y.c.1222[1]). And in return Fleay could ask for a testimonial for his application for a Professorship of Modern History and English Literature at Bristol (21 May 1876; LOA 222:35).[278] Halliwell could also be tolerant or understanding of attacks on his work, albeit so sensitive that he could never forget errors which he noted (or were noted) in his work and constantly sought criticism and correction from his close friends, such as Ingleby and Charles Roach Smith. He was even incensed if the errors were perpetuated. "A very curious instance" of the "importance of careful acknowledgement," he illustrated to Fleay, "is in a new fact in Shakespeare's life discovered by me many years ago. In

---

278. Fleay, who had profited from information Halliwell had given him and had had from him at least such polite reactions to his work as "I can see at a glance that it will be very interesting" (10 July 1882; Folger Y.c.1222[15]), did not hesitate to criticize Halliwell very shortly after his death. In an unpublished manuscript, an address entitled "On Certain Modern Shakespeariana" (Folger S.b.81), he praised the "late Mr Halliwell Phillipps" as the "most generally esteemed of all writers in Shakesperian historical matters" but took exception to Halliwell when he "attempts the higher duties of the biographer or historian" due to his "absolute inability to coordinate his materials." That "inability," it should be noted, was communicated to Fleay in a letter from Halliwell himself on 31 March 1879 (Folger Y.c.1222[9]) and was a common complaint and not necessarily to be taken at face value. Edward Dowden was another who disagreed with Halliwell on many points and would not break with Furnivall, but he was smooth enough to maintain good relations with both men.

printing it I made a hideous blunder. Dozens of others have since used it–e.g. Dyce, Staunton, Neil, Furnivall &c.–in no single instance has the discoverer been named, *in no single instance has the blunder been suspected*!!!!!" (17 March 1880; Folger Y.c.1222[10]).

What Halliwell could not accept–or deal with internally–was an attack on his person and integrity. It was not simply that he was upset by the lack of good manners. He knew Furnivall only too well, and besides he had himself sought and cultivated the informality and directness of rustic life. What seems to have been at the heart of Halliwell's conflict with Furnivall may well have been his insecurity about his relationship with Swinburne, which feeling was then immersed in the larger swell of resentment against Furnivall's profane language and ruffian behavior and the clash of scholarly objectives and methodology.

For all his modesty about his reputation and for all his avowals against titles, Halliwell was pleased and proud to receive honors. From the beginning of his career he advertised his associations in lists of societies of which he was a member; on his wife's gravestone his name was followed by F.R.S; the testimonials he had received from Stratford were glazed and framed and hung prominently in his study. That Swinburne chose to dedicate his *Study of Shakespeare* (1880) to him was enormously flattering. Swinburne was, after all, a major personality in English letters and doubtless (along with Robert Browning) the most illustrious figure with whom Halliwell was ever to be connected. His relationship with Swinburne could not be termed personal. In the 1870s they courteously exchanged information and opinion, after Halliwell had sent Swinburne a copy of his *Illustrations* and had complimented him on the first installments of his studies of the text of Shakespeare. Recalling these events in a letter to Halliwell of 23 September 1879 (LOA 253:56), Swinburne cautiously and with elaborate ceremony approached the matter of the dedication of his new book, "then begun & since postponed by various interruptions ... now completed & in the press":

Disliking as I do the appearance, & disapproving the custom, of dedications 'by permission', I do not (after the usual form) solicit your leave to inscribe my 'Study of Shakespeare' to you in token of obligation and respect; nor on the other hand would I take upon myself to dedicate the book without notice or warning to an elder & a better Shakespearean scholar than myself.

Swinburne did not avoid a "word of warning"–that he was continuing "with some vigour of expression" his attack on German commentators, "but more especially on their English disciples of the 'New Shakspere Society'," and hoping that the "attacks" have the "good fortune to commend themselves to your good opinion." Halliwell answered immediately and elaborately (preserving a copy, as was his wont with important matters) that the "proposed dedication ... coming from you ... is ... the greatest compliment I have ever received, & although I feel that I am not deserving of it, laying claim to little more than being an earnest student with an endeavour to keep within the bounds of common sense criticism, the temptation to receive it is irresistible, & if you do so honour me I can only accept the distinction with gratitude" (25 September 1879; LOA 255:33). In his immediate reply–the work was after all in the press–to Halliwell's acceptance, Swinburne described his dedication: "I have simply placed your name at the top & mine at the bottom of a few sentences expressing my reasons of general & also of personal gratitude which have together made it proper that the book should be inscribed to you, without any common epistolary flourish of elaborate address & signature" (27 September 1879; LOA 255:31). The dedication itself was something Halliwell may not have fully expected:

TO
JAMES ORCHARD HALLIWELL-PHILLIPPS.
That a sample or excerpt given from this book while as yet save in design unfinished should have found such favour and won such approval at your hands as you then by word alike and action so cordially expressed, is reason enough why I should inscribe it with your name: even if I felt less pleasure in the reflection and the record that this little labour of a lifelong love had at once the doubly good fortune and the doubly grateful success, to be praised by those who have earned the praise and thanks of all true Shakespearean scholars, and dispraised by such as have deserved their natural doom to reap neither but from the harvest of their own applause or that of their fellows. It might be hard for a personally unbiassed judgment to strike the balance of genuine value and significance between these two forms of acknowledgment: but it will be evident which is to me the more precious, when I write your name above my own on the votive scroll which attaches my offering to the shrine of Shakespeare.
ALGERNON CHARLES SWINBURNE.

Although Swinburne's admiration of Halliwell was doubtless genuine, and even allowing for his characteristic rhetorical flourish, it is difficult not to suspect that Swinburne was seeking an ally and that Halliwell was being lured ("temptation" was his word) into a contentious position that he would otherwise have avoided. His praise of the work was for him uncharacteristically lavish: in his "honest opinion" it was a book in which "greater powers of genius are displayed than in any other work on the subject," and the extent of his submissiveness is glaring in the closing words of his letter to Swinburne: "If you feel that you can tolerate for a few hours a very dull person, unendowed with the slightest powers of conversation, I should feel so very much gratified & flattered by a visit whenever you happened to be at Brighton, & at least there will be some Shakean curiosities that cannot fail to interest you" (1 January 1880; Folger Y.d.329[11]).

When Furnivall urged him to disclaim the dedication, Halliwell could not. Trapped, he could only stiffen up and, defensively, argue pitifully that he "had never heard before of the dedicatee of a book sharing in the remotest degree in either the honours or responsibilities of its contents," suppressing the fact that Swinburne had written him on 1 December 1879 (LOA 257:25), "I trust the printers & publishers will soon at last enable me to send you the completed study which while yet incomplete was distinguished by your approval." He may not have even comprehended the full extent of what was to occur when he wrote to Francis Bedford: "It is a serious evil to me having through no fault of my own got into anything like even a small literary squabble, as I seem to have done. I find as I get into the last stage of life a wish for quiet & to be friendly & kindly to everybody, & take the most generous view of everything" (29 January 1880; Folger Y.c.1191). But, and inevitably, the conflict escalated. The fiery Furnivall spat flames and bad language in every direction. The apprehensive Halliwell responded rigidly and, cornered (as it were), struck back with a number of public letters and pamphlets. That both men were personally and deeply hurt is easily measured not merely by the intensity of their assaults but by its level. The main topic of the paper war was profane language and bad manners: Furnivall slung foul mud and Halliwell countered with prim respectability. The issue of literary criticism was no longer in the foreground.

For Halliwell the result was not a happy one. There were, to be sure, numerous resignations from the New Shakspere Society. One printed letter of 17 April 1881 (LOA 246:25) listed fifteen very prominent figures: Edwin A. Abbott, M. Creighton, [the Duke of] Devonshire, J. G. Fitch, H. Buxton Forman, R. C. Jebb, John W. Hales, J. Newby Hetherington, C. M. Ingleby, Henry Morley, H. A. J. Munro, Henry Sidgwick, William Smith, Leslie Stephen, W. H. Thompson. But in a very long letter to F. A. Marshall (1 March 1881; Folger W.a.73[22]) Halliwell painfully detailed the whole affair, concluding with the disappointing official response to his public letters:

Not caring to hold any communication with Mr Furnivall & feeling that some notice should be taken of his extraordinary behaviour, I ventured to address a temperate remonstrance to the Committee, under whose publicly announced approval the series in which his work appeared, was being undertaken; the Committee, however, were indifferent to the insults which had been publicly issued as written by the founder & Director of the New Shakspear Society.–for, in a curt reply denying their responsibility, they had not even the ordinary courtesy to express regret for the treatment to which I had been subjected.

It is not of course pretended that the Committee are immediately responsible for language printed without their knowledge, but their responsibility does arise–& a heavy responsibility it is in respect to what is neither more nor less than a literary outrage–if, now being well acquainted with the character of that language, they do not demand its immediate & public withdrawal. In the absence of such a demand, it must be assumed that their sanction is tacitly given to the obscenities by which Mr Furnivall has insulted me & dishonoured the New Shakspear Society, while the public will be very slow indeed to believe in the genuine Shakespearean spirit of a Society the members of which do not unmistakably manifest their indignation at the introduction of low scurrility into Shakespearean criticism.

There was even more to be grieved at: the loss of a longtime friend and the gain of a short-term acquaintance; the loss of a lively, if turbulent, relationship and the gain of a polite but essentially static series of mutual compliments on exchanges of published works. The effect on his scholarly work was also marked. Halliwell's strenuous efforts to reduce the number and scope of his activities and to concentrate on his literary life of Shakespeare were sharply undermined by the series of open letters in various forms he was obliged to undertake. He printed and circulated an exchange of correspondence with Robert Browning, president of the New Shakspere Society, dated 26, 27, and 31 January and a letter to the members on 4 February 1881.[279] Halliwell was doubtless justified in protesting in his letter of 26 January 1881 against Furnivall's preface to his facsimile of the second quarto of *Hamlet* in which he was described as a "leading member of the firm of Pigsbrook and Co." and some of his observations "denounced as 'porcine vagaries,' and others as being promulgated 'on the prongs of a dung-fork'." But it is disappointing that

279. The manuscripts of his letters to Browning are in the Folger Shakespeare Library: Y.c.1195(1,2); the letter from Browning of 27 January 1881 is LOA 247:2.

he objects only to the "phraseology of Billingsgate" (in which, naturally, he is not versed), the "offensive vulgarities," the "disreputable language." No mention is made of the substance of Furnivall's attacks. And Halliwell's already waning energy was more than casually employed in an extensive correspondence with numerous sympathizers and some dissenters. He was called upon to renew the methods he had employed and abandoned in seeking and managing subscriptions to his various works. To accompany his publications, he prepared form letters expressing, as in one devised to be sent with his "little work on *Hamlet*, his "kind thanks for your sympathizing note" and his view that Furnivall is "vulgar & makes himself so ridiculous." To this form letter of 8 February of 1881 (LOA 247:45) he added the note: "*Similar* letters sent to" eight named recipients. The immediate effect of the controversy on Halliwell's literary work was pronounced. Because he was forced to write so many letters, he confided to Ingleby, "my darling Shakespeare studies are shortened" (13 December 1881; Folger C.a.11[37]). "Abandoned" would be a more appropriate word if the reference is to the series of monographs on individual plays called "Memoranda" in which he had dealt with ten plays (in four volumes) in 1879 and three plays (in three volumes) in 1880, for Halliwell had "little doubt that [Furnivall's] insolent eccentricities will put a stop to the series of books I am now printing ... & [bitterly, no doubt] so I shall save a pot of money. Fortunately I can garden & enjoy a glass of old port" (27 December 1879; Folger C.a.11[16]). Six months later he sardonically informed Ingleby, "I am amusing myself just now by destroying nearly all my immense MS. collections on the plays, not wanting them after my death to be travestied used & misrepresented by an insolent lunatic" (11 June 1880; Folger C.a.11[20]).

After the vacuum in publications in 1877 and 1878, after the death of his wife and his remarriage in 1879, Halliwell's "new life" was to a certain extent stalled or diverted by his preoccupation with the professionally, if not essentially, marginal Furnivall affair. Halliwell's correspondence with William Aldis Wright is so typical of the overweighted emphasis and the mutual concerns of all who were directly or indirectly involved that it is worth a brief excurse.

It began in 1876 with a letter from Wright, continued with another from him in 1879, and then was concentrated in 1880 and 1881 with seven letters from Wright and one from Halliwell. Since Wright's Cambridge edition of Shakespeare was completed in 1866 and Halliwell's folio Shakespeare in 1865, and there were no startlingly new or controversial editions to attract wide attention, other Shakespearean topics occupied them. And from the dates of the letters it is not surprising that Shakespearean politics was central–namely, the New Shakspere Society and its "Champion," as F. J. Furnivall was titled by Wright.

There are only ten letters in all between them, and so it is relatively simple to describe them and outline the relationship they portray. Four deal exclusively with Wright's thanks for publications Halliwell had sent him and a few comments derived from a usually cursory "dip" into them. The rest, longer and certainly more spirited, deal in the main with Furnivall. Wright's thanks for Halliwell's *A Catalogue of the Shakespeare-Study Books*, 1876 (16 April 1876; LOA 227:40), for the *Memoranda on the "Midsummer Night's Dream*," 1879 (9 November 1879; LOA 248:43), for the second edition of *New Lamps or Old?*, 1880 (18 June 1880; LOA 256:50), for the *Memoranda on "Love's Labour's Lost*," 1879 (22 June 1880; LOA 248:3), and for the *Outlines of the Life of Shakespeare*, 1881 (14 July 1881; LOA 251:71) establish a relationship which was at once professional in the scholarly exchange of opinion and also of increasing cordiality. From the first brief response (16 April 1876; LOA 227:40) in which, in a birdlike neat script, he seemed to venture to comment–"If I were a book collector I should be inclined to envy you the possession of so many rare and curious works but my madness has not yet taken that form & therefore without envy I thank you most sincerely"–Wright proceeded a few years later, in a somewhat bolder script, to add more than the obligatory or automatic frill to his expression of thanks. Responding to the *Memoranda on the "Midsummer Night's Dream*," he commented approvingly on the "parallelism between the Fairys song and the Faery Queen," saying it "must 'give pause' to those who argue for an earlier date ... than 1596." Still, for his "own part" the evidence "would have more weight if it did not occur in a song" since "we know so little about the songs which Shakespeare brings in to his plays." Until it can be proved that the song is older than the play, Halliwell's "argument holds good"–Wright adding a statement of critical position which signalled a strong bond with Halliwell at a time when Furnivall was rampantly challenging the older establishment: "& it [the argument] has the great advantage that fact always has over theory."

In his very brief response to the *Memoranda on "Love's Labour's Lost"* half a year later–Halliwell's "benefits come faster than my acknowledgements"–Wright provided information about his own activities, another aspect of the correspondence: "The relation between the quartos and folios of Richard III is occupying me just now and I do not see my way to a satisfactory solution" (22 June 1880; LOA 248:3). Wright's final letter (14 July 1881; LOA 251:71)–and the last of pure thanks–although opening with the customary excuse of being so busy that he has "only had time to cut the leaves [of the *Outlines*]" (as in the previous letter he had only "just dipped into [the *Memoranda on "Love's Labour's Lost"*] in the midst of other work"), continued his habit of commenting on some point and then posing a larger question concerning a critical stance. Accepting Halliwell's "curious point ... about the editions of North's Plutarch which Shakespeare did not use"–"I have entered [it] in my Coriolanus"–Wright asked: "Might he not have had access to the ed. of 1579?" From this now accepted view he proceeded to the larger matter: "The whole question of the variations in copies of the same edition of 17th cent. books is worth looking into," adding a further bit of information about his own work, "My attention was called to it in editing Bacon's Essays from the ed. of 1625."

The remaining five letters of 1880 and 1881 focus on Furnivall and the unrest emanating from his managing of the New Shakspere Society and inciting the Pigsbrook affair. In them Wright displays more than mere sympathy with Halliwell's position; he demonstrates his own irritation with Furnivall's behaviour towards him as well as others and finally his growing realization that no compromise with Furnivall is possible. Wright's thanks (3 January 1880; LOA 250:31) for Halliwell's "protest against the new lights of the Shakspere Society"–his *Which Shall It Be? New Lamps or Old? Shaxpere or Shakespeare?* (1879)–combines the main elements of Wright's correspondence with Halliwell's: gratitude, an appraisal of a particular issue, a more general critical strategy–and, Furnivall being his irascible self, a more temperamental assertion of his own feelings. Furnivall's intransigent spelling of Shakespeare's name, "Shakspere," irritated Halliwell, who propagated "Shakespeare" from the very beginning of his career. Wright's rejection of the "new lights"–"They are great at teaching their grandmothers"–is based not on emotion but, as was his wont, on his own careful study of their "cheval de bataille," the signature on Shakespeare's will. Independent as always, Wright came to differ with the "greatest weight" of the "opinion of Sir Frederic Madden in matters of paleography," acknowledging that "at the British Museum the latest view is that there are traces of an 'a' in the last syllable," and having "long thought that the symbol following 'k' is the abbreviation for 'es' and not simply 's'." For the moment at least he concluded, "But as I love peace and quietness I shall just hold my tongue about it all." Although conceding that Halliwell had been "treated ... with scant courtesy," Wright asserted his "rule," which "is to have nothing to do with them and I find that I get on better with them & their Director in consequence."

This position, however, became difficult to sustain. In his next letter

(18 June 1880; LOA 256:50) Wright's thanks for the second edition of
New Lamps or Old? (1880) were followed immediately by his commitment
"to continue to spell Shakespeare as I wish it to the last in spite of or
rather in consequence of what Furnivall and his company say." Moreover,
stung personally, he termed Furnivall a "nuisance" for the "ridiculous
preface to the facsimile of the Hamlet of 1604 in which [ix-x, n. 3] he
attacks me like an angry monkey." Although Wright had "warned him to
keep his hands off me and to go his own way which is not mine ... he will
not be persuaded." Levelling his aim at Furnivall, he questioned ("curious"
is his understated adjective) the attempt to "reproduce Shakespeare in the
'old spelling'," but found that "it is impossible to make Furnivall
understand that the spelling of the books of that time was the spelling of
the printers and not of the authors." At any rate, Wright concluded, with
angry exasperation: "The modern Bottom feels too confident of his own
ability to play many parts to allow of his being instructed in any."[280]

In his longest letter (8 February 1881; LOA 252:3) Wright gave up the
attempt to counter Furnivall's criticism, not caring to "read any more of
his ejaculations" evoked by Wright's expression "'sign-post criticism'
which has penetrated even his rhinoceros-hide of self conceit and
ignorance."[281] He vowed to "take no notice of any thing he may do or say
believing him to be half mad and wholly contemptible." Although "no
admirer of Swinburne's whose own language is none of the choicest," he
could not condone Furnivall's language in the note on Swinburne in the
facsimile of *Love's Labour's Lost*.[282] Strengthening his bond with Halliwell,
Wright aligned himself with those who "would mark their sense of the

280. In 1880 Furnivall issued a circular, "Proposed Edition of Shakspere in Old
Spelling," to the members of the New Shakspere Society.

281. A sample of Furnivall's "ejaculations" from the infamous footnote (ix-x,
n. 3) of his "foreword" to the facsimile of the second quarto of *Hamlet* (1604):
"Men who dub our school the 'sign-post' one, who write inane and feeble
allegories to show that the labourers at Shakspere should remain mere labourers,
and never strive to become gardeners, much less, scientific botanists [...] must not
be surprised if we call their school the 'woodenhead' one, and treat it with the
contempt it deserves, when it steps outside the province which it has wisely
declared that it is alone fit for."

282. Troubled by Furnivall's intentions (7 February 1881; LOA 246:10 and 19
February 1881; LOA 246:2), William Griggs, the photo-lithographer, finally
informed Halliwell that "personally I will not continue to be the means of
diffusing anything that will give pain to you or others. I have not only cut out all
pages referring to you, but Mr. Swinburne as well" (24 March 1881; LOA 244:23).
Halliwell congratulated him on the "gentlemanly & honorable step" he had taken
(21 March 1881; LOA 252:1).

impropriety of Furnivall's proceedings by withdrawing publicly from the [New Shakspere] Society." That action came swiftly. A week later Wright informed Halliwell that as soon as he had received Furnivall's "offensive rejoinder" to Halliwell's "remonstrance,"[283] he "at once requested the Secretary to remove my name from the list of members." And he concluded this brief, hard-hitting note: "The Committee can no longer plead that the quarrel is a private one of which they have no cognisance, for he cons[t]itutes himself the Champion of the Society" (17 February 1881; LOA 252:26). Halliwell, obviously moved by Wright's strong expression of sympathy and "valued support," answered immediately (and thought it fit to keep a copy of this, his only, letter to Wright in the Edinburgh collection), condemning Furnivall as "singularly incorrigible," and stressing that "were it not indeed that he means to be offensive, his utterances in his incomprehensible Hamlet preface would be simply ludicrous" (19 February 1881; LOA 252:28).

In one further letter a few months later (9 July 1881; LOA 251:19) the split with Furnivall was complete on all fronts.[284] "Furnivall," Wright informed Halliwell on the same day as he had received a note from him asking where to send a copy of his *Outlines*, "I hear is proposing to found a Browning Society–for what purpose who can tell? He has not asked me to join." The bond between Wright and Halliwell, on the other hand, was confirmed, since Halliwell's note of 9 July 1881 and then another of 12 July 1881–both in the library of Trinity College Cambridge–do not name Furnivall but are concerned with mundane matters of scholarly exchange.

The demise of the New Shakspere Society was not far off. In the years that followed the number of its *Transactions* fell sharply and by 1892 it was defunct. (Alone among major countries, England or Britain has not had another national Shakespeare organization.) For Halliwell, had he lived to

---

283. The "Co." of Pigsbrook & Co. was issued in two editions in 1881; the second and enlarged one was the response to Halliwell's "remonstrance," *A Letter from Mr. J. O. Halliwell-Phillipps to the Members of the New Shakspere Society, with a Copy of a Correspondence on the Extraordinary Language Used under the Apparent Sanction of That Society*, 1881.

284. Furnivall being the man he was, there were of course numerous further irritations. In an amusing letter to Wright years later, his friend, H. H. Furness, wrote from London on 12 June 1905: "Dearest Wright: Sh–Sh–not a word! I never imagined that you would divine my secret. I am *in hiding*. Don't tell, but I have just murdered Furnivall! and left him in his gore. I bribed his servant to conceal his body for three days, and by that time I shall be on the ocean and safe." *The Letters of Horace Howard Furness*, ed. H[orace] H[oward] F[urness] J[ayne] (2 Vols., Boston, 1922), II:143.

1892, the demise would not have been a victory, nor even a relief. The Furnivall affair weighed heavily upon him. Although he vowed to Ingleby, "I never mention his name either in print or MS. or bother my head about his nonsense" (27 April 1880; Folger C.a.11[19]), he could never do so. True, the burst of letters of sympathy and his responses in 1881 fell off drastically thereafter. But Halliwell's personal letters are full of Furnivall. Hardly an exchange with Ingleby, a major correspondent, is without a mention of Furnivall. In a way the man, if not the matter, was his albatross. It was as if Halliwell could not forget Furnivall's plea, albeit in a totally different context before the split: "Open your heart, & at least disclose all the facts you know that can correct the wrong beliefs" (4 May 1879; LOA 256:66). There was even a touch of grim and unrelieving humor along the way which seemed to counterpoint the "dismal vulgarity" (Edmund Gosse's phrase) of the wordplays Pigsbrook and Brothelsdyke. It ranged from Henry Stevens's grinning coinages "in-Furni*vile*" and "Infurn[iv]all" (28 January 1880; LOA 257:18) to Halliwell morosely signing himself "J. O. H. Phillipps alias Hell-P!!!" (10 August 1883; Folger Y.d.5[48b]) and found a climax of sorts in the dreary doggerel (copied in what appears to be the hand of his daughter Katie) which Halliwell included in his literary legacy (LOA 254:24):

Swinburne versus Furnivall.

Thanks 'Benefactor' and kind friend
     For all you 've writ to me,
Of how my name's derived from 'Swine'
     And *yours* less Piggishly!
Though from your style and nature too,
     One easily can see
That wallowing in *most* slimy ways,
     Befits a brute like thee!

And though you feebly try to pain
     You miserably fail,–
For what can filthy Ghouls like you,
     Do in a Ferny vale?
Rather the Grave yard is the place
     Where bodies foul and stale
Furnish with food thy thieving brood,
     After some funeral!

Throughout the 1880s till the time of his death, the trauma appeared and reappeared in the form of disquisitions of self-justification. On 16 November 1888 (Folger Y.c.1297[17]), long after the smoke had cleared and less than two months before his death, in the longest letter Halliwell admitted to have written in six months, he assured Henry Wheatley that his association with the New Shakspere Society would in no way affect their friendship,

especially when, after such a lapse of time, you or any one else would have taken it for granted that Furnivall would have been anxious that people should not be reminded of his furious attacks on me in former days by the present exhibition of an unprovoked animosity. Ever since his quarrel with me, now over seven years ago, I have been most careful not to make the faintest movement either against him or that Society, & more than one worker for it are numbered amongst my very good friends ... But ever since Furnivall in 1881 reached the climax of offence in an attempt to prejudice my own daughter against me, there has been & will be an inflexible determination to the end of my life, *so far as I am personally concerned*, to avoid even *the most remote or indirect* communication with him or his alter ego, the said Society.

And this was not the last of the bitter disappointments and sad farewells.

Stratford-upon-Avon: Not in Single Spies

As if Pigsbrook were not enough to unsettle his composure and to divert him from his main professional aims, Halliwell had at the same time an even more turbulent and distressing conflict with the city fathers of Stratford-upon-Avon. Tregunter Road and Hollingbury Copse were homes for his body and to an extent for his heart. But Stratford was where his soul lived. From the late 1840s Stratford was the center of Halliwell's professional and spiritual life. It was never an easy life, but it was one that Halliwell lived intensely, with great and generous engagement. If Stratford without Halliwell, as Blight had said, would not be Stratford, then Halliwell without Stratford would not be Halliwell. But the fateful year in which Halliwell lost his wife and Furnivall and was to give up Middle Hill, 1879, was also the year in which his ties with Stratford, already strained, began to give way.

It all began where it always began, with Shakespeare's Birthplace, in which Halliwell was instrumental in founding a Shakespeare library and museum. Founding is, of course, an understatement, for Halliwell came to regard it not merely as his creation but also as his very own possession. With the local help of W. O. Hunt, he was in one way or another its proprietor, patron, advocate, guarantor, donor, and more. In matters of policy and of plumbing, of structure and of staff, of construction and of contributions, Halliwell was its champion. But if he assumed all the attributes of a landlord, he had become in the late 1870s an absentee landlord. And although he maintained good relations with Thomas Hunt, who had succeeded his father as town clerk, and other Stratfordians, the local scene had changed. W. O. Hunt, Halliwell's great friend and ally, had died in 1873, and Edward Fordham Flower, the former mayor and benefactor who had played so great a role in the Tercentenary Celebration, had suffered a stroke in 1866, was forced to the sidelines, and died in 1883. Halliwell himself did not attend meetings of the Trustees from 1877 to 1880, having vowed, for a number of reasons,[285] "in future"

285. See pp. 389-92.

not to "interfere in any sort of way, & ... even sedulously avoid attending the meetings of the Board of Trustees" (13 January 1877; LOA 240:63). But on 7 June 1880 he returned to discuss the appointment of a librarian. The tension, however, had begun earlier; in fact, it was always present in one form or another.

The mayor of Stratford in 1879 was Charles Edward Flower, and his pet project was the Memorial Theatre, which opened officially on Shakespeare's birthday in 1879 with a performance (prophetically or not) of *Much Ado about Nothing*, starring Helen Faucit, aged sixty-seven, as Beatrice. Flower was the major patron of the Theatre, initially donating £1000 and the two-acre site on the Bancroft. Further donations were disappointing, and attempts to divert funds from the Birthplace, which Halliwell had passionately resisted in the mid and late 1870s, did not cease. On 7 May 1879 Frederick Haines, like Halliwell a Trustee, reported that a resolution on diverting money had been withdrawn but only by the barest margin and counselled that the "only safe course eventually will be to apply to the court for directions" since the trust deed was "so very poor thin, and flimsy" (LOA 271:65). And in another of the same day (LOA 277:74) he confirmed Halliwell's estimation of the local Trustees, who "begin to get most restless & fidgetty apparently because we are becoming so well off ... [and are] becoming as frantic as the lions & tigers in the Zoological Gardens when the feeding time approaches–to get the money for their different *town projects*. As for Shakespeare he is only the dress they put on to make themselves look in character. It is Stratford *not* Shakespeare they care for." Halliwell was so incensed that he informed Flower that "it is a good thing that the resolution was withdrawn, having been fully prepared, had it been carried, to have at once applied to the Court of Chancery for an injunction. So long as I live & have health & strength," he vowed, "I will do my utmost to prevent a shilling of the Birth-Place fund being applied to any other object than the preservation of the memorials of the personal history of Shakespeare" (14 May 1879; LOA 277:22).[286] To this vow he voiced his indignation that the "ordinary rules of business" had not been observed: a letter of his had not been "officially acknowledged and replied to immediately after the meeting" and reports of the meetings had not been circulated promptly, as they had been in the days of Hunt. This issue was to remain a constant source of stress, however. Three years later, in the face of another such attempt Haines wrote that it was a "great relief to know that you intend to be so

286. On 28 April 1879 (SBT TR 10/2/2/21) he had written as much to J. S. Leaver, secretary to the Trust.

firm with regard to the proposed 'breaches of trust' ... [and was] glad you have had the opinion of counsel. Pray be armed with this powerful weapon at Stratford" (1 May 1882; LOA 288:76).

This was only one of the continuing problems. In a letter to Flower of 11 June 1879 (LOA 277:26) Halliwell protested that he would be "decidedly against any proposal having even the appearance of a desire to supersede" the Misses Chattaways, who were employed as custodians in the museum. Lest a decision be made prematurely, Halliwell pointed out that it would be nearly a year before the next meeting of the Trustees, by which time "if life & health be spared, I may be able to resume some part of a Trustee's duty." And not only in the matter of the Chattaways but also, he did not hesitate to add, to counter "so terrific a blunder" as to take away part of the New Place Garden in order to widen Chapel Lane. Upset by the way the local Trustees were dominating the crucial matters, Halliwell, as one of the founders and "survivors" of the project, sought to prevent further encroachments by issuing a printed letter "To the Trustees of Shakespeare's Birth-Place," dated 1 August 1879, in which he underlined "the necessity of the removal of a large number of the modern books and manuscripts from the Birth-Place, an exigency which must arise sooner or later from sheer want of room." In suggesting the removal of certain classes of material–later portraits of Shakespearean actors, modern pictures, engravings representing scenes in Shakespeare, books and manuscripts relating to Warwickshire with no notes on Stratford or its neighborhood, and editions of and works on Shakespeare published after the seventeenth century–Halliwell was attempting to focus on the "biographical treasures," which of course was his own focus. He was willing as well to include among the removals the bookcase which was devoted to his own unpublished notes on the text. To insure the "strictly biographical character of our trust," he proposed a position for a librarian who would have a "perfect acquaintance with these [treasures], united with paleographical ability and topographical knowledge ... one on whom the trustees might rely for advice in the selection of articles from the Sight-Museum, and relieve us from the censure we at present so richly deserve for the public exhibition of absurdly spurious or trivial objects that are fitted only for a rag-and-bottle shop." In the following year, before the annual meeting of the Trustees, Halliwell recommended Bruce Tyndall for the position of librarian (4 May 1880; SBT TR 10/2/2/22). To be absolutely certain to be informed, Halliwell sent J. S. Leaver, secretary of the Trust, a card for him to fill in the day of the next meeting (18 May 1880; SBT TR 10/2/2/22). Of the meeting itself on the next day, Haines, along with Ingleby the only ones present representing the

Trustees "from a distance," reported that they had to be "very careful" since the real business was being done by an Executive Committee consisting only of locals who "take interest only in *themselves* and *Stratford*" (8 May 1880; LOA 277:20).

Complying with the request of the Executive Committee, Halliwell, in a printed letter of 31 May 1880 to the Executive Committee, announced that he had interviewed Tyndall, who was willing to accept the post for not less than £1 a year. He took the occasion to press on with his campaign of reform by "earnestly" advocating a reduction of the opening hours from "10 to 4 in summer and 11 to 3 in winter, with an interval for luncheon" (p. 6). His suggestion was not based on relieving the strain on the staff or even on the "few sixpences" which might possibly be lost, but on his desire to raise the level of the museum and to appeal to a "larger number of visitors making a more intelligent examination of the local memorials of Shakespeare than is now usual" (p. 6). In an ingenious blend of intellect and economics Halliwell reasoned:

Nowadays, the chief object of nearly all strangers is to rush through and 'do' Stratford in as brief a time as possible. Any measure which would tend to arrest this mischievous tendency to merely useless and ignorant sight-seeing would surely in the long run be beneficial, and probably would tend to accomplish this object more than the proposed reduction in the hours of attendance. Visitors for the Birth-Place who arrived in the town after four o'clock would have to remain until the next morning, and do them good too (pp.6-7).

Halliwell did not hesitate to mention once again his proposal on the removal of the modern articles, his willingness to return to Stratford to assist in their selection, and, in a cunningly diplomatic rhetorical question, recommending that a complete catalogue should be postponed in favor of two catalogues, one of the articles at New Place and another of those at the museum.

Striking while the iron was hot, Halliwell immediately followed up his meeting with the Executive Committee "on Monday," 7 June 1880, at which the removal of the modern articles (with the exception of the portrait of Garrick) was unanimously resolved, with another of his printed "fly-leaves." Dated 6 July 1880, the *Second Letter* lists nineteen items (some consisting of two or three sketches each) which Halliwell thought "might take the place of the modern fanciful etchings and similar objects now exhibited in the Museum" (p. 5). Again, Halliwell did not hesitate to carry his campaign further by also suggesting that there was much "rubbish" which was not worth cataloguing at all. Halliwell's efforts were strenuous but evidently taking effect. His advice was sought and followed. Asked by Tyndall about the arrangement of the titles of the new catalogue, for example, Halliwell wrote to Leaver (3 August 1880; SBT TR 2/1) that he was "altogether perplexed by the supposed necessity of any being required of the printed books," since there already existed a printed catalogue of 1868 and he himself would be happy to do his best to bring it up to date the next time he was in Stratford. The removal of the modern articles from the museum was not without problems since two Shakespeare museums "cannot be wanted at Stratford," Halliwell wrote to James Cox, now mayor, on 5 April 1881 (LOA 266:54). He then suggested to the Executive Committee a "consulting strictly Shakespearian library in the present Museum at New Place," with the cases from Henley Street and a few others as starters, to which he added another "new proposal ... which will be most highly useful": transcripts of the Captain Saunders MSS. and Wheler's *Collectanea de Stratford*. The move had a tactical element, as well as the scholarly one of a clearly defined biographically Shakespearean focus: "keeping our objects entirely distinct from & more limited in view than those are of the Memorial Theatre, with which indeed our present acquisitions & collections could not legally in any way be amalgamated." The reference was to the library in Charles Flower's Memorial Theatre and obviously reflected Halliwell's fear of a kind of fusion or takeover. Anxious to make concrete progress, Halliwell, in compliance with the instructions of the Trustees," printed and submitted to the Executive Committee on 13 May 1881 *A Brief Report on the Interchange of Books, Relics, &c. between the New Place and the Birthplace Museum, and on the Rearrangement of the Library*. It contains a list of fifteen objects (a knife, coins, a pocket ring-dial) and a list of sixty-one duplicates and titles of no value or importance or not connected with Shakespeare or Stratford (mainly works of the eighteenth and nineteenth centuries). In addition there is a description of the arrangement of the printed works and of the more important deeds and manuscripts. To give the whole the needed professional appearance, Halliwell suggested that "a volume should be provided in which every applicant should enter his or her name and address, before any volume is brought out for inspection" (p. 15).

Interesting was Halliwell's tactic, once his own needs had been made known, of adding a carefully generous gesture towards Flower's library: "It will be observed from the above list [of sixty-one titles] that there are about sixty volumes of absolute duplicates, which, with the consent of the donors, might appropriately be transferred to the elegant library-room at the Memorial theatre" (p. 11). As was to be expected, Flower reacted by seeking a further and more extensive transfer. In a detailed reply of 16 January 1882 (LOA 277:18) Halliwell "quite agree[d] ... [that] it would be better if all the critical works were removed to [Flower's] new library" and said he "will do everything in my power to aid the transfer, feeling convinced that the Henley Street collection will be materially improved by being restricted to its invaluable assemblage of rarities, deeds, drawings, engravings & early documents." His resolution to that effect was carried by the Trustees at their annual meeting on 5 May 1882. Halliwell did, however, make it clear that "dangers may arise unless we are very careful to avoid breaches of trust or unauthorized deviations from the wishes of the donors." Halliwell was, of course, referring to a possible diverting of funds by Flower in mentioning, "It was only at the last meeting of the Trustees that a vigorous effort was made to obtain a vote of money for the Grammar School, an object altogether out of the power of the Trustees." Illegal acts, he stressed prophetically, cannot be tolerated. If once a departure be made, one will want money for one pet object & one for another. If the Grammar School is to [be] assisted, why not the Chancel of the Church, Anne Hathaway's cottage, a monument on the side of the Globe Theatre & so on." On the same day, 16 January 1882 (LOA 271:7), Halliwell made the same point to W. C. Perry, the headmaster of the Grammar School. Although acknowledging that Henry Kingsley and J. J. Nason at the Executive Committee meeting had made "in exceptionally able speeches, whatever could be advanced in favour of the project ... all the eloquence in the world will not avail in opposition to the provisions of the Trust. The Birth Place deed of trust is most explicit on the direction that no money whatever be diverted to any other object. The Trustees have in short no power in the matter."

The pressure, however, increased. Although Halliwell had the support of his lawyer, George Ade, who was certain that the Court would prevent the Trustees from an "illegal resolution to deal with the income of the Trust Property" (24 April 1882; LOA 271:77), Frederick Haines, just a few days later (1 May 1882; LOA 288:76), was so alarmed at what had come up at the meeting of the Executive Committee that he was "quite prepared to apply at *once* for an Injunction to restrain any payment out of trust funds." Indeed, at the annual meeting of the Trustees on 5 May 1882 the motion "that a grant be made in aid of a fund to endow a Shakespearian Scholarship in connexion with the Stratford-upon-Avon Grammar School" was followed by a "very lengthy discussion ... resulting in Dr. Kingsley consenting, with the concurrence of the seconder [Arthur Hodgson], to withdraw it." The situation remained precariously unstable and threatening, as evident in such typical exchanges as Halliwell asking

Leaver whether a single member of the Executive Committee constitutes a quorum (9 October 1882; LOA 271:5) and Robert Gibbs's retorting why the funds already accumulated should not be devoted to certain purposes (11 January 1883; LOA 281:15). So frequent and disturbing were such exchanges that it must have been a certain relief for Halliwell to be informed by George Godwin of the inadequate hot water system and the danger of fire at the Birthplace (7 February 1882; LOA 277:34). Nor could the mounting crisis be forgotten while Halliwell was "in a regular whirl receiving guests & preparing things for [his] daughter's wedding, which takes place *today!* (25 April 1883; Folger Y.c.1240[30b]). Unable to attend the meeting of the Trustees, Halliwell issued on 1 May 1883 *Memoranda on the Present State of the Birthplace Trust*, whose subjects were "*The expediency of obtaining a private Act of Parliament for the legalization of the double trust*" and "*The desirability of forming a descriptive calendar of the voluminous contents of the Library and Museum.*" In the first matter Halliwell argued against the diverting of funds to the Grammar School and cited a supporting opinion of counsel by A. J. Wood. Further, he proposed to legalize the "illegal" amalgamation by unanimous vote of the Trustees of the New Place and the Birthplace Trusts (the double trust) since both estates were "so exactly analogous in their relation to the biography of Shakespeare ... [for] *both include existing remains that are absolutely connected with his life-career*" so that "it is not likely that the amalgamation will ever be seriously opposed" (p. 10). In the second matter Halliwell urged that a librarian be engaged at a moderate salary to calendar the old documents. The latter proposal was accepted by the Trustees. A letter of 30 March 1884 from Halliwell and Ingleby stating that George F. Warner of the British Museum had been selected and offered the post of calendarist was entered into the minutes of the meeting of the Trustees in 1884.

The "victory" was, however, only a temporary cessation of hostilities. The same minutes recorded the appointment of Richard Savage as librarian and the resignation of the "late librarian" Bruce Tyndall. For two years after his appointment in 1880 Tyndall took advantage of being granted a "tolerably long vacation." On 23 June 1882 he notified Leaver, the secretary, that he would be absent for three weeks from 24 June, "the height of the season ... throwing the whole work [as guide] upon the Lady Custodians [the Misses Chattaway]," so the statement of 6 February 1884 of the Executive Committee. On the same afternoon of 23 June, the statement continued, Charles Flower volunteered to audit the cash accounts and, being told of Tyndall's absence, "declined to take upon himself ... the responsibility of signing [erroneously, "singing"] a cheque for the Librarian's salary." At the meeting of the Committee on 2 August it was decided that "in consequence of his having taken his vacation without a special warrant, the payment of his quarter's salary on the 5th inst. would be withheld for the present," to which Halliwell continued in his printed *To the Trustees of the Shakespeare Birth-Place* of 4 May 1883, "the generous intimation being added that consideration would be given to a doubt as to whether three weeks' remuneration should not be deducted from the amount." Tyndall resigned three months later, the period stipulated in his contract. Halliwell was incensed at what he felt was the cruel treatment of his "friend and nominee,–one of the most amiable and conscientious of men," most particularly at the decision of the Committee to lay the whole irritating correspondence before the Trustees instead of a "mere announcement of his resignation, accompanying the notice with some kind expressions towards Mr. Tyndall that might tend to obliterate the recollections of the past."

The situation was complex. For one thing, it is not clear to what extent Tyndall ignored the authority of the Committee. Halliwell mentions "the mischief done by relying on verbalities" (7 May 1883; Folger C.b.17[141]), verbal agreements and understandings: Leaver reportedly told Tyndall not to go away without asking leave (SBT TR 10/2/2/24). The Committee refers to resolutions supposedly known and accepted by Tyndall. Equally unclear is the role–or complaints–of the Misses Chattaway, the custodians. In Halliwell's view, "For two years the Misses C. used to extol Tyndall to the skies, but the poor fellow managed to offend them, & since then——!!" (9 May 1883; LOA 287:69). Doubtless too the frantic reaction of Tyndall contributed to the general turmoil: "he was in such a distracted state of mind & so ill (Harry Hunt told me he looked so thin & ill he thought he could not live)–it is very possible that he often did not know what he was about," Halliwell continued to Ingleby. In Halliwell's mind must also have been an echo of his own situation in the British Museum affair, for in his letter of 30 August 1882 (SBT TR 10/2/2/24) to the Trustees Tyndall complained of their "outrageous conduct" in condemning him "without giving me a chance of speaking for myself." And there could not be any doubt that there was always tension between the Stratfordian Executive Committee and the Trustee "from a distance," Halliwell. Whatever the exact cause or more likely combination of causes, Halliwell felt it necessary once again–as he had throughout his career–to come to the aid of one unfairly treated. "There I am," he wrote to Charles Roach Smith, "with the now great object of my life to keep out not only of 'rows' but even of acrimonious discussion, *compelled* to *fight* on behalf of a friend" (7 May 1883; Folger C.b.17[141]). It was a war which could not be won, even if Halliwell had diagnosed it accurately: "It is a case exactly of this. A insults B and B in consequence writes a strong letter about A, whereupon A turns round on B & says you're a pretty sort of fellow to write a letter like that—why, you deserve to have been insulted" (23 May 1883; Folger C.a.11[59]). Halliwell vowed "to refrain from taking the remotest part in the appoint[men]t of a new one [librarian]" (18 July 1883; LOA 259:67*). The Committee sought to vindicate itself by recommending that the Trustees publish all the minutes and letters bearing on the subject. They did not succeed, however. Instead, at their meeting of 5 May 1884, at which Halliwell was not present, the Trustees were "*nem. con.*" of the opinion that "no blame is to be attached to the members of the Executive Committee ... [and] also desire to express their sense of the services rendered to the Trust by the Committee, and to thank the members thereof for the same."

The vindication of the Executive Committee thus fell short of the desired fulfillment. Flower, who had put forward the resolution to publish, could not be satisfied by Halliwell's decision to refrain form participating in the selection of the new librarian, nor by the fact that in mid 1883 some 650 volumes had been removed to his Memorial Library. It was not simply a clash of personalities but of one aggravated by a tangle of interrelated issues. The ongoing disagreements on the constitution, management, and aims of the Shakespeare enterprises in Stratford—barely patched at best—contained still another and potentially explosive element. In its statement to the Trustees of 6 February 1884 the Committee sought to be publicly vindicated from further charges made by Halliwell in his pamphlet entitled *The Shakespeare-Autotype Committee at Stratford-on-Avon.*

It all began innocently—nay, promisingly—enough. Ever alert to new developments and techniques, and learning of the British Museum's ordering of autotypes of the Shakespeare estate-deeds to be made for public sale, Halliwell was "led ... to think that a similar course might be advantageously furnished in respect to some of the valuable papers preserved amongst the archives of the [Stratford] Corporation" and recommended it to mayor W. G. Colbourne (15 February 1883; LOA 271:50). He even offered to pay the expenses himself, with the proceeds (after he had been repaid for the autotyping and printing) to be "of course at their [the Counsel's] sole disposal." Colbourne answered immediately, hoping confidently that the Council "will see the advantage of so doing and also accepting your very generous and valuable assistance" (17 February 1883; LOA 299:25). The Council unanimously resolved to accept the offer on 6 March 1883 (LOA 281:23). The project was then swiftly implemented; at its annual meeting in May the Trustees considered it "desirable ... to form a descriptive Calendar of the Records" with

Halliwell and Ingleby to "be requested to assist the Committee."

The advancement of the undertaking was somewhat diverted by a conflict between the city fathers and Ingleby, who had proposed in 1883 that the grave of Shakespeare be opened for the reason explicit in the title of his tract, *Shakespeare's Bones. A Proposal to Disinter Them, Considered in Relation to Their Possible Bearing on His Portraiture. Illustrated by Instance on Visits of the Living to the Dead.* A controversy arose, not in the least mitigated by "their friend and colleague" Ingleby's dedication of the work to the mayor and the Corporation of Stratford and the vicar of Holy Trinity, who were predictably appalled and denounced Ingleby's project as "impudent," "base," and "foolish," among other objecting adjectives. Although he felt Ingleby had been "wantonly grossly & out of the mark insulted" (5 September 1883; Folger Y.c.1238[2]), Halliwell nevertheless himself opposed the undertaking in a temperately worded public letter of 1 September 1883 *To the Mayor and Corporation of Stratford-on-Avon.* The vehemence of public and press sentiment, as well as that of the city fathers, damned the proposal. Ingleby took Halliwell's opposition gracefully: "Your dignified & gentlemanly protest gave me far more pleasure, than annoyance at your opposition" (6 September 1883; LOA 276:27). But Ingleby, also a Life Trustee and one of those "from a distance," was also a friend of Halliwell's. And as far as the Stratfordians were concerned, there were hard feelings remaining after harsh words.

Ingleby was also interested in autotyping, and Halliwell offered to make available some of the negatives he had already produced and was careful to mention the restrictions—e.g. autotyping allowed only in Stratford—and the necessity of approval by the mayor (4 October 1883; Folger C.a.11[67]). On the same day (Folger C.a.11[68]) he enclosed a letter to help Ingleby get permission to do selected leaves from the diary of Thomas Greene in the museum. Not unexpectedly, there was resistance, notably from Charles Flower: "My autotypes," Ingleby informed Halliwell, doubtless aware of the production fees, "must be *all* or none" (12 October 1883; LOA 276:43). While Ingleby continued to seek approval, and the Tyndall affair was still brewing, Halliwell was having his own problems with the autotyping and, once again, with Flower. In November 1883 he issued the twenty-three page *The Shakespeare-Autotype Committee at Stratford-on-Avon. Transformation Scenes. And a Retrospect.* And a month later there came a second edition of fifty-nine pages (reprinting pp. 7-23 of the first edition). The title page notice "Printed for the Use of Stratford-on-Avon" signalled not so much beneficence as bellicosity. It must be remembered that in seeking vindication for its action against Tyndall, the Executive Committee also sought to be publicly vindicated from the charges made against it by Halliwell in the second edition of his pamphlet *The Shakespeare-Autotype Committee at Stratford-on-Avon*.

In the opening section of the first edition, "The Autotype Committee," Halliwell presents the relevant correspondence on the constitution of the Committee and singles out points of contention. For one, Halliwell insists there "was nothing ... to suggest that a supervision over my preliminary work was contemplated" (p. 8). For another, because of Flower's treatment of Tyndall, Halliwell was compelled to inform Colbourne that "it will not be agreeable for me to meet Mr. Charles Flower under conditions partaking of a personal conference" (p. 10). In "Transformation Scenes," the next section, Halliwell reiterates his refusal to accept the supervision and control of his work by the Committee. And furthermore he objects to a situation in which "instead of proposing to lend me the documents, the Council is staggered at the idea of their being carefully taken the distance of a few hundred yards, and pass a resolution that none shall be removed from the Birth-Place, thus practically rendering the autotyping an impossibility" (p. 12). "A Retrospect" summarizes Halliwell's efforts over the years to arrange and catalogue the records of the Corporation and recounts what he has done. When it was discovered that the autotyping could not be done satisfactorily in the record room, he decided to supervise the temporary transfer to the artist's studio. Using the keys left for him by the town clerk, Halliwell "took the documents, one at a time, to the studio, and, in this way, in the course of a few days, fourteen of them were successfully and beautifully facsimiled" (p. 18). But Flower characterized the proceeding as "irregular," although, so Halliwell charging bias if not ignorance, Flower "during the more than a quarter of a century that I have been at work on them [the records] ... has never appeared on the scene to study or consult a single document,–has never, until within the last few days, given the remotest indication that he cared a halfpenny about them" (pp. 19-20). Finally, in "The Record Room," Halliwell points to the absurdity of the Counsel's granting Ingleby permission to autotype leaves of Greene's diary and at the same time passing a resolution that no documents are to be taken from the record room, which is totally unsuited and unequipped for autotyping.

The response was immediate. Having received a copy of the pamphlet, Flower replied on 1 December 1883 (LOA 294:63), confessing that he was "amazed to learn for the first time, that there is a quarrel between us" and, as far as the treatment of Tyndall was concerned, stressing that the Committee had not had the "slightest intention to treat that gentleman uncourteously and that his nervous temperament and vivid imagination has caused him to misconstrue matters." Asserting that Halliwell's autotyping had received his "hearty support" and that "as always" he "most thoroughly appreciated what have and you are doing," Flower proposed to withdraw "at once" from the Committee and "so avoid being the cause of there being any difficulty in your working with–*not under*–that Committee which was appointed to assist you." But Flower's blandishments and Henry Holl's gleeful approval of Halliwell's having "so completely demolished them [the Stratford "set of cads–cads of the worst description, and fitter to be called *hounds*"] ... Mr Charles Flower too!" (4 December 1883; LOA 271:40) did not prevent the matter from escalating. Newspaper reports of a speech made by Flower at the Council meeting of 4 December 1883, in which it was denied that the word "irregular" had been used and asserted that Halliwell "had drawn largely on his imagination, and possibly his conscience might have told him that 'irregular' was the milder term that could have been applied to those proceedings," were confirmed as "substantially correct" by Flower in a brief reply to Halliwell (8 December 1883; LOA 285:64). Brief, it should be noted, because he did not think "I am called upon to answer yours of yesterday which is written in a very different tone" from his own of 1 December, "which was couched in the terms of that friendship which I supposed had hitherto existed between us" and which Halliwell "did not think fit to answer."

Stung–"to my utter astonishment, he has made a rabid attack on me in a speech as reported in a Birmingham paper," he wrote to Ingleby, "quite as bad if not worse than that vulgar idiot Colbourne characterizing your proposal as impudent" (7 December 1883; Folger C.a.11[75])–Halliwell fired back with a second edition of December 1883 of his pamphlet, reprinted the first edition and adding thirty pages more. "Mr Charles Flower's Speech" (pp. 27-9) is a verbatim rendition of the report in the Stratford *Herald.* 'The Library Question" (pp. 31-43) is a detailed defense of both Tyndall and Halliwell with a transcript of his long letter to the mayor of 24 April 1883 and in the end an attack on Flower for misrepresenting his position and, since he was the "only member of the Committee present when the suspension of the librarian's salary was ordered" (p. 43), thus meriting sole responsibility for acting arbitrarily. In "Very Irregular Indeed" (pp. 45-6) Halliwell, having investigated the newspaper reports, concludes that "there was no evidence ... which excluded the possibility of the use of the word *irregular.*" Reviewing the exchange of letters between Halliwell and Flower, "A Variation" (pp. 47-52) deals with Halliwell's feeling that Flower has returned "to the attack with redoubled severity, and virtually own[ing] that he regrets not having used a stronger term" than *irregular* (p. 47). Two further charges in the report are dismissed summarily in "The Copyright Question" (p. 53): 1. That Halliwell had allowed the photographer to retain the negatives: "Of course I had. The diminutive negatives taken in the first instance are of no practical use until they are enlarged"; 2. that he had allowed the photographer to register the copyright in his own name: "All that I have got to say to this is that I have never had any communication whatever with the photographer upon the subject" (p. 53). Finally, in "Red-Tape Amenities" (pp. 55-8) Halliwell repeats his view that he did not need a "special application" because, "in the exceptional position" he "had so long occupied in respect to the records" (p. 56), he was very well aware of his responsibility for their safety.

In this concluding section Halliwell refers to the "last scene of this 'strange eventful history'." It was not the last, however. A more accurate metaphor might be Rosencrantz's "massy wheel / Fix'd on the summit of the highest mount, / To whose huge spokes ten thousand lesser things / Are mortis'd and adjoin'd, which, when it falls, / Each small annexment, petty consequence, / Attends the boist'rous ruin." The wheel had begun to fall, gathering speed and momentum, losing control and direction, and did not come to rest until all had been boisterously ruined some years later. In the years that followed to the time of his death in 1889, no amount of persuasion or reason could restore Halliwell's injured pride. Neither Samuel Timmins's attempt at mediation if not reconciliation (5 January 1884; LOA 287:29), nor Ingleby's appraisal, "I really don't think the game (as *bird*) worth the powder, nor (as *play*) worth the candle" (29 February 1884; LOA 287:73), could controvert Halliwell's rigid position. "Kindly recollect that the Committee's statement was censorious against me, & absolutely demanded an vigorous exposure," he answered Ingleby, "it is nothing to the rodding I could give them" (2 March 1884; Folger C.a.11[80]). Appeals by others, soft and stern–by Dillon Croker, J. W. Jarvis, Joseph Mayer, Thomas Hunt, Frederick Kendall–were of no avail. For Halliwell it was not a simple private quarrel, "though it turns on semi-public affairs," as Ingleby had judged in advising Halliwell not to be "so vehement, or so sarcastic" (29 February 1884; LOA 287:73). For Halliwell it was a cause, a battle against the unjust and oligarchical, personified in "His Imperial Majesty Charles the Third of Stratford" (12 January 1884; Folger C.a.11[78]). And so the letters continued abundantly, carrying messages of meetings and maneuverings of cliques and factions. Political issues were degraded to petty stratagems. Halliwell decided not to send any more books to the Memorial Library (5 April 1884; LOA 292:67); he reprimanded Leaver for addressing him as "Dr." (6 May 1884; LOA 292:54); he complained that his name had been misspelled (5 January 1885; LOA 299:70*); he declined an invitation of the Shakespeare Club (27 April 1885; LOA 286:2); he could not accept an offer by Richard Savage to do a transcription for him (7 December 1885; LOA 291:21); he asked on 3 September 1886 (SBT TR 10/2/3) for the names of the members of the Executive Committee who had been present at a meeting on 3 January 1884, two years earlier.

Halliwell was desperate for vindication. It was as if he were replaying the trauma of the British Museum affair some forty years earlier. But then he was anxious to appear before the Trustees of the Museum, to confront them in person, and to effect justice. Over the years, however, he had become less confident of his person, sought privacy and retreat. He would not, could not, face Flower or the Committee. "With my thorough inaptitude for public speaking of the most limited kind, I should be no match for some of the astute & practised speakers belonging to the Executive Committee," he confessed to Ingleby. "But I flatter myself that I shall be able to reply effectively, if necessary, before the general public" (3 May 1884; Folger C.a.11[82]). And that meant using his pen, and thus risking substituting repetition for intensity, sarcasm for substance–in short, art for matter. There were long letters of self-justification to Edgar Flower, Charles's brother (15 November 1884; Folger W.b.90[17]), and Samuel Timmins (23 November 1884; Folger C.a.11[92])–which were earnest and factual but essentially retrospective and static with no new hint of resolving but mainly intensifying his dilemma. Halliwell was trapped in his mind as in his position with regard to Stratford. He was determined not to resign as Trustee of the Birthplace: "I don't see why I should, any more than that Gladstone should resign because he is badgered by two or three Irish cads" (12 April 1885; Folger C.a.11[103]). And yet he could vow: "My literary connexion with Stratford-on-Avon, excepting so far of course as it may be involved in my action as independent critic, must be considered to be terminated" (15 March 1886; LOA 296:18). He remained a Life Trustee but he no longer attended annual meetings. His selection of George Warner to calendar the Birthplace collection was approved by the Trustees; he responded to the appeal of the Misses Chattaway to arbitrate their "annoyance at being requested by the local Committee ... to answer the door at Shakespeare's House for the Librarians private business, and to secure messages from his tradesmen" (16 December 1884; LOA 294:59). All such duties–important or trivial–he fulfilled conscientiously and willingly. And he never rescinded on the bequests he had made to the Birthplace. But he conducted most of the business by post. Stratford was too important to his work and his soul for him to break with it totally and finally.

His resentment at the treatment he had received was never still. And so he continued to stress his indignation not with his person but with his pen. In December 1884 he issued *A Brief History of the Ancient Records of Stratford-on-Avon, Chiefly in Reply to a Leading Article That Recently Appeared in the Stratford-on-Avon Herald*, to counter imputations made by the Council and the *Herald* that he had been a "bad workman and an unreasonable grumbler," by outlining the nature and care of the Stratford records over the forty or so years since he was introduced to them. To this fairly restrained pamphlet of twenty-one pages came a snowballing series of highly charged and lengthy pamphlets entitled *The Stratford Records and the Shakespeare Autotypes. A Brief Review of Singular Delusions That Are Current at Stratford-on-Avon. By the Supposed Delinquent*, in which Halliwell attempted, so the preface, to correct "singular misconceptions being prevalent at Stratford respecting my record-work and the treatment I have met with in that town" (p. 7). As in his earlier pamphlets, the issues themselves are more matters of personal pique than public concern. And as before, Halliwell's charges are in the main repetitive, a mixture of seriousness and sarcasm, the increasingly strident tone excluding any possibility of reconciliation. Halliwell produced six editions (including a "suppressed" one): the suppressed and the first in 1884, the second and third in 1884-85, the fourth in 1886, and the fifth in 1887. In general, each incorporated the previous one, occasionally deleting and always adding a bit more. Singly, they grew from an initial twenty-eight pages to a final 111 pages—for a grand total of almost four hundred pages. And as if this were not enough, in late 1887 Halliwell produced a supplement to the fifth edition called *The Executive Committee of Shakespeare's Birth-Place and Mr. Halliwell-Phillipps* in two editions. In the first he reproduced an exchange of four communications between Richard Savage, librarian and secretary of the Trust, and himself between 3 and 7 November 1887; in the second, he added three more between 8 and 10 November. In a sad comedy of misconceptions, Halliwell purchased sixty-six documents at the Severne sale, unaware that the Trustees had instructed Savage not to bid against him, leading Halliwell to criticize them for not bidding: although the documents had little to do with Shakespeare, he was ludicrously disappointed that they had not continued their policy of buying "worthless medieval documents." And as far as Shakespeare was concerned, he was equally disturbed at their failure to bid, which enabled him, "to my utter amazement, to secure all of them [the Shakespeare lots] for what was, for unique relics of the most interesting description, the nominal sum of Six pounds two shillings" (p. 15). Charges and countercharges followed. Be that as it may, the insistence on nuances led to the inevitable resolution of the Committee quoted by Halliwell in Savage's letter of 8 December 1887: "It is useless attempting to convince him that his attitude towards the Committee and its individual members is founded upon an entire misapprehension of facts." There is little need to analyze what is in essence a rehearsal of things past with no opening to the present. His fervent engagement and the sheer volume of his pamphleteering do not represent one of Halliwell's best moments. And there were numerous other charges in addition to the "*collective injustice* with which [Halliwell felt to] have been treated" (19 November 1886; Folger W.b.90[70]): the investment of the Trust Funds (7 May 1885; LOA 299:34); the waste of money in printing the Guild Records (22 June 1886; Folger W.b.90[68]); the "mischievous alteration made in the direction of the southern fence at New Place" (13 September 1886; Folger W.b.86[53]). Still, It is difficult not to conclude that most of it was more small-minded than generous, more a nagging tooth than a major calamity.

It is equally difficult to overlook the spectacle of personal decline in Halliwell's persistent concentration on small details and petty prejudices. Yet all things considered there is a certain sadness in the words appearing on the title page of the fifth edition of *The Stratford Records and the Shakespeare Autotypes*: "*To which is Prefixed the Farewell of the oldest living Shakespearean Biographer to the Shakespeare-Councils of the Town which should be, but which is not, the chosen Centre of Shakespeare-Biographical Research.*" And there is a kind of noble pathos in Halliwell's conclusion:

Let me here mention that, until impelled by recent occurrences, I never dreamt of alluding to any services that I may have rendered the town of Stratford, but there are circumstances under which a little egotism is not only excusable but a necessity in self-defence. As a well-known author lately observed under conditions similar to those in which I am now placed,–'when a man is attacked in the way I have been, he must say something for himself' (p. 91).

More than the pain of unjust treatment, more than the discontent with the way things were going, was perhaps the actual separation from the everyday and human routine of Halliwell's Stratford experience. It is evident in the touching reminders, the "General Notes for Stratford-on-Avon," undated but doubtless from his last years, found among Halliwell's assorted papers (SBT ER 135:19):

1. Beware of Tom Hunt's dogs.
2. See as to good ink.
3. Robinson ... lucifers in Birth-Place cellar.
4. Ask Peter Hunt to a liquor up.
5. C. W. Smartt, 2. Colonnade, Leamington, & Ivy Cottage, Stratford-on-Avon, offers to do the autotype or the Collotype. May be very useful to me.
6. Only those papers &c. marked '&&' [deleatur] are thoroughly done.
7. Hydrosulphuret of ammonia to restore faded writing. *Very* smelly.
8. Call on Loggin & the Sloane St. Pastry-cook.
9. Mind head if I go into the B. P. cellar, especially in returning.
10. In consulting local registers look for bur. of R. Tyler from 1610.
11. G. F. Kendall & family *very* friendly.
12. Always note commencing dates of the parish-registers.
13. Timmins says he will meet me at the B. P. at a short notice at any time. Nov. 1887.
14. See List of Addresses in my Brighton Address-Book.
15. Maude Warrilow, 0.10.0.

Stratford may have been Halliwell's problem, but it was also his passion and his profession. "Only fancy my working again at the Record Office as hard as ever!" he exclaimed in planning a visit (24 April 1880; Folger C.a.11[18]). Despite his difficulties and growing disenchantment, Halliwell continued his scholarly investigations and publications concerning Stratford and its environs. His focus was the one he stridently advocated for the library and museum: biographical research. But it was not narrow. It was in fact a gathering of material which ultimately amounted to a socio-economic history of Stratford. And the objects assembled–artifacts, maps, deeds, and suchlike–contributed an archaeological and cultural dimension as well. Halliwell was collecting material for his life of Shakespeare, but was at times so excited by his discoveries that he had them reproduced and privately published without much in the way of discussion or explanation beyond the fact they were interesting enough in themselves to be published in advance of the larger work, following in a way the procedure of his early days when the book-publishing societies were flourishing. Since Halliwell had found and bought many of the documents, their publication was also a token of the possessor's pride in showing off his rarities to those who could not come to see them at Hollingbury Copse, "the quaint bungalow on the Brighton Downs," he proclaimed in introducing one of them, "which has the honour of sheltering, amongst others, the valuable relic here given in facsimile."

Among those which are not directly connected with Shakespeare but mainly with his environment is Halliwell's transcription *of An Inventory of the Goods and Chattels of Ann Shaw, the Friend and Neighbour Of Shakespeare, at Stratford-upon-Avon, Taken in the Year 1630* (1880), which lists her apparel, the objects in the "Chamber over the hall," another unidentified room, the "Litle Chamber," the hall, and the cellar. Of interest are not only the items themselves—"redy mony" and jewellery, beds and chests, candlesticks and warming pans, pigs and pails, tables and barrels—but also the monetary value assigned to them: a "gould ring," 13s.4d.; a court cupboard, 6s.8d.; 2 brass pots, 13s.; a close stool, 6s.; a parcel of "furse and od" wood, 10s. Another transcription is *Shakespeare's Grave. Notes of Traditions That Were Current at Stratford-on-Avon in the Latter part of the Seventeenth Century* (1884), Halliwell's transcription of a letter in the Bodleian Library written about December 1694 by William Hall to Edward ("Neddy") Thwaites, a well-known Anglo-Saxon scholar at Queen's College Oxford containing the earliest known notice of the epitaph Shakespeare ordered to appear on his tombstone. Halliwell also published facsimiles for private circulation: *A Facsimile of an Indenture Executed by Sir John and Lady Barnard, in October 1652* (1883) concerns New Place and the land Shakespeare had purchased from the Combes in 1602 and a companion *Facsimile of the Original Indenture of the Conveyance of Over a Hundred Acres of Land, Which Was Made by William and John Combe, of Stratford-on-Avon, to Shakespeare, on the First of May, in the Year 1602* (1884). Although not a transcription or facsimile, Halliwell's *Observations on the Charlecote Traditions, and on the Personation of Sir Thomas Lucy in the Character of Justice Shallow* (1887) is in the same mode, being a kind of narrative of collected memoranda most of which are found in Halliwell's larger life but a "few scraps [of] which are peculiar to and may be thought to justify this extremely limited separate impression" (p. 5). In November 1887 he contributed a pleasant preface to a reissuing of Fairholt's *Home of Shakespeare*, which had first appeared in 1847, affording him the chance to honor his dear friend professionally and personally not only in a gracefully phrased recollection and appraisal but in the conditions under which he agreed to undertake the assignment. For one thing, he stipulated that Fairholt's name must not take a "subordinate position under that of another writer using, as I think, ungenerously, Fairholt's capital title of the book & also his leading idea"; for another, "To prevent misapprehension, I should decline to receive any remuneration for editing" (6 February 1882; LOA 259:69). Halliwell's insistence on the integrity of the original work was consistent with his devotion to authenticity. Only the "most insignificant" alterations were permitted, most of them confined to the spelling of Shakespeare's name.

Transcriptions and facsimiles of old documents of this sort are essentially passive in orientation, having little or no direct relevance to the present. As long as Halliwell was able to continue burrowing for this form of authenticity he was content. But the problem in Stratford was the collision of the authentic past with the real present. Once again, in the twilight of his life, just short of a year before his death, Halliwell took up his pen against an action he felt to be historically unjustified. His method, as was his wont, was the open letter: a copy "for circulation in the United States" of a Letter to the Editor of the *Times* of 30 January 1888 entitled *The Proposed So-Called Restoration of the Church of the Holy Trinity At Stratford-on-Avon, Its Ancient Charnel-House, and Shakespeare's Grave*. In it Halliwell responded to an appeal for funds made by the vicar of Stratford, the Reverend George Arbuthnot, "in aid of the so-called restoration of his most deeply interesting Church," Holy Trinity. Most certainly motivated by his continuing aversion to the modernization and vulgarization of Stratford and the "irremediable mischief which occurred through local management on previous occasions" (p. 3), Halliwell deplored the lack of historical information and a "protective schedule of the monuments affected by the repairs" (p. 5)–despite his warnings and offers of assistance. Some years earlier, on 13 September 1886 (Folger W.b.86[53]), he had protested to Charles Flower that there was "a radical defect in the various actions respecting the Stratford ancient buildings & monuments being taken without a very minute *preliminary* investigation into the history & topography ... if, indeed, I had to draw up an indictment against Stratford for errors that have been unconsciously committed through a defective study of local history & Shakespearean biography, it would be as long as an American President's Message." Further correspondence–offers of assistance, appeals, and threats–with Arbuthnot and others[287] brought no satisfactory results. Most objectionable to Halliwell–a "serious piece of Vandalism"–was the proposal to remove the ancient charnel-house crypt to make room for a modern addition to the northern exterior of the church. As always, Halliwell could not be shaken from his programmatic declaration that he would "jealousy guard the absolute integrity of every vestige of Shakespeare's town–that is to say, of the town that existed from 1564 to 1616–instead of encouraging designs that promote its obliteration" (p. 8).

What is clear–what was always clear–is that Halliwell's struggle was not

287. See 29 October 1887; Folger W.b.90(84); 11 November 1887; Folger W.b.90(80); 13 February 1888; Folger W.b.90(95); 14 February 1888; Folger W.b.90(96); 10 March 1888, Folger W.b.90(101).

so much against Charles Flower or the ignorance and greed of some citizens of Stratford; it was more even than an attempt to defend his personal dignity and professional accomplishments. Halliwell's greatest obstacle was his unattainable dream of protecting what *was*–Stratford in the lifetime of Shakespeare. A breach with contemporary Stratford was inevitable. "The more I think of it," he wrote to George Boyden (1 October 1887; Folger W.b.90[81]), "the more I see the impossibility, even under the most encouraging conditions, of my taking in the future any active part in the Shakespearean deliberations of your town." Melancholy and frustrated, he concluded: "This is an end of our epistolary troubles & of my connexion with modern Stratford." His bitterness towards certain individuals was unrelieved but at the same time his relative powerlessness as "independent critic" was exposed in his heavy-handed sarcasm and wishful threats, as in his remarks to Frederick Haines (10 May 1888; Folger W.b.90[103]):

I suspect you have been 'talked over' by that ignorant & pompous lump, Sir Arthur Hodgson, K.C.M.G., K - a Knight C - Collared M - a peace-loving Man and G - Gammon'd him. No, no! My temperament, extra placid & diffident as a rule, is not adapted to Being humble Unto Bumble & a finer specimen of a quasi-aristocratic Bumble was never met with ... To such a fellow I'll not budge one single inch. If I am worsted it is no great matter. I've nothing to gain from S.O.A. & can better support the real Shakespn interests as an independent critic. But I fancy that victory is not utterly outside my reach. At all events I have a few unflung bits of peel of a curiously slippery nature, & if I throw them out broadcast the great K.C.M.G. had better be careful in his steps or he may come a cropper that might spoil his cocked hat & impair his official dignity.

"Nothing to gain from S.O.A."–but there was a world elsewhere: the quaint wigwam of Hollingbury Copse with its rarities, mementoes of bygone days and "with annually diminishing working powers that must be primarily devoted to the study of my still very large unused collections on the Life of Shakespeare" (1 October 1887; Folger W.b.90[81]).

· 23 ·

The Library and Museum
in the Rustic Wigwam

Hollingbury Copse was peculiar not merely in its architecture but in its contents as well. It was Halliwell's personal library and museum. Its rarities, the result of years of searching and dealing and collecting, were the illustrations for all the works he was planning, especially the new life of Shakespeare. The way they were assembled and arranged is typical of Halliwell's employment of his skills as bookman, researcher, and organizer. Although literally thousands of books, manuscripts, and other relics passed through his hands from the time he began collecting in the mid 1830s, and concentrating on Shakespeare in the 1840s, he was in the last decade of life certain of what he wanted, how to obtain it, and how to deal with it. Generally speaking, Halliwell followed a plan he had formulated some years earlier: he was interested only in articles printed or produced before 1660. In the various circulars to booksellers which he issued periodically he specified his wants. Typical of their direction and extent is one of July 1887 addressed "To Booksellers" and appended (pp. 167-8) to his *Calendar of the Shakespearean Rarities: Drawings and Engravings Preserved at Hollingbury Copse, Near Brighton* (1887):

Being pretty widely known as a Shakespearean collector, hardly a week passes by without my having offers of articles which are illustrative, in one way or other, of either the works or the life of the great dramatist. Collecting, however, only in special directions, the large majority of these offers refer to objects that are outside my line of research; and, in the belief that trouble will often be saved on both sides by an indication of the nature of that limit, I would venture to submit the following memoranda:–

I do *not* want offers of the following articles:–

1. Printed books or tracts of any description whatever that were printed either before the year 1564 or after the year 1660.

2. Painted portraits either of Shakespeare or of any other member of his family.

3. Mulberry-tree or Herne's Oak relics.

4. Shakespearean engravings that have been *published* after the year 1660.

But I should feel particularly obliged by offers of the following articles:–

1. Editions of Shakespeare, and books mentioning Shakespeare, that were printed before the year 1660.

2. Popular English literature, especially plays, story-books, and poems, printed during the Shakespearean period, 1564 to 1616. With the exception of editions of the plays or poems of Shakespeare which were published before the year 1660, I do not care for any books or tracts that were printed either before 1564 or after 1616.

3. Views or plans of London that were issued before the great fire of 1666, especially any which include the Southwark theatres.

4. Original sketches of objects at Stratford-on-Avon and its neighbourhood, as well as old deeds and MSS. relating to those localities.

5. Any MSS. on Shakespearean subjects by the late Edmond Malone, who died in 1812.

6. Manuscript plays written before the year 1660.

7. Autograph letters or MSS., written before the year 1840, which refer in any way to the *life* (not the works) of Shakespeare.

"*The London auctions are well looked after by myself for everything of the kind,*" Halliwell added in a very generous understatement. For in addition to his vast traffic with prospective sellers from all over the country, Halliwell–who rarely attended a London sale himself in his later years–entertained an enormous correspondence with numerous dealers and agents in England and America who represented him at various sales. In the Edinburgh collection there are thirty letters to him from James Coleman, twenty-five from J. W. Jarvis, eleven from John Pearson, among others; in the Folger Shakespeare Library there are sixty-three from Coleman, fifty-one from Jarvis, and over two hundred letters written by Halliwell between 1879 and 1888 to an unnamed agent who has been identified as John Pearson of the Booksellers J. Pearson & Co.[288]

288. See Birgit H. Beile, "James Orchard Halliwell-Phillipps's Agent at Auction," *The Library*, VI, 13 (1991), 262-5.

And since his passion for collecting was insatiable–"I want Shakespeare Shakespeare Shakespeare SHAKESPEARE [written an inch high]," he declared to Coleman (26 February 1880; Folger Y.c.1206[23])–and he now had the means to satisfy it. "I do not spend all my income, *so I always have ready cash*" (8 January 1880; Folger Y.c.1206[21]), and he could maintain, "If I *really* want anything I will pay *very* liberally." Again and again, the passion is pronounced: "I should go out of my mind (or what is left of it) if I missed any theatrical MS. I really wanted" (12 November 1884; Folger 1241[1]); "If I really want it, I won't haggle about price" (4 June 1884; Folger Y.d.5[56b]); "I am not *at all* particular about price if I *really* want anything" (2 October 1887; Folger Y.c.1288[3b]). And the price could be high; "I cannot (& indeed it is an inflexible rule with me not to) name a price for anything I want myself," he wrote to William Downing, "but ... I am not within a few pounds for anything I really want" (23 July 1883; LOA 281:55). He paid £60 for the deed of bargain and sale of Shakespeare's Blackfriars estate. He wished Coleman would offer him "sommat" he could pay £1 for (14 January 1884; Folger Y.c.1206[46]). He was interested in a collection of books of a county gentleman in North Wales for which he would pay £10 or more (23 December 1887; Folger W.b.90[89]). And since his collection was considerable and its limits defined, Halliwell's passion and purse were directed at very special items. His motto might well have been his words to Jarvis & Son: "Something Shakespeareana very early & unique, worth a hundred pounds or so, much wanted" (2 November 1888; Folger Y.c.1241[11]). "My great fancy–or rather one of them–is for old Latin grammars *printed in England before 1610*," he informed Jarvis. "I do also want to buy an old MS. play of Shakespeare's time" (10 December 1882; Folger Y.c.1240[27b]). "*Do* get something early & dramatic, there's a good boy," he encouraged Coleman (12 February 1883; Folger 1206[33]). Towards the end of his life his wishes were enormously refined. He was not interested in the Third Folio, he wrote to Charles Lowe, but "if you had an imperfect copy I should like to buy the leaf containing the portrait but I don't want the complete book" (26 April 1887; Folger Y.c.1249). "I will give a hundred guineas," he declared shortly before his death, "for any sort of copy of the first folio of 1623, no matter how dirty or imperfect, *provided* only that it has a nice impression of the genuine engraved portrait" (9 November 1888; Folger W.b.90[112]). Ever searching for a MS. play of Shakespeare's time, he informed Coleman two weeks later, "*even a single leaf of one would be worth having*" (23 November 1888; Folger Y.c.1206[63]). Lest Halliwell's passion and purse be misunderstood as crass possessiveness and greed, it is well to mention that his motivation may, in large part certainly, be attributed not merely to his work-in-progress but certainly also to the attitude expressed in his thanking Ingleby for a book: "No reprint can bring the very times before one like the original. It is a delightful addition to my iron-safe rarities" (29 April 1883; Folger C.a.11[57]). As for his dealings, his relations with dealers and agents were always flexible, cordial, and correct. And as far as private offers were concerned, Halliwell was often gallant: "where a purchase is solicited from a private owner as a favour," he wrote to the Reverend Thomas Helmore, "I should of course be willing to give much more than I should to a dealer" (30 December 1886; Folger W.b.85[46]).

To these more or less official channels of advertising and commissioning must, of course, be added Halliwell's own browsing which, although decreasing as he grew older, was still capable of a happy discovery, as was the case in describing with great glee his finding "a jewel in the dust-heap":

In the midst of a collection of the veriest rubbish was an engraved view of old London in a black frame, the whole measuring about eight feet in length. Although it was begrimed and covered with dust, it required no great penetration in a lover of old engravings to see that it was, in all probability, a valuable relic. And so it turned out to be when the dirt and some old varnish had been removed. It was not only an original early work by Visscher, executed about the year 1625, but an unique edition differing from all other known engravings of London by the same artist. The saleroom was filled with furniture-dealers,–there was no one who appeared to take the smallest interest in the lot, and the hammer fell to me at fifteen shillings. This was a high price as things went, but in those days I was fool enough to be a bit of a dandy, and the unwashed company were probably disinclined to allow a 'swell' to march off with anything for the nominal price of the frame.[289]

Another possible source of augmentation stemmed from his years-long search of the corporate records of England and Wales for material likely to be illustrative of Shakespearean biography and the history of the contemporary stage. His searches did not produce much in actual additions to his own collection, but they did illuminate sources and illustrate methods. Halliwell was not passive in dealing with record offices and parish registers. He pointed out to local communities (such as Barnstaple) how important and valuable their records were, and urged that

289. See the preface to *Two Old Theatres* (1884).

they be well protected and catalogued efficiently, as he had attempted to do in Stratford. Moreover he appealed to his countrymen not to neglect their attics, so to speak, ever hoping for some important finds, such as his "dream" of a copy of a 1602 quarto *Hamlet* being found: "If preserved anywhere, it will be found in one of the closets or lofts of an old county family," he had remarked to Charles Roach Smith (3 October 1867; Folger W.a.81[51/2]). And to enlist and assist them, he published in 1884 *Memoranda, Intended for the Use of Amateurs, Who Are Sufficiently Interested in the Pursuit, to Make Searches in the Public Record Office, on the Chance of Discovering New Facts Respecting Shakespeare and the Contemporary Stage.* With sportive enthusiasm Halliwell invited the reader to join in the "sport" of record-hunting, "the only game followed by the Hollingbury Copse Hunt." In the "immense forest—belonging to the nation and called the Record Office ... are undiscovered notices of Shakespeare amidst millions of papers" (vi), he pointed out. Experience had taught him the arduousness of the game: as he had advised the impatient Furnivall some years earlier, "to be successful require not only a long course of training in research, but an acquaintance with the subject so special that the minutest clue may be at once detected, & not only detected but followed up inductively by the aid of that special knowledge" (12 March 1879; LOA 250:17). Halliwell's was no simple or general call to the hunt—as was his controversial piece of juvenilia, *A Few Hints to Novices in Manuscript Literature*, some forty-five years earlier—but a specific list of thirty "memoranda" (pp. 13-24) which he suggested as subjects for investigation. They range from 1. Burbage, Robinson and Hemings v. Sir Matthew Brend, to 12. The Corporation of Stratford-on-Avon v. William Shaw and others, a Chancery suit, 1626, to 24. Pasch. 29 Eliz. Johannes Shakespeare protulit breve domine regine de habeas corpus cum causa, Stratford MS., to 28. Documents respecting Phillip Rosseter, temp. Jac. I. In addition there is an alphabetical list (pp. 25-7) of names "likely to prove of Shakespearean interest," including charming "memorial verses" on the names of important actors by his then thirteen-year-old daughter Ellen,[290] "nearly as indispensable as those of the Thirty Days Hath September," followed by a list of seventeen records already printed (p. 29) and an index of all the names in the work (pp. 31-2). Halliwell also published two further research tools in the last decade of his life: *Regnal Years List of Law terms, &c., During the Shakespeare Period* (1883) and *A Dictionary of Misprints, Found in Printed Books of the Sixteenth and Seventeenth Centuries. Compiled for the Use of Verbal Critics, and Especially for Those Who Are*

290. See n. 212 for the full text.

Engaged in Editing the Works of Shakespeare and Our Other Early Dramatists (1887). The tables in the former are followed by a "Nominal Index" (pp. 61-80) of Elizabethan persons and places and Shakespearean characters, ranging from Abhorson and Adams, John, 1588, to Disley or Distle, 1582 and Dogberry, to Paris Garden and Parr, William, 1594, to Yohan or Vaughan and Yorick. The latter work, also recalling Halliwell's youthful *Few Hints* (1839), is a "mere instalment, of what I hope will some day, if life be spared, be expanded into a larger work" (p. 5). It may well be the first large-scale attempt to assemble, systematize, and, in an all-too brief note (pp. 91-4), to discuss the source and nature of errata.

To the outlines of the what, where, and how of collecting materials for the life of Shakespeare and the history of the early English stage Halliwell also provided a system of arranging and cataloguing. He had, of course, done so before. In "A List of the Contents of the Drawers in my Study and in two other Rooms" (1870)[291] he specified by room and subject the data he had assembled in 328 drawers at 11 Tregunter Road: in the drawers on the west side of the Biography Room were 145 subjects; on the west side, twenty-eight; on the east side of the ante-room, eighteen; in the middle case of drawers on the east side of the ante-room, twenty-eight; in the upper case, twenty-eight; as the contents of the flats, five; under the oak book-case on the west side of the study, drawings, engravings, &c., A-U; on the south side of the study, thirty-two; in the oak case on the east side of the study, A-Q. In 1880 Halliwell issued a *Rough List of Shakespearean Rarities and Manuscript Collections, at Hollingbury Copse, Brighton, April, 1880*, which his prefatory note described as a "hand list of books, manuscripts, engravings, parcels, &c." The arrangement is according to location and subject. In "Brown-Paper Parcels" are 134 subjects, ranging from 1. The Hathaways to 19. The Will to 32. Lord Southampton to 45. The Fortune Theatre to 71. Actors in Theatres to 92. Taverns at and near Stratford-on-Avon to 111. Residences in London to 116. Treatment of Wife to 134. Troilus and Cressida. Under Portfolios of Engravings are eighteen subjects, from 1. Facsimiles to 11. Charlecote to 16. Journeys to 18. Facsimiles of Stationers' Register. Under "Manuscript Memoranda Books" are thirty-two topics, from 1. Audit Office to 9. Star-Chamber to 19. County Records to 31. Middlehill Library to 32. Private Collections, 2 vols. Under "Books, Manuscripts, &c." are eighty-eight titles, from 1. King Lear, ed. Furness to 7. Alleyn's Memoir and Papers, in 1 vol. to 14. Morley's Ayres, 1600 to 26. Comical Gallant, 1702 to 35. Destruction of Troy, 1607 to 45. Gull's Hornbook, 1609 to 56. Faire Em,

291. See pp. 407-8.

1631 to 62 Satiromastix, 1602 to 77. England's Parnassus, 1600 to 88. The Comedy of Errors in the Guise of a Dictionary, fol. And in 1883 Halliwell produced a brief *Inventory of a Selected Portion of Manuscripts and Printed Books, Chiefly Relating to Shakespeare and the Old English Drama, in the Library of J. O. Halliwell-Phillipps, at Tregunter Road, London, and at Hollingbury Copse, Brighton,* in which he listed sixty-seven lots, beginning with Nos. 1 to 40: "A series of forty folio volumes of Collections [of notes and cuttings] on the Life of Shakespeare, the History of the early English Stage, the Topography and History of Stratford-on-Avon," followed by forty topics ranging from Actresses to Costume to Globe to London to Printing to Shakespeare Errata to Various Companies. The remaining items consist largely of modern editions of Shakespeare–including the twenty-one-volume Variorum edition of 1821, the nine-volume Cambridge edition of 1863-1866, and the twelve-volume Riverside edition by Richard Grant White–as well as further collections of modern works and some manuscript material on topics already mentioned.

There were a number of reasons for this kind of arrangement. It was obviously practical, a personally conceived subject index being superior to all other systems. It conformed to the way the material was dealt with in the publications Halliwell was preparing. Furthermore, it made no distinction between books and manuscripts assembled through purchases and Halliwell's own notes, both considered worthy of collection and preservation. Halliwell, of course, was aware of what he wished to preserve for himself and what was dispensable, what was to be sold and what was to be donated. He had all along been thinning out and donating parts of his collection in order to control and direct his energies–always mentioning their diminution–towards his announced goal. In both these publications he noted his motivation: the first of 1880 "was printed for a very special object in reference to their [the relics] probable destination at some future period"; the second of 1883 was "drawn up for a special purpose,–an eventual deposition of the volumes in a permanent library." One may speculate on a possible psychological motivation: for one thing, Halliwell's increasing sense of his mortality evidenced in his desperation about putting his material in proper order and seeing that it is well looked after; for another, his desire to erect a memorial to his efforts and, for all his self-effacement, to himself. This glance to the future, to the destiny of his collection, was already apparent in his early will and its bequests to his family and favored institutions. He was so concerned about the safety of his bequest to Edinburgh University, for example, that he made it a condition that it not be sent by sea. There was, finally, a very practical reason for having a rigidly restricted collection. Halliwell's "spacious" study, so the sale prospectus after his death, "a most pleasant and well-lighted Room, having windows on Three Sides of it, with a Fine Prospect over Land and Sea, and a pretty outlook over the Plantation and Grounds" where his "wonderful Collection of Shakespeare Rarities was preserved," measured about 24 by 15 feet. In area it was second only to the drawing room. But since it had windows on three sides, it may not have been able to accommodate much in the way of large bookcases, hence Halliwell's references to parcels, portfolios, memoranda books, which could lie flat or in drawers in cases in the center of the room (referring to his print collection, he said, "I have three drawers full" [3 April 1881; Folger Y.c.1268])–as do many today, such as those which found their way into the Folger Shakespeare Library. This, in fact, was compatible with Halliwell's system of cutting out relevant passages and then pasting them up in indexed sections. As one visitor described it: "The supreme interest of this English interior centres on the Study, a treasury of Shaksperiana, which is separated from the rest of the mansion by doors of iron. Along one side of its antechamber stretches what Mr. Phillipps has named his 'book bin.' Every afternoon his habit is to look over a score of books, cut out of each the fractions he can use, and throw the rest as refuse into his mammoth waste-basket."[292] And the system was

292. J. D. B., "Hollingbury Copse and Its Shaksperiana," *Book-Lore*, 1 (Dec. 1884-May 1885), 139. Reprinted from the New York *Nation* of 26 February 1885. For his cutting up of books Halliwell has been charged with vandalism. To reply that this was Halliwell's system in lieu of index cards, or that the practice was not uncommon, would not satisfy the accusers. Nor would the fact that he made no secret of his practice or that he seems not to have suffered any contemporary rebuke. His wife records one typical instance in her diary entry for 16 October 1863: "James also went to an old book stall & quite astonished Mr B[light] by buying a sixpenny book, then tearing 3 leaves out of it, & then throwing it down again. This is what J. frequently does when he wants only a leaf or two of a book." And Halliwell was in the habit, as well, of sending odd leaves to friends as gifts. But since Halliwell was a bookman, it would be illogical to believe that he would willingly emasculate or destroy when he could sell or exchange. From his overall concern for books and his utterances in print and letters, it seems not unreasonable to believe that–apart from an oversight here or there–he used imperfect copies or loose leaves. And, of course, he was only too well aware of the larger implications; as he stated in prefacing his *Early Editions of Shakespeare* (1857), "it has been the fashion to form perfect copies from imperfect fragments, and as in some cases different early editions of the same play correspond exactly in catchwords, signatures, and head-lines, deception has been practised in the sale of copies presumed to be perfect; though it may be that, in the generality of instances, nothing fraudulent has been intended."

also compatible with the way Halliwell showed his rarities, as he "unweariedly turned over the portfolios." As for artifacts–rings, pieces of the mulberry tree, seals, and the like–he had boxes made especially for them if none were available, for "one of my fancies," he wrote in thanking Jarvis for a small box in which "the animal" was sent to his daughter, "is to collect small slender boxes of which I have hundreds" (22 February 1881; Folger Y.c.1240[23b]).[293] Thus, to put it another way, matters of aim, method, and space combined to determine what remained in Tregunter Road and what was to be admitted into the inner sanctum at Hollingbury Copse.

Needless to say, Halliwell was very proud of his rarities both in themselves and in their contribution to his "darling studies." Year for year, from 1884 to 1887, he produced a series of catalogues announcing and describing his treasures but, unlike his earlier catalogues, with no indication that any were for sale. They were self-advertising and also, if somewhat indirectly, an advertisement for items of a similar nature which Halliwell, always on the lookout for additional items, might consider buying.

In 1884 Halliwell published *A Hand-List of the Drawings and Engravings Illustrative of the Life of Shakespeare, Preserved at Hollingbury Copse, Near Brighton*. It is interesting in a number of ways, despite its admittedly "very limited circulation." It is in essence a museum catalogue, listing 1093 articles, among which Halliwell singled out (pp. 6-7) such "noticeable" ones as Visscher's original drawings of the paintings in the Guild Chapel, the London Arches of Triumph (1604), Norden's original plan of Middlesex (ca. 1593), the earliest engravings of Shakespeare's Cliff near Dover, sketches by Hollar (ca. 1640), the oldest view of Herne's Oak, Winter's plan of Stratford (ca. 1760), and the "gem" of the collection, the engraving of Shakespeare by Droeshout (1623). Needless to say, the collection was not, as Halliwell points out, "the result of a mere desire for accumulation" but "has been with the definite purpose of illustrating the Life of Shakespeare" (p. 8). What is striking is Halliwell's admission that the illustration extends to "representations of every morsel that could be found of his [Shakespeare's] own contemporary England,–that is to say, of every object that he himself was likely to have seen" (p. 8). Thus conceived, the collection attempts a kind of total topographical representation of all the places and objects of Shakespeare's lifetime and of such in his works as well. Since the range is extensive, its value to many

293. Many of the objects which found their way into the Folger Shakespeare Library are in the original portfolios and boxes.

groups–historians, geographers, archaeologists–increases. So dedicated was Halliwell to presenting a complete picture of what the historian Leopold von Ranke termed "wie es eigentlich gewesen"–and as always determined to rescue vestiges of that world from oblivion–that he engaged the draughtsman J. T. Blight to make sketches: "Not only every corner of Stratford-upon-Avon and its neighbourhood explored, but we followed as far as we could the routes known to have been taken by the poet in his various journeys, anxiously searching for remains that could be positively assigned to his own times, and carefully excluding those which had passed through the hands of the modern restorer" (pp. 8-9).

The biographical information to be deduced from the years of dedicated collecting and exploration is complemented by direct autobiographical assertions. Looking back becomes a feature of Halliwell's work in the last decade of his life, just as the word "memoranda"–"notes" blending with "memory"–becomes a favored descriptive title of a whole series of works, replacing such earlier ones as "notes" and "notices." The limited audience which understands and appreciates the process and results of collecting–and Halliwell's "chief pleasure of having rarities is to show them to those who really appreciate them" (19 September 1885; Folger S.b.128[15])–would doubtless understand and appreciate Halliwell's personal reflections on the past, present, and future:

A large work on the lines above indicated could hardly fail to be welcome to the student, but, as is so often the case, the time occupied in gathering together the necessary artistic and literary material has practically excluded the collector himself from the opportunity of making an effective use of his accumulations. As our Brighton whip, in the old days of coaching, used to say,–"tempus will fudgit,"–and it has fudgited with me until there is but a little working slice of it left. That slice is insufficient for the due execution of such an undertaking. In a very few years, half a century will have elapsed since my first work on Shakespeare was published, and the termination of that period must also, if I survive, be that of my student work. If the fate of the Archbishop of Grenada is to be escaped, this should be the resolve not merely of those who have traversed the higher walks of literature, but of the lesser votaries who, like myself, lay claim to nothing beyond a capacity for research and the ability of utilizing its products.

Little autobiographical reflections of this kind might anyhow be excused in a privately-printed brochure of very limited circulation, but they are in fact given as the most effectual method of advising a younger enthusiast that he can, without lack of courtesy to the originator, carry out an important design. When such a one arises with the large means that will be requisite to complete the work in a satisfactory manner, the artistic materials catalogued in the following pages cannot fail to prove of essential service (pp. 9-10).

The sense of the old passing the baton on to the young and so continuing the tradition of research and preservation is undeniable.

In 1885 Halliwell carried on in that spirit by producing *Brief Notices of a Small Number of the Shakespeare Rarities That Are Preserved in the Rustic Wigwam at Hollingbury Copse, Near Brighton* in which forty-eight of the more than 1500 separate articles in the collections are briefly described in general terms for the benefit of visitors. There are in fact four versions of this work: an elegantly printed pamphlet, with the added title page *A List of Shakespeare Rarities. Compiled for the Use of the Members of the British Archaeological Association on the Occasion of Their Visit to Hollingbury Copse, Saturday, August the 22nd, 1885*; the same but *Printed for the Use of Literary Visitors*; a second edition of September 1885, "nearly an exact reprint, but it has a few corrections and additions"; and an article with the identical content entitled "Shakespeare Rarities" which appeared in *Book-Lore*, 2 (June-November 1885), 121-31. Although Halliwell "selected from those [articles] that are likely to be of the most general interest," the objects are among the rarest and those he himself most treasured. Heading the list are the unique Droeshout portrait, the conveyance to Shakespeare of the house in the Blackfriars that he purchased in 1613, and the original deed transferring the legal estate of the house in 1617-18. Since such an exhibit made the "turning over of portfolios" impractical, the most important documents (such as Norden's plan of London, 1593) and engravings (such as Visscher's view of London) were complemented by printed works, among which were the First Folio (1623), *Palladis Tamia* (1598), Shakespeare's *Poems* (1640), *England's Parnassus* (1600), *Loves Labors Lost* (1597). Thomas Morley's *First Booke of Ayres* (1600), and *England's Helicon* (1600). Only one object is represented, a "square of glass ... in which a circular piece is leaded, having the letters W. A. S. for William and Anne Shakespeare, tied in a true lover's knot, and the date, 1615." Though not completely authenticated, it must certainly have been a curiosity which appealed to the general visitor.

In 1886, in connection with a meeting of the British Medical Association in Brighton, Halliwell prepared an exhibition and published *A Brief List of a Selected Portion of the Shakespeare Rarities That Are Preserved in the Rustic Wigwam at Hollingbury Copse, Brighton*. The forty-seven items listed are essentially the same as in the previous year's catalogue, though the

First Folio is missing, and the descriptions are in most cases simple reprints. Four items, printed in italics, were recent acquisitions exhibited for the first time: the first of the two editions of *Pierce Penilesse* of 1592, the head of Shakespeare in an oval, engraved by John Stafford in 1655; three of the original deeds of Shakespeare's residence of New Place; and two original indentures of a fine that was levied on New Place between Shakespeare and Hercules Underhill in 1602. Interesting in addition to the fact that the collection was growing is the fact that all the items were exhibited "In the Study" with the exception of the Droeshout portrait (its fuller description also a reprint), which was located "In the Dining Room."

Finally in 1887 Halliwell issued *A Calendar of the Shakespearean Rarities, Drawings and Engravings, Preserved at Hollingbury Copse, Near Brighton*. It lists 805 items, a collection (but for the sketches by Blight) formed within the past fifteen years and in the main the items already listed in the *Handlist* of 1884. Like that earlier work, its casts a brief glance to the past, depicts the present, and opens to the future. But the preface is more extensive than before, as was Halliwell's experience. The opening is personal and revealing:

For nearly half a century I have been an ardent Shakespearean collector, being most likely the only survivor of the little band who attended the sale of the library of George Chalmers somewhere about the year 1840. But for a long time, attempting too much in several directions with insufficient means, and harassed, moreover, by a succession of lawsuits, including two in the Court of Torture,–I mean Chancery,–I was unable to retain my accumulations: and thus it came to pass that bookcase full after bookcase full were disposed of, some by private contract, many under the vibrations of the auctioneer's hammer. This state of affairs continued till February, 1872, but since that period, by a strict limitation of my competitive resources to one subject,–the Life of Shakespeare,–I have managed to jog along without parting with a single article of any description,[294] nor is there a probability that the collection described in the following pages will ever be dispersed (p. 5).

The preface is also evaluative: the collection "already stands pre-eminent amidst the libraries of the world in no less than four of the most

294. In a letter to Ingleby of 22 January 1886 (Folger C.a.11[111]), Halliwell recalled that "many years ago" he vowed "never again to sell a book, nor have I done so over fourteen years."

important divisions of Shakespeareana" (p. 5). It is analytic: the four divisions are "1. Early engraved portraits of Shakespeare.–2. Authentic personal relics.–3. Documentary evidences respecting his estates and individuals who are connected with his biography.–4. Artistic illustrations of localities connected with his personal history" (pp. 6-9). It is descriptive, providing a narrative connecting the members within the divisions. And in typical Halliwellian manner it recycles material when necessary: it repeats the remarks about employing Blight in the *Handlist*, but, taking into account Blight's sorry end, adds a personal tribute ("a thorough good fellow in every sense of the word"); and with customary husbandry does not shy away from a word-for-word repetition of the memorable "tempus will fudgit" conclusion. Looking forward, Halliwell appends an address "To Booksellers" (quoted above), indicating articles not wanted and wanted (pp. 167-168).

The presence of a detailed index of names and places is striking. It is the first and only one Halliwell ever provided for his collection. Of course it may be said that catalogues do not ordinarily have indexes, especially when a collection is being formed and growing: Halliwell put off doing a index to his ever-expanding *Outlines*, which he was updating year for year from 1881 to 1887. One reason he gave, lack of time and energy, is understandable, but then again an index is the logical ending of a completed work and he did ultimately provide one. And although Halliwell is very explicit that he has "managed to jog along without parting with a single article of any description" and there is no "probability that the collection described ... will ever be dispersed," a sense of finality is inescapable. Halliwell's death a year or so later was sudden but perhaps not unexpected. "If life be spared" was a common refrain in his writings. What was to become of the collection which was not to be dispersed? Halliwell was ever the planner, cautious in regard to the future. His will had provided for his children; a marriage settlement provided for his wife as well. He had made an ongoing bequest to the University of Edinburgh and, should that not be accepted, for the British Museum. Various libraries around the country and Stratford had received much, and circumstances made it unthinkable that Stratford could receive more. There were hopes that Halliwell might bequeath his "jewels to America–that utmost corner of the West where the majority of those who speak the tongue of Shakspere are already resident, where that majority daily grows, and where all helps to the appreciation of that prince of dramatists will accordingly do the most good." The English periodical, *Book-Lore*, which had so cordially described the collection, could not of course "be expected ... to endorse the suggestion." Still, "the proposition struck him [Halliwell] as equally new and startling, but he promised he would take it into consideration."[295]

Two further catalogues in 1887 add to the sense of an ending. *An Inventory of Certain Books and Manuscripts, Including Notes for Shakespearean Researches, Preserved at Hollingbury Copse, Brighton* is a simple list of ten lots, of which the first, containing twenty-five collections of his notes on various subjects (such as Private Collections, Provincial Researches, Wills, London) are announced as bound in quarto volumes, along with other printed works and manuscripts (notably the four-volume diary of his first wife). The spareness of the inventory would seem to indicate that the items have been sorted out, bound, and prepared for a certain destination. They did indeed find their way to the University of Edinburgh. Similarly, *A Hand-List of Sixty Folio Volumes, Containing Collections Made by J. O. Halliwell-Phillipps, from 1854 to 1887, on the Life of Shakespeare, and the History of the English Stage* contains Halliwell's notes and cuttings on a range of Shakespeareana—such as 1. Brearly, 9. Companies of Actors, 19. London, 27. Stratford Index, 36. John Shakespeare, 44. Southwark, 51. Tarlton, 60. Third Electro Ultimates. The dates 1854 to 1887 signify finality. The volumes are itemized, bound, and ready for shipment. They are next to be found "by Order of the Executors of the Late J. O. Halliwell-Phillipps, the eminent Shakspearian scholar," as lots 666-673 in the sale at Sotheby, Wilkinson, & Hodge from 1-4 July 1895.

At the summit of his age and career Halliwell was, as his wife Henrietta often wrote in her diary on returning home after a long journey, putting things to rights.

---

295. "Hollingbury Copse and Its Shaksperiana," 1 (Dec. 1884-May 1885), 141.

24

Last Works: *Outlines* and Outlook

Hollingbury Copse was in many respects idyllic, a retreat, with curious architecture and decoration, horticultural delights and evergreens threaded with labyrinthine paths, and stone-curbed fish-pond. It was ideal for putting things to rights, and, for Halliwell, now assured of domestic peace and financial security, it was the place where he was to proceed with his research and produce what was doubtless the most important work of his life. It was not, however, without problems. Hollingbury Copse was sheltered and Halliwell was determined to withdraw. But the world elsewhere was not to be denied. There was Furnivall and the New Shakspere Society and Pigsbrook: Halliwell entered that fray, unwillingly perhaps but, once in, fervently and at great cost to his emotional well-being. The affair diverted him from his main objective, since it meant letters and discussions and factions and all the rest of the political ramifications. But it did have a scholarly focus and was not simply a matter of personal or party-political power struggles. It concerned Shakespeare and the direction of Shakespeare studies: both formed the content of Halliwell's life and career. And for him even the spelling of Shakespeare's name was not trivial but fundamental. It was, in a way, the focal point of historical accuracy and veracity. In short, the proper spelling of the name was intimately connected with the comprehension and preservation of the way things were, "wie es gewesen."

Furnivall provoked a good part of the Shakespeare world with the spelling *Shakspere*. The move was deliberate, and sides were quickly drawn up. "We unfortunate Conservatives of Shakespearean orthography," Swinburne wrote to Halliwell, "are held up to the divine wrath of the Neo-Chaxpurian Radical" (26 January 1880; LOA 255:53). For Halliwell the situation was not new: he had taken his position publicly some fifty years earlier, at age twenty-one, advocating the spelling *Shakespeare* in his *Introduction to A Midsummer Night's Dream*. Then, in 1841, he was involved in a great controversy, being held, it would appear, as radical and not conservative because of his age and assertiveness, at least by his opponents and seniors, Frederic Madden and Bolton Corney. But he had support, for on his side in the public controversy were Isaac Disraeli, Collier, Dyce, Bruce, and Hunter. The conflict was fierce; Halliwell held fast to his position throughout his entire life. And it is difficult not to believe that enduring grudges were borne. It is equally difficult not to believe that Furnivall's stance was for Halliwell not unlike Madden's stance, and that there was not a repetition of what was undeniably a traumatic scholarly and personal experience. In 1841 Halliwell was motivated to a considerable extent by attacks on Isaac Disraeli; in 1879 he was acutely conscious of criticism of his friend Ingleby, whose *Shakespeare: The Man and the Book* (1877) opened with a chapter, "The Spelling of the Surname," in which Halliwell's position was defended against that of Furnivall. As in 1841, so in 1879, a similar drama emerged. Sides were drawn up according to party lines: for *Shakespeare*, Halliwell, Swinburne, Ingleby, and others who disapproved of Furnivall (like W. A. Wright) or were obligated to Halliwell (like Furness); for *Shakspere*, Furnivall, Dowden, Knight, Fleay, and cohorts. Of course, there was more to it than the spelling of the name or of the Society. Until the Pigsbrook affair Halliwell was skeptical but not condemning of the Society and its aims. He took its spelling of the name and the objectives of the Society with critical good humor: Responding with a wait-and-see attitude to the prospectus of the New Shakspere Society, Halliwell informed Furnivall, "In the mean while I shall, nothing daunted, go on quietly with my work, leaving you & your colleagues to determine what plays Chakespeare wrote when he was in a good humour, those that were composed when he was teased by Mrs Shakespeare & those that were written under the deteriorating influence of a stomach ache" (13 May 1879; LOA 256:62). Still, in what seems a knee-jerk response to Furnivall's request of 2 November 1879 (LOA 245:5*) that Halliwell decline if not renounce Swinburne's dedication to him of his *Study of Shakespeare*, Halliwell issued (with a preface dated 4 November) his pamphlet *Which Shall It Be? New Lamps or Old? Shaxpere or Shakespeare?* Since only three pages are devoted to the study—an indication that it was produced for the occasion[296]—Halliwell can only admit the lack of uniformity in the spelling

---

296. Pages 9-12 are paginal reprints of pages 77-80 of *Memoranda on All's Well That Ends Well, The Two Gentlemen of Verona, Much Ado about Nothing, and on Titus Andronicus*, which appeared around the same time. Its position at the end of a volume, which has a different subject-matter, also confirms its connection to the occasion.

of names[297] and support his preference for the spelling *Shakespeare* by its appearance in the "only two works we can safely believe to have been printed under his own superintendence" (pp. 10-11), in the dedications of *Venus and Adonis* and *The Rape of Lucrece*. And, interestingly enough as testimony to Halliwell's persistent scholarly and emotional adherence to his position, he reprints (with some modification) in four pages (13-16) of small print what he had written "many years ago," in his *Life of William Shakespeare* in 1848 (pp. 278-83).

As the controversy heated up, the spelling of the name became the trophy that was battled for. In January 1880 Halliwell responded to a "score" of notices in newspapers and journals–"no one would have imagined that such an enquiry [his "tentative little pamphlet"] could have raised the smallest of storms in the minutest of teapots"–by publishing *New Lamps or Old? A Few Additional Words on the Momentous Question Respecting the E and the A in the Name of Our National Dramatist*. He was unquestionably stung by

One writer, indeed, in a letter in the Daily News of December the 20th, [who] was positively stimulated to compare the reluctance to adopt the shorter form of the poet's name with the fearful obstruction of 'Toryism' to everything that is correct and proper. From the expressions used by the individual in question it may be inferred that, in his opinion, the Tories, having done their best to prevent the introduction of Free Trade and the Reform Bill, are now completing their iniquities by spelling the name of the great dramatist in the way in which he himself printed it in the first editions of his own poems; that the vagabonds who write *Shakespeare* are bucolic and pig-headed Conservatives, and that the angels who prefer *Shakspere* are advanced and enlightened Radicals (pp. 3-4).

Now expanded to twenty-three pages, the pamphlet adds details, such as another instance of the spelling *Shake-speare* following his poem "Threnos" in Robert Chester's *Love's Martyr* (1601), which "could hardly have been inserted without his direct sanction" (p. 14), as well as an analysis of the five extant signatures. But Halliwell's position does not change. It is underlined by his cheerfully hyperbolic conclusion:

297. In Folger W.b.188:154-168 Halliwell listed "Forms of Name." They extend from Those commencing with *Sha* not followed by *k*, nor by *c*. (154) to Those *not* commencing with *S*. (156) to Those commencing with *Shas* (160) to Those commencing with *Shax* not followed by *p*. or *s*. (162) to Those commencing with *Shakes*. (165) to Those commencing with *Shaxs*. (168). In most cases each spelling is given a manuscript source.

Now, in conclusion, with a flourish of magnanimity. If it be possible that any student, after perusing the above luminous exposition, can wish to discard the e and the a, he has my solemn assurance that I shall not have the slightest inclination either to roar him down or quarrel with him on that account. On the contrary, if such an individual appear and will favour me with a visit, he shall be received with all the attention due to a rara avis at my primitive and ornithological bungalow ... And the feast of reason shall be irrigated by the flow of poet, claret, or madeira, and by what is not now to be seen every day of the week, really old sherry. If, unfortunately, he has forsworn racy potations and not discovered that good sherris-sack 'ascends into the brain and dries there all the foolish, and dull, and crudy vapours which environ it,' then are there our deep chalk wells yielding an inexhaustible supply of the pure aqueous element as bright and sparkling as the waves and atmosphere of Brighton herself (pp. 22-3).

Halliwell's employment of a kind of merry and inflated disinterestedness is, as was his wont, an indication of how deeply he felt. And the reference to drink is certainly aimed at Furnivall the teetotaller. And if style alone were not enough to illustrate his unshakable stance, then Halliwell produced still another pamphlet in 1880 with the same title, a "second edition" (with a preface dated 3 April), in which the January work is reprinted (pp. 5-27), "Notices of the Press" on the controversy are added, and—ever practicing good husbandry—a reprint of his letter of 3 April to the *Athenaeum* announcing *The Life of Shakespeare* (pp. 33-8), a "Note" modifying the mode of production (p. 39), and a letter to him of 11 May 1880 from Col. J. L. Chester with three variant spellings by the same scribe of the name *Wiltshire* in three consecutive lines. Emphasis by incremental repetition was as much a Halliwell trademark as his jovially sarcastic tone. In fact, the juggling with Shakespeare's name was a fitting complement to the mischievous wordplay on the names Swinburne and Furnivall, apparently lighthearted but deadly earnest. All the names appear on the title page of a projected attack which was given to Halliwell by Furnivall in "1879 or 1880." It reads: *The Spelling of Shakspere's Name as Shake-speare Illustrated by That of Algernon G. Pigs-brook or Swine-burne, etc.*

The impact of Halliwell's conflict with Furnivall inspired some works and put an end to others. Halliwell was intimidated by Furnivall's harsh criticism and shocked by its boisterousness. He was appalled by Furnivall's unhesitating attack on Swinburne's "personal character in print," he wrote to Ingleby, continuing, "I have little doubt that his insolent eccentricities will put a stop to the series of books I am now printing—the 4th by the way is nearly out." His conclusion, "& so I shall save a pot of money" (27 December 1879; Folger C.a.11[16]), is cold comfort against the deepest distress of his abandoning of literary pursuits. He could not shake off the threat and his fear. He will complete his "little book" on *Love's Labour's Lost*, he confessed to Ingleby a short while later,

& then I shut up. I shall still go on collecting for the sake of summat to do, but as for publication, not for Joe so long as one is to be subjected to Furnivall's ungentlemanly criticism. I shall give him as good as he gives me, but what I mean is that, pursuing these matters for recreation, it is not worthwhile by printing more to further encounter a rusty lance because one is too independent to acknowledge the aesthetic charms of his Dulcinea del Toboso. Shut up in my own windmill he will be a deuced clever fellow if he ever gets further than the sails. It is a pity, for my inedited collections on the life and history of the stage are enormously valuable & include so much that no one could now attain for love or money. If they are lost for ever to the Shakespeare student, he has only to thank the insolence of F.J.F. for the result (14 February 1880; Folger C.a.11[17]).

Months later Halliwell is still harping on the same theme: "Perhaps, however, I ought not to complain of him, for he is rapidly weaning me from the love of my once favourite studies & by putting a stop to further printing of Memoranda &c. is saving me a good lot of money" (16 October 1880; Folger C.a.11[23]). He is even more virulent in a letter to Ingleby of 7 January 1881 (Folger C.a.11[26]), in which he concludes: "to his vulgar insolence you & others are indebted for the change of my printing 250 copies to give away into printing 16 copies of each not to be either sold or given away until my death."

The immediate works in question were nine volumes, seven of which belonged to a series entitled "Memoranda," and two similar ones.[298] The first of the four which appeared in 1879 treats *All's Well That Ends Well*, *The Two Gentlemen of Verona*, *Much Ado About Nothing*, and *Titus Andronicus*; a second, *Love's Labour's Lost*, *King John*, *Othello*, and *Romeo and Juliet*; a third, *Hamlet*; and a fourth, *A Midsummer Night's Dream*. In 1880 one deals

298. They are not all of uniform size or decoration. Six are quartos, two printed in 1880 by Whittingham and Co., are small quartos, and one on *The Tempest* in 1880 is explained by Halliwell in his presentation copy to Swinburne as "a disreputable piece of book-making, three pages of text expanding into a quarto volume!!" In 1868 Halliwell produced two volumes of "Selected Notes," of a projected thirty-six, but abandoned the undertaking. See pp. 361-2.

with *Measure for Measure*, another with *Troilus and Cressida*, a third with *The Tempest*, a fourth, "cursory memoranda," with *Macbeth*, and a fifth, "discursive notes," with *Romeo and Juliet*. It is not too much to say that these volumes do little to advance or enhance Halliwell's reputation. They are doubtless part of his effort to put things to rights–to sort out and order the countless notes he had assembled during his career. "Most of my Shakespeare notices are *cuttings from the original books* and are now in the process of binding," he informed Ingleby (7 January 1881; Folger C.a.11[26]), referring to the scrapbooks which were to be sold at auction after his death. The "Memoranda" volumes, while not composed of cuttings, are similar, in being collections of notes and "observations" (the description Halliwell most often uses) assembled over the years, some in fact transcriptions of what must have been cuttings. Halliwell makes no attempt to disguise their provenance. For example, he added at the end of the discussion of *All's Well That Ends Well*: "*The above observations on All's Well that Ends Well were written by me in the year 1857, and out of a mass of subsequent notes I do not find any worthy of preservation*" (p. 22). Going further, he prefers to juxtapose "memoranda" of an earlier period with those of the present. Thus "Introduction. A.D. 1855" of *Much Ado about Nothing* is followed by "Memoranda.–1879." Nor does Halliwell hesitate to confess, "The preceding observations on Much Ado About Nothing were written by me in the year 1855, and I am sorry to find that there is nothing of very much value or importance amongst my papers of a later date" (p. 47). The same procedure and much the same qualification hold for *Titus Andronicus*, *Love's Labour's Lost*, *King John*, and *A Midsummer Night's Dream*. In the preface to the *Hamlet* volume Halliwell is even bolder by admitting reservations about his procedure–"Had I consulted my own reputation, or now cared much for the slender credit attached to works on Shakespearean criticism, it would have been better to have framed the notes into a connected essay"–and attempting specious logic, to salvage the effort thus, "but the stealing steps are now in rapid movement and warn me that, unless this and similar contributions to Shakespearean literature are produced in a slipshod and uncorrected fashion, they will never see the light at all" (p. 5).

The "observations" are diverse. They may include a character portrayal (Bertram in *All's Well*), matters of dating (*Two Gentlemen*), of source (*Much Ado*), of authorship (*Titus*), of locality of performance (*Love's Labour's Lost*), of historical truth (*King John*), of legal statutes (*Othello*), of name invention (*Romeo*), of poetic style (*Midsummer Night's Dream*), of date of performance (*Macbeth*), of date of composition (*Tempest*). The appropriately titled *Discursive Notes on Shakespeare's Tragedy of Romeo and*

Juliet is a distilled anthology of the topics of all the volumes. There is no discernible order or discussion, only what amounts to an indiscriminate listing of items, some only a sentence or two long, some several pages. In their order of appearance are the following: a dropped "h" in "this" in some copies of the 1609 quarto; a Spanish translation of Bandello's novel; the story in various works, with a long quotation from its appearance in an unpublished manuscript of the seventeenth century; remarks on a copy of the quarto of 1599; references to a copy of the title page of *Romeus and Juliet* of 1587, to a work in which the Montagues and Capulets are introduced with torchbearers, to two metrical epistles in imitation of Ovid, to names in other works, to a mention of the play in a manuscript of 1660, to the notice of a stone coffin, with a long quote from Breval (1726), to early notices of the story, to a copy of the 1599 quarto with manuscript notes and an emendation proposed by Halliwell.

Hamlet receives the longest treatment of all the plays. Halliwell is cautious and self-protective enough to warn the reader of the difficulty, if not impossibility, of grasping the entire play. "Let me add," he concludes his preface,

that the more I read of the tragedy of Hamlet the less I really understand it as a whole, and now despair of meeting with any theories that will reconcile its perplexing inconsistencies, making of course allowances for those that are most likely intentional. It should not be supposed that, in any of the following scattered notes, written at various times, I have the presumption to imagine a success in mastering its difficulties. There may be a few suggestions worthy of consideration, and my readers, if I have any, must not expect to find much more (pp. 6-7).

His "scattered notes," however, are so connected as to form a coherent whole. And he is not reluctant to address that "fatal Cleopatra" of questions, the character of Hamlet, and to challenge existing interpretations. "The reason of the general failure in Hamlet criticism," he holds, "is no doubt chiefly to be traced to the want of ability to enter fully into the inspiration of the poet's genius. It may, however, be safely asserted that the simpler explanations are, and the less they are biased by the subtleties of the philosophical critics, the more they are likely to be in unison with the intentions of the author" (p. 13). Halliwell's own appraisal—"There seems to have been in Hamlet ... an almost perpetual conflict between impulse and reason, each in its turn being predominant" (p. 16)—is not unfamiliar, nor is its criticism of the "present favourite idea" propounded by Goethe of Hamlet as "an irresolute mind oppressed by the weight of a mission which it is unable to accomplish" (pp. 13-14). What distinguishes Halliwell is not so much the interpretation as his attention to a listing of older versions of the subject and quoted early allusions to the play. This, in turn, leads to the main objective of the entire tract, the relationship of the three existing versions, Q1 (1603), Q2 (1604), and F1 (1623), to each other and especially to the existence of an older play, the so-called Ur-Hamlet. Less crucial than Halliwell's argumentation in favor of the existence of the older play–a view more or less dismissed by textual critics–is Halliwell's critical orientation. In his concentration on "substantial" evidence–be it internal textual evidence, such as verbal repetition and errors, or external, such as publication and performance practices–Halliwell was affirming his kind of archaeological criticism and confuting the stance of the New Shakspere Society. For it must be remembered that the date of the preface, November 1879, was coincidental with his conflict with Furnivall over the Swinburne dedication. And to make sure that his critical point of view would not be missed, Halliwell added a section entitled "Aesthetic Criticism" (pp. 75-8), in which he attacked with a kind of pastoral ridicule those who, not content with sign-posts (bad enough) to what they considered worthy of attention, took to a balloon for a bird's eye view, "one in which the entire region [i.e. Shakespeare] and the supposed consonance of its various districts could be comprehended in one glance" (pp. 76-7) and then asserted his unshakable view that "the works of Shakespeare are involuntarily adapted to the various hearts and instincts of us all, and any system which disturbs that adaptation enervates and cripples the freedom of individual thought" (p. 78).

Not surprisingly, Halliwell's position, not altered since his *Introduction to Shakespeare's Midsummer Night's Dream* in 1841, serves to explain his reaction to some contemporary approaches, such as his questioning of relying "*chiefly* on metrical percentages" to determine the authorship of Henry VIII (20 July 1881; Folger C.a.11[33]), his "cheering" response the ridiculing of the "metrical nonsense" of the New Shakspere Society (9 January 1882; Folger Y.c.1211[155], and his "fiery" rejection of the "Bacon theory" as "an idiotic hypothesis, one impossible to be held by any sane person who has studied the history of our early stage & dramatic poetry" (13 August 1881; Folger Y.c.1208[1]) and devoid of "the least particle of substantial evidence" (12 January 1883; LOA 261:7). P. A. Daniel's endorsement of Halliwell's position–"with your remarks on sign-post–or as it is polite to call it–aesthetic criticism I feel more free to express my hearty sympathy; for I am one of those benighted beings who think it possible that on the whole Shakespeare himself may be the best exponent of his own meaning and therefore that the first and highest duty of a critic is to endeavour at a true version of his words" (6 January 1880; LOA 280:39)–is also testimony to the deepening split among Shakespeareans, both within the New Shakspere Society and without. Also receiving a copy was Edward Dowden (ever mindful of bridges as friend of both Furnivall and Halliwell), who responded that the *Hamlet* "contains much that interests me, a good many things new to me, some things I cannot wholly accept, & nothing I am not greatly pleased to have read." This elegantly phrased diplomacy was matched by his graciously accepting that the "last three lines on p. 78 seem to me full of wisdom & of warning, & I shall try to make them my own" (14 January 1880; LOA 255:35). The lines form the conclusion of Halliwell's "Aesthetic Criticism": "Those who have lived as long as myself in the midst of Shakespearean criticism will be careful not to be too certain of anything." Only Furnivall was certain of everything. And in his treatment, in his facsimiles of *Hamlet*, of Halliwell the critic and Halliwell the person, his trumpeting use of the first person pronoun and the absoluteness of his assertions could not but do great damage to persons and the profession. It is little wonder that the bookseller Alfred Russell Smith should come to the "conclusion that the study of Shakespeare is steadily on the *de*crease, notwithstanding the efforts of a few noisy persons to revive it. Interest in any study leads to book buying, and I judge of Shakespearian interest by a corresponding demand for Shakespeare books. I have more of the latter than all the booksellers in London put together, and the books lie on my shelves & rot" (4 January 1881; LOA 257:36).[299]

Uncontroversial for Halliwell was his collection of substantial evidence for his life of Shakespeare and the publication of such as might be of general interest. A few were slight. One, in 1882, "A Shakesperian Ballad Book," is a brief description and list of content of a unique copy of Thomas Morley's *First Booke of Ayres* (1600), which Halliwell had acquired.[300] Another, in 1883, is *The Fool and the Ice: A Brief Account of a Singular Adventure Which Occurred at Evesham in the Reign of Queen Elizabeth, and Which is Supposed to Be Alluded to by Shakespeare in His Drama of Troilus and Cressida*, a four-page-long transcription of an episode involving Jack Miller, the popular Fool of Evesham, witnessed by Robert Armin, who collected it in the *Nest of Ninnies* (1608). Two further works, also

---

299. Two years later Samuel Timmins confessed to Halliwell, "Herr [Albert] Cohn does contrive to make up a very curious Bibliography. I confess I feel ashamed when I see his List & the Shakespeare Jahrbuch that we here do so little in that way" (19 August 1883; LOA 261:47).

300. *The Bibliographer*, 1 (Dec. 1881-May 1882), 12-13.

illustrating Halliwell's habit of publishing items from his own collection, are facsimiles of rare documents. Halliwell was especially proud of one document, having "for years been on the search for this desirable treasure, and was at length, a few months ago, fortunate enough to secure it": *A Facsimile of the Deed of Bargain and Sale of Shakespeare's Blackfriars Estate, That Which Was Conveyed to the Poet and Trustees on March the 10th, 1613* (1884). Although it is not clear why Shakespeare purchased the property for the stately sum of £140–whether for investment or conversion into a residence–the document was undoubtedly authentic, and the day on which he bought it from William Tite (for £60[301]) Halliwell described as "an epoch in my Shakespearean life." A second facsimile, also published in 1884, is *Two Old Theatres. Views of the Globe and the Bear Garden ... a Wood Engraving, Taken from an Unique View of London, Published by Visscher in the Early Part of the Reign of Charles the First.*

Of more substance are two volumes of notes, memoranda, and "literary scraps," further instances of Halliwell's attempt to sort out the material he had accumulated and to publish what might not find a place in his life of Shakespeare. In 1880 he issued *A Budget of Notes and Memoranda on the Life and Works of Shakespeare, and of the History of the Early English Stage.* Almost half of the forty-eight pages is devoted to the nature and relationship of the six versions and their authorship of the *Henry 6* plays, a subject Halliwell had treated in his editions in 1842 for the Shakespeare Society of *The First Part of the Contention ... and The True Tragedie of Richard Duke of Yorke* under the collective title *The First Sketches of the Second and Third Parts of King Henry the Sixth.* Adding detail to his earlier presentation of their publishing history, reviewing again and doubting such theories as Malone's (that Shakespeare reworked a pair of older plays, p. 14) and Dr. Johnson's (that the quartos were memorial reconstructions, p. 15), omitting the earlier direct criticism of Charles Knight, including favorable remarks on Swinburne's view that Marlowe was "at least the chief writer of the three original plays amended by Shakespeare" (p. 13), and adding further details from their theatrical history, as well as allusions and analogues, Halliwell recognized the immense complexity of the authorial history and conceded that "No one has yet suggested a theory which satisfies all the conditions of the problem, but the hypothesis that the above-named two histories published by Millington are surreptitious, blundering and imperfect, copies of the original plays after the latter had been at least partially altered by Shakespeare appears to be the explanation which involves the fewest

---

301. See 19 August 1883 (LOA 269:52).

perplexities" (p. 6). And in the end, convinced that the problem is unlikely to have an absolute answer, he cautiously concluded: "Although of course it is a matter of speculation, the probability is that, if Shakespeare had lived to have superintended an edition of his works, he would have followed the example of Ben Jonson and excluded from the series any compositions that were not entirely his own" (p. 21). The rest of the volume is devoted to paragraphs on performances of plays, such as *Ignoramus* in March 1615 in Cambridge, and the closing of the theaters in 1594 for fear of the plague (pp. 21-4); transcriptions of records concerning the Earl of Pembroke's Company (pp. 24-8); the publishing history and abdication scene of *Richard II* and Heywood's account (pp. 28-32); the publishing history of *Richard III* and other versions attesting to its popularity (pp. 32-40); dramatic versions of the story of Troilus and Cressida (such as that by Dekker and Chettle) and its transmission from Chaucer (pp. 40-5); and Shakespeare's hand in *The Taming of the Shrew* and his use of Gascoigne's translation, *The Supposes*, of Ariosto's work for certain names and incidents (pp. 45-8). Halliwell had dealt with most of these works during his career, and these notes do little to further the discussion.

In one of his last publications, *The Visits of Shakespeare's Company of Actors to the Provincial Cities and Towns of England, Illustrated by Extracts Gathered from Corporate Records* (1887), Halliwell printed the notes he had accumulated in his researches in the archives of "upwards of seventy towns," having devoted a portion of every summer of the past twenty years to the "prosecution of the task" (p. 5). The notices are arranged alphabetically according to towns ranging from Barnstaple and Bath to Shrewsbury and Worcester. They consist normally of brief transcriptions and vary in length from a sentence or so—as in the case of Rye, Co. Sussex: "Shakespeare's Company visited this town in the month of August, 1597. 'Paid for a reward given to my Lord Chamberlens players at the assignement of Mr. Maior, xx.*s*.'—chamberlains' accounts, August, 1597" (p. 35)—to a six-page narrative indicating the depositories of records and Halliwell's own experience in such places with large amounts of material which require patience, a precisely defined objective, and a measure of good luck, as in the case of Worcester and its neighboring localities (pp. 41-7). If Halliwell is careful to point out that "strict accuracy has been sacrificed to convenience in the use of the expression Shakespeare's Company,—words that are to be taken for the company to which he belonged," he is nevertheless certain that "the poet was never manager either of a theatre or of a company. As a dramatist he was the chief writer for the Lord Chamberlain's or the King's Servants, but as an actor he was never more than a sharer" (p. 9). The notices Halliwell provides are of varying quality and interest: that, for example, the company most frequently visited Oxford, but Cambridge is not mentioned despite the fact that the title page of the 1603 quarto of *Hamlet* says it was performed there; or that the company received a grant of thirty shillings from Bristol in September 1597 and only "xiij.*s*.iiij.*d*." in the same month from Dover. Although concluding that "comparatively little of worth has been found in those towns the records of which might reasonably have been expected to have yielded a harvest" (p. 5)–such as Worcester, Gloucester, Warwick, and, to his "great disappointment," Coventry–and no mention of Shakespeare himself was found, Halliwell was nevertheless content with his findings and encouraged by the work of the Historical Manuscripts Commission. In any event, the information, although admittedly incomplete, has been accepted by Shakespeare scholars and incorporated into modern comprehensive research instruments, such as the Records of Early English Drama project. And Halliwell's ever-present appeal to scholars, town clerks, and historical commissions to follow his lead in searching out, organizing, and preserving records of the national heritage has not gone unheeded.

The climax of more than forty years of research was his *Outlines of the Life of Shakespeare*. It began inconspicuously enough in 1881 as a slight volume of 192 pages "printed for the author's friends," privately, as was Halliwell's custom. On the surface at least this might be considered an anticlimax after the ambitious *Illustrations*, whose imposing size and expensive makeup seemed more appropriate to what came to be generally regarded as the *summa* of Halliwell's career. There is even some uncertainty of purpose and direction preceding its appearance. In an announcement entitled "The Life of Shakespeare" appended to the second edition of his *New Lamps or Old?*, a letter of 10 April 1880 that he had sent to the *Athenaeum*, he made it known that

Under the title of *Contributions towards a Life of Shakespeare*, it is possible, health, strength, and inclination permitting, that I may some day commence a series of folio volumes in which I shall hope to fully investigate the truth or probability of every recorded incident in the personal and literary history of the great dramatist, and include a vast mass of correlative information, the accumulation of many years' researches, the whole to be copiously illustrated with wood engravings and fac-similes. Amongst the latter would be fac-similes of every known contemporary document in which the name of the poet appears (p. 33).

A few pages later Halliwell, after asserting that "the first volume of the projected series could not be completed at the earliest before the Spring of next year ... [and] would be obtainable only through a special London agent, and the impression will be extremely limited," admits that he is attempting to ascertain "whether there is sufficient interest taken in the subject to encourage the commencement of so large and costly an undertaking" (pp. 37-8). Yet, one page later and doubtless only a short time later, reacting to what he regards as the "wholly ... gratifying and encouraging character" of the response to the announcement, Halliwell, "on careful enquiry" and desiring to retain "a perfect independence of action, with freedom from all subscription and publishing troubles," proposes another course:

a number of small occasional volumes, of various sizes and of limited impression, each one to be a separate work in itself. Thus, there will be one volume on the Davenant scandal, another on the Globe Theatre, a third on the deer-stealing adventure, another on the poet's last illness, and so on. These will be submitted at intervals to public auction in London, so that an intending purchaser can give a commission to his bookseller even for a single volume (p. 39).

Like so many of Halliwell's works—his *Life of William Shakespeare* (1848), the *Life* in the folio edition of Shakespeare (1853), the numerous catalogues, inventories, and handlists—the lodestar of his researches was the "life." But as the years progressed, the focus seemed to become a frame: from the concise title *A Life of William Shakespeare* through the roomy *Illustrations of the Life of Shakespeare* and expanding to the ample *Outlines of the Life of Shakespeare*.

His material had, of course, increased considerably over the years. But it would be unconvincing to attribute his widening spectrum to quantity alone, much less to his penchant for serial publication by subscription. Halliwell's acute and much-reported awareness of growing old and his fragile health and failing memory, moreover, had only a relatively small influence as well, as had his increasing anxiety and confusion about all his scattered and unordered notes. Perhaps a major reason, however much submerged, may have been not merely his admiration of Shakespeare but his identification with him. In 1875 he had jocosely compared the events of Shakespeare's life with his own. "A List of a few parallel Circumstances in the Lives of Shakespeare and Mr. J. O. Halliwell-Phillipps" (LOA 230:77) begins:

He was descended from very small country farmers.   So am I.

With no pretensions to an aristocratic pedigree.   Neither have I.

Nor with any really good claim to the use of coat-armour.   Neither have
I.

But he purchased a grant of arms from the Heralds' College.   So have I.

His father, not being satisfied with the poverty of his rural life, left the
country & commenced business in a town as a glover.   So did mine.

and continues through:

He married very early in life.   So did I.

And without a sixpence on either side.   So did I.

He obtained his marriage licence at Worcester in a great hurry & in the
midst of family disagreements.   So did I.

He was persecuted by Sir Thomas, a country squire.   So was I.

And after numerous parallels:

He sometimes drank a little too much at a merry meeting.   So do I.

He bought one house in London.   So have I.

One of his friends wanted to borrow thirty pounds of him.   So has one
of mine.

His eldest daughter married a gentleman of the name of Hall.   So did
mine.

Still, he gallantly concludes:

The chief difference between us in our respective careers appears to be
that he knew how to write plays and I don't.[302]

In his list of thirty-three parallels Halliwell smiled away literary pretensions
and serious comparisons. But one parallel is missing from the rich list. In
the announcement of the work appended to the second edition of *New
Lamps or Old?* Halliwell defends Shakespeare against those who attack his
character:

That he was wild in his youth, that he sometimes drank a little more than
was good for him, and that he occasionally flirted with the young ladies
at the Bankside more freely than Mrs. Shakespeare at Stratford-upon-

302. The entire list is printed in *Shakespeariana*, 7 (1890), 6-7.

Avon would have approved of, may be conceded by those who do not consider it requisite to assume that the greatest of poets must necessarily be the greatest of saints. But that he deliberately would either have ruined the character of another, or betrayed the domestic confidence of a friend or host, is too inconsistent with the contemporary opinions of his character to be at all credible. With the exception of a tale that is a palpable fabrication, the Davenant story is the only recorded one respecting Shakespeare which, if true, would really involve an accusation of criminality; but so difficult is it to eradicate scandal, however, baseless, that the tale has been accepted as truthful for many generations and by even recent writers. It is, therefore, with peculiar satisfaction that, after the lapse of nearly three centuries, I can announce the discovery of contemporary evidences which prove decisively that there is not a word of truth in the libel (pp. 36-7).

The motif is a familiar one: Halliwell coming to the defense of those, like himself, unjustly maligned because of their origin or profession or some act they were purported to have committed. The motif is found in his choice of subjects. There were literary and historical persons, such as Samuel Morland, Simonds D'Ewes, Francis Douce, and Edward Capell; there were those of his immediate circle, such as Ashbee and Bumstead. And for Halliwell himself there was the scandal of the British Museum and the victimization by Thomas Phillipps. He had been libelled, he felt, and struggled to maintain a good reputation, acknowledging the difficulty of doing so. Revealingly, but not surprisingly, his biography of Shakespeare sets out not merely to provide the essential information with which his personality is to be accurately perceived but also to defend Shakespeare from unjust accusations. The motive, in short, has become a motif.

Underlining his critical approach, the main reason, however, may be found in the motto appearing on the title page, the first three lines of Sonnet 30. The third line, "I sigh the lack of many a thing I sought," is the key. Putting it more directly, Halliwell felt it "scarcely necessary to observe that the compilation of a satisfactory life of Shakespeare is an impossibility. A biography without correspondence, without details of conversation, and without any full contemporary delineations of character, must necessarily be fragmentary" (p. 33). Thus the biographical researches could at best be only illustrations, contributions leading to outlines to be filled in. A "life" thus conceived can only be understood as from a distance, directions often by indirections found, through the accumulation of data of the widest scope from which specific characteristics may be deduced and accepted or rejected, as the case may be. In any event, the "life" would be a library or research center in itself, self-contained and providing all the possibilities extant. The vastness of the material would afford the biographer to draw conclusions, although it must be stressed that Halliwell was, consistent with his approach, of the opinion that there could be no binding or final conclusions, no finished portrait. It is little wonder that Halliwell should quote Dickens, who, "in one of his hasty letters," wrote, "The life of Shakespeare is a fine mystery, and I tremble every day lest something should come up" (p. 36). It is even less wonder that Halliwell himself, the greatest authority of his time on the life of Shakespeare, should be so devoted an advocate of that mystery. After about half a century of Shakespeare research he did not miss the forest for the trees; for him the trees were the forest.

This was Halliwell's position all along in his scholarship. He was presenting caviare not to the general but to the limited few who shared his archaeological point of view and were able to pay for it. As always, private publication was financially risky and involved a considerable amount of personal engagement in its administration–both of which Halliwell had always, and willingly, accepted. In this instance he was quoted as remarking, not untypically, that "he would as soon think of making money by keeping a yacht as by the sale of his Shakespeare *Outlines*."[303] But then he was master of his own fate, as it were, independent of advice from unwanted sources and, in most cases, from what might be hostile reviews in journals, and could thus avoid rows and controversies. To advertise was infinitely better than being reviewed.

What did emerge punctually, almost exactly a year after the announcement, was neither the first or a series of folio volumes nor of a number of "small occasional volumes, of various sizes ... each one to be a separate work in itself." Instead, *Outlines of the Life of Shakespeare*, its preface dated 8 April 1881, was described as "a mere unfinished instalment of what may ultimately be expanded into a much larger work; this fragment of a design being thus prematurely issued in the hope of eliciting, before I proceed further, the opinions of my literary friends and correspondents on the novel treatment of the subject here initiated" (xv). "Novel" is certainly hyperbolic, for Halliwell's approach had not changed. "In the absence of some very important discovery," he was, as ever, committed to the fact that the "general and intense desire to penetrate the mystery which surrounds the personal history of Shakespeare cannot be wholly gratified." He was, as ever, convinced that "something, however,

303. *Book-Lore*, 3 (Dec. 1885-May 1886), 56.

may be accomplished in that direction by a diligent and critical study of the materials now accessible, especially if care is taken to avoid the temptation of endeavouring to decipher his inner life and character through the media of his works" (vi-vii). The sketch of Shakespeare's personal history which Halliwell proposes to construct is, as always, to be derived "strictly out of evidences and deductions from those evidences" (xiii). Not a small amount of that information had been seen before in Halliwell's publications, and a good deal based on recent researches was to come. There was, as well, the "negative" data resulting from Halliwell's provincial tours and personal examination of the municipal records of thirty-three cities and towns which yielded "no single instance [of] ... a notice of the poet himself," although "curious material of an unsuspected nature respecting his company and theatrical surroundings has been discovered" (xiv-xv).

Halliwell's presentation, in his customary "plain and unobtrusive language," is not to be understood as simple prose connecting selected quotations and reprinted documents, the scissors-and-paste method he had recommended to John Fenwick in constructing a catalogue.[304] Halliwell had opinions, and his narrative consists of an evaluation of the data and the various opinions already surrounding them. He is constantly engaged in proving or disproving individual points. Thus he is able to correct John Aubrey's view that Shakespeare's father was a butcher and Dyce's that he had "tried sundry occupations" by referring to the Corporation books of June 1556 and a "recognizance" in the "Controlment Roll of the twenty-nine of Elizabeth" that he was known as a glover. In another instance, he is able to give further evidence of the popularity of *1 Henry 4* by quoting a private letter from Toby Matthew to Dudley Carleton written in September 1598. He can also be skeptical, as in his evaluation of a notice of *Romeo and Juliet* in Weever's *Epigrammes* of 1599. And he can be diffuse, as in his doubtless correct but certainly peripheral conclusion, pointed out by the *Athenaeum* reviewer,[305] that "there was a far greater extent of moisture in the land than would now be thought possible, and streamlets of a water-power sufficient for the operation of corn-mills meandered through the town [of Stratford]." From this hint of the range of Halliwell's approach, it is easy to understand Collier's comments and preferences in his manuscript diary:[306] "very industrious, and labouriously accurate: no body more accurate, or

304. See p. 407.
305. 4 June 1881, p. 743.
306. Folger M.a.38.

painstaking to be so. It is a bad title but a good book. He seems to think the minutest fact important; as if the accuracy of the text were a matter comparatively of little consequence. I would give up all the facts of Shakespeares life, if I could only correct one word of his text" (3 July 1881, p. 57). And on 6 July 1881 (p. 60) he continued: "Halliwell has done admirably in his 'Outlines', 1881, as regards dates, and his is almost invariably to be trusted; but he does not by any means sufficiently apply them to the great political incidents of the time when the passages were written. I have gone through his book with great admiration for its fidelity industry & acuteness."

Collier's assessment is accurate and genuine, well beyond the requirements of a long friendship and his own predilections.[307] In the main, the relatively slight *Outlines* of 1881 cannot be considered the culmination of a lifelong occupation with the biographical details of the life of Shakespeare. Nor can it be considered a kind of magisterial summing-up of a life's work by one who has absorbed all the scrupulously assembled data and then abstracted a short view as a "present" for his friends and colleagues. Such an objective might suit the reclusive Hermit of Hollingbury Copse, rusticating amid his rarities and birds and flowers. But it would hardly be appropriate for the restless literary archaeologist if he could not present the evidence he had collected in so many places over so many years. Besides, the first edition of the *Outlines* lacked not merely details and records but left many gaps in the personal history of Shakespeare and the wider environment Halliwell considered so vital for the understanding of that history. And it could hardly be doubted that Halliwell, the proud possessor of rarities, was always anxious to display his finds, to show his treasures. If he could produce a *Life* in 1848 of some 350 pages, with seventy-six illustrations and eighty-nine documents, he could surely be expected to do more some thirty years later.

He did so—and immediately—in a second edition, whose preface was dated April 1882 and was thus already well underway along with the first edition, whose preface was dated 8 April 1881. And he did so massively, for after a paginal reprint of the preface the second edition is expanded to 703 pages, whose object, so the publisher's blurb,

is to supply for the use of students of English literature the ascertained facts of Shakespeare's life and the known particulars respecting the

---

307. On p. 59 of his diary he stated there was "*ample room* for a good book 'On the Life and language of Shakespeare' showing how public events operated upon his mind."

sources and the production of his plays, in a connected outline narrative, divested of all commentary, critical, argumentative or controversial. In every instance, the documents and extracts are given *verbatim et litteratim* in chronological order, and the explanatory and connecting matter is confined to essentials. It seems superfluous to add that if any contemporary literary and personal biography of Shakespeare, however meagre, had come down to us with the stamp or look of authenticity, or if any recognized bibliography were in existence, however brief or imperfectly executed while his works were still fresh, no necessity could exist for such a volume as the present. The plays might still appear overloaded with superfluous and repulsive commentary, but there could be no field for the conjectural and imaginary biographies which at greater or less length encumber every edition of the works.

The change was not simply cosmetic. For one thing, the narrative of the life is developed: page 90 of the first edition is equivalent to page 174 of the second. Most typically and significantly, in the second edition Halliwell begins to treat individual topics, those presaged as matter for individual volumes in his appended "Note" in *Which Shall It Be?*. There are twenty-three topics covering almost the entire range of Shakespeare studies: After the Funeral, The Two Noble Kinsmen, The Spurious Plays, Illustrative Notes, North's Plutarch, Early Notice of Hamlet, Lord Pembroke's Actors, Symbols and Rules, The Coventry Mysteries, The Theatre and the Curtain, Shakespeare's Neighbours, The New Place, The Chapel Lane, The Mulberry-Tree, The Ratsey Episode, The Only Shakes-scene, The Later Theatres, The Davenant Scandal, Contemporary Notices, Theatrical Evidences, The Copyright Entries, Life-time Editions, and the First Folio. And, as was his wont, Halliwell provided a Documentary Appendix which contains transcriptions of fifty documents of Shakespeare's time. Furthermore the publication of a work of this scope may well have been beyond the powers of Halliwell or his Brighton printers. For one reason or another he was no longer willing or able to take on the arduous business of soliciting subscriptions and the complicated bookkeeping involved. A few years earlier Longmans had published the first part of his luxurious *Illustrations of the Life of Shakespeare*. Halliwell had abandoned the second part "although a good bit" had been printed, "owing to more than one circumstance, but chiefly to a diminishing power for mental labour" (25 October 1876; LOA 238:63). Although his financial and domestic situation had improved dramatically by 1882, Halliwell's concern about his failing mental powers had increased. Besides, he seemed anxious to reach a larger audience–his preface addresses "students of English literature"–

than the relatively few for whom he published privately. His decision to employ a commercial publisher, Longmans, Green, & Co., was both a relief and a boon.

An analysis of the exact contents and issues of the seven editions which appeared during Halliwell's lifetime–one per year from 1881 to 1887–is a study in itself and must be done separately and in detail. For the nonce it is perhaps sufficient to point out a number of salient features and personal characteristics. On the whole, Halliwell's approach is recognizable. It is at once additive, expansive, and analytical, in the manner of both his larger enterprises, which were more often than not collections of essays or works, and of his participation in continuing controversies, as in the series of pamphlets on his conflict on autotyping with the Executive Committee of the Shakespeare Birthplace Trustees which ran parallel with the Issuance of the *Outlines*. The vast expansion of the second edition has already been touched upon. An illustration of the nature of the development of the *Outlines* is apparent in the differences between the second edition of 1882 and the third of 1883. Although its preface is dated December 1882, barely nine months after the second edition, the third edition contains a new and much expanded preface (twenty-one pages where there had been ten) in which various sources of information from early manuscripts to Nicholas Rowe are mentioned and evaluated. The narrative of the *Outlines* is extended from 171 to 241 pages. New material is added on Shakespeare's marriage, on Tarlton's performance for the Queen's Players, on Shakespeare's knowledge of fruits and flowers, among other matters. The treatment of Shakespeare's correspondence with Richard Quiney is expanded from eleven lines to seven pages; the discussion of Shakespeare's will is also enlarged. Notes are added on, for example, Sir William Davenant, Elizabeth, Susanna Hall's daughter, and Shakespeare's drinking bout at Bidford. New are a separate chapter called "Records of Affection," a few illustrations (e.g. a view of Stratford in 1749), and facsimiles of early documents (e.g. a letter of Richard Quiney to Shakespeare). The most striking changes, perhaps, are in the appendix. The Documentary Appendix of the second edition is divided into three parts: Domestic Records, Biographical Records, and Estate Records. Instead of fifty documents there are now thirty-six, but two new ones are added. This newly structured documentation, as well as the redistribution of the data under more precise headings, became the model for all following editions.[308] It was also a practical model, enabling

---

308. For a more detailed description of the changes in the first five editions, see "The Story of a Great Biography," *Shakespeariana*, 3 (1886), 1-7.

Halliwell to add, delete, reprint, and shift material with great ease and flexibility. Flexibility, in fact, was essential, for the enterprise was not static. Halliwell was constantly evaluating his material, seeking advice, asking for correction, and, as need be, reinforcing or modifying his opinions. For one thing Halliwell attempted to keep up-to-date: in the second edition, for example, in discussing "The Old and New Styles," he added the comment, "Consult Mr J. J. Bond's Handy-Book of Rules and Tables for Verifying Dates, 8vo Lond. 1866, by far the ablest and most important work that has ever appeared on this and kindred subjects" (p. 16). He was ever reviewing his material, hardly ceasing until he felt it to be right: having added "After the Funeral" to the second edition as a continuation of his discussion of the last days of Shakespeare in the first, in a typical instance, he kept on modifying it substantially and stylistically until the fifth edition, after which he was content with a paginal reprint in the following editions. Even as late as the seventh edition of 1887, which had reached two volumes and 848 pages, he was adding plates and expanding the Illustrative Notes. And with characteristic husbandry he was recycling material he had used earlier, incorporating the tracts on "The Theatre and Curtain" and "The Coventry Mysteries" which had appeared in the *Illustrations* and reprinting *The Fool and the Ice* (1883), as well as numerous documents from the *Life* of 1848 and engravings and drawings from other of his earlier works.

As always, he implored his friends to point out errors, so anxious was he to achieve the highest degree of accuracy. In a typical response to observations and corrections on the fourth edition that he had received from Ingleby, his main correspondent in the matter, he could only "earnestly hope [they were] the precursors of many more" (21 August 1884; Folger C.a.11[87]). And he was not merely receptive, for he went on, again typically, to discuss four details. He took time with his correspondents, effecting a dialogue on various points. Responding to the "memoranda" on the sixth edition that he had received from the Reverend H. P. Stokes, Halliwell, "like Oliver Twist ... never ... tired of 'asking for more' from your pen respecting my oversights in any of the editions from Nos. 1 to 6," wrote a four-page letter dealing with twenty-five points (giving volume and page number), defer[ring] "any remarks about the coat-armour" until he had "fully studied" the matter, and extending his "grateful thanks" for the valuable and useful criticisms (2 August 1886; Folger W.b.83[25]). In a Memorandum (xx) inserted in the fifth edition and dated April 1884 Halliwell publicly acknowledged his gratitude for their continuous assistance to Stokes, Ingleby, and W. J. Rolfe; in the seventh he extended it to J. Chancellor Smith and Herbert

A. Evans. Halliwell was so strenuously engaged in achieving the absolute authority of his work that a presentation copy of the edition of 1887[309] even contains three letters (two of 1884, one of 1887) from him to Professor Henry Bedford on his treatment of religious history with a note on the cover to the relevant passages. And, as always, he was responsive to the wishes of his public. Throughout his career his correspondence with subscribers was understanding and cordial: he offered extensions of payment and discounts. When he discontinued the *Illustrations* he not merely regretted the inconvenience he had caused the publishers, Longmans, Green, & Co., but even offered to return the "full publishing price" to "meet any complaints that might arise from purchasers of Part I being dissatisfied with having an incomplete work" (25 October 1876; LOA 238:63). He was attentive to the requirements of the users of the *Outlines* as well. Along the way he supplied marginal numbers in the text corresponding to the numbered illustrative Notes; he patiently explained to one buyer that the third edition was not a mere reprint of the second, that "none of it can be had separately nor would an efficient separate Appendix be practicable" (30 March 1883; Folger Y.c.1252[1]). Since his bare two-page indexes to the first five editions were a constant source of irritation to many, especially Ingleby, who badgered Halliwell about their inadequacy for years, Halliwell conceded:

Your previous complaints about the want of an index to Outlines did not fall on heedless ears. I had not intended to say anything about it, but astonish you in the 5th ed. as with a display of fireworks! When you next come here you will see a folio volume of MS. Index in preparation & being done in a careful manner, but I need not say that I shall be most thankful for your suggestions. It is no easy matter to decide on some of the entries, & there are many that I shall be anxious to consult you about (3 September 1884; Folger C.a.11[88]).

A year later, he was still at work. "I felt that I could not even bring myself to copy out & arrange the elaborate index I have so nearly completed," he assured Ingleby. "It [the 5th edition] is now all done & off my mind, & I must try & not think of it or its subject for a few months" (19 June 1885; Folger C.a.11[107]). In the sixth edition of 1886 he replaced the two-page index with a detailed fourteen-page Biographical Index.

And, as always, he was active in the propagation of his work. He chose not to send copies to any journals, but did forward to Norman Maccoll

309. In Special Collections, Edinburgh University Library, JA 3460.

of the *Athenaeum* pages which might be of general interest, like the "refutation of the Davenant, the only serious scandal against our national poet," diplomatically remarking, "no possible harm arising if you consign them to your voluminous paper-basket," and cleverly suggesting, "they contain however materials that could be boiled up into an interesting article" (25 June 1882; Folger Y.c.1253[1]).[310] He realized the importance of advertising and sought to have the *Outlines* mentioned in *Notes and Queries*. "The grand thing is with me," he informed Ingleby, "to make the book known & there is nothing like an exposé *in a journal* for that" (23 August 1882; Folger C.a.11[45]).

"Lord! how the youth has grown!" was Arthur Bullen's response on receiving the second edition of the *Outlines* (29 June 1882; LOA 262:69). Producing yearly expansions was not simple. Halliwell was too scrupulous, too anxious (as numerous letters testify) to avoid errors and inaccuracies, to take the task lightly. Moreover, he was ever sensitive to how potential critics might react. He trusted Ingleby and sought his criticism, to be sure. But in sending Dowden a copy, he was careful to say that he had mentioned him "in a manner that I hope will not be disagreeable" (12 August 1884; Folger 1214[1]). Fearful of Fleay, he confided to Ingleby: "You have correctly hit the right nail on the head when you conjecture that if I had spoken of him in my Outlines in connexion with his theories he might have been more indignant at my criticism than he is now at my silence" (23 January 1886; Folger C.a.11[113]). Earlier, he had found it necessary to refute Fleay on the nature of the publication of the *Outlines* and its price:

I never before heard that an author was called upon to supply purchasers of old editions with the new matters of new ones—it would be a troublesome business & put practically a stop to improvement & alteration. You seem to be under an error as to the price of my Outlines, the publishing price of which has never exceeded 7s.6d.–to be got with disct. off for about 5 shillings & 8d. or thereabouts (3 October 1884; Folger Y.c.1222[16]).

In any case the pressure on Halliwell was immense. The scholarship was strenuous enough, but the personal stress was even greater, especially at a time when Halliwell was passionately involved in a conflict with the

310. This, however, did not preclude his work from being reviewed in the *Athenaeum*. A favorable review of the first edition appeared on 4 June 1881 (pp. 743-4), written most likely by Maccoll himself.

Stratford authorities over the autotypes. His health suffered. He was not well, he informed Ingleby: he was suffering from "something very like nervous exhaustion & ... have been compelled to wind up my 5th ed. very hurriedly" (19 June 1885; Folger C.a.11[107]). Apologizing to Professor James Davie Butler for not having responded sooner, he explained that, "warned by my sudden break-down last year," he had devoted himself entirely to completing the sixth edition (3 June 1886; LOA 286:34). He gave the same explanation to Appleton Morgan, referring also to his "*incessant* work" and "intense labour" on the new edition, "much enlarged & is in 2 vols." (3 June 1886; Folger Y.c.1257[1]).

Halliwell persevered and the enterprise prospered. Cecil Harrison, of the printers Harrison and Sons, was impressed:

Longmans & the British Public are like Oliver Twist, they are still asking for more. Yesterday they sent to enquire whether you had made any arrangements as to the next edition, so I presume the whole of the present Edition has gone off, on which fact I send my congratulations. The man who can sell the whole Edition of his works within a few weeks of its issue must obviously be amassing a colossal fortune (3 May 1883; LOA 268:70).

Thanking Halliwell for the fourth edition, a "monument of scholarship and learning," Ingleby commented:

I don't know how many copies you print: but if not beyond 500, the Edition at its present ridiculous price will be soon exhausted: I say *at present* because every copy sold at 7/6 will directly become worth 10/ when the 5th Ed. is called for (13 August 1884; LOA 274:34).

It is not clear how many copies of the first edition were printed as presents—a hundred would seem a reasonable estimate. Longmans' records show that it sold 791 copies on commission from June 1882 to June 1883, 153 in 1884, 445 in 1885, 437 in 1886, and 189 in 1888. In 1889, after Halliwell's death, Longmans bought the copyright, electroblocks and plates for £50, produced an eighth edition at their own expense, and printed 1000 copies in four equal batches in August 1889, February 1890, March 1898, and October 1907, and there were still 200 copies on hand in June 1912 when there occurs a break in the records.[311]

311. This information was kindly supplied by Michael Bott, Keeper of Archives & Manuscripts in the library of the University of Reading.

Halliwell could not hide his satisfaction at the success of his venture, although the publication apparently brought him no financial gain,[312] since Longmans was merely distributing the work and deducting fifteen percent for handling, advertising, and the like, while Halliwell paid for the paper, printing, and binding. Responding to his brother Thomas's "friendly & gratifying notice [in the *Daily News*] of the Outlines on Monday last," Halliwell confessed: "I will not be so affected as to give the remotest hint that I did not deserve it, for in truth the book cost incessant & anxious labour in the endeavour to reach truth & accuracy" (7 July 1886; Folger Y.c.1289[3]). Graciously, he informed Appleton Morgan that the seventh edition was "already nearly exhausted, a result I have reason to believe I owe mainly to your countrymen" (4 February 1888; Folger Y.c.1257[2]).

He was working away with his customary intensity, "working up" (as he was fond of saying) a new edition as fast as he finished one. "I have to get through a new ed. of my Outlines by the end of April–although the last ed. came out but last May, & I only put in five advertisements," he continued to Appleton Morgan, having recovered from a month of influenza and hoping Morgan would visit him in the summer. Other matters were occupying him as well. Late in the year he issued a pamphlet, *A Letter to Professor Karl Elze, Respecting Certain Views That Are Advocated in the Recently Published English Version of His Literary Biography of Shakespeare*, in which he refuted one of Elze's charges–that he had said Shakespeare's wife was mentally afflicted–and more important that Elze conveyed

an erroneous idea of the system under which [Halliwell] attempted to work,–a system set out in the following words,–'subtle and gratuitous assumptions of unsupported possibilities will be rigidly excluded, and no conjectures admitted that are not practically removed out of that category by being in themselves reasonable inferences from concurrent facts ... that precedence will be always given to early testimonies over the discretionary views of later theorists, no matter how plausible or how ably sustained those views may be' (pp. 7-8).

Refuting other specific criticisms, such as the legacy of the second-best bed or the real birthplace of Shakespeare, was less important than the defense of his "system," one which had put him at odds with much of the scholarship being promulgated by the New Shakspere Society. What is

---

312. In his obituary of 12 January 1889, p. 53, the *Athenaeum* asserts that he published "at a loss."

notable too is that Halliwell did not answer the gratuitously unkind remark
on a Halliwell facsimile which was not available because "according to the
intolerable [the German adjective is "unleidlich"] English custom [it] was
printed in ten copies only,"[313] nor that the facsimiles of the quartos are
"not altogether free from faults," are printed only in small numbers, and
are thus merely "gratifying the fancy of bibliophiles."[314] Halliwell passed
over the fact that Elze was one of the founders of the Deutsche
Shakespeare Gesellschaft, which had elected him an honorary member in
1869). He preferred to counter such sniping not with snips or sarcasm but
with restraint and facts. He did not even make use of the fact that Elze's
work was written twelve years earlier, in 1876, long before the appearance
of the *Outlines*. And a good measure of the intensity of his engagement is
evident in his very typical habit of carefully revising and refining his
viewpoints, very much in the manner of his expanding the *Outlines* and the
Stratford Records and the Shakespeare Autotypes, albeit on a smaller scale.
Although the preface is dated 19 December 1888 there exist (Folger
W.a.81) a version whose pages 31-4 become pages 7-10 in the separate
publication *New Evidences in Confirmation of the Traditional Recognition of
Shakespeare's Birth-Room* (1888) and another with corrections in Halliwell's
hand, as well as his note (most likely to Ernest Baker) on the flyleaf,
"Proofs only. Kindly return this when you come here on Monday, & if
time permits look closely after any flaw there may be in the argument."
Appleton Morgan describes the Halliwellian process of composition
vividly:

And so, indeed, the dainty little book [*New Evidences*] was issued. But
scarcely had its author opened the first copy ... when he determined to
make it larger; call it 'Letter to Professor Elze' (as indeed it was), and his
shears soon demolished the book: and he had pasted its pages on great
sheets of paper for elaboration. (No man was Mr. Halliwell-Phillipps's
equal for cutting up bound books, throwing away the books and saving
a scrap, to be mounted and written to, until morsels became portly
quartos and folios.) According to the Brighton printers, accustomed to
drop all other work when 'copy' from Hollingbury Copse arrived, had
hardly distributed the type of '*New Evidences*' before they were again at
work upon '*Letter to Professor Elze*.' Halliwell-Phillipps always found it the
hardest task of his long life to satisfy Halliwell-Phillipps, and it is doubtful

313. Karl Elze, *William Shakespeare, A Literary Biography*, trans. L. Dora Schmitz
(London, 1888), p. 133, n. 1.
314. Ibid., p. 280.

if he ever saw any of his own work in print without longing to cut it to pieces, to rearrange and rewrite it.[315]

The date of the proofs was 22 December 1888. On the same page is a handwritten remark by Appleton Morgan, who had received the proofs from Baker: "The above was the last autograph of J. O. Halliwell-Phillipps made on what proved to be his death bed." Not quite and not so dramatically. For on 23 December 1888 Halliwell, ever occupied with his rarities, wrote a cheerful letter to T. N. Brushfield:

Since I had the pleasure of seeing you here (pray never come to Brighton without paying me a visit) I have often thought which predominated, my impudence in asking you to let me have the Birth-Place drawing in exchange for a five guinea Devonshire book or your cruelty in refusing. I hope not the impudence!![316]

On the next day, Christmas Eve, however, in the midst of readying still another edition of the *Outlines*, of revising his *Letter to Elze*, of attending to his collection of rarities, and doubtless of preparing for Christmas—"in harness," so his American admirer, Appleton Morgan—Halliwell caught a chill, went to bed, and died on 3 January 1889.

315. "Halliwell-Phillipps's Last Manuscript–The Letter to Dr. Elze," *Shakespeariana*, 7 (1890), 16.
316. Tipped into the Folger copy of the *Gentleman's Magazine*, 77 (1807), on a front flyleaf.

25

Death and Afterlife

Although Halliwell's health had been failing, his death was sudden and surprising. In June 1888, ironically enough, he caught cold while working in the Record Office, and the chronic illness which had plagued him for years—on 20 October 1883 (Folger C.a.11[170] he referred to hydrocele, later to his "urethral complaint" (11 April 1885; Folger C.a.11[102])–was aggravated. By November, however, he could inform Richard Savage that he was "very much better," while admitting that he was "not as yet up to the mark & [was] find[ing] the utmost difficulty in attending to matters while clearing off the most urgent of the arrears that six months of enforced inaction have accumulated" (9 November 1888; SBT TR10/2/5). But on Christmas Eve he caught cold and went to bed, and on Christmas Day W. H. Nicholls, surgeon of Waterloo-place, Brighton, who had been attending the family for years, was sent for. On the following Saturday, 29 December, Halliwell's condition worsened, and the surgeon Arthur Edward Durham of Guy's Hospital in London was telegraphed for and, after visiting Halliwell on Sunday, took a favorable view of the case. But serious complications set in, and on Thursday afternoon, 3 January 1889, Halliwell died. At his deathbed were his wife, her mother and sister, and W. H. Hunt of Stratford, the son of W. O. Hunt, who was visiting the Halliwells at the time. The death must have been very sudden, for his brother, Thomas, one of the curates of St. Andrew's Church in Brighton, was not present, nor were any of his daughters.[317] The official cause of death, as certified by Nicholls, was

---

317. The suddenness of Halliwell's death had one serio-comic consequence. Officials at Stratford informed his executor, Ernest Baker, that they did not have the keys to open the bookcase Halliwell had bequeathed. After a considerable search by Baker and Fred Hall, Halliwell's son-in-law, the keys were found and the case was ceremoniously opened at a meeting of the Committee in the presence of the mayor and Hall on 13 February 1889. It contained 186 volumes. The correspondence is in SBT TR10/2/6.

chronic cystitis and syncope.[318]

On Wednesday, 9 January, Halliwell was buried in the graveyard attached to the ancient Church of All Saints' in the village of Patcham, the parish in which Hollingbury Copse was situated. "The funeral cortège," so the *Brighton Herald* of 12 January (p. 1),

left Hollingbury Copse shortly before twelve o'clock, and reached the Church soon after noon ... The coffin, borne on an open car, was of polished oak, with brass handles and fittings, and a breast plate, inscribed with the names of the deceased, and the dates of his birth and death. It was covered with wreaths of flowers placed there or sent by Mrs Owen Walcot ([Charlotte] daughter of the deceased), Miss Hobbes, Mr and Mrs William Black, Miss Nellie Slack, Miss Allela Morgan, Mr William Rendle, historian of Southwark, Miss Winstone, Miss Smith, Mr and Mrs W. H. Nicholls, Mrs Cecil R. Harrison, Miss Hopper, the Copse servants, and the Misses Chattaway, who will be remembered by visitors to Stratford-upon-Avon, as the custodians of the birth-place of the poet ... The mourners, who arrived in three carriages, were (in the first carriage) the Reverend Thomas Halliwell, curate of St. Andrew's Church, Brighton, brother, and three of the sons-in-law of the deceased, namely, Mr O. C. Walcot, Lieut. F. C. N. Hall, R.N. [husband of Henrietta Somerset] , and Colonel [F. L.] Graves [husband of Ellen];[319] in the second carriage, the Rev. J. E. Halliwell, nephew, Mr E. Baker, brother-in-law, Mr Ernest Edward Baker, of Weston-super-Mare, nephew, Mr John Robinson, of West Brompton, and Mr W. H. Nicholls, for many years the medical attendant of the family; and in the third carriage, Mr W. H. Hunt, of Stratford-upon-Avon, Mr Dillon Croker, the dramatic and literary author, Mr Cecil Harrison, and Mr G. R. Wright, F.S.A. Among those who had assembled in the Church to pay a last mark of respect to the memory of the deceased were Mr H. Griffith (representing the Sussex Archaeological Society and the Society of Antiquaries), Mr W. J. Smith, Mr John William Jarvis, of Holloway, Mr J.. G. Bishop, Mr J. Haines, Mr Henry Davey, Mr H. Choal, Mr Charles Hindley, Mr William Murray, Mr Skevington, and a few others. The mayor of Stratford had written [actually telegraphed on 5 January[320]], intimating a desire to attend the ceremony, but, it being wished that it should be as far as possible of a private character, no

318. These details are taken from the report in the *Brighton Herald* of 5 January 1889, p. 3, doubtless written by the editor, Halliwell's friend J. G. Bishop.

319. Halliwell's youngest daughter, Katie, who had married John C. Walcot, was in Australia.

320. SBT TR 10/2/6.

invitations were issued ... The second portion of the funeral service was carried out at the graveside, during a shower of rain and hail, which added a last touch to a mournful scene. The grave itself had been hung with Hollingbury Copse ivy (the deceased's favourite plant).

Public tributes followed swiftly. So "large and continuous" was the demand for the two numbers containing the obituary notices that the *Brighton Herald* reprinted them in a separate form (at one penny each). The *Athenaeum* (12 January 1889, pp. 59-60) referred to Halliwell as "the last of the brilliant band of scholars who founded the Shakespeare Society." Of a more personal nature than this or many of the other obituaries in numerous newspapers and journals, and perhaps more touching because he was not of Halliwell's immediate circle, was J. Woodfall Ebworth's communication in *Notes and Queries* (19 January 1889, p. 59):

Let me, who seldom intrude myself into any of the public journals, give a few words in humble praise and reverence of the good and learned man whose loss must be deeply mourned by all who had enjoyed the privilege of his friendship. To other and better hands I leave the record of his lifelong labour, work unceasingly pursued for its own sake and neither for fame nor profit, though fame was not withheld and the highest profit reached him in his perfect independence. Yet his own private correspondence showed, when writing freely to me for many years, in the confidence of friendly sympathy, that he well knew all the imperfections of his past achievements; and to the very last he was unflagging in his efforts to secure more thorough accuracy and extended knowledge. I never knew a man of equally great attainments who was at heart so humble-minded. Of his unfailing courtesy, the sweet and genial nature of this true-hearted and chivalrous gentleman, which never failed to sustain him on the few occasions when ungenerous conduct rewarded his hospitality, all of us can bear witness. He has speedily followed his friend William Chappell, and not long after John Payne Collier, earnest ballad-lovers and faithful friends, who will together be remembered lovingly.

More extensive and despite its hyperbole doubtless heartfelt was the tribute paid by the Shakespeare Society of New York. First, in its immediate editorial reaction, less reserved than those in England:

Halliwell-Phillips [*sic*] is dead! ...
To speak of the close of such a life, requires more than the impulse of a moment. To speak fittingly of it, who will dare? Later we shall try to dwell

on his noble manliness, his inexhaustible patience, his magnificent hospitality, his large, unfailing friendliness—which, even more than his achievements in the great field of history he had made his own, and to which he gave life, time, fortune, and strength—crowd upon us. Just now we can only bend to the blow.[321]

To the lavish praise which completed this initial reaction came a more significant gesture: forty-seven pages of the next number of its journal, *Shakespeariana* (7 [1890], 1-47), devoted to the career and personality of Halliwell, to reminiscences and recollections of him, and to photographs of him and Hollingbury Copse. There followed tributes from longtime friends and colleagues: George R. Wright's *A Brief Memoir of the Late J. O. Halliwell-Phillipps* (1889), Charles Roach Smith's *Retrospections, Social and Archaeological* (1891, vol. 3, pp. 75-87), and John Cordy Jeaffreson's *A Book of Recollections* (1894, vol. 2, pp. 167-232). There were honors from abroad as well as at home. Halliwell was an honorary member of the Shakespeare Society of New York and of the Deutsche Shakespeare Society. He was granted the freedom of the City of Penzance (in July 1888, the illuminated certificate reached Hollingbury Copse after his death). A window in the chancel of Holy Trinity Church in Stratford was dedicated to his memory. To perpetuate his life-work the Shakespeare Birthplace Trust Bill was presented to the House of Commons, received the Royal Assent on 26 March 1891 and became law.[322] In the major works dealing with the sources for the biography of Shakespeare Halliwell's work takes a prominent place. In the index to E. K. Chambers's *William Shakespeare: A Study of Facts and Problems* (1930) Halliwell, with twenty-three references, far outranking all others (the closest being Collier with nine). In S. Schoenbaum's *William Shakespeare: A Documentary Life* thirty-eight references to Halliwell far exceed all others but those to Shakespeare himself and Stratford-upon-Avon (among modern critics the nearest rival is Chambers with twenty-one).

But the sunset cannot be described as golden. However well intentioned (and most likely inspired by Halliwell's wife[323]), the stately stone cross atop a three-step pedestal of Halliwell's tomb would not seem to be consonant with his oft-expressed preference for "something durable & *flat* on the earth," like the flat slab he had put over his parents and his

---

321. *Shakespeariana*, 6 (1889), 40.

322. An early draft is reprinted in *Shakespeariana*, 8 (1891), 95-100.

323. Her own tombstone in West Moors, Dorset, is also a granite cross atop three steps.

first wife Henrietta and recommended for Fairholt, "which will last humanly speaking for ever, & requires no repairs" (3 July 1866; Folger W.a.81[49/1]). And the inscription "IHS" must be considered unusual for one, who, though a churchgoer (often for the music or the sermon) and early on the founder of the English Theological Society and author of *An Introduction to the Evidences of Christianity*, never showed signs of the kind of piety such an inscription presupposes. Furthermore its suggestion of Roman Catholicism could only be considered an embarrassment (if not irony) to one who at one point denied rumors that he had joined the Church of Rome in a public letter to the editor of the Sussex *Daily News* (4 August 1882, p. 2). Moreover, in the very shadow of Halliwell's death, the Paris correspondent of the *Times* (11 January 1889, p. 14), was "reminded" of an "incident which might have materially affected his career," reporting that Thomas Phillipps had intended to adopt one Henry Ward de May and concluding, "How many things might have been different had the adoption been carried out!" This oblique and tasteless questioning of Halliwell's legitimacy evoked an immediate and sharp reply from his daughter Charlotte (12 January 1889, p. 6), who pointed out that "Sir Thomas ... had only a life interest in the property." Disappointing too might well be the announcement just three months after Halliwell's death of the sale at auction of his beloved Hollingbury Copse and "bought in at the upset price of 6,000 guineas." It found no buyer even at that bottom price, for Mrs. Halliwell was still living there in 1891. She remarried in 1892, and then moved to Dorset. Within a few years the rustic wigwam and its string of curious one-storey shanties at the center of Hollingbury Copse were torn down and disappeared. Halliwell's tombstone still stands, however, overgrown and forlorn.

Halliwell's collections did not fare very well either. The four-day sale from 1 July 1889 at Sotheby's of 1291 items fetched only a mildly respectable £2298.10.6. Disappointing, in a way, was the fate of his treasured rarities. For one thing, he had stipulated in his will that the material described in his *Hand-List of Sixty Folio Volumes, Containing Collections Made ... from 1854 to 1887, on the Life of Shakespeare and the History of the English Stage* (1887) and also all the unbound papers in eight drawers indicated alphabetically A to H in his largest safe at Hollingbury Copse were to be deposited at the Chancery Lane Safe Deposit until they were sold for £1200 or more, or, if such a price could not be obtained within twelve years, to be sold at auction in one lot. Yet they appear "by order of the executor" as lots 666 and 667 in the catalogue of the auction at

Sotheby's on the third day of the sale begun on 1 July 1895.[324] In the priced catalogue they are marked as "withdrawn," and in a letter of 7 July 1895 Henry Sotheran, the agent, informed the buyer, Henry Folger, who had paid £1200, that the lots were being shipped to him at 212 Lefferts Place, Brooklyn, New York. For another thing, Halliwell also stipulated that his most treasured possessions–described in his *Calendar of the Shakespearean Rarities, Drawings and Engravings, Preserved at Hollingbury Copse, Near Brighton* (1887)–which he regarded as "unrivalled and of national interest," be offered to the Corporation of Birmingham for £7000, which, if not accepted within one year of his decease, were to be deposited until sold for £10,000 or more, or, if not sold within twelve years, to be put up in one lot at public auction. Birmingham declined the rarities for financial or legal reasons. They appear, however, as items 668-673 in the same auction sale of July 1895 and are also marked as "withdrawn." Through Sotheran, Folger offered £11,000 for them, but was told (in a letter of 13 July 1895) the owner had replied that they were not for sale at any price. The implication would have to be that they may have already been promised or sold privately. Folger was persistent and finally succeeded in acquiring them (and seven quarto volumes) in 1908 for $69,000 from the owner, Marsden Perry of Providence, Rhode Island (from whom he had also bought items 666-667), who (so Sotheran to Folger on 18 January 1908) had been "affected by the financial disturbances in America."[325] In a word, the letter of Halliwell's will may not have been quite observed, and this despite his executor Ernest Baker quoting in his own *Few Notes on a Selected Portion of the Halliwell-Phillipps Library* (1889) an extract from a memorandum left by his late uncle in November 1888: "Pray sell no books, nor engravings, nor manuscripts, nor old deeds, &c., by private contract. If you do, you will be 'done' as sure as a whistle."[326] Sadder still was the fact that Halliwell's wish that the collection be kept in England was not fulfilled. And, as is often the case in the dispersal of so vast a number of possessions, there are many that are not to be found.

Halliwell's reputation lost its glow as well, owing in great part to the "knot intrinsicate" of his scholarship and personality. As a young man he

324. Yet the cover of Ernest Baker's reprint of the *Hand-List* in 1889 reads "Referred to in Clause 11 of the Will," in which a public auction was to be held twelve years after Halliwell's death.

325. The correspondence between Folger and Sotheran is in the Folger Shakespeare Library.

326. Halliwell's estate was valued at £31,073. 2s. 8d. (*Times*, 12 March 1889, p. 11), which would be the equivalent today of about £1,855,059, a sum that seems to have eluded surviving relatives.

was regarded by many of his seniors as pushy and aggressive. This led to suspicion and mistrust. His hasty marriage to the daughter of Thomas Phillipps and the ensuing British Museum affair did much to stigmatize him, it seems, forever–despite the fact that Phillipps's motives were not benevolently parental and the purported theft of the Trinity College manuscripts never stood any legal test. Much of all the furore subsided as Halliwell grew older and came to be regarded as the most eminent Shakespearean of his time. Still, for Victorians, as for their heirs, sensationalism was magnetic. Even book collecting was no dusty pastime: forgery was fascinating, and theft was thrilling. It is not surprising that Sidney Lee in his *Dictionary of National Biography* (*DNB*) article on Halliwell could not resist mentioning Halliwell's involvement in the theft of the Trinity College manuscripts (although word had it that Jaggard moved his valuable items to the back room when Lee entered his shop) and erroneously stating that Halliwell's exclusion from the British Museum had not been rescinded. Even the indignant correction and defense of Halliwell against an "injustice to [his] memory in the *Athenaeum* review of the *DNB* (16 May 1891, pp. 628-9) and elsewhere–which resulted in Lee's altering the order for exclusion as "not rescinded" to "readmission would be granted him if application were made"[327]– may have served more to keep the matter alive rather than squash it. In 1932 E. V. Lucas, in his *Reading, Writing and Remembering: A Literary Record*, reported what he "chiefly" remembered of his meeting with Halliwell, his "second author to speak with ... [who] was then about sixty, a big man with a white beard":

He showed us many rare books and documents, but what I chiefly remember of this meeting is his remark that if he ever chanced to see anything in anyone else's house or in a museum that he thought he was more worthy to possess, and (obviously) more able to protect, than its owner, he had no scruples about taking it. This may have been a humorous and idle boast; but he said it (pp. 47-8).

Halliwell's passion for collecting–well documented not merely by his doing but even more perhaps by such utterances as "I want Shakespeare, Shakespeare, Shakespeare, SHAKESPEARE" (the last written at least an inch high) (26 February 1880; Folger 1206[23]) or "I will go down on my knees for it [a 1602 *Hamlet*]" (30 October 1867; Folger W.a.81[51/2])–seems to have licensed a stream of accusations that theft

327. In the reissue of the *DNB* in 1908.

was Halliwell's ruling passion. A hundred years after the British Museum affair a member of the staff the Bodleian Library deduced that a single missing leaf seen by Halliwell some hundred years earlier must have been stolen by him.[328] A hundred years after the case against him was dropped and Halliwell had his reader's ticket restored, D. A. Winstanley reopened the case and came to the involutedly expressed conclusion that "it is impossible not to believe that he stole the manuscripts from the college library."[329] Once a rogue always a rogue seems to be the logic of W. A. Jackson's insinuating "Did Halliwell Steal and Mutilate the Phillipps Copy of Hamlet, 1603?"[330] and of W. H. Bond's attempt to unmask Halliwell's questionable "tactics" in defending himself against the charges of theft and his coupling his remark that later Halliwell's conduct was "apparently exemplary" with an insidious footnote, "But there may well have been incidents that were not discovered" [and *pace* Lucas] "Halliwell in his later years is quoted as saying he would never scruple to steal anything 'he thought he was more worthy to possess ... than its owner'." A myth of sorts was firmly established by Schoenbaum, who somewhat gleefully was convinced that there was a "streak of larceny in his character,"[331] a conclusion which persists and is apparently irrevocable. It even spreads to a charge of vandalism: instead of index cards, Halliwell cut passages from books and pasted them under specific headings in his appropriately named scrapbooks and also in the manuscripts he himself was writing. The charge is modern and myopic since it was not an unusual procedure in its time and none of Halliwell's friends and colleagues (who received gifts of single leaves) or enemies for that matter seemed to have objected. Besides, it is difficult to believe that Halliwell's passion for books was so unruly as to cause him to destroy anything but relatively worthless or defective copies.

Inextricable from assessments of Halliwell's character is the criticism of his scholarship. His energy and productivity, especially in his youth, led to accusations of carelessness and unprofessionalism. They were not unjustified, even if they came from the same senior establishment that disapproved of his character and from his avowed rivals and apparently stand in contradiction to the decision of his father, experienced in the intricacies of business matters, to make his youngest son sole executor of

328. See pp. 139-40.
329. See pp. 141-2.
330. See p. 140.
331. *Shakespeare's Lives*, p. 290. This view is perpetuated by Richard Maxwell, "James Orchard Halliwell Phillipps," *Dictionary of Literary Biography*, 184 (1997), 202-18.

his considerable and complex estate. Whatever the reason, there can be little doubt about Halliwell's unquenchable desire, as the years progressed, to achieve perfect accuracy. But first impressions do not fade, and in modern times have led to anything from an unsupported and incorrect charge that his Latin was poor[332] to a certain coolness even towards Halliwell's major accomplishments. After the fullest use of Halliwell's records in his *Life of Shakespeare*, Chambers comes to a less than enthusiastic assessment in his *Sources for a Biography of Shakespeare*: "The sources, so far as known to him, were fully set out by J. O. Halliwell-Phillipps in his *Outlines of the Life of Shakespeare*, which took its final form in 1887. It is a useful, but rather ill-arranged and imperfectly indexed work."[333] For all his sympathetic and extended treatment of Halliwell, Schoenbaum in his *Shakespeare's Lives* tends to seesaw. On the one hand, Halliwell's style is "spare, dry, graceless—rarely rises to the level of banality" (p. 291), and "the records unearthed by Halliwell's diligence are uniformly unspectacular" (p. 293). On the other, Halliwell is the "greatest of the nineteenth-century biographers of Shakespeare in the exacting tradition of factual research which extends from Malone to Chambers" (p. 290), and of course though Halliwell's scholarship is dull there are always for Schoenbaum his attractive "eccentricity and ... the streak of larceny in his character" (p. 290).

It is easy to understand Schoenbaum's rejection of Halliwell's picture of a "Shakespeare of the middle class imagination ... the image of Shakespeare as a stout burgher" (p. 296), even if the records seem to reinforce that image. More difficult to understand is his doomsday assertion that the "achievements of scholarship are notoriously ephemeral, consigned as they are to oblivion by new information and improved methods of research" (p. 290), especially since he would agree with Chambers and most others that the material Halliwell provided for a life of Shakespeare more than a hundred years ago is still valid and essential. For underlying Schoenbaum's assertion is a questioning of the methodology or ideology of scholarship. In his own day Halliwell clashed with Furnivall and his New Shakspere Society. The battle was of the minute and heated. In the late twentieth century Halliwell's records remain in use, but his kind of scholarship, while not yet in oblivion, has suffered neglect and abuse. Times change, and often for the better. But they are

332. Arthur Gray and Frederick Brittain, *A History of Jesus College Cambridge* (London, 1960), p. 84, commenting on Halliwell's edition of John Sherman's *Historia Collegii Jesu Cantabrigiensis*: "it teems with errors, and has little value." Halliwell was twenty years old when it appeared.

333. (Oxford, 1946), p. 7.

not helped by an inability or unwillingness to understand (if not appreciate) earlier premises. If charges of vandalism are based on a certain ignorance of conventions, so too are such self-contradictory overstatements as "James Halliwell, who contributed more to our knowledge of Shakespeare's life than any other nineteenth-century scholar, contributed nothing to the history of criticism and precious little to the history of editing."[334]

Still, and not surprisingly, Halliwell might well agree. A mere bookworm and a recluse, as shy in public as he was gregarious in private, he had few pretensions to greatness. He was too much the doer, his days were too full, for him to court celebration, much less to contribute consciously to the history of anything. And for all his incessant professional activity—not to mention his evenings in song with his family, his jaunts to music halls, his holidays by the sea, his gardening, his proud displaying of his rarities to countless visitors from home and abroad—he was a deeply private man. He wrote voluminously, but kept no private diary. He recorded his scholarly tasks and objectives and his expenditures with passionate detail, but the touches of his private self he put only sporadically in letters which were then scattered to many destinations. In the sifting of the thousands of them are to be found the outlines of his life. In one, in fact, is to be found his opinion of biography itself. Having heard that James Prior was writing a life of Malone, Halliwell, at the peak of his life and career, wrote to Fairholt: "To my mind the biography on a large scale of mere literary men of talent is an absurdity. You & I are as clever as Malone, & in one way or other will have done as much. The rage for disturbing privacy is fearful. Who ought to care what Malone had for dinner, what women he kept, what prosaic letters he wrote, &c." (19 January 1860; Folger W.a.81[21/7]). Halliwell was exaggerating, to be sure. But he was certainly setting priorities, exalting unselfconscious accomplishments in the spirit of his age and by no means simply disregarding or diminishing the singularity of the private and the strength of the domestic. And if he was unwilling or unable to appraise the exact value of his accomplishments in his own day, and the contribution of his private life, then he was only too aware, as in his critical stance, of the futility of fancy and the perils of prediction.

Since we too cannot read the book of fate and see the revolution of the times make mountains level, that tale we have of a remarkable scholar and notable personality is best told which is told round and unvarnished.

---

334. Gary Taylor, *Reinventing Shakespeare* (London, 1989), p. 189.

Index

Brown, Henry, 347, 374, 375
Brown, Ivor, 385 n.223
Browning, Robert, 508, 511, 514,
514 n.279
Bruce, John, 23 n.17, 24, 40, 54, 89,
97, 106, 120, 161, 214, 214
n.130, 217, 227, 228, 269, 346,
410 n.237, 557
Brushfield, Thomas N., 582
Bryan, Mr., 368 n.212
Bryant, Mrs., 450
Buccleuch and Queensberry, Duke
of, 364
Budworth, John Philip, 450
Bulkeley, John, 44
Bullen, Arthur Henry, 474, 479, 490,
578
Bumstead, George, 238, 274, 285,
357, 403, 404, 405, 408, 480,
488, 570
Burbage, Mrs. Richard, 343
Burbage, Richard, 200, 368 n.212,
402, 546
Burdett-Coutts, Angela Georgina,
118, 311, 316, 317, 317 n.184,
382, 395
Burgon, John William, 113, 115, 116
Burr, Mr., 348
Burr, Mrs., 348
Bury, M. E., 134 n.75
Butler, Catherine S. E., 4, 5, 7 n.4,
13
Butler, Charles, 6, 7, 7 n.4, 8, 10, 12,
13, 72
Butler, James Davie, 579
Butler, Joseph, 38
Butler, Mrs. William Henry, 7
Butler, William Henry, 4, 5, 7, 10
Byron, Lord, 38
C., W. B., 254 n.149
Caesar, Julius, 4
Caffin, Charles S., 427
Cagzini, Jacques, 9
Caius, Dr., 171
Caldecott, Thomas, 256

Caligula, 155
Camden, William, 23, 38
Campbell, Alexander, 397
Campbell, Thomas, 83, 84
Canton, Alfred, 326, 455
Capell, Edward, 49, 139, 216, 221,
273, 281, 282, 374, 570
Capulets (family), 562
Carew, Lizzy, 122
Carleton, Dudley, 572
Carr, Samuel, 38
Carter, Maria, 464
Cartwright, Thomas, 23
Casley, David, 81 n.51
Cato the Elder, 63
Cavalieri, Bonaventura, 20
Cavendish, Charles, 44
Cawdrey, Robert, 178
Celsus, 270
Chalmers, Alexander, 57
Chalmers, George, 57, 553
Chambers, E. K., 222, 586, 591
Chandos, Duke of, 315
Chappell, William, 23 n.17, 77, 78,
346, 459, 585
Chard, Sarah, 165, 454
Charlemont, Lord, 360, 409
Charles I (king of England), 69, 151,
158
Charles II (king of England), 278,
279, 345
Charles, Samuel, 40, 62, 138, 489
Chasles, Michel, 15
Chatham, Lord, 203
Chattaway, Caroline and Maria, 524,
528, 529, 535, 584
Chatto & Windus, 360, 361, 408
Chaucer, Geoffrey, 48, 53, 55, 96
n.57, 176, 494, 496, 566
Chester, Joseph Lemuel, 559
Chester, Robert, 281, 558
Chettle, Henry, 61, 355, 566
Choal, H., 584
Christie's, 408
Churchyard, Thomas, 255